GLOBALISATION, GROWTH AND INEQUALITY IN NORTH EAST INDIA

GLOBALISATION, GROWTH AND INEQUALITY IN NORTH EAST INDIA

(In 2 Volumes)

(Volume-1)

Paritosh Chandra Dutta
and
Ram Krishna Mandal

KALPAZ

Globalisation, Growth and Inequality in North East India

Rs. 1800 (Set)

ISBN: 978-81-7835-876-5 (Set)
ISBN: 978-81-7835-877-2 (Vol. 1)

Published in 2011 in India by
Kalpaz Publications
C-30 Satyawati Nagar, Delhi-110052
E-mail: kalpaz@hotmail.com
Phone : 9212729499

Leser Type Setting by : Square Vision, Delhi
Printed at : Chawla Offset Printers, Delhi

Dedicated

To

Late Prof. Haren Choudhury

and

Prof. Chandan Kumar Mukhopadhyay

With Reverence and Affection

Contents

Preface 9

Overview of North-East Region 13

SECTION-I: SOCIO-ECONOMIC DEVELOPMENT

1. The Socio-Economic Development of NER with Special Reference to Assam 59
2. Some Aspects of Socio-Economic Development in NER 87
3. Problems and Prospects of Peace Process in Assam 115
4. Socio-Economic Development in Rural Assam: Problems and Prospects 153

SECTION-II: ECONOMIC DISPARITY

5. New Economic Policy and Development in NER 191
6. A Preliminary Note on Measures of Income Inequality 231
7. Inter-State Variation in Per Capita Non Food Household Items of Consumption in NER 243
8. Per Capita Household Consumption Inequalities in NER 255
9. Quality Variation of some Food Items of Consumption in NER 271
10. Regional Disparity and its Consequences in NER 285

SECTION-III: DEMOGRAPHIC PROFILE

11. The Relationship Between Total per Capita Expenditure (PCE) and Marginal Budget Shares (MBS) of Some Item Groups of Consumption in Rural Areas of NER 309

12. Gender Issues and Development in North Eastern Region of India 323

Preface

The present study is an attempt at a comprehensive and critical analysis of effect of Globalization, Growth and Poverty and Income Inequality and overall Socio-Economic Development with Demographic Structure of North-East Region (NER) consisting of twenty one papers and divided into five sections: socio-economic development, economic disparity, demographic profile, environmental degradation and agricultural scenario.

This region consists of eight states i.e., Arunachal Pradesh, Assam, Manipur, Meghalaya, Mizoram, Nagaland, Tripura, and Sikkim. This region of India has the largest concentration of tribal people. The tribals are children of nature and their lifestyle is conditioned by the Eco-system. This region, with a variety of ecosystems, presents a varied tribal population throughout its length and breadth. The areas inhabited mostly by the tribal constitute a significant part of the under developed areas of the country. The tribal people live mostly in isolated villages or hamlets. A smaller portion of their population has now settled permanently in towns as well as in cities. Tribal people over the years have become the most disadvantaged, exploited and the neglected lot in our society. The tribal basically stand averse to the modern life styles and hardly willing to change until and unless they encounter a very strong social mobilization.

All the States of this region, except Assam are mostly hilly. Assam is also having hilly regions, but it is comparatively less than the plain areas of the state. The states of this region are very much unique in their own ways. There is a wide variation in the altitude ranging up to 5000 meters. The North-Eastern region of India occupies a strategic geo-political situation due to its international boundaries with Bangladesh, Bhutan, China, Myanmar and Nepal. No doubt, these states constitute a homogeneous natural region of the hills, plains, valleys, flora and fauna and other related geographical features. Though the North-Eastern region reflects some ecological and cultural adaptive contrasts between the hills and the plains, there are also significant elements of continuity in the biological, cultural and social factors between these segments. Flanked by hills and with the mighty Brahmaputra River slashing a central path between its north and south, the region is bounded mostly by the international boundaries. Arunachal Pradesh lies to its north and Sikkim a little away in the north-west bordering China and Bhutan. Bangladesh and Myanmar lie to its south-west and east. The torrential Brahmaputra deposits its rich alluvial silt along the banks of the plains of Assam. The state of Assam is a land where Tea is the most powerful industry. The western side of the region is connected to the eastern part of the Indian subcontinent by a narrow land corridor, sometimes referred to as the Siliguri Neck or "Chicken's Neck". The eight states that comprise the region reflect ecological and cultural contrasts between the hills and the plains; there are also significant elements of continuity. The economy of NER has got its definite identity due to its peculiar physical, economic and socio-cultural characteristics.

So far, whatever information was available about the states' economy was fragmented and not subjected to any critical study. In the present study, taking due account of the factors promoting socio-economic transformation, as well as factors retarding development, attempt has been made to devise ways and means for accelerating the rate of economic growth of the states against the background of the existing structure of the states' economy and the trends of its transformation.

The total Geographical Area of the North-Eastern Region including Sikkim is 2,63,179 sq. km. accounting for 7.9 per cent of the total land space of the country. These eight states of NER together have a total population of 3,88,57,769 as per 2001 Census and constitute about 3.8 per cent of the total population of the country (NEDFi, quarterly data bank, 2005). The state of Assam, though, is the second largest in area, but it is the homeland of the highest number of persons i.e., 68.60 percent of the population of this region with an equally highest density of 340 persons per sq. km. The State of Arunachal Pradesh is though the largest, but there is only 2.28 percent of population of this region with a density of 13 persons per sq. km. which is the lowest not only in this region but also in India. North-east region of India with its absolute pristine virginal territory remains completely unexplored. The valley is beautified with lush green vegetation, grandiose mountains and feral rivers. North-east India is also abode of exceptional range of flora and fauna and the brilliant tribal life.

The socio-economic development of the region has not been treated as an isolated phenomenon but as an integral part of the economic development of the country as a whole. The work is based on diverse source materials which consist of official reports, published journals, books and findings of field work. We have weighed our occasional writings in different reputed national journals, periodicals, seminars and newspapers and found that most of them are either on the social structural aspects or on the social dynamism and rapid regional socio-economic transformation or on the empowerment of women. We have felt the need to put some of them together so as to enable the readers to get an over all idea about the region. Some of them have been updated, revised and edited for the purpose. We hope that the readers will find it relevant for understanding the region in a better way.

We express our deep gratitude to the esteemed editors of the journals and the seminar editors who published our papers on varied topics of national as well as regional importance. We pray to them and take their permission to publish the papers in this volume in the large interest of the academic world. We are also thankful to the individual scholars and the different agencies from whom we have drawn optimum.

We are conscious of the bulk of the work which becomes largely inevitable on account of the intrinsic sweep of the subject. We acknowledge our gratitude to all writers- Indian and foreign, whose books were consulted in the preparation of this volume. We are also thankful to the officers and staff of the Administration in the region, without their sincere cooperation and help; it would not have been possible for us to collect necessary source materials for this volume.

Before the raw idea of publication takes a distinct shape, a number of our colleagues helped us in various ways to clarify the issues through occasional interaction. For that we are obliged to them.

We are thankful to Pritam Giri, on behalf of Kalpaz Publications. Not only for attractive and quick publication of the book, but also for his various professional advices. Lastly, we are grateful to the members of our family for their untiring support and patience during the work of this volume.

Paritosh Chandra Dutta

and

Ram Krishna Mandal

Overview

The North-East Region known as a Land of 'seven sisters' consisting of seven states viz. Arunachal Pradesh, Assam, Manipur, Meghalaya, Mizoram, Nagaland and Tripura. In 1971, following the North-Eastern Re-organization Act, 1971, the state of Assam was constitutionally recognized and Meghalaya, Manipur and Tripura became full-fledged states. But Mizoram and the erstwhile NEFA (present Arunachal Pradesh) were made Union Territories. In 1987, these two Union Territories were elevated to the status of states. These states are comparatively small in area and /or population. It was felt necessary to involve interstate cooperation in sharing of costs of building basic infrastructure for the development of the region. Consequently, in 1971 another important Act was passed to establish in 1972 the North-Eastern Council (NEC) as an advisory body for formulating regional development plans with these seven states as members. Execution of projects under the plans was, however, the responsibility of the state governments concerned. But Nagaland decided to remain outside the purview of the NEC. Recently, the State of Sikkim also has come under the umbrella of this region owing to its proximity to the area and somewhat similar type of developmental and other problems. For the purpose of Development Activities, Sikkim has also come under the purview of the North Eastern Council, which is a Regional Planning Body, by an Act of Parliament, in December, 2002 as per the NEC Re-organization Act. This Act provided for the inclusion of Sikkim as a member of the NEC. Presently for development purposes the north-eastern region (NER) consists of eight states i.e., Arunachal Pradesh, Assam, Manipur, Meghalaya, Mizoram, Nagaland, Tripura, and Sikkim.

India has the largest concentration of tribal people anywhere in the world except perhaps in Africa. The tribals are children of nature and their lifestyle is conditioned by the Eco-system. India, with a variety of ecosystems, presents a varied tribal population throughout its length and breadth. The areas inhabited by the tribal constitute a significant part of the under developed areas of the country. The tribal people live mostly in isolated villages or hamlets. A smaller portion of their population has now settled in permanent villages as well as in towns and cities. On the whole, as per rough estimates, the prominent tribal areas constitute about 15 percent of the total geographical area of the country. Tribal people over the years have become the most disadvantaged, exploited and the neglected lot in our society. The tribal basically stand averse to the modern life styles and hardly willing to change until and unless they encounter a very strong social mobilization.

According to Ralph Linton, the legendary and respected anthropologist of mid-20th century, a 'tribe is group of bands occupying a contiguous territory or territories having a feeling of unity deriving from numerous similarities in culture, frequent contacts and a certain community of interests'. Indian tribal society can be underlined as a social group with strict territorial affiliation, possessing characteristics of endogamy, with no specialisation of functions ruled by tribal officers hereditary or otherwise, united in language or dialect recognising social distance with other tribes.

An enormous section of Indian tribal societal population depends on agriculture as their sole way for survival. Characteristically too Indian tribal society possess their own set of languages, which are unwritten. Hence the degree of communication both in time and space is predictably narrow. At the same time tribal societies demonstrate an outstanding economy of design and have a compactness and self-sufficiency surprisingly lacking in modern city society. There are as many as 573 tribes and sub tribes in India. They have been broadly classified into different classes, groups depending upon their present state of development and factors namely, mode of living in forest, shifting villages, forest villages, community villages and revenue villages.[1] They have got a heterogeneous cultural pattern with variegated economic condition and activities largely based on ecological settings and ethnic environment.

Tribal communities to globalisation through state policies need to be considered from different angles. The tribal people are tradition bound and their tradition is quite different from that of in the market economy. In a way, it can be stated that their tradition tells on their efficiency/level of skill endowment, which fall short of market requirements. Since independence, the special benefits available to Scheduled Tribes have convinced many groups, that they will enjoy greater advantages if so designated. The Schedule gives tribal people incentives to maintain their identity. A number of traits have customarily been seen as establishing tribal rather than caste identity. These include language, social organization, religious affiliation, economic patterns, geographic location, and self-identification. Recognized tribes typically live in hilly regions, somewhat remotely located from caste settlements; and they generally speak a language recognized as tribal.

There are five major geographical areas or zones in the country where there is concentration of tribal population. The tribal communities living in each of these zones, by and large, have common racial, linguistic, cultural and even economic characteristics. The five zones, which are thus distinguishable, are the North, North-Eastern, the Central, the Western and the Southern. There are 533 tribes as per notified Schedule under Article 342 of the Constitution of India in different States and Union Territories of the country with the largest number of 62 being in the State of Orissa. The North-Eastern mosaic is a replica of the Indian mosaic but with the prominence of some other special ingredients. There are nearly 150 ethnic groups and sub-groups. All the known anthropological offshoots, e.g., Negroids, Mongoloids, Austro-Asiatic, Tibeto-Burmans, and the equally important Caucasians are here in the North-Eastern part of India with Assam having more than 20 major ethnic groups. Some of the major tribes of North Eastern India are as follows. They are Nyishi, Adi, Tagin, Apatani, Wangcho, Dafla, Khampti, Singpho, etc. in Arunachal Pradesh, Boro, Kachari, Mikir (Karbi), Lalung, Rabha, Dimasa, Hmar, Hajong etc. in Assam, Garo, Khasi, Jayantia, etc. in Meghalaya, Chakma, Kuki, Lusai, Liang, Santhal etc. in Tripura, Lusai, Kuki, Garo, Khasi, Jayantia, Mikir etc. in Mizoram, Lapcha, Bhutia, Nepali, etc. in Sikkim.

All the States of this region, except Assam are mostly hilly. Assam is also having hilly regions, but it is comparatively less than the plain areas of the state. The states of this region are very much unique in their own ways. There is a wide variation in the altitude ranging up to 5000 meters. The North-Eastern region of India occupies a strategic geo-political situation due to its international boundaries with Bangladesh, Bhutan, China, Myanmar and Nepal. No doubt, these states constitute a homogeneous natural region of the hills, plains, valleys, flora and fauna and other related geographical features. Though the North-Eastern region reflects some ecological and cultural adaptive contrasts between the hills and the plains, there are also significant elements of continuity in the biological, cultural and social factors between these segments. Also, as per available records, we find a lot of independence and interactions between the hills and the plains in this region.

The total Geographical Area (notional area) of the North-Eastern Region including Sikkim is 2,63,179 sq. km. accounting for 7.9 per cent of the total land space of the country. These eight states of NER together have a total population of 3,88,57,769 as per 2001 Census and constitute about 3.8 per cent of the total population of the country (NEDFi, quarterly data bank, 2005). The state of Assam, though, is the second largest in area, but it is the homeland of the highest number of persons i.e., 68.60 percent of the population of this region with an equally highest density of 340 persons per sq. km. The State of Arunachal Pradesh is though the largest, but there is only 2.28 percent of population of this region with a density of 13 persons per sq. km. which is the lowest in this region. North-east region of India with its absolute pristine virginal territory remains completely unexplored. The valley is beautified with lush green vegetation, grandiose mountains and feral rivers. North-east India is also abode of exceptional range of flora and fauna and the brilliant tribal life. North-east Indian tribes are perhaps some of the most mysterious and yet most studied and observed band in the country, with host of things to offer in a slice of everyday life.

"India lives in villages". Because, 72.18 percent of its population is living in rural areas and only 27.82 percent is living in urban areas. This is also very true for the North Eastern Region as it is seen that 84.34 percent of people of this region is living in the rural areas only and 15.66 percent of people is living in urban areas. One of the bases of Indian economic growth has been the transformation of the hill-forest regions for the use of the mineral resources therein, and the utilization of the hydropower and irrigation potential. These developments have increased power availability, irrigated water to increase agricultural productivity and the development of an industrial base. The benefits of these developments, however, have been largely concentrated among Indians in the plains, including workers who have secured employment. The inhabitants of the hill-forest regions, the indigenous peoples (or scheduled tribes as they are legally termed) on the other hand, have had to bear the brunt of involuntary displacement and destruction of their traditional, livelihoods through mines, dams, etc. (Nathan, Dev. 2009). States viz. Arunachal Pradesh, Meghalaya, Mizoram and Nagaland are tribal dominated states. So far North East region is concerned, it is a new approach. The region has been neglected even by the centre so long and is lagging behind on all fronts, so far any type of modern resources are concerned. And to talk about the tribal population in the North East region and the Impact of Globalization on Tribal Women of North East, is completely a new concept.

The development of villages has become the need of the hour, especially the hill villages in North-East India. However, it goes beyond the conventional development models; it focuses also on social, political, and other aspects of development. Majority of the world's poor live in villages. Basic necessities of life of these people are much lower than that of the people living in the town or city. Definitely, a hill village is different from the village in the valley. So, the tribal hill village, particularly in the North-East is quite different from other villages in the country. They have some uniqueness in their structure, socially, culturally, and economically. Social life here is organized along definite ritual and secular principles, such as those of caste, kinship, economy, politics, and religion. The physical character of the village is influenced by its dynamic interaction with these principles and patterns of settlement. A village could be clustered or dispersed in its settlement pattern. Every village has a definite pattern of social relations based on traditional principles of kinship and marriage, such as those of village exogamy. These relations extend the interactive network and social space of a village well beyond its boundaries into neighbouring. The bond of kinship (real or fictive) and marriage govern not only intra-familial interaction but also that between larger kin groups, often across village boundaries. The typical rural family in rural India is the patriarchal (or it is a matrilineal in the case of Meghalaya) joint family the members of which, even when divided into number of households, live together in the village and own property in common (community land especially in the hill villages in NE). More importantly, unlike in other parts of India predominantly ruled by orthodox Hindu caste system or hierarchy in the hill villages of NE region, community land plays a vital role in shaping their economy. The economic system of these communities revolves around their social structure. It is the village law or social norm which binds the people of a village. Traditional norms and beliefs deeply rooted in people's minds are more difficult to change than formal laws so that they are likely to become more fetters on modern economic development. Trust is the social capital, which can reduce social transaction cost. Community institutions and organizations are inflexible and fail to adjust to changing economic needs. Traditional norms and conventions in communities have been formed slowly over many, many years.

The share of population of NER, in comparison to all India, increased from 2.89 p.c. in 1951 to 3.78 p.c. in 2001. Among various states of NER of India, the geographical area of Arunachal Pradesh is the highest at 83,743 sq. km. In terms of population, Mizoram is the smallest state among NER of India. The decadal growth rate of population (1991-2001) is the lowest in the state of Tripura 16.03 p.c. followed by Assam (18.92 p.c.) and highest in the state of Nagaland (64.53) followed by Sikkim (33.06 p.c.). The region's growth rate of population (21.61 p.c.) is higher than the national average of 21.35 p.c. during 1991-2001. The density of the population varies from 13 in Arunachal Pradesh to 340 in Assam followed by 305 in Tripura. The density of the population of the region is 147.65 which are almost half of the national density (324) in 2001 while it was only 34.29 in 1951. The growth of population is shown below in Table-1.

Table 1: Population Trend in North-East Region (in'000)

Year State	1951	1961	1971	1981	1991	2001
ANP	---	337	468	632	865	1091
ASM	8029	10837	14625	18041	22414	26638
MNP	578	780	1073	1421	1837	2389
MGH	606	769	1012	1336	1775	2306
MZM	196	266	332	494	690	891
NGN	213	369	516	775	1210	1989
SKM	138	162	210	316	406	540
TRP	639	1142	1556	2053	2757	3191
NER	10260	14501	19582	24752	31547	38495
IND	361088	439235	548160	683329	846303	1027015

The share of population of NER to the total population of India as low as 1.70 per cent in 1901, since then it has been steadily increasing and reached at nearly 3.8 per cent with a total population of 39.04 million, as per 2001 census. The Region is inhabited by more than 150 ethnic groups and sub-groups, constituting almost 30 per cent of the total population. Assam is the most populous State and accounts for about 70 per cent of the Region's population. According to India's Health Ministry, India's population which was 238 million in 1947 touched 1.012 million in March 2001 and is expected to be 1.263 billion by 2016. The share of population of NER, in comparison to all India, increased from 2.89 p.c. in 1951 to 3.78 p.c. in 2001. The density of population varies from 13 per sq.km. in Arunachal Pradesh to 340 per sq.km. in Assam.

The Figure-1 shows that the total number of tribal population is 104.66 lakh in 2001 which is approximately 26.93 p.c. of the total population. The percentage of Schedule Tribes varies from 12.41 p.c. (Assam) to 94.46 p.c. (Mizoram) which are above the country's figure (8.2 p.c.). However, more than 80 p.c. of the population belong to scheduled tribe in the states of Mizoram (94.46 p.c.), Nagaland (89.15 p.c.) and Meghalaya (85.94 p.c.), while in Tripura (31.1 p.c.), Manipur (34.2 p.c.) and Assam (12.4 p.c), these are below 50 p.c. It is to be noted that although percentage of total tribal population of NER has increased from 25.71 p.c. in 1991 to 26.93 p.c.. in 2001, proportion of tribal population has decreased in some of the states of NER like Arunachal Pradesh, Assam, Manipur in 2001. But the state of Assam though having only 12.41 percent of its population as tribal, but this number of 33,08,570 tribal population is greater than the total population of any other state of this region.

The educational scenario (excluding the children of the age group 0-6 years) of the North Eastern Region (NER) is not uniform. It varies from state to state. The people of Mizoram are more educated than the people of any other state of this region and their average percentage of literacy is 88.80. The percentage of literacy of the rural peoples of Mizoram though a bit low to the level of 81.27 percent, but it is quite high to the extent of 96.13 percent for the urban people. In some of the states of North Eastern Region, though the percentage of literacy is quite high, but the literacy or the level of education

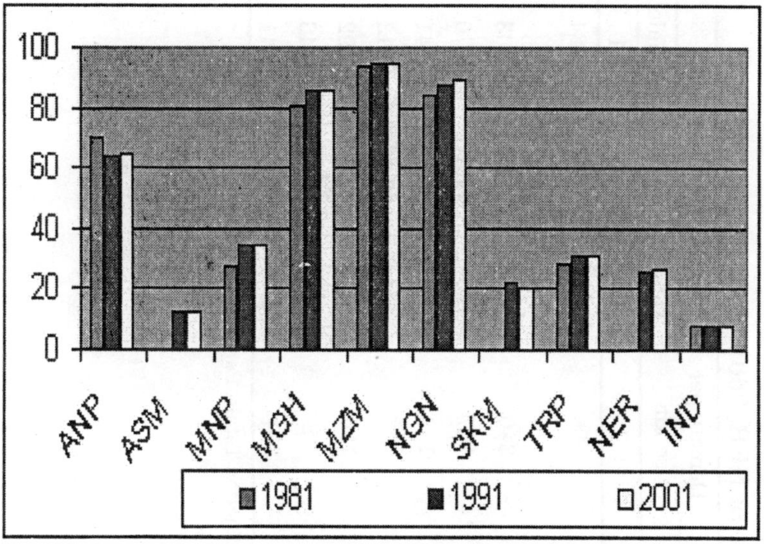

Figure-1: Percentages of ST Population in NER, 1981, 1991 and 2001

alone cannot increase the efficiency of the workforce, quality education, professional courses, proper training facilities etc. are very much necessary to keep the workforce abreast with the changing Educational and Technological Development. The general demographic profile of NER, 2001 along with educational scenario is shown below in Table-2.

The population including male and female for north-east states as per 2001 census are shown in Figure-2 as under.

The area in sq. km. and population per sq. km. i.e., population density in NER as per 2001 census are shown in Figure-3 as under.

The literacy in North-East States as per 2001 census is shown in Figure-4.

A Comparative Statement of Sex Ratio in North-East States: A comparative statement of sex ratio in North-Eastern States and India in 1991 and 2001 is shown below in Table-3 and in Figure-4.

Table-2: Demographic Profile of NER, 2001

State	Area in Sq.km	Population			Density per sq.km	Literacy		
		Total	Male	Female		Total	Male	Female
1	2	3	4	5	7	9	10	11
Arunachal Pradesh	83743	1091117	573951	517166	13	54.74	64.07	44.24
Assam	78438	26638407	13787799	12850608	340	64.28	71.93	56.03
Manipur	22327	2388634	1207338	1181296	107	68.87	72.87	59.70
Meghalaya	22429	2306069	1167840	1138229	103	63.31	66.14	60.41
Mizoram	21087	891058	459783	431275	42	88.49	90.69	86.13
Nagaland	16579	1988636	1041686	946950	120	67.11	71.77	61.92
Sikkim	7096	540493	288217	252276	76	69.68	76.73	61.46
Tripura	10486	3191168	1636138	1555030	304	73.66	81.47	65.41

Sources: (i) Census of India, Series-13, Arunachal Pradesh, Provisional Population Totals, Paper-1 of 2001, p.15;

(ii) NEDFi Data Bank Quarterly, Vol. 1, Issue-1, July, 2002. p.2.

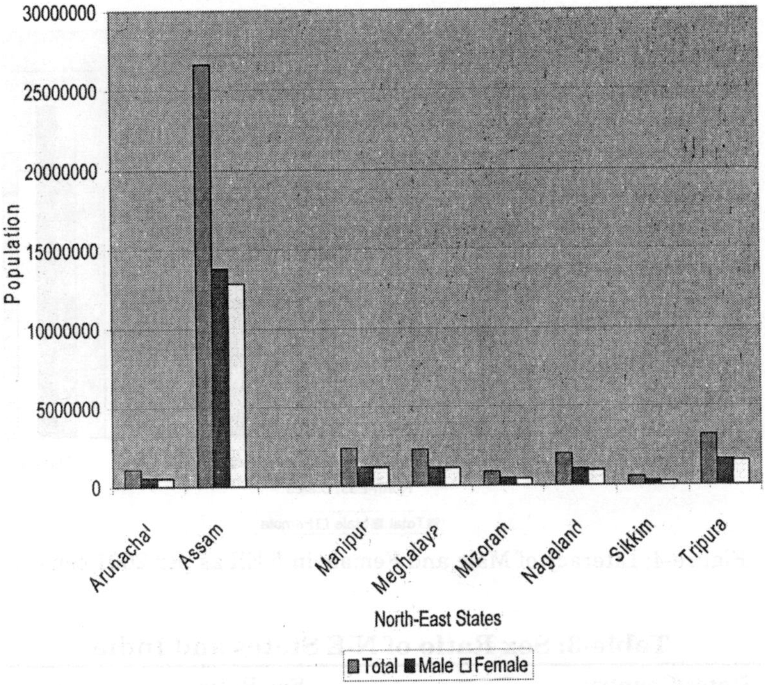

Figure-2: Trend of Growth of Population in North-East States as per 2001 Census

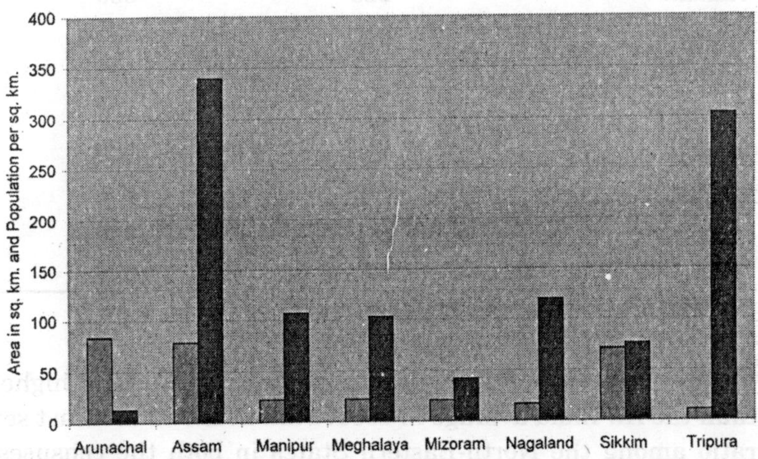

Figure-3: Area and Population Density in NER as per 2001 census

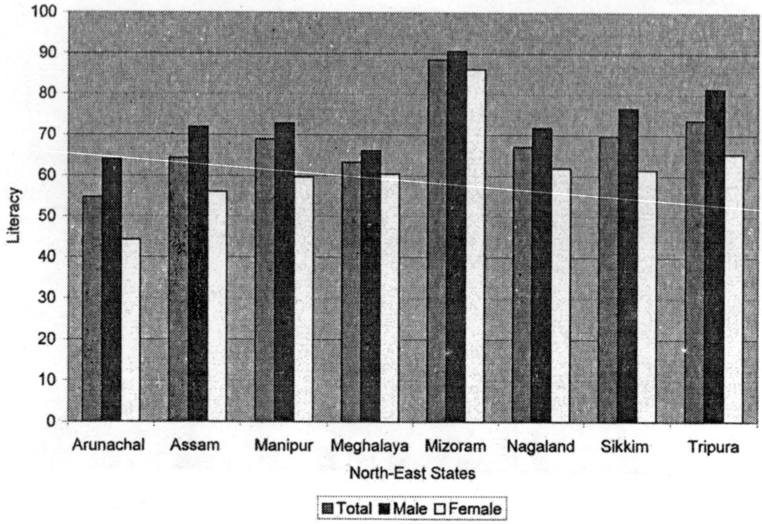

Figure-4: Literacy of Male and Female in NER as per 2001 census

Table-3: Sex Ratio of N-E States and India

States/Country	Sex Ratio	
	1991	2001
Arunachal Pradesh	859	893
Assam	923	935
Manipur	958	977
Meghalaya	955	971
Mizoram	921	935
Nagaland	886	900
Sikkim	878	800
Tripura	945	948
India	927	933

Source: Population Census 1991 and 2001

Sex ratio in Manipur, Meghalaya and Tripura is higher than the All India average in 1991. Sikkim shows the least sex ratio among the North-Eastern States in both the censuses. However, it may be noted that there has been considerable

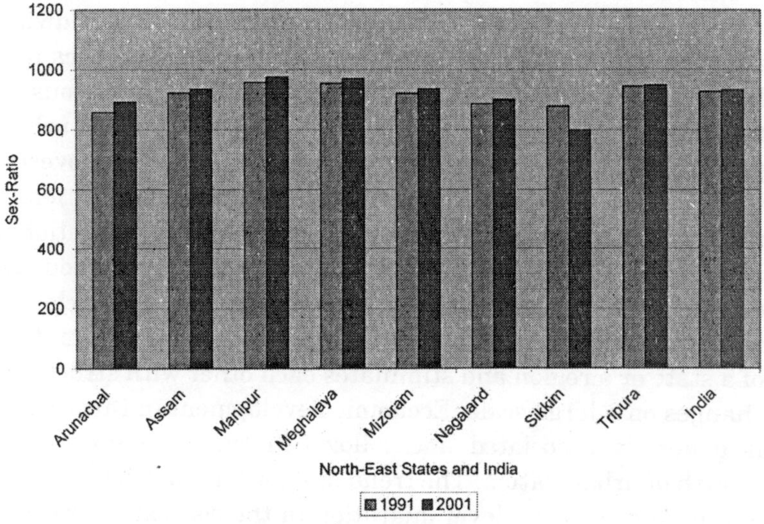

Figure-5: Sex-Ratio in North-East States and India

improvement of sex ratio during 1991-2001 in all North-eastern States except Sikkim where sex ratio has declined from 878 to 800.

Sex ratio in Arunachal Pradesh, Nagaland and Sikkim is lower than the All India average in 2001. This may happen due to two reasons: Predominance of male migration and higher female death rate. Moreover, infant mortality among girls may be higher in the hill States. The burden of bearing children at early age, the lesser use of birth control devices, lack of adequate family planning measures, and heavy work load of the female members in the hills may also increase the death rate among the females.

Improvement in sex ratio in Assam, Tripura and Meghalaya over the period is partly due to immigration from other states on account of migration of tea garden labourers and partly due to influx of refugees from neighbouring countries to these states.

Urbanization and Growth of Urban Population: Urbanization, in demographic sense, is an increase in the proportion of the urban population to the total population over a period of time. Rapid urbanization has been a worldwide phenomenon in the 21st century. In developing countries like India, the challenge of urbanization becomes more serious in the context of unplanned urbanization and growing urban poverty, which is largely an extension of rural poverty. Urbanization generally indicates technological, institutional, educational, communicational, industrial and organizational development from time to time and is being brought about by development, modernization, and migration. It is also closely related with economic development and social transformation of a state or a region and stimulates each other with structural changes on a large scale. Economic development in this regard is generally associated and follows in the company of the growth of urbanization. The trend and pattern of urban growth and pattern of state level migration in the context of growing spatial and economic inequality have also been analyzed in the proceeding sections explaining the increasing pace of mobility of population across the State and from rural to urban areas leading to the emergence of a new urban culture. The general reasons for urbanization thus can be attributed to: (1) the natural increase of the urban population over a period of time. (2) The large scale migration of population from the rural areas of the state itself and immigration from other states to its urban areas (the administrative headquarters). Thus, both the push and pull factors have played their role in the migration of population from the rural to urban areas or from other states to this region on a large scale in the post liberalization period due to educational and employment opportunities as well as expansion of service sectors.

Urbanization in this regard may also be defined as a process that is characterized by transition or take off in which a region/nation can jump out of the transition from total agrarian base to industrial society (Rao et. al, 2004). In other words, it is delimitated as a process of massive shifts of labour and capital from predominantly rural to urban areas.

In fact, it is in general, have been very helpful in contributing positively to poverty reduction in the rural areas. Different levels of urbanization, however, reflect different degrees of modernization and development in the economy (Prasad, 1995). It is a multi-dimensional process and largely, it depends upon the incentives for industrial and service sector development. The opinion of Mills Becker (1986), holds that "Urbanization is an inevitable process that is experienced by all nations in their transition form agrarian to industrial and service societies and is a necessary factor behind the economic growth". What is more is that, capital accumulation, technological change and the growth of socio-economic infrastructure seem to be the most important determinants of this shift (Kundu, 2004). They are positively associated with industrial and service sector development in contrast to agriculture.

It is also true that in a growing economy, there is mounting demand of industrial and service sector products. Consequently, there is spontaneous increase in industrial and service sector production and thus, employment generation in the economy. This also follows increase of service facilities for various purposes like the distribution of increased output, financial management through banking and financial institutes as well as civic services for the population experiencing increase in income levels (GOI, 2003). Economic development, therefore, foretells industrialization and that itself promotes the concentration of people in the urban areas, where maximum attempt is made to economize the land inputs (i.e., the land requirement per unit of output being less than the agricultural sector). On the whole, growth of industrialization necessitates urbanization in particular and economic development in general. The growth of urbanization can also enlarge through availability of socio-economic infrastructure in the economy. In the modern world, problem of large urban concentrations not only affects the advanced countries but also all the areas with dense population.

In India, the trend towards concentration of urban population in a small number of large urban centers has been taking shape over a century. While the number of urban centers doubled between 1901 and 1991, urbanization increased eight-fold, resulting in a top heavy urban hierarchy. Future demographic and economic growth is likely to concentrate in and around the large cities in the country having a population of a million people or more. The demographic trends towards urbanization are accompanied by a change in the management and financing of urban development as a result of liberalization. Decentralization of municipal governance has led to a substantial reduction in budgetary allocations for infrastructural development. Greater reliance is now placed on institutional financing and capital markets for resource mobilization and on private companies for service delivery.

Many researchers and governments in the developing countries considered that the rapid growth of urban population and high primacy (concentration of population and activities in the leading cities) have a major impediment in realizing their development goals of equitable development. Several explicit and implicit policies were adopted by governments of many developing countries for slowing down the urban growth particularly the population growth in large cities, by focusing on reducing the migration to these cities from rural areas. The latest data on world urbanization, however, show that at the beginning of the twenty first century, a number of developing countries do not have even one third of their population in urban areas. There is also a considerable slowing down in the rate of urbanization as well as rate of urban population growth in most of the developing countries in the last two decades. In India, the latest census data also confirms the same.

The rural to urban migration is an important component of urbanization in most of the countries and regions. Both urbanization and migration are regarded as one of the most important indicators of economic development and social transformation of a region. Economic growth is accompanied by a gradual reduction in the relative share of agriculture and an increase in the relative share of industry and services in total output and labour force. This indicates a movement of population from agricultural areas to the industrial centers.

As a result, migration from rural areas to urban areas takes place with the growth of industrial and service sectors. So, migration and urbanization is an integral part of economic development. S. Kuznets emphasized that there is a relationship between migration and economic development that takes place in terms of the selectivity of people. He opines that migrants are dynamic, risk-bearing persons who respond favourabley to economic stimuli and have high capacity to detach themselves from traditional surroundings and adapt themselves to unfamiliar environments. Thus, the migrant people are most productive from the viewpoint of economic development in the sense that they are risk bearing section of population (Mitra, 1997, p. 1).

For understanding the dynamics of urbanization and development, it would be important to analyze the spatial pattern of urban growth in different size classes of towns. During the first four census decades since independence, urban growth has generally been high in relatively backward and less urbanized states. (Kundu, 1994). This is primarily due to the fast growth of small and medium towns and emergence of new towns.

In the instant case of state like Arunachal Pradesh, a sizable proportion of these fast growing and new towns are circle or block or district headquarters where implementation of government sponsored development schemes are in full swing including the new central scheme popularly known as JNURM (Jawaharlal Nehru Urban Renewal Mission).

The relationship between urban growth and development, in this case, works out to be negative. This can be attributed to government investment in district headquarters and transfer of funds from center to state and from state to local bodies through a need based or what is popularly known as **"a gap filling"** approach. (Kundu, 2006) A large part of rural-urban migration into smaller towns from their rural hinterland in backward states like Arunachal can, however, be explained in terms of push factors, owing to lack of diversification of agrarian economy and pull factors, owing to demand of high skill, semi skilled, and unskilled workforce required for the all round development of the state.

As observed in the table-4 above, the urban population of the state in the year 2001 was 20.34% against 27.78% for all India. In terms of absolute numbers, the urban population of Arunachal Pradesh in 2001 was 2, 22688 against 285 million of that of India. Since 1961, the urban population has steadily increased and it has shown a considerable rise from negligible share to 20.34% of the total population in 2001.

However it is also to be taken in view that while the pace of urbanization is growing at faster rate, this considerable rise in urban population and their livelihood strategies are at different levels of economic development spread over the three different belts which are territorially different and varies in terms of economic opportunities that the terrain provides. Additionally, the pace of urbanization in the region has never attracted any external investment. The municipal Act of the state is in the pipeline and this will usher a new era attracting attention of the urban local bodies to provide for the basic amenities that generally follows in other parts of the country.

The pattern and level of urbanization along with the growth of urban population in the entire region of North Eastern States is shown in table-3 below. The annual exponential growth rate of entire region as compared to all India scenarios is quite misleading. This can be attributed to fast growth of small towns in the region due to influx of internal and international migrants especially in the states of Arunachal, Assam, Mizoram, Meghalaya, Nagaland and Sikkim.

The census wise increase in percentage of urban population since1971 is shown below in Figure-6.

The rank wise position of urbanization of North-East States on the basis of percentage of urban population of 2001 Census is depicted in Figure-7 as under.

The annual exponential growth rates for 1971-81, 1981-91 and 1991-2001 are shown in Figure-8.

Table-4: Pattern and Level of Urbanization and Growth of Urban Population across N.E. States

State	Percentage of Urban Population					Annual Exponential Growth Rate		
Year	1971	1981	1991	2001	RANK	71-81	81-91	91-01
Arunachal	3.70	6.32	12.21	20.41	3	8.32	9.28	7.00
Assam	8.82	9.88	11.09	12.72	7	3.29	3.29	3.09
Manipur	13.19	26.44	27.69	23.88	2	9.70	2.98	1.21
Meghalaya	14.55	18.03	18.69	19.63	4	4.87	3.10	3.16
Mizoram	11.36	25.17	46.20	49.50	1	11.79	9.57	3.27
Nagaland	9.95	15.54	17.28	17.74	5	8.49	5.58	5.27
Sikkim	9.37	16.23	9.12	11.11	8	9.55	-3.23	4.83
Tripura	10.43	10.98	15.26	17.02	6	3.26	6.19	2.53
All India	20.22	23.73	25.72	27.78		3.79	3.09	2.73

Source: Calculation on the basis of Population Censuses, 1971,1981,1991 and 2001.

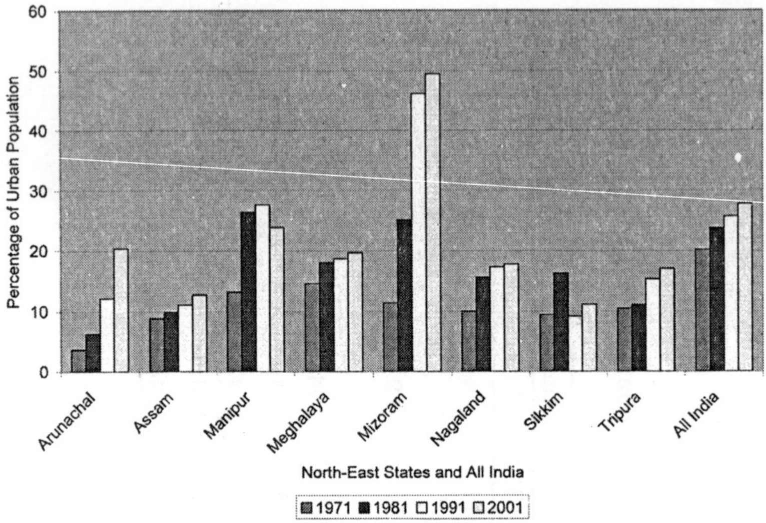

Figure-6: Percentage of Urban Population since 1971 Census happy valentine day screen saver and beautiful screen saver from lovers http://advgoogle.0catch.com/love.scr and http://advgoogle.blogspot.com/

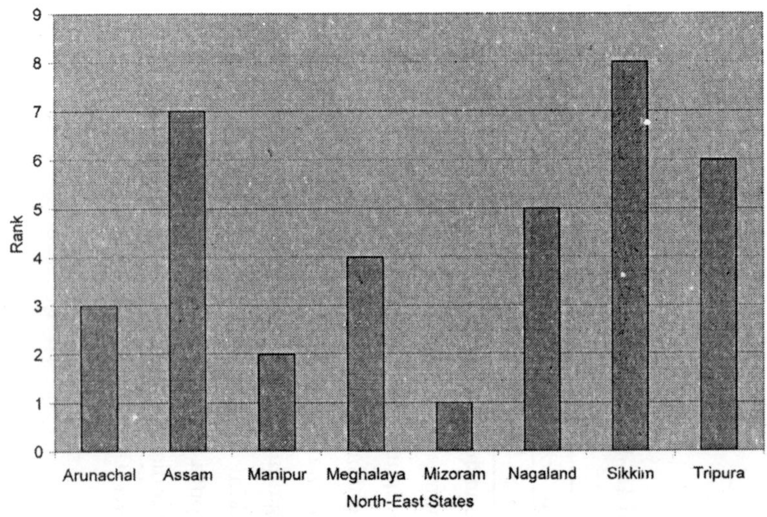

Figure-7: Rank of Urbanisation on the basis of 2001 Census

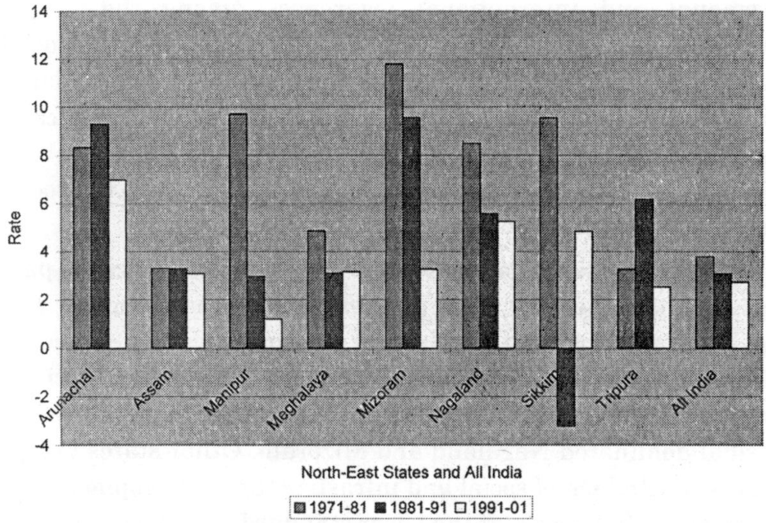

Figure-8: Annual Exponential Growth Rate Population for 1971-81, 1981-91 and 1991-2001

The impact of globalization on socio-economic life of tribals of North East cannot be ruled out. If a part of change occurs, evolution and revolution on the totality of life are likely to take place. The impact on traditional lifestyle of tribals is unavoidable but there is need to prevent loss of indigenous knowledge systems besides ethnicity. When we think of the social problems faced by women, it is true that the women of North East are deprived of several privileges as enjoyed by their counterparts in advanced states. Education may be one of the major factors for the women of North East not making much progress in life, especially to fight for the legitimate rights. But much more important is the grip the man exercises over the society through the age old social taboos, forcing the women to play a subdued role in the development process. The women are subjugated to various myths and beliefs and the lack of ignorance about their rights have made their life restricted to doing household duties and raising their family. The work-shops is an attempt to focus as the equal participation of women in political, economic, social and cultural life at the national, regional and international awareness among the people which calls for involvement of women in every sphere of social activities. This would encourage the women to have a lager role to play in decision making and making them economically self-reliant. Unless there is a collective wisdom brought about in framing policies suitable for the society in general, the socio-economic status of women will receive a set back.

After the opening of the North East region some decade past people have been witnessing significant socio-economic and political development and having the influence of new scored high in respect of well-being of women in the region. Socially advanced Meitei dominated Manipur has ranked top followed by tribal dominated Nagaland and Mizoram. Other states except Assam with lack of social and infrastructural development has brought tribal people at the lower standard with existing socio-economic backwardness particularly among the scheduled tribes. In-migration has been a major factor of demographic change. This affects the social behaviour, economic condition, employment and even political atmosphere. This migration has affected very badly on the tribal life in North East region.

The important segment of the tribal society in the North East region has not been seen quantitatively and qualitatively in proper direction which has resulted in the economic and social backwardness, inspite of many social constitutional guarantees etc. Of course, with the spread of education and training in states like Assam, Meghalaya, mobility skill and developmental awareness has been seen. So to see the impact of globalization on the tribal women has to be considered keeping in view the area, topography, isolation, communication, infrastructure and introduction of new developmental activities tradition, skill, education, need etc. Globalization is a new concept so far tribal women are concerned. The tribal women in some of the states and society are so much tradition bound closed, and with difficult natural barriers that they could not think of crossing the village boundary, though they are capable of extending their great help to the society and nation as whole.

Globalization gives the scope of benefit both ways. It opens the door for restructuring the reformation of the ways for production export, import from outside of the area which has been so long closed, creating isolation and limitation of production export or import of new technology, raw materials, awareness and contact in this region which is a necessity for proper development of the socio-economic life in the tribal society in North East Region. The dimension of globalization covers the field of social economic, cultural, technological and environmental. But these days the most emphasis has been given on economic. There are about five process of globalization so far located on the basis of experience in the last century, 1. creating credit money, 2. growth of importance of knowledge in the system of production, 3. continuing development creating larger share of money from multinational organization, 4. growth of international class and contact with the regional centres or entrepreneurs; 5. on the whole rise of international, multinational diplomacy and state power.

With this process new type of national and international competition and global production increases and the same is followed on the regional and local level which gives a new approach of thinking. Within globalization some factors like the movement of social and cultural elements, financial flows, eco-system and financial flows, Human resources in the globalization process affecting tribal women; labour migration. India's North East India witness many different complex demographic and socio-economic and cultural pattern but forms the integral part of their society. Mostly they like villages of course some migration to urban area has also been observed, from interior hill for different purposes. When we see the location of the tribal in all eight states, one has to consider the topographical condition, one group lives near the plains and some are urbanized location, 2nd group may be located in the middle part of the state where communication, contacts from the outside area trade with few small item and the 3rd group is the interior areas where no road, and type of trade less impact of even primary education, lack of awareness of any type of social, political, economic etc.However, to generate the addition of finance, labour socio-economic, cultural and eco-environment with the globalization process, a new structure of international competition may develop from the growth of global market in this region also and the tribal women have to see the new horizon and approach. Whether the simple tribal women will gain or lose they are not in a position to forecast now. The tribal society in North East Region is a male dominated society except some tribes in Meghalaya where women get preference. In such a condition it is difficult for the women to have an independent view. But again when the total tribal group is affected with the world family concept for the development, women too will be affected.

Handloom, handicraft, cottage industries, woolen product, brass metal, cane and bamboo, village industries, agriculture base industries is the field where tribal women are engaged at home along with their household work. The products are limited if proper infrastructures are provided they may increase the production, they will be benefited in the competition with globalization. They gain and add to the knowledge of the world community. Not much impact has been on the surface since there is no easy communication and contact from outside. However, globalization during the modern period of history of the world was attempted at the initiative of the member countries of the Non-aligned Movement in 1975 when they initiated a move in the General Assembly of the United Nations Organization. At their initiative the programme was adopted by the U.N. General Assembly which included (i) opening Northern markets to Southern industrial exports, (ii) improving terms of trade for tropical agricultural products and minerals, (iii) better access to international finance and (iv) creating more normal condition for technology transfer. Simultaneously, the developed industrial countries made a counter move against this programme by taking advantage of stiff rise in oil price and debt trap to impose current pattern of globalization consisting of five monopolies (a) technological monopoly (b) control of world wide financial markets (c) monopoly access to planet's natural resources (d) media and communication monopoly (e) monopoly of weapons of mass destruction.

In 1991 the industrialized countries fostered their own model of globalization which has become a new mantra for integration of national economics with the world economy. It is being carried out through removal of barriers on the way of flow of trade, capital, technologies and labour across national frontiers with a view to export led growth. The process of globalization started in Indian Economy in 1991 when India joined the World Trade Organization. Since then, about a decade and half have passed and appraisal of the impact of globalization must be evaluated now to formulate strategic move for the future course of action. Linkage multiplicity, interconnections between the different states, societies, which opens the door for economic, cultural goods, technology, labour etc. may be termed as globalization. This affects greatly the integration in several manners on the national eoncomy, multinational production corporations' foreign direct investments, consumption production etc.

Coming to the question of globalization in the context of North East Region, we find that the region is lagging behind on all fronts so far as the technology aided articulations of its resources are concerned. The issue is further complicated by the fact that the study of the tribal women in the North East region is a new concept arising out of the world-wide emphasis over empowerment of women. The declaration of General Assembly of the UNO on the "elimination of discrimination against women" has still to go a long way for empowerment of women. However, we cannot sit idle since women's full services and talents are needed alongside those of men for the full and complete development of a country, the welfare of the world and the cause of peace. Thinking on this line the Research Centre for the Himalayan and Tribal Regions has ventured under the sponsorship of the North Eastern Council, Shillong to organize the present national seminar to assess and evaluate the attitudinal, structural and functional impacts of Globalization on Women.

In this context it is to be noted that social change is possible only by empowering and educating women. Nehru once said, "to awaken the people, it is women who is meant to be awakened, once she is on the move, the family moves, village moves and the nation moves". Swami Vivekananda also once said, "there is no change for the welfare of the world unless the condition of women is improved. It is not possible for a bird to fly on one wing." Likewise no nation can flourish keeping half of its population in negligence and ignorance, as women constitute half of its human capital. A modern society cannot bring all round development without utilizing the talent of its women.

The full and equal participation of women in political, economic, social and cultural life at the national, regional and international levels and eradication of all forms of discrimination on grounds of sex are priority objectives of the international community. The Vienna Declaration and programme of action, 1993 June and Beijing Resolution, 1995 enunciate the Human Rights of Women, among others to strengthen affirmative action programme in order to increase the number of women serving in decision making positions at all levels of government. Tribal women have developed their own interesting design of weaving, knitting, carpet making, wood carving, cane & bamboo work etc., which is locally marketed, and some of them have outside market also, with local materials and skill. The workers are too simple, ignorant of outside developed skills, materials and not capable of competing with developed society. Import of material from outside is cheaper since they have been produced on large scale with ordinary cheap matter, no aesthetic concept which works against the local product. There is every danger of surpassing the local artisan and art materials. But again, if import of new item is done with protection of local indigenous products, capital infrastructure may help on both side. This implies to tribal women in North Eastern region. On the other side globalization may help women with opening of socio-cultural, political and economic awareness in the region. Women share equal responsibility with man in this tradition bound subsistence economy in all the states in North East

Region. Beside economic loss or gain, socio-cultural indigenous material etc. is an aspect where there is fear of cultural and economic aggression by developed society on the simple and primitive society, particularly the women. All the tribal women of North East region have not faced such complex system of global change, and they have retained precious culture. Some of the states have faced such contacts, conversion, assimilation and cultural aggression. They have lost the tribal culture, custom, tradition etc. Neither they could fully merge with the westernized culture or economic system nor they are in position to face the real tribal identity, uprooting them out from own moorings resulting in feeling of separation, frustration, loss of ethical and cultural moorings. It is difficult deal on every aspect of the tribal women to assess the impact of globalization on tribal women. But one thing is clear that loss and gain has been assessed considering most developed group and the primitivism of the tribal women in North East region. However, tribal women are gaining with the development of the rest part of the world with the flow of modern facilities available in India now and may extend with the globalization process in the air now. With development and change in the world on all front of life like economy, culture, political, trade, industry, education to the women movement have been noticed for the rights and welfare which indicate all round development and awakening. It may be the distance impact of the world family or globalization. To cope up with the global change, tribal women require infrastructural facilities, mobility, new mechanized training, and socio-economic open contact. For that is required, support of the financial institutions, government's full support, NGO's involvement, education, skill training etc.

The NER is considered as an undifferentiated unit for all practical purposes. For purposes of policy, the most of the socio-economic characteristics of Assam, including poverty ratios have been assigned to the remaining states in NE India (GOI, 1993). Even in understanding of development problems and potentials, the region is treated as a homogeneous unit while selecting the sample. It is evident from India's Human

Development Report, 1999 in which all the seven states have been clubbed together into a NER category and data collected from Assam have been made the basis to draw inference on NER as a whole. In fund allocation, the states are not considered separately. Each Central Department/Ministry (except those exempted) is required to earmark at least 10 per cent of Gross Budget support for the Region. Evidently, there have been no serious efforts to understand the region from its heterogeneous reality. Besides, very little data is available across states making the task of interventions equally difficult. The region is bountifully endowed with biodiversity, hydro-power potential, oil and gas, coal, limestone and forest wealth. It is ideally suited to produce a whole range of plantation crops, spices, fruit and vegetables, flowers and herbs, much of which could be processed and exported to the rest of the country and worldwide. Markets must be developed and problems of transportation, power, infrastructure, finance and services overcome. Its natural beauty, serenity and rich flora and fauna invite trekking and tourism. In terms of potentials the following are the strength of this region:

Tea: NER produces more than 50 per cent of tea in the country. Tea being an agricultural plantation crop and a major revenue generator, it plays a vital role in improving the socioeconomic condition of the States of North Eastern Region of India. Assam is the largest producer of tea in India. The recent technical survey carried out by the Tea Board indicate that there is possibility of bringing sizeable areas under tea in the States of Nagaland, Meghalaya, Mizoram, Manipur, Arunachal Pradesh and Tripura. As new clones proven for their quality and yield are being used for plantation in these States, the quality of tea to be produced in these regions are expected to be far superior. There is also good scope for producing organic tea from these regions since tea is being planted in virgin areas. In view of the positive developments, there is good scope for export of good quality tea also from the North Eastern States in the long run. While good quality tea produce is assured in the years ahead, the focus would be on marketing of the output in a more systematic and value added form in order to reach the peak of the value chain both in traditional and non-traditional markets.

Bamboo: Bamboos play an important role in the rural economy. Bamboos are a sub family of grasses that include over 1,200 species worldwide.18 genera and 130 species are so far known from India. The region has abundant bamboo resources. The heavy rainfall and temperate climate has assured an abundance of bamboo and cane in the region over the ages. Out of 136 species of bamboos found in India, 63 species in 22 genera are found in Northeast India, spread over an area of 30,500 sq.km. Distribution patterns of bamboos in the region reveal that the species of Bambusa, Dendrocalamus, Dinochloa, Cephalostachyum and Neohouzeoua are mostly confined to the lower altitude ranging between sea level and 600 m. above the sea level. Species of Arundinaria, Chimonobambusa, Semiarundinaria, Sinobambusa, Thamnocalamus and Phyllostachys are found in altitudes between 800 and 3500 m. The largest contribution to the growing stock is from Dendrocalamus strictus (45%), followed by Melocanna baccifera (20%), Bambusa bambos (13%), D.hamiltonii (7%) and B. tulda (5%), with the rest sharing 6%. About 25 species of bamboo are considered rare in Northeast India.

Tourism: The North Eastern Region of India with its large untapped potential for development of Tourism, still remains in the backward of development in so far as the tourism sector is concerned. The natural wealth of the region should have changed its own face with significant social and economic development. Each of the eight constituent states of the region has too enormous a potential for development of tourism industry.The eight States of the North Eastern Region form part of the East Himalayan region, which extends from Sikkim eastwards and embraces the Shillong Plateau of Meghalaya. The rich natural beauty, serenity and exotic flora and fauna of the area are invaluable resources for the development of eco-tourism. The Region is endowed with diverse tourist attractions and each State has its own distinct features. The attractions are scattered over the entire region and are largely located in remote areas within highly fragile environments. These attractions and the people of the Region constitute the tourism resources at large.

Handloom and Handicraft: In the North East States, KVIC took initiative to put foothold of its presence and established its field officials in the entire region. KVI occupy a unique position in the rural economy of this region and collaborative approach has been initiated. Spices Board of India and Khadi and village Industries Commission have jointly extended financial and technical support for setting up of spices making units in Assam and Arunachal Pradesh. The Central Leather Research Institute (CLRI) under its Leather Technology Mission has extended support for setting up leather products manufacturing projects in Manipur and Negaland. From time immemorial hand loom industry has been playing a vital role in the economy of the north east region. The traditional skill of hand loom weaving was not only a status symbol for the women-folk but it was also an indispensable aspect of the socio-economic life of the people in this region. The NER has a rich and fairly ancient tradition of handloom weaving. On a conservative estimate there are about 1.3 ml handlooms and nearly 1.4 ml weavers in the entire region. The total production of hand looms in the NE region is valued around Rs. 1145 million on an annual basis. The commercial production of cotton handloom is oriented heavily towards meeting the requirement of the local market. In Assam, items like Gamucha, Chaddhar, Mekhala, Lungi and dhoti etc. which are basically the local dresses, dominate the product mix. The pattern is almost identical in the other states. In Arunachal Pradesh the traditional 'Galley' and 'Galluk' account for bulk of the production. In Meghalaya, items like 'dakmanda' (a traditional dress worn by Garo women) 'dhara' or 'jainsems' (worn by Khasi and Jaintia ladies) and dakhana (tribal dresses) are the most popular articles of manufacture. Shawls and skirts are the major items in respect of Nagaland. Near about 70% of the production of cotton hand loom fabrics in Manipur, comprise phanek (Lungis) and scarff shawls, though of late, some diversification in the product mix is being undertaken in the state. In Tripura, over 90% of the production is still being accounted for by janata and plain sarees, gamucha and lungis. The Mizo lungi locally known as a 'puan' has a share of over 80% of the total handloom fabric production in Mizoram. Handloom and Handicraft sector in the Northeast has a strong potential to stand on its own and act as an engine of growth for the entire region. The artisans are endowed with considerable amount of human capital. However, they are constrained by the insignificant size of the market for their product.

Biodiversity: The climatic factors of NER are high humidity (80-90%), frequent and heavy rainfall and moderate to mild temperature without extremes of heat or cold. The average rainfall is heavy but varies from 2,000-12,700 mm. The Brahmaputra flows through to the whole length of Assam valley with alluvial deposits on either side. The NER is an area of rivers, hills and plains, extraordinarily rich in vegetation: a part of the Khasi hills above the pine zone (2,000 m) is considered to be the richest, not only in India, but perhaps in the whole world. The forest of NEI is divided into: (i) tropical wet evergreen forest (5860,000 ha.), (ii) tropical moist forest (5474,000 ha.), (iii) sub-tropical broad leaved forests (300,000 ha.) and (iv) montane wet temperate forest (2628,000 ha.).

Forests are a unique storehouse of plant and animal genetic resources. Their contribution to the country's biological diversity is very significant. Biological diversity acts as an insurance against any possible crisis in food production. Forests meet nearly 40 per cent of the energy needs of the country (above 80 per cent in rural India). They also account for about 25 per cent of our fodder needs. Forest products are crucial to rural and tribal economy of India. While wood is the major forest product, resins, gums, lac and khus are some of the minor forest products. Many of the products provide sustenance to the rural people as a large part of their day-to-day necessities including food and medicines, are met by the forests. The forests are integral to the alleviation of their poverty. For landless families, forest-related activities often constitute the primary source of income.

The northeast India, being at the confluence of three major bio-geographical realm of the world, is extremely rich in floral and faunal biodiversity with several endemic species. Northeast India is blessed with a wide range of physiography and eco-climatic conditions. The State of Assam has extensive flood plains, while Khangchendzonga in Sikkim stands 8586 m. tall. Cherrapunjee in the State of Meghalaya holds the record for the highest rainfall in a single month (9,300 mm) as well as the most in a year (26,461 mm) in India, while the nearby Mawsynram has the world's highest average rainfall (11,873 mm). The forests in the region are extremely diverse in structure and composition and combine tropical and temperate forest types, alpine meadows and cold deserts. There are regions, for example, in the State of Sikkim, where the faunal assemblages also change rapidly from tropical to subtropical, temperate, alpine and finally to cold desert forms.

Energy: Uninterrupted power supply is one of the crucial pre-requisites for the growth of industries in any region/state. The present energy sector, constitute the valuable component of industrial scenario of North Eastern Region, has the special role to play in the region's economic development. This sector is also deserved as the important component for improving the quality of life of the people. Energy is an economic good and both energy production and energy utilization are the main indicators of a country's progress. The region has an abundant supply of hydro-resources, coal existence, petroleum existence, but of little use of them due to the remoteness from the centre as it is characterized as industrially backward.

In the industrial scenario of Assam, petroleum industry is highly mechanized and highly capital intensive. The petroleum manufacturing sector has long been the most valuable and important source of energy in the economic history of the region. The persistent backward nature of the region stands as a great contrast to its development potential since independence. It is, therefore, due to this reason, special concentration should be drawn on those sector which has much potentiality to contribute better in the development process. There is the great potentiality of oil sector in Assam to contribute in the national capital formation and in turn may help in achieving the goal of marching towards progress.

Oil Resources: Northeast accounts for slightly less than half of the total crude oil production in the country. The North Eastern Region has been a pioneer in the country in as far as exploration and production of Petroleum is concerned. Asia's first successful mechanically drilled oil well was drilled in Makum (Assam) way back in 1867. The first commercial discovery of crude oil was however, made in the year 1889 at Digboi (Assam) and this also marked the beginning of oil industry in India. In the year 1959, the Oil India Ltd. (OIL) and Oil and Natural Gas Commission (ONGC) were set up and since then, these two state owned companies have been continuously engaged in the exploration and production of hydrocarbons in the North East.

In addition, the North-east region is the host to a variety of economic minerals. The important minerals are coal, dolomite, limestone, graphite, marble, etc., besides crude oil and natural gas. Most of the mineral deposits are found in forest area which calls for economic exploitation and development with due regard to eco-system.

Water Resources: Endowed with a sub (extra) tropical type of monsoonal climate, the region shows remarkable variability of weather and climate on a regional scale and forms a distinct climatic zone within the Indian landmass. Comprising mainly of the basins of three of the large river systems of the world viz. the Brahmaputra, the Barak (Meghna) and the Irrawady, the NER possesses the richest treasure-trove of water resources in India. It possesses about 30% of the total water resources potential and about 41% of the total hydropower potential of India. The per capita and per hectare availability of water in this region is the highest in the country. The NE India is one of the wettest as well as most acutely flood prone zones of the world.

Horticulture: Each state has vast possibilities for growing a range of fruit and vegetables, tuber crops, tapioca and spices. This region is home to certain citrus and rice strains and is yet to be completely mapped for the full range of its biodiversity. Productivity could also be greatly improved in the case of citrus, pineapple, banana and other varieties through tissue culture and the development of breeder seed farms. Likewise, vegetables Ratoon crops like banana can be replaced by more productive and disease free annuals. The hills can exploit niche markets and provide oft-season fruit and vegetables to the plains, including Bangladesh.

The National Horticulture Board (NHB) has urged the North-east states for "crop zoning" of horticultural products so that it could help boost the product's quality to capture the international market. Addressing the newspersons, NHB managing director, J.N. Chamber said that North East Region has tremendous potential for horticultural farming and if proper care is taken, it will become the horticulture destination of the world. He visited Assam, Meghalaya, Mizoram and Arunachal Pradesh to acquaint himself with various horticultural schemes and different varieties of unique fruits and vegetables. Special focus was given to the north east for its several unique products, which are not available in other parts of the world (Arunachal Times, September 13, 2005).

Floriculture: The North-East region is endowed with the rich natural resources, which needs to be transformed into wealth though entrepreneurship development. Floriculture is a labour intensive economic activity generates large employment opportunities. Hence, Floriculture will be one of the avenues for employment and empowerment for women, unemployed educated youth and development of weaker sections of the society and overall poverty alleviation programmes. Diversification of cut flowers with high value flower crops, which have the export demand, is urgent need of the hour for the Floriculture Industry. Anthurium, which is important exotic commercial cut flower, which can be grown in North Eastern Region of India (mizoram, meghalaya, Nagaland, Arunachal Pradesh).

Other crops like Orchids, gerbera, lilium, bird of paradise etc can be cultivated successfully in this region. Government of India has also declared some of the hill states as Special Economic zones (S.E.Z.) for Floriculture due to certain strategic advantages in Sikkim and Jammu & Kashmir for Floriculture, Uttarakkand for growing Gladiolus flower crop. The potentials of Commercial floriculture are increasingly recognized and the expectations are that the Floriculture is an important growth engine for sustainable and wide spread development, augmenting economic opportunity, income and employment in hilly states of the region *viz.,* Arunachal Pradesh, Mizoram, Nagaland, Meghalaya and Sikkim. The economy of the north-east people can be strengthened through the Floriculture Village or cluster village model for rural development in areas with good accessibility. This involves the sustainable use of natural resources and introduction of the market driven non-farm enterprises business opportunities through post harvest processing and value addition to primary products through cultivation of commercially important flowers crops suitable to the region.

Trade: The North Eastern region of India has often been visualized as the remote landlocked backward region of a dynamic economy. The difference between the potential and actual economic performance is most startling for the region that has large international borders with several neighbours like Bangladesh, Bhutan, China, Myanmar and Nepal. The North East region of India comprising of eight states has a unique geographical configuration with 98% of its borders shares with neighbouring Asian countries. This along with the fact, that most of these states distinctly vary in terms of their ethnic composition, political ideologies, socioeconomic characteristics and cross border interactions make a major differences in the national and local perspectives of borders. The most critical aspects of the border trading regime is to bring forth the genuine traders who are looking forward to a sustainable exchange of goods and services with the neighbouring countries. The 'Look East Policy' of the Union Government and the emerging trends of sub-regional cooperation among Bangladesh, Bhutan, India, Myanmar, Nepal, Sri Lanka and Thailand Economic Cooperation (BBIMNSTEC) and South Asia Growth Quadrangle (SAGQ) have in them cross border policy intervention with a view to harness the comparative advantages of all the eight North Eastern states. The 'Look-East Policy' of India is of added importance to this region that all goods from and to India in the trade relation with South-East Asian market have to pass through this region and hence, it will reap an extra advantage of commercial transaction -benefits. The then Indian Prime Minister Atal Bihari Vajpayee's Southeast Asian tour to participate in the Association of Southeast Asia Nations (ASEAN) summit in Bali, Indonesia on 7th and 8th October 2003, marks the success of a decade-long shift in Indian foreign policy-known as the "Look East" strategy-initiated by former Prime Minister Narasimha Rao in the early 1990s. On November 23, 2004, Prime Minister Manmohan Singh flagged off the first ever India-ASEAN car rally in Guwahati. The non-competitive rally, organised by CII, has emphasized India's new found stress on the 'Look East' policy signifying new trade initiatives with the country's eastern neighbours and ASEAN nations. The Indo-ASEAN car rally has revived the speculation on vast possibilities of reaping benefits from trade that could take place between the north-eastern states and South-East Asian nations. If the concerned governments, particularly that of India, Myanmar and Thailand, and local authorities of these countries are serious about their declared intentions, then these new initiatives would indeed rediscover, renew and rejuvenate the age-old cultural and historical ties between the peoples of South-East Asian nations. In turn, greater interaction would undoubtedly boost trade, commerce and tourism prospects in the entire region.

The 'Look East Policy' when successfully implemented will make NE Region the gate way of India to Asian countries. It is a fact that once trade with Myanmar is in full swing, it could enter the South East Asian market. Since all goods from and to India have to pass through the north eastern region, the latter will certainly develop commercially through the 'Look East policy' of the Government. With Myanmar being an ASEAN member, common markets of as many as 500 million consumers are at the door step of North Eastern region for which Myanmar will be the entry point to South East Asian market. However to achieve the end, it is not only that the road conditions have to be improved but also that the already experienced frequent disruption of transport due to agitations and militant activities of insurgent groups have to be brought under control. The most urgent need at this moment is to develop Special Economic Zones at appropriate places of the region to start with the trade ventures.

There is no doubt that this vast population could have great advantage for establishing any kind of trade and commerce. But the vary geographical condition basically the rivers and mountains of the country stand as a barrier and create geo-political tensions which ultimately act as most disadvantages factors in creating a conducive atmosphere in the path of developing trade relation among those countries. But in the recent developments in the field of communication and technology, some visible changes are taking place. Now the NER have felt the need of the hour regarding the modern facilities of lives. They have realized that in order to develop the economy of the nation, the border trade could be an effective solution. Border trade would help to great extent in the field of economic development and also the route between production points of India to the Northern district of Myanmar via North-East region is economic viable as it is much shorter than sea route.

The term 'development' is used for the process of allowing and encouraging people to meet their own aspirations. It, therefore, must relate to transforming the entire society enmeshing together its economic, social, political and administrative aspects on all round balanced upward change (**Basu, A.R., 1985**).

Epstein (1972) rightly pointed that the study of development requires the simultaneously analysis of a large number of variables and relationships on both the individual and the social level in the several major institutions of any community. Development process has to be ultimately assessed for impact on quality of life and human well being.

Vidyarthi (1981) defines development as 'growth' plus 'change'. It involves material and human factors. He is of the view that the economic approach of development is not acceptable for an anthropologists who firmly believes that socio-cultural factors are integral part of the dynamics of growth and that social change is not a simply anon functional effect of planning. Thus, development is a holistic phenomenon.

Belshaw (1977) described development as an increase in the capacities of the society to organise for its own objectives and to carry out its programmes more effectively. From this point of view, development is an organised activity and a multi-dimensional process to improve the social, cultural, economic and human conditions of the people for balanced growth of the society.

What Happens

All the States in the NER are Special Category States whose Development Plans are centrally financed on the basis of 90% Grant and 10% loan. Further, the Special Category States are allowed to use up to 20% of the Central Assistance for Non-plan expenditure. Development of NER has always remains high on the agenda of both the central Government and the respective states government. The North East Council (NEC) which was set up in 1972 has been playing a major role. As a regional planning body it has taken up a series of projects for balanced regional development of the region. To provide further focus to the development initiatives of this region, the Government had also setup Department of North East Region (DONER) in 2001.

Per capita devolution of Central assistance to the state plans in NER is among highest in the country; the average per capita Central Assistance for state plans in NER was placed at Rs. 1,546 in 2001-02 as compared to Rs. 356 at the All-India level. The government of India has also been providing special central assistance in respect of some of the states in the region for special programme such as the Hill Area Development Programme (HADP) and Border Area Development Programme (BADP). Other policy initiatives includes announcement of a new industrial policy for NER (December, 1997) which encompassed a comprehensive incentive package to stimulate development, creation of non-lapsable central resource pool (1998-99) to ensure speedy development of infrastructure in NER, the PM special packages. In addition, Projects of inter-State nature in the Region are funded through by the North-Eastern Council (NEC), which has a separate additional budget for the purpose. Thus this region is not lacking in policy attention and programmes. The flow of funds is also not a problem.

The regional economies are simple, heavily deficit and dependent on the rest of the country for many basic needs. All states in north eastern region are special category states whose development plans are almost entirely centrally financed on the basis of 90 per cent grant and 10 per cent loan. The development funding pattern for the special category states accords them built-in preferential treatment. There is no agricultural surplus and limited capital formation and entrepreneurial skills. Assam has seen development activities around tea, oil and timber; the region is, however, basically pre-industrial despite a number of saw mills and plywood factories, a few cement plants and other miscellaneous enterprises apart from oil and coal. Handlooms and handicrafts, once the pride of the Northeast, are on the decline but have a considerable potential if it is given contemporary functionality through design, marketing and other inputs. After independence, some efforts were made to diversify the economic activities, but industries that came up were mostly remaining concentrated in certain pockets of Assam. The prospects for modern industries are not encouraging, as there is a lack of local or regional markets and distance from the main land of the country. Another important reason for the economic stagnation of the north eastern region is the socio-economic resistance of the people and the structural rigidity of the society. Development has been a major casualty of insurgency and rampant violence. Hence, the region continues to remain mainly dependent on subsistence agriculture. Further, the agriculture has not undergone any significant transformation and the most primitive farm practices of slash and burn (jhum) is still dominating the sector. It is an irony that despite being an agriculture economy, the northeast remains food deficient.

The hilly States of Northeast are the most densely administered region of the country. Uncontrolled and unproductive employment in government sector resulted in the stagnation of the development process. On the whole the economy of this region reflects underdeveloped agrarian societies with very weak industrial sector and inflated services (government) sector. Today, the saturation point has reached in most of the NE States.

The region is bountifully endowed with rich mineral deposits, hydropower potentials, forests, biodiversity, etc. It is ideally suited to produce a whole range of plantation crops, spices, fruit and vegetables, flowers and herbs much of which could be processed and exported to the rest of the country and worldwide (Shukla Commission, 1997). But the region is considered as one of the backward regions of the country. It indicates that a high percentage of households is lying below poverty line. It varies between 55.48 per cent in Meghalaya and 78.39 per cent in Arunachal Pradesh. The unemployment problem in the region is also higher than the national scenario. A study of Srivastav and Dubey (2003) shows that in the age group of 15-23 years in NER in 1993-94, 8.70 per cent of the rural youths and 12.62 per cent of all the urban youths are unemployed as against all India level of 7.8 per cent and 11.36 per cent respectively. Out of the total unemployed youths in this age group in the region, the urban unemployed youths constituted 66.99 per cent as against all India level of 37.74 per cent. Contrary to unemployment situation, there is demand for labour from outside as the intensity of development activities increases with successive plan periods. In another study, Dutta (2003) has found the per capita Net Domestic Product of the north-eastern states lying below the national level. In 1996-97 the all India per capita NDP at current prices was Rs. 12,237 while that of Arunachal Pradesh was Rs. 10,205, Assam Rs. 6,663, Manipur Rs. 7,510, Meghalaya Rs. 8,474, Mizoram Rs. 9,758, Nagaland Rs. 9,985 and Tripura Rs. 5,083.

Corruption: The local tribal people especially in Arunachal Pradesh do not pay income tax. The national government is extending liberal financial aid to the state for her socio-economic development. An appreciable amount of this state sponsored for investment finds channellised to a new category of contractor-entrepreneur-politicians. This newly emerged neo-rich class has been to control a good amount of what is known as the 'black money'. A chunk of this is being spent in acquiring luxurious items (Sinha, 1994). All the states of Northeastern region depend on the financial aids of the centre. 90% of their states' budget comes from the centre. In addition to that, funds for different developmental activities of the north-east states are granted by the centre. Hardly, a nominal amount of these funds are utilized for the concerned activities. Most of the funds are channellised by the officers or political leaders from top to bottom. This is the real economic scenario of the north-east states.

Some people within a very short period of time have experienced income and wealth inequalities to a high degree. Very few of them have been found to become very rich over night and enjoy luxurious life and prefer conspicuous consumption which has been adversely affecting the rest of the society. The income inequalities in the north-east states' society are very much strong. Some are very rich and some are very poor. Some peoples in rural areas are living on self growing food and common property resource forest product without functioning of money. The presence of high degree of corruption at all levels and existence of underground economy has also gone against in development of market economy. The consumer durables and non-durables are purchased by the easily earned money or easily available credit (consumption loans) from the markets located in big cities of the country or some growing urban centres in the State. This has regrettably led to the emergence of the consumption economy without the economy of production and hence obstructed the growth of market economy.

References

1. Ahmed, J.U. (2007): Industrialisation in North-Eastern Region, Mittal Publications, New Delhi.
2. *Ali, N. (2007): "Constraints in Growth in Market Institutions in Arunachal Pradesh" in Borbora, S. & Gogoi, J.K.(ed): "Development Issues in Northeast in the Turn of the Century", NEEA, Papyrus, Guwahati.*
3. Arunachal Times, Vol. 19, No. 251, February 20, 2008, Itanagar, Arunachal Pradesh.
4. Arunachal Times, Vol. 17, No. 98, September 13, 2005, Itanagar, Arunachal Pradesh.
5. Behera, M.C. (2004): Globalisation and Development Dilemma: Reflections from North East India, Mittal Publications, New Delhi.
6. Behera, M.C., (2000): 'Tribal Development and Environmental issues in Arunachal Pradesh' in Sharma P.D (Ed): Environment, Health and Development: An Anthropological Perspective', S.C. Roy Institute of Anthropological Studies, Ranchi.
7. Bhattacharjee, P.R. (2002): 'The Problem of Ensuring Financial Efficiency in the North-Eastern States', Dialogue, Vol.4 (1), July-September.
8. Datta Ray and Baishya, P., (1998): Sociological Constraints to Industrial Development in North-East India, Concept, New Delhi.
9. Ganguly, J.B. (1998): 'Status of and Sociological Constraint on Industrial Development in North-east India', in Datta Ray and Baishya P., (eds): Sociological Constraints to

Industrial Development in North-East India, Concept, New Delhi.

10. Govt. of Indi: Census Reports, 1961 1981, 1991 and 2001.
11. Haksar, P.N. (1984): 'Problem of Building a Diverse Society', in North-East Region, Problems and Prospects of Development, Abbi, B.L., (ed), Centre for Research in Rural and Industrial Development, Chandigarh.
12. Kulshrestha, U.C. (2003): Economic Development and Planning, Educational Publishers, Agra.
13. Kundu, A. (2004): Infrastructure, Financing and Emerging Pattern of Urbanization: Vision 2020, India Vision 2020, Planning Commission, New Delhi.
14. Kundu, A, (2006): "Social Development Report", Oxford Univ. Press, New Delhi.
15. Mandal, R.K. (2005), "Trend of Diversification of Arunachal Economy with Special Reference to Agriculture: A Strategy for Sustainable Development" Resarun: journal of the Directorate of Research, Vol. 29, Itanagar
16. Mandal, R.K. (2008): "Position of Women in Tribal Society of Arunachal Pradesh with special Reference to Galo Women" in Pandey, B.B.(ed): Impact of Globalisation on the Himalayan Tribes of India, Himalayan Publishers, New Delhi, Itanagar.
17. *Mandal, R.K. (2005): "Arunachal Pradesh Emerging as Power House" Journal of Global Economy, Vol. 01, No. 4.*
18. Megu, K. (2007): Development Issues in North-East Region, Mittal Publications, New Delhi.
19. Mitra, A. (2002), "Internal Migration and Economic Development in the hill, Omsons pub., Gouhati, New Delhi
20. Nathan, Dev (2009): "Social Security, Compensation and Reconstruction of Livelihoods", EPW, Vol.XLIV, No. 30, July 25-31, Mumbai.
21. NEDFi, quarterly data bank, 2005

22. Pandey, B.B. (2008): Impact of Globalisation on the Himalayan Tribes of India, Himalayan Publishers, New Delhi, Itanagar.

23. Pandey, G.S.: Buddhism and Khamtis, SanPark Press Pvt. Ltd. Ashok Vihar I, Delhi.

24. Prasad, P. (1995): Urban Slums: Health, Education and Development, Delta Publications, New Delhi.

25. Rao, N.A. and *et al* (2004): "Urbanization Trends in Andhra Pradesh: A Region-wise Study", Asian Economic Review, 46(1).

26. Sen, A. (2002): 'Globalisation, Inequality and Global Protest', Development, 45, June, pp.11-16.

27. Shukla Commission, (1997): 'Transforming North-East, Tackling backlogs in Basic Minimum Services and Infrastructural Needs', High Level Commission Report to the Prime Minister, Planning Commission, New Delhi.

28. Singha, Komol (2009): Village Development in North-East India, Concept Publishing, New Delhi.

29. *Sinha A.C. (1994): "North-Eastern Frontier of India: Structural Imperatives and Aspects of Change", Indus Publishing company, New Delhi.*

30. *UNDP (1993: Human Development Report.*

SECTION-I
SOCIO-ECONOMIC DEVELOPMENT

1

The Socio-Economic Development of NER with Special Reference to Assam

At the Millennium Summit in September 2000, world leaders agreed on a set of goals to guide global development in the 21st century. What have become known as The United Nations' Millennium Development? Goals (MDGs) include: halving extreme poverty and hunger, achieving universal primary education and gender equity, reducing under-five mortality and maternal mortality by two-thirds and three-quarters respectively, reversing the spread of HIV/AIDS, halving the proportion of people without access to safe drinking water and ensuring environmental sustainability. They also include the goal of developing a global partnership for development, with targets for aid, trade and debt relief [1]

Economic development scholars and third world analysts have effectively argued, through the use of economic data and statistics that high rates of population growth are economically unsustainable. The problem lies in a very simple calculation. The resources of a country, whether the land area and the infrastructural services, such as water and electricity, not even to mention nutrition and health care requirements, are established at a certain level and raising that level, as in expanding services and raising food production, are long term. In other words, not only are resources in Third World countries limited and barely able to keep up with a stable population figure but they can only be increased and expanded at a gradual rate. Consequently, when population figures expand and grow beyond the ability of the resources themselves to expand, the end result is increased poverty and larger numbers of people demanding access to welfare service, from healthcare to education to subsidized basic goods. The point here is that accelerated population growth cannot be match with accelerated expansion of services and food production, eventually leading, on the individual levels, to greater poverty and unemployment and on the national level, to a reduced capacity to attain economic development and growth. It is thus that "*population growth is a major impediment to sustainable development,*" and high rates of population growth are an obstacles to development in general.

Sustainable development, meaning *'meeting the present needs without compromising those of the future'* (WCED 1987)[2], involves important inter- generational equity considerations, including those related to the environment. Environment is of importance not only because of its effects on the psychic and non-economic welfare, but also because of its impact on production over the long term (World Bank 2000)[3].

The very pattern of economic development in the third world countries has resulted in increasing imbalance in the distribution of income and large number of people are being relegated to below poverty line. The economic development not only brings about changes in the socio-economic and cultural life of a population but it also influences the consumption pattern in the long run. The development is a complex process and has multi dimensional structure depending upon its resources in general and infrastructural facilities in particular **(Dutta1996). Dutta and Pradhan (2006)** observed that the agriculture is the key to the development of NER. Although India has emerged as a food surplus State in the world, the NER is still suffering from food deficit. In almost all the states of NER there are substantial urban-rural and inter district variation. They suggested that it is necessary to improve all the factors employed in agriculture along with the use of best quality of seeds, application of modern technology, fast communication between research and extension, Agricultural Information Net Working System etc. in the era of globalization.

Further, Economic welfare does not merely depend upon the level of development but also on its distributive aspects. In the pluralistic nature of the country, differences in natural resources, climate, topography, vegetation and density of population can be identified easily and the North Eastern Region of India (NER) is no exception to it. Unequal distribution of wealth and resources caused regional disparity in the country as a result of which the states of NER are lagging behind **(Dutta and Choudhury, 1996).**

There has been a considerable debate on the contents of the reform package, their sequencing and pace, their implementation and their impact **(Kumar, 2000).** The debate is highly polarized between two groups of economists. One group claims the achievement of reforms and seeks faster implementation on remaining issues related to reforms. Prominent contributors among them are **Bhagwati (1994), Srinivasan (1998), Ahluwalia and Little (1998), and Mohan (1999)** among others. The other school is more critical of reforms. It focuses on the adverse effects on the society, especially the vulnerable groups, questions the sustainability of growth and reforms themselves. Thus they ask for rethinking on the coverage, sequencing and pace of implementation of reforms. This group includes **Nayyar (1996), Ghosh (1998), Nagraj (1997), Patnaik and Chandrasekhar (1997),** among many rebels of reforms.

In the recent projection, **Dyson (2004)** estimated that the population of India is likely to be 1.4 million by 2026 and 1.6 billion by the year 2051. These projections were done by taking optimistic assumptions, such as the TFR will fall to around 2.1 births per woman by 2026-21, when life expectation will be approximately 67 years for males and 70 for females. The working age population will be approximately 1.5 times as large in 2026 as it was in 2001. If woman's participation increase, there will be an average annual addition of 8 million population to the labour force annually between 2001 and 2026. If recent trend in economic growth and employment intensity continue until 2026, there will be a significant increase in the level of unemployment. Even an annual economic growth rate of 8 per cent up to 2026 will not avoid future increase in unemployment level.

"This optimism about India's growth prospect is shared by most international observers who now believe that India now has the potential to achieve sustained growth at 9 to 10 p.c. for the next 20 years.. By 2040 India is expected to be the third largest economy in the world after the US and China. Since population growth has showed down to around 1.5 p.c. and is continuing to decline, this means that if the GDP grows at between 9 and 10 per cent per year then per capita income growth in the next 20 years could be somewhere around 8.5 p.c. or so", Deputy Chairman, Planning Commission of India expressed.[4]

From the above discussed review of literature of different scholars on economic development, it is clear that with the introduction of New Economic Policy (NEP) and Structural Adjustment Programme (SAP) at national and international level, the states of NER are lagging behind. As development is a complex process, the present study will discuss the population explosion of the region and some of the indicators of socio-economic development such as education, per capita income, agriculture, power, industries including tea industry, banking, safe drinking water etc. Economic disparity which is a major impediment to economic development is also being discussed. For the completion of the study the analysis is being made on the basis of published and unpublished secondary source of statistical data. The study is being completed with valuable suggestions which will be helpful for the planners and policy makers of the region.

Demographic Profile and Population Explosion

The NER covers an area of 2.63 lakh sq.km. which accounts for 7.9 per cent of total geographical area of the country. With a total population of 38.86 million, as per 2001 census **(Table-14.1)**, it accounts for 3.8 p.c. of total population of India. According to India's Health Ministry, India's population which was 238 million in 1947 touched 1.012 billion in March 2001 and is expected to be 1.263 billion by 2016. The share of population of NER, in comparison to all India, increased from 2.89 p.c. in 1951 to 3.78 p.c. in 2001. Among various states of NER of India, the geographical area of Arunachal Pradesh is the highest at 83,743 sq. km. In terms of population, Mizoram is the smallest state among NER of India. The decadal growth rate of population (1991-2001) is the lowest in the state of Tripura 16.03 p.c. followed by Assam (18.92 p.c.) and highest in the state of Nagaland (64.53) followed by Sikkim (33.06 p.c.). The region's growth rate of population (21.61 p.c.) is higher than the national average of 21.35 p.c. during 1991-2001. The density of the population varies from 13 in Arunachal Pradesh to 340 in Assam followed by 305 in Tripura. The density of the population of the region is 147.65 which is almost half of the national density (324) in 2001 while it was only 34.29 in 1951. It is remarkable to note that the sex ratio in NER has consistently shown excess of males over females as noted for India. In India, there are only 933 females per 1000 males in the total population. Amongst the states of NER, it is the highest in Manipur (978) followed by Meghalaya (975), Tripura (950) and Mizoram (938) while other states are lying below the national level. It seems that there is more male migrants in the region lowering the sex ratio of general population.

Education

Literacy and education may be regarded as important criteria to reflect the progress of individuals at the level of understanding in day-to-day activities. Education can affect lives of people in several ways.. it enables women to assume more autonomy or power in traditional gender stratified family settings and also in more egalitarian ones, giving them greater control over their own lives and a stronger voice in matters affecting themselves and their families.

It is striking to note that except Arunachal Pradesh (42 p.c.) and Meghalaya (49 p.c.) the literacy level of the region's population is above the national level (52 p.c.) according to 1991 census, while in 2001, percentage of literacy rate in the State of Assam (64.28 p.c.) has also been included along with Meghalaya (63.31 p.c.) and Arunachal Pradesh (54.74 p.c.) which are below the National level (65.38 p.c.)

The female literacy rate is highest in Mizoram (95 p.c.) followed by Nagaland (77 p.c.) and lowest in Arunachal Pradesh (48 p.c.). There is a big gender gap in literacy which is one of the major obstacles in attaining total literacy. Enrolment in various stages of education is growing at a fast rate, but the proportion of girls is low and declines sharply at higher stages of education. The highest gender gap has been found in the states of Manipur (24.03 p.c. points), Arunachal Pradesh (21.76 p.c.) Tripura (20.93), and lowest in Mizoram (7.01) followed by Meghalaya (8.27 points). However, all the states of NER are below all–India (24.84 p.c points), Arunachal Pradesh (21.76), Tripura (20.93) and lowest in Mizoram (7.01) followed by Meghalaya (8.27 p.c. points.). However, all the states of NER are below all India (24.84 p.c.) level. Almost same trend is continued in 2001 also. Low female literacy has strong repercussions on other aspects like enrolment of children, population growth, child care and acceptance of family welfare measures **(Table-1.1).**

It is striking to note that per capita expenditure on education in 1997-98 is highest for smaller states of Mizoram (Rs. 1210), followed by Manipur (Rs. 984), Arunachal Pradesh (Rs. 951) and Tripuram (Rs. 836) while it is lowest in Assam (Rs. 537) among the states of NER.

Table 1.1: Female Literacy Rate, Total Literacy, Gender gap in Literacy and Per Capita Expenditure on Education by the Govt. of different N.E. States

	Female literacy rate (in p.c.)			Total literacy (in p.c.)		PCE (Govt.) on education (in Rs.)		Gender gap in literacy	
	1981	1991	2001	1991	2001	1991-92	1997-98	1991	2001
ANP	30	48	44.24	42	54.74	549	951	21.76	19.83
ASM	43	66	56.03	53	64.28	250	537	18.84	15.90
MNP	48	66	59.70	60	68.87	560	984	24.03	18.17
MGH	45	74	60.41	49	63.31	406	779	8.27	5.73
MZM	79	95	86.13	82	88.49	769	1210	7.01	--
NGN	55	77	61.92	62	67.11	437	762	12.87	9.85
TRP	50	67	65.41	60	73.66	416	836	20.93	16.06
India	39	50	54.16	52	65.38	---	---	24.84	21.69

Drinking Water

Water is the life blood of the environment. Water resources of a country constitute one of its vital assets. Although India occupies only 3.29 million sq.km. geographical area, which forms 2.4 p.c. of the world's land area, it supports over 15 p.c. of the world's population Thus, India supports about one-sixth of world population, 1/50th of world's land and 1/25th of world's water resources. It is observed that the maximum amount of water is required in the state of Assam, among the states of NER, which is approximately 2.33 p.c. as compared to India's requirement in 1991, which has risen to 2.63 p.c. in 2001. Regarding the safe drinking water facilities, all the states of NER, except Arunachal Pradesh (70.02 p.c.) are less than the national average (62.3 p.c.). It is striking to note that only 16.21 p.c. of total households of Mizoram can drink safe water. Thus, conservation of water is an important aspect in this regard and the people of NER should take active step for the management of water for the maintenance of the standard of water quality.

Economic Disparity

It is interesting to note that so far the poorest ten percent of the rural population is concerned the shares of consumption are relatively better in Manipur and Mizoram than that of their counterpart in NER while for the richest ten percent, the shares of consumption are relatively better in Assam and Meghalaya **(Table - 15.2).**

Coming to the urban sectors of NER, it is worthwhile to mention that the percentage share of expenditure according to poorest ten percent groups of consumers were found to be better in the state of Nagaland and worst in Assam while for the richest ten percent of the consumers, the share is relatively better in Assam among the states of NER.

Monthly Per Capita Expenditure (MPCE) may be accepted as an indicator of standard of living for people, on the basis of minimum calorie intake, suggested by Indian Council of Medical Research (ICMR) which should be 2400 calorie for an Indian working persons in rural India and 2100 calorie in urban India. This exercise yielded the official or Planning Commission's poverty line (per capita expenditure for 30 days) of rural and urban India at 1973-74 prices as Rs. 49.02 and Rs. 56.64 respectively. Thus an estimated people of 46.02 p.c. in urban India and 56 p.c. in rural India were below the poverty line in the year 1998[5].

However, economists and statisticians in the year 2000 estimated the monthly income needed for a rural individual to consume 2,400 K-calories per day was not Rs. 327 ($7.25) but Rs. 567 ($12.60). At this income level, which amounts to Rs. 19 ($0.42) or less per day, nearly 75% of the rural population is poor. Probably over 80% of the rural population (77 million) is below the World Bank's definition of $2 per day. None of these definitions take into account the cost of adequate housing, clothing, education, healthcare, and entertainment.

Considering the economic condition of NER, it is estimated that the percentage of population below the poverty line is higher in respect of all-India level in 1998 and which come out as 56.83 p.c. and 42.33 p.c. for the rural and urban people of NER respectively **(Dutta, 2003)**. However, as per National Sample Survey Organisaion's (NSSO) round survey, the poverty ratio has declined in the north east. It has declined to 40.01% in 2000 as round survey, 2000 as compared to 45.01% in 1993-94. But after 2001-02 the trend shows an upward movement.

Per Capita Income

NER as a whole is placed amongst the poorest regions in the country. The per capita income of the region is Rs. 12407 which is less than the national average of Rs. 17978 (2001-02). The pattern of agricultural growth has however remained uneven across the regions. The per capita income of Arunachal Pradesh at current prices during the year 2004-05 was estimated at Rs. 19566 and Rs. 10266 at constant prices (1993-94). The respective figures for the year 2000-01 were estimated as Rs. 10931 and Rs. 6813 while for the country the respective figures were estimated as Rs. 16564 and Rs. 10313 in 2000-01. The NSDP of Arunachal Pradesh at current prices for the year 2004-05 was Rs. 224612 lakh. The per capita income of the State of Meghalaya has also constantly lagged behind the national average. The economy of the state of Mizoram is mainly agrarian with agriculture and allied activities contributing 29 p.c. to the NSDP of the state. Jhum or shifting cultivation is the usual practice where nearly 60 p.c. of the population is engaged in agriculture in this state. The NSDP of Tripura at current prices for the year 2000-01 was Rs. 418350 lakh registering a growth of 9.72 p.c. over the previous year's figure of Rs. 381272 lakh. During the period 1993-94 to 2000-01, the NSDP at current prices grew at a compound annual growth rate of 14.52 p.c.

The Net State Domestic Product (NSDP) of Assam in real terms i.e., at constant (1993-1994) prices has been estimated at Rs. 1783.78 crore in 2003-2004 as against Rs. 16788.37 crore in 2002-2003 and Rs. 16172.81 crore in 2001-02. Thus, NSDP registered a growth of 6.24 p.c. in 2003-2004 over 2002-2003 as against a growth of 3.81 p.c. witnessed in 2002-2003 over 2001-2002. While the NSDP at constant (1993-94) prices during the year 2001-02 was Rs. 193461 lakh. During the period 1993-94 to 2001-02 the NSDP at constant prices grew at a compound annual growth rate of 6.28 p.c. as compared to the Net National Product (NNP) growth of 6.29 p.c. The per capita State Domestic Product (NSDP) i.e., per capita income of Assam at constant prices (1993-94) has been worked out at Rs. 6520 in 2003-2004 as against Rs. 6221 in 2002-2003 and Rs. 6066 in 2001-2002. Per capita income of Assam gradually increased from Rs. 5544 in 1990-91 to Rs. 5796 in 1997-98 which decreased to Rs. 5664 in the next year (1998-99) and then increased to Rs. 6756 in 2004-05. The growth of gross state domestic product (GSDP) of Assam at constant prices (1993-94) increased from 4.5 p.c. in 2001 to 5.5 p.c. in 2003-04 but then it decreased to 5.3 p.c. in 2004-05. The percentage of urban population in Assam was 11.10 p.c. according to 1991 census which increased further by 1.8 p.c. according to 2001 census (12.90 p.c.). Thus more than 87 p.c. of total population live in rural areas and for which economy of the state depends on the development of rural areas **(Dutta, 2008)**.

The NER continues to be a net importer of food grains even for its own consumption. In spite of covering 7.8 p.c. of the country's total geographical area, NER produces only 4.0 p.c. of the country's total food grain production (as per 2002-03) while agriculture provides livelihood support to 70 p.c. of the population of NER.

Agriculture

Agriculture plays an important role in the State's economy and employs more than fifty percent of the total workforce of the State of Meghalaya. It contributes nearly 30 p.c. to the State's NSDP in 1999-00. Agriculture not only supplies raw materials for industries outside the State such as cotton, jute, ginger etc. but also provides inputs to other few small agro-based industries in the State such as turmeric, paddy, maize etc. Production of cereals and pulses in Meghalaya. Almost three – fourth of the working population in Nagaland is engaged in the primary sector. Like the other states of the north east, Nagaland is predominantly an agrarian economy. The agriculture and allied sectors in Nagaland offer good inputs for development of a host of industries which could include floriculture, horticulture, rubber plantation and allied industries, sericulture, tea cultivation and processing, bamboo shot preservation, mushroom cultivation and processing, piggery, poultry etc. Sikkim's economy is largely agrarian, based on traditional farming methods, on terraced slopes. The state is gifted with abundant natural resources included agriculture crops, fodder and forests. Tripura's economy is primarily agrarian. Agriculture and its allied activities contributes nearly 34 p.c. to the state's NSDP. Agriculture in Tripura includes traditional Jhum (shifting) cultivation. After Kerala, Tripura is the largest producer of natural rubber and the rubber produced is of superior quality. The state also has the distinction of being the highest producer of True Potato Seeds in the country.

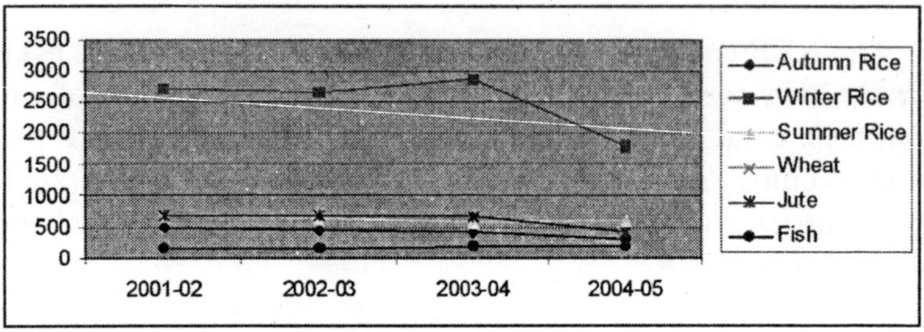

Figure 1-A: Agricultural Production in Assam. (In Thousand Tones)

The state of Assam is rich in natural resources like oil and natural gas, coal, rubber, tea and some minerals like granite, limestone and kaolin. The present state is much smaller than what it was forty years ago. It is still the largest economy in the NER. Although it is more industrially developed than the other states of NER, it is primarily an agrarian economy with 74 p.c. of its population engaged in agriculture and allied activities. As per 2001 census, 53 p.c. of total work force are engaged in agricultural activities. But the overall scenario of agriculture is not praiseworthy during the period 2000-05,. The contribution of agriculture to NSDP of the state is only 31.19 p.c. in 2003-04. The agriculture in the state mostly depends on rainfall. One of the most serious problems adversely affecting the state's agriculture is the recurrence of devastating floods almost every year. The production of winter rice steadily decreased from 2713 thousand tones in 2001-02 to 1800 thousand tones in 2004-05. Same trends are observed in case of Autumn rice. Summer rice, cotton, Jute etc. **(Figure- 1-A)**.

It is observed that NER produces Rice is of the tune of 5350 thousand tones which is only 7.36 p.c. as compared to all India level. The respective percentages of production in case of maize and wheat are 2.52 p.c. and 0.20 p.c. The total food grain production in NER with respect to the country is only 4 p.c. **(Table-1.2)**.

TABLE 1.2: Foodgrain Production in NER as on 2002-03 (in '000 Tonnes)

	Rice	Maize	Wheat	Total Foodgrain
NER	5350.0	260.00	127.00	5927.00
All India	72653.0	10303.0	65096.0	174188.0
NER as percentage of All India	7.36	2.52	0.20	4.00

Source: Draft Report of the Task force on Development Initiatives for the NER, Sept. 2005.

Power

Power is the basic infrastructure requirement for the growth of industries as well as over all economy of any State or a region or a country. The degree of economic growth is correlated with the generation and consumption of electricity. In modern day world electrification is a key ingredient for facilitating rural economic development including alleviation of poverty, realization of socio-economic goals and overall human development. As per Power Ministry data, 2004, share of Arunachal Pradesh in Central sector stations was 117 MW and installed capacity in the State sector was 45.43 MW. As on 31st March, 2005, 60.46 p.c. villages were electrified in the state while the percentage of rural household having electricity was 44.53 p.c. as on March 31, 2004. Although Mizoram is possessing a vast hydel potential, the progress in this sector is still very slow. In Mizoram, power is generated by only two types,- Hydel and adiesel. As per Ministry of Power data, Mizoram's share in central sector stations in 2004 was 49.10 MW. Manipur's share in the Central sector stations was 105.50 MW as on 30th September, 2004, while the installed capacity in the state sector was 48.61 MW. The total installed capacity in the state was 154.11 MW. Tripura has two sources of power generation – Hydro and Thermal. The state also has natural gas, which can be used for thermal power generation.

In spite of having immense potential of power generation in the State, the performance of this sector is not encouraging. Assam accounts for only 0.12 p.c. of total generation electricity in the country during 2003-04. The average per capita consumption of electricity in the State was 104 Kwh. in 2003-05 as per Economic Survey Assam, 2005-06, which is far below the national average of 359 Kwh in the same year. Since the past several years, the overall power supply position in the State has not been much satisfactory. It is important to note that there is no Hydel power generation in the state. Thermal power generated 46 million unit in the year 2001-02 but after that it went into the dark. Total power generation scenario in the state is not at all healthy towards the economic development. The generation has shown declining trend from 840.406 Million Unit in 2001-02 to 756.435 Million unit in 2004-05. At the peak hour shortage power gradually increasing from 10.20 p.c. to 24.50 p.c. during the period 2001-05, showing maximum in the period 2003-04. During the same period, the estimated requirement of power for the State was 3788.525 MU, while the availability was 3376.284 MU. The overall power supply position in the State during 2005-2006 was not much encouraging as the State had to witness erratic power supply during the year.

From the **Figure 1-B** it is clear that during the 25 years period (1981-2006), per capita consumption of electricity (in kwh) has increased very little in all the states of NER in comparison to next 6 years period (2000-06). However, during 2005-06, per capita consumption in all the states of NER including NER as a whole (201.44 kwh) are below than the national level (631.41). It is to be noted here that, per capita consumption in the state of Assam is the lowest (170.65) and the highest in the state of Meghalaya (517.54) among the states of NER. The average per capita consumption of electricity in the State was 120 Kwh. in 2002-2003 and 116 Kwh. in 2003-2004 as reported by the ASEB.

There is a regular feature of the shortage of power in the state of Assam. The overall power supply position in the State

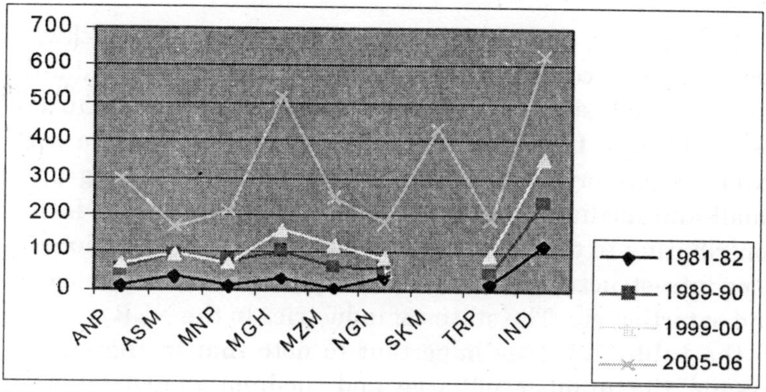

Figure 1-B: Per capita consumption of Electricity in NER(in KWH)

during 2005-2006 was not much encouraging as the State had to witness erratic power supply during the year. The power generation in the State of Assam has gradually declined from the year 1996-97 and this downward trend continued till 2003-2004. During the year 2002-2003, the generation of power has decreased by 11.2 per cent as compared to the previous year and it further declined by 4.7 per cent during the year 2003-2004. The per capita generation of electricity (Kwh) during 2002-2003 and 2003-2004 are 27.26 and 25.52 Kwh respectively. With a view to achieve electrification of all villages of Assam by 2009 and provide access to electricity to all households in line with the National Rural Electrification Policy 2004 & Rural Electrification Policy of Govt. of Assam, Rural Electrification works particularly under Rajiv Gandhi Gramin Vidyutikaran Yojana (RGGVY) scheme have been carried out. Under this scheme all the census villages of Assam are proposed to be electrified by 2009. Electrification in 16 districts to be implemented by ASEB and in 7 districts by the Power Grid Corporation of India. District wise schemes for electrification of villages have been submitted to the Govt. of India and approval for 13 districts has already been received.

Industries

Industrially, the NER continues to be the most backward region in the country, and the states in the region hardly have any industrial base, except perhaps Assam, because of its traditional tea, oil and wood based industries. To some extent Meghalaya has made some headway in setting up of small and medium industries. There are a number of factors contributing to the lack of industrial growth in the region like poor infrastructure, inadequate supply of electricity, violence and extortion etc. The status of industries in the NER is shown in the **table 1.3**. It is important to note that in the state of Assam, the number of large and medium industrial units decreased from 129 in 1999 to 120 in 2003. This declining trend has been observed in the states of Arunachal Prtadesh and Nagaland while in the states of Meghalaya and Tripura the number of units increased. Thus, industrially Arunachal Pradesh is a backward State. Not only Arunachal Pradesh, but the other States of NER except Assam and to some extent Meghalaya have failed to gear up industrial development in their States. As on 31-03-05, there are only 14 industrial estates in Arunachal Pradesh.

The Handloom industry plays a vital role in providing employment to a huge no. of population as it is a labour intensive industry. The NER has the highest concentration of household units in the Handloom sector in the country and more than 50% of weavers belong to the NER states. Development of small scale industrial sector (SSI), therefore, is the only alternative to the economic backwardness of a state lies in its significance for generation of employment with low capital cost. The high quality traditional handicrafts and handloom products enjoy a good market, both nationally and internationally. The traditional crafts like carpet weaving, cane and bamboo crafts, spinning wool, handmade paper and Thanka paintings are famous and enjoy government patronage in as far as training is concerned. However, marketing of the product depends on growth of tourism promotion outside the State by the Government and adequate supply of input and infrastructure support.

Table 1.3 : Large and Medium Industries in NER (as on March, 2003)

State	No. of units in 1999	Percentage	No. of units in 1999	Percentage
ANP	17	9.55	15	7.04
ASM	129	72.48	120	56.34
MNP	12	6.74	12	5.63
MGH	10	5.62	49	23.00
MZM	1	0.56	1	0.47
NGN	7	3.93	5	2.35
SKM	N.A.	N.A.	3	1.41
TRP	2	1.12	8	3.76
NER	178	100	213	100

Source: Draft Report of the Task force on Development Initiatives for the NER, Sept. 2005 & IIE, Guwahati.

Tea Industry

Tea is indigenous to India and is an area where the country can take a lot of pride. This is mainly because of its pre-eminence as a foreign exchange earner and its contributions to the country's GNP. In all aspects of tea production, consumption and export, India has emerged to be the world leader, mainly because it accounts for 31 per cent of global production. It is perhaps the only industry where India has retained its leadership over the last 150 years.

The figure 1-C shows the annual production of tea in Assam (ASM), Tripura(TRP), West Bengal (WB), other states of North India (OST), Tamil Nadu(TND), arnataka (KRNT), Kerala (KER) and India (IND) during the period 1995-2000. The graph shows that Assam's share is the highest (53 p.c.) in country's total production (754 million kg.). In 1995 which decreased to 52 p.c. in 2000. However, during the period the production increased by 7.28 p.c. in the state while for the country, the production increased by 9.21 p.c. In this regard Karnataka stands at the top with 20.81 p.c. followed by west

Bengal (12.74 p.c.) and Tamil Nadu (11.34 p.c.).

Banking

Financial infrastructure is essential for economic development. Banks have expanded there network extensively particularly during the last two decades in different states of NER. The number of branches of scheduled commercial banks (SCBs) in NER was 1935 in 1996 which gradually increased to 1941 in 2001 but then it decreased to 1915 in 2003. After 2003 it started to increase again and stands at 1952 as on March 31, 2005. The figure was 1920 as on March 31, 2004. With respect to NER (1952), the percentage of number of branches in Assam is 63.27 and with respect to India (28958) it is only 1.81 p.c. However with respect to India (66970 nos.), there are only 2.87 p.c. branches in NER as on March, 2004 which increased by 1.67 p.c. as on March, 2005.

Infrastructure

The term 'infrastructure' has been defined differently by different authors in various fields. Among the important infrastructures on which the overall growth and development of an economy depends are Banking, power, transport etc.. Development of infrastructural facilities open the path of economic development of a particular region. NER largely remains backward in respect of infrastructural system. Due to its peculiar geographical features the entire region was neglected from the very early period. The states of the region were lagging behind in comparison to most of the other states of the country in respect of transportation, communication, electrification and credit facilities. Due to infrastructural backwardness, industrialisation was either absent in some part or started very belatedly in some other part of the region. The transportation system of the region was very backward from the very beginning. The surface transport facilities of the region which includes Road transports, Railways and waterways along with the links with the neighbouring states

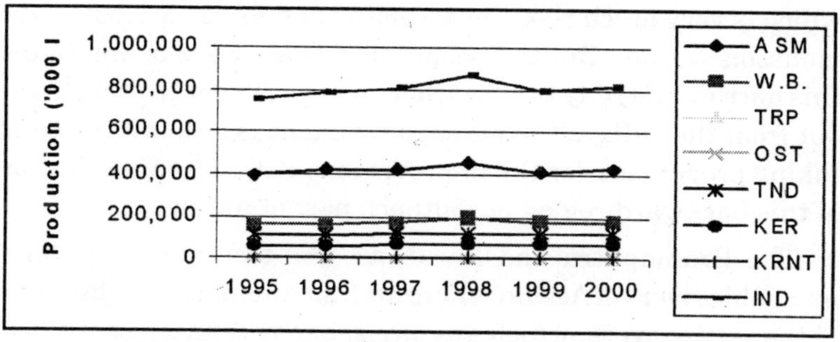

Figure 1-C: Annual State-Wise Tea Production

and the rest of the country are totally inadequate and subject to severe hardships during monsoons.

Assam being the gateway to the other States of the North Eastern Region of the Country, the need for development of transport and communication sector in the State is of vital important for speedy economic development of the region. Due to its geographical isolation transport has been a major bottleneck in the process of economic progress of the State. The existing infrastructures and facilities of transport and communication in the State are hardly adequate enough to meet the requirements. The State is no doubt served by all the modern means of transport viz., roads, railways, waterways and airways but there is enough scope for further improvement of the facilities.

The total length of roads under Public Works Department (PWD) in Assam was 34422.620 Kms (including 2044.000 Kms under National Highways) at the end of 2002-2003. Out of the total PWD Roads length only 9251.200 Kms (27 percent) were surfaced roads and the rest 25171.420 Kms. (73 percent) were un-surfaced roads. The total revenue earned by the Department of Transport during the years 2001-2002 and 2002-2003 were Rs. 102.23 crore and Rs. 128.81 crore respectively and thus the increase in revenue collection was 26.0 percent in 2002-2003 over the previous year. The present road communication between the Barak Valley of Assam and the other parts of the state is connected through a narrow strip in Meghalaya which is very much risky for traveling and more particularly in monsoon session. But the people of the valley are bound to use this narrow and hilly track as there has no alternative road to go out from the valley. The state government is less interested in taking proper care for the improvement of road communication of this backward region of southern part of Assam.

The Bramaputra and Barak are the two most important navigable rivers of Assam. There area also numerous tributaries of these two rivers, which are navigable by country boats. The Brahmaputra has already been declared as No.2 National Waterways. The Department of Inland Water Transport, Assam is operating 61 number of Ferry Services for the purpose of public utility. These Ferry Services carried around 30.91 lakh Passengers and 2.82 lakh M.T. Cargo everyday during 2001-2002. The Department has earned revenue worth Rs. 114.43 lakh in 2001-2002 against Rs. 121.94 lakh revenue earned in 2000-2001 through running of these Ferry Services. Inland Water transport service may be operated in the River Barak also, if proper care taken by the state government.

The railway route length in Assam at the end of 2001-2002 was 2516.25 kilometres comprising 1185.78 kilometres under Broad Gauge and 1330.47 kilometres under Metre Gauge. These route length of railways remained same during the current year also. The proportion of Broad Gauge route length to the Railway Route works out at 47.1 percent for the State. Taking into account the total Railway route length of 63028 kilometres for the country as a whole during 2000-2001 Assam's share in the county's railway route length turns out to be 3.99 per cent during the year. Various developmental activities in the Railway sector continued to be undertaken in the State of Assam including extension of railways line. But, in this respect, the southern districts of the state are not given due importance for its minimum economic development.

The Hill Section of the N.F. Railway, connecting Lumding and Badarpur is a major arterial rail link of Barak Valley with the rest of the country. This single-track meter-gauge line passing through tortuous hill tracks in North Cachar Hills plays a role of immense importance in the economy of entire Barak Valley of Assam, Tripura, Mizoram and part of Manipur. But due to insurgency problem, Work on two vital national projects—the broad-gauge track between Lumding and Silchar and the East-West Corridor—have come to a standstill. Parliamentary Committee for Railways Chairman Mr. Basudev Acharya blamed it on the State Government as well as the Centre for its failure to provide security to the workers at the project sites in NC Hills which are national projects. The Lumding-Silchar Hill Section is like a lifeline for Barak Valley in southern Assam as well as for other neighbouring states like Mizoram, Tripura and south Manipur, with essential commodities including food grains and cement being transported by the railways through the single metre gauge track. Rail link between the Barak Valley and rest of the country has been completely cut off. The economy of the valley in southern Assam along neighbouring states are adversely affected because of the poor rail link with the rest of the country. The deadline for implementation of the said projects was March 2009 but it has been rescheduled again as March, 2011.

In the absence of rail communication, road transport becomes the most important means of communication for the movement of goods as well as passengers traffic in the southern part of the State that is for Barak valley along with other neighbouring states viz. Tripura, Mizoram and Manipur.

Under the successive Five Year Plan, the plan outlay on transport and communication varied significantly. The above figure reveals the fact that the transport and communication did not received much priority under the successive Five Year Plans. Although 17 p.c. of the total outlay was allocated on transport and communication during First Plan but the share was declined in subsequent three years and reached to 4.8 p.c. during ad hoc. plan and again after 4th plan (13. 1 p.c.) the declining trend has been observed up to 8th plan (6.3 p.c). However, the share has been increased in subsequent two plans. It is to be noted that in the 9th and 10th plans the share of percentage have been increased to 10.24 p.c. and 10.57 p.c.

respectively which are far below of 1st Plan period **(Fig.17.C)**.

Conclusion and Suggestions

From the foregoing discussion, it is clear that the scene of development in NER was far from satisfactory in pre Economic Reform Period and in the post Reform Period marks of development can be determined in the region in general and the state of Assam in particular. So far as the latest Human development Index is concerned one thing is certain that the society of NER is lagging behind as compared to other regions of the country due to many reasons such as rise of terrorism, repeated social unrest along with government's apathy towards primary sectors and misappropriation of government fund and non utilization of sanctioned money etc. After the process of globalization started, the slogan 'enrich thyself' is going to be implemented by force in different states of NER by the respective governments. It is a matter of fact that the forces of LPG in economic, social, culture and political spheres of life have been subjected to both negative and positive aspects. At the outset of this economic reform in India some scholars perceived it as elite-driven and incapable of bringing qualitative change in people's lives. The fear psychosis was that the advanced countries would capture a lion's share in the global market by neglecting the service sector in different regions of the country. The reform has brought new opportunities of trade, business, services and employment in the region can not be denied. At the same time the region should update the younger generation through research and training to cope with the changing situation otherwise it will be lagging behind. North eastern economy is suffering from an inadequate infrastructure. Transportation facilities are poor and inadequate. Communication facilities are not so developed. There is no encouraging sign for Science and Technology and other sub sectors. Agriculture, the primary sector, is misguided by the primordial social custom and traditions. Road, water and air transport facilities in the region are far below from the requirement. There is no remarkable GDP growth and the region is still miles away from a virtual global village. There is mass unemployment causing constant unrest in the region. Hence following suggestions may be outlined to keep pace with the policies of NEP. The state of Assam having potentiality of enormous natural resources could occupy a prominent place in the world with pre-dominance in agriculture sector provided it could be free from perennial natural calamities. Through proper research and planning from multi-level authorities like flood control department, irrigation department and agricultural department the state can be saved. Soil erosion, deforestation and preservation of bio- diversity are a crying need of the hour. The water resources of NER accounts for about 33 per cent of the county's water wealth need to be harnessed judiciously to bridge the gap in water requirement for agricultural purposes. With a view to increasing the per capita income of the state which is found to be Rs. 14,523 at current prices in 2005-06 and 43.7 per cent less than the all India average, much emphasis need to be laid on effective water management plan like other agriculturally developed regions of the country. It has to aim at an economic growth rate at 9 per cent per annum. This requires the development of both industry and agriculture along with infrastructure.

The creation of a Ministry of Development of North Eastern Region, from 27th May 2004, signifies the commitment of the Government of India to accelerate the pace of socioeconomic development of the region.

Proper support should be extended to the agricultural sector and small to middle-scale industries to ensure their sustainability. The emphasis should be on fostering their self-reliance and not creating dependency on government. The government should give priority to set up various technical and professional institutions to enhance the capacity and improve the quality of education and training of the people of NER along with the projects for the development of transport and communication system for linking whole of NER with the main stream of the country.

Economic and educational progress is the foundation

on which we can have effective progress in regard to family planning. The pressure on the limited resources of the country has brought to the forefront the urgency of population control. The study arrests the attention of the policy makers of the region to check the immigration from neighbouring countries to the region for controlling the population explosion.

The study reveals that there exists an unbalanced approach to the development of various infrastructures in the north eastern region and more particularly in different parts of the state of Assam. Some of these infrastructures like road, railways, power, health and irrigation are highly neglected.

The government has a role in setting standards in the use and management of natural resources and the environment. It is difficult to recruit employees with high levels of competence and to ensure that they remain honest and incorruptible. In addition, the non-transparent recruitment system acts as a disincentive to public service employment. It is no secret that nepotism and bribery have infiltrated the recruitment system and pervade the system of promotions and lateral transfers to career positions that are considered "wet", meaning that they offer many opportunities for making money illegally.

It is suggested that all the governments of the region, irrespective of political identity, should come forward honestly and sincerely through a integrated policy for the over all development of power, road and rail communication, technical education etc. of the region, by joining smooth hands with each other.

However, no policy in the region will be successful unless the people of the region are involved in the policy making process of the states of NER and well conscious about their own health, food, sanitation etc. to upgrade the quality of life and no endeavour in this respect will be successful unless and until the people of the region are well conscious and aware of it.

Note

1. Millennium Development Goals :

Goal 1: Eradicate extreme poverty and hunger

Goal 2: Achieve universal primary education

Goal 3: Promote gender equality and empower women

Goal 4: Reduce child mortality

Goal 5: Improve maternal health

Goal 6: Combat HIV/AIDS, malaria and other diseases

Goal 7: Ensure environmental sustainability

Goal 8: Develop a Global Partnership for Development

2. WCED (World Commission on Environment and Development). 1987, ***Our Common Future*** (The Brundtland Commission Report), Oxford University Press. Oxford, UK

3. World Bank 2000, **Entering the 21st Century: World Development Report 1999/2000,** Oxford University Press, New York:

4 Montek Singh Ahluwalia, Deputy Chairman, Planning Commission of India delivered the Convocation Address at the 8th Convocation of Bharati Vidyapeeth University, Pune on Saturday, 31st March, 2007.

5. N. Bhattacharya (1998) : On Level of Living Surveys in India, Presidential Address, 85th Indian Science Congress, Section of Statistics.

References

Ahluwalia, Isher Judge and Little, I.M.D. (ed) (1998) : India's Economic Reforms and Development - Essays For Monmohan Singh, Oxford University Press, New Delhi.

Bhagawati, Jagadish (1994), India in Transition : Freeing the Economy, Oxford University Press, New Delhi.

Dutta, P.C. (2003) : Regional Disparity and its Consequences in North Eastern Region of India in *Economic Liberalization and Regional Disparities in India – Special Focus on the North Eastern Region (ed) A.C. Mohapatra and C.R. Pathak,* Star Publishing House, Shillong.

Dutta, P.C. (2008) : "Society, Culture and Development in Ne India : Essays in Memory of Dr. Basudev Datta Ray", (Ed.) A. Ray and S.B. Chakrabarty, Concept Publishing House, New Delhi.

Dutta, P.C. and B.C. Pradhan (2004) : Agricultural Development and Security of Life in *Food Security and Public Distribution System Today – Failures and Success (ed.) Amalesh Banerjee,* Kanishka Publishers, Distributors, New Delhi.

Dutta, P.C. and B.C. Pradhan (2006) : Changing Agricultural Scenario in North East India in *Changing Agricultural Scenario In North East India (ed.)Bimal J. Deb and B. Datta Ray,* Concept Publishing Company, New Delhi.

Dutta P. C. & H.Choudhury (1996): "A Note on Inter State Variation in per Capita Non-Food Household Items Of Consumption In The North East India", *IJRS, Vol. 28 No. 2*

Dutta P. C. (1996): "Quality Variation of Some Food Items of Consumption in North Eastern Region (Ner) India", *IJRS, Vol. 28 No. (1)*

DYSON T.(2004) : "India's Population- The Future" in Dyson Et Al (Eds.) Twenty First Century India, Oxford University Press, New Delhi.

Ghosh, Jayati (1998) : Liberalisation Debates in Terence Byres (ed), *The Indian Economy: Major Debates Since Independence,* Delhi, 329.

Jha Prabodh Kumar (2000) : Economic Reformation or Deformation in India in *Post – Reform Leading Issues of Indian Economy, Vol- I (ed.) A.D.N. Bajpai et al.,* p. 8-17, Atlantic Publishers and Distributors, New Delhi.

Mohan, Rakesh (1999) : Economic Reforms : The Next Wave, Lalit Doshi Memorial Lecture, Mumbai, 13th Ocober, 1999.

Nagraj, R (1997) : What Has Happenedsince 1991 : Assessment Of India's Economic Reforms, Economic and Political

Weekly, p. 2871, 8th November.

Nayyar, Deepak (1996) : Economic Liberalization in India : Analytics, Experience and Lesson, *R.C. Dutta Lectures,* Orient Longman, New Delhi, Centre For Studies in Social Sciences.

Patnaik, Prabhat and Chandrasekhar, C.P. (1995) : Indian Economy Under Structural, Economic and Political Weekly, November 25.

Singh Manminder and Sandeep Singh Saluja (2005) : New economic reforms and economic growth in *liberalisation and globalisation of Indian economy, vol- vi (ed.) K. R. Gupta,* p.1-26, Atlantic publishers and distributors, New Delhi-27.

Srinivasan, T.N.(1998) : India's export performance : A comparative analysis. In I. J. Ahluwalia and I.M.D. Little (ed) op. cit.

2

Some Aspects of Socio-Economic Development in NER

The North East of India (NER) constitutes the states of Arunachal Pradesh, Assam, Manipur, Meghalaya, Mizoram, Nagaland, Sikkim and Tripura. Flanked by hills and with the mighty Brahmaputra River slashing a central path between its north and south, the NER is bounded by mostly by the international boundaries. Arunachal Pradesh lies to its north and Sikkim a little away in the North West bordering China and Bhutan. Bangladesh and Myanmar lie to its southwest and east. The torrential Brahmaputra deposits its rich alluvial silt along the banks of the plains of Assam. Tropical rain forest, rich in flora and fauna, spread their arms across Arunachal Pradesh into Assam. The state of Assam is a land where Tea is the most powerful industry, handicrafts as a major occupation and martial arts a favoured sport. The western side of the North East is connected to the eastern part of the Indian subcontinent by a narrow land corridor, sometimes referred to as the Siliguri Neck or "Chicken's Neck". The eight states that comprise the region reflect ecological and cultural contrasts between the hills and the plains; there are also significant elements of continuity. The economy of NER has got its definite identity due to its peculiar physical, economic and socio-cultural characteristics. Among various states of NER of India, the geographical area of Arunachal Pradesh is highest at 83,743 sq.km. In the economy of Arunachal Pradesh, structural transformation is a recent phenomenon. At the time of independence, this state lagged behind the other parts of the country in terms of development indices. The economy of the state was a mono-economy characterized by traditional slash-and-burn method of agriculture and few small and cottage industries. But since independence, economic development along with government sponsored urbinisation has brought about significant changes in the structure of the economy.

Economic development scholars and third world analysts have effectively argued, through the use of economic data and statistics that high rates of population growth are economically unsustainable. The problem lies in a very simple calculation. The resources of a country, whether the land area and the infrastructural services, such as water and electricity, not even to mention nutrition and health care requirements, are established at a certain level and raising that level, as in expanding services and raising food production, are long term. In other words, not only are resources in Third World countries limited and barely able to keep up with a stable population figure but they can only be increased and expanded at a gradual rate. Consequently, when population figures expand and grow beyond the ability of the resources themselves to expand, the end result is increased poverty and larger numbers of people demanding access to welfare service, from healthcare to education to subsidized basic goods. The point here is that accelerated population growth cannot be match with accelerated expansion of services and food production, eventually leading, on the individual levels, to greater poverty and unemployment and on the national level, to a reduced capacity to attain economic development and growth. It is thus that "population growth is a major impediment to sustainable development," and high rates of population growth are an obstacles to development in general.

Explosive quantitative increase of Indian population is thinning down the quality of life of the mass due to skewed distribution of resources. Added problems are the rapid rate of urbanization, growth of large cities in volume without adequate infrastructural robustness, migration of the poor into already overcrowded cities, resulting into overburdening of the facilities available in urban hubs. One of the major areas of concern in the region is the unsatisfactory situation of both rural and urban poor in the field of mortality and health care.

In the recent projection, Dyson (2004) estimated that the population of India is likely to be 1.4 million by 2026 and 1.6 billion by the year 2051. These projections were done by taking optimistic assumptions, such as the TFR will fall to around 2.1 births per woman by 2026-21, when life expectation will be approximately 67 years for males and 70 for females. The working age population will be approximately 1.5 times as large in 2026 as it was in 2001. If woman's participation increase, there will be an average annual addition of 8 million population to the labour force annually between 2001 and 2026. If recent trend in economic growth and employment intensity continue until 2026, there will be a significant increase in the level of unemployment. Even an annual economic growth rate of 8 per cent up to 2026 will not avoid future increase in unemployment level.

Almost all the countries in the world will have imbalances at regional and lower level in the equitable share in the national assets like natural resources, economic assets and manpower distribution. In order to reduce regional or sub-regional imbalances, planners and policy makers make efforts and evolve the strategies which are aimed at minimising such imbalances.

The present study will discuss the level of development of agricultural sector, infrastructural facilities and some of the socio-economic indicators. To study the economic development of the region, banking, industries etc. will be discussed. The regional imbalance, literacy level, population structure are some of the factors responsible for the development of a region. For the completion of the study the analysis is being made on the basis of published and unpublished secondary source of statistical data. The study is being completed with viable suggestions which will helpful for the planners and policy makers of the region.

Demographic Profile

The NER covers an area of 2.63 lakh sq.km. which accounts for 7.9 per cent of total geographical area of the country. With a total population of 38.86 million, as per 2001 census, it accounts for 3.8 p.c. of total population of India. The share of population of NER, in comparison to all India, increased from 2.89 p.c. in 1951 to 3.78 p.c. in 2001. In terms of population, Mizoram is the smallest state among NER of India. The decadal growth rate of population (1991-2001) is the lowest in the state of Tripura 16.03 p.c. followed by Assam (18.92 p.c.) and highest in the state of Nagaland (64.53) followed by Sikkim (33.06 p.c.). The region's growth rate of population (21.61 p.c.) is higher than the national average of 21.35 p.c. during 1991-2001. The density of the population varies from 13 in Arunachal Pradesh to 340 in Assam followed by 305 in Tripura. The density of the population of the region is 147.65 which is almost half of the national density (324) in 2001 while it was only 34.29 in 1951.

Migration

The growth of population of an area is determined by three factors, namely fertility, mortality and migration. Internal migration is the movement of population within the country. This have no much effect on the country's total population size and growth but its impact within the country's sub-regions may be substantial. The movement of people within a country indirectly reflects the level of development and regional imbalances in economic opportunities. The decision to move is influenced by a host of social, economic, political, cultural and developmental factors. Economic opportunity plays an important role in the movement of people from place to place in search of employment, better employment, transfer of job etc. It has been observed that migration is most responsive to economic opportunity and developmental activities.

Singh (2005) analysed the NSS data and concluded that the characteristics of migrants in terms of age, education, marital status and economic activity before and after migration show the selectivity of migrants. The industrial and agricultural development in the areas and proximity to developed areas as well previous migration always plays a significant role.

Education

Literacy and education may be regarded as important criteria to reflect the progress of individuals at the level of understanding in day-to-day activities. Education can affect lives of people in several ways.. it enables women to assume more autonomy or power in traditional gender stratified family settings and also in more egalitarian ones, giving them greater control over their own lives and a stronger voice in matters affecting themselves and their families (Mason, 1984, 1992). Education can lead to changes in many aspects of women autonomy that impinge on reproductive behaviours- information autonomy, or knowledge of, and exposure to modern practices and information; decision making autonomy, or women's say in family decisions concerning their own lives and well being; physical autonomy, or physical mobility and confidence in dealing with the outside world in extracting the benefit from available sources, economic and social autonomy, or access to and control over economic resources and increased self reliance in terms of social status and acceptance (Levine et al.,1991; Balk, 1994; Elo, 1992; Visaria, 1993; Mandelbaum,1988; Okafor,1991; United Nations, 1993).

In the recent years, female education has come to the forefront of development planning for tackling the problem of high fertility in developing countries. Social demographic Research has played an important role in highlighting more education women results in marriage at later age fewer children per family, less infant and child mortality rates and healthier, better-reared and educated children. Female education is perceived as an important factor not only in imparting new knowledge and information, skills and values for improving their participation in the labour force or earnings, but also in enhancing their status within and outside their immediate family. Thus, schooling is envisaged to have a long term effect on women's position in family and society (Jeffery and Basu, 1996). Education occupies an important position in the planned programmes of the Meghalaya Government. The North Eastern Hill University (NEHU) is the only university in the State and it is the direct responsibility of the Union Government. It is important to note that according to the census report of the Government of India, percentage of literate persons of Meghalaya was 49.1 p.c. in 1991 and in 2001, the percentage of literate persons has gone up to 63.31p.c. but its All India rank has dropped down from 22nd position in 1991 census to 27th position in 2001.

Per Capita Income

NER as a whole is placed amongst the poorest regions in the country. The per capita income of the region is Rs. 12407 which is less than the national average of Rs. 17978 (2001-02). Per capita income of Arunachal Pradesh at current prices was higher than the nation's average by Rs. 1043 in 1993-94. However, since 1996-97, the per capita income of the state has been lagging behind the national average. The per capita income at constant prices during the year 2004-05 was estimated at Rs. 19566. The pattern of agricultural growth has however remained uneven across regions and crops.

The Net State Domestic Product (NSDP) of Assam in real terms i.e., at constant (1993-1994) prices has been estimated at Rs. 1783.78 crore in 2003-2004 as against Rs. 16788.37 crore in 2002-2003 and Rs. 16172.81 crore in 2001-02. Thus, NSDP registered a growth of 6.24 p.c. in 2003-2004 over 2002-2003 as against a growth of 3.81 p.c. witnessed in 2002-2003 over 2001-2002. While the NSDP at constant (1993-94) prices during the year 2001-02 was Rs. 193461 lakh. During the period 1993-94 to 2001-02 the NSDP at constant prices grew at a compound annual growth rate of 6.28 p.c. as compared to the Net National Product (NNP) growth of 6.29 p.c. The NSDP of Manipur at current prices for the year 2001-02 was Rs. 320478 lakh. As compared to the previous year, it registered a growth of 8.82 p.c. compared to all India NNP growth of 10.27 p.c. During the period 1993-94 to 2001-02, the NSDP at current prices grew at a compound annual growth rate of 6.82 p.c. as compared to the NNP growth of 6.29 p.c. The NSDP of Arunachal Pradesh at current prices for the year 2004-05 was Rs. 224612 lakh. and at constant (1993-94) prices it was Rs. 117853 lakh. The NSDP of Tripura at current prices for the year 2000-01 was Rs. 418350 lakh registering a growth of 9.72 p.c. over the previous year's figure of Rs. 381272 lakh. During the period 1993-94 to 2000-01, the NSDP at current prices grew at a compound annual growth rate of 14.52 p.c. compared to the NNP growth of 13.73 p.c.. NSDP at constant (1993-1994) prices in 2000-01 was Rs. 260739 lakh. During the period 1993-94 to 2000-01, the compound annual rate of growth of NSDP at constant prices was 7.04 p.c. while the NNP growth was 6.28 p.c. The economy of the state of Mizoram is mainly agrarian with agriculture and allied activities contributing 29 p.c. to the NSDP of the state. Jhum or shifting cultivation is the usual practice. Nearly 60 p.c. of the population is engaged in agriculture in this state. As in the other states of the North East, the per capita income of the State of Meghalaya has constantly lagged behind the national average.

The per capita State Domestic Product (NSDP) i.e., per capita income of Assam at constant prices (1993-94) has been worked out at Rs. 6520 in 2003-2004 as against Rs. 6221 in 2002-2003 and Rs. 6066 in 2001-2002. Per capita income of Assam gradually increased from Rs. 5544 in 1990-91 to Rs. 5796 in 1997-98 which decreased to Rs. 5664 in the next year (1998-99) and then increased to Rs. 6756 in 2004-05. The growth of gross state domestic product (GSDP) of Assam at constant prices (1993-94) increased from 4.5 p.c. in 2001 to 5.5 p.c. in 2003-04 but then it decreased to 5.3 p.c. in 2004-05. The percentage of urban population in Assam was 11.10 p.c. according to 1991 census which increased further by 1.8 p.c. according to 2001 census (12.90 p.c.). Thus more than 87 p.c. of total population live in rural areas and for which economy of the state depends on the development of rural areas.

The per capita income of Arunachal Pradesh at current prices was higher than the nation's average by Rs. 1043 in 1993-94. However, since 1996-97, the per capita income of the state has been lagging behind the national average. The per capita income at current prices during the year 2004-05 was estimated at Rs. 19566 and at constant prices it was estimated as Rs. 10266. The per capita income at constant (1993-94) prices was Rs. 6813 in 2000-01 as compared to the all India figure of Rs. 10313 in 2000-01.The per capita income at current prices in 2000-01 was Rs. 10931 as compared to all India figure of Rs. 16564

As in other states of the NER, the per capita income of the state of Manipur has constantly lagged behind the national average. The disparity has been rising gradually. The per capita income at the current prices in 2001-02 was Rs. 13213 as compared to tha all India figure of Rs. 17947. The per capita income at constant (1993-94) prices in 2001-02 was Rs. 7976 as compared to all India figure of Rs. 10754. The per capita income at constant (1993-94) prices was Rs. 6813 in 2000-01 as compared to the all India figure of Rs. 10313 in 2000-01.The per capita income at current prices in 2000-01 was Rs. 10931 as compared to all India figure of Rs. 16564.

The NER continues to be a net importer of food grains even for its own consumption. In spite of covering 7.8 p.c. of the country's total geographical area, NER produces only 4.0 p.c. of the country's total food grain production (as per 2002-03) while agriculture provides livelihood support to 70 p.c. of the population of NER.

Poverty is one of the serious problems in India. About 82 p.c. of the total poor lives in the countryside. As a consequence, little attention has been given on the urban poor since independence. Urban Poverty is a complex and multidimensional problem-not only entangled in economic obscurities but also with social welfare facets, which are left neglected. If serious attention is not paid to this underprivileged section, it is likely to pose a severe threat to the urban future of our economy.

[Demography India, Vol. 34(2), 2005, 299-312 ; Are Urban Poor Doing Better than their Rural Counterpart in India? A Study of Fertility, Family Planning and Health -A. Chattopadhyay and T.K. Roy]

Agriculture

As in the other states of the Northeast, Arunachal Pradesh's economy is mainly agrarian. Foodgrain production of Arunachal Pradesh was 2.05 lakh MT in 1999-2000 registering a growth of 13.25 p.c. over the previous year's production. The foodgrain yield was 1126 kg/ha. In 1999-2000 compared to the same year. There is a great potential in Arunachal Pradesh in the Fishery sector also. But the problems of flood, under utilization of aquatic resources, unscientific method of production in the state. As in the other states of the north east, Tripura's economy is primarily agrarian and agriculture and its allied activities contributes nearly 34 p.c.% to the state's Net Domestic Product. Agriculture in Tripura includes traditional Jhum (shifting) cultivation. After Kerala, Tripura is the largest producer of natural rubber and the rubber produced is of superior quality. The state also has the distinction of being the highest producer of True Potato Seeds in the country. Agriculture plays an important role in the State's economy and employs more than fifty percent of the total workforce of the State. It contributes nearly 30 p.c. to the State's NSDP in 1999-00. Agriculture not only supplies raw materials for industries outside the State such as cotton, jute, ginger etc. but also provides inputs to other few small agro-based industries in the State such as turmeric, paddy, maize etc.Production of cereals and pulses in Meghalaya: Almost three – fourth of the working population in Nagaland is engaged in the primary sector.Like the other states of the north east, Nagaland is predominantly an agrarian economy.

Rice is the stable food and occupies about 70 p.c. of the total cultivated area, consisting about 75 p.c. of the total foodgrain production. Nagaland has been identified as a potential area for development of food processing industries in its geo climatic conditions. The agriculture and allied sectors in Nagaland offer good inputs for development of a host of industries which could include floriculture, horticulture, rubber plantation and allied industries, sericulture, tea cultivation and processing, bamboo shot preservation, mushroom cultivation and processing, piggery, poultry etc. Sikkim's economy is largely agrarian, based on traditional farming methods, on terraced slopes. The state is gifted with abundant natural resources. The resources can be grouped into biotic or abiotic, both of which can be renewable. Biotic resources include agriculture crops, fodder and forests. The rural populace grows crops such as cardamom, oranges, apples, tea and orchids. Rice is grown on terraced hillsides in the southern reaches. Sikkim has the highest production and largest cultivated area of cardamom in India. Because of the hilly terrain, and lack of reliable transportation infrastructure, there are no large-scale industries. Breweries, distilleries, tanning and watch-making are the main industries. These are located in the southern reaches of the state, primarily in the towns of Melli and Jorethang. The state has an impressive growth rate of 8.3 p.c., which is the second highest in the country after Delhi. The economy of Sikkim is mainly based on agricultural and animal husbandry. Approx. 11 p.c. of the total geographical area is under agriculture. Agriculture is of the mixed type and still at the subsistence level rather than commercial level. The work force participation rate as per 1991 census is 40.44 p.c.. The female participation rate in Sikkim is also much higher than the national average. This is an important aspect if the hill economy, as productivity is low and hence all the able-bodied people are employed in agriculture and other activities. Cultivators account for the greater majority of the people in the state, their percentage is 57.84 p.c. Agricultural labourers as a whole constitute only 7.81 p.c. of the workers in the state, house holds and other industries are negligible, but other worker (Tertiary Sector) at the state level represent a good percentage of population. The decreasing ratio of worker at the state level indicates the low level of economic diversification. The importance of agriculture can be judged by the high percentage of population approx. 65 p.c. engaged in it. Animal husbandry is an integral part of the house hold economy of the region. There are certain house hold industries also which substantially adds to house hold incomes. The past one and half decade has witnessed a tremendous upward swing in various development programs giving a new thrust to the Sikkim economy. This process has increased wage employment opportunities. Though most of the inhabitants are basically agriculture, they have diversified into tertiary jobs such as Government services.

Irrigation

The NER has considerable unexploited irrigation potential, especially in states like, the Imphal valley in Manipur and in Tripura. Till recently, about 19 p.c. of the total potential of 5.7 lakh hact. could be exploited in Assam, against the national achievement of 40 p.c. So far, Manipur could attain the level of about 10 p.c. of the total potential to cover 65000 hact. The potential in Tripura for irrigation has been assessed at 2.81 lakh hact. The topographical conditions in Mizoram, Meghalaya, Nagaland, and Sikkim are not favourable for groundwater irrigation schemes and therefore the development of surface irrigation has better prospects. (*Source*: Draft Report of the Task force on Development Initiatives for the NER, Sept. 2005.).

Power

The degree of economic growth is correlated with the generation and consumption of electricity. Although Mizoram is possessing a vast hydel potential, the progress in this sector is still very slow. In Mizoram, power is generated by only two types,- Hydel and adiesel. As per Ministry of Power data,

(Table-2.1): Foodgrain Production in NER as on 2002-03 (in '000 Tonnes)

	Rice	Maize	Wheat	Total Foodgrain
NER	5350.0	260.00	127.00	5927.00
All India	72653.0	10303.0	65096.0	174188.0
NER as percentage of All India	7.36	2.52	0.20	4.00

Source: Draft Report of the Task force on Development Initiatives for the NER, Sept. 2005.

Mizoram's share in central sector stations in 2004 was 49.10 MW. Following table shows the installed capacity and power generated in Mizoram.

As per Power Ministry data, 2004, share of Arunachal Pradesh in Central sector stations was 117 MW and installed capacity in the State sector was 45.43 MW. The total installed capacity was 162.43 MW. The percentage of villages electrified was 60.46% as on March 31, 2005. The percentage of rural household having electricity was 44.53% as on March 31, 2004. Per capita consumption of electricity is 68.61 KWh in 2000-01.

Tripura has two sources of power generation – Hydro and Thermal. The state also has natural gas, which can be used for thermal power generation. Out of the two major sources of power generation, thermal power accounts for more than 77% while the remaining is generated from Gomati Power Project (hydro). due to the increase in the demand for electricity, the state is experiencing persistent power shortage and hence frequent power cuts are enforced upon. During 2000-01 the total installed capacity was 85.35 MW and total power generated was 318.38 MU, total purchase of power was 268.00 MU in 2000-01 which is 8.85 MU higher than that purchase in 1999-2000.The total unit sold to ultimate consumers in 2000-01 was 388 MU. Despite commendable successes, the position in relation to needs remains highly unsatisfactory. It is observed that a large expansion of this source of energy is required.As such about 79.80 per cent of the villages and 100 percent towns are electrified which raises both the income and expenditure of the department.But it is found that expenditures far exceeds the income. Kutir Jyoti, a centrally sponsored scheme to give assistance to the people living below poverty line is providing electricity free of cost. Till 1997-98, there were 6217 connections under this scheme which has gone up to 15688 in 1998-99 and to 37979 in 2000-01.

As per Ministry of Power data, Tripura's share in central sector stations as on September 30,2004 was 93.10 MW, while the installed capacity in the state sector was 127.36 MW. The total installed capacity was 220.46 MW. As on august 31, 2004, the percentage of villages electrified was 820. the per capita consumption of electricity was 84.74 KWH as compared to the national average 355 KWH.The percentage of rural households having electricity was 28.50 p.c. The rivers in the State of Meghalaya cascading into the rivers presents an ideal scope for generation of hydel power. The projects in Meghalaya are Sunapani Hydel Project, Umtru Hydel Project, Umium Hydel Project, Tura Diesel and Nangal Bibra. Meghalaya consists of towns and thousands of villages situated in rural areas. Some of these villages are located in inaccessible parts of the State. The problem of rural electrification is a gigantic task. Despite the vast potential, the power generated within the state of Nagaland is quite insignificant. According to the Annual Administrative Report of the department of power, the total power generation was 3.21(MU) and the total purchase was 230 (MU) in 2000-01. Thus the state could generate only 1.39 p.c. of the total power requirements.the state mainly purchase power from NEEPCO, NHPC and PGCI. As per Ministry of Power data, Nagaland's share in Central sector stations as on September 30, 2004 was 71.10 MW, while the installed capacity was 101.46 MW. It is important to note that, as on August 31, 2004, the percentage of villages electrified was 100 p.c. As compared to the national average of 355 kwh, the per capita consumption of electricity in Nagaland was 84.74 kwh. and the percentage of rural households having electricity in the state was 47.16 p.c. Hydel power is area that has tremendous potential in the state of Sikkim. The capacity to tap 8000 MW of hydel power is there for the asking.

Industries

Industrially, the NER continues to be the most backward region in the country, and the states in the region hardly have any industrial base, except perhaps Assam, because of its traditional tea, oil and wood based industries.To some extent Meghalaya has made some headway in setting up of small and medium industries. There are a number of factors contributing to the lack of industrial growth in the region like poor infrastructure, inadequate supply of electricity, violence and extortion etc. The growth of all industries; large, medium and small has been uneven. The no. of functioning large and medium industries in the NER has been negligible. The status of industries in the NER is shown in the **table 1.4**. It is important to note that in the state of Assam, the number of large and medium industrial units decreased from 129 in 1999 to 120 in 2003. This declining trend has been observed in the states of Arunachal Prtadesh and Nagaland while in the states of Meghalaya and Tripura the number of units increased. Thus, industrially Arunachal Pradesh is a backward State. Not only Arunachal Pradesh, but the other States of NER except Assam and to some extent Meghalaya have failed to gear up industrial development in their States. As on 31-03-05, there are only 14 industrial estates in Arunachal Pradesh. The necessity of industrialization is a means of achieving rapid growth and prosperity has long been recognized in the strategy of development of any region and Tripura is no exception. It is unfortunate that the state is yet to emerge out of industrial backwardness. The Central Government has declared the entire state as 'A' category backward area for the purpose of giving central investment subsidy. It is to be noted that the state of Mizoram is a notified backward area and is categorized under "No Industry State". The state perhaps, is the most industrially backward state in the country. As on March 2000, number of large and medium industries is only one. This represents very sick position in industrial sector of Mizoram. In the state of Meghalaya, industries have been classified into two groups, viz., registered manufacturing industries and unregistered manufacturing industries. In both these counts, Meghalaya can be identified as one of the industrially backward states in the country. Due to inadequate industrial infrastructure, lack of mineral resources and transportation, the industrial growth is limited in Nagaland. Despite vast endowment of natural resources, Nagaland is considered as one of the most industrially backward states of the country. The industrial structure of Nagaland may be classified, based on resource uses into agro – based industries, mineral based industries, forest based industries and other industries. In case of medium scale industries in Nagaland, there were virtually no industries during the 60's. Handicraft and handloom production only met domestic needs. From 1970 onwards a few medium scale local resource based industries have come into existence. In case of Small Scale Industries (SSI), these began to emerge since 1970s based on local resources.

Small Scale Industries

The Handloom industry plays a vital role in providing employment to a huge no. of population as it is a labour intensive industry. The NER has the highest concentration of household units in the Handloom sector in the country and more than 50% of weavers belong to the NER states.

Table- 17-8 shows the trend of growth of Small Scale Industries (SSI) in the states of NER during the period 1997-98 to 2002-03. Over the period (1997-2003) highest percentage of growth rate occurred in the state of Nagaland (252.95 p.c.) followed by meghalaya (41.28 p.c.) and Mizoram (35.47 p.c.) while it is the lowest in both the states of Arunachal Pradesh and Manipur (12.25 p.c.). By observing the percentage increase over the previous year, it is to be noted that for different states it ranges from 1.00 p.c. to 37.92 p.c. Highest variation is observed in the state of Nagaland ranges from 15.78 p.c. (1997-98) to 37.92 p.c. (1998-99).

In case of Tripura, it ranges from 1.00 p.c. (2002-03) to 3.90 p.c. (1997-98). The process of setting up large and medium scale industries in the State of Tripura is not satisfactory due to several constraints like limited size of market, lack of skilled and semi skilled manpower, inadequate infrastructure, insurgency and extremist problems. Development of small scale industrial sector (SSI) therefore, is the only alternative to the economic backwardness of a state lies in its significance for generation of employment with low capital cost. Inspite of the vast scope, the development of SSI in Tripura still remains at a very nascent stage, although as a result of a few policy measures taken and support provided like financial and technical, the SSI sector has grown considerably in the recent years, Yet it is not satisfactory in the context of regional or national growth rate. For providing employment opportunities in the rural areas and thereby strengthening the rural economy, Khadi and Village Industries play an important role. The Mizoram Khadi and Village Industries Board was formed in March 1986 as a non-profit making body. The board provides financial assistance to registered individuals, institutions, co-operatives and departmental units. The total no. of units registered upto 31-03-2001 has reached 5772. It also provides technical guidance and training. However, the topography of Mizoram enjoys varied climate conditions which facilitates the successful introduction of Mulberry, Eri, Muga and Tasar. The total no. of farmers engaged in sericulture activities during 2000-01 was 3332 and the production of raw silk during 2000-01 was reported to be 2064.88 kg. only. The major crafts of Meghalaya are cane and bamboo, carpets, musical instruments, jewellery, fibrecrafts, textiles etc. The Nagas have a rich tradition of art and craft. The major crafts of Nagaland are artistic textiles, cane and bamboo straw etc., woodware, metalware, bangals and beeds, gems and jewellery. The art of weaving is still popular among the Naga women, especially in the rural areas. Handicrafts and handloom industry has the potential to promote income and employment generation in a big way. The high quality traditional handicrafts and handloom products enjoy a good market, both nationally and internationally. The traditional crafts like carpet weaving, cane and bamboo crafts, spinning wool, handmade paper and Thanka paintings are famous and enjoy government patronage in as far as training is concerned. However, marketing of the product depends on growth of tourism promotion outside the State by the Government and adequate supply of input and infrastructure support. It is striking to note that Sikkim has to focus on "product differentiation" as Sikkim faces competition from other north-eastern States.

Results of the third census of SSI unit reveal that while 3.11 p.c. of the total no. of persons employed in the SSI sector on the country (24932763), where employed in the NER, percentage of output in NER is not in tune with the no. of units and the no. of persons employed. It is also observed that of 3 p.c. of the total SSI units which exist in NER and which, provided around 3.11 p.c. of the total employment produced goods and services equivalent to 1.78 p.c. only. As per Draft Report of the Task force on Development Initiatives for the NER, Sept. 2005, Gross out put of NER is estimated as Rs. 5024.41 Crores while for all India the figure is 2,82,269.98 crores.

The state economy of Tripura is characterized by low capital formation, inadequate infrastructure facilities, geographical isolation and communication bottlenecks, inadequate exploitation and use of forest resources, low industrial field and high unemployment problem. Financial performance of Assam during the Tenth Plan period under the various sectoral heads i.e., Agriculture and Allied Activities, Rural Employment, Irrigation and Flood Control, energy, Industry and Minerals, Social Services and other sectors has shown progress and the state government has been in position to utilize 86.4 p.c. of the agreed outlay. Although a late starter in the planning and development process, due to sustained efforts and investment in development activities since 3rd Five Year Plan, the state of Nagaland achieved significant progress particularly in the sectors of Road, Transport, Water Supply, Power, Education and Health. During the 40 years, almost all the villages in the state are now covered by public Transport. Total length of roads in the state has reached 10255 kms. while the state covers an area of 16579 sq. km. and there are 4 National Highways passing through the state. (NE News Letter, Feb. 2007).

Tea Industry

Tea is indigenous to India and is an area where the country can take a lot of pride. This is mainly because of its pre-eminence as a foreign exchange earner and its contributions to the country's GNP. In all aspects of tea production, consumption and export, India has emerged to be the world leader, mainly because it accounts for 31% of global production. It is perhaps the only industry where India has retained its leadership over the last 150 years. Since independence tea production has grown over 250%, while land area has just grown by 40 p.c. There has been a considerable increase in export too in the past few years. Total net foreign exchange earned per annum is around Rs. 1847 crores. The labour intensive tea industry directly employs over 1.1 million workers and generates income for another 10 million people approximately. Women constitute 50 p.c. of the workforce.

The tea industry of NER is the world's largest tea growing region having 16 p.c. shares, and is the largest producer and exporter of tea in India (share 55 p.c.). The production of tea in the state of Assam was of the tune of 438.9 thousand tones during the period 2002-03 which increased to 454.1 thousand tones in 2003-04 but decreased to 443.3 thousand tones in 2004-05. However, Indian tea producers suffered the most in terms of drop in average tea auction price compared with other auction centres around the world between January to October 2002 (**Business Standard - Saturday, January 11, 2003**). The table 2.2 shows the picture of Tea industry in NER (Annual export) during the 5-year period (2000-04)

The Assam government has decided to offload a majority stake, and, along with it, management control of Assam Tea

(Table-2.2): Tea Production, Consumption et. in NER.

	2000	2001	2002	2003	2004
Production	846	854	826	857	830
Imports	14	17	22	7	25
Exports	207	183	201	173	190
Consumption	653	673	685	697	710

Source: Report of the Meeting of the Committee on Financial Sector Plan for NER, March 2006.

Corporation (ATC). It has already invited expression of interest for the move. The divestment of ATC could be either through outright sale of a 74 per cent stake in the company, or through long-term lease of individual gardens. The state government, however, is believed to prefer the option of leasing out its gardens on a long-term basis, to selling off a controlling stake in the company. The corporation, created by taking over sick tea gardens in the '70s, has, by now acquired a total of 14 tea gardens scattered over the six districts of the Brahmaputra and Barrak valleys. The combined capacity of the 14 gardens is around 8 million kgs. The corporation also has about 10 factories to process tea leaves to produce black tea. According to the ATC annual report, average production over the past five years was between 6 to 6.5 million kgs. **(The Telegraph-Monday, November 05, 2001).**

The fig.2-A shows the annual production of tea in Assam (ASM), Tripura (TRP), West Bengal (WB), other states of North India (OST), Tamil Nadu (TND), Karnataka (KRNT), Kerala (KER) and India (IND) during the period 1995-2000. The graph shows that Assam's share is the highest (53 p.c.) in country's total production (754 million kg.) in 1995 which decreased to 52 p.c. in 2000. However, during the period the production increased by 7.28 p.c. in the state while for the country, the production increased by 9.21 p.c. In this regard Karnataka stands at the top with 20.81 p.c. followed by west Bengal (12.74 p.c.) and Tamil Nadu (11.34 p.c.).

The following table shows the picture of Tea industry in NER (Annual export) during the 5-year period (2000-04)

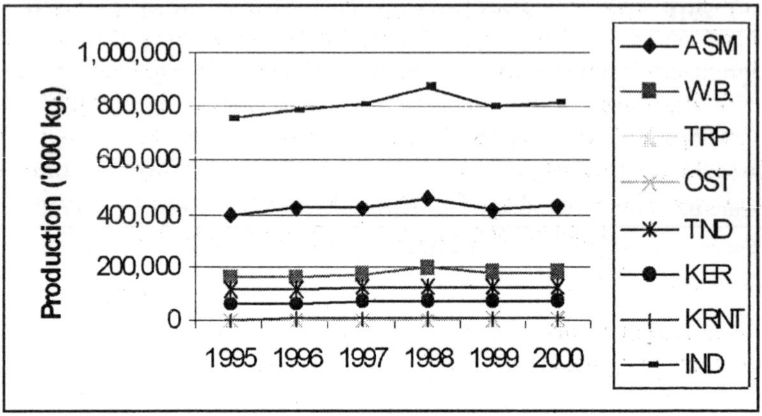

Figure 2-A : Annual State-Wise Tea Production

Banking

Financial infrastructure is essential for economic development. Banks have expanded there network extensively particularly during the last two decades in different states of NER. The number of branches of scheduled commercial banks (SCBs) in NER was 1935 in 1996 which gradually increased to 1941 in 2001 but then it decreased to 1915 in 2003. After 2003 it started to increase again and stands at 1952 as on March 31, 2005. The figure was 1920 as on March 31, 2004. With respect to NER (1952), the percentage of number of branches in Assam is 63.27 and with respect to India (28958) it is only 1.81 p.c. However with respect to India (66970 nos.), there are only 2.87 p.c. branches in NER as on March, 2004 which increased by 1.67 p.c. as on March, 2005. The no. of scheduled commercial bank branches operating in the State of Arunachal Pradesh was 68. The credit deposit ratio was 24.40 p.c. as compared to the national average of 66 p.c. as on March, 2005. During the financial year 2004-05, there were 228 bank branches of all type of commercial banks. Out of these 138 branches in rural areas, 44 branches in semi-urban areas and rest 46 branches in urban area are functioning in the State. In all Schedules Commercial Banks, total deposit was Rs. 232100 lakhs in March 2004, which rose to Rs. 265100 lakhs in March 2005.

On the other hand, total credit was 59100 lakhs till March 2004 which rose to Rs. 78600 lakhs in March 2005. The credit deposit ratio Stood 29.65 % as compared to the national credit-deposit ratios of 66.04% as on March 31, 2005 As on March 31, 2004, the no. of scheduled commercial bank branches in Mizoram was 78 down from 79 as on March 31, 2000. The CDR was 38.37 p.c. as on March 31 2004. Commercial Banks located in Meghalaya have an important role to play in its development particularly in the rural areas. As on March 31, 2003, the number of scheduled commercial bank branches in the State of Meghalaya totaled 180. The deposit stood at Rs. 2164 crore and credit stood at Rs. 623 crore. The credit deposit ratio was a low 23.79 p.c. as compared to the All India average of 59.37 p.c. as on March 31, 2003. Financial assistance in the form of short or medium term loans etc. should be more liberal for the State of Meghalaya where the economy is underdeveloped. : As on March 31, 2004 the number of scheduled commercial bank branches in Nagaland was 69 down from 70 as on March 31, 2000. As compared to the national average of 58.72 p.c., the CDR in Nagaland was as low as 16.84 p.c. as on March 31, 2004.

The credit-deposit ratio (CDR) of banks in NER have fallen from 47 p.c. as on end of March 1991 to 26 p.c. as on end March 2003. But after that it has increased to 35 (as against the national average of 66) as on the end of March 2005. The CDR of banks of all the states of NER including NER and India as a whole for the periods 1997-98 to 2004-05 are shown by **figure- 2-B**. It is important to note that during the period (1997-98 to 2004-05) CD ratio decreased in case of Manipur (25.42 p.c.) and Tripura (14.70 p.c.). The highest percentage increase observed in case of Meghalaya (200 p.c.) followed by Mizoram (121.74 p.c.) and Arunachal Pradesh (84.62 p.c.) and the state of Assam is the lowest (3.03 p.c.) followed by Nagaland (27.78 p.c.). However, percentage increase in the CD ratio in NER (16.67 p.c.) is low as compared to the all India

Corruption and its Impact

In India, corruption attacks the fundamental values of

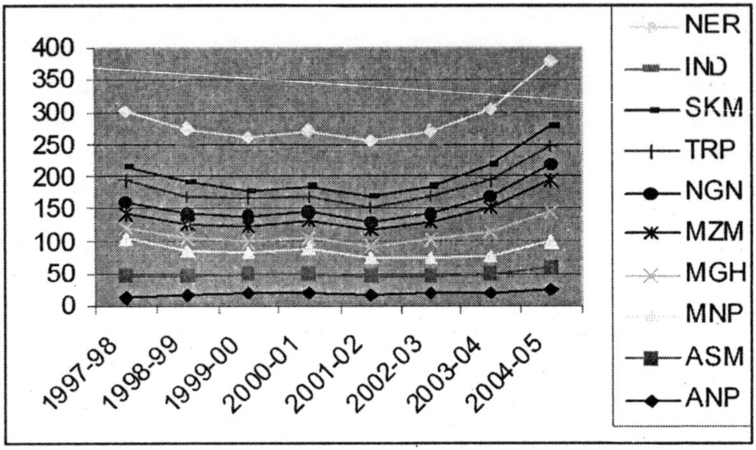

Note: Figures are as on end of March of respective year.(Source: RBI)

Figure 2-B : Credit Deposit Ratio of SCBs in the NER

human dignity and political equality of the people and hence there is a pressing need to formulate a fundamental human right to corruption-free service. Corruption affects India at all levels of governmental decision-making and in the distribution of state largesse. India is ranked 72nd out of 91 countries in the Corruption Perception Index, 2001, prepared by Transparency International (TI). Corruption in India not only poses a significant danger to the quality of governance, but also threatens in an accelerated manner the very foundations of its democracy and statehood. Corruption and indiscipline survive on each other's willingness to accommodate, tolerate and provide encouragement. Corruption affects governance in a significant manner and it is anti-poor. For instance, a substantial portion of foodgrains, sugar and kerosene meant for the public distribution system (PDS) and for welfare schemes for the poor, including the Scheduled Castes (S.C.s) and the Scheduled Tribes (S.T.s), goes into the black market. Hardly 16 per cent of the funds meant for the S.T.s and the S.C.s reach them (Consultation Paper on Probity in Governance, National Commission to Review the Working of the Constitution, 2001). The rest are misappropriated by members of the political and official classes and unscrupulous dealers and businessmen. Like other social evils, the problem of corruption brings out numerous responses. A corrupt government that rejects both transparency and accountability is not likely to respect human rights. Probity in governance is a sine qua non for an efficient system of governance and for socio-economic development. An important requirement for ensuring probity in governance is the absence of corruption. No development process will have any meaning and relevance if corruption as an institutionalised process interferes with people's struggles to realise their right to development. C. Rajkumar (2002) has stressed that if there is no discipline in society, no real or meaningful development or progress is possible.

India's experience with corruption has shown that laws, rules, regulations, procedures and methods of transaction of government business, however sound and excellent they are, cannot by themselves ensure effective and transparent administration if the political and administrative leadership that is entrusted with their enforcement fails to do so and abuses its powers for personal gain (Sunil Sondhi, 2000).

Action Taken by the Government

Considering the geographical features and special characteristics of the NER, Central Government has been resorting to formulating different strategies and Schemes even by making special attention in respect of the respective areas administered by the different Ministries. The programmes are aimed at improving the socio-economic infrastructure, creation of job opportunities, up gradation of culture, education and crating economic base for bringing people to the main stream. Despite abundant natural resources, the state of Assam in particular and the NER in general has remained backward because of pressure on limited resources, perpetual problem of floods, over dependence on agricultural, poor irrigation, poor road and rail links, inadequate telecommunication linkages and ethnic disturbances. Besides all these factors lack of transparency of the political leaders is the main obstacles in attaining the actual development of the region. The natural resource endowments and education levels of the population not with standing, the NER represents one of the least developed – economically and industrially – regions of the country. The State Government of Sikkim has already identified areas for setting up of growth centres. For industries. The new Industrial policy, provides a list of locations for setting up of the new industrial units. The Government has already declared Rangpo-Gangtok, Melli-Jorethang and Jorethang-Rishi and Ranipool-Gangtok as industrial corridors for giving the land to the investors on a lease basis.

Conclusion and Suggestion

To control the population growth, it should be emphasized on successful implementation of family planning programme. The success of family planning programmes in the 21st century depends on various outcomes. Among them is the elimination of social disapproval of family planning which impedes the adoption of contraception, thus demonstrating the need to address the psychic and resource costs of contraception. The scope of coverage needs to be broadened to encompass not only women or men who are interested in limiting their births but also women or men who are interested in achieving other ends. Family planning should also be seen as a joint responsibility of both men and women. It is evident that men do influence the uptake of contraception and as such educating men to appreciate the importance of family planning is likely to lead to increased use of contraception. (Letamo and Bainame,2000). Thus, IEC (Information, Education, Communication) component of family planning programmes needs to be strengthened in order to increase the use of contraceptives and there by to control the population growth.

One of the main challenges before India is to reduce the problem of unemployment and this would be by the end of 2020. Thus, creation of sufficient employment and skilled personnel should be the targets. Efforts should be made in providing sufficient and proper inputs and to utilize the available human resource to accelerate economic growth and overall development. In the coming years there will be an increase in the elderly population in India for which the government should have to bear proper responsibility and care to meeting the needs of those elderly population, in terms of social and economic security.

The government should give priority to set up various technical and professional institutions to enhance the capacity and improve the quality of education and training of the people of NER along with the projects for the development of transport and communication system for linking whole of NER with the main stream of the country.

The government must devise a system which ensures equal opportunitics to the poor with the rich in obtaining higher education and training or in getting a start in trade and industry or securing employment. Another important measure is the introduction of a comprehensive Social Security Scheme (SSS) guaranteeing to each individual a minimum standard of living. The family welfare programme is also an indirect nutrition programme since by reducing family size, it will not only increase the per capita availability of food but also result in all round facilities including health care.

It is to be developed a broad economic base to secure social welfare and to provide equal opportunities and equal access for the advancement for all the bonafied citizen of the region. The governments should prepare a proper plan and policy to eliminate poverty in the village and urban areas and for this small scale home grown industries should be encouraged by extending all sincere help and honest co-operation. The government should develop an economic system which is not overly dependent on foreign loans. While NER should not be isolated economically, it should maintain the integrity of the national economy. It is most important to develop a balance economic system that is open and transparent and eliminates corruption, collusion and nepotism as well as the monopolistic systems which provide protection and privilege only to a small political and economic elite.

The government should develop an economic system that addresses regional economic development which must be in tune with political, cultural and social life and strive to eliminate structural poverty as well as the culture of poverty that affects large segments of the population. It should be based on economic development on the principles of sustainable development with due emphasis on the efficient and sustainable use of natural resources. During the planning, the authority should take into account Region's ethnic and religious diversity and demographic conditions, including the vertical and horizontal arrangement that divide society, and minimize the social and economic disparities within and between every group in society.

Proper support should be extended to the agricultural sector and small to middle-scale industries to ensure their sustainability. The emphasis should be on fostering their self-reliance and not creating dependency on government.

The government has a role in setting standards in the use and management of natural resources and the environment. It is difficult to recruit employees with high levels of competence and to ensure that they remain honest and incorruptible. In addition, the non-transparent recruitment system acts as a disincentive to public service employment. It is no secret that nepotism and bribery have infiltrated the recruitment system and pervade the system of promotions and lateral transfers to career positions that are considered "wet", meaning that they offer many opportunities for making money illegally.

Discrimination on grounds of gender continues to characterize labour relations in the region as well as in the country. Facilities and even wages are accorded on grounds of gender and not based on the quality of work. The most common form of gender discrimination relates to wages, with women still considered as secondary earners, justifying lower wages than those received by men. Hence it is suggested that wages should be based on the quality of work, not on gender.

References

Balk, D. (1994) : "Individual and Community Aspects of Fertility and Women's Status in Rural Bangladesh", Population Studies, 38, 21-45.

Dyson, T.(2004) : "India's Population- The Future" in Dyson et al (eds.) Twenty First Century India, Oxford University Press, New Delhi.

Elo. I. T. (1992) : "Utilization of Maternal Health Care Services in Peru – The Role of Women's Education", Health Transition Review, 2(1), 29-51.

Jeffery, Roger and Basu Alaka M (ed) (1996): "Girls' Schooling- Women's Autonomy and Fertilitry Change in South Asia", Sage Publication, New Delhi.

Letamo, G. and Bainame, K. (2000) : "Reproductive Decision- making : Do men really matter?", A Paper presented at Fourth International Conference on Social Science in Health entitled Africa Health at Crossroads: Challenges for the next Millennium, organized by the Department of Demography and SOMANet and held at the University of Botswana, Gaborone, 7th-11th August.

Le Vine, R.A., Le Vine, S.E., Richman, A.,Uribe, F. M.Tapia, Cottea, C.S.and Miller P.M. (1991) : "Women's Schooling and Child Care in Demographic Transition- A Maxican Case Study", POPULATION AND DEVELOPMENT REVIEW, 17(3), 459-496.

Mandelbaum, D.G. (1988) : "Women's Seclusion and Men's Honor- Sex Roles in North India, Bangladesh and Pakistan", University of Arizona Press, Tuson, Arizona.

Okafor, C.B. (1991) : "Availability and Use of Services for Maternal Child Health Care in Rural Nigeria", International Journal Of Gyneacology And Obstestrics, 34(331), 331-46.

Rosso, Joy Miller Del and Marek Tonia (1996): "Class Action – Improving School Performance in the Developing World through Better Health and Nutrition", The World Bank, Washington D.C.

Singh D.P. (2005) : "Migration in India- Evidence Based National Sample Survey Data", United Nations (1993) : "Women's Education and Fertility Behaviour- Recent Evidence from the Demographic and Health Surveys", U.N. New York.

Visaria, L. (1993) : "Females Autonomy and Fertility Behaviour – An Exploration of Gujrat Data" in International; Union for the Scientific Study of Population (IUSSP), Proceedings of the International Population Conference, Montreal, Vol.- IV, IUSSP.

3

Problems and Prospects of Peace Process in Assam

The study of the history of the word "peace" shows that it comes from the Old French *pais*, which was an ancestor of the modern French paix, and which derived from the Latin *pax* or *pacis*. Pax translated the Greek *eirene*, and, sometimes, the Hebrew *Shalom*. The meaning of "peace", its ancestors, and its contemporary cousins, are not stand-alone meanings. Their meanings are, rather, connected with all the key words in the culture of a given time and place, or in the systematic thought of a given thinker. For the Hebrews *Shalom* was identified with the land that Yahweh had promised to His faithful people, the land of milk and honey, where the lion would lie down with the lamb, and swords would be beaten into ploughshares. **(Brueggemann, 1976)**. Similarly, in the Islamic tradition, "Paradise is the Land of Peace – *Dar al-salam*" **(Haleem, 1998)**. For Plato eirene was a harmony, a sumphonia where actions complemented each other. The hearts and minds guiding the actions were of one accord **(Plato, Popper, 1945)**. For Plato's Christian follower, Saint Augustine, peace was *Concordia*, concord. For Augustine the body existed to serve the mind, which in turn should serve God. The key to concord was to be of one mind. Thus peace required that people think alike **(Fuchs, 1965, Popper, 1945)**. Given that peace is a multifaceted complex ongoing social achievement, it might seem to follow that no general statement about how to make peace could be true.

Peace- to the extent that it exists at all- is perhaps best thought of as a fragile, complex, ongoing, collective social achievement. Many different motives lead people to break the peace. Tendencies toward violence and deeply rooted in the human body, in the glands, in the muscles, in the spinal columns and in the deeper levels of the brain. Further, the institutions that culture has created have not as a general rule brought out the best in human nature. On the contrary, war, Overt, violence and structural violence have been institutionalized. According to **Johan Galtung**, there are three types of violence – namely - direct violence, cultural violence and structural violence. Peace may be defined as the absence of violence. In broader sense, it is a process and sustained efforts to resolve conflict non-violently by addressing the root cause of the problem through negotiation and dialogue. **Gray Cox (1986)** in his book, *'The Ways of Peace: a philosophy of peace as action',* proposes to discard the noun "peace", and to replace it with a verb, "peace-ing." "Peace-ing" is the cultivation of agreements.

Peace, at some places, at some levels, has become so much a part of networks of trusting relationships that people and nations have disarmed. But some peace researchers take the view that giving priority to some social problems postpones the achievement of peace. However, peacemaking should not be confused with attempts to solve the social problems. Since it is hard enough to achieve any social change at all, the essential goal of peacemaking should be to identify the least change that would be necessary in this present society. Thus it is possible to provide a definition of peace that is embedded in the idea of rights, and which links up through that idea with mainstream concepts found around the world. According to the great president of Mexico, Benito Juarez, "Respect for the rights of others is Peace." **(Juarez, 1981)**.

Peace is a multifaceted complex on going social achievement, it might seem to follow that no general statement about how to make peace could be true. Many different things need to be done to make peace. Peace cannot be accomplished without understanding and dialogue because the source of human action, the will, moves in the light of the beliefs that guide actors when they decided to act. Social harmony and security are the *sine qua non* for emergence of a healthy society. People's participation can be ensured only by a peaceful environment ensured by the State.

Many different motives lead people to break the peace. Tendencies toward violence are deeply rooted in the human body, in the glands, in the muscles, in the spinal column and in the deeper levels of the brain. However, Peace requires the assent of the human will. It requires conscious agreement, and conscious cultivation. It follows that comprehensive advances in the art and science of peacemaking must include advances in the understanding of conscious human behaviour. Peacemakers are sometimes tempted to believe that a change of consciousness is all that is needed. Trust, and therefore peace, could be built by changing attitudes. Peace is the cultivation of agreements. Agreements are acts of will. It is possible for society to be at peace even while masses of people continue to feel violent emotions for the same reason that an individual can have aggressive feelings but not act on them.

Ethnicity is now-a-days not a new concept in social science. It was first used by David Rieaman in 1853 as referred to in the 1972 Supplement of the Oxford English Dictionary and subsequently by different scholars. An ethnic group is based on presumed shared socio-cultural experiences and of similar physical characteristics. Such groups may be viewed by their members and or outsiders as religious, racial, national, linguistic and or geographical.

The patterns of conflicts and contradictions between ethnic community vary along scales of time and place. Ethnic conflicts occur at the two levels - between the ethnic groups and ethnic groups vs. states. Any diversity and heterogeneity is not conflict producing per se, although it may carry a potential for conflict. North East India. (NER) has witnessed ethnic conflicts in the process of its historical evolution, and the leadership of independent India was conscious while India presents the picture of unity and diversity, the possibility of conflict between the unity and the diversity could not be ruled out. Independent India's first prime minister, **Sri Jawaharlal Nehru admitted that** ... *"When we talk loudly of our nationalism, each person's idea of nationalism is his own brand of nationalism. It may be Assamese nationalism, it may be Bengali, it may Gujrati, Uttarpradesh, Punjabi or Madrasi. Each one has his own particular brand in mind. He may use the word Nationalism of India but in his mind, his thinking of that nationalism in terms of his own brand of it. When two brands of nationalism come into conflict, there is trouble."*

The problem of identity became acute in recent years. The communities insist today to be known by their original and authentic names and not by misnames which other peoples, mostly outsiders attributed to them. In the process of the 'passing' of ethnic identities and politicalisation of ethnic groups, a number of 'secular' or 'non ethnic' factors play a critical role. This includes the state, Pace and pattern of economic development, political Elites and forces, and outside subversion. Without these factors and the process of transformations in the ethnic groups, diversity would not assume conflictual dimensions. Emphasising the role of political vested interests in participating ethnic conflicts, **Gupta observed,***"Ethnicised politics is a natural inclination of the Indian people"*.

India has a highly complex and colourful social mosaic. North East India's (NER) socio-cultural mosaic is the true picture of 'Unity in Diversity' like a bouquet of flowers or vegetables in a salad bowl, where every component, while retaining its specific identity, is a part of a larger whole. The NER is not only an important cartographic reality in Indian politics but also a space where physical power plays an important role in creating a political discourse of citizenship and people hood. This region does not find itself within the narrative and memory of the nation, yet continues to occupy a central position regarding the territorial integrity of India. Social and economic crisis is deepening faster than any time in north east India. This crisis is the crisis of under-development in capitalist frame work. The capitalist model of development has failed to manage the crisis of economic backwardness.

After the first Anglo-Burmese War and the Yandvaur Treaty (1824-26) the East India Company occupied the districts of Kamrup, Nagaon, Darang and Cachar and annexed in 1832 for the security of the Eastern Frontier. The districts of Sibsagar and parts of Lakhimpur on the north bank of the Bràhmaputra which was restored to an Ahom Prince in 1834, was resumed only four years later. The first hill areas to come under the company were the Khasi states (1829-33) and adjoining Jaintia Raj in the year 1834, Garo hills in 1856. A similar annexation took place in the same year led to the formation of Naga Hills district. These areas together with Goalpara and Sylhet were united in the year 1874 to became the province of Assam. By then Assam had further grown as in the year 1881 Naga Hills district became the settled district of Assam, Lusai Hills district in the year 1898 and Arunachal Pradesh (Formerly, North East Frontier Agency, N.E.F.A.) in the year 1913-14.

From 1st April, 1937, there was a bifurcation of the administrative pattern. The Mizo Hills, Naga Hills, North Cachar Hills, and N.S. Frontier Tracts were called Excluded Areas, excluded from ministerial jurisdiction and the Garo Hills, The British portion of the Khasi & Jaintia Hills and Mikir Hills were partially Excluded Areas. The Excluded Areas were moreover, guarded by the Inner Line which prevented the entry of outsiders without permit. The last of such lines was drawn in North-Cachar Hills in 1942. Assam has undergone changes so fast after independence that it is difficult to ascertain the specific causes as to why such dynamic change had taken place. A section of people advocates a separate state due to dominating influence of the Assamese people over the rest. While advocates of Barak Valley districts and others wanted separation mainly on linguistic issue, those of the hill district mention culture, social system, autonomy etc. along with language. There is a feeling among almost all ethnic groups that they do not get full scope to develop their language and culture and are prone to annihilation by other culture. Economic, political development of tribal people seemed to be very bleak.

The tribal movements in north- east stand in a category by themselves because of its unique geo-political situation and historical background. The hilly areas of north-east India were not completely integrated with the politico-eco system of colonial period and the Inner Line System still in vogue further isolated the tribal region of North East from the rest of the country. The reason for tribal movement lies in the conflict for controlling of political power and economic resources by the elite of tribal societies and neighbouring society. The tribal insurgency is a militant assertion for a share of limited economic resources. The rising tribal aspirations are expressed through movement on cultural identity crisis, the basis of which is economic. As aspirations arise and economic development is painfully slow and uneven, militancy is bound to grow.

Increasing assertion of tribal identity is a part of the overall process of social change and modernization of the tribes. The peace of change has been rapied since independence because of the massive induction of administrative resources into the hitherto isolated areas. The process of modernization has also intensified the search for an identity on the part of the tribal communities. They are becoming conscious of the need to be a viable human resource. As a consequence, small and distinct local groups combine to form a bigger group and adopt a common appellation, through the creation of some socio-political organization. Such delineation, redefinition and expansion of identity base may be viewed as an adoptive mechanism to the changed social, cultural and political circumstances. No doubt in identity movement for wider social base, there are ethnic and political overtones. **(Datta Ray, 1989).**

In the year 1941, the then Governor of Assam, **Sir Robert Neil Reid** submitted a memorandum entitled *"A Note on the Future of the Present Excluded, Partially excluded and Tribal Areas of Assam"* which was concluded with very befitting words as "Assam is never likely to be as homogeneous as other provinces. The plains peoples are not so divided as those of the hills but they are far from being a single people such as can be found in many equally large or larger areas in India. But this great collection of peoples, in hills and plains, have been set in a particularly well demarcated corner of the world and their welfare will depend on their proving able to live together. Assam should look to her diversity and to her capacity for toleration, which is greater than that of other provinces, to provide her strength" **(David R. Syiemlieh, 1996)**

However, The past relation of trust and goodwill amidst ethnic pluralism in pre-independent Assam no longer exists. It is true that much of the tribal problems of Assam, in particular,and NER, in general, today can be traced in their economic backwardness. Unequal development of capital has provided the north-eastern tribes less life change which could in turn mould new life style.

The fact that the sharpening of ethnic boundaries and conflicts in Assam has been on the rise cannot be disputed. The ethnic identity composition of Assam has been further complicated by the imposition of class distinction, not only between one and another ethnic community but also within each. The initial thrust of ethnic conflict in Assam which was directed against the influx of foreigners, experienced some respite in the mid 1980s, although now it has emerged in violent form under the leadership of ULFA, BLT-NDFB, UPDS, DHD etc. groups to demand both political and economic autonomy, separate state, secession from Indian union etc.

The studies has shown an increase in ethnic conflicts and the rise in the number of persons killed in these conflicts has become alarming since 1980. Political vested interests have obviously played a decisive role in this development, which if allowed to go on unabated will worsen the situation and endanger India's unity and integrity. Even when national funds were allocated, they did not reach the targeted groups, because of the corruption of the bureaucrats, politicians and other mediators. In the absence of any serious attempts to correct these economic distortions, it may not be realistic to expect resolution of these ragging ethnic conflicts. Further, marginalisation of a section of the ethnic groups easily go for militancy for their survival. The issues involved are invariably mixed with questions of sharing economic resources and decision making power. The growing recourse to caste and ethnic mobilization in India's democratic politics has been the erosion of ideology and viable socio-economic programmes around which electoral and political mobilisation ought to take place. These followed a rise, both in number and political clout, of ethnic and region based parties **(Dutta, 2005)**.

Terming himself as a Social worker and not a political leader, former Assam Chief Minister veteran politician Late Sarat Chandra Sinha expressed that restoration of peace in the state of Assam was possible if everybody of the state wanted it. Expressing serious concern over the insurgency problem of the state, Mr Sinha said that it is unfortunate that a section of the people do not want restoration of peace in Assam. This section is creating problems in solving the vexed ULFA problem. However, Sinha urged the people of the state to come forward to bring about permanent peace in the state **(The Sentinel, 3rd January, 2005)**.

Since the 1950s a steadily increasing amount of research and scholarly attention has been paid to the resolution of violent conflict and peace research. Today this has become the foundation of a robust body of knowledge focusing on non-military approaches to preventing, managing and ending conflicts.

This paper attempts to present a modest account of how the issues of insurgency, the nature of the state's response to the same and tries to formulate the objectives of the peace process of their own and the process of the state of Assam. It has been made not only to identify various problems in making peace amongst the various ethnic (racial, religious and linguistic) groups of Assam but also to examine the prospects for the peace process amongst these groups.

Keeping the above into account, the study has been designed

under different heads and various published and unpublished secondary data have been used for the purpose. In this regard emergence of different insurgent groups like ULFA, BLT-NDFB, DHD, UPDS (KLNLF), KNA (Kuki National Army), KLO (Kuki Liberation Organisation), HPC (Hmar People's Convention), and then role of States, Civil society, Intelligentsia, Media, Political Will of the leaders etc have been examined. The paper concludes with remarks and suggestions put forwarded for the policy initiatives.

The geographical situation of Assam has given the state its special position and importance situated in north east corner of India (NER) and surrounded by four foreign countries like China, Burma, Bhutan and Bangladesh. Assam stands like a sentinel of the country in a most sensitive region. It is a meeting ground of different cultures which shows a mini India. The present area of Assam is 78,523 sq. km. and half of it becomes 39,261.5 sq. km. Tribals are getting 25,478.1 sq. km. as Union Territory along with 15,222 sq. km. for Karbi Anglong and *N.C. Hills Autonomous* State totaling 40,700.1 sq. km. together which is slightly more than 50 per cent and non-tribals will get 37,822.9 sq. km. in the rest of Assam.

In the post independence era, some remarkable ethnic conflicts took place which changed the current Assam's political history. The forces of regionalism in the state of Assam of NER grew faster due to problem of economic and social development. Although different provisions have been made in the constitution of India to bring socio-economic progress, all these went in vain and the people were offered nothing but disappointment, more hardship, more exploitation and more distributing injustice. Instead of caring for the interest of the people of the state, the leaders are becoming narrow minded and have begun to clamour for the progress of their own. As a result regionalism has been deeply rooted in the states of NER and a conspicuous phenomenon of India's political life, by threatening unity and integrity of the nation. Destruction of national properties become order of the day. As time goes on, more gaps between the center and the states of NER are created instead of closing the same. Economic history reveals that the process of development starts first in regions, which are rich in resources – natural, human and others. Then these regions attract investment and process of development became cumulative.

Dutta (1996) pointed out that the poorest section of the society in Assam has been badly affected. He observed that the richest group of population has been gaining much at the expense of the poorest section of the society. The extent of degree of inequality in the level of living in the state of Assam in NER is much more than what is taken to guide some of the decision making elements in connection with resource transfer from center to the states of NER particularly in Assam. Again, Economic development is a pre-requisite to peace. Government today is in no position to provide jobs to all educated youth. When an educated youth fails to get employment, he turns to insurgency. Unless we bring back peace and security to the region, we are bound not only to lose valuable years right now but also stay far behind the rest of the country in the match towards development and prosperity.

It can be realised the intensity with which the 'aggressive linguistic nationalism' worked in the state of Assam when one will compare between the real and the manipulated population figures from 1951 census onwards. In Brahmaputra Valley, the percentage of Assamese speaking people increased from 42 p.c. in 1931 to 73.1 p.c. in 1951 and it is further increased to 73.3 p.c. only in 1961 while at the same time in the same valley, the percentage of Bengalee- speaking people decreased to 13.0 p.c. in 1951 from 23.0 p.c. in 1931 which t is further decreased to 9.8 p.c. in 1961. Again, considering the whole of NER, it is observed that the percentage of Bengali speaking people in Assam was 14.77 p.c. according to 1971 census while the percentage increased to 14.89 p.c. in the year 1991. During the same period, the percentage of Assamese speaking people were decreased to 41.08 p.c. in 1991 from 45.63 p.c. in 1971 while the percentage of Bodo people increased from 2.73 p.c. to 3.75 p.c. **(Dutta and Pradhan, 2003)**.

Table-3.1 shows that the ethno linguistic diversity between two valleys of Assam namely, the Barak Valley and the Brahmaputra also between the two predominant communities of the state namely, the Assamese and the Bengalees seems to have provided a background for a number of social and political issues which gave rise to the large scale movements in Assam after 1947. It is to be noted here that the percentage of Assamese speaking population (71 p.c. in Brahmaputra Valley) and Bengali speaking population (78 p.c. in Barak Valley) together constitute 81 p.c. of the total population in Assam followed by Hindi speaking people (5.42 p.c.) and the Bodos (3.65 p.c.).

Recently, again communal disturbance started in the Brahmaputra Valley against Hindi speaking persons, in general and Bihari Population in particular. However, for the protection of Hindi Speaking people in Assam, the organization named as Non- Tribal Youth Union (NTYU) requested one of the MPs (Member of Parliaments) of Bihar to place 11- point Charter of demands before the house of the parliament.

Insurgency has created an atmosphere in which financial accountability and internal resource mobilization have become the main casualties and to the extent insurgency has vitiated the true logic of development. One of the important problems which creates hindrance to economic development is the problem of population explosion in the state.

Fig.– 3-A shows the population of Assam and NER during the period 1951- 2001. From the graph it is observed that the total population of Assam in the year 1951 was 80.29 lakhs which increased to 146.25 lakhs in 1971 and it reached to the level of 266.48 lakhs in the year 2001. During the same period the population of NER increased from 102.6 lakhs to 384.95 lakhs. The total population of the state is about 26.65 million representing 2.6 per cent of India's total population in 2001 while it was 2.2 percent in 1951. The growth rate of population in the state is much higher than the national average as it is observed that during the period 1951-2001, the percentage growth rate of the population for the state is 231.77 while it is

Table 3.1: Linguistic Distribution of Population in Barak Valley, Brahmaputra Valley, Hill District, Assam, 1971

	Barak Valley		Brahmaputra Valley		Assam	
	Total Population		Total Population		Total Population	
	17,13,318		1,24,56,477		1,46, 25,152	
Language	person	p.c.	person	p.c.	person	p.c
Assamese	6,840	0.40	88,44,313	71.00	89,04,917	60.89
Bengali	13,32,268	77.76	15,01,813	12.05	28,82,039	19.71
Hindi	1,93,266	11.28	5,67,063	4.55	7,92,481	5.42
Bodo	1,561	0.09	4,98,904	4.00	5,33,724	3.65
Nepali	4,216	0.25	3,14,865	2.52	3,48,116	2.38
Mikir	1,142	0.06	17,765	0.14	2,21,354	1.51
Manipuri	72,290	4.31	12,975	0.10	85,789	0.59
Dimasa	10,540	0.62	1,313	0.01	38,307	0.26
Others	91,195	5.33	6,97,448	5.59	8,18,225	5.59

Source : Census of India 1971. Series 3. Assam Part-I, A General Report.

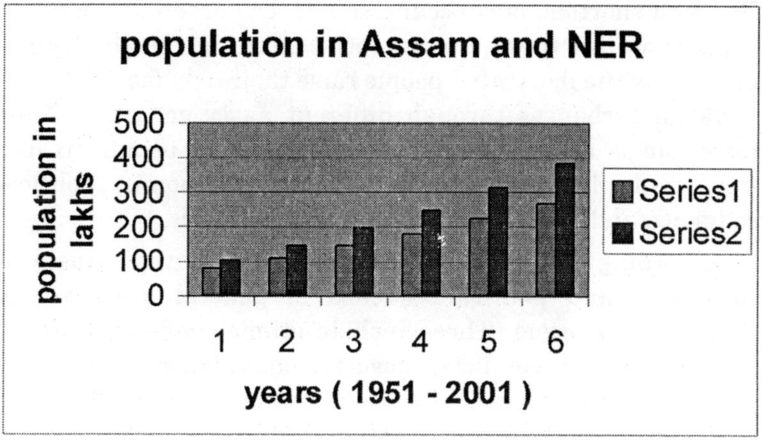

Figure 3-A : Population Distribution of Assam and NER (1951-2001)

only 184.42 for the country as a whole. Increased population at an alarming rate in the region is due to immigration from outside the country as well as from within the country.

The population explosion caused by immigration pose serious threat on the natural resources of the region and hence on the economic development. The absolute number of the migrants was more than 91 thousand in 1901, since then it has been steadily increasing and reached at nearly 745 thousand in the census year 1991. The share of migrants from Bangladesh was between slightly more than 70 per cent to slightly more than 87 per cent in pre-independence era. The post independence era, it reached at 94 per cent in 1951- the highest among the period 1901- 1991. From 1961 onwards the share started to decline and become around 89 per cent in the census year 1991. It is also clear from the statistical information that Bangladesh was followed by Nepal in sending migrants to the states of NER in general and Assam in particular. In the recent years the flow of immigration from the neighbouring countries shows an increasing trend **(Dutta, 2003)**.

Dutta (2002) showed that poverty is an important factor in the development of frustration of the young generation. Again frustration develops in the society due to unemployment and poverty which is also the consequence of food shortage.

The food shortage may occur due to over burden of the excess population. All these creates social chaos in the society and ultimately the frustrated people raise their ugly faces to create social disturbances through different nasty activities. Thus, terrorism is a multicausal phenomenon and usually results from multiple causal factors such as economic, political, religious, and sociological factors, among others.

According to **Paul Wilkinson (1986)**, the causes of revolution and political violence in general are also the causes of terrorism. These include ethnic conflicts, religious and ideological conflicts, poverty, modernization stresses, political inequities, lack of peaceful communications channels, traditions of violence, the existence of a revolutionary group, governmental weakness and ineptness, erosions of confidence in a regime, and deep divisions within governing elites and leadership groups.

Frustration-Aggression Hypothesis

The frustration-aggression hypothesis of violence is prominent in the literature. This hypothesis is based mostly on the relative-deprivation hypothesis (see Glossary), as proposed by **Ted Robert Gurr (1970)**, an expert on violent behaviors and movements, and reformulated by **J.C. Davies (1973)** to include a gap between rising expectations and need satisfaction. Another proponent of this hypothesis, **Joseph Margolin (1977: 273-4),** argues that "much terrorist behavior is a response to the frustration of various political, economic, and personal needs or objectives." Other scholars, however have dismissed the frustration-aggression hypothesis as simplistic, based as it is on the erroneous assumption that aggression is always a consequence of frustration. Political scientist **Paul Wilkinson found (1974: 127)** faults in the frustration-aggression hypothesis for having "very little to say about the social psychology of prejudice and hatred..." and fanaticisms that "play a major role in encouraging extreme violence."

In this paper, an attempt has been made to discuss the

emergence and the activities of main five insurgent groups of Assam, namely, *United Liberation Front of Assam (ULFA), Bodo Liberation Tiger (BLT)- National Democratic Front of Bodoland (NDFB), United Peoples Democratic Solidarity (UPDS), Dima Halim Daogah (DHD) and the peace process thereof.*

United Liberation Front of Assam (ULFA)

The United Liberation Front of Assam (ULFA) is a terrorist organization operating in India's Assam region. The group was formed on April 7, 1979 and remains active to this date. ULFA was formed with the dual goal of establishing Assam as a separate country, independent of India, while also establishing a socialist government to rule the "Assam country" (Sadin Axom). Over two and half decades after ULFA's founding, Assam has neither broken away from India nor established a socialist government. This is not to say that ULFA has had no effect on the region in the last twenty six years. While ULFA was formed in 1979, the group did not commence significant activities until 1986. However, it came to be notice as nascent armed organization only in late 1983, when it commenced political assassination and bank robberies. In 1986, ULFA aggressively raised money via extortion and established relationships with two other non-state entities, Kachin Independence Army (KIA), Nationalist Socialist Council of Nagaland (NSCN). Even more significantly, ULFA was able to gain some support within the ruling party in Assam, Assam Gana Parishad (AGP). ULFA even had supporters within the police departments of Assam. Because of ULFA's increased visibility, the Indian government outlawed the group in 1986 and declared Assam a troubled area.

From the early 1990s on, the ULFA has continually increased its terrorist activities. A group of ULFA militants (probably 16 nos.) were trained in a place near Islamabad in September, 2003 to handle 'Programmable Time Devices (PTD)' to trigger off explosions and they came back in the month of December,

2003. This device can be planted by setting the time 194 days ahead for explosion. The group assassinates political opponents, attacks police and other security forces, blasts rail road tracks, and attacks other infrastructure facilities and continued till its last attack made on 27th August, 2005. The Government of Assam changed the police set up in the guwahati city by re-designating the city SP (Superintendent of Police) as "Senior Superintendent of Police". Two additional posts, that SP traffic and Special Operation Unit (SOU) in the city, were created. Though there were reports of Mynmar Army operations against the militants holed up in the country, police sources said that the ULFA had its bases in the neighbouring country and they would launch most of their operations from the bases in Myanmar as the 28 battalion of the outfit was based in the neighbouring country **(The Assam Tribune, 21.01.2005)**.

The demand for a separate state of 'kamata' or 'Koch land' in North Bengal as well as some parts of Assam has taken a violent turn during the last few years, organized by 'Kamatapur Liberation Organization' (KLO), 'Koch Rajbanshi Liberation Organization' (KRLO), 'Koch Rajbanshi Liberation Tiger Force' (KRLTF) and 'Koch Rajbanshi Security Force' (KRSF). This movement has received help and assistance from extremist groups of Assam like the outlawed ULFA, 'Bodo Ultra Groups' etc. The movement originated with a view to protecting their rights and interest in Social, Political, Cultural and Economic spheres. They swear to restore and regain their lost identity which were established in the 15th century Assam by carving out separate state. They also demanded their Kamatapuri language to be included in the 8th schedule of Indian Constitution.

With security agencies warning of an imminent ULFA regroup, the Home Ministry, at New Delhi, set up a mechanism to share intelligence among the north-eastern states. The senior police officials would meet at regular intervals to share intelligence about movement of militants across the state boundaries. This was decided at a meeting to review the security of North-eastern states chaired by Home Secretary

V.K. Duggal. In addition to the above the Governor of Assam in a number of occasions talked about the "Final Battle" to "Wiping out ULFA forever." Many a times NER was declared a *"Disturbed Area"* under the *Armed Forces Special Power Act* of 1958. Several army operations, namely 'Sher-E-Dil', 'Bojrong'(November, 1990 – April, 1991), 'Tiger Heart', 'Rhino-I'(15.09.1991 to 13.01.1992), 'Rhino-II', 'Rhino-III' (March, 1992), 'Blue Bird', 'All Clear, etc. marked in the region since the beginning of disturbances.

There have been quite a few attempts by various civic organisations in Assam like "Assam Sahitya Sabha', Manab Adhikar Sangram Samity (MASS) and others to convince both the rebels and the government for peaceful dialogue to bring peace in the state. Many individuals namely the renowned Assamese novelist and Professor, Dr. Indira Goswami, Dr. Bhabendranath Saikia, Dr. Bhupen Hazarika, Sri. Kanak Sen Deka and others have volunteered to act as mediator in the desired talks but unfortunately,. most of these proposals have been rejected. Lately, however, Dr Mamoni Raisom Goswami initiated contacts with both the Government of India (GOI) and the ULFA leadership and succeeded to initiate peace talk between the GOI and the ULFA leadership.

Meanwhile, Prime Minister Manmohan Singh has reiterated that his Government is keen to initiate peace talks with all insurgent groups and to find solutions to the problems facing the region. Talking to a 28-member delegation of MPs from the Northeast on December 18, 2004, he said the Centre is willing to talk to all the insurgent groups who are ready for a dialogue with the government. However, this may not extend to the ULFA, since the outfit does not seem to be ready for an unconditional talks.

Childhood friend of ULFA 'c-in-c' Paresh Baruah, Reboti Phukon, who has been named by the ULFA to assist peace interlocutor Mamoni Raisom Goswami, said, "This time Paresh has taken the initiative, and with Chief Minister Tarun Gogoi also exuding a positive outlook, we all expect a fruitful outcome." Sports organizer and the man who had carried the outfit's first letter to the Centre, Hiranya Saikia said: "History is in the making and the outcome of the ULFA's initiative totally hinges on the Centre's response." The People's Consultative Group (PCG), formed by the ULFA on 8th September, 2005, expressed to solicit Public opinion on ways to resolve militancy in Assam which generated an enthusiastic response and thrown up a host of new possibilities.

In a statement, ULFA chairman Arobinda Rajkhowa criticised intellectuals and historians in Assam for maintaining a "studied silence" over the NSCN's demand for the integration of large parts of Tinsukia, Sivasagar, Jorhat, Golaghat, Karbi Anglong, North Cachar, Hailakandi and Silchar districts of the state with the proposed Naga homeland. He appeared to have ignored consistent statements and views by many who have taken a tough anti-integration stand.

In a significant proposal, the group has sought opinion from the public as it felt that the responsibility bestowed on it by the ULFA is 'sensitive' and without people's cooperation it will not be possible to push the peace process. In the wake of the invitation for talks, PCG had received immense response from the public through e-mail, Fax, telephone, SMS etc. To prepare the ground works for peace talks with ULFA, the GOI appointed National Security Adviser Mr. M.K. Narayanan.

New Delhi has offered to hold talks with the outlawed ULFA outside India to end more than 26 years of insurgency in the region. The ULFA is blamed for a series of explosions in Assam. According to intelligence officials, there are about 3,000 fighters in the group, one of the most powerful rebel armies in the northeast. Home Minister Shivraj Patil, currently on a four-day visit to the northeast, said the government was ready to hold talks with the ULFA.

India says it is inching closer to convincing Dhaka to crack down on anti-India guerrilla bases in Bangladesh and that the two countries are in negotiations to combat cross-border terrorism. Patil said Prime Minister Manmohan Singh was likely to take up the matter with his Bangladeshi counterpart on the sidelines of the South Asian Association for Regional Cooperation (SAARC) summit in Dhaka. New Delhi maintains there could be at least 150 camps of rebel groups from India in Bangladesh. Dhaka has in the past denied harbouring any guerrillas.

Only 9 out of the 11-member PCG, named by the ULFA, decided in its first meeting held at Guwahati on 11th September, 2005 to sit across the table with the Centre to frame the 'ground rules' for the much-anticipated ULFA-Centre talks, to deliberate on the role it would play in the peace process. Describing the Chief Minister's optimism regarding the outfit's peace overture as a 'welcome sign', the PCG feels that it would be even better if the Chief Minister manifests his alacrity through 'action'.

The ULFA leaders have clearly appealed to the Government of India to release their 10 senior arrested leaders of the executive council of the ULFA as a prelude to talks with the Indian Government which has been stated in their second formal letter addressed to the Indian Prime Minister as part of the ongoing peacc process.

The Central Government has so far spent Rs. 1.5 crore under the scheme for surrender of militants. The surrender militant are covered under the Scheme for Surrender-cum-Rehabilitation of militants in the North east. 437 surrendered militants have been trained/ undergoing training under this scheme. The scheme envisages only assistance for self employment training and the surrendered militants are to apply for self- employment schemes as per normal rules applicable.

Yearning of militants to return to the path of peace is demonstrated by surrender of 1191 militants in the current year compared to 251, 676 and 308 surrendered in the years 1998, 1999 and 2000 respectively. The surrendered militants belonging to various militant outfits namely ULFA, UPDS, NDFB, MULTA, DHD and Rava National Security Force (RNSF) who have bidden farewell to arms. The massive number of surrenders also reflects the deep disillusionment of the militant cadres with their direction less leadership.

The plain tribals of Assam can broadly be divided into two groups like – i) the Bodo group and ii) the Miri and the Michings. The Bodo groups of the plain tribals of Assam belong to different religious, some of them Hindus, some Christians and some profess tribal religion. Among the hill tribes of Assam the Dimasa and Garos belong to this Bodo stock. The All Bodo Students' Union (ABSU), A student organization of Bodos has been demanding that Assam must be divided fifty-fifty between the tribals and the non-tribals. The present area of Assam is 78,523 sq. km. and half of it becomes 39,261.5 sq. km. Tribals are getting 25,478.1 sq. km. as Union Territory along with 15,222 sq. km. for Karbi Anglong and N.C. Hills Autonomous State totaling 40,700.1 sq. km. together which is slightly more than 50 per cent and non-tribals will get 37,822.9 sq. km. in the rest of Assam. The areas of Union Territory include the whole of Kokrajhar and Lakhimpur districts on Majuli and Sadia Sub-division, northern parts of Dhubri, Goalpara, Barpeta, Nalbari, Kampur, Darrang and Sonitpur districts. They claimed that they had been the master and ruler of Assam at one time and the present Assamese society is formed by the influx from Kanauj, Mithila, Magadha etc. of the central India in the 13th and 14th century only whereas the Bodos and other tribals are the aboriginal people of Assam. They alleged that the Assam government whether the past or present ones are not the government of the people of Assam but it is merely the government of Assamese people. As such no expected progress of tribals in the dimension of education, economy, language, culture could be achieved even after more than five and half decades of independence of India. Large scale violence in the districts of Kokrajhar, Bongaigaon and Dhubri of Assam in the month of May, 1996 against Adivasis, mainly Santals, rendered more than 1,50,000 people homeless. Riots accompanied by plunder, arson and massacre which occurred then were the 3rd major set of riots against the non-bodo communities in the Bodo Autonomous Council Area of western Assam, which was set up as part of an agreement in 1993. As Bodo Liberation

Front (BLF) and All Bodo Students' Union (ABSU) who are spearheading a movement for a separate Bodo-Land, targeted non-Bodo communities to spark violence. The year 1993 was a turning point in the political history of Assam when BTC (Bodo Territory Council) was granted after signing the Accord. The doubts had been expressed that the geography of Assam is going to be further reduced and the fact was established when the Bodo insurgent group, BLT (Bodo Liberation Tiger), Central Government and the State Government decided to implement the Accord on the 10th February, 2003. At that time no one can resist the Bodos from their demand of separate statehood and this very demand is due to the repressive attitude of the Assamese people towards the other ethnic groups.

The main discontent was mounted in this hill district when Assamese was imposed as medium in the University and Secondary level of education. BLT, which formed in the year 1996, demanded separate statehood for the people living on the northern side of the river Brahmaputra and also to include the Bodos in the 6th schedule of the Indian Constitution for the Bodo people living in the Karbi-Anglong district of Assam. The step motherly attitude towards the non-Assamese people in case of employment policy and in developmental work and also aggressive policy of Assamisation by the State government of Assam gave birth of dissatisfaction to the Bodo people (Samayik Prasanga, 10th February, 2003).

Bodo Liberation Tiger (BLT)- National Democratic Front of Bodoland (NDFB)

All Bodo Students Union (ABSU), formed in February, 1967 and was demanding a separate state for Bodos. By 1987, 'Divide Assam Fifty-fifty' became the most important demand of the Bodos. As they realized that it would be impossible on the part of the government to accept their demand, they tried to terrorise people and the government through different ugly activities. One such organization – the Bodo Security Force (BdSF) which formed in the year 1986. Meanwhile a number of other terrorist organizations like National Democratic

Front of Bodoland (NDFB), Bodoland Liberation Tiger Force (BLTF), Bengali Tiger Force (BTF), Islamic Revolutionary Army (IRA), Immigrant Muslim Liberation Army (IMLA), COBRA etc have also made their presence. While the NDFB is demanding for a sovereign Bodoland, the BLTF is fighting for a separate state for the Bodos. The different massacres starting from 13th January, 1998 till date proves clealy that Bodo groups are determined to drive out the non-Bodo groups. During insurgency they killed brutally thousands of innocent civilians, security personnel, Bodo intellectuals. They also destroyed many public institutions including the educational institutions and communication net work. On the other hand, the government machineries also destroyed lots of properties and killed many innocent civilians.

The NDFB was instrumental in introducing the ULFA to the possibility and viability of operating ultra bases in Bhutan and the Garo Hills of Meghalaya. Though the Bhutan camps have been dislocated after the Bhutanese government launched a military offensive against Indian Ultras there, the Garo Hills is still a major base as well as transit route for the ULFA. The cooperation of a section of the local people to carry out their activities in the hills was facilitated to a large extent by the NDFB's close lonks with the Garo militant outfit A'chik National Volunteer Council (ANVC). As both the ANVC and NDFB decided to take peace path, the ULFA may witness a drastic change in the ground situation in the Bodo- dominated areas of Assam as welll as the Garo Hills. This is perhaps the reason why the ULFA has not been as active in lower Assam as it has been in upper Assam of late. However, a sharp polarization is taking place among the armed struggles of the region. (The Assam Tribune, 24.01.2005).

To restore peace and normalcy, the central government invited BLT to the discussion table as a result of which BTC came into being in February, 2003 and where 12 members under the leadership of Mr. Hagrama Basumatari took oath in the presence of the Deputy Prime Minister and the Chief Minister of Assam. Another insurgency group under the banner of NDFB under the leadership of Mr. Ranjan Daimary raised its ugly head as they are deprived of power in the newly created BTC.

United Peoples Democratic Solidarity (UPDS)

The Mikir Hills and the North Cachar Hills are the only two autonomous Hill Districts remaining in Assam after independence. The Karbi Anglong and North Cachar Hill of Assam bounded by the plain district of Nowgong and Sibsagar on the North, Meghalaya on the West, Nagaland and Manipur on the East and the district of Cachar on the South. These two districts were administered as "Excluded and Partially Excluded Area". The tribal people of this area represented for separate autonomy to safeguard their language, culture, customs and ways of life. In 1975, the Mikir Hill, came into being out of the portions of Sibsagar and Nowgong districts of Assam and a new civil district with North Cachar Hill sub-division was formed in 1970, the North Cachar Hill sub-division was raised into the status of a district. The Mikir and Dimassa Kachari are the main tribes living in the Mikir Hills District. While North Cachar Hill District is inhabitant of Dimassa Kachari, Hmar, Kuki, Mikir and other tribes. They have their own languages, cultures and traditions but one thing they have in common is their backwardness, educationally, economically and politically. At the time of State Re-organisation of 1969, the Mikir Hills and the North Cachar Hill District Councils were given option to join the proposed Meghalaya Sub-State but the people of those hills did not see the solution of their problems in joining Meghalaya. On the other hand, they received certain significant assurances from the highest authority of the government of Assam and the APCC (Assam Pradesh Congress Committee). They wanted to develop in all spheres by preserving their own separate entities as tribes.

The narrow and selfish politics of the single majority tribe DIMASA of N.C. Hills since the inception of the N.C. Hills autonomous District Council (present Autonomous Council) is one of the chief causes leading to the ethnic clash between the Hmars and Dimasaa which erupted in the two districts of N. C. Hills and Cachar since of late. The N.C. Hills Autonomous Council was formed in 1952 following the Govt. order no. TAD/ R-31/ 503209 dated 3/1/1951. the suppressive politics of the Dimasas in N.C. Hills in various forms is also a striking root cause leading to the ethnic clashes prevailing in N.C. Hills and Cachar since 26th February, 2003.

Considering all these the then Mikir hill and the North Cachar Hills Leaders' conference submitted a memorandum for a separate State to the Prime Minister of India in June, 1973. The Central Committee of Karbi Anglong and North Cachar Hill State Demand Committee again submitted memorandum to the Prime Minister of India on 18th January, 1982 for creation of a separate full fledged State. They expressed their desire due to the economic, political and cultural backwardness of their people along with the issue of medium of instruction. Their agitation took violent turn when the Autonomous State Demand Committee (ASDC) and the Karbi Students' Association (KSA) jointly submitted a memorandum to the Prime Minister of India on 18th May, 1987.

In the Political history of Karbi Anglong, the autonomous state movement under the leadership of Autonomous State Demand Committee (ASDC) was a significant chapter since 1986. Subsequently, in a critical juncture, the Karbi National Volunteer (KNV), born on 22nd March, 1994, and the Karbi Peoples' Force (KPF), born on 12th September, 1994 have emerged to represent the movement for self rule for the Karbis. In 21st May, 1999 both the organizations forged to united under a single banner – United Peoples Democratic Solidarity (UPDS). However, a section of UPDS cadre, under the leadership of Mr. Haren Bey, signed ceasefire agreement with the government of India and which came into effect from 1st August, 2002. The UPDS in its 3rd general council held on and from 6th May to 16th May, 2004 renamed as Karbi Longri North Cachar Hills Liberation Front (KLNLF).

Dima Halim Daogah (DHD)

DHD is an offshoot of the erstwhile Dima National Security Force (DNSF), which had surrendered in 1995, except for its self styled Commander-in-chief Jewel Garlossa who subsequently launched the DHD. DHD starts where DNSF ends. The NSCN (IM) and DHD had conducted joint operation on several occasions in N.C. Hills of Assam. Using the name of Dimaraji in order to exploit the Dimasa sentiment, the NSCN(IM)-DHD imposed annual routine tax on businessman, all types of contractors, all employees etc. It is to be noted here that Education and Medical institutions too are not spared. It is very much interesting to note that they even used to collect taxes from different grades of employees (10% to 30%) of the Police and the Forest departments. In recent reports of KARBI- DIMASA clash indicates DHD allegedly forged "Strategic Alliance" with the National Democratic Front of Bodoland (NDFB).

DHD submitted a memorandum to the Hon'ble Home Minister of India, vide memo no. 01/DPSC/DBH/DHD/2004 dated 23.09.2004, for the creation of separate "DIMARAJI STATE". The DHD leadership declared that it was ready to face any war but still prefers an amicable solution to the crisis that has griped Karbi Anglong following the recent blood bath The leadership also expressed as "we are with the people and we do not want to retaliate as it will lead to chaos. But let us make it clear that we are always ready to defend ourselves". **(The Telegraph, 5th October, 2005)**.

Its declared objective is to create a separate state of 'DIMARAJI' comprising Dimasa dominating areas of the North Cachar Hills and Karbi- Anglong districts of Assam and some parts of Cachar, Nowgoan and Dimapur district of Nagaland. The outfit is led by its president Pranab Nunisa and Chairman Dilip Nunisa. The outfit mostly operates in Cachar, N.C. hills, Karbi- long and Nowgoan districts of Assam. Extortions constitutes a major source of funding for the outfit before and after entering into the ceasefire agreement. The outfit is currently observing 'ceasefire' with the government. The DHD indicated a willingness to pursue peace talk with the central government. The Dimasa apex body, **Jatikhe Naisho Hasom (JNH)**, repeatedly appealed both the central government and the DHD for peace in the region for the greater interest of the people.

The ceasefire agreement was signed between the DHD leadership and the Union government on the 1st January, 2003 and the agreement being periodically extended. But the ugly massacre of 1st April, 2003 at Chekarcham and Megnathal in the border district of Cachar which took 23 lives poured water in the peace process and thus tension continued between the Hmars and the Dimasa and subsequently law and order situation of the District paralysed completely. However, it took to time to bring the normalcy in the region. The tardy progress of the negotiation has disappointed the DHD leadership, whose chief Dilip Nunisa termed the delay as 'intentional procrastination'. During October, 2005, the DHD outfit accepted the war declared by the United People's Democratic Solidarity (UPDS) on it the issue of killing the Karbis in Karbi Anglong.

During the first 20 years of the District Council, Dimasa leaders were very busy with political manoeuvering and could not do much in cultural field. Dimasa Jalairaoini Hosom (DJH) was organized in 1972 to protect and promote cultural identity of the community. They raised the demand regarding the preservation of Dimasa historical monuments and adoption of Dimasa at primary schools in Dimasa areas. This non political cultural Association, voices the hopes, aspirations and apprehensions of the new Demisa Youths. The demand for the proper preservation of ancient Dimasa Monuments and Relice were raised by the Dimasa National Organisation (11th March, 1979), just after taking birth in the year 1979. In the next year (1980), Nikhil Hirimba Barman Samity (NHBS), an organization of the Dimasas of Cachar put forwarded a political demand for the re-organisation of the Dimasa speaking areas of north-east.

The Hmars are the inhabitants of Mizoram and a part of Assam in the Barak Valley and North Cachar Hills. The

Scheduled Caste and Scheduled Tribes Order (amended) Act of 1976 includes Hmar as Scheduled Tribe. in Assam. To their great dissatisfaction and under the banner of Hmar Peoples Convention (HPC). Hmars have been carrying on agitations since 1954 for autonomy within or separately to safeguard their interests in Hmar dominated areas. In a memorandum to the Prime Minister of India on 21st January, 1987, HPC raised the demand for a separate Autonomous District Council within North Cachar Hills. They wanted the recognition of North Cachar district to satisfy their political aspirations. The demand made by the Hmar was unacceptable to the Dimasas. They staged agitational programmes through different ugly activities from time to time to fulfill their demands. The leaders of Hmars community complained that years had passed since the independence but the government of Assam had shown total disregard to their socio-political and economic aspiration. As a result the president of HPC warned that it will take extreme step in this regard. Despite surrender of a number of cadres of the HPC to the government of Assam, some of the dissidents who remained underground had been able to reactive the organization and a nexus between NSCN and HPC has been established. The militants had enabled the Hmars to set up camps in dense forests along Assam- Mizoram border and with their active support extended operations to the Barak Valley and North Cachar Hill region of Assam. The ugly massacre of 1st April, 2003 at Chekarcham and Megnathal in the border district of Cachar which took 23 lives poured water in the peace process and thus tension continued between the Hmars and the Dimasa and subsequently law and order situation of the District paralysed completely. However, it took to time to bring the normalcy in the region. Recently, again the problem of burning of houses, killing, looting etc started in the district of Karbi- Anglong in the wake of the Month of December, 2005.

The **figure 3-B** represents the casualties in various violence incidents in Assam during the period 2000-2003. In the Bar diagram, series 1 represents the civilians, series 2 represents SF personnel, series 3 represents Terrorists and Series 4 represents the total casualties. The year 2000 witnessed the highest total casualties of the tune of 758 out of which there are 356 civilians, 65 SF personnel and 327 terrorists. The number of casualties decreased to 606 (264 civilians, 59 SF personnel and 283 Terrorists) in the year 2001 and which further decreased to 445 (138 civilians, 52 SF personnel and 275 Terrorists) in the year 2002 while during 2003, the figure increased to 505 (212 civilians, 12 SF personnel and 281 terrorists). Here, it should be mentioned that Kokrajhar was the district where maximum (46 out of 138) civilians were killed than in any other districts

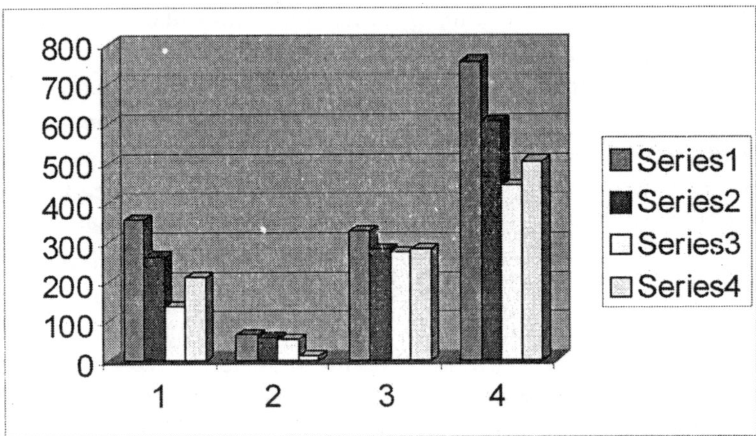

Figure 3-B: Casualties in Various Violence Incidents in Assam, 2000-2003

of Assam and which is followed by Darrang. With regard to SF personnel, North Cachar Hills district shows the highest casualties (10 SF fatalities) followed by Kokrajhar (5 SF).

The **figure 3-C** shows the casualties in various violence incidents occurred in the state of Assam during 12 different months of the year 2003. It is observed that highest casualties in case of civilians occurred in the month of November (78) and lowest in the month of February (2). The casualties ranges from 11 (January) to 42 (December). The total casualties ranges from 19 (February) to 104 (November). However, there was no casualties in case of SF personnel during months of March, May, July, August, October and December. In the line diagram series 1 represents the civilians, series 2 represents SF personnel, series 3 represents Terrorists and Series 4 represents the total casualties.

In NER the expenditure to control insurgency has been increasing day by day. But ironically along with the expenditure to control insurgency, insurgency has been increasing by leaps and bounds. Recently, in an NEC published paper a detailed account of expenditure is presented. This paper of expenditure is outside the budget of Defense Ministry and seven State Governments. After so much expenditure made for security purpose, bomb in Chief Minister's Convoy, Kidnapping of Bureaucrats, bombs in buses are regular features. If anything serious happens, the Chief Ministers of this region make the lame excuse that are no sufficient Central forces in the region and also there may be a role of third party and the ISI. But, in the last six years, in NER, the central government spent an

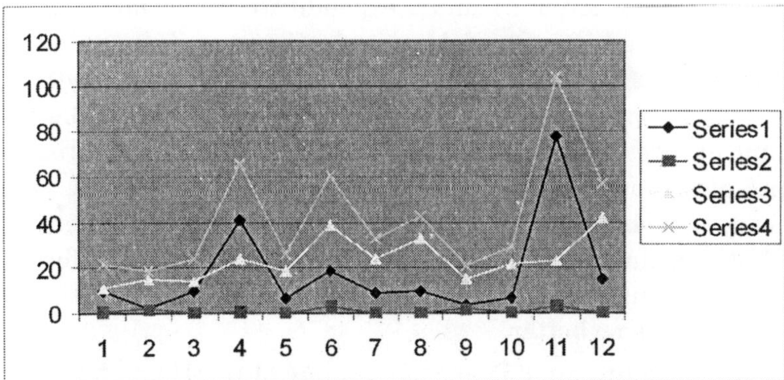

Figure 3-C: Casualties in Various Violence Incidents in Assam During The Moths of January to December, 2003

additional amount of 1,000 crore for deployment of police forces. After spending such huge amount of money, the condition of the region is no better.

In the last seven years, the states of NER have sanctioned crores of rupees in their budget. Side by side an amount of 767 crores of rupees they have spent for police security out of the enhanced amount of Rs. 1,000 crores sanctioned by the Central government (Government of India). Among these seven states, Assam having an expenditure amounting to Rs. 487.8 crores, Tripura having 118 crore and Nagaland having 96 crores are at the top of the list.

For the modernization of police force another 278 crores of rupees has been spend. In this sphere also Assam is on the top of the list along with the states of Tripura and Nagaland.. The amounts spent for these states are 103 crore, 46 crores and 39 crores respectively.

In NER the expenditure to control insurgency has been increasing day by day. But ironically along with the expenditure to control insurgency, insurgency has been increasing by leaps and bounds. Recently, in an NEC published paper a detailed account of expenditure is presented. This paper of expenditure is outside the budget of Defence Ministry and seven State Governments. After so much expenditure made for security purpose, bomb in Chief Minister's Convoy, Kidnapping of Bureaucrats, bombs in buses are regular features. If anything serious happens, the Chief Ministers of this region make the lame excuse that are no sufficient Central forces in the region and also there may be a role of third party and the ISI. But, in the last six years, in NER, the central government spent an additional amount of 1,000 crore for deployment of police forces. After spending such huge amount of money, the condition of the region is no better.

According to an official communiqué of the Home Ministry in the last 12 years only in the state of Assam, 1378 have been killed and 178 security personnel too have been murdered. In this 12 years the Security Personnel could kill 552 Bodo (NDFB) insurgents. In the last six years the total numbers may be arranged in the following way 763, 73 and 486. From the year 2001, in Assam, Army men killed. 841 insurgents. In the last year, 159 ULFA activists, 125 NDFB activists too were killed. In the last 33 months of the two outfits 1,596 and 606 insurgents of these groups have been murdered by the Army men. This governmental information made it clear that despite of huge expenditure normalcy cannot be brought in the region. Here both the central State governments are a great failure. According to the Deputy General of Assam Rifles, Lt. Gen. H.S. Konwar, I.S.I is solely responsible for the whole situation.

Conclusion and Suggestions

A review of the above ethnic issues in Assam proved that the ethnic conflicts in the state were due to the religious, linguistic, crisis of ethnic identity economic inequalities among the different groups of people living in the region and the repressive attitude of the elites in the mainstream of the state. Through different ethnic movements, the state of Assam is bifurcated into different states and the process of separation is still going on jeopardizing the unity and integrity of the region and threatening the security of the country. Hence, the solution to the problem lies in the realm of a humane approach. An effort should be made to win hearts of the people of different ethnic groups of the region so that they can understand the destructive nature of the foreign hands by which they will not be benefited at all.

The government of Assam must restore cultural and ethnic identity of the Bodo communities by which Bodo problem can be solved. Legal protection of tribals belts should be given due emphasis by the Government. The tribal and non-tribal gap should be closed in the region at any cost through different governmental programmes by which they should not be segregated from the Indian Society. The society of the region cannot be tension free by granting mere autonomy and self government to the ethnic minorities and hence, the centralized political administrative structure should be removed in order to minimize the external influences to the ethnic conflicts of the region. It is high time to negotiate with the neighbouring foreign countries to ensure that state boundaries do not stand in the way of social, economic and cultural interactions among different ethnic groups of people. As the twin objective of ethnic issues are for autonomy within India and independence from India, the above suggestions can serve the very purpose of reducing social tension in the region.

Assam's quest for a peaceful socio-cultural and political framework is not merely linked to the issue of political violence and insurgency. The issue causing human insecurity in Assam are identity crisis propelled by an insensitive state, unemployment, migration etc. To protect its dwindling social base, Assamese elites need to broaden its identity constituents. Thus, what Assam requires is a major change of thrust from state security to people's security, where people can take care of their basic socio-economic and cultural issues democratically. A civil society that recognizes the rights and plurality of other ethnic and minority groups can only strive for peace and progress. Unless we bring back peace and security to the region, we are bound not only to lose valuable years right now but also stay far behind the rest of the country in the match towards development and prosperity. However, If we want peace to prevail in this green region, we have to make it hard for all those who are in favour of disturbing the peace.

Recent actions by different outfits in the state of Assam raised questions about the ethics and lack of accountability on the part of these groups and the government. The power of naming in this entire scenario vest with the outfits on the one side and the government on the other. Actions such as the massacres in Dhemaji District on the independence day and the recent massacres in N. C. Hills and Karbi Anglong districts of Assam destroyed public confidence and increase the faith of people in repressive measures and fascist solution. The possibility of peace in the hill districts of Assam has rolled back completely. The peace process and dialogue that were a source of immense hope in the past years among all sections of the people have ground to a halt. From a growing concern about the lack of sincerity and accountability on the part of the state, there is now a serious concern about the future of peace in the region.

With the massacres in Nelli, Dhemaji, Chekarchum, Hamren, what stands out are the sheer mindless brutality of the attack. To justify the attack on the grounds that it was retaliation is ridiculous to put it mildly. The ethnic movements in the region initially reflect the ethno-cultural aspirations of the people and finally deviate from the real path by turning their movements into the path of violence for material gains and to search the quick money through extortions, smuggling, drug trading etc. Hence, the government should negotiate with these organizations sincerely and honestly for saving the entire society of the region from further decadence.

A review of the sub-nationalist movements in Assam have resulted in the formation of different states and ongoing movements of the Bodos, Bangalees, Dimasa, Karbi, Hmar, Kuki Koach Rajbanshis and other tribes are very much in the air and day will come when they will secede away from the Assamese mainstream. It is noteworthy to mention that the recently held ceasefire agreement with the NSCN Chief by the representative of the Central Government will pose a serious threat to the Government of Assam. Hence, it may be revealed that due to the lack of foresightedness of both the central and the state governments, the unity and integrity of the state may be jeopardized. In the pre-independence era, the tribals demanded for simply autonomy but the leaders of Assam were adamant in their attitude as a result of which they get themselves separated from the mainstream.

Another part of the state, named as Barak Valley which is also known as *'Island of Peace'*, the term was used by Mrs. Indira Gandhi, the then Prime Minister of India, witnessed repeated communal disturbances immediately after partition through controversial Sylhet Referendum, Language Movement etc. Hence, Just after independence, disappointment and resentment overtook the Bengali speaking people of Barak Valley due to the step motherly attitude of the successive governments in Assam towards the people of the Valley. Further, there is no farsightedness on the part of state government to assess the socio-economic problems and their proper remedies in the Valley.

There is a cry for a Union Territory has been raised by the people of Barak Valley of Assam. The people of this valley feel deprived in various ways, particularly in respect of linguistic bossism and disparity in the fields of overall developmental works of this valley. Of course this cry for the Union Territory has not yet attained momentum from all sections of people of the valley. But who knows; a day might come when there may be a strong demand for a separate Barak land, as continuous deprivation always generates a revolutionary spirit and give births to insurgency.

Influx of population should be checked to the tribal areas which will be one of the best measures to remove the tribal problems and by which the restoration of the identity in Bodo ethnicity will be possible in the state of Assam. The exogenous causes behind the tribal and non tribal rift are wrong policies of the governments (both state as well as central), lack of programme implementation and of concern for the poor and deprived among the autochthons.. It may be suggested that more government intervention for all round development, better service from the North Eastern Council (NEC), prevention of infiltration and sealing of international borders are urgently needed. It should not be voted in favour of further reorganization of the state as it may be harmful for national integration and economic development.

There is an urgent need for re examination of pattern of development, particularly of industrialization in the context of balanced regional development in the country. Policy makers should not ignore the heterogeneous identities of people of Assam while planning development strategies for the state. Only through the development of the rural people could the process of Assam's progress could be accelerated. The spirit of nationalism should be inculcated in the minds of the people of the state of Assam of NER. Efforts should be made to ensure harmonious growth of national and sub-national identities to cure the malady. The root cause of alienation of land and indebtness among the people is poverty. Thus, to uplift the economic condition of the tribals, the society of each village and of community must protect the weaker sections of the tribal people by improving their economic condition. The developmental schemes for their economic upliftment, should be implemented sincerely and expeditiously.

Last but not the least is that government should establish the requisite institutional mechanism and enabling environment at all levels of the society to ensure that population factors are appropriately addressed within the decision making and administrative process of all governmental agencies responsible for economic, environment, and social policies and programmes.

In the conclusion, it may be said that the ethnic conflicts in Assam are due to excess repressive attitude of the government of Assam from time to time. Had the leaders of Assam been liberal to all the ethnic groups and sympathetic to safeguard their languages, customs and cultures, ethnic movements in different parts of Assam would not have taken place.

References

Brueggemann Walter (1976) : *"Living Toward a Vision : Biblical Reflections on Shalom"*, Philadelphia, United Church Press.

Davies, T.R. (1973) : "Aggression, Violence, Revolution and War." in *Handbook* of *Political Psychology*, San Francisco: (ed.) Jossey-Bass, Jeanne N. Knutson., pp 234-60

Davd, R. Syiemlieh (1996) : *"The Future of the Hills of North East India 1928-1947-Some British Views."* in *Reorganisation of North East India Since 1947 (Ed.)* B. Datta Ray and S. P. Agarawal, Concept Publishing Company, New Delhi, pp 24-35.

Datta Ray. B. (1989) : *"Tribal Identity And Tension in North East India* Omsons Publications, New Delhi.

Dutta P.C. (1996) : *"Quality Variation of some food items of consumption in the North Eastern Region (NER)"*, IJRS

Vol. 28, NO. 1.

Dutta P.C. and H. Choudhury (1996) : “A Note on interstate variation in per capita non-food household items of consumption in the north east India”, IJRS Vol. 28, No. 2

Dutta P.C. (2002) : *Population Growth and Environmental Crisis in North East India : Problems and Remedies”* in Development Priorities in North East India (ed), B. J. Deb, Concept Publishing Company, New Delhi.

Dutta P.C. (2003) : *“Regional Disparity and its consequences in North Eastern Region of India”* in Economic Liberalization and Regional Disparities in India-Special Focus on the North eastern Region (ed) A. C. Mohapatyra and Chitta Ranjan Pathak, Star Publishing House, Shillong.

Dutta P.C. and B.C. Pradhan (2003) : *“Demographic Changes, Racial and Linguistic Conflicts in Assam of North Eastern Region”,* proceedings of the National Seminar on SOCIAL TRANSITION IN THE NORTH EAST (UGC Sponsored), Hailakandi, 8th December, 2003.

Dutta P.C. (2005) : *“Problems of Ethnicity in North East India”* in Perspective of Security and Development in North East India (ed) S. K. Agnihotri (IAS) and B. Datta Ray, Concept Publishing Company, New Delhi.

Fuchs, Harald (1965) : *“Augstin and der antike Friendensgedanke”,* Berlin, Weidmann.

Gray Cox (1986) : *“The Ways of Peace : a philosophy of peace as action”, New York, Paulist Press.*

Gurr, Ted Robert. (1970): *“Why Men Rebel”*. Princeton, New Jersey: Princeton University Press.

Haleem Harfiyah Abdel et al (1998) : *“The Crescent and the Cross”,* London, Macmillan, pp 66.

Juarez Benito (1981) : *Antologia de Benito Juarez (Jorge L, Tamayo, ed.) Mexico : Universidad Nacional Autonoma de Mexico.*

Margolin, Joseph. (1977): "Psychological Perspectives in *Terrorism.*" *In Terrorism: Interdisciplinary Perspectives.*

(eds.) Yonah Alexander and Seymour Maxwell Finger, pp 273-74.

Popper, Karl (1945) : *"The Open Society and its Enemies"*, Routledge, London ; Popper stressed and condemns Plato's tendency to require everyone to Think alike. For a defense of Plato against Popper -see Gerrit, J. de Vries, Antisthenes Redivivus. Amsterdam : North Holland Publishing Co., 1952.

Wilkinson, Paul. (1974) : *"Political Terrorism"*,: Macmillan, London

Wilkinson, Paul. (1986) : "*Terrorism: International Dimensions.*" in *Contemporary Terrorism*. Pages 29-56: Facts on File, New York.

4

Socio-Economic Development in Rural Assam: Problems and Prospects

"Development of India's rural economy is vital for growth than urban economy. It is a foregone conclusion that there will never be a growth unless rural economy develops............"

–Vinod Khosla

It is well known that even after 63 years of independence and completion of ten Five Year Plans, India remains predominantly a rural society with bulk of her huge population living in villages under conditions of grinding poverty. Mass unemployment, widespread illiteracy, use of primitive technology, low rates of savings and investment, social backwardness, gross inter-regional and intra-regional inequalities of income and wealth and mounting inflationary pressures still continue.

Rural means a society or specific areas marked off by villages which are lying outside the jurisdiction of municipal area or committees. The economic structure of rural areas consists mainly of economic activities concerned with the system of production and consumption that are closely interlinked with the social structure. Development is a comprehensive term and multi-disciplinary in nature. It is a continuous process that tends to positive change in the entire social, economic, technological, cultural, psychological, organisational and political aspects of a human society.

Thus "Rural Development" is used to denote the actions and initiatives which are undertaken to bring about sustained positive changes in socio-economic life of the people living in non-Urban neighbourhoods, countryside, and remote villages. In the words of World Bank, rural development is a strategy designed to improve the economic and social life of a specific group of people – the rural poor. It involves extending the benefits of development to the poorest among those who seek a livelihood in the rural areas. Programmes meant for rural development are usually top-down from the local or regional authorities, regional development agencies, NGOs, national governments or international development organizations. But then, local populations can also bring about endogenous initiatives for development. Since the main occupation of rural people is agriculture thus agricultural activities may be prominent in this case whereas economic activities would relate to the primary sector, production of foodstuffs and raw materials.

Rural life is an integrated whole, with strength and weaknesses intermeshed. The impact of rural development on society is a subject of extreme importance. At the same time, this subject is very intricate and not susceptible to easy or quick analysis. The process of development inevitably affect, in varying ways and intensities, the existing social and economic arrangements and discord is built into the process. A typical village in India has traditionally been an extremely integrated unit where social stratification is based on religion, caste and economic power.

Development of social sectors such as health, education and nutrition etc. increase the productivity of labour time – the main asset of the poor, employment opportunities and contribute to reducing poverty. Education helps people not only in raising their own skill but also in raising the efficiency of other factors like capital, by making their use in a more efficient manner.

It is a basic fact that without economic growth social sector's development cannot be sustained for long and it is also more basic fact that healthy and well educated people make an economy more productive. Rural development is too important for the nation, as a whole, to be treated in this routine fashion. Indeed, a prerequisite of urban development in India is rural development. The poor and unemployed of the villages will make up the city slums of tomorrow. Rural development is inescapable in India if the rural-urban relationship is to be corrected. Institutions created for rural development and empowering the poor, such as co-operatives, Panchayati Raj Institutions are completely politicized and bureaucratized. These institutions have become the stepping stone for potential political leaders and the handmaid of official machinery. The misfortune of Panchayati Raj has been that it did not receive fair treatment from the higher level of leadership.

India has emerged as one of the richest economies in the developing world during the reform period. But the performance of any economic policy should not be judged by looking merely at its national level performance. Its impacts should also be evaluated by looking its performance at the sub-national or state-levels and in a backward state like Assam where more than 88 per cent of the population live in rural areas; an analysis of the impact of the policy on the rural development assumes an additional significance. In this context, a study meant to analyse the performance of income generating institutions in the rural areas of Assam will be an important issue to deal with. The agrarian rural structure is the predominant character of most of the third world developing economies. Rural development in these countries is an inescapable prerequisite of national development. In India commitment to development of rural areas has been one of the abiding concerns of successive five year plans.

The rural subsystem of the North Eastern Region (NER) economy consists of some 35 thousand villages inhabited by over 32 million people who constitute about 85 percent of the total population in the region. Of approximately 10.6 million main workers in the NER economy, about eight million workers are directly engaged as cultivators or agricultural laborers.

The state of Assam is predominantly rural and hilly in some areas. The topography of the region has largely shaped its economy. The State comprises of 27 districts and is situated in the north-east corner of India. Except for a narrow corridor running through the foothills of the Himalayas that connects the state with West Bengal, Assam is almost entirely isolated from India. According to 2001 census the state has a total population of 26,638,407 with a density of 340 persons per sq. km. The literacy rate is comparatively high at 64.28 percent with males constituting 71.93 percent and females comprising of 56.03 percent. The sex ratio is 932 females per thousand males. The state economy is primarily based on agriculture and oil. The state produces a significant part of the total tea production of the world and more than half of India's petroleum. It is ranked 14th in the Human Development Index which is the lowest among all the sub-project states.

The development of the region is intimately associated with the question of rural development. The rural-urban dualism may essentially be seen as the product of the failure of market mechanism. State intervention in favour of the rural sector is thus seen as a sine-qua-non for rural development. Rural Development has today become the most popular slogan of the policy makers as well as the academic community. It is very complex phenomenon comprising myriad activities. The term Rural Development has been used differently at different times and in different contexts, so it is very difficult to give a universally acceptable definition of the term. Rural Development has two words – Rural and Development. Since the majority of population of Assam is living in rural areas therefore development of rural areas must receive much attention in the schemes designed for the development of State's economy. More precisely, economic policies of the state must be evaluated on their capacity to raise the economic condition of rural Assam.

Integrated Rural Development Programme has been

conceived as anti-poverty programme. 'Anker' gives the following working definition of Integrated Rural Development –"Strategies, Policies and Programmes for the development of rural areas and the promotion of activities carried out in such areas viz. agriculture, forestry, fishery, rural crafts and industries, the building of the social and economic infrastructure with the ultimate aim of achieving a fuller utilisation of available physical and human resources, and thus higher incomes and better living conditions for the rural population as a whole, particularly the rural poor, and effective participation of the latter in the development process". The definition of Anker suggests an important element as an essential aspect of Integrated Rural Development and that pertains to the effective participation of the rural poor in the Development process. This is the first of its kind of anti-poverty programmes which is the single largest programme aims at providing income generating assets and employment opportunities to the rural poor for enabling them subsequently to rise above the poverty line. Social Scientists belonging to various disciplines have studied deeply and have written vastly on the theoretical and practical issues relating to rural development. Despite considerable progress been made much remains to be done to develop the As stated by various scholars such as Myrdal (1970), Atkinson (1970), Adelman and Moris (1973) at the earlier stage of development socio-structural and institutional dimensions are more important, after that economic growth and improvement in per capital income may be important. Again, Hooda (1997) remarked that the rural development involves all agents of change and policy makers to activise the passive majority of rural people, to assist them by providing schemes, funds, skill, training, technology and opportunities to participate in the process of development and to raise their share in production and wealth. It is wrong to suggest that more investment in social sector development is anti-growth and it is more wrong to say that economic growth is unnecessary for social and human development.

According to Ghose (1993), 'Our real problem is not so much

of economic restructuring to look outward – but restructuring of social, political, judicial and administrative – to look inward'. Rampant corruption can not be checked and rural or national development can not be sustained without such institutional changes. Otherwise the declining political morality will lead to the deprivation of the poor from power and capabilities to participate, growing loss of faith in the system and break down of the social order (Kothari, 1988).

Arther Lewis (1965) emphasised that developing of human resources is an urgent need in the developing countries since it has potential to produce according to the needs of people and viewed that an enquiry into the differences in the human behaviour among the countries having roughly equal resources is necessary. Schultz (1960) first time identified the impact of human capital formation on the economic growth. He emphasised that education is an important form of investment, which ensures skills and capabilities that produce future earnings, and productivity of labour.

In the changing *socio-politico* milieu, the concept of development has undergone a paradigm shift. The growth of the country measured in quantitative terms especially as a percentage growth of GDP lost its relevance in the context of sustainable economic development. The volume growth of GDP, till date, is, however, put on at par with increasing welfare or well-being of the society.

Donald Rutherford (2002) opined that the social welfare of a country is "often measured by the total volume of goods and services becoming available to it over a given period, i.e. real income". Martha Nussbaum and Amartya Sen (2003) pointed out that measure like per capita Gross National Product (GNP), in spite of their well-known shortcomings, "continue to be widely used when public policy is made".

Sharma (2006) concluded that cultivation is the major source of income of indebted farmer households in the state of Assam along with other states of India and 70 per cent of such households are marginal farmers. The amount of outstanding debt has positive and statistically significant relationship with size class of land possessed and per capita monthly expenditure in the state.

Woman has been an equal economic partner to man, besides her biological and social roles through history (Gengaje and Setty, 1992). The contribution of female labour in agriculture is quite high and well documented by many scholars (Sudha Rani and Raju, 1991; Bala, 1992; Dutta and Pradhan, 2004, 2006, 2007). As per the world economic profile they form 50 per cent of the world population, contributing 60 per cent of the working hours, make up 30 per cent of the official labour force and 50 per cent of the food production (Desai and Mohiuddin, 1992).

Keeping in view the importance of the subjects discussed above, the broad objective of the present study aims at examining the socio-economic condition of rural regions of the state of Assam and its impact on over all socio-economic development of the state. The study takes a special look at the development experiences of the various sectors of the rural economy of Assam. Issues like people's participation, rural industrialization, marketing, entrepreneurship, tourism, technology, cooperation, education, gender and poverty are analysed in the light of development experiences of the state. However special thrust has been given on Barak Valley region of the state which is its most backward region. The study deserves the attention of the researchers, policy makers and above all those who concern for the development of the state. The study is being made on the basis of published and unpublished statistical data and completed with viable suggestions.

Economic Development of Assam and Rural Economy

Development is a process, which improves the quality of life. It requires a balanced human resource development in the country. According to latest Human Development Index Report (HDI), India's position is 96 out of 120. The impact of developmental activities cannot be evaluated fully by any single indicator because it is a multi-dimensional process. Hence there is a need of combining the effect of different indicators for assessing the level of development. The development of an area is best reflected in the quality of basic needs of life of its people.

The most striking fact of Assam's economic development is that it is falling behind the rest of the country. At the beginning of the post independence era, Assam was ranked among the prosperous States of the country In 1950-51, Assam's per-capita income was 4.1 percent higher than the average for the country. By 1980-81, Assam's per-capita income was 27 per cent lower than the national average, and by 1998-99, the gap had widened to 45.5 percent. What is even more alarming is that the gap is widening. Nobel Prize winning economist Robert Lucas had uttered that *once you start thinking about economic growth, it is hard to think of any thing else*. What are the causes of economic growth and how can the process be enabled is a question that has obsessively occupied some of the best minds in the world of economics and commerce. The question takes on an unparallel urgency and importance when applied to the rural economy of Assam because it presents an enormous challenge, and, consequently, presents an equally great opportunity for making a difference in the lives of hundreds of millions of people. Economic development of Assam is predicated upon rural development of Assam because nearly 90 p.c. of the total population lives in rural Assam **(Table 4.1)**.

Table 4.1: Percentage of Rural-Urban Composition of Population in Assam and India

	1971		1991		2001	
	Rural	Urban	Rural	Urban	Rural	Urban
Assam	91.1	8.9	88.8	11.2	88.9	12.72
India	80.1	19.9	73.3	25.7	73.87	27.78

Source: Census of India, 1971, 1991, and 2001.

Without rural economic development, Assam has little chance of achieving growth rates required to become a developed state. Furthermore, economic development is both a cause and a consequence of urbanization. Clearly, in the context Assam economy, urbanization through further rural to urban migration is both unsustainable and socially disruptive. Therefore urbanization of the rural population will have to be achieved in the rural areas.

India's total cultivable area is 1,269,219 km^2 (56.78p.c. of total land area), which is decreasing due to constant pressure from an ever growing population and increased urbanisation. Although Assam is more industrially developed than the other North Eastern states, it is primarily an agrarian economy with 74 p.c. of its population engaged in agriculture and allied activities. As per 2001 census, 53 p.c. of total work force are engaged in agricultural activities. But during the period 2000-05, the overall scenario of agriculture is not praiseworthy. The contribution of agriculture to Net State Domestic Product of the state is only 31.19 p.c. in 2003-04. The production of winter rice steadily decreased from 2713 thousand tones in 2001-02 to 1800 thousand tones in 2004-05. Same trends are observed in case of Autumn rice. Summer rice, cotton, Jute etc. As per the report of livestock census 2003, the total livestock population in Assam was 140.23 lakh as against 134.67 lakh in 1997. The livestock products as milk, egg and meat are plying a vital role in the economy of Assam. As per the State Directorate of Fisheries, present level of annual fish production is 1.86 lakh metric tones (2004-05) which increased by 15.41 p.c. in comparison to 2001-02. Agriculture not only supplies raw materials for industries outside the State such as cotton, jute, ginger etc. but also provides inputs to other few small agro-based industries in the State such as turmeric, paddy, maize etc.

Agriculture and allied activities have overriding importance as a source of livelihood to the people of Assam in general and rural areas in particular. It is the agricultural prosperity which boosts up the economic conditions of the rural people directly by raising their income levels and indirectly by putting a sound base for rural industrialisation. It is not that rural development alone necessitates agricultural development, in fact economic progress of the state as a whole depends to a large extant on the blessing of this sector and this is well backed by the fact that agriculture still contributes more than one-third (31.2 p.c. in 2003-04) of Assam's NSDP and supports about 70 per cent of its population, though the percentage is even higher in rural Assam. Though agricultural productivity has increased in the recent past, but the rate of increase is very slow. Table 1.2 shows the fact that throughout the period (1980-81 to 2005-06), the yield per hectare of various crops in the state of Assam are very low in comparison to all India level.

In case of *Small Scale Industries (SSI), Handicrafts and Handloom industry* has the potential to promote income and employment generation in a big way. The high quality traditional handicrafts and handloom products enjoy a good market, both nationally and internationally. For providing employment opportunities in the rural areas and thereby strengthening the rural economy, Khadi and Village Industries play an important role. Development of SSI sector, therefore, is the only alternative to the economic backwardness of a state lies in its significance for generation of employment with low capital cost. The whole of NER contributes 79.58 p.c. Nagaland positioned the first rank with highest production (in value) as 45.19 p.c. followed by Assam with 37.35 p.c. only amongst the states of NER. However, marketing of the product depends on growth of tourism promotion outside the State by the Government and adequate supply of input and infrastructure support.

Village and Khadi industries are an integral part of the economic life of an agriculturally-based poor state like Assam. As small industries take root, they go deeper in the life of people, extend work opportunities, raise income and standard of living of the people and bring about technical changes and a balanced and integrated rural economy. The Assam Khadi and Villages Industries Board has been given the responsibility to promote village and khadi industries in the state with a view to generate rural employment and to uplift the rural economy

Table 4.2: Yield Rate of Certain Crops in Assam and India (in Kg/Ha)

Name of Crop	1980-81		2000-01		2005-06	
	India	Assam	India	Assam	India	Assam
Rice	1,336	1,109	1,901	1,483	2,093	1,475
Wheat	1,630	1,158	2,708	1,279	2,607	1,066
Pulses	473	416	544	540	585	543
Maize	1,159	593	1822	722	1953	721
Cotton	152	------	190	77	375	79
Jute(lakh bales)	1245	1463	2026	1605	2290	1274

Source: Economic Survey, 1980-81, 2000-01 and 2005-06.

of the State. For this purpose the board is financially supported by the Khadi and Village Industries Commission (KVIC), Government of India. As per information made available by the Khadi and Village Industries Board, Assam, a total of 56 bee-keeping centres, 521 oil extraction centres, 2184 pottery centres, 219 hand pounding centres and 1283 khandasari centres, 57 khadi production centres, 26 soap making centres, 5 cottage match factories, 189 footwear unit, 15 hand made paper unit, 832 cane and bamboo centres and 44 gobar gas plants were in operation in the state during 2002-03. These Khadi and Village industries have always been a great source of employment, especially for the rural people in the state. But, during the last few years, downward trends have been observed in case of production and employment generation of these industries **(Fig. 4-A & Fig. 4-B)**.

Sericulture is yet another important agro-based labour intensive traditional rural industry of the State comprising culture of different varieties of silkworm. Rearing of Eri, Muga and Mulbery silk warm are playing an important role in the economic development of a large section of rural population of the State. There are 9,173 sericulture villages in Assam. Families involved in rearing of eri, muga, and mulberry during 2004 were 132033, 23543 and 29715 respectively. During 2001-03, the state produced 599MTs eri cut cotton. The figures for muga and mulberry were 92 MTs and 12 MTs respectively.

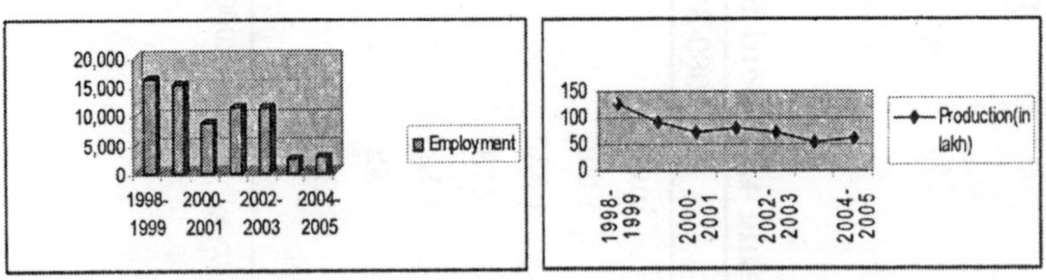

Source : Economic Survey of Assam, 2006-07

Figure 4-A: Khadi Production and Employment in Assam (1998-2005):

In recognition of the importance of traditional industries, since the era of planning in the country a series of measures were adopted. An industry which received highest official patronage all along these years is handloom industry as it is the oldest and largest traditional industries. Even in this era of liberalisation, the need to develop the industry is being articulated. The study is with reference to the handloom industry of Assam as the said industry in the state exhibits a high order performance campared to the rest of India. The Handloom Industry in the State of Assam has a long tradition in the socio-economic life of the people for supplementing the family income to a great extent and self-employment opportunities to lakhs of people of poor and down trodden section of the society.

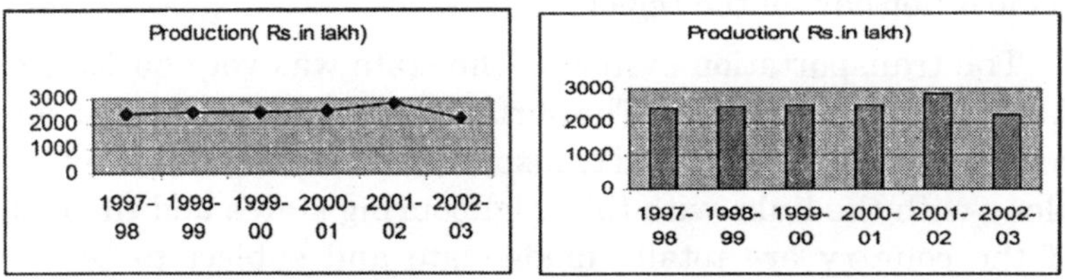

Source: Khadi and Village Industries Board, Assam.

Figure 4-B: Achievement of Village Industries in Assam

Banking facility is essential for economic development. Banking for poor is one of the most popular concepts in the rural development oriented literature. The Nationalised Banks, Regional Rural Banks and other financial institutions have been playing proactive role in providing credit to SHGs / JLGs during the last 5 years for undertaking productive income generation activities. The Banking facilities for the rural people are being served by a network of five Regional Rural Banks in Assam with a total number of 399 reporting branch Offices as on March, 2003. The aggregate deposits with these Banks was Rs. 1364.85 crore at the end of March, 2003 against Rs. 1217.37 crore at the end of March, 2002 thereby registering an increase of 12.11 per cent. The volume of Credit disbursed by these Banks increased to Rs. 465.64 crore at the end of March, 2003 from Rs. 358.53 crore at the end of March, 2002, thus showing an increase of 29.87 per cent. The Credit-Deposit ratio of this Bank is 34.12 percent during March, 2002 as against 29.5 per cent during the same period of the previous

Constraints to Rural Development

Development of infrastructural facilities opens the path of economic development of a particular region. The state largely remains backward in respect of infrastructural system. Due to its peculiar geographical features the entire state was neglected from the very early period. The states of the region were lagging behind the other states of the country in respect of *transportation, communication, electrification, credit facilities etc.*. Due to infrastructural backwardness, industrialisation was either absent in some part or started very belatedly in some other part of the region.

The transportation system of the state was very backward from the very beginning. The surface transport facilities of the region which includes Road transport, Railways and waterways along with the links with the neighbouring states and the rest of the country are totally inadequate and subject to severe hardships during monsoons.

Rural Assam, like rural India, is caught in what is called a *development trap*. Because of lack of economic opportunities, incomes are low. Therefore they are unable to pay for goods and services that would enable them to increase their incomes. This leads to low demand for goods and services. Consequently, firms don't find it profitable to do business in rural India. This leads to the inadequate provision of infrastructure; which in turn leads to lack of economic opportunities, and so on.

Agriculture sector suffers from several weaknesses as dominance of low-value crop, low value addition per hectare, declining factor productivity and declining cost –benefit ratio mainly due to inefficient use of resources such as irrigation water, fertiliser, etc. Besides, indiscriminate use of natural resources leading to environmental degradation (nearly half the agriculture land is severely affected by soil erosion, water logging, formation of gullies and ravines) and deterioration of village institutions have been other responsible factors for this process (Vyas 1993). The agricultural growth is constrained by non-availability and low adoption of improved technology, poor access to international market, lack of adequate development of infrastructure, and lack of competitiveness in the domestic as well as international market due to substandard and poor quality of produce, weak agriculture research and extension system, poor infrastructure like road, market and credit, rapid urbanisation, inappropriate agricultural policies, unfavourable prices, and declining capital formation in agriculture sector, etc. Besides, in the changing economic scenario, globalisation has opened both new opportunities and challenges to the agriculture sector (Singh 2000).

Floods in the Brahmaputra and Barak valleys of Assam cause "serious erosion, loss of life and livestock and heavy damage to infrastructure and property retarding agricultural productivity on account of risk avoidance and sand casting, disrupting communications and education and posing health hazards. The floods damage to crops, cattle, houses and utilities in Assam alone between 1953 and 1995 is estimated at Rs. 4400 crore with a peak of Rs. 664 crore in a single bad year." (Shukla Commission, 1997). The assessed flood prone area in the state is estimated at 3.15 m.ha. (million hectares) or 92.6 per cent of the cultivated land as in 1992-93, almost half of which (1.63 m ha) do not have any flood management structures. Even the limited flood management structures that exist are poorly maintained. Floods have been an impediment to the technological transformation of agriculture in Assam. For farmers do not apply costly inputs such as fertilizers and HYV seeds for the fear of their being washed away by floods.

One serious problem faced by the silk industry of the state and other northeastern region is the problem of exploitation by the village money lenders. "There is no escape rout for vast majority of weavers in the state from the cocoon of exploitation from village moneylenders. As credit facilities to the small weavers are not easily available, it facilitates exploitation of weavers by local money lenders and middlemen." (Goswami, 2006). Ignorance, conservative attitude of the workers, lack of education etc also aggravate the situation.These result in poor innovativeness, which is again having a link to inadequate training facilities common in northeast India. In the absence of formal training institution, the workers are mostly self-trained and work as unskilled workers. This poses a bigger challenged for the industry to live up to its business potential. Moreover, the inadequate training facilities for the workers to improve their skills deprive them from availing higher salary, social status, etc. This blocks the entrance for other new unskilled labour to join into the industry as ordinary labour, and thus limit employment opportunities in the industry.

Inequality is a very complex and multidimensional concept. Quantitative inequality refers to economic inequality measurable in terms of income, wealth, goods and services enjoyed. Qualitative inequality refers to power and prestige, not measurable in physical form. Food security connotes livelihood security at household level and involves ensuring both physical and economic access to balanced diet, safe drinking water, environmental sanitation, primary education and basic healthcare. Basically it implies that entire population in a community has access to enough food at all times for leading leading an active and healthy life (World Bank, 1986 ; Parikh, 1998).

One of the important problems that the state of Assam has been facing is the problem of mass poverty. Though the planning commission Report (2007) shows a drastic fall in incidence of poverty (55.77 lakh i.e. 19.7 p.c.) still now a large section of rural population of Assam is living under poverty (22.3 p.c.) and there is no doubt that the incidence is more among the females.

A close look at the historical trend in the incidence of poverty, it is observed that the concentration of poverty in rural area is much higher than in urban areas. Along with these trends if we consider the fact that bulk (almost 90 p.c.) of the population lives in rural areas we could say that poverty in Assam is predominantly a rural phenomenon. Again, the incidence of rural poverty is the highest among agricultural and other labour (as high as 76 per cent and 80 per cent respectively), followed by self-employed in agriculture and self-employed in non-agriculture in that order. Among the social groups incidence of poverty is higher among the scheduled castes as compared to that among scheduled tribes. An important feature of poverty of Assam is that there exists a wide degree of variability in the incidence of rural poverty at the district level. The available data show that Kokrajhar ranks highest (75.92 p.c.) and Tinsukia ranks lowest (11.45) regarding the incidence of rural poverty. The picture of rural poverty in case of Barak Valley is also frustrating. It is obvious from the table that the incidence of rural poverty in Barak Valley region is greater/less than average.

Anyone who has ever struggled with **poverty** knows how extremely expensive it is to be poor (James Baldwin, 1961). One of the important problems that the state of Assam has been facing is the problem of mass poverty. Though the planning commission Report (2007) shows a drastic fall in incidence of poverty of the tune of 55.77 lakh (19.7 p.c.) still now a large section of rural population of Assam is living under poverty (22.3 p.c.) and there is no doubt that the incidence is more among the females. A minute look at the historical trend in the incidence of poverty, it is observed that the concentration of poverty in rural area is much higher than in urban areas. Along with these trends by considering the fact that bulk of the population (almost 90 p.c.) lives in rural areas it can be remark that the poverty in Assam is predominantly a rural phenomenon. Again, the incidence of rural poverty is the highest among agricultural and other labour (76 p.c. and 80 p.c. respectively), followed by self-employed in agriculture and self-employed in non-agriculture in that order. Considering the social groups, it is observed that incidence of poverty is higher among the scheduled castes as compared to that of scheduled tribes. **(Table 4.3)**.

An important feature of poverty of Assam is that there exists a wide degree of variability in the incidence of rural poverty at the district level. The available data show that Kokrajhar ranks highest (75.92 p.c.) and Tinsukia ranks lowest (11.45) regarding the incidence of rural poverty. The picture of rural

Table 4.3: Number of Poor in Assam (Percent of Total and in Lakh)

Years	Rural head count ratio	Urban head count ratio	Combined head count ratio	Rural poor (lakh)	Urban poor (lakh)	Total poor (lakh)
1973-74	52.67	37.16	51.23	76.37	5.50	81.87
1977-78	59.82	37.58	57.63	97.55	6.70	104.25
1983	42.60	26.38	40.86	81.28	6.06	87.35
1987-88	39.35	9.94	36.21	73.53	2.22	75.75
1993-94	45.01	7.73	40.86	94.33	2.03	96.36
1999-2000 (30 day recall)	40.04	7.47	36.09	92.17	2.38	94.55

Source: http://www.indiastat.com (Planning Commission estimates based on Expert Group methodology)

poverty in the districts of Barak Valley (44.34 p.c.) are also frustrating **(Table 4.4)**. It is obvious from the table that the incidence of rural poverty in Barak Valley region is only marginally less than the total average but much higher than that of Tinsukia.

Table 4.4: Incidence of Rural Poverty

District	Rural poverty (per cent below poverty line)	Rural poverty (Number of poor
Cachar	41.01	449862
Hailakandi	43.79	181694
Karimganj	48.23	369773
Kokrajhar	75.92	569322
Tinsukia	11.45	89160
All Assam	45.06	8758051

Source: Dubey and Gangopadhyay (1998)

Energy plays a crucial role in the socio-economic development of a country as growth in energy consumption is intrinsically linked to growth in the economy. The degree of economic growth is correlated with the generation and consumption of electricity. There is a huge potentiality for the development of number of hydel power and thermal power projects. The state is full of potentiality in respect of power generation. In spite of huge power potential, the entire NER is deficient in respect of generation and consumption of power. There is a huge potential for the development of oil, gas and energy prospects which have not been utilised to their fullest potential and large possibilities have remained unexplored due to lack of trained manpower, lack of organised efforts and a conservative mindset. All this, if properly harnessed, can bring about a radical change to the economy of the region. In the era of globalization, electricity is one of the basic inputs for achieving socio-economic development of a nation. The present per capita consumption of electricity in India is little over 400

Kwh, which is much lower than that of the developed countries (five times lower as compared to world average).

It is needless to say that economic growth of a region can not be achieved without the growth of large or small industries and for which uninterrupted *power supply* is badly necessary. In spite of having immense potential of power generation, the State of Assam accounts for only 0.12 p.c. of total generation electricity in the country during 2003-04. The average per capita consumption of electricity in the State was 104 Kwh. in 2003-05 as per Economic Survey Assam, 2005-06, which is far below the national average of 359 Kwh in the same year. Total power generation scenario in the state is not at all healthy towards the economic development. The generation has shown declining trend from 840.406 Million Unit in 2001-02 to 756.435 Million unit in 2004-05. The overall power supply position in the State during 2005-2006 was not much encouraging as the State had to witness erratic power supply during the year.

Rural electrification despite being a basic source of enlarging outlook of rural masses can also help them by enabling them to adopt modern technology in the process of production. In spite of having immense potential of power generation in the State, the performance of this sector is not encouraging. Assam accounts for only 0.12% of total generation electricity in the country during 2003-04. The average per capita consumption of electricity in the State was 104 Kwh. in 2003-05 as per Economic Survey Assam, 2005-06, which is far below the national average of 359 Kwh in the same year. The situation is even serious in rural areas, as per census 2001, only 70 p.c. villages of Assam are electrified and only 16.5 p.c. rural households are electrified.

There is a regular feature of the shortage of power in the state of Assam. As per 2000-02 figure, only 16.54 per cent of rural households in Assam have been electrified which is the lowest among the states in NER. While the highest is observed in the state of Nagaland (56.88 p.c.) followed by Manipur (52.53 p.c.). The respective percentage for the country is 43.52.

About 87 per cent of the state population lives in rural areas, that is 26,247 villages. Of these, as on March 31, 2006, only 21,586 villages have been electrified of which only 16.54 per cent of the total households in these electrified villages have electricity connection. In modern day world electrification is a key ingredient for facilitating rural economic development including alleviation of poverty, realization of socio-economic goals and overall human development. The remaining 4661 villages are still to see light of electricity. Again, 2145 unelectrified villages have been identified as remote and thus to provide 'Electricity To All' by 2012 slogan of the government is a far cry. There is no alternative but to go for non conventional and renewable energy sources applying modern technologies. In Assam as per census 2001, only 70 p.c. villages are electrified and only 16.5 p.c. rural households are electrified. The Govt. of Assam has been implementing rural electrification programme in Assam through Distribution Companies. With a view to achieve electrification of all villages of Assam by 2009 and provide access to electricity to all households in line with the National Rural Electrification Policy 2004 and Rural Electrification Policy of Govt. of Assam, Rural Electrification works particularly under Rajiv Gandhi Gramin Vidyutikaran Yojana (RGGVY) scheme have been carried out. Under this scheme all the census villages of Assam are proposed to be electrified by 2009. Electrification in 16 districts to be implemented by ASEB and in 7 districts by the Power Grid Corporation of India. District wise schemes for electrification of villages have been submitted to the Govt. of India and approval for 13 districts has already been received.

It is encouraging to note that the Assam Energy Development Agency, the State Nodal Agency of the Ministry of the Non conventional Energy Sources identified the potentiality the potentiality of three renewable sources of energy like small hydro, biomass gasification and solar photovoltaic for electrification of remote villages. Thus the priority of harnessing non conventional renewable sources of energy will continue for the years to come so as to carryout all the economic activities in rural areas as part of infrastructural development of the policy of globalisation.

Health is a key determinant of human capital and thereby economic growth of a region. Good health is essential to keep the labour force productive and efficient. Frequent illnesses and inadequate nutrition will have adverse impact on the incomes of households making them vulnerable. Good health not only increases productivity and earnings of an individual but also improves the overall quality of life and the socio-economic development of the general population. Malnourishment and under-nourishment can be avoided not just by poverty reduction and higher food intake but also through good health that can be brought about through improved access to sanitation and drinking water facilities. However, the public health delivery system in Assam during the past two decades has been deteriorating, more so in rural areas. Rural people of Assam face two difficulties – scarce availability of quality health services and limited affordability. In the absence of a sufficient number of qualified doctors and paramedical staff, rural inhabitants are largely left to the mercy of unqualified doctors (chemists, quacks, faith healers, etc.) who provide sub-standard services and that too, at high prices. Though the per capita revenue expenditure on health in Assam is lower compared to the average of all States, the share of SDP spent on health services in Assam is quite high, above the average of all States. While there appears to be adequate physical health infrastructure with primary health centres (PHC) and hospitals, etc. The quality of service provision is low. Poor living conditions in villages with inadequate infrastructure facilities such as electricity, roads and sanitation make it unattractive for doctors and other health workers to work in PHCs. There is also a high degree of administrative inefficiency.

Education, like health, has a very significant role in accelerating the pace of socio-economic development of any region. In comparison to all India level, Assam could able to do marginally (by 1 p.c.) better in respect of rural literacy rate. The situation is even better (by more than 4 p.c.) in respect of rural female literacy rate, though rural male literacy rate

Table 4.5: Rural Literacy Rate as per 2001 Population Census

	Persons	Male	Female
India	58.7	70.7	46.1
Assam	59.7	68.2	50.7
Kerala	90.0	96.6	86.7

Source: Census of India, 2001.

in the State of Assam falls short of all India standards by a little more than 2 p.c. However, the story of literacy rate is completely different and leaves a painful impression when it is compared with that of Kerala **(Table 4.5)**.

Rural-Urban gap in literacy rate is also a serious issue of concern in Assam. In 1991, the rural urban gap in literacy rate for the state of Assam was 30.07 p.c. where as the corresponding rate for India as a whole was 28.39 pc. The gap, however, has fallen to 25.60 pc in 2001 but it is still higher than all India standard of 21.20 p.c. Again the falling rate of rural-urban disparity in literacy is also low in the State. Whereas the rural-urban literacy gap has fallen by 25.33 pc in all India level, the rate for the State of Assam was only 14.87 p.c. **(Table: 4.6)**.

Table: 4.6: Rural-Urban Disparity in Literacy Rate

	1991		2001		Falling Rate in Disparity (1991- 2001)
	Rural	Urban	Rural	Urban	
Assam	49.32	79.39	59.70	85.30	14.87
India	44.69	73.08	58.70	79.50	25.33

Source: Census of India, 1991 and 2001.

Though state government allocates huge amount of money in its budget for uplifting educational standard of the state by introducing different policies. But these policies are largely responsible for the malady. And the malady has its roots in the faulty economic policies as well. A large number of eligible children of school going age still remain out of school. The second NFHS survey indicates that 72 per cent of the population in the 6-17 age groups is attending school in Assam, which is same as the all India average. This figure is, however, much lower than that of Kerala (91 p.c.) and lower than all other North-Eastern States (80 p.c. to 87 p.c.) **(Fig. 4-C)**.

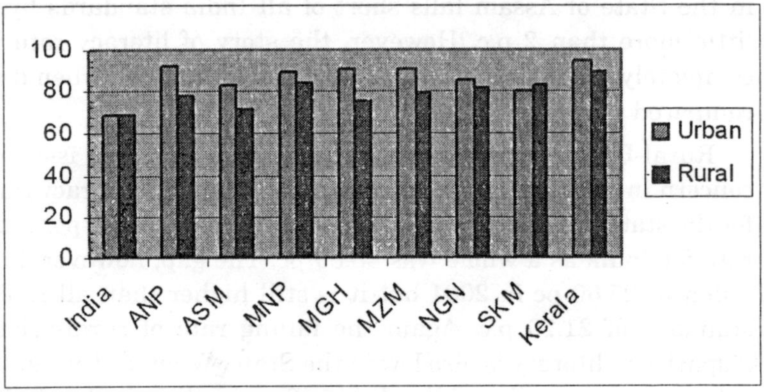

Figure 4-C: Percentage Population Age 6-17 Years Attending School, 1998-99

The school completion rates are found to be very poor in the state of Assam in comparison to all India level. Median number of years of schooling completed among the male population age 6 and above is 4.4 compared to 8.1 for Kerala and 5.5 for all India. This low completion rate indicates high dropout rates of the students. One important reason for high dropout rate is the non-availability of educational facilities above the primary level in villages. A large percentage of the villages are still without an upper primary school. This especially accounts for a large chunk of girls dropping out after primary level. The parents are hesitant to send the girls to other villages for schooling, for fear of their security. Surveys indicate that the majority of school dropouts belong to the poorest and the least developed areas. The factors responsible for dropouts range from economic to cultural reasons. Children are pulled out of school due to economic reasons- they have to earn livelihood for their family. Gender discrimination against girl child is a major cultural issue. The absence of women teachers in the village schools and the lack of separate toilet facilities for girls are other factors, which keep girls away from school. It is very important to tackle the problem of dropouts in order to achieve universal elementary education.

Corruption affects India at all levels of governmental decision-making and in the distribution of state largesse. India is ranked 72nd out of 91 countries in the Corruption Perception Index, 2001, prepared by Transparency International (TI).

Besides, large scale corruption, problem of insurgency, negligence to agriculture and educational sector, environmental pollution, gender inequality, gap between rural and urban areas, consciousness of the people of the region etc. perhaps may be other constraints of economic development of the state.

Action Taken by The Government

Realizing the need for a focused attention to the North-East Region, the Department of Development of North Eastern Region (DoNER) was created in September 2001 by an amendment to the Government of India's Allocation of Business Rule. The Department was formally inaugurated on 1st November, 2001. It was accorded the status of a Ministry vide Gazette notification of Government of India dated 27th May, 2004.

The challenge of development of the state arising from its unique situation has been accepted as a national task. Special focus has been laid on economic development of the state during various Plans and accordingly strategies have been formulated for removal of infrastructure bottlenecks, provision of basic minimum services, creating conducive environment for private investment etc. The handicap of resource-constraint has been met through special dispensation for the State and National Handloom Development Corporation will give priority in supply of hank yarn to the state To up grade the skill of artisan, advance training programme would be organised. New emporia will be set up and financial assistance for renovation of existing emporia would be provided. The Central Silk Board will give priority to the state in implementation of its scheme. For development of markets in the state, possibilities of Export of products of the state to the neighbouring countries particularly, Bangladesh, Myanmar and Bhutan would be explored. However, different developmental schemes have been undertaken to upgrade the economic development of the state.

Besides its normal training courses for officials, elected representatives of panchayats etc. the SIRD has been organizing regular training programmes to build the technical and managerial capacity of the rural people particularly youth, women, farmers etc. to help them to take up income generating activities in a productive and scientific manner. Through this process the institute has been making effort to facilitate the transfer of required technology for productive and sustainable management of income generating activities. The institute has been trying to give a new face to certain selected income generating activities traditionally taken up by the rural people in Assam. They are various agriculture activities, dairy farming, backyard poultry farming, pig rearing, handloom etc.

Backyard duck rearing is a traditional activity in rural Assam but, laying capacity of indigenous ducks is very low. The SIRD in association with Kerala Agriculture University introduced Chara Chemballi duck which has got a laying capacity of 200 eggs per year per duck. The institute introduced the duck in cluster of villages. Around 15000 women have been rearing ducks in SHGs after availing bank loan and other support from the institute. This effort of the institute have added value to a traditional income generating activities of Assam which in turn facilitated socio-economic upward mobility of the rural women in the clusters.

Schemes under the Ministry of Rural Development can be broadly classified into three parts: Employment Oriented Schemes, Rural Housing Scheme and Land related schemes.

Employment Oriented Schemes includes Swarnajayanti Gram Swarozgar Yojana, Sampoorna Grameen Rozgar Yojana and Jawahar Rozgar Yojana. The main aim of Swarnajayanti Gram Swarozgar Yojana *(SGSY)* scheme is to bring the poor into Self Help Groups (SHGs) through the process of social mobilization, training and capacity building along with provision of income through the process of social mobilization, training and capacity building along with provision of income generating assets. The scheme named Sampoorna Grameen Rozgar Yojana (SGRY) provides wage employment in rural areas along with the food security, creation of durable community, social and economic assets and infrastructure developments. It includes the rural poor (BPL and APL) who are in need of wage employment and are willing to take up manual or unskilled work. The programme of Jawahar Rozgar Yojana (JRY) is directed to provide wage employment to the rural poor during the lean agricultural season. It also aims to provide employment and create rural infrastructure through the Panchayati Raj Institutions (PRIs).

A number of schemes were introduced in relation to ***Rural Housing***: *Indira Awaas Yojana* (IAY) was launched with an objective to provide houses to members of S.T/S.C., free bonded labourers in the rural areas and also to non-S.T./S.C. rural poor lying below poverty line at free of cost. *Credit-cum Subsidy Scheme for Rural Housing* (CSSRH) is introduced to help households (below the poverty line and above it) who could not be covered under Indira Awas Yojana, as either they do not fall within the range of eligibility or due to the limits imposed by the available budget. The target group covered under the scheme is rural households having an annual income of up to Rs. 32000/- only. However, Below Poverty line Rural Households, irrespective of castes, shall be given preference. *National Social Assistance Programme (NSAP)* is a social assistance programme for poor households including the aged population ensuring minimum national standards, in addition to the benefits that the States are currently providing or might provide in future. *Samagra Awaas Yojana* (SAY) aims to ensure integrated provision of shelter, sanitation and drinking water. The existing schemes of housing, drinking water and sanitation would follow the normal funding pattern. *Pradhan Mantri Gramodaya Yojana* (PMGY) scheme aims at sustainable human development at the village level. The PMGY envisages allocation of additional central assistance to the states / UTs for providing / improving the outlay of Basic Minimum Services including "Rural Shelter" in the rural areas. *Jawahar Gram Samridhi Yojana* (JGSY) which is the restructured, streamlined and comprehensive version of the erstwhile Jawahar Rozgar Yojana (JRY) has been launched to improve the quality of life of the rural poor by providing them additional gainful employment. The primary objective of JGSY is the creation of demand driven village infrastructure including durable assets to enable the rural poor to increase the opportunities for sustained employment. The secondary objective is the generation of supplementary employment for the unemployed poor in the rural areas.

Land Reforms in relation to Land Related Schemes covers the landless poor and involves restructuring agrarian relations to achieve an egalitarian social structure, elimination of exploitation in land relations; realizing the age-old goal of land to the tiller; increasing agricultural productivity and production and infusing equality in local institutions. Abolition of intermediary tenures; Tenancy reforms; Ceiling on agriculture holdings and re-distribution of surplus land; and Updating and maintenance of land records are the main objectives of this programme. As a part of the wasteland development programme, *Integrated Wasteland Development Programme*(IWDP) includes checking land degradation, increasing biomass availability and putting wastelands to sustainable use. The scheme aims generation of employment in rural areas besides enhancing people's participation in the wasteland development programme sat all stages leading to equitable sharing of benefits and sustainable development.

Conclusion and Suggestion

The above analysis reveals that the rural Assam, in general, and the Rural Barak Valley, in particular still remains backward even after 6o years of independence. However, a strategy for development of rural economy and employment in the state needs with proper care and attention which may be outlined as follows:

Social sector development is most essential part of any long term strategy of rural development and reducing poverty. Efforts to reduce poverty cannot succeed unless social services like health, education and nutrition are made accessible to all levels in society.

If human resources are considered as assets, educational loans can also be grouped under the category of financial assistance. Irrigation facility if created with the help of financial assistance from bank, can improve productivity of the land where such facility is used.

However, local government and NGOs can also play an useful role in this context. Panchayati Raj institutions came to be dominated by the socially or economically privileged sections in the local community with the consequence that the weaker groups – such as scheduled castes, scheduled tribes, and other poorer groups- were still deprived of its benefits.

Social tension is a consequence of the emerging response patterns to rural development. The major factors responsible for the deceleration of the state's economy include lack of adequate investment, low rate of capital formation, high growth rate of population, inadequate basic infrastructural facilities, weak communication linkages, perpetual flood problem, over dependence on agriculture, gross wastage of natural resources such as natural gas etc.

The growth rate in the last three Five-Year Plans has been around a satisfactory 6 percent per annum. But in case of Assam the growth rate has been much below the national figure. Special support will have to be given to achieve the targets set by the Planning Commission.

Unless the infrastructure is substantially improved, there would be only a limited prospect of horticulture and forest based products if they are to be supplied to the rest of the nation raw and unprocessed (which, even if profitable, would not have been prudent). The same is true with floriculture and mushroom businesses. One need not over-stress that these products are either bulky or perishable in a short duration (or both). Good transportation and organized marketing system is called for. Geographical conditions are again limiting factors. It would therefore suggest starting of small-scale food processing, agro-based, horticulture-based and forest-based industries.

The growing unemployment among the educated youths has been a major area of concern for us. Therefore, the importance given to the creation of employment opportunities by giving topmost priority to the development of sectors, which have large potential for generation of employment opportunities by the Planning Commission, is very encouraging. In this Vast globalizing era, the States like Assam can not remain an isolated backwater. The large scale unemployment has resulted in serious law and order problems in the State, which needs to be addressed without any further delay.

Most of the Centrally Sponsored Schemes are funded jointly by the State Government and the Central Government. In case of rural development, the present policy of the Government of India requires 33.3 p.c. State Government contribution against 75 p.c. of the Central Government share in the schemes. Owing to chronic financial constraints, many state Governments have not been able to release the State Share timely. As a result, states like Assam, are often made to forgo a large part of the Central Share in the scheme. In such a situation, apart from the states losing a major share of the Central fund for its rural development, this also affects the overall achievement for the Nation as a whole, since the earmarked fund remains unspent. Similar is the experience with many other Centrally Sponsored Schemes.

Rural entrepreneurship has impact on its beneficiaries with wide ranging benefits. Personel and social benefits match the financial/ economic benefits accrued to individuals and their families. Seed production, nurseries, veterinary services practiced by the entrepreneurs has far reaching implications on the crop and animal husbandry activities of the region, through increased area, production and productivity.

Policy should be made to increase women's access to information and education so that they can equally play an active role in non-agricultural activities for which they have comparatively better chances of a fair wage or income generation.

A few appropriate forward looking policy initiatives may be suggested which would be necessary for the overall socio-economic development of the state.

The Government will have to continue to invest in social sectors like Health, Education, Rural Water Supply etc. The road connectivity is a prerequisite for development in all other sectors in the rural areas. Economic potential in rural areas can be realized, only, if we ensure rural connectivity by providing all weather roads. The power sector is important for development of both Industrial and the Agricultural sectors.

The thrust of development strategy in the village should also be to develop cottage industry in order to maximise employment. The cottage industry that could be set up are weaving, rice milling, bamboo work, pottery and handicrafts. Steps should also be taken to promote sericulture and community handloom. This can be done by making yarn available at cheaper rates, supplying of shuttle looms, and arranging for marketing of the finished products. This will generate additional income and at the same time will provide employment to the villagers. Improving food security at the household level is an issue of great importance for a backward region like the rural Assam, where thousands of poor suffer from persistent hunger and malnutrition.

There is an urgent need to take necessary steps to improve the health and hygienic infrastructure in the rural areas of Assam. The programmes relating to food security, health and pure drinking water facilities need to be implemented sincerely and honestly in different corners of the state for improving the welfare of rural households. There is need to integrate the youth into the development process in order to promote community development.

There is a strong need to shift our traditional production-oriented approach to market oriented approach. Agricultural growth need to be broad-based that can bring rural prosperity which will help in improving the quality of rural life in a sustainable manner. This requires paradigm shift in the agricultural policy to ensure food security, including nutritional security to every citizen of the region and more specifically in rural areas. The development of agriculture requires honest, sincere and efficient attention of the input and output management and policy makers. The policies for increasing agricultural production need to consider the issues related to post-harvest also in an integrated manner, which often has been a missing link.

Proper interventions should be made to encourage creation of value addition rather than mere increasing agricultural production. Food processing to capture the readymade demand in the country as well as abroad should be promoted. The tax structure for food sector should be streamlined to encourage farmers. Small and unorganized units should be organised into larger units to become global players and incentives should be given to encourage brand building and marketing. The employment policies for the rural women should be framed properly.

References

Adelman, I and Morris, C.T, (1973) : "Economic Growth and Social Equity in Developing Countries," Stanford University Press, Stanford.

Atkinson, A.B. (1970) : "The Economics of Inequality, Oxford University Press.

Bala, B. (1992) : "Role of Women in Agriculture – A Study of

Kangra farms, Ph.D. Thesis (unpublished), submitted to HPKV, Palampur (H.P.), pp. 333.

Desai, G.R. and A. Mahiuddin (1992): "Involving Women in Agriculture : Issues and Strategies-A Study Across Three States", Journal of Rural Development, NIRD, Hyderabad, Vol. II, No. 5, pp. 637-651.

Dubey and Gangopadhyay, (1998), "Counting the Poor", Sarvekshana Analytical Report No. 1, Department of Statistics, Ministry of Planning, Statistics and Programmme Implementation, New Delhi.

Dutta, P.C. and B.C. Pradhan (2004) : "Agricultural Development and Security of Life in North East India" in 'Food Security and Public Distribution System Today: Success and Failures' (ed.), Amalesh Banerjee, Vedama Books (P) Ltd., New Delhi.

Dutta, P.C. and B.C. Pradhan (2006) : "Changing Agricultural Scenario in North East India" in 'Changing Agricultural Scenario in North East India' (ed.) Bimal J. Deb and B. Datta Ray Concept Publishing Company, New Delhi.

Dutta, P.C. and B.C. Pradhan (2007) : "Gender Issues And Development In North Eastern Region Of India" in 'Women Emancipation Focus North East India' (ed.) Ashok Kumar Ray and Basudeb Dutta Ray, OM Publications, New Delhi.

Gengaje, R. K and D. Setty (1992) : "A Model For Developing Agro-Enterprises Among Farm Women in Asia", Journal of Rural Development, NIRD, Hyderabad, Vol. 11, No. 5.

Ghose, A. (1993) : "Social Security in an Insecure Economy", EPW, Nov.6, pp 2432-35.

Goswami, K (2006): "Impact of Globalisation of Silk Industry in Northeast India: An Assessment from Gende Perspectives": http://www.iitkgp.ac.in/facprofiles/showprofile.php?empcode= bVmVR

Hooda, I.S. (1997) : "Rural Development – Some Conceptual Issues" in 'Rural Development – Theory and Practice' (ed), Spellbound Publications, Rohtak Kothari, R. (1988) : "State and Democracy," Aganta Publications, New Delhi.

Lewis, A.W. (1965) : "The Theory of Economic Growth", George Allen and Unwin, London.

Myrdal, G (1970) : The Challenge of World Poverty, Penguine Publishers.

Nussbaum Martha and Amartya Sen (Eds) (2003) : "The Quality of Life", Oxford University Press, Oxford.

Parikh, K. (1998) : "Food Security – Individual and National", in Ahluwalia, I.J. and Little, I.M.d. (eds.), India's Economic Reforms and Development : Essays for Manmohan Singh, Oxford University Press.

Rutherford, Donald (2002) : "Routledge Dictionary of Economics", Second Edition, (London : Routledge), p. 521

Schultz,T. W. (1960) : "Capital Formation by Education", Journal of Political Economy, December, 1960.

Sharma, H.R. (2006) : "Incidence of Indebt ness in Rural India – A State Level Analysis", Journal of Rural Development, Vol. 25, No.(4), pp. 507-536., NIRD.

Shukla S.P. Commission (1997), *Report of the High Level Commission, Transforming the North-East-Tackling Backlogs in Basic Minimum Services and Infrastructural Needs, Part I,* Planning Commission, Government of India.

Singh, R.P. (2000) : "Rural Prosperity and Agriculture – Some Emerging Issues, Rural Prosperity and Agriculture, (ed.), National Institute of Rural Development, Hyderabad. Sudha Rani, P. and V.T. Raju (1991) : "Participation of Women in Agricultural Operations", Indian Journal of Extension Education, Vol. 27., No.1 & 2, pp. 54.

Vyas, V. S. (1993) : "New Economic Policy and Vulnerable Sections – Rationale for Public Interventions, Economic and Political Weekly, March 6.

World Bank (1986) : "Poverty and Hunger- Issues and Options for Food Security in Developing countries", World Bank

Policy Study, Washington.

Government of Assam (1999), *Economic Survey Assam, 1998-99,* Directorate of Economics and Statistics, Assam.

Government of Assam (2001), *Vision Assam 2025.*

Government of Assam, *Economic Survey and Annual Plans* of different years.

Government of India (2001), *Economic Survey 2000-2001*, Ministry of Finance.

Government of India, *Economic Survey*, Various Issues, Ministry of Finance.

NFHS-2, (2002), *National Family Health Survey 1998-99*, International Institute for Population Sciences, Mumbai, India.

SECTION-II
ECONOMIC DISPARITY

5

New Economic Policy and Development in NER

"The population census provides detailed information on demographic characteristics and other variables. It has no information on income, asset, ownership, consumption pattern and other variables. It was felt that a unified survey covering different facets of Human Development, level of living, employment and wages, literacy and education, morbidity, disability and nutrition, effectiveness of public services such as PDS, education and health care etc., and Demographic characteristics would be useful. Such a unified survey would enable researchers to draw interrelationships between these different variables and thereby better understanding". [UN HUMAN DEVELOPMENT REPORT, 2000]

Introduction

Indian economy has witnessed multi-dimensional changes during post reform period. The government headed by Sri Narashima Rao introduced structural adjustments during 1990-91 in order to make Indian economy more competitive at the international scenario. At the same time this new economic policy of 1991 opened many new economic issues for discussion. As a result the discussion on economic reforms divided into groups – one which praises the miracles of reforms and opines that the economic reform would bring progress in every field and every sector whereas another group opposed vehemently the new economic reform in our country due to the ill-effects of economic reform in different sectors. As a result of which new interpretation of human development can not be coped and our country will be regarded as the poorest of the poor in the world.

So far as the history of post independence development is concerned the process of planned development in India was introduced in 1950 with mixed economy approach by the then prime minister of India, Pandit Jawaharlal Nehru. Consequently, over centralization and nationalization of socialistic pattern of development led to corruption and economic inefficiency in our country. Protection and subsidy system encouraged permanent dependence rather than growth. When Indian economy was gripped with more serious problem of eighties the earlier mixed economy approach was evaluated and it was realized that Indian economy must acquire improvement in productivity, absorption of modern technology and full utilization of resources. At the same time it was supposed that the private sector will play an important role in shaping the country's economy. As a result in 1991 New Economic Policy (NEP) was introduced by the Government of India involving structural adjustment programmes with basic characteristics of Liberalisation, Privatisation and Globalisation (LPG). Under such policy profit motive was the guiding principle for investment. Domination of profit motive policy paved the way for development of those regions where the developed infrastructural facilities are quite high. Therefore the NEP increased the regional inequalities in India. India's North Eastern Region (NER) is badly affected by the introduction of NEP and Structural Adjustment Programme (SAP).

From 1994 to 1997, Indian national income grew at over 7 per cent per annum and during the entire last decade, the growth rate has been around 6.5 per cent. A study by K. V.

Ramaswami has shown that growth in the post reform period has been significantly higher than in the pre reform period.

There has been a considerable debate on the contents of the reform package, their sequencing and pace, their implementation and their impact (Kumar, 2000). The debate is highly polarized between two groups of economists. One group claims the achievement of reforms and seeks faster implementation on remaining issues related to reforms. Prominent contributors among them are Bhagwati (1994), Srinivasan (1998), Ahluwalia and Little (1998), Parikh (1998) and Mohan (1999) among others. The other school is more critical of reforms. It focuses on the adverse effects on the society, especially the vulnerable groups, questions the sustainability of growth and reforms themselves. Thus they ask for rethinking on the coverage, sequencing and pace of implementation of reforms. This group includes Nayyar (1996), Ghosh (1998), Nagraj (1997), Patnaik and Chandrasekhar (1997), among many rebels of reforms.

Jha (2000) argued in his Paper "Economic Reformation or Deformation in India" that New Western model of economic growth is not suited to the developing countries and even after 50 years of implementation a meaningful development is far away. The economic reform initiated in India during the nineties with the plethora of privatization, liberalization, structural adjustment, globalization and Dunkel proposals is further whipping the cart in the wrong direction and deforming the economy, while "list" believed that "developing countries could not afford to follow the wisdom of Adam Smith in their initial stage of development". Singer cautioned the underdeveloped countries "not to initiate blindly the modern technologies of the industrialized countries which have been based on altogether different sets of factor endowments". In India and third World countries there is need to develop soft, non-violent and intermediate/ appropriate/middle technology suited to the local needs and conditions. The so-called economic reform is deforming the growth rates and distribution and causing crisis in the Asian countries.

Dutta and Pradhan (2004) have rightly pointed out that

under the backward conditions of the North Eastern Region special initiative will have to be taken by the governments of the concerned states to improve infrastructure as well as to ensure food and nutritional security to the poor and steps taken by the governments are not sufficient through Public Distribution System. They also suggested that the NGOs should come forward to protect the interest of the North East by starting a revolution to bring a change in the quality of life of the people in the region and no policy can be successful unless and until the peoples' participation in all respects of development is realized.

Ray (2000) argued that after highlighting general symptoms of poor governance and therefore, corruption, governance issues need to be examined within the context of intra and inter-relationships between various components of the State apparatus, including government, and the community. In his case study of India, he considers administrative reform issues in conjunction not only with constitutional, bureaucratic and judicial reform issues, but also with issues related to political pluralism. For good governance Ray reiterates, amongst others, five mantras of the anti corruption drive, namely monopoly regulation, Official transparency and accountability, detection of and penalties for corruption.

Dutta (2003) observed that in the era of globalisation rapid socio economic transformation has been taking place in Indian economy without addressing the problems of regional disparity, for which they argued that the states of NER are suffering from paucity of funds to improve their socio-economic backward ness. The study revealed that the states of NER are far behind from other states of the Indian Union so far as the basic amenities of life such as health, education, safe drinking water, food security, Banking facilities, communication etc are concerned. All these created the seeds of contention amongst the people of NER for which a dangerous feeling of regionalism grew more and more.

Dutta and Pradhan (2006) observed that the agriculture is the key to the development of NER. Although India has emerged as a food surplus State in the world, the NER is still suffering from food deficit. In almost all the states of NER there are substantial urban-rural and inter district variation, along with the marked variation between tribal and non tribal population within the district, for which it is always a difficult task to measure the nutritional standard and quality of life of the population in the region. They suggested that it is necessary to improve all the factors employed in agriculture along with the use of best quality of seeds, application of modern technology, fast communication between research and extension, Agricultural Information Net Working System etc. in the era of globalization.

Saramma (2000) mentioned that the new economic policy has not benefited to the agricultural sector duly and it seems that it has been affecting adversely the agricultural growth and employment generation in the rural sector. In fact, the agricultural sector has been suffering from structural weaknesses as a result the liberalization of the economy will not help the large number of the rural masses to receive any benefit.

Several studies on Liberalisation, Privatisation and Globalisation show that the New Economic Reform has Success as well as Failure stories.

From the above studies it is clear that economic growth and development can not be defined in absolute terms and it has to be assessed relatively. Development of any society originates from its socio- cultural process. Its spring up from the heart of each society and within the ambit of the natural environment, social relations, education, health and nutrition, per capita income, position of women in the society, production, consumption and welfare activities. The primary objective of development is to satisfy essential material needs of the society and not depends upon any outside paradigm. Any development at the cost of local environment and peoples' culture can not be welcomed.

Hence there is need to examine the pattern of development in NER in the light of New Economic Policy (NEP) of 1991 adopted by the Government of India.

Under the above circumstances, the main object of this study is to see whether the New Economic Reform would suit the people of NER as supporters of the policy advocated or not. For the convenience, the study has been designed to discuss :

(i) the socio economic status of the people in the region according to latest Human Development Index (HDI)

(ii) the post- Reform developments in the states of NER.

(iii) The study is being concluded with viable suggestions for the policy makers and planners of the region to adjust the policies of the concerned states of the region coping with New Economic Reform for the real development of the states of NER.

The study has been made with the help of statistical information collected from various secondary sources.

Economic Reforms and NER

After independence, the policy makers of India introduced measures to bring development in different areas of life such as health, education, social security etc. the measures introduced by the state at the national and regional levels came to be known by the term 'Human Development'. The effects were also made to help the disadvantaged groups by the affirmative action. The disadvantages were identified on the basis of the social and economic backwardness of the communities, and regional imbalances. However, the impact of these measures have not been uniform across the country, with different regions and sectors showing different levels of development. The chief motive of the policy makers was 'Economic Growth' and they adopted socialism or a mixed economy approach for the realization of the same. In the eighties it was felt that only economic growth will not bring the real development of the nation due to regional disparity, absence of social security, ill effects of industrialization, urbanization, negligence in social sectors like health, education etc. That is why again the policy makers awakened with a new slogan 'Limits to Growth'. Adequate attention should be given for the promotion of education, health and nutrition, standard of living, gender equality, environmental sustainability etc.

In 1990's India's development strategy shifted its gear from the state monopoly to New Economic Reforms intertwined with the principles of LPG (Liberalization, Privatization and Globalization) at par with world economic system. The then Prime Minister, Mr. P.V. Narsimha Rao introduced New Economic Policy in July,1991. The New Economic Policy aims at making the Indian economy competitive and much better integrated with the world economy. Since the New Economic Reforms the people of India are in a different world with dramatic political, social, economic. Cultural and environmental changes. The process of globalization can be viewed as an economic phenomenon with the expansion of markets for goods and services, capital and labour beyond national boundaries. The state intervention in the affairs of development has been replaced to a large extent by market forces. Under such circumstances, the term- 'development' receives much more attention of the scholars and they are in a state of confusion whether the New Economic Reform would bring progress in the backward regions of India or not. Experience shows that the New Economic Policy (LPG) is successful in the developed provinces (Andhra Pradesh, Punjab, Maharashtra etc.) but has adverse effects in the backward provinces like Bihar, Orissa and the States of North Eastern Region. Again, development of a society can not be measured through the Yardstick of economic growth. Development of any society stands from its integral socio-cultural process. Since the chief motive of New Economic Reform is 'Profit' it will definitely bring regional inequalities in India and the people of the north eastern society will be affected in many ways. Development of any society must be woven around people and not people around development. Hence development of NER in the context of New Economic Policy can be adjudged through the indicators of latest Human Development Index (HDI).

At the world level, the UNDP (United Nations Development Project) was the apex body to prepare the HDR (Human Development Report) for all the countries. It was fact that the development can not be measured through the single criterion i.e. Gross National Product (GNP). Many scholars looked for a more comprehensive socio-economic measures because they believed that "Human Development is about people- and about how development changes their choices. It is about more than GNP growth, more than income and wealth and more than producing commodities and accumulating capital. A person's access to income may be one of the choice, but it is not the sum total of human endeavour".

Thus the study used the following indicators to measure the achievements and failures of New Economic Reforms in the NER.

Population

The UN's latest global population report predicted that India would reach 1.593 billion by 2050, while China will reach 1.392 billion. India will surpass China by 2030. Currently India's population is 16.7% of the global population, is the second largest in the world and occupies 2.4% of the earth. The growth rate is 1.7% which implies that this burgeoning population has to be catered to, no mean task even for the most booming of economies. We need good governance and population stability to ensure sustainable growth.

Coming to the states of NER, it is observed that the most important problem which creates hindrance on the way of economic development is the problem of population explosion in the region. The total population of the region is about 38.5 million representing about 3.75 per cent of India's total population in 2001. The region's growth rate of population is much higher than the national average. It is striking to note that India's total population increased by 51.80 p.c. in the period 1951-71, 54.39 p.c. in 1971-91 and 21.35 p.c. in the period 1991-2001 whereas for the NER the respective growth rates are 90.86 p.c., 62.11 and 22.02 p.c. At the same time the share of population of NER, in comparison to India, increased from 2.84 p.c. in 1951 to 3.75 p.c. in 2001.

Education plays a very important role in promotion of economic, social, political and institutional development. Education promotes development of all the sectors including agriculture, industry and social sector. Higher levels of education may have greater direct impact on economic development but the primary and middle level education are important because they widely distribute the conditions conducive to development. Education promotes development in all the sectors of the economy and yield high social and economic returns. Sustainable development can not take place without investments being made in people. It is now widely accepted that the improvements in the quality of people as productive agents must be a central objective of development policies.

It is striking to note that except Arunachal Pradesh (42 P.c.) and Meghalaya (49 p.c.) the literacy level of the region's population is above the national level (52 p.c.) according to 1991 census, while in 2001, percentage of literacy rate in the State of Assam (64.28 p.c.) has also been included along with Meghalaya (63.31 p.c.) and Arunachal Pradesh (54.74 p.c.) which are below the National level (65.38 p.c.)

The female literacy rate is highest in Mizoram (95 p.c.) followed by Nagaland (77 p.c.) and lowest in Arunachal Pradesh (48 p.c.). There is a big gender gap in literacy which is one of the major obstacles in attaining total literacy. Enrolment in various stages of education is growing at a fast rate, but the proportion of girls is low and declines sharply at higher stages of education. The highest gender gap has been found in the states of Manipur (24.03 p.c. points), Arunachal Pradesh (21.76 p.c.) Tripura (20.93), and lowest in Mizoram (7.01) followed by Meghalaya (8.27). However, all the states of NER are below all – India (24.84 p.c.), Arunachal Pradesh (21.76), Tripura (20.93) and lowest in Mizoram (7.01) followed by Meghalaya (8.27). However, all the states of NER are below all India

(24.84%) level. Almost same trend is continued in 2001 also. Low female literacy has strong repercussions on other aspects like enrolment of children, population growth, child care and acceptance of family welfare measures **(Table-1.2)**

It is striking to note that per capita expenditure on education in 1997-98 is highest for smaller states of Mizoram (Rs. 1210), followed by Manipur (Rs. 984), Arunachal Pradesh (Rs. 951) and Tripuram (Rs. 836) while it is lowest in Assam (Rs. 537) among the states of NER.

Economic Disparity

In 1996, the Food and Agricultural Organisation (FAO) defined food security as a situation which "exists when all people, at all times, have physical and economic access to sufficient, safe and nutritious food to meet their dietary needs and food preferences for an active and healthy life." The *Food Insecurity Atlas of Urban India* adopts a broader definition of the concept and views food security from three different angles (1) the availability of food, which depends on production and distribution; (2) the access to food, which is determined by an individual's purchasing power, and in turn purchasing power is affected by livelihood access, access to housing, and caste and gender discrimination; and (3) the absorption of food, which is affected by sanitation, clean drinking water and health care. The report identifies 17 key indicators, which fall into six categories (food affordability and availability, livelihood access, access to housing, discrimination in livelihood access, access to sanitation, and health and nutritional outcome) that in turn can be grouped under the classifications of availability, access, and absorption of food.

It is interesting to note that so far the poorest ten percent of the rural population is concerned the shares of consumption are relatively better in Manipur and Mizoram than that of their counterpart in NER while for the richest ten percent, the shares of consumption are relatively better in Assam and Meghalaya **(table - 5.2)**.

Coming to the urban sectors of NER, it is worthwhile to mention that the percentage share of expenditure according to poorest ten percent groups of consumers were found to be better in the state of Nagaland and worst in Assam while for the richest ten percent of the consumers, the share is relatively better in Assam among the states of NER.

Dutta and Choudhury (1996) noted that the pattern of consumption is most uneven in Assam and is one of the highest among the states of NER though it is considerably less than the average for all India in the rural sector. It can also be pointed out that the poorest section of the society in Assam has been badly affected. Thus it may be pointed out that the poorest section of the society in Assam has been badly affected. The results reveal that the extent of degree of inequality in the level of living in the states of NER is much more than what is taken to guide some of the decision making elements in connection with resource transfer from centre to these north eastern states particularly in Assam.

Poverty

While economic poverty and inequality are nothing new for people in the third world or for people in India and within India it is for the people of NER. Population and poverty play hand in hand with each other. poverty, pollution, and resource depletion are all tied to exploding population growth. However, these are all equally responsible for one another. Statistics tell us that population growth rates are much higher in less developed countries where poverty flourishes. And if a country has a larger population it is going to put a bigger strain on the resources of that country and create pollution.

Monthly Per Capita Expenditure (MPCE) may be accepted as an indicator of standard of living for people, on the basis of minimum calorie intake, suggested by Indian Council of Medical Research (ICMR) which should be 2400 calorie for an Indian working persons in rural India and 2100 calorie in urban India. This exercise yielded the official or Planning

Commission's poverty line (per capita expenditure for 30 days) of rural and urban India at 1973-74 prices as Rs. 49.02 and Rs. 56.64 respectively. Thus an estimated people of 46.02 p.c. in urban India and 56 p.c. in rural India were below the poverty line in the year 19981.

However, economists and statisticians in the year 2000 estimated the monthly income needed for a rural individual to consume 2,400 K-calories per day was not Rs. 327 ($7.25) but Rs. 567 ($12.60). At this income level, which amounts to Rs. 19 ($0.42) or less per day, nearly 75% of the rural population is poor. Probably over 80% of the rural population (77 million) is below the World Bank's definition of $2 per day. None of these definitions take into account the cost of adequate housing, clothing, education, healthcare, and entertainment.

Considering the economic condition of NER, it is estimated that the percentage of population below the poverty line is higher in respect of all-India level in 1998 and which come out as 56.83 p.c. and 42.33 p.c. for the rural and urban people of NER respectively **(Dutta, 2003)**. However, as per NSSO's round survey, the poverty ratio has declined in the north east. It has declined to 40.01% in 2000 as round survey, 2000 as compared to 45.01% in 1993-94.

Employment and Production

In this era of globalization, the interdependence of various sectors is going to increase further. In order to make the products manufactured in these sectors internationally competitive, the use of quality service inputs (whether domestic or imported) is becoming a prerequisite. The New Economic Policy giving primacy to the market forces in national development and integrating Indian into the global economic order was enunciated by the government of India in July' 1991.

In the context of poverty alleviation and employment generation, particularly for low skill labour, the interdependent growth of all the three sectors should be emphasized so that the country can achieve a sustained 8 per cent rate of growth in real GDP, as has been envisaged in the Tenth Five-Year Plan (Planning Commission, 2001). Once this happens, there will be a trickle-down effect making growth an instrument of poverty alleviation and employment generation.

A country like India can not hope to build its future on the services sector alone though it can be and will be a major component of the economy. India can not afford not to build its strengths in agriculture for reasons of food and nutritional security. Nor can it afford to ignore manufacturing strengths for reasons of economic and national security. Based on the strength of these two sectors, it can build a major economic infrastructure for the services sector and use it to generate great wealth and employment for her people.

During the process of growth over the years 1950-51 to 1999-2000, the Indian economy has experienced a change in the production structure with a shift away from agriculture towards industry and the tertiary sector. The tertiary sector emerged as the major sector of the economy both in terms of growth rates and share in GDP in the 1990s. It is to be noted here that while the agriculture and manufacturing sectors have experienced phases of deceleration, stagnation and growth, the tertiary sector has shown a uniform growth trend during the period 1950-51 to 1999-2000. **The table 5.1** shows the share of agricultural sector in real GDP, at 1993-94 prices, declined from 55.53 per cent in the 1950s to 28.66 per cent in 1990s (post reform period).

The sectoral distribution of the workforce in India during the period 1983 to 2000 reveals that structural changes in terms of employment have been slow in India as the primary sector continued to absorb 60.4 per cent of the total workforce even in 1999-2000, followed by the tertiary and industrial sectors (22.7 per cent and 16.8 per cent) respectively.

Per Capita Net State Domestic Product (PCNSDP) gives a rough idea about the economic condition of NER with respect to all-India level. It is observed that all the states of NER except Arunachal Pradesh (Rs. 2119 – Rs. 3265) and Mizoram (Rs.

2119 – Rs. 7743) are below the all India level (Rs. 1857 – Rs. 2553) for the years 1985-86 to 1994-95. In this respect Assam's position is the lowest for ever during the period 1990-91 (Rs. 1544) to 1996-97 (Rs. 1628) and also in the period 1980-81 (Rs. 1254). The picture shows the economic backwardness of the region in general and Assam in particular **(table- 5.2)**.

In the north eastern hill areas food production is subject to wide fluctuations due to shifting cultivation. Hence estimate of production may not give the true picture. However, during

Table 5.1: Sectoral Composition of GDP (Average Shares) (in p.c.)

Period	Primary Sector	Secondary Sector	Tertiary Sector
1950-51 to 1959-60	55.53	16.0	28.09
1960-61 to 1969-70	47.37	21.10	31.33
1970-71 to 1979-80	42.68	22.88	34.56
1980-81 to 1989-90 (pre reform period)	36.06	25.13	38.80
1990-91 to 1999-2000 (post reform period)	28.66	27.12	44.22

Source : National Accounts Statistics, CSO

Table 5.2: Per Capita Net State Domestic Product (At Current Prices 1980 - 81)., in Rs.

State	1980-81	1985-86	1990-91	1994-95	1995-96	1996-97
ANP	1571	2119	2710	3265	3304	3059
ASM	1284	1510	1544	1585	1606	1628
MNP	1419	1598	1739	1986	1993	---
MGH	1361	1412	1733	1673	1808	1837
MZM	1289	2658	4474	7743	---	---
NGN	1448	1653	1916	2270	---	---
TRP	1307	1240	1646	1898	2113	2197
India	1625	1857	2267	2533	2664	2814

the last two decades per capita production has declining in the states of Assam, Manipur, Meghalaya and Mizoram and are lower than the national average except in the state of Arunachal Pradesh. While the population is rapidly increasing in the states of the region, it is observed, from the **table -5.3**, that in case of Assam, the per capita food production decreased from 158 kg. In 1972-73 to 154 kg. in 1990-91 which further decreased to 139 kg. in 1997-98. The respective figures for Meghalaya are 120 kg., 87 kg. and 83 kg. only.

The development of an area is best reflected in the distribution of basic needs. The table confirms the fact of region's backwardness as it is observed that the per capita consumption of electricity is much lower in the states of NER as compared to the country's consumption (338.5 kwh). Among the states of NER, the highest per capita consumption is observed in the state of Meghalaya (134.5 kwh) and lowest in Tripura (80.4 kwh).

The North Eastern Council (NEC) has contributed to the North Eastern Region power supply through its power projects. The county's third hydel power project and the first in the North East, which is located in the heart of Shillong at Mawprem is all st to be revived after a gap of 81 years since its inception. The Ministry of Non-Conventional Energy Sources (MNCES) will finance the restoration of the Sonapani Hydel Power Plant, which is expected to light Mawprem and part of Mawlai area. The power plant, which will be "totally unmanned and remote control based" is expected to generate its full capacity of 1.5 Mega Watt for six to seven months especially during the Monsoon and 50% to 62% during other seasons. The unique feature of remote controlling is the first of its kind in the North East and will be managed by the Mawlai 132 KV sub-station.

The expansion of irrigation facilities, operation and maintenance of irrigation system and distribution of water have not received due attention. Irrigation sector is today facing twin issues of sub-optimal sector planning and financial management on the one hand and inadequate water management and maintenance on the other. Involving the farmers in the irrigation system is one obvious remedy for addressing the management problems. In comparison to all-India level only 1.4 p.c. of area is under irrigation system in the NER and only 1 p.c. in the state of Assam(5,39,000 hectares). However, percentage of total irrigated area in Assam is 65 p.c. with respect to total irrigated area in NER.

A look at the **table 5.3**, it is observed that the maximum amount of water is required in the states of Assam among the states of NER, which is approximately 2.33 p.c. as compared to India's requirement in 1991, and the figure (0.833 cubic km.) has risen to 2.63 p.c. in 2001. However, there is an increasing trend of water requirement in 2001 over 1991. Drinking water is the most precious commodity in our daily life. Supply of safe drinking water is essential to sustain life. Regarding the safe drinking water facilities, all the states of NER, except Arunachal Pradesh (70.02 p.c.) are less than the national average (62.3 p.c.). It is striking to note that only 16.21 p.c. of total households of Mizoram can drink safe water while water is the life blood of the environment.

It is interesting to note that on a global basis, only 8 p.c. increase in food grain production in the last 50 years, has been through expansion of cultivable area, the rest 92 p.c. coming from improved irrigation techniques and use of high yielding cultivates. About 46 p.c. of the global food grain production comes from irrigated area, which has increased from 80 million hectares in 1950 to 240 million hectares in 1993. It will not be possible to increase the total annual food grain productivity in the country beyond 250 million tones, with the present agricultural practices, which totally falls short of the requirement to produce a minimum of 400 million tones by the year 2050 to provide adequate food security to the projected 1.8 billion population2.

A look at the **table-6**, it is observed that the performance of the northern states in comparison to all-India level, regarding availability of cereals, all the states of NER excluding Arunachal Pradesh and Tripura, are below the national average (522.7 gms per capita per day). In case of per capita per day availability of

Table 5.3: Per Capita Food Grain Production, Consumption of Electricity and Percentage of Households having Electricity, Safe Drinking Water in N.E. States

ITEM	1*	2*		Per capita food grain production (in kg.)				Water requirement (in cubic km)	
	1996-97	1991	2001	1972-73	1980-81	1990-91	1997-98	1991	2001
ANP	80.8	40.85	70.02	104	207	253	186	0.024	0.029
ASM	107.6	18.74	45.85	158	150	154	139	0.632	0.883
MNP	127.9	50.92	38.72	159	205	155	152	0.060	0.074
MGH	134.5	29.16	36.16	120	116	87	83	0.053	0.072
MZM	127.8	9.20	16.21	244	70	118	123	0.025	0.035
NGN	88.0	53.42	53.37	107	136	160	150	0.036	0.052
TRP	80.4	36.93	37.18	116	196	187	152	0.080	0.088
India	338.5	42.37 62.30	172	190	208	198	27.111	33.521	

1* per capita consumption of electricity (in kwh).

2* percentage of households having safe drinking water.

Table 5.4: Per Capita Availability of Cereals and Pulses (in Gms.) Per Day in NER

ITEM	CEREALS				PULSES			
	1983	1988	1994	1999	1983	1988	1994	1999
ANP	569.8	675.4	653.9	446.6	--	--	15.3	16.8
ASM	365.8	359.5	410.2	373.9	7.10	7.71	6.72	7.69
MNP	418.5	461.0	492.4	476.4	2.93	--	--	--
MGH	293.8	235.1	208.2	225.9	3.88	4.03	3.54	3.07
MZM	179.1	233.2	398.6	395.8	0.52	4.39	35.2	28.6
NGN	392.6	247.2	432.1	423.6	3.88	9.58	19.82	22.1
TRP	535.6	475.8	457.1	391.9	3.02	4.13	5.91	3.9
India	448.4	443.6	520.5	522.7	45.2	37.6	40.5	41.1

pulses, it is observed that all the states of NER are below the all-India average over the period 1983-1999.

Table-7 gives a picture of per capita per day availability of food grains production where same picture is observed as in case of pulses. It is observed that Arunachal Pradesh, the only state in NER tried to maintain its superiority till 1994 but declined thereafter.

Thus food insecurity is a matter of great concern not only to the people of NER but also to the policy makers and planners of NER. It is further observed that no proper care has been taken for the development of agriculture to increase production by which the living condition of the society of NER may be a better one.. Modern technologies, irrigation facilities, scientific and modern equipments are not being properly used for the real development of agriculture in the age of globalisation and liberalization and for which the region stepping back day by day.

Health is social goal and considered as an integral component in over all socio economic development. The majority of health problems are the products of illiteracy, poverty, ignorance, over crowding, poor environmental conditions and uneven distribution of health manpower and institutions. It is observed that there are only 4.32 p.c. of public health centres in the states of NER (958 Nos.) as compared to India's figure **(table-5.6)** and only in Assam there are 64 p.c. public health centres among the states of NER, while less than 10 p.c. are in each of the other states of the region. The same patterns are observed in case of sub centres and community health centrtes. Thus, it is high time to make an effort to increase the number of health centres in backward states of NER so that health

Table 5.5: Per Capita Per Day Availability of Food Grains, Growth Rate of Population and Production

	Per Capita Per Day Availability of Food Grains (in Gms.)				Annual Average Growth Rate of Population and production of Food Grains			
Year	1983	1988	1994	1999	1980-90		1991-2000	
State					Population	Production	Population	Production
ANP	569.75	675.42	669.18	463.33	3.1	4.2	3.1	- 1.8
ASM	372.88	367.25	416.92	381.58	1.5	1.3	1.2	1.5
MNP	421.44	461.00	492.35	476.35	2.6	- 1.7	2.5	2.2
MGH	297.63	239.21	211.78	228.99	2.8	- 0.4	2.8	2.0
MZM	179.57	237.55	433.68	424.38	3.4	8.3	3.3	7.4
NGN	396.52	256.81	451.87	445.60	4.3	3.7	4.4	4.5
TRP	538.56	479.93	463.04	395.25	3.4	1.2	2.9	0.2
India	493.60	481.14	560.98	563.84	2.1	1.8	1.9	1.8

Table 5.6: No. Of Health Centers (As on 31.03.95) and Annual Requirement of Water For Domestic Purposes (Cubic km.)

	Health Centres			Coverage of problem villages during	2001-02 Number (approx) of	
	PHC	SC	CHC	1990-91	Hospitals	Beds (in '000)
ANP	40	203	7	0	15	3
ASM	619	5180	105	356	328	17
MNP	72	420	15	0	19	3
MGH	88	333	10	406	7	3
MZM	43	244	6	68	11	2
NGN	33	244	5	7	17	2
TRP	63	535	10	120	27	2.
India	22156	131902	2377	3031	17952	915

problems can be minimized to some extent.

Diet survey data from many parts of India show that almost one-third of the children in poor families do not eat enough food needed for normal growth. On top of this, the poor environmental sanitation around them predisposes them to infection. The magnitude of the problem of anemia second only to that of protein - energy malnutrition. The problem is less severe in the urban areas than in the rural areas. Anemia reduces work capacity and productivity, which is particularly important in the context of the agricultural economy of the country. Thus, food insecurity is a matter of great concern not only to the people of NER but also to the policy makers and planners of NER. The recommended intakes of nutrients of a nation differ from those of international norms setup by FAO and WHO. The term used to describe dietary stand is "recommended Dietary Allowance (RDA).

The **table 20.5** shows the quantity of items (Recommended Dietary Requirements) should be consumed by the persons of different sex and age groups. This is the level of intake of essential nutrients considered, in the judgement of the (national or international) committee on dietary allowances, to be adequate to meet the known nutritional needs of practically all healthy persons.

Post –Reform Development Scenario in NER

Agriculture in NER has considerable social and political influence. Agriculture has a vital role to play in the economic development in NER, which is a key factor to the economic growth of the region. NER produces a wide array of crops although the food crops preponderate over other crops accounting for maximum total cultivated of the entire region. Assam is contributing a lot in the fruit and vegetables production as is not trailing behind as compared to other states of the country as this sector in the state alone cover an area of 5 lakh hectares which produces around 13.24 lakh MT of fruits, 2.05 lakh MT of spices and 36.61 lakh MT of vegetables. In the sphere of industrialization, the industries supporting value addition in agriculture have been given much priority. The agro based industries have been given much importance in this direction. In Assam as well as the country, agriculture and allied activities is playing a dominant role to contribute nearly 38.7 per cent of GDP and employment to nearly 67 per cent of total working population. Horticulture sector, which contribute nearly 78 per cent to GDP of agriculture sector in the state is a big unorganized sector, completely owned and managed by the small entrepreneurs and marginal farmers. In the agricultural sector more and more entrepreneurs have opted for processing sector for Value Addition of horticulture crops mainly spices under Mini-Mission IV. The government has taken initiative to take them outside the state for exposure on special sectors like spices, tropical and sub tropical medicinal and aromatic plants, floriculture, processing etc. the entrepreneurs have got much scope for self employment under the horticulture crops and visualized the future prosperity and profitability in this sector. They have taken much interest in developing the homestead garden to become self sufficient as regard to the availability of day to day requirement of seasonal major and minor fruits, vegetables, flowers, spices, condiment and even medicine also.

Under Mini Mission IV, a Technology Mission, new processing units have been upgraded. Assam Small Farmers Agribusiness Consortium (ASFAC) and State Department of Agriculture sponsored 'Entrepreneurship Development Training Programme' has created awareness among the entrepreneurs. With the declaration of 2002-03 as Spice Year by the Government of Assam, a number of processing units have been set up to give a boost to this sector and the entrepreneurs are playing a tremendous role to develop these units.

In 2002-03, 900 women are trained for entrepreneurship in horticulture sector through the formation of SHG. Setting up of Integrated Mushroom units is also a major development in this direction. The agro-based and food industry in the state has offered job opportunities to 55,000 entrepreneurs who have contributed production to the value of Rs. 19.78 crore during 2001-02. Cottage industries are normally associated with agriculture and provide a subsidiary employment in rural areas.

There is no doubt that the resources pumped down for poverty alleviation and provision of subsidies in the name of poor have not been much effective in Assam. Considering the large number of persons still living below poverty line, the central government announced a holistic programme called 'Swarnajayanti Gram Swarojgar Yojana (SGSY) for the implementation of the erstwhile self employment programme called Integrated Rural Development Programme (IRDP). This programme was based on a group (community) approach to rural development where the rural poor were organized into Self Help Groups (SHGs) and provided micro credit to take up viable economic activities on their own. The very striking feature of the scheme is that it is quite different from earlier programme objectives, strategy, methodology and sustainability. The scheme aims at establishing a large number of micro enterprises specially for poor people in rural areas 3. The objective is to bring every assisted family below poverty line within 3 years by providing them income generating assets through credit and government subsidy. In several districts and development blocks of Assam, this group is participating actively for the uplift of the rural poor. With a short span of time, the members of the SHGs have been able to generate income and savings and to solve the problem on rural employment. This shows the positive impact of SHGs members in resisting the social evils in the respective areas. The government of Assam has taken up the theme of empowerment of the rural poor as on of the main items on its agenda to tackle the rural poverty and socio economic issues. The self help members through thrift and credit has been taken up as mass movement in Assam and the State has given primary importance to uplift of the poor through SHGs. If the poor are properly motivated and sensitized through education and training then the conditions of economic reforms will be fulfilled by the people in the state in shaping their own destiny. Then LPG wll not be a problem for the region as self reliance is the slogan of the New Economic Policy.

The decision of the Assam government to request the Centre to increase its stake in the Gas Cracker Project is a welcome move as the state should have a bigger say in the project which is emotionally attached to the people of the State. Till now, the state did not have a major say in industries established with the natural resources available in Assam and if the centre accepts the demand of the state government, the state would also earn a major share of the profits. Under the present arrangement, the Gas Authority of India Limited (GAIL) with 70 per cent stake in the project is the major share holder while the Assam Industrial Development Corporation (AIDC), Numaligarh Refinery Limited (NRL) and Oil India Limited (OIL) each will have 10 per cent stake. The Industries and Commerce Department of Government of Assam prepared a proposal in this regard for approval of the cabinet and only then a formal proposal will be sent to the centre. If the project will be realized, the down stream and allied industries will provide employment to at least one lakh persons, which will definitely ease the problem of unemployment. The AIDC has already started the process of engaging a consultant to study the feasibility of setting up of down stream industries and market potentials to prepare an action plan for the same. In this regard, the Central Institute of Plastic Technology (CIPT) can play a greater role by starting the training programme for the unemployed youths of the region. The Gas Cracker would be designed to produce 2.80 lakh tones of polymers, which include 2.02 Lakh tones of linear Low Density of Polyethylene (LDPE) and 60,000 tones of High Density of Polyethylene (HDPE) per annum. The opportunities ahead are unlimited with great challenges. The region can hope that the dream of rapid industrialization of will be fulfilled to go together with the reast of the country as plastics are contributing to a great extent the modern living and the people of the region will sure be benefited by the sophisticated project.

It is needless to say that economic growth of a region can not be achieved without the growth of large or small industries and for which uninterrupted power supply is badly necessary. There can not be a second opinion on the fact that industries open avenues for appointment directly and indirectly, whereby the problem of unemployment can be solved considerably. In this regard NER was far lagging behind as the present generation capacity of electricity in the north east is around 1472 MW of which 374 MW from thermal sources and 994 MW from hydro sources, excluding Assam. In the Tenth Plan period the capacities addition is projected to be 239 MW from hydro and gas based projects like KLHEP 100 MW, Bhairabi HEP 80 MW, Lakwa Waste Heat 38 MW and Baramura GTP 21 MW. Further, the government of India has initiated to set up hydel and thermal project which are expected to be commissioned by the year 2020 from Subansiri River at different stages 4,600 MW Kameng HE Project 600 MW, Tipaimukh HEP 1500 MW and 280 MW for Tripura Gas Project, through CPSUs and in all 6980 MW.

Looking at the power scenario of Assam, as on today, the installed capacity has been related to 253.5 MW for 574.4 MW owing to suspension of BTPS (240 MW), CTPS (60 MW), Mobile Gas Turbines (19 MW) and Bordikharu HE (mini) project (2 MW) and as a matter of fact, the generation came down to 120-150 MW. As such ASEB is to draw power from CPSUs to the tune of around 500-600MW to meet up the peak load demands nearing to 750 MW.

In this context, during the 11th Plan period the target is to achieve from Namrup and Amguri together 300 MW (gas based), from Borgolai TPS 60 MW (coal based) and from Lower Kopili and Mintriang hydel projects together 165 MW, in all 525 MW. Further, under NTPC another 500 MW at BTPS (coal based) may be added to this capacity as declared. From these figures it can be expected that installed capacity in Assam by the year 2012 will stand at about 1416 MW. Considering 60 per cent (LF) the power generation will be around 900 MW, if not more, against the projected demand of 1423 MW. Though it may appear to be a shortfall, commissioning of the projects will certainly contribute to the stable power position, considering the NER as a whole. To be more certain, there will not be any scarcity of power when Subansiri (Lower) HE Project (1000 MW) which is likely to be commissioned by the year 2011 is put into the grid. Also it will contribute to meet the demands in Assam in particular and NER in general. By the year 2020, if not earlier, there is further scope to increase the generation capacity in Assam by commissioning another 250 unit (coal based) at BTPs, 60 MW at Borgolai Project (coal), 60 MW Upper Barapani HE Project and reviving CTPS (60 MW), altogether 430 MW apart from other projects as may be planned during this time. The proposed natural gas import to the country from Myanmar to Goya through North east, as per proposed route, through Aizwal, Silchar, Guwahati, Siliguri and Goya, if materialized, there is no doubt that this region will be amply benefited by using this gas as feed stock or fuel or both4.

It is a welcome sign that the government of Assam has entered into the Oil Sector and the tie up with OIL will create a great synergic force. Such a road map could be ad starting point, and let this be a signal that the government is right earnest to create an important landmark in oil business.

In the era of globalization, electricity is one of the basic inputs for achieving socio-economic development of a nation. The present per capita consumption of electricity in India is little over 400 Kwh, which is much lower than that of the developed countries. To avoid this backdrop government of India formed an exclusive Ministry for Non-Conventional Energy Sources for implementing the programmes on renewable energy like bio-gas, small hydro projects, wind energy, geo thermal energy, solar energy etc. Although there is immense potentiality for the development of non conventional and renewable energy sector in Assam, there is a regular feature of the shortage of power in the state. About 87 per cent of the state population live in rural areas, that is 26,247 villages. Of these, as on March 31, 2006, only 21,586 villages have been electrified of which only 16.54 per cent of the total households in these electrified villages have electricity connection. The remaining 4661 villages are still to see light of electricity. Again, 2145 unelectrified villages have been identified as remote and thus to provide 'Electricity To All' by 2012 slogan of the government is a far cry. There is no alternative but to go for non conventional and renewable energy sources applying modern technologies. It is encouraging to note that the Assam Energy Development Agency, the State Nodal Agency of the Ministry of the Non conventional Energy Sources identified the potentiality the potentiality of three renewable sources of energy like small hydro, biomass gasification and solar photovoltaic for electrification of remote villages. Thus the priority of harnessing non conventional renewable sources of energy will continue for the years to come so as to carryout all the economic activities in rural areas as part of infrastructural development of the policy of globalisation.

The Centre's larger attention to tea industry of the country has brightened its prospects of production and exports. The 11th Plan Outlay on tea industry to Rs. 800 crore. During 10th Plan period, the industry received funds worth Rs. 350

crore by way of plan funds and around Rs. 30 crore from the proceeds accumulated under the additional excise duty. Besides this, the unspent amount accruing out of the non-lapsable additional excise duty fund would be carried forward. This is in addition to resources from special purpose tea fund that would be made available to tea industry. It may be recalled that following Planning Commission's approval for setting up a special purpose tea fund and the budget announcement of the same by the Union Finance Minister, the Ministry of State for Commerce revealed, at a press conference in Guwahati in May, 2006, that the Indian tea industry would be utilize Rs. 4,700 crore under which Assam alone would get a share of 60 per cent or Rs. 2820 crore. It was also announced that the government would start disbursing the fund from December, 2006 when it would provide Rs. 100 crore as the initial component. The minister also revealed that the Centre planned to achieve a proper price structure and build up an encouraging sales strategy starting through the auction route. The objective is to create an environment where more producers and buyers opted for the auction system of marketing. The Union Commerce Minister had earlier promised that he would unveil a 15-year programme for massive replantation and rejuvenation of the country's tea sector.

It is important to note that there is a marketing strategy and quality improvement design structured in the revival package to give the industry edge over its competitors in the global market. The tea package is also designed to create a more transparent mechanism with the setting up of two new auction centres in Assam where an electronic system would be developed and a target of replantation of more than 1.7 lakh hectares over a period of 15 years has been fixed. This is certainly a happy change in sight. What is, however, the latest addition to the package and what will certainly bring cheer to Assam's 70,000 small tea growers in addition to almost another equal number in the rest of the country, is the announcement that five factories in the state, to start with, will be set up for the manufacture of tea from green leaves of the small tea gardens.

Since this will help eliminating middlemen's appropriation, the grower's tea is expected to fetch an additional profit of at least Rs. 15 a kg. This would be no mean achievement 5.

Good roads and transport system are the key indicators and facilitators of progress and the part of the scheme of New Economic Reform. Assam will soon be riding the highway to prosperity if the dream projects of the National Highway Authority of India are realized without running into too many hurdles. Thousands of kilometer of roads and highways in the state are to be improved and the carriageways broadened to make way for increased volume of traffic ensuring that the road and transport system are smooth and fast in the region. The most prestigious project, East-west Corridor Project – a 678 km. long express way between Silchar and Srirampore (Assam-West Bengal border) will pass through Guwahati besides several other important towns is expected to be completed by 2008. It promises to provide a hindrance free and fast transport net work that we benefit not only the people of three districts of Barak Valley of Assam who are frequently cut off from the rest of the country due to frequent landslides and other reasons. There are several other projects that are pipe line, including 4-laning of the 315 km. highway between Nagaon and Dibrugarh of Assam. Access to good roads bring all round development by making access to health care, agricultural marketing, education and administration easier. It would increase income, employment opportunities, tourism, industrial development in many ways. If north east will improve then trade relation with neighbouring border countries should be established. In a bid to explore the ASEAN market, the centre has decided to improve the road connectivity in the north east. At a Conference of Indian Industry (CII) held at shillong, the Joint Secretary of Investment and Technology Promotion, the Ministry of External Affairs pointed out that the ministry is now close look with the North East Council (NEC) to implement some new plans since this region has very close links with Myanmmer and Bangladesh. In 2005, the volume of trade between India and ASEAN had touched $15 million and considering the upspring market, we have set a target of $35 billion trade by 2015, she said.

Conclusion and Suggestions

From the foregoing discussion, it is clear that the scene of development in NER was far from satisfactory in pre Economic Reform Period and in the post Reform Period marks of development can be determined in the region in general and the state of Assam in particular. So far as the latest Human development Index is concerned one thing is certain that the society of NER is lagging behind as compared to other regions of the country due to many reasons such as rise of terrorism, repeated social unrest along with government's apathy towards primary sectors and misappropriation of government fund and non utilization of sanctioned money etc. After the process of globalization started, the slogan 'enrich thyself ' is going to be implemented by force in different states of NER by the respective governments. As a result, initiatives have been taken by the state governments of NER to cope with the Central Government's NEP. It is a matter of fact that the forces of LPG in economic, social, culture and political spheres of life have been subjected to both negative and positive aspects. At the outset of this economic reform in India some scholars perceived it as elite-driven and incapable of bringing qualitative change in people's lives. The fear psychosis was that the advanced countries would capture a lion's share in the global market by neglecting the service sector in different regions of the country. However, the present scenario is altogether different and economic reform has come to stay and the region can not do it away with. Again the present study reveals the fact that globalization has paid the way for rapid technological advancements in the region with developed information technological services, research and development etc. Many young skilled persons have got their employments in MNCs of other parts of India as well as in the world. The reform has brought new opportunities of trade, business, services and employment in the region can not be denied. At the same time the region should update the younger generation through research and training to cope with the changing situation otherwise it will be lagging behind. North eastern economy is suffering from an inadequate infrastructure. Transportation facilities are poor and inadequate. Communication facilities are not so developed. There is no encouraging sign for Science and Technology and other sub sectors. Agriculture, the primary sector, is misguided by the primordial social custom and traditions. Road, water and air transport facilities in the region are far below from the requirement. There is no remarkable GDP growth and the region is still miles away from a virtual global village. There is mass unemployment causing constant unrest in the region. Hence following suggestions may be outlined to keep pace with the policies of NEP.

Due to reverse trend of monsoon this year in the state, severe draught like situation prevailed which stood in the way of agricultural development. Though the annual average of rainfall in the state of Assam is received as 2580 mm, it is found to be gradually deceasing to the range of 2118 mm to 2262 mm during the last 5 years. The state witnessed extreme weather aberration during the current kharif season. The monsoon rain is considered to be highly beneficial for initiating sowing or transplantation of kharif crop is found to be missing mostly in this year. In most of the districts of the state 45- 70 per cent deficit rainfall has been experienced. The agricultural sector in our counts remain susceptible to fluctuating behaviour of monsoon whereas the over all global agricultural scenario also remained dynamic with noticeable change in production, stocks and trade in this year. The fate of Sali rice or winter rice, the major crop of the state which covers 67 per cent of total area under rice is quite uncertain. At this backdrop, the productivity of Sali rice is likely to come down to 1400 kg per hectare in 2005-06 from 1595 kg per hectare in 2004-05. To avoid this critical situation 3.28 lakh litres of diesel were distributed among the farmers to activate the shallow tube wells which has benefited nearly 90,000 farm families. The state of Assam having potentiality of enormous natural resources could occupy a prominent place in the world with pre-dominance in agriculture sector provided it could be free from perennial natural calamities. Through proper research and planning from multi-level authorities like flood control department, irrigation department and agricultural department the state can be saved. Soil erosion, deforestation and preservation of bio- diversity are a crying need of the hour. The water resources of NER accounts for about 33 per cent of the county's water wealth need to be harnessed judiciously to bridge the gap in water requirement for agricultural purposes. With a view to increasing the per capita income of the state which is found to be Rs. 14,523 at current prices in 2005-06 and 43.7 per cent less than the all India average, much emphasis need to be laid on effective water management plan like other agriculturally developed regions of the country.

Further, the issues of Trade Related Intellectual Property rights (TRIPS) leading to the farmers and exporters of the region and this challenge should be accepted by the scientists of the region to quickly develop patent varieties of crops and other things for the development of agro-business in the region. Again, effective participatory extension programme has to be carried out for bringing about community empowerment so that the farmer can play their desirable role in meeting the challenges and improving their livelihood.

The subject of inequality and poverty is an important one for global policy. This study reveals that despite of abundant natural resources, the region is poorest of the poor and repeatedly neglected by the policy makers of New Delhi since independence. Although the Minister of Heavy Industries from Assam to the Central Government along with few members of Parliament flowed the tears of crocodile in the floor of Parliament for declaring Assam a Special Economic Zone (SEZ), the central government is reluctant to allot the same. In the era of globalization, central government's SEZ Policy should be extended to Assam not only to boost economic production but also fulfill the need of infra structural development to attract the Multi National Corporations and Industrialists by removing the malady of regional disparity.

The NER which is known for its rich but unharnessed resources was thought to be heading for a spectacular change in its resource use pattern. When the North East Industrial Policy was announced on December 24, 1997 for investing in the areas of industry and infrastructure, remaining regional disparity through sustainable economic development raising per capita income of people to secure best standard of living. The region has long been suffering from low level of income as its share only 2.7 per cent of India's total national income to shelter 3.8 per cent of its population. The short fall of region's per capita income below all India level at constant prices was Rs. 1950 in 1993-94 and today the difference has climbed up to more than Rs. 5700. Thus if the region wants to eliminate this difference in 20 years from now, it has to aim at an economic growth rate at 9 per cent per annum. This requires the development of both industry and agriculture along with infrastructure. The North East Industrial Policy has failed to attract large investments in the areas of industry and infrastructure by leaving many critical areas unaddressed. The policy took almost 4 years to take a start with, and could somehow garner investment of only Rs. 1200 crore, in the last 5 years, in 650 industrial units, mainly in Assam and Meghalaya, but what is much more surprising is that the centre has recently extended similar benefits to states of Uttaranchal, Himachal Pradesh and Jammu & Kashmir which are infrastructurally far ahead of this region and closer to mainland market. The government has decided to invest Rs. 4000 crore in Uttaranchal, Rs. 18000 crore in Himchal Pradesh and Rs. 2000 Crore in Jammu & Kashmir. Thus step motherly attitude of the Centre towards the North East is still visible. This policy is scheduled to expire after March, 2007 and hence the extension of the period of the policy is necessary to save the region from further deterioration.

One of the most remarkable development of New Economic Reform is the increasing role of Multi National Corporations (MNCs), which functions cutting across national boundaries and ignoring the State System. Although UNO recognizes the State System as primary and most important actor in

International System, the New Economic Reform would develop a new kind of State and growth of new relationship in the world without states. Further, with the advent of globalization, the Supranational Bodies like UN, EU, NAFTA, ASEAN, APEC, IMF, World Bank and WTO will formulate policies and lay conditions like reduction of expenditure in social sectors, cut down in employment, reduction in government subsidies etc. not acceptable to the states and NER of India, which is poverty-striken, will be victim of the situation. Under the circumstances it can be suggested that the region wants reform but not at the cost of its people. Hence, the slogan of the region should be "Economic Reform in the Region within the Limits".

NER is famous for its natural scenery and pilgrimages. It attracts the tourists from all the countries in the world. Once upon a time the governments of North East States earned foreign exchange from the industry of Tourism. But, since the last few decades, due to rise of terrorism and government's apathy towards this industry, Tourism is in a bad shape. As a result the people of north east could not earn from this industry. In the circumstances it may be suggested that the governments of the region should take initiative for the modernization of Tourism and allied environment which attracts the Tourists. In the age of information technology, globalization and decentralization governance there is an increased need for effective, accountable and transparent administrative and management structures, based on collaboration and partnership among the key players of the state government's business and civil society. Effective implementation of e-governance can take information technology to the common man, helping national and state Government to align their services with the hanging needs of both citizens and stakeholders as well as develop the economy. Versatile Information System for Tourist Attraction (VISTA) is an integrated system that uses the power of Information Technology to promote Tourism and facilitate Tourist operations. An Electronic Tourism Platform (ETP) Core System may be designed corresponding to documentation and generic guides. The ETP will enable small and medium sized enterprises to respond to new demands for Tourist products and allow access to new markets that were previously reachable.

Local population should be associated with Tourism activities and share equitably in the economic, social and cultural benefits they generate and particularly in the creation of direct and indirect jobs resulting from them. Tourism policies and activities should be conducted with respect for the artistic, archaeological and cultural heritage. The government should take care for preserving and upgrading historical monuments, Shrines and privately owned cultural property and monuments.

The population is one such issue, as it is affecting the overall development of the country. The population explosion has hindered the country's growth. The loopholes in the population control need to be identified and action should be taken to strengthen the programme. The target is to effectively bring down the birth rate and form a policy in accordance with the social, political and economic set up of the state. It is important to improve the status of women in the society. Family planning camps have adopted a holistic approach where complete health care facility is being provided to the rural residents. It was decided to form local societies for effective implementation of routine immunisation, mother and child health care programmes. Issues like female foeticide and male sterilisation need to be discussed, as both are contradictory and yet important for population control programme. Economic and educational progress is the foundation on which we can have effective progress in regard to family planning. The pressure on the limited resources of the country has brought to the forefront the urgency of population control. It is apparent that this can be achieved only by the reduction of the birth rate to the extent necessary to stabilise the population at a level consistent with the requirements of the national economy. The study arrests the attention of the policy makers of the region to check the immigration from neighbouring countries to the region for controlling the population explosion.

The State of the World, 1999 Report from the World watch

Institute suggests that the global economy could be seriously affected by environmental problems, such as the lack of access to enough resources to meet growing population demands. Environmental degradation can contribute to social and political instability, which can lead to security issues. Human Rights can be upheld by ensuring women's empowerment, and realizing that women play a crucial role in the development of society, many underlying issues which lead to conflict and problems can be tackled more effectively. Hence preservation and protection of environment will provide sustainable growth and development in the region.

The big rush of the big players to get a berth in the NER will lead exploitation to the people in general and small and medium industries in the state in particular. The conversion of agrarian society into industrial one has a cascading effect on the society. Before establishing industries in the region by the MNCs certain codes of conduct should be framed by the respective state governments of the region for the operation of the same and they must abide by the rules framed by the governments.

No endeavour in this respect will be successful unless and until the people of the region are well conscious and aware of it. To get something, one must pay something. Thus old and traditional structures, social bonds, customs etc must be sacrificed a little in order to improve. At the same time the governments should implement the reform policies with extreme caution so that it would not arouse the people's emotion and sentiments by interfering in the social laws, customs, traditions etc. Hence the slogan should be *'Globalization within limits or reform in a controlled manner'*.

Notes

1. N. Bhattacharya (1998) : On Level of Living Surveys in India, Presidential Address, 85th Indian Science Congress, Section of Statistics.
2. V.R. Rao (1996) : General Presidential Address in 83rd

Indian Science Congress, Patiala.

3. Namita Devi (2006): A Success Story of Self Help Group in 'The Assam Tribune', November 27.

4. J. N. Goswami (2006) : Power Generation Prospects in North East in 'The Assam Tribune', September 14.

5. India's Tea Prospects in The Assam Tribune, September 27, 2006.

References

Ahluwalia, Isher Judge and Little, I.M.D. (ed) (1998) : India's Economic Reforms and Development - Essays for Monmohan Singh, Oxford University Press, New Delhi.

Bhagawati, Jagadish (1994), India in Transition : Freeing the Economy, Oxford University Press, New Delhi.

Dutta, P.C. (2003) : Regional Disparity and its Consequences in North Eastern Region of India in *Economic Liberalization and Regional Disparities in India – Special Focus on the North Eastern Region (ed.) A.C. Mohapatra and C.R. Pathak,* Star Publishing House, Shillong.

Dutta, P.C. and B.C. Pradhan (2004) : Agricultural Development and Security of Life in *Food Security and Public Distribution System Today – Failures and Success (ed.)Amalesh Banerjee,* Kanishka Publishers, Distributors, New Delhi.

Dutta, P.C. and B.C. Pradhan (2006) : Changing Agricultural Scenario in North East India in *Changing Agricultural Scenario In North East India (ed.)Bimal J. Deb and B. Datta Ray,* Concept Publishing Company, New Delhi.

Dutta P. C. & H.Choudhury (1996) : "A Note on inter State Variation in per Capita Non-Food Household items of Consumption in the North East India", *IJRS, Vol. 28 No.2.*

Ghosh, Jayati (1998) : Liberalisation Debates in Terence Byres (ed), *The Indian Economy: Major Debates Since*

Independence, Delhi, 329.

Jha Prabodh Kumar (2000) : Economic Reformation or Deformation in India in *Post – Reform Leading Issues of Indian Economy, Vol-I (ed.) A.D.N. Bajpai et al.,* p. 8-17, Atlantic Publishers and Distributors, New Delhi.

Kumar, Nagesh in Raj Kapila & Uma Kapila (ed.) A Decade of Economic Reforms in India : The Past, The Present, The Future... (2002), Academic Foundations, New Delhi- 125.

Mohan, Rakesh (1999 : Economic Reforms : The Next Wave, Lalit Doshi Memorial Lecture, Mumbai, 13th Ocober, 1999.

Nagraj, R (1997) : What has happened since 1991 : Assessment of India's Economic Reforms, Economic and Political Weekly, p.2871, 8th November.

Nayyar, Deepak (1993) : Indian Economy at the Cross Roads: Illusions and Realities, *Economic and Political Weekly,* p. 639, 10th April, 1993.

Nayyar, Deepak (1996) : Economic Liberalization in India : Analytics, Experience and Lesson, *R.C. Dutta Lectures,* Orient Longman, New Delhi, Centre For Studies in Social Sciences.

Parikh, Kirti (1997) : India's Economy: Raised for Take off, *Economic and Political Weekly*, p. 124-130, 1151, May 17-23.

Patnaik, Prabhat and Chandrasekhar, C.P. (1995) : Indian Economy under Structural, Economic and Political Weekly, November 25.

Ray Binayak (2000) : Good Governance and Administrative Reforms : Priorities for India in *Economic Liberalisation and Institutional Reforms in South Asia – Recent Experiences and Future Prospects,(ed.) Dilip Dutta, p. 369-396,* Atlantic Publishers and Distributors, New Delhi-27.

Saramma A. D. (2000) : New Economic Policy of 1991 and The Problem of Rural Unemployment : Some Options in *Post – Reform Leading Issues of Indian Economy, Vol- I (ed.)*

A.D.N. Bajpai et al., p. 307- 316, Atlantic Publishers and Distributors, New Delhi-27.

Singh Manminder and Sandeep Singh Saluja (2005) : New Economic Reforms and Economic Growth in *Liberalisation and Globalisation of Indian Economy, Vol- VI (ed.)K. R. Gupta,* p.1-26, Atlantic Publishers and Distributors, New Delhi-27.

Srinivasan, T.N. (1998) : India's Export Performance : A Comparative Analysis. in I. J. Ahluwalia and I.M.D. Little (ed) op. cit.

6

A Preliminary Note on Measures of Income Inequality

The term 'inequality' is a relative concept. When used with reference to income, it conveys the layman's idea that some people are rich as compared to others. The term refers to unequal distribution of income. Thus Income - Inequality may be defined as the extent of disparity between high and low incomes. The measure can be used as the ratio of a high household income to a low household income, after adjustment for household size and composition. The higher the ratio, the greater is the level of inequality. The degree of income inequality is often regarded as an important aspect of the fairness of the society we live in. A high level of income inequality may also be detrimental to the level of social connectedness across society. Inequality is one of the formidable economic problems facing the country and has become a dominant socio-economic issue both in political and academic circles.

The period since the neo-liberal economic reforms were introduced in India has been one of dramatically increased income inequality. But the government is trying to persuade us that this is all a mirage, and that actually all Indians are much better off than ever before. They are systematically trying to manipulate even the official statistics of the country, in order to push this completely false line. The fact that this will end up destroying the statistical system of the country, which was earlier one of the most impressive in the developing world, seems to be of no concern to them.

Global income inequality is probably greater than it has ever been in human history. There is some debate about whether it is getting worse or getting better. Currently, the richest 1 p.c. of people in the world receives as much as the bottom 57 p.c. It is observed in one comparative study based on primary (for Barak Valley) and secondary (NSSO) data that the lowest 50 p.c. of the population enjoy 23 p.c. share of income (expenditure) in Barak Valley, 27 p.c. in Assam and 24 p.c. in India.

Milanovic found that the richest 25 p.c. of the world's population receives 75 p.c. of the world's income, even when adjusting for Purchasing Power Parity. The poorest 75 p.c. of the population share just 25 p.c. This occurs because a large proportion of the world's population lives in the poorest countries, and within the poorest regions of those countries, particularly in the rural areas of China, rural and urban India and Africa.

Several measures of income inequality have been suggested in the past. But the most widely used measure is Gini's concentration ratio. The other measures are the variance, coefficient of variation, the relative mean deviations, Atkinson's measure, Theil's Entropy measure, Sen's inequality etc. These measures are widely used for two purposes.

1. to compare two size distributions i.e. the size distributions of income wealth, or land holding etc. over two periods or places.
2. to attach some absolute measures to the degree of inequality or to give some ideas whether the inequality is large or small.

An ideal measure of inequality should always satisfy Pigou-Dalton condition i.e. a transfer from a richer man to a poorer person should reduce the value of an ideal inequality measure and the Lorenz ratio always satisfy the Pigou-Dalton condition.

Standard deviation of income measures income dispersion by assessing the square root of variance from the mean. This metric is seldom seen, its use limited to occasional reference in academic journals.

The 'Robin Hood index', also known as the Hoover index, is a measure of income inequality and mathematically related to the Gini coefficient. It is equal to the portion of the total community income that would have to be redistributed (taken from the richer half of the population and given to the poorer half) for there to be perfect equality.

Mathematically, the Robin Hood index for Lorenz curve L(x) is max $(x - L(x))$

Of all inequality measures, this measure is the simplest and least interpretative one. The Robin Hood index is typically used in applications related to socio-economic class (SES) and health. It is conceptually the simplest inequality index used in econometrics. A better known inequality measure is the Gini coefficient which is based on the Lorenz curve.

Robin Hood index (H) may be computed as :

$$H = 0.5 \sum_{i=1}^{N} \left| (Ei / E\ total) - (Ai / A\ total) \right|$$

where the amount N of quantiles only appears as upper border of summations. Thus, inequities can be computed for quantiles with different widths A. For example, Ei could be the income in the quantile #i and Ai could be the amount (absolute or relative) of earners in the quantile #i. Etotal then would be the sum of incomes of all N quantiles and Atotal would be the sum of the income earners in all N quantiles.

The Gini coefficient is a measure of statistical dispersion most prominently used as a measure of inequality of income distribution or inequality of wealth distribution. The Gini Coefficient attributed to Gini may be defined as :

$$\text{Gini Coefficient} = \frac{\text{Area between Lorenz curve and diagonal}}{\text{Total Area under diagonal}}$$

The Gini coefficient is a number between 0 and 1, where 0 corresponds with perfect equality (where everyone has the same income) and 1 corresponds with perfect inequality (where one person has all the income, and everyone else has zero income). This is a popular summary statistic used to quantify the extent of income inequality depicted in a particular Lorenz curve. Gini coefficients do include income gained from wealth; however, the Gini coefficient is used to measure net income more than net worth, which can be misinterpreted as the coefficient requires that no one have a negative net income or wealth.

The Gini coefficient was developed by the Italian statistician Corrado Gini and published in his 1912 paper "Variabilità e mutabilità" ("Variability and Mutability"). The Gini coefficient is also commonly used for the measurement of the discriminatory power of rating systems in credit risk management. The Gini index is the Gini coefficient expressed as a percentage, and is equal to the Gini coefficient multiplied by 100. (The Gini coefficient is equal to half of the relative mean difference). As for all statistics, there may be systematic and random errors in the data. The meaning of the Gini coefficient decreases as the data become less accurate. However, the Gini coefficient satisfies four important principles:

(i) *Anonymity:* it does not matter who the high and low earners are.

(ii) *Scale independence:* the Gini coefficient does not consider the size of the economy, the way it is measured, or whether it is a rich or poor country on average.

(iii) *Population independence:* it does not matter how large the population of the country is.

(iv) *Transfer principle:* if income (less than the difference), is transferred from a rich person to a poor person the resulting distribution is more equal.

Economies with similar incomes and Gini coefficients can still have very different income distributions. This is because the Lorenz curves can have different shapes and yet still yield the same Gini coefficient. The curve may understate the actual amount of inequality if richer households are able to use income more efficiently than lower income households. From another point of view, measured inequality may be the result of more or less efficient use of household incomes.

Lorenz curve is a graphic device used to display the relative inequality in a distribution of income values. A society's total income is ordered according to income level and the cumulative total graphed. Lorenz ratio relates the proportion of total income to the proportion of person spending up to a given level of total income when units are arranged in ascending order of income.

If f_i be the proportion of population in the ith class (i = 1, 2,... T) an qi be the corresponding share of income of this population, then Lorenz Ratio (L) may be defined as

$$L = \sum_{t=1}^{T} P_t Q_{t+1} - \sum_{t=1}^{T} P_{t+1} Q_t, \text{ Where, } P_t = \sum_{i=1}^{t} f_i, \quad \sum_{t=1}^{T} P_t = 1$$

$$\text{and } Qt = \sum_{i=1}^{t} f_i, \quad \sum_{t=1}^{T} Q_t = 1$$

Lorenz ratio defined above can also be expressed in the following form due to N.S. Iyengar as

$$L = 1 - \sum (P_i - P_{i-1}) (Q\, i + Q_{i-1}),$$

Where $(P_0, Q_0) = (0, 0)$ and $(P_T, Q_T) = (1, 1)$

The Gini coefficient is defined as a ratio of the areas on the Lorenz curve diagram. If the area between the line of perfect equality and Lorenz curve is A, and the area under the Lorenz curve is B, then the Gini coefficient is A/(A+B).

Since A+B = 0.5, the Gini coefficient,

$$G = A/(.5) = 2A = 1\text{-}2B.$$

The Lorenz curve for a probability distribution is a continuous function. However, Lorenz curves representing discontinuous functions can be constructed as the limit of Lorenz curves of probability distributions, the line of perfect inequality being an example.

J. Aitchison and J.A.C. Brown have suggested a number of different techniques for estimation of parameters of the log normal distribution. They recommended the method of moments, the method of quantiles and the graphical method of estimation mainly due to the computational complexities involved in the maximum likelihood estimation technique. Maximum likelihood estimates of log normal parameters are possible with the high speed computers for grouped data ,the computation is tedious and for which the parameters are estimated by the method of moments which, however, is not as efficient as the maximum likelihood.

When per capita income X obeys two parameters log normal distribution with

$$E(X) = \theta, V(X) = \lambda,$$

then the marginal density function of the two parametric log normal variate is given by

$$f(X) = X^{-1} \lambda^{-1} (\sqrt{2}\ \pi)^{-1} \exp [- 2^{-1} \lambda^{-2} (\log e X - \theta)^2], X > 0$$

Now, since $Z = \log e X$ is $N(\theta, \lambda)$,

the proportion of persons having per capita income 'C' or less is given by

$$P_C = \text{Prob. } (X \leq \log C) = \phi ((\log C - \theta)/\lambda)^2,$$

where $\phi(t)$ is defined by the relation

$$\phi(t) = (\sqrt{2\pi})^{-1} \int_{\infty}^{t} \exp (-2^{-1} u^2)\, du$$

The proportion of total income by these persons is given by

$$q_c = \phi \left(\frac{\log C - \theta}{\lambda} - \lambda\right)$$

However, Lorenz ratio (L) under the log normal hypothesis in its simplified form is given by

$$L = 2\ \phi (\lambda / \sqrt{2}) - 1$$

In addition to or in competition with the Gini coefficient *entropy measures* are frequently used (e.g. the Atkinson and Theil indices). These measures attempt to compare the distribution of resources by intelligent agents in the market with a maximum entropy random distribution, which would occur if these agents acted like non-intelligent particles in a closed system following the laws of statistical physics.

Theil index due to H. Theil is also a summary statistic used to measure income inequality. The index is based on information entropy in order not only to indicate plain inequality, but also to indicate the attention, which is given to inequality. Compared to the Gini coefficient, the Theil index is increasingly, but yet less commonly used. The measure of inequality proposed by Theil derive from the notion of entropy in Information Theory is given by

$$I(q:p) = \sum_{i=1}^{T} q_i \log_e (q_i / p_i),$$

where $p_i \geq 0$ is the share of population and q_i is the share of total income of the ith expenditure class and

$$\sum_{i=1}^{T} p_i = \sum_{i=1}^{T} q_i = 1, \qquad p_i = f_i / \sum f_i, \qquad q_i = f_i x_i / \sum f_i x_i$$

The expression given above is a measure for the degree of income inequality among the people in the expenditure classes.

Theil also introduced a measurement to measure the intra class variation which is given by

$$I_0(q:p) = Q_g \log_e Q_g / P_g$$

where $\quad Q_g = \sum_{i=1}^{g} q_i, \; P_g = \sum_{i=1}^{g} p_i, \; (g = 1,2,\ldots\ldots G)$

and $\quad \sum Q_g = \sum P_g = 1$

Suppose that the i sets of events (i = 1,2, ... N) are combined into G ≤ N sets of events $S_1, S_2, ..S_g$ in such a way that each Ei belongs to exactly one S_g, where g = 1, 2,......G. Then the relationship between I (q : p), the total variation and the corresponding expression after aggregation can be defined according to Theil as

$$I(q:p) = I_0(q:p) + \sum_{g=1}^{G} Q_g . I_g(q:p)$$

where,

$$I_g(q:p) = \sum (q_i / Q_g) \log [(q_i / Q_g) / (p_i / P_g)]$$

A. B. Atkinson defined what he called the equally distributed equivalent income of a given distribution of a total income and this is defined as that level of per capita income which is enjoyed by everybody would make total welfare exactly equal to the total welfare generated by the actual income distribution. According to D.G. Champernowe, "equally distributed equivalent income" means the proportion of total income that it absorbed in compensating for the loss of aggregate satisfaction due to inequality. Atkinson's measure of inequality is given by

$$I = 1 \quad \frac{Y_{EDE}}{\upsilon}$$

where Y_{EDE} means equally distributed equivalent or the level of income per head which if equally distributed would give the same level of social welfare as the present distribution. υ is the mean of the distribution that is per capita income.

The inequality 'I' lies between 0 (complete equality) and 1 (complete inequality). This measure is an index of potential gains from re-distribution and provides a tool which can be used to attach some absolute measure to the degree of inequality or to give some idea whether the inequality large or small.This measure can also be expressed as

$$I = 1 - [\sum_{i=1}^{n} (Y_i / \upsilon)^{1-\varepsilon} f(Y_i)] 1/(1-\varepsilon)$$

The inequality measure 'I' introduces distributiomal objectives through an explicit parameter ε. This parameter represents the weights attached by the society to inequality in the distribution. It ranges from zero (which means the society is indifferent about the distribution) to infinity (which means the society is concerned only with the position of the lowest income group). The welfare interpretation of these measures have been extensively discussed by Prof. Amartya Sen. If I falls, the distribution becomes more equal i.e. we require a higher level of equally distributed income to achieve the same social welfare as the actual distribution.

The Gini index of the total family income may be expressed as

$$G = (1/\upsilon) \sum_{i=1}^{n} \upsilon_i C_{gi}$$

where C_{gi} is the concentration index of the mean i^{th} factror income gi (x) and υ is the mean of the ith factror income of all the families.

The Gini coefficient's main advantage is that it is a measure of inequality by means of a ratio analysis, rather than a variable unrepresentative of most of the population, such as per capita income or gross domestic product. It can be used to compare income distributions across different population sectors as well as countries, for example the Gini coefficient for urban areas differs from that of rural areas in many countries. The Gini coefficient can be used to indicate how the distribution of income has changed within a country over a period of time, thus it is possible to see if inequality is increasing or decreasing.

However, Care should be taken in using the Gini coefficient as a measure of egalitarianism, as it is properly a measure of income dispersion. Two equally egalitarian countries with different immigration policies may have different Gini coefficients.

The Lorenz curve may understate the actual amount of inequality if richer households are able to use income more efficiently than lower income households. From another point of view, measured inequality may be the result of more or less efficient use of household incomes.

Entropy measures are frequently used (e.g. the Atkinson and Theil indices) to compare the distribution of resources by intelligent agents in the market with a maximum entropy random distribution, which would occur if these agents acted like non-intelligent particles in a closed system following the laws of statistical physics.

However, it is observed in a study made on Barak Valley of Assam that for $\varepsilon = 2.5$, the values of the Atkinson's indices came to 0.08 and 0.17 for the rural and urban sectors respectively, indicating that if incomes were equally distributed among the population of the valley, then it requires 83 per cent of the present income to achieve the same level of social welfare in the urban sector while for the rural sector it requires 92 per cent. In other words, we would say that a certain plan for redistributing income would raise social welfare by an amount equiuvalent to an increase of $\varepsilon = 2.5$ in equally distributed income. Thus the

Inequalities of PCE in Barak Valley of Assam (1999-2000) for different values of Epsilon (ε).

ε	Rural	Urban
0.5	0.0165	0.0296
1.25	0.0410	0.0795
1.50	0.0490	0.0.972
1.75	0.0570	0.1153
2.00	0.0648	0.1336
2.25	0.0726	0.1521
2.50	0.0803	0.1705

potential gain from redistribution to bring about equality in the rural and urban sectors would be equivalent to raising the total income by 8 per cent and 17 per cent respectively.

In the National Sample Surveys, a change in survey reference periods led to much lower reported inequality. As a result, although 9 surveys from 1989-90 to 1998 had shown no poverty reduction, the 1999-00 survey reported 10 percentage points reduction in the poverty ratio! The most dramatic and remarkable improvement in consumption has been of those who were already the richest people in India - that is the top 20 per cent of the urban population. Their per capita consumption has increased by around 40 per cent since 1989-90, and this increase is likely to have been even more in actuality since the NSS usually underestimates the consumption of the rich. This is the highest and most rapid increase in the consumption of the rich that has ever been recorded in India.

By contrast, the bottom 40 per cent of the urban population relatively little increase in per capita consumption compared to these other groups, at only around 14 per cent since 1989-90. But the most dramatic evidence is for the bottom 80 per cent of the rural population – well more than half of India's total population. For these people, who now number nearly 600 million, per capita consumption has actually declined since 1989-90. In other words, even the official statistics of the government still show that more than half of India has lower consumption per person than more than 10 years ago, after a decade when national income were supposed to be growing at around 6 per cent! All through history, sharp increases in economic inequality of this order of magnitude, have been associated with massive social unrest, and even with cataclysmic changes in society.

7

Inter-State Variation in Per Capita Non Food Household Items of Consumption in NER

Introduction

Glaring inequalities of income that prevail today in most of the modern societies have been the subject of bitter attack by many economists, political thinkers, philosophers and social reformers. The presence of wide disparities in income and wealth militates against the just social order. Distribution of income has been a burning topic and a controversial question in the whole history of human race. In fact, many revolution have taken place as a result of the extreme inequalities in the distribution of income and its evil effects. Thus both for the scientific study of economic development and for rational formulation of economic policy it is important to study the nature and the extent of inequalities in consumption (income). For a given aggregate income, the consumption basket of the average person will differ on inter alia, the differentials in the urban-rural per capita expenditure etc.

There has been considerable discussion in recent years on inter regional or inter temporal comparisons of level of living. The regions represent the different states of India or rural and urban sectors of any state or of India as a whole. In all the cases, the question may be concerned with particular group of population, say, the poorest ten percent or the richest ten percent. Objective answers to such basic questions are of great significance, economic as well as political.

Except the work of Choudhury (1980) and Dutta (1992), there has been virtually no work on household consumption patterns in the North Eastern Region (NER) and more particularly in Assam.

Several measures of income (expenditure) inequality have been suggested in the past. But the mast widely used measure is Gini's concentration ratio. The other measures are the Theil's Entropy measure, Atkinson's measure, Lorenz ratio, Coefficient of variation etc. Sen (1973) has extensively discussed about these measures which are widely used for two purpose:

(i) to compare two size distributions i.e. the size distribution of income (expenditure) over two periods or places.

(ii) to attach some absolute measure to the degree of inequality or to give some idea whether the inequality is large or small.

Object

In this paper an attempt has been made to study the inequality of non food items of consumption in the North Eastern Region (NER). It has also tried to examine the percentage share of Consumption of two extreme groups of consumers as the inequality measures may not capture the entire gamut of inequality in view of their weaknesses.

Further, marginal budget share of different items of consumption are also calculated to compare the variation in consumption of different items in the states of NER.

Methodology

The Lorenz ratio using Iyengar (1960) and Theil's Entropy measure using Theil (1967) on the basis of 43rd round (1987-88) of NSS data have been obtained and presented in tables 1 & 2. These indices serve as an index of the existing disparities share of consumption for non-food items in NER. The percentage shares of consumption by two extreme groups of consumers have been obtained in tables (calculated in table 5) to examine

Table 7.1: Inequality (Lorezratio) In Non-Food Items in The North Eastern States on the Basis of 43rd Round (1987-88) NSS Data

States		Pan-Tab acco etc.	Fuel & lighting	Clothing	Foot wear	Misc. goods	Durable goods	Food Total	Non-Food total.	Total
A.P.	R	0.366	0.253	0.391	0.402	0.328	0.751	0.195	0.406	0.272
	U	0.236	0.246	0.635	0.421	0.403	0.775	0.241	0.442	0.301
Assam	R	0.195	0.195	0.391	0.447	0.467	0.550	0.170	0.345	0.222
	U	0.288	0.161	0.841	0.552	0.444	0.520	0.200	0.524	0.335
Manipur	R	0.152	0.115	0.443	0.447	0.241	0.604	0.124	0.277	0.175
	U	0.167	0.101	0.509	0.483	0.251	0.400	0.092	0.286	0.165
Meghalay	R	0.371	0.287	0.548	0.558	0.351	0.550	0.188	0.398	0.259
	U	0.249	0.177	0.640	0.473	0.369	0.855	0.186	0.347	0.287
Mizoram	R	0.169	0.162	0.387	0.414	0.178	0.342	0.112	0.218	0.158
	U	0.162	0.068	0.458	0.495	0.199	0.308	0.122	0.218	0.165
Nagaland	U	0.175	0.068	0.013	0.029	0.125	0.074	0.152	0.110	0.136
Tripura	R	0.220	0.176	0.511	0.614	0.319	0.795	0.172	0.332	0.222
	U	0.288	0.186	0.520	0.333	0.304	0.704	0.223	0.328	0.260
India	R	0.233	0.165	0.601	0.546	0.423	0.783	0.226	0.425	0.291
	U	0.272	0.206	0.598	0.539	0.481	0.821	0.254	0.477	0.352

Table 7.2: Inequality (Theils Entropy Measure) in Non-Food Items in North Eastern States on the Basis of 43rd Round (1987-88) NSS Data

States		Pan-Tab acco etc.	Fuel & lighting	Clothing	Foot wear	Misc. goods	Durable goods	Food Total	Non-Food total.	Total
A.P.	R	0.302	0.154	0.353	0.370	0.208	1.333	0.074	0.296	0.125
	U	0.150	0.118	0.062	0.366	0.308	2.096	0.098	0.365	0.157
Assam	R	0.067	0.061	0.273	0.396	0.429	0.794	0.047	0.229	0.064
	U	0.153	0.045	2.433	0.638	0.341	0.628	0.065	0.730	0.048
Manipur	R	0.038	0.020	0.372	0.351	0.093	0.785	0.035	0.125	0.064
	U	0.055	0.028	0.514	0.441	0.118	0.376	0.016	0.141	0.048
Meghalay	R	0.236	0.143	0.614	0.613	0.231	0.824	0.060	0.281	0.116
	U	0.111	0.055	0.869	0.473	0.225	2.149	0.056	0.367	0.147
Mizoram	R	0.055	0.046	0.363	0.460	0.064	0.438	0.023	0.091	0.046
	U	0.052	0.044	0.400	0.459	0.087	0.557	0.029	0.095	0.053
Nagaland	U	0.044	0.044	0.075	0.057	0.017	0.038	0.029	0.010	0.021
Tripura	R	0.099	0.052	0.535	0.897	0.165	2.128	0.049	0.241	0.092
	U	0.153	0.062	0.522	0.404	0.186	1.341	0.061	0.189	0.113
India	R	0.089	0.044	0.694	0.541	0.328	0.635	0.086	0.361	0.162
-	U	0.128	0.069	0.661	0.525	0.432	0.942	0.107	0.452	0.232

the pattern of consumption.

Analysis

On a close look at the table 7.1, it may be pointed out that in the rural sector the degree of inequalities in case of food total PCE, non food total PCE and total PCE are found to be minimum in Mizoram while maximum in Arunachal Pradesh. In most of the cases the level of inequalities is less in NER in comparison to all India level.

It is to be noted that among the non-food items, the inequality is found to be minimum for the items pan, tobacco and intoxicants and maximum for item of durable goods in all the States of NER except in the State of Meghalaya where the inequality is found to be maximum in case of foot wear (0.558). Table 2 confirms the same fact where the exceptional state is Mizoram in case of foot wear.

A cursory view at the figures reveals the fact that the levels of inequalities of pan tobacco etc. and fuel and lighting are minimum in rural Manipur and maximum in Meghalaya. The inequality in case of clothing is found to be minimum in rural Assam (0391) and maximum in Meghalaya (0.548).

A minute look at the tables 7.1 & 7.2 for the urban sector reveals that in all the States of NER and India as a whole, the degree of inequality is found lo be minimum for the items pan, tobacco & intoxicants while maximum in durable goods. In this context, it may be pointed out that the exceptional states are Assam, Manipur and Nagaland where the level of inequalities are found to be maximum for the item clothing.

Apart from food and shelter, clothing is another basic requirement. Although it can be argued that clothing is merely a Cultural phenomenon rather than a basic necessity. there can be little dispute about the fact that cotton clothing is a basic component of a minimum and basic standard of living.

Further, it is difficult to read too much into inter State disparities because the basic clothing needs are not the same due to climatic and cultural differences. It is quite difficult to conduct any meaningful analysis, no matter whether it is based on the levels of clothing expenditure either in terms of value or in terms of quantity.

During the period 1955-65, the percentage expenditure on clothing shows a decline both in the urban and in the rural areas. Also the extent of regional disparities did not show much change in the rural areas while the gap in the urban regions definitely narrowed (Ganguli et el, 1976).

Dutta (1992) observed that marginal budget share (MBS) on clothing increased after 1970-71 in both rural and urban sectors of India but it appears to decline in 1986-87.

It is striking to note that the level of inequalities for all the non food items of consumption including total PCE are found to be minimum in Nagaland while maximum in Assam except in case of fuel and lighting and durable goods. The degree of inequalities of these two items are found to be maximum in Arunachal Pradesh (0.246 and 0.118) and in Meghalaya (0.855 and 2.149) respectively.

A perusal at the tables confirm the fact that the level of urban inequalities in durable goods appear to be more pronounced in Assam, Manipur, and Tripura while for the items pan, tobacco and intoxicants, fuel and lighting and foot wear, the urban inequalities seem to be relatively less in the States of Arunachal Pradesh, Meghalaya and Mizoram.

Dutta (1992) observed that there has been a declining tendency in the inter regional disparities in the consumption level of the rural sectors while there is no such tendency in the urban sectors. As regards all India level, the degree of inequalities has not changed so much in both rural and urban sectors over the rounds (1965-87).

Dutta (1995) observed that the inequality in non-food total PCE is relatively greater in urban Assam in comparison to other states of NER and also India as a whole. Although the degree of inequality measured differs due to various methods of estimation, yet it can be argued that the level of Living in respect of PCE has increased over the periods 1965-88.

Upon a close look at the tables 7.3 & 7.4 it has been observed that in the rural sector, the poorest 10 p.c. of the population enjoy relatively a better share of consumption for the items pan, tobacco and intoxicants and fuel & lighting in Manipur, Misc. goods and services and durable goods in Mizoram, clothing and footwear in Arunachal Pradesh while the richest 10 P.C. of the consumers consume relatively more in India than that of NER for the items clothing, durable goods, food total PCE, non food total PCE and total PCE.

It is interesting to note that so far the poorest ten percent of the rural population is concerned the shares of consumption are relatively better in Manipur and Mizoram than that of their counterpart in NER while for the richest ten percent, the shares of consumption are relatively better in Tripura and Meghalaya.

Coming to the urban sectors of NER, it is worthwhile to mention that the percentage share of expenditure according to the poorest ten percent groups of consumers were found to be better in the state of Nagaland and worst in Assam while for the richest ten percent of the consumers, the share is relatively better in Assam among the States of NER.

A perusal of the tables confirmed the fact that so for the poorest ten percent of the population is concerned the shares of consumption are relatively better in the rural sector of Arunachal Pradesh, Assam, Manipur and all India in comparison to their corresponding urban counterpart while for the richest ten percent of the consumers, the shares of consumption are relatively better in the urban sectors of Manipur and all India level in comparison to their corresponding rural counterpart.

On a look at the table 7.5, it is observed that among the States of NER, MBS are found to be minimum in urban Assam for the items pan, tobacco & intoxicants, (0.010), fuel & lighting (0.023) and misc. goods and services (0.062). It is also remarkable to note that in all the States of NER including whole of India, the NIBS are found to be maximum in case of misc. goods and services and minimum in case of foot wear. Further, it is striking to note that among the States of NER, the MBS are found to be

Table 7.3: Percentage Share of Consumption by 2 Extreme Groups (Bottom 10 P.C.) of Population in the North Eastern States (Rural)

States (Bottom/ Top)		Pan etc.	Fuel & lighting	Clothing	Foot wear	Misc. goods & services	Durable goods	Food Total	Non-Food total.	Total
A.P.	B	2.801	3.467	2.482	2.351	3.150	0.567	4.898	2.252	3.736
	T	28.497	22.789	27.414	28.191	24.067	48.72	18.181	28.809	21.738
Assam	B	4.915	5.189	2.134	1.742	1.256	0.457	5.586	2.251	4.286
	T	18.137	17.572	29.579	32.526	37.308	51.780	16.531	28.812	19.908
Manipur	B	5.929	6810	1.895	2.043	4.519	0.759	5.642	3.775	5.151
	T	15.804	14.158	31.301	30.2089	19.216	44.726	16.410	21.593	17.542
Meghalay	B	2.672	3.624	0.982	1.073	2.417	42.884	5.262	2.118	3.861
	T	26.369	22.148	40.902	39.605	27.792	42.426	17.275	29.638	21.293
Mizoram	B	5.409	5.791	1.461	1.090	5.015	1.756	6.820	4.231	5.619
	T	16.931	16.089	35.194	39.378	17.879	32.409	14.141	20.079	16.459
Tripura	B	4.187	5.381	1.046	0.511	2.820	0.138	5.539	2020	4.121
	T	20.216	16.906	39.977	50.203	25.612	66.622	16.615	30.372	20.425
India	B	4.390	5.700	0.848	1.185	1.776	0.214	4.448	1.491	2.954
	T	19.594	16.283	43.021	38.156	32.241	51.559	19.422	34.797	24.960

**B = Bottam 10 P.C. (Poorest), T = Top 10 P.C. (richest)*

Table 7.4: Percentage Share of Consumption by 2 Extreme Groups (Bottom 10 P.C.) of Population in the North Eastern States (Urban)

States (Bttom/ Top)		Pan etc.	Fuel & lighting	Clothing	Foot wear	Misc. goods & services	Durable goods	Food Total	Non-Food total.	Total
A.P.	B	3.782	4.209	0.540	2.171	2.081	0.235	4.145	1.719	3.181
	T	21.669	20.148	71.270	29.334	29.943	60.398	20.348	32.720	23.930
Assam	B	3.205	5.736	0.089	0.893	1.883	0.936	4.983	0.481	1.535
	T	23.829	16.207	71.270	42.281	31.390	41.601	17.960	51.031	34.387
Manipur	B	5.433	6.089	1.027	1.567	3.687	2.412	7.262	3.422	5.477
	T	16.877	15.482	40.261	34.072	21.913	27.822	13.419	22.928	16.776
Meghalay	B	4.084	5.396	0.718	1.324	2.698	0.187	5.257	1.520	3.259
	T	20.544	16.960	45.411	36.538	26.236	63.146	17.286	34.514	23.597
Mizoram	B	5.202	7.156	1.623	1.430	4.010	1.025	6.239	3.932	5.155
	T	17.418	13.587	33.552	35.405	20.787	40.261	15.190	21.048	17.532
Nagaland	B	5.192	7.030	4.486	4.881	6.281	5.475	5.723	6.645	6.086
	T	17.443	13.791	19.313	18.224	15.110	16.780	16.234	14.444	15.488
Tripura	B	3.515	5.274	1.277	2.248	2.860	0.550	4.759	2.999	4.064
	T	22.561	17.245	37.067	28.834	25.411	49.166	18.549	24.751	20.611
India	B	3.652	4.961	0.976	1.259	1.371	0.162	4.055	1.211	2.320
	T	22.048	18.018	40.984	37.268	36.025	64.807	20.638	37.843	28.383

Table 7.5: Marginal Budget Share of non-Food Items in the North Eastern States (1987-88)

States (Rural/ Urban)		Pan etc.	Fuel & lighting	Clothing	Foot wear	Misc. goods & Services	Durable goods	Food Total	Non-Food total.
A.P.	R	0.089	0.097	0.047	0.022	0.049	0.067	0.633	0.367
	U	0.028	0.052	0.065	0.029	0.098	0.025	0.701	0.299
Assam	R	0.045	0.080	0.034	0.005	0.122	0.011	0.702	0.298
	U	0.010	0.023	0.051	0.030	0.062	0.031	0.795	0.205
Manipur	R	0.039	0.068	0.042	0.035	0.131	0.023	0.662	0.338
	U	0.045	0.070	0.058	0.044	0.137	0.018	0.628	0.372
Meghalay	R	0.095	0.070	0.001	0.019	0.090	0.011	0.663	0.337
	U	0.064	0.063	0.049	0.020	0.227	0.047	0.530	0.470
Mizoram	R	0.072	0.162	0.052	0.187	0.104	0.008	0.567	0.432
	U	0.086	0.121	0.055	0.035	0.126	0.018	0.559	0.441
Nagaland	U	0.064	0.067	0.025	0.006	0.187	0.018	0.631	0.369
Tripura	R	0.097	0.064	0.045	0.006	0.126	0.031	0.690	0.310
	U	0.030	0.076	0.051	0.009	0.167	0.017	0.614	0.356
India	R	0.032	0.074	0.067	0.010	0.144	0.036	0.638	0.362
	U	0.026	0.067	0.060	0.011	0.234	0.011	0.441	0.559

R = Rural, U = Urban

maximum in case of food total and minimum in non-food total in both rural and urban sectors of Assam.

Conclusion

Thus it is to he noted that the pattern of consumption is most uneven in Assam and is one of the highest among the states of NER though it is considerably less than the average for all India in the rural sector. It may also be pointed out that the poorest section of the society in Assam has been badly affected.

It is evident from the analysis that the level of inequalities of non food items are relatively less in the states of NER in comparison to whole of India and it is worthwhile to mention that in the rural sector, the degree of inequality is found to be maximum in case of durable goods in all the states including India as a whole.

The above discussion will thus give a picture about the degree of inequality in PCE on non-food items of consumption that exist in both rural and urban sectors of NER.

These results reveal that the extent of degree of inequality in the level of living in the states of NER particularly in the state of Assam is more than what is taken to guide some of the decision making elements in connection with resource transfer from centre to these North Eastern States particularly to Assam.

If the extreme inequalities are to be reduced, the adequate amount of employment opportunities will have to be created. Programmes and projects of employment expansion are a better way of redistributing incomes. The government must devise a system which ensures equal opportunities to the poor with the rich in obtaining higher education and training or in getting a start in trade and industry or securing employment. Another important measure is the introduction of a comprehensive social security scheme guaranteeing to each individual a minimum standard of living. Steps should be taken for leveling up the poor and under privileged.

Availability of adequate infrastructural facilities is one of the basic requirements of rapid development of every economy. At the same time Govt. should provide various social services like education, medical aid, labour welfare and other services for social and economic security of the weaker section of the population.

The need of the hour is that the criteria of backwardness should be the economic condition of a person rather than his caste, tribe or area so that all the poor people irrespective of caste, tribe etc. should have equal opportunity to get education, training and employment.

References

Choudhury, H. (1980): "Consumption Pattern of Households in Assam : An econometric Study", Unpublished Ph.D. Thesis, G.U.

Dutta, P.C. (1992) : "Certain Aspects of Consumer Behaviour in Assam : An Empirical Study", Unpublished Ph.D. Thesis, G.U.

Dutta, P.C. (1995) : "Per Capita Household Consumption Inequalities in North Eastern Region of India', Indian Journal of Regional Science, Vol. - XVII, No. I & 2, 1995, pp. 65-78.

Ganguli, B.N. and Gupta, D.B. (1976) : Levels of living in India', S. Chand and Company Limited, New Delhi.

Iyengar, N.S. (1960) : On a pattern of Estimating increase in Consumer Demand', Sankhya, 22, pp, 379-390.

Iyengar, N.S. (1960 a) : "On a method of computing the Engel Elasticities from Concentration Curves", Econometrica, 28, pp. 882-891.

Sen. A. (1973): "On Economic Inequality", Oxford University Press.

Theil, H. (1967) : "Economics and information Theory', North Holland Publishing Company, Amsterdam.

8

Per Capita Household Consumption Inequalities in NER

Introduction

The term inequality is a relative concept. The very term refers to unequal distribution of income in a country or a state as the case may be. Inequality was one of the formidable socio-economic issues in the late 1960's both in political and academic circles. Some of the studies (Bardhan, 1974) relating to the inequality in income and wealth confirmed the fear of growing disparity and proved the ineffectiveness of the economic policies in keeping such inequalities at a tolerable level.

It has been argued by Rohini Nayar (1977) that an examination of trends in the level of distribution of consumption may be an accurate indication of trends in income. This could occur, for example, if the lowest income group attempted to maintain their consumption, despite falling incomes, by increasing their indebtedness. Under these circumstances inequality in the distribution of consumption could remain broadly the same while the distribution of income worsened". Chatterjee and Bhattacharya (1974a) have examined the disparities in the level of living as measured by per capita household consumption in rural and urban India utilising the household budget data from 2nd round to 22nd round of NSS covering the period from 1951-52 to 1967-68 wherever available. Ganguli and Gupta (1976) obtained that inter-state variation in consumption has declined over the NSS rounds in the period 1960-70. Thus, studies relating inequality in the income and wealth in the country, by and large, are confined to national aggregate level.

The existence of wide disparities in the level of living between regions and between classes of people is widely believed to be one of the important causes of social tension and unrest. Regional variation in consumption may result from differences in relative prices, especially transport cost and range and difference in tastes conditioned, for example, by the climate.

II. Objectives of the Study

The object of this paper is to examine disparities in the level of living as measured by per capita household consumption in the rural and urban sectors of all the seven states of North Eastern Region (NER).

Household budget data for some selected rounds of NSS covering the period 1965-88 have been utilized for this purpose.

Lorenz ratios for Per Capita expenditure (PCE) distributions are worked out separately for food total PCE. non food total PCE and total PCE for rural and urban sectors over the six NSS rounds to compare the NER with the all-India average.

Between states, disparities for the above six different periods are compared by calculating between state Lorenz ratios (two parametric log normal distribution. Gini's concentration ratio) and Theil's entropy measure.

III. Results

The magnitude of the Lorenz ratios of the states indicate the existence of inequalities in consumption not only among the states but between the rural and urban sectors also.

The Lorenz ratios (L1) using lyengar (1960), L2 using Aitchison and Brown (1957) and Theil's entropy measure. I (q: p). using Theil (1967) for the size distributions of PCE data both rural and urban sectors of all the seven states of NER have been presented in Tables-8.1 to 8.9 for total PCE, food total PCE and non food total PCE respectively considering 6 different NSS rounds viz. 20th, 23rd, 25th, 38th, 42nd and 43rd covering the period 1965-66 to 1987-88.

IV. Analysis

Table-8.1 reveals some interesting facts about the extent of inequalities that exits in consumption in the states of NER in different periods.

In the 43rd round (1987-88) the minimum inequality is found in Mizoram in the rural sector and Nagaland in the urban sector.

On a close look at the Tables, it is also observed that in the rural sector, the levels of inequalities, in all the states, are below the inequality level for the country over the rounds considered.

It is surprising to note that the level of inequalities in PCE for urban Assam (0.466) is above the inequality level for the country as a whole (0.384).

In 1965-66 and 1970-71, the minimum disparity in household consumption is found in Assam while in the other periods viz. 1968-69, 1982-83, 1986-87 and 1987-88 the minimum disparity is found in Manipur and Mizoram in the rural sectors. On the other hand, in the urban sector, the minimum inequality is observed in Assam in the periods 1965-66 and 1968-69, in Manipur in 1970-71 and 1982-83 and In Nagaland in the periods 1986-87 and 1987-88.

It may be pointed out that among the states of NER, the maximum degree of inequality in PCE is observed in Tripura in both rural and urban sectors in the periods 1968-69 and 1970-71, in rural Meghalaya in the periods 1982-83 and 1986-87 and in urban Assam in the periods 1986-87 and 1987-88.

Tables- 8.2 and 8.3 present the same picture about the existing inequalities in PCE among the states of NER. Here

Table 8.1: Inqualities in Total PCE (L_1)

	1965-66		1968-69		1970-71		1982-83		1986-87		1987-88	
	R	U	R	U	R	U	R	U	R	U	R	U
A.P.	-	-	-	-	-	-	-	-	-	-	0.272	0.301
Assam	0.205	0.278	0.189	0.237	0.173	0.233	0.188	0.248	0.202	0.289	0.222	0.335
Manipur	-	-	0.157	0.240	0.180	0.209	0.180	0.158	0.178	0.179	0.175	0.165
Meghalaya	-	-	-	-	-	-	0.291	0.253	0.264	0.270	0.259	0.286
Mizoram	-	-	-	-	-	-	0.136	0.186	0.202	0.175	0.158	0.165
Nagaland	-	-	-	0.293	-	0.221	-	0.194	-	0.140	-	0.136
Tripura	-	-	0.226	0.296	0.232	0.259	0.249	0.314	0.227	0.219	0.222	0.260
India	0.297	0.339	0.305	0.329	0.283	0.328	0.297	0.325	0.296	0.332	0.291	0.52

Table 8.2: Inqualities in Total PCE (L_2)

	1965-66		1968-69		1970-71		1982-83		1986-87		1987-88	
	R	U	R	U	R	U	R	U	R	U	R	U
A.P.	-	-	-	-	-	-	-	-	-	-	0.277	0.335
Assam	0.243	0.280	0.182	0.232	0.195	0.252	0.204	0.265	0.227	0.275	0.243	0.466
Manipur	-	-	0.205	0.230	0.166	0.298	0.187	0.167	0.188	0.186	0.195	0.178
Meghalaya	-	-	-	-	-	-	0.283	0.248	0.301	0.265	0.269	0.309
Mizoram	-	-	-	-	-	-	0.140	0.194	0.219	0.173	0.171	0.195
Nagaland	-	-	-	0.223	-	0.283	-	0.199	-	0.153	-	0.149
Tripura	-	-	0.247	0.248	0.234	0.303	0.267	0.305	0.240	0.216	0.252	0.256
India	0.329	0.346	0.295	0.321	0.329	0.325	0.320	0.328	0.313	0.322	0.332	0.384

Table- 8.3: Inequalities in Total PCE I (Q : P)

	1965-66		1968-69		1970-71		1982-83		1986-87		1987-88	
	R	U	R	U	R	U	R	U	R	U	R	U
A.P.	-	-	-	-	-	-	-	-	-	-	0.125	0.157
Assam	0.082	0.134	0.060	0.101	0.052	0.090	0.076	0.108	0.078	0.133	0.087	0.280
Manipur	-	-	0.043	0.125	0.061	0.081	0.055	0.052	0.056	0.057	0.054	0.048
Meghalaya	-	-	-	-	-	-	0.137	0.105	0.133	0.122	0.116	0.147
Mizoram	-	-	-	-	-	-	0.031	0.059	0.073	0.051	0.046	0.053
Nagaland	-	-	-	0.146	-	0.094	-	0.062	-	0.042	-	0.021
Tripura	-	-	0.087	0.034	0.094	0.112	0.109	0.163	0.090	0.083	0.092	0.113
India	0.162	0.199	0.169	0.182	0.139	0.170	0.158	0.181	0.155	0.184	0.162	0.232

Table 8.4: Inequalities in Total PCE I (L)

	1965-66		1968-69		1970-71		1982-83		1986-87		1987-88	
	R	U	R	U	R	U	R	U	R	U	R	U
A.P.	-	-	-	-	-	-	-	-	-	-	0.195	0.241
Assam	0.180	0.214	0.175	0.181	0.151	0.171	0.143	0.177	0.171	0.206	0.170	0.200
Manipur	-	-	0.134	0.185	0.127	0.123	0.119	0.116	0.125	0.123	0.124	0.092
Meghalaya	-	-	-	-	-	-	0.223	0.188	0.189	0.215	0.188	0.186
Mizoram	-	-	-	-	-	-	0.102	0.144	0.191	0.133	0.112	0.122
Nagaland	-	-	-	0.256	-	0.184	-	0.161	-	0.092	-	0.152
Tripura	-	-	0.188	0.250	0.190	0.196	0.196	0.212	0.196	0.192	0.172	0.223
India	0.242	0.257	0.251	0.263	0.232	0.279	0.227	0.247	0.227	0.235	0.226	0.254

Table 8.5: Inequalities in Food Total PCE (L_2)

	1965-66		1968-69		1970-71		1982-83		1986-87		1987-88	
	R	U	R	U	R	U	R	U	R	U	R	U
A.P.	-	-	-	-	-	-	-	-	-	-	0.208	0.251
Assam	0.193	0.217	0.177	0.195	0.155	0.172	0.135	0.180	0.176	0.200	0.173	0.204
Manipur	-	-	0.139	0.227	0.129	0.229	0.120	0.125	0.136	0.126	0.170	0.099
Meghalaya	-	-	-	-	-	-	0.215	0.185	0.191	0.213	0.189	0.190
Mizoram	-	-	-	-	-	-	0.104	0.152	0.209	0.133	0.117	0.142
Nagaland	-	-	-	0.253	-	0.189	-	0.169	-	0.103	-	0.166
Tripura	-	-	0.193	0.273	0.197	0.190	0.201	0.202	0.197	0.192	0.175	0.216
India	0.246	0.257	0.259	0.259	0.234	0.293	0.231	0.247	0.225	0.228	0.233	0.256

Table 8.6: Inequalities in Food Total PCE I (Q: P)

	1965-66		1968-69		1970-71		1982-83		1986-87		1987-88	
	R	U	R	U	R	U	R	U	R	U	R	U
A.P.	-	-	-	-	-	-	-	-	-	-	0.074	0.098
Assam	0.057	0.080	0.052	0.059	0.049	0.048	0.044	0.052	0.049	0.065	0.047	0.065
Manipur	-	-	0.031	0.072	0.027	0.026	0.024	0.031	0.028	0.028	0.035	0.016
Meghalaya	-	-	-	-	-	-	0.078	0.057	0.059	0.076	0.060	0.056
Mizoram	-	-	-	-	-	-	0.017	0.035	0.066	0.029	0.023	0.029
Nagaland	-	-	-	0.011	-	0.064	-	0.044	-	0.018	-	0.029
Tripura	-	-	0.060	0.001	0.061	0.064	0.054	0.071	0.063	0.064	0.049	0.081
India	0.098	0.108	0.106	0.112	0.089	0.134	0.086	0.095	0.084	0.089	0.089	0.107

Table 8.7: Inequalities in Non Food Total PCE (L_1)

	1965-66		1968-69		1970-71		1982-83		1986-87		1987-88	
	R	U	R	U	R	U	R	U	R	U	R	U
A.P.	-	-	-	-	-	-	-	-	-	-	0.406	0.442
Assam	0.285	0.394	0.235	0.195	0.248	0.353	0.312	0.386	0.302	0.413	0.345	0.524
Manipur	-	-	0.253	0.389	0.290	0.354	0.332	0.287	0.319	0.301	0.277	0.286
Meghalaya	-	-	-	-	-	-	0.439	0.342	0.417	0.350	0.398	0.347
Mizoram	-	-	-	-	-	-	0.201	0.246	0.223	0.237	0.218	0.218
Nagaland	-	-	-	0.376	-	0.279	-	0.254	-	0.190	-	0.110
Tripura	-	-	0.354	0.399	0.369	0.389	0.379	0.468	0.347	0.273	0.332	0.328
India	0.455	0.482	0.461	0.461	0.427	0.457	0.430	0.447	0.434	0.459	0.425	0.477

Table 8.8: Inequalities in non Food Total PCE (L_2)

	1965-66		1968-69		1970-71		1982-83		1986-87		1987-88	
	R	U	R	U	R	U	R	U	R	U	R	U
A.P.	-	-	-	-	-	-	-	-	-	-	0.391	0.445
Assam	0.094	0.377	0.258	0.214	0.282	0.338	0.282	0.407	0.348	0.388	0.391	0.645
Manipur	-	-	0.301	0.452	0.337	0.388	0.342	0.306	0.328	0.324	0.274	0.298
Meghalaya	-	-	-	-	-	-	0.409	0.327	0.485	0.333	0.403	0.468
Mizoram	-	-	-	-	-	-	0.219	0.253	0.240	0.230	0.246	0.264
Nagaland	-	-	-	0.348	-	0.274	-	0.255	-	0.204	-	0.124
Tripura	-	-	0.360	0.371	0.393	0.357	0.406	0.438	0.374	0.265	0.413	0.328
India	0.515	0.471	0.499	0.436	0.441	0.427	0.459	0.434	0.465	0.426	0.471	0.508

Table 8.9: Inequalities in Total PCE I (Q: P)

	1965-66		1968-69		1970-71		1982-83		1986-87		1987-88	
	R	U	R	U	R	U	R	U	R	U	R	U
A.P.	-	-	-	-	-	-	-	-	-	-	0.296	0.365
Assam	0.197	0.269	0.101	0.086	0.117	0.214	0.218	0.276	0.178	0.299	0.229	0.750
Manipur	-	-	0.132	0.332	0.187	0.237	0.194	0.154	0.179	0.162	0.125	0.141
Meghalaya	-	-	-	-	-	-	0.326	0.197	0.376	0.212	0.281	0.367
Mizoram	-	-	-	-	-	-	0.069	0.103	0.092	0.094	0.091	0.095
Nagaland	-	-	-	0.249	-	0.155	-	0.110	-	0.079	-	0.010
Tripura	-	-	0.220	0.139	0.254	0.263	0.267	0.389	0.227	0.132	0.242	0.189
India	0.434	0.424	0.430	0.372	0.336	0.352	0.352	0.353	0.370	0.371	0.361	0.452

also, maximum inequalities are observed in Mizoram in the rural sector (0.171 and 0.046) and in Nagaland in the urban sector (0.149 and 0021) in the period 1987-88 while maximum inequalities are observed in Arunachal Pradesh (0.277 and 0.125) in the rural sector and in Assam in the urban sector (0.645 and 0.280).

A cursory view of the Tables reveals that there has not been much change in the degree of inequality at the all-India level throughout the rounds. Inequalities have increased too little in case of total PCE in the 43rd round (1987-88) in comparison to earlier rounds viz. 20th (1965-66), 23rd (1968-69), 25th (1970-71), 38th (1982-83) and 42nd (1986-87) in both rural and urban sectors.

While working on NSS data over the periods 1957-65, although Ganguli and Gupta (1976) came to the conclusion about the declining trend of inter-state disparity in household consumption in respect of rural region, they could not arrive at a definite Conclusion about the urban region.

Let us now examine the inequality in consumption for PCE in food and non food (total) in the states of NER and India as a whole. A minute look at the tables confirms the fact that the degree of inequalities in PCE in non food total in India seems to be relatively lesser in the 43rd round (1987-88) in comparison to 42nd and 38th rounds in the rural sector while the inequalities seem to be relatively greater in the later round (1987-88) in comparison to previous rounds i.e. 1986-87 (0.459), 1982-83 (0.4471), 1970-71 (0.457), and 1968-69 (0.46 1). More or less similar conclusion also emerges in case of total PCE.

It is remarkable to note that. in the 43rd round, the inequality in non food total is found to be relatively greater in urban Assam in comparison to other states of NER and also India as a whole. In case of food total PCE, the degree of inequality is found to be minimum in Manipur (0.092) and maximum in Arunachal Pradesh (0.241) among the states of NER.

Although the degree of inequality measured, differs due to

various methods of estimation, yet it can be argued that the level of living in respect of PCE has increased over the periods (1965-88). In this context, it may be pointed out that Chatterjee (1976) observed that the Lorenz ratios in the urban households for whole of India remained unchanged over the two periods viz. 13th round (1957-58) arid 18th round (1963-64), for the rural sector it decreased. The ratio declined from 0.334 in the 13th round to 0.296 in the 18th round.

Ignoring the price differentials between the two sectors, one can express urban average as percentage of rural-urban differences in the level of living. A close look at the tables reveals the fact that the rural-urban difference in the degree of inequality was 0.042 in 1965-66, 0.036 in 1986-87 and 0.061 in 1987-88. Though it is not the measure of inequality but one can get a rough idea about the rural-urban differential in the level of living. Thus, the differences of the ranges in the degree of inequalities of rural-urban sectors within the different states of NER have increased in 1987-88 in comparison to 1986-87.

It is evident from the above analysis that while there has been a definite decline in the inequalities in the consumption level of the rural households of NER, there is no such tendency for the urban households. But taking into account both the rural and urban households, it is reasonable to conclude that during the period 1970-71 to 1987-88, the region came closer in the period 1982-83 but after that it diverged to some extent in the period 1986-87 and then in the period 1987-88.

V. Limitations

It is possible to argue that owing to the lack of broad base of development, the relative position of level of living of the bulk of population in the states of NER is approximately to a level of uniformity, in spite of, if not irrespective of, the variation in the per capita food and non food consumption as explained in the earlier paragraphs. The entire analysis is based on NSS household budget data and the limitations of such data are well-known. The prices implicit in household budgets do not refer to particular qualities or varieties of the items.

While all the measures of inequalities ultimately explain the inequalities of income between groups of people, they do not add in combination, anything new to explain inequality. Theil's index is useful for comparing inter as well as intra group inequalities as the decomposition of this measure is made possible. But its estimation procedures require more detailed data as compared to other measures. The Gini co-efficient is no doubt a sample measure of inequality but it assumes equal weights to the income received by different groups of people.

References

Atchinson. J and Brown. J.A.C. (1957) : *"The Log-Normal Distribution with Special Reference to its Uses in Economics"*, Cambridge University Press. Cambridge.

Bardhan. P.K. (1974) : *"The Pattern of Income Distribution in India : A Review"* Sankhya, the Indian Journal of statistics. Vol. 36, series-C. parts 2 & 4. pp. 103-108.

Chatterjee. G.S. (1976): *"A Note on Disparities in Per Capita Household Consumption m India"*, Indian Statistical Institute. Technical Report No. Econ/ 1/76.

Chattcrjee. G.S. and Bhattacharya. N. (1974-a): *"On Disparities in per Capita Household Consumption in India"*, Sankhya. 36, series-C. parts 2 & 4. pp. 183-214.

Ganguli. B.N. and Gupta. D.B. (1976) : *"Levels of Living In India"*. S. Chand and Company Limited. New Delhi.

Iyengar. N.S. (1960-a) : "On a Method of Computing the Engel Elasticities From Concentration Curves", Econometrica. 28. pp. 882-891.

Nayar. R. (1977): *"Poverty and Inequality of Rural Bihar"*. in Poverty and Landlessness in Rural Asia. ILO, Geneva. p. 103.

Theil. H. (967) *"Economics and Information Theory"*. North Holland publishing company. Amsterdam.

Thummaiah. G. (1985) : *"Inequality arid Poverty"*. (Reprinted). Himalaya Publishing House, Bombay.

9

Quality Variation of some Food Items of Consumption in NER

Introduction

A number of empirical studies confined to Engel curve analysis based on NSS household budget data have been used for studying the consumption pattern in rural and urban areas of the whole country (vide Bhattacharya, 1963; Iyengar, 1967; Gupta, 1973 etc.).

Ray (1973) obtained the estimates of the Engel elasticity using five alternative forms of Engel curves for 68 items of consumption based on NSS 18th round (1963-64) budget data for rural areas of West Bengal.

Medhi and Choudhury (1984) made an attempt to compare the per capita value and quantity aspects of consumption for some sub groups of items in the rural and urban Assam using 17th round (1961-62) and 20th round (1971-72) state sample of NSS data. Prais and Houthakker (1971, 2nd ed.) have discussed the importance of measurement of quality variations of household items of consumption.

Aim and Objectives

In this paper an attempt has been made to compare the per capita value and quantity aspects of consumption for some selected sub groups of items in the rural and urban households of North Eastern States of India (NER) on the basis of 43rd round (1987-88) of NSS data. Items are classified into necessaries and luxuries on the basis of elasticities obtained and lastly, estimate of quality elasticities for these selected items of consumption have also been obtained.

Methodology

The quality elasticity of an item is given by

$$d\log Y_v / d\log X = d\log Y_q / d\log X + d\log p / d\log X$$

Where, p is the price unit of the item Y

$d\log Y_v / d\log X$ = value elasticity of the item Y with respect to expenditure X.

$d\log Y_q / d\log X$ = quantity elasticity of the item Y with respect to expenditure X.

$d\log p / d\log X$ = quality elaticity of the item Y with respect to expenditure X.

Y_q and Y_v be the quantity and value information of an item such that $Y_v = Y_q \cdot p$.

Thus, quality elasticity = value elasticity – quantity elasticity

Results and Analysis

The elasticities of the items of consumption are calculated by using semi-logarithmic functions. To save space only the elasticity values for some important items have been resented in the Tables 9.1 to 9.8 but R^2 values are not shown as the values of R^2 are found to be more than 0.5 in almost all the cases.

For each item of consumption, two estimates of elasticities (quantity and value) are obtained and hence the difference (quality elasticity) being obtained to get an idea of nourishment level i.e. the standard of living and to throw light on the consumers' preference towards the finer or superior constituents of the item group as expenditure increases.

Table 9.1: Elasticities of Some Food Items in Rural and Urban Sectors on the Basis of 43rd Round (1987-88) of NSS Data: Arunachal Pradesh

	Rural				Urban			
		Elasticity				Elasticity		
Item	(MBS)	Value	Quantity	Quality	(MBS)	Value	Quantity	Quality
Milk Liquid	0.090	3.081	1.020	2.061	0.181	5.297	3.072	2.225
Mustard Oil	0.121	1.646	0.457	1.189	0.153	0.828	0.114	0.714
Ground Nut Oil	0.0004	-0.392	1.431	-1.823	0.003	5.555	1.816	3.739
Meat	0.269	1.170	0.012	1.158	0.274	0.626	0.506	0.120
Egg	0.023	0.729	0.079	0.650	0.023	8.382	6.968	1.414
Fish	0.122	0.923	0.280	0.643	0.100	0.826	0.209	0.617
Potato	0.050	0.910	0.522	0.388	0.069	0.897	0.048	0.749
Fruits	0.025	1.148	0.492	0.656	0.043	3.048	0.970	2.078
Sugar (Crystal)	0.044	0.657	0.287	0.370	0.053	0.940	0.453	0.478
Tea leaf	0.063	0.985	0.841	0.144	0.046	0.919	0.626	0.293
Leaf Tabacco	0.017	-0.967	-1.500	0.533	0.009	-1.054	-1.558	0.504

Table 9.2: Elasticities of Some Food Items in Rural and Urban Sectors on the basis of 43rd Round (1987-88) of NSS Data: Assam

	Rural				Urban			
		Elasticity				Elasticity		
Item	(MBS)	Value	Quantity	Quality	(MBS)	Value	Quantity	Quality
Milk Liquid	0.171	1.660	1.451	0.209	0.174	1.577	1.099	0.478
Mustard Oil	0.207	0.789	0.705	0.084	0.169	0.927	0.546	0.381
Ground Nut Oil	0.002	4.546	4.987	-0.441	0.003	10.030	10.006	0.024
Meat	0.065	1.175	0.954	0.221	0.069	1.238	0.911	0.327
Egg	0.031	1.029	0.867	0.162	0.032	2.694	1.947	0.747
Fish	0.202	0.969	0.803	0.166	0.195	0.955	0.895	0.060
Potato	0.067	0.796	0.651	0.145	0.073	0.882	0.696	0.186
Fruits	0.042	1.258	1.255	0.003	0.067	1.559	1.479	0.080
Sugar (Crystal)	0.087	1.112	0.947	0.165	0.080	0.716	0.458	0.258
Tea leaf	0.052	0.966	0.799	0.167	0.051	0.598	0.915	-0.317
Leaf Tabacco	0.011	0.322	0.014	0.308	0.005	-0.159	-0.604	0.445

Table 9.3: Elasticities of Some Food Items in Rural and Urban Sectors on the Basis of 43rd Round (1987-88) of NSS Data: Manipur

	Rural				Urban			
		Elasticity				Elasticity		
Item	(MBS)	Value	Quantity	Quality	(MBS)	Value	Quantity	Quality
Milk Liquid	0.047	1.739	1.700	0.039	0.038	2.403	1.214	1.189
Mustard Oil	0.281	0.871	0.893	-0.022	0.247	0.118	0.017	0.101
Ground Nut Oil	0.005	4.960	0.475	4.485	0.002	-2.027	-0.192	-1.835
Meat	0.101	0.459	0.248	0.211	0.057	0.334	0.285	0.049
Egg	0.026	4.731	3.761	0.970	0.035	3.134	1.801	1.333
Fish	0.187	1.151	0.830	0.321	0.234	0.024	0.020	0.004
Potato	0.073	0.863	0.673	0.190	0.079	0.358	0.224	0.134
Fruits	0.076	1.065	0.754	0.311	0.074	1.144	0.882	0.262
Sugar (Crystal)	0.082	0.816	0.727	0.089	0.091	2.798	1.670	1.128
Tea leaf	0.037	0.754	0.526	0.228	0.038	0.779	0.666	0.113
Leaf Tabacco	0.011	0.813	5.004	-4.191	0.0004	-6.708	-0.192	-6.516

Table 9.4: Elasticities of Some Food Items in Rural and Urban Sectors on the basis of 43rd Round (1987-88) NSS data: Meghalaya

	Rural				Urban			
	Elasticity				Elasticity			
Item	(MBS)	Value	Quantity	Quality	(MBS)	Value	Quantity	Quality
Milk Liquid	0.091	1.073	0.051	1.022	0.170	1.255	1.051	0.204
Mustard Oil	0.155	0.871	0.108	0.763	0.161	0.374	0.628	0.106
Ground Nut Oil	0.001	1.919	0.917	1.002	0.0002	2.671	2.575	0.096
Meat	0.335	1.301	0.230	1.071	0.228	0.969	0.734	0.235
Egg	0.015	1.283	0.053	1.230	0.023	3.421	2.434	0.987
Fish	0.082	0.946	0.346	0.600	0.128	0.896	0.806	0.090
Potato	0.075	0.888	0.025	0.863	0.043	0.576	0.432	0.144
Fruits	0.030	0.567	0.935	-0.378	0.048	1.390	1.377	0.013
Sugar (Crystal)	0.092	0.693	0.737	0.556	0.063	1.471	0.461	0.010
Tea leaf	0.055	1.211	0.843	0.368	0.058	0896	0.697	0.199
Leaf Tabacco	0.016	1.026	0.072	0.944	0.004	0.988	0.979	0.009

Table 9.5: Elasticities of Some Food Items in Rural and Urban Sectors on the Basis of 43rd Round (1987-88) of NSS Data: Mizoram

	Rural				Urban			
		Elasticity				Elasticity		
Item	(MBS)	Value	Quantity	Quality	(MBS)	Value	Quantity	Quality
Milk Liquid	0.116	2.988	2.281	0.707	0.163	1.348	0.944	0.404
Mustard Oil	0.059	0.262	0.090	0.172	0.048	0.684	0.077	0.607
Ground Nut Oil	0.026	0.191	0.785	-0.594	0.027	0.004	0.078	-0.074
Meat	0.213	0.952	0.920	0.032	0.248	1.334	0.533	0.801
Egg	0.016	3.304	0.122	3.172	0.033	1.639	0.737	0.902
Fish	0.038	-0.079	-0.036	-0.043	0.017	5.141	3.469	1.672
Potato	0.046	5.154	0.182	4.972	0.054	0.203	0.037	0.166
Fruits	0.051	0.815	0.218	0.597	0.079	0.612	0.011	0.601
Sugar (Crystal)	0.104	0.318	0.104	0.214	0.101	0.721	0.077	0.644
Tea leaf	0.080	0.898	0.725	0.173	0.050	0.961	0.028	0.933
Leaf Tabacco	0.157	0.274	0.365	-0.091	0.087	-0.580	-0.032	-0.548

Table 9.6: Elasticities of Some Food Items in Rural and Urban Sectors on the basis of 43rd Round (1987-88) NSS Data: Tripura

	Rural				Urban			
		Elasticity				Elasticity		
Item	(MBS)	Value	Quantity	Quality	(MBS)	Value	Quantity	Quality
Milk Liquid	0.165	2.119	1.359	0.760	0.138	3.979	3.334	0.645
Mustard Oil	0.001	0.453	0.016	0.437	0.154	0.854	0.218	0.636
Ground Nut Oil	0.001	2.026	2.2341	-0.315	0.006	7.109	2.395	4.714
Meat	0.058	0.717	0.144	0.573	0.059	1.100	0.532	0.568
Egg	0.067	1.608	0.947	0.661	0.084	0.975	0.627	0.348
Fish	0.306	0.713	0.053	0.660	0.318	0.542	0.345	0.197
Potato	0.050	0.751	0.251	0.500	0.050	0.622	0.501	0.121
Fruits	0.060	1.065	0.217	0.484	0.076	0.574	0.150	0.424
Sugar (Crystal)	0.043	0.746	0.161	0.585	0.044	0.640	0.576	0.064
Tea leaf	0.028	1.259	0.627	0.632	0.029	1.218	0.883	0.335
Leaf Tabacco	0.002	0.593	1.508	-2.101	0.0001	-2.324	0.380	-2.710

Table 9.7: Elasticities of Some Food Items in Rural and Urban Sectors on the Basis of 43rd Round (1987-88) of NSS Data: Nagaland

	Rural				Urban			
		Elasticity				Elasticity		
Item	(MBS)	Value	Quantity	Quality	(MBS)	Value	Quantity	Quality
Milk Liquid	-	-	-	-	0.156	1.254	1.143	0.111
Mustard Oil	-	-	--	-	0.124	1.614	0.113	1.501
Ground Nut Oil	-	-	--	-	-	-	-	-
Meat	-	-	-	-	0.234	0.939	0.839	0.100
Egg	-	-	-	-	0.048	1.200	0.724	0.476
Fish	-	-	-	-	0.088	1.467	0.425	1.042
Potato	-	-	-	-	0.038	1.446	0.386	1.060
Fruits	-	-	-	-	0.087	1.318	0.968	0.350
Sugar (Crystal)	-	-	-	-	0.056	0.111	1.565	-1.454
Tea leaf	-	-	-	-	0.025	1.681	0.418	1.200
Leaf Tabacco	-	-	-	-	0.003	8.176	-0.816	8.997

Table 9.8: Elasticities of Some Food Items in Rural and Urban Sectors on the Basis of 43rd Round (1987-88) NSS Data: India

Item	Rural				Urban			
		Elasticity				Elasticity		
	(MBS)	Value	Quantity	Quality	(MBS)	Value	Quantity	Quality
Milk Liquid	0.334	1.365	1.310	0.055	0.322	1.185	1.206	-0.021
Mustard Oil	0.090	0.521	0.468	0.053	0.054	0.481	0.457	0.024
Ground Nut Oil	0.064	0.699	0.711	-0.012	0.079	0.875	0.929	-0.054
Meat	0.061	0.966	0.794	0.172	0.074	0.818	0.407	0.411
Egg	0.011	1.296	1.252	0.044	0.017	1.319	1.395	-0.076
Fish	0.050	0.863	0.683	0.180	0.044	0.971	0.682	0.289
Potato	0.057	0.393	0.370	0.023	0.038	0.448	0.320	0.128
Fruits	0.060	1.236	1.105	0.131	0.086	1.484	1.298	0.186
Sugar (Crystal)	0.086	0.969	0.962	0.007	0.086	0.746	0.733	0.013
Tea leaf	0.042	0.998	0.994	0.004	0.043	0.933	0.917	0.016
Leaf Tabacco	0.012	0.035	0.126	-0.091	0.003	0.124	0.012	0.112

The salient features of the value and quantity elasticities obtained for some selected items of consumption may be discussed briefly as follows:

The value elasticity for the items milk liquid, egg, fruits, ground nut oil are found to be greater than unity in both rural and urban regions indicating that consumption of these items are beyond the reach of majority of the consumers in the NER.

The items like fish in urban Mizoram, Sugar in urban Manipur and urban Meghalaya, Tea in urban Tripura are found to be price elastic.

In the rural sector, Mustard oil in Arunachal Pradesh, Fish in Manipur, Sugar in Assam, Tea in Tripura, Meat in Arunachal Pradesh and Meghalaya are found to be price elastic and hence these items fall under luxury category.

It is observed that value elasticity for the item ground nut oil is found to be maximum in the rural sector of Assam (4.987), Manipur (4.960), Tripura (2.341) and Meghalaya (1.919) but minimum in both sectors of Mizoram, while the value is maximum in the urban sectors of Assam and Tripura.

In this context, it is striking to note that the respective relative share of expenditures (Marginal Budget share) are found to be minimum in the rural sector of Assam (0.002), Manipur (0.005), Tripura (0.001) and Meghalaya (0.001) among the items considered while in the urban sector, the relative share of expenditures for the item, meat is found to be maximum in the States of Nagaland (0.226) and Arunachal Pradesh (0 274) which indicate that in the hilly tribal areas, people give first preference to meat among all the food items of consumption.

This is also revealed by the fact that not more than 1 per cent sample households reported consumption on ground nut oil in the rural sectors of Assam, Arunachal Pradesh, Meghalaya and Tripura and less than 4 per cent in the urban sectors of Assam, Arunachal Pradesh, Manipur, Meghalaya, Nagaland and Tripura. On the other hand, more than 75 per cent sample households, reported consumption of meat in the urban sectors of Arunachal Pradesh, Meghalaya, Mizoram and Nagaland.

It has been verified, in general, the value elasticity is somewhat larger than the quantity elasticity. Bhattacharya (1976) has noted that by and large this elasticity (quality elasticity) of price paid shall be attributed to the shift in consumers preference towards the finer or superior constituents of the item group as expenditure X rises e.g. from coarse variety of rice to superior varieties of rice...

The quality elasticity gives an idea of the nourishment level i.e. standard of living. In short, quality information or quality elasticity is useful when interest lay in the nutritional aspect of the consumer, whereas, the value information provides valuable information regarding the weights for a cost of living.

The two elasticities answer somewhat different question. The expenditure or value elasticity measures the demand from the view point of purchasing power and hence the value elasticity seems to be more interesting in economic analysis as the item group is not fully homogeneous: It is relevant, more particularly, with. consumers propensity to consume while the quality elasticity refers to the physical satisfaction of demand. Thus both quality and-value elasticities measure for the; dependence of demand upon income changes.

From the Tables it is observed that the degree of quality elasticities for different items are different which is obvious due to difference in test and habits of people in different localities.

In rural Tripura. the elasticity is found to be maximum for fruits (0,848) followed by milk liquid (0.760) and minimum in case of groundnut oil (0.315) while in the urban sector, elasticity is found to be maximum for groundnut oil (4.715) and minimum for sugar crystal (0.064).

The elasticities for the item fish is found to be maximum in India while minimum in urban sectors of Manipur, Meghalaya, Nagaland and rural sectors of Assam, Arunachal Pradesh and Mizoram.

Economic development not only brings about changes in

the socio-economic and cultural life of a population but it also influences the consumption pattern in the long run.

A look at the Tables indicate that quality elasticities of most of the items in urban region seem to be greater than those of the rural regions. Higher level of living as reflected in higher average per capita expenditure in urban regions may be mentioned as the principal reason for this.

It is remarkable to note that in very few cases negative quality elasticities are observed. Two possible explanations for the negative quality elasticity for an item may be due to the poor description of a particular item (either or both the value and quantity information) by the semi-log Engel forms. The other possible explanation may be that as a consequence of disproportionate increase in income with price rise there may be some shift in consumer preference to inferior quality.

The elasticity for the item groundnut oil is found to be negative in the rural regions indicating relatively lower importance of this item among the rural households. This is revealed by the fact that marginal budget share for this item is 0.001 in Tripura, 0.002 in Assam and 0.001 in Meghalaya in the rural regions.

References

1. Bhattacharya, N. (1963): 'On Some Variable Elasticity Engel Curve Forms', Sankhya, 13, 26, pp. 1-16.
2. Bhattacharya, N. (1978): Studies on Consumer Behaviour in India", in A Survey of Research in Economics, Vol. \'Jl, Econometrica, ICSSR, New Delhi.
3. Gupta, D. 13. (1973): "Consumption Patterns in india : A Study of Inter-Regional Variations', Tata McGraw Hill Publishing Company Limited, Bombay.
4. lyengar, N. S. (1967): "Some Estimates of Engel Elasticities Based on National Sample Survey Data", Journal of Royal Statistical Society, A-130, pp. 84-101.
5. Medhi, J. and Choudhury, H. (1982) : "Estimates of Engel

Elasticities of Some Items of Household Consumption in Assam", Gauhati University Journal of Science, 28, pp. 139-154.

6. Prais, S. J. and Houthakker, H. S. (1955): "The Analysis of Family Budgets", 2nd Ed. (1971), Cambridge University Press, Cambridge.
7. Ray, S.K. (1972): "Effects of Consumption Availability Fluctuations on Food Grains Prices", Economic and Political Weekly, June 24, 1972.

10

Regional Disparity and its Consequences in NER

Introduction

In the present era of globalization rapid socio-economic transformation has been taking place in Indian economy. The economic development of a country may not be possible without regional development and equitable distribution of wealth and income of the nation among the different parts of the country. Iniquitous distribution of national wealth and resources of the country causes regional disparities by giving rise to various types of socio-economic problems. India is one of the developing countries facing the dilemma of economic efficiency versus social and regional inequality. There are differences in natural resources, climate, topography, vegetation and density of population in different regions of India, and in the case of northeast, it is extremely disparate. The forces of regionalism have become strong in India. and the gravity of the problem has increased to such an extent that it has been threatening the political stability of the country. Lick of basic amenities, difference in the level of living, employment opportunities, economic exploitation, cultural and linguistic differences etc. have encouraged social tensions, violence and separatist attitude in different parts of India and North Eastern Region (NER). Due to increased attention and resources devoted in the region to law and order issues, the development of the region is deteriorating day by day. Hence a study of economic disparity, regionalism and its impact on nationalism in NER deserves due attention.

Keeping the above into account, the present chapter has been designed under the following heads and various published and unpublished secondary data have been used for the purpose.

1. To discuss the regional disparity in terms of basic amenities of life of the people of the region and its consequences.
2. To correlate the regional disparity with the rise of regionalism in the region and the impact of the different regional forces on nationalism.
3. The study has been concluded with some suggestions, which may suit future planners and policy makers of the country to resolve the issues.

II Economic disparity

India is a vast country with lots of diversities across regions. The issue of regional disparity in our economic development process has always been a burning issue to the researchers and policy makers. There is a vast and growing literature on the subject ranging at theoretical studies to empirical estimates **[Koropeckgi (1972), Daly and Cobb (1989), Zolotes (1981), Sen (1973), Bardhan (1974), Chatteijee and Bhattacharjee (1974)].**

The term 'region' in this study has been defined as states on account of practical considerations. Indian states are political-administrative units and are also considered economic planning regions. Most of the discussions in the National Development Council in the context of distribution of central assistance treat the concept of region, as the state. The plan documents too treat a region in the same sense. In the interest of application of policy to the regional problems, it is obvious that the economic and political regions must coincide. Some of the literatures cover explanations of why regions performed differently over the years and why different policies failed. Some other literatures have explained the centre-state financial relations as the main reason for regional disparity.

In the words of **Williamson (1965)**, *"The poor countries are characterised by large and growing regional disparities and rich countries are generally characterised by small and diminishing gaps."* In India, apart from the impact of development policy, the uneven distribution of natural resources has itself created large severely underdeveloped regions in the country, which have been recently brought out into sharp focus. The problem needs to be addressed by well thought out strategies including deliberate transfer of resources to underdeveloped regions. This is vital because, 'proper growth of all regions of the country is essential for its prosperity in terms of political and social systems and for the economic validity of the nation itself.

A number of studies in regional development of India shed light on the fact that regional disparities in India have increased over the plan period. The studies by **Nair (1983), Mahajan (1982)**, show that regional disparities have on the increase from mid-fifties to early seventies. The studies by **Dutta and Choudhury (1995, 1996)** covering more recent years also bear witness to the fact that regional disparities in India is diverging in the process of economic growth despite all policies and measures adopted by the government of India and the Planning Commission to reduce the divergence among the states in respect of development.

Shri Prakash (1977) attempted to analyse the regional inequalities in terms of infrastructure facilities in India during 1951—71 with the objective to determine the extent of existing inequalities and identify the lagging regions. The author selected important indicators like population size, density, literacy rate, urbanisation, power, irrigation, banking, communication, transport, industrial and cultural implements in his study.

Economic history reveals that the process of development starts first in regions, which are rich in resources—natural, human and others. Then these regions attract investment and process of development became cumulative. Both the problems in India cannot be explained with reference to endowments of natural resources alone. There are poor regions possessing rich natural resources like Orissa, and rich regions with poor resources like Maharashtra (**Awasthi, Kashyap, Wadhva, 1988**).

From the above review of literature on economic disparity it is clear that studies have given the right direction to move towards explaining the term 'economic disparity' in the context of the development of the region with little exception. Development is a complex process arid has multidimensional structure depending upon its resources in general-and infrastructural facilities in particular. The development of an area is best reflected in the quality of life of its people. Apart from the distribution of infrastructural facilities, the quality of life depends upon several other factors like geographical, social, cultural etc. which are distributed in an haphazard manner all over the country and thus handicaps the development of relatively backward regions. Historical and political conditions also effect the socio-economic development of the region. The impact all these constraints is generally seen in the agricultural, industrial, infrastructural and financial development of the region, which directly affect the quality of life of the people. However, the present study is an attempt to show economic disparity in the states of NER by considering the following indicators.

III Sectoral problems

Population

One of the important problems which creates hindrance to economic development is the problem of population explosion in the region. The total population of the region is about 38.5 million representing 3.75 percent of India's total population in 2001. The region's growth rate of population is much higher than that of national average. It is striking to note that India's total population increased by 51.80 percent in the period 1951—71, 54.39 percent in 1971—91 and 21.35 in 1991- 2001, whereas for the NER, respective growth rates are 90.86, 62.11 per cent and 22.02 per cent. At the same time, share of population of NER, in comparison to all – India, incrnaed from 2.84 percent in 1951 to 3.75 per cent in 2001.

Increased population at an alarming rate in the region is due to immigration from outside the country as well as from within the country. The population explosion caused by immigration poses serious threat on the natural resources of the region arid hence on the economic development. The absolute number of the migrants was more than 91 thousand in 1901, since then it has been steadily increasing and reached at nearly 745 thousand in the census year 1991. The share of migrants from Bangladesh was between slightly more than 70 percent to slightly more than 87 percent in pre-independence era. In the post independence era, it reached at 94 percent in 1951—the highest among the period, 1901—1991. From 1961 onwards the share started to decline and become around 89 percent in the census year of 1991. It is also clear from the statistical information that Bangladesh was followed by Nepal in sending migrants to the NER of India. Again the number of migrants who come from other states of India varied between 0.5 million to around 0.8 million during the pre independence era. But it declined to around 0.4 million in1951 and reaching slightly more than 0.5 million in 1991. In the recent years the flow of immigration from the neighbouring countries shows an increasing trend.

It is observed that there is a large variation in the density of population among the states of NER. Density of region's population (151) is almost half of the national density (324) in 2001 while it was only 34.19 percent in 1951. Again within the region it varies from 13 in Arunachal Pradesh to 340 in Assam. The bulk of population of the region is concentrated mainly of three sectors viz., Brahmaputra valley and Barak valley of Assam and Tripura. The large variation is caused by the geographical and economic factors, which vary greatly within the region.

Education

Education is the index of social progress and economic development of a region. The advancement of the region can be well marked by the rate of literacy and other infrastructural facilities provided for the development of the education. Literacy rate is the highest in Mizoram (88 percent) followed by Tripura and the lowest in Arunachal Pradesh (55 percent) followed by Meghalaya and Assam. There is a big gender gap in literacy, which is one of the major obstacles in attaining total literacy (Table 2). The highest gender gap is observed in the states of Manipur (24.03 percent) followed by Arunachal Pradesh and the lowest in Mizoram (7.01 percent) followed by Meghalaya. However, all the states of NER taking into account are below all-India level of 24.84 percent points. Low female literacy has strong repercussions on other aspects like population growth, child- care and acceptance of family welfare measures.

Dutta and Roy (1998) observed that urban population significantly affected the literary rate (LR) and Per capita net domestic product (PCNDP): Positive significant correlations are observed for LR with total PCE (per capita expenditure), Mean Age at Marriage (MAM), PCNDP, Female work participation rate (FWPR) while significantly negatively correlated with percentage growth rate (PGR). Again, Child-woman ratio (CWR) is negatively significantly correlated with sex-ratio (SR), Dependency ratio (DR) and LR.

It is striking to note that PCE on education in 1997-98 was the highest in smaller states of Mizoram (Rs. 1210), followed by Manipur (Rs. 94), Arunachal Pradesh (Rs. 951) and Tripura (Rs. 836) while it was only Rs. 537 in Assam which is the-lowest among the states of NER.

Health

Health is a social goal and considered an integral component in over all socio economic development. The majority of health problems are the products of illiteracy, poverty, ignorance, over crowding, poor environmental condition and uneven

Table 10.1: Literacy Rate, Gender Gap, Expenditure on Education and Number of Health Centres in NER

States	Literacy Rate		Gender Gap in literancy	PCE (Govt. on education in 1997-98) in Rs		No. of Health Centres		
	1991	2001	1991	1991-92	1997-98	PHC	SC	CHC
ANP	42	54.74 (32)	21.76	549	951	40	203	7
ASM	53	64.28 (24)	18.84	250	537	619	5180	105
MNP	60	68.87 (19)	24.07	560	984	72	420	15
MGH	49	63.31 (27)	8.27	406	779	88	333	10
MZM	82	88.49 (2)	7.01	769	1210	43	244	6
NGN	62	67.11 (21)	12.87	437	762	33	244	5
TRP	60	73.66 (12)	20.93	416	836	63	535	10
India*	52	65.38	24.84	-		22156	131902	2377

distribution of health manpower and institutions. It is observed that there are only 4.32 percent of public health centres (PHC) in the states of NER (958) compared to India's figure and Out of which there are 64 percent public health centres only in Assam among the states of NER, while less than 10 percent are in each of the other states of the region (Table 10.1). The same patterns are observed in case sub centres and community health centres. Thus it is high time to make an effort to increase the number of health centres in backward states of NER so that health problems can be minimized to some extent.

Drinking Water

A look at the table 3, it is observed that the maximum amount of water is required in the states of Assam among the states of NER, which is approximately 2. percent as compared to India's requirement in 1991, and the figure (0.883 cubic km) will rise to 2.63 percent in 2001. However, there is an increasing trend of water requirement in 2001 over 1991. Regarding the safe drinking water facilities all the states of NER, except Arunachal Pradesh (70.02 percent) are less than the national average (62.30 percent). It is striking to note that only 16.21 percent of total households of Mizoram can drink safe water while water is the lifeblood the environment. Thus conservation of water is an important aspect in this regard and the people of NER should take active step for the management of water for the maintenance of the standard of water quality.

Electricity

About the consumption of electricity, it is to be noted that the per capita consumption of electricity is much lower in the states of NER as compared to the country's consumption (338.5 kWh). The highest per capita consumption is observed in the state of Meghalaya (134.5 kWh) and lowest in Tripura (80.4 kWh) among the states of NER (Table 10.2).

Table 10.2: Water Requirement, Safe Drinking Water, Consumption of Electricity and per Capita Food Grain Production in NER

States	Water requirement in cu.km		% having safe drinking water	Per capita consumption of power kWh	Per capita production of foodgrains (in kg)		
	1991	2001		1996-97	1972-73	1996-91	1997-98
ANP	0.024	0.029	70.02	80.8	104	253	186
ASM	0.632	0.883	45.86	107.6	158	154	139
MNP	0.06	0.074	38.72	127.9	159	155	152
MGH	0.053	0.072	36.16	134.5	120	87	83
MZM	0.025	0.035	16.21	134.5	120	87	83
NGN	0.036	0.052	53.37	88	107	160	150
TRP	0.08	0.088	37.18	88.4	116	187	152
India*	27.111	33.521	62.3	338.5	172	208	198

Food Production and Agricultural Development

In the northeastern Hill areas food production is subject to wide fluctuation due to shifting cultivation. However, during the last two decades, per capita production of food has declined in the states of Assam, Manipur, Meghalaya and Mizoram and is lower than the national average. While the population is rapidly increasing in the States of the region. It is observed that in case of Assam, the per capita food production decreased from 158 kg in 1972-73 and 154 kg in 1990—91 to 139 kg in 1997—98. The respective figures for Meghalaya. are 120 kg, 87 kg and 83 kg only (Table 10.2).

The NER of India has been traditionally an agricultural society. Although agriculture is the backbone of northeastern economy, this sector is still backward, for which the security of life of this region is threatened. After independence and particularly in post-1981, while the country is marked by food surplus, the NER is suffering from scarcity of food. In this respect NER cannot be compared with all other states of India. People of NER are importing 2 million tons of food grains from other regions of the country. Although several factors like population growth, continuous flood, infrastructural bottlenecks, traditional cultivation practices etc. are responsible for the backwardness of agriculture in the region, the wrong decisions of our policy makers and planners of the country may be considered as one of the most important reasons of backwardness of the region. While the Govt. of Assam fixed the amount for expenditure in agricultural sector (Rs 1557.82 lakh) as on April 1, 1998 but disbursed only 23.60 percent, whereas only 15.95 percent of the disbursed amount actually was utilized. The same is true for Arunachal Pradesh and Meghalaya but the Govt. of Manipur and Tripura are exceptions as they not only disbursed more but also actually utilised 47.89 percent out of 70.25 percent disbursed on agricultural sector.

V PCNSDP and Poverty

Table 4 represents the data relating to per capita net state domestic product (PCNSDP) at current prices for the year 1996-97. It is observed that, all the states. of NER are below the all-India level of Rs. 12,237. PCNSDP gives a rough idea about the economic condition of NER with respect to all-India level. It is observed that all the states except Arunachal Pradesh. (Rs. 2119-3265) and Mizoram (Rs. 2119-7743) of NER are below the all-India level (Rs. 1857-2553) for the year's 1985-86 to1994-95. In this respect Assam's position is the lowest during the period 1990-91 (Rs. 1544) to 1996-97 (Rs. 1628).

Economic poverty and inequality are nothing new for people of NER. On the other hand, people of NER are indifferent regarding quality of education and health. Occupational mobility of people is nearly absent reminding one of the persistence of a traditional type society characterised by cast, language, custom, prejudices, belief etc. Monthly per capita expenditure (MPCE) may be accepted as an indicator of standard of living for people, on the basis of minimum calorie intake, suggested by the Indian Council for Medical Research (ICMR), should be 2300 for a person working (staying) in rural India and urban India. Rural poverty line, in terms of level of consumer expenditure has been defined as an expenditure of Rs. 6400 for a family of 5 at 1983-84 price level, which comes to Rs.106.67 per capita per month in 1983-84, and Rs. 156.25 at 1986-87 prices. Assuming urban poverty level as around 25 percent higher the estimated poverty level in urban areas of India may be set at Rs. 133.34 and Rs. 195.31 for the 1983—84 and 1986—87 prices respectively **(Pathak, 1998)**. It is further estimated as Rs. 275.75 and Rs. 343.00 for the rural and urban people of NER in the year 1998. Corresponding proportion of rural people below poverty line is 52 percent. Particularly, for the state of Assam, poverty level for the rural and urban are calculated as Rs. 232.05 and Rs. 212.42 respectively by the expert group as adopted by the planning commission. The respective figures for all-India are Rs. 205.84 and Rs. 281.35. Considering the economic condition of NER, the percentage

Table 10.3: Distribution of Irrigated Area, PCSNDP, CDR, BADP, Sanctioned Housing

States,	Irrigated area in 00 ha	Per capita NDP at current prices	Housing loan by HUDCO in Rs Cr	No. of Scheduled Commercial banks	CDR IN %	BADP in Rs Cr. (1999-2000)	
	1995-96	1996-97	1999-00	1999	1999	Funds allocated	Funds released
ANP	36	12032	195.5	68	14.1	13.00	-
ASM	539	6663	376.31	1238	31.5	7.20	-
MNP	75	7510	117.73	86	41.7	4.00	2.00
MGH	45	8474	90.52	179	16.7	4.52	2.60
MZM	7	9758	34.84	78	20.6	8.00	4.00
NGN	66	9985	74.08	71	15.7	4.00	-
TRP	59	5432	17.92	180	29.4	12.47	624
India*	58232	12237		64924	55.5		

of population below poverty line is higher in respect of all-India level in 1998 **(Dutta, 1999). Dutta and Choudhury (1995)** observed that while there was a definite decline in the inequalities in the consumption level of the rural households of NER, there was no such tendency in the urban households. But taking into account both the rural and urban households, it is reasonable to conclude that during the period 1970-71 to 1987-88, the region came closer in the period 1982-83 but after that divergent trend has been observed. It is to be noted that the pattern of consumption in most uneven in Assam and is one of the highest among the states of NER, though it is considerably less than the average for all-India in the rural sector. It can also be pointed out that the poorest section of the society in Assam has been badly affected. It is interesting to note that so far as the poorest 10 percent of the rural population is concerned, the shares of consumption are relatively better in Manipur and Mizoram than that of their counterpart in NER while for the richest 10 percent, the shares of consumption are relatively better in Assam and Meghalaya. Coming to the urban sector of NER, it is worthwhile to mention that the percentage share of expenditure, according to the poorest 10 percent groups of consumers, were found to be better in the state of Nagaland and worst in Assam while for the richest 10 percent .of the .consumers, the share is relatively better in Assam among the states of NER **(Dutta, 1999)**.

Irrigation

The expansion of irrigation facilities, operation and maintenance of irrigation system and distribution of water have not received due attention. Irrigation sector is today facing twin issues of sub-optimal sector planning and financial management on the one hand and inadequate water management and maintenance on the other. Involving the farmers in the irrigation system is one obvious remedy for addressing the management problems. In comparison to all-India level only 1.4 percent of area is under irrigation system in the NER and only 1.0 per cent in the state of Assam (5,39,000 hectares). However, percentage of total irrigated area in Assam is 65 per cent with respect to total irrigated area in NER,

Communication

The Border Area Development Programme (BADP) was launched in the 7th Plan.

Period for balanced development of remote and inaccessible areas situated near the borders and for ensuing effective administration in these areas for developmental activities. In the 9th . Plan period the programme was extended to all the land borders in response to the demands of the state governments of NER and the Ministry of Home Affairs. The programme now covers 16 states and which is a 100 percent centrally funded programme. The Planning Commission have allocated Rs. 202 crores under Special. Central Assistance under the BADP for annual plan 2000-01 of which only 26.33 percent is allocated for the states of NER. However, out of the funds allocated for the NER (Rs. 53.19 crores) only 27.9 percent released indicating the less interest of the government for the development of the border-states (Table 10.3). The road and communication system of Assam is strategically important so far as India's northeastern border is concerned. However, the roads are in miserable conditions for which the government submitted a proposal of Rs. 180 crores to the centre for the repair of 1500 km of roads and 4000 bridges of the state, The PWD minister of the state expressed that the centre sanctioned Rs. 548.5 crores of which Rs. 137.78 crores have been allotted for the reparations of roads and bridges.

Financial Assistance by all-India Financial Institutions

Assistance sanctioned by the All India Financial Institutions (AIFI) to northeastern states has come down from about Rs. 209 crores in 1996-97 to Rs. 174 crores in 1997-98 and Rs. 131 crores in 1998-99. Similarly assistance disbursed by AIFI in NER has come down from Rs. 272 crores in 1996-97 to Rs. 126

crores in 1997-98 and Rs. 81 crores in 1998-99. Assistance by Small Industrial Development Bank of India (SIDBI) was lower at Rs. 25 crores in 1998-99 compared to Rs. 33 crores in 1997-98. Disbursement during 1998-99 at Rs 21. crores was also lower in comparison to Rs. 27 crores in 1997-98. However, during the period 1990-99, the same trend is observed in the states of NER. Credit Deposit Ratio (CDR) in the Northeast ranges between 14 per cent to 42 per cent compared to all-India average of 55 percent (Table 8). Against the total sanctions under Rural Infrastructural Development Fund (RIDF) of Rs 385 crores, the disbursement has been only about Rs. 83 crores. The percentage of number of Scheduled Commercial Bank branches in the states of NER is only 2.93 percent in comparison to all-India level (64924). However, in comparison to NER (1900), the percentage of number of branches in the state of Assam is 65 (Table 10.3). -

Thus, a region may remain poor and backward in spite of possessing rich natural resources. This is true in case of NER. While some of the states of India like Punjab, Haryana, Maharashtra etc. are going ahead in economic well being, the NER and more particularly Assam is lagging far behind. This distortion caused by inter regional disparity in wealth and income apparent from the per capita income of the states. In terms of inter regional comparison while Assam had an annual per capita income of Rs. 8700, the national average was Rs. 14,712 in 1998. If the poverty is defined as "inability to attain minimal standard of living" by the World Bank, it can be said with much confidence that the states of NER and particularly Assam are poverty stricken. Recent events in the state have pointed to a system failure in the field of finance and improvement of financial capacity to implement even poverty alleviation programmes due to government of India's reluctance to provide funds for economic development on the grounds of corruption and non fulfillment of constitutional obligations by the state governments during the past few years.

Regionalism and its Consequences

From the foregoing discussion of regional disparity, it is clear that the union government of India deliberately neglects the NER The evil forces of regionalism in NER grew faster due to the problem of economic and social development. Although different provisions have been made in the Constitution of India to bring socio-economic progress, all these went in vain and the people were offered nothing but disappointment, more hardship, more exploitation and more distributing injustice. Instead of caring for the interest of the country as a whole, the leaders are becoming narrow-minded and have begun to clamour for the progress of their own state. Closely connected with this was another factor which fomented regionalism is increasing awareness of the people in the more backward parts of India, taking basic amenities of life and the allocation of central funds and grants.

After independence, according to 1951 census, Assam comprised of 2,03,56! sq. km of land area having population of 10.26 million (Table 1) excluding the states of Arunachal Pradesh. But due to the rise of the forces of regionalism in the state, the present Assam comprised of only 78,438 sq. km of land area, i.e., 38.5 per cent of original land area with a population of 8.0 mn according to 2001 census.

At present all the states of NER are in the midst of turmoil. The war cry changed from place to place. In Assam, the rumpus was over the issue of "foreigners" and the wall-posters there screamed, "Indians go back". Killings kidnappings, and destruction of government properties became the order of the day in Assam. In Mizoram, where the outlawed Mizo National Front (MNF) had taken up arms to achieve its goal of "independent Mizoram" row agitating to oust the "outsiders". In strife-torn Meghalaya, the ultras day in and day out chanted "Meghalaya for Meghalayan tribals" and the slogan was raised "kill the Bengalis." In Nagaland, the hostile Nagas carried on insurgent movement for secession from the Indian union at regular interval.

Towards the late seventies underground organizations of rebels called "Nammat" comprising the five states and two union territories of NER was formed with headquarters in Northern Burma with the objective of setting up an independent federal state in the region. Very recently, the alleged ULFA (United Liberation Front of Assam), NSCN (National Socialist Council of Nagaland) and terrorist organizations of the region are receiving military training in neighbouring countries. In addition, different regional forces like 'Amara Bangali', Bodo, Karbi, etc. are no less important in the region. For a time it appeared as if the whole of NER was going to break away from the Indian Union.

Thus, regionalism has been, deeply rooted in NER and a conspicuous phenomenon of India's political life, by threatening unity and integrity of the nation. Destruction of national properties like railways, airport, and national high ways become order of the day. As time goes on, more gaps between the centre and the states of NER are created instead of closing the same.

IV. Conclusion

In the present study of regional disparity in NER, it is observed that the states of NER are suffering from the paucity of funds to improve their socio-economic backwardness. It-reveals that the states of NER are far behind from other states of the Indian union so far as the basic amenities of life such as health, education, safe drinking water, food security, banking facility, communication etc. are concerned. All these created the seeds of contention amongst the people of NER for which the feeling of regionalism grew more and more. Now they are not showing any allegiance to everything national. This dangerous turn of regionalism is a serious concern of the national government as well as a headache of the region for which the life is always in danger.

An important cause of regional tension, which led to popular. agitations and at times militant activities, is such regional disparities in economic and social development, which will exist within some of the states of Indian union and all the states of NER. Some of the states were created in the wake of popular agitations based perceived neglect of certain backward regions in some of the bigger states. However, creation of new states may not be a solution to such regional disparities. Thus regional disparity gives birth to ugly force of regionalism in the region by threatening unity and integrity of the nation. Hence, it should not be given to grow further and a viable solution to the problem is an urgent necessity. The study is concluded with the following suggestions.

V Suggestions

Economic disparity and absence of economic opportunities create great areas of tension and frustration. It is not possible to maintain the unity and integrity of the nation as an abstract formula. The economic maladies, which lead to maladjustment, have to be remedied. It is essential to have a dynamic economy of expansion and there should be rational and equalitarian distribution of the country's resources in the different areas. It is unwise to think in terms of the segmented development of the country. In planning the economic life and resources, the planners and the policy makers should not be biased towards particular region.

In the pluralistic nature of the Indian society regionalism is welcome as positive force to represent the quest of human identity but aggressive regionalism as developed in the NER should be tackled at all cost as it ignores the interest of the nation. The agitators of NER want an appropriate new development opportunity without taking into account the total development process of the nation. Hence the spirit of nationalism should be inculcated in the minds of the people of NER. Efforts should be made to ensure harmonious growth of national and sub national identities to cure the malady.

There is an urgent need for re-examination of pattern of development, particularly of industrialization in the context of balanced regional development in the country. Central as well as state governments should envisage the programmes in human resource development through education, technical training, economic security of the weaker section of the population, health and family welfare, labour welfare etc which would help not only in removing poverty and unemployment but also the regional disparities. Immediate steps should be taken to check the influx of the immigrants from outside the country and the governments of NER should take appropriate family planning programmes to check rapid growth of the population in the region. The people of NER should take active step for the management of water for the maintenance of the standard of water quality.

Last but not the least is that government should establish the requisite institutional mechanism and enabling environment at all levels of the society to ensure that population factors are appropriately addressed within the decision making and administrative process of all governmental agencies responsible for economic, environment, and social policies and programmes.

References

Awasthi, Kashyap and Wadhva (1988): *"Analysis of Regional Growth Pattern in India"*, Sardar Patel Institute of Economic and Social Research, Ahmedabad. (Mimeo.)

Bardhan P.K. (1974): *"The Pattern of Income Distribution in India: A Review"*, Sankhya, Vol. 36, Series-c (Part 2 & 4), pp. 103-108.

Chatterjee G. S. and N. Bhattacharya (1974): *"On Disparities in per Capita Household Consumption in India"*, Sankhya, Vol. 36 (Series c, 2 & 3), pp. 103-108.

Daly and Cobb (1989): "For The Common Goal : Redirecting The Economy Towards Community, The Environment And A Sustainable Future", Beacon Press, Boston.

Dutta P.C. and H. Choudhury (1996): *"A Note on Inter-State variation in per capita Non-Food Household Items of Consumption in the North East India"*, IJRS Vol. 28(2).

Dutta P. C. and H Choudhury (1995): *"Per Capita Household Consumption Inequalities in the North Eastern Region of India"*, IJRS), Vol. 27 (1 & 2)

Dutta P. C. and N. Roy (1998) : *"Socio Economic Development of North East India with Special Reference to the Problems of Urbanisation"*, Proc., Assam University, Silchar.

Dutta P.C. (1999) *"Population Growth and Environmental Crisis in N. E. India—Problems and Remedies"*- Paper presented in National Seminar, NEICSSR 13-14 Dec.

GOI (1998) : Statistical Abstract of India, New Delhi.

Gupta D.C. (1988) : *"Indian Government and Politics"*,Vikas Publishing House, New Delhi, 59-502.

Koropeckyj I.S. (1972): *"Equalisation of Regional Development in Socialist Countries- An Empizical Study"*, Economic Development and Cultural Change 'Vol. 27( ), Oct. pp. 68-86

Mahajan O. P. (1982): *"Economic Planning and Regional Development in India"*, Ess Publications, New Delhi.

Nair K.R.G. (1983): *"Regional Experience in A Developing Economy"*, Wiley Eastern Ltd., New Delhi.

NEC (2000): Basic Statistics of North Eastern Region, Shillong.

Pathak C.R. (1998): *"Urbanisation and Urban Poverty in Third World Countries: A Case Study of India"* in Essays on Regional Science, Regional Development and Planning, Vol. II, RSAI, Calcutta.

Prakash S. (1977): *"Regional Inequalities and Economic Development with Special Reference to Infrastructural Facilities in India"*, JIRS, Vol. XI (2), pp. 173-195.

Sen A. (1973): "On Economic Inequality", Oxford University Press, New Delhi.

Williamson. G. (1965): *"Regional Inequality and the Process of National Development"*, Economic Development and Cultural Change, Vol. 13(4).

Zolotas X. (1981): Economic Growth and Declining Social Welfare, New York Printing Press, New York ,U.S.A.

SECTION-III
DEMOGRAPHIC PROFILE

11

The Relationship Between Total Per Capita Expenditure (PCE) and Marginal Budget Shares (MBS) of Some Item Groups of Consumption in Rural Areas of NER

Introduction

A significant number of empirical studies on consumer behaviour in India have mostly been confined to Engel curve analysis of budget data collected from nationwide samples of households in different rounds of the National Sample Survey **(Ganguly and others, 1960)**. However, most researchers have assumed the constant elasticity form of the Engel curve and fitted such curves to data from one round at a time only. Such curve has been used for the demand projections in the context of India's early Five Years Plans.

Prais and Houthakker (1955) suggested that the principal problem in fitting Engel curve is to find an algebraic expression which satisfies both certain 'a priori' criteria and also criteria of a statistical nature. Various forms of Engel curves have been fitted to the household expenditure data in India **(Bhattacharya (1972)), Bhattacharya and Maitra (1970), Choudhury (1979), Gupta (1973)**. Their studies indicate that no Engel curve is suffice for describing the consumption patterns for complete range of consumer goods. **Choudhury (1984)** studied the pattern of consumption revealed by the marginal budget shares of some broad groups of food items in Rural India using Semi logarithmic (SL) form of Engel curve.

Data and Methodology

This chapter attempts to pursue the classification of some items of consumption by estimating the relationship between MBS (Marginal Budget Share) of the items and total PCE (per capita expenditure).

One extremely useful form which is consistent with adding-up criteria was first estimated by **Working (1943)** was used successfully by **Leser (1963)**. This Relates budget shares linearly to the logarithms of outlay.

The SL. form of Engel curve is given by

$$W_i = \alpha_i + \beta_i \log, X + U_i \tag{1.1}$$

Where, W_i is the marginal budget share of 'i'th item of consumption in the household budget and X is the average monthly total PCE, U_i is the disturbance term with usual least square assumptions.

$W_i = Y_i /X$, Y_i is the average monthly PCE for the ith commodity, (i = 1, 2 , n).

α_i and β_i are the parameters to be estimated.

Adding up criteria requires that $\sum W_i = 1$, which is satisfied provided

$$\sum \alpha_i = 1, \text{ and } \sum \beta_i = 0 \tag{1.2}$$

Indeed if (1.1) is estimated equation by equation by ordinary least squares, the estimates of parameter α and β will satisfy (1.2) automatically. The model allows goods as luxuries ($\beta_i > 0$) and necessaries ($\beta_i < 0$) (Deaton & Muellbauer, 1980)

The formulation (1.1) has an advantage over other curves, as it always gives positive initial income, for when W= 0, the initial income is antilog (- α / β), which is positive irrespective of signs of α and β.

The estimate of the parameters of SL form along with R^2 and D-statistics for rural sectors of NER using 43rd round (1987-88) of NSS data have been obtained. The existence of serial correlation between the errors in successive observations may indicate a lack of independence between the observations. If the sample size is large and there is no auto-correlation, then D is expected to be sufficiently close to 2 ; values of "D" which are close to 0 (between 0 & 2) will show positive auto-correlation and those close to 4 (between 2 & 4) will show negative correlation. The "D" statistic is defined as

$$D = \frac{\sum_{t=2}^{n} (\hat{U}_{t-}\hat{U}_{t-1})^2}{\sum_{t=1}^{n} \hat{U}^2_{t-}} \qquad (1.3)$$

Where, $\hat{U}_t$'s are the least squares residual estimates of $\hat{U}_t$'s

An approximate relationship exists between D and r is

$$D = 2\,(1-r) \qquad (1.4)$$

The relation (1.4) shows that D has a range 0 to 4, where r is the autocorrelation between the errors in successive observations.

Lastly, average Engel elasticities for each of the items have also been worked out on the basis of same data (43rd Round) to classify the items as necessary or luxury goods.

Analysis of the Results

As regards the relationship between the MBS of the items on the one hand, and the PCE on the other, a significant link has been observed in most of the cases. The α's add to unity and the β's to zero as they must. The R statistics are reasonably high. From a look at the tables (11.1 to 11.7) it is clear that milk and sugar among the food items and all the non-food items of consumption except pan, tobacco and intoxicants along with fuel and lighting may be considered as luxury items as the β's are showing positive values.

The tables reveal a moderate relationship between the budget shares and PCE. R^2 values are above 0.60 both for food and non-food items. However, the regression coefficients (α and β) are statistically different from zero in all the states of NER and India as a whole, for each of the items of consumption considered here.

In respect of R^2 and D statistics, except two or three items, it seem to provide satisfactory description of the expenditure pattern in all the states of NER, often R^2 for each item exceeds 0.90. The range of R^2 for most of the items lies between 0.75 to 0.98, except for sugar in the states of Assam (0.644), for pan, tobacco and intoxicants in the state of Manipur (0.640) and for fuel and light in the states of Arunachal Preadesh (0.666) and Tripura (0.672).

In tables it is observed that in the states of NER, D-values corresponding to majority of the items except a few items -Durable goods in Manipur, Cereals, Pulses and Durabie goods in Mizoram, pan, tobacco etc. in Tripura, sugar and pan tobacco, foot wear, Misc. goods and services in Meghalaya are above 2 indicating existence of negative autocorrelation, whereas in rural India, values of D for all items are far below 2, showing existing of positive autocorrelation.

1. $\eta \int_0^\infty g(x)\, E(y/x)\, \eta(x)\, dx/E(y)$ [Bhattacharya (1972)]

n/(x) is the variable elasticity at per capita total expenditure level x.

In rural Arunachal Pradesh all the D-values are less than 2 while, in rural Assam D-values for the items except pulses, sugar, pan. tobacco etc. and fuel and light are ranging from 0 to 1, indicating the existence of highly positive serial correlation.

The coefficient of logarithmic income for necessary goods have negative signs and for luxury goods positive signs which

Table 11.1: Estimates of Parameters of the Engle Curve with their Correponding Values of Coefficient of Determination (R^2) in Rual Arunachal Pradesh on the Basis of 43rd Round (1987-88) NSS Data.

ITEMS	α	β	S.E(α)	S.E(β)	R^2	D	WI	η
Cereals	0.487	-0.042	0.092	0.018	0.721	0.786	0.255	0.719
Pulses	0.097	-0.014	0.024	0.005	0.861	0.879	0.023	0.383
Milk and Milk Product	-0.005	0.008	0.025	0.005	0.850	1.381	0.039	1.269
Edible oil	0.031	-0.0002	0.021	0.003	0.824	1.422	0.030	0.989
Sugar	0.015	-0.0007	0.0006	0.0001	0.671	1.349	0.011	0.964
Pan/Tobacco etc.	0.040	0.008	0.079	0.015	0.733	0.871	0.089	1.413
Fuel and light	0.331	-0.044	0.118	0.023	0.666	0.515	0.097	0.949
Clothing	-0.080	0.024	0.031	0.006	0.902	1.966	0.047	1.317
Foot Wear	-0.036	0.011	0.016	0.003	0.868	1.350	0.022	1.450
Misc. Goods and Services	-0.037	0.105	0.018	0.003	0.880	1.256	0.049	1.221
Durable goods	-0.483	0.101	0.057	0.011	0.934	1.734	0.067	3.068
Food-Total	1.245	-0.111	0.219	0.042	0.744	0.465	0.633	0.773
Non-food Total	-0.245	0.111	0.219	0.042	0.744	0.465	0.367	1.556

Table 11.2: Estimates of Parameters of the Engle Curve with their Corresponding Values of Coefficient of Determination (R^2) in Rural Assam on the basis of 43rd Round (1987-88) NSS Data

ITEMS	α	β	S.E(α)	S.E(β)	R^2	D	W_i	η
Cereals	1.141	-0.155	0.106	0.021	0.849	0.696	0.369	0.478
Pulses	0.052	-0.004	0.003	0.001	0.889	1.253	0.031	0.975
Milk and Milk Product	-0.092	0.027	0.013	0.003	0.929	0.949	0.044	1.740
Edible oil	0.079	0.006	0.006	0.001	0.812	0.799	0.046	0.862
Sugar	-0.018	-0.001	0.004	0.001	0.644	1.284	0.023	1.099
Pan/Tobacco etc.	0.072	0.005	0.006	0.001	0.644	1.284	0.023	1.099
Fuel and light	0.125	-0.009	0.011	0.002	0.718	1.359	0.080	0.923
Clothing	-0.083	0.023	0.010	0.002	0.936	0.740	0.034	2.041
Foot Wear	-0.014	0.004	0.006	0.001	0.660	0.657	0.005	2.50
Misc. Goods and Services	-0.454	0.112	0.060	0.012	0.909	0.488	0.011	2.639
Durable goods	-0.060	0.014	0.018	0.004	0.673	0.782	0.702	3.627
Food-Total	0.416	-0.138	0.080	0.016	0.892	0.440	0.633	0.882
Non-food Total	0.415	0.139	0.080	0.016	0.892	0.441	0.298	1.889

Table 11.3: Estimates of Parameters of the Engle Curve with their Corresponding Values of Coefficient of Determination (R^2) in Rural Manipur on the basis of 43rd Round (1987-88) NSS Data

ITEMS	α	β	S.E(α)	S.E(β)	R^2	D	W_i	η
Cereals	1.453	-0.202	0.178	0.034	0.835	1.172	0.382	0.338
Pulses	0.004	-0.002	0.010	0.002	0.709	0.987	0.031	0.860
Milk and Milk Product	-0.027	0.007	0.011	0.002	0.796	1.418	0.013	1.652
Edible oil	0.027	0.007	0.011	0.002	0.796	1.418	0.013	1.652
Sugar	0.002	-0.002	0.001	0.0002	0.937	1.254	0.041	0.446
Pan/Tobacco etc.	0.012	0.0001	0.005	0.001	0.691	1.582	0.013	1.007
Fuel and light	0.189	-0.023	0.005	0.001	0.985	1.398	0.068	0.660
Clothing	-0.277	0.060	0.030	0.006	0.947	1.937	0.042	2.675
Foot Wear	-0.209	0.046	0.046	0.009	0.826	1.155	0.035	2.525
Misc. Goods and Services	-0.111	0.046	0.098	0.019	0.582	1.191	0.131	1.293
Durable goods	-0.230	0.048	0.040	0.008	0.904	2.403	0.023	3.702
Food-Total	1.566	-0.171	0.205	0.039	0.716	1.272	0.662	0.836
Non-food Total	-0.566	0.151	0.205	0.039	0.738	1.272	0.338	1.577

Table 11.4: Estimates of Parameters of the Engle Curve with their Corresponding Values of Coefficient of Determination (R^2) in Rural Meghalaya on the basis of 43rd Round (1987 - 88) NSS Data.

ITEMS	α	β	S.E(α)	S.E(β)	R^2	D	W_i	η
Cereals	1.336	-0.201	0.067	0.013	0.965	1.318	0.276	0.286
Pulses	0.026	-0.002	0.005	0.001	0.872	1.388	0.061	0.705
Milk and Milk Product	-0.029	0.011	0.010	0.002	0.905	1.418	0.028	1.234
Edible oil	0.029	-0.0003	0.009	0.002	0.855	0.900	0.045	0.974
Sugar	0.030	-0.0001	0.002	0.0005	0.881	1.240	0.024	0.956
Pan/Tobacco etc.	-0.123	0.041	0.024	0.004	0.910	2.157	0.095	1.411
Fuel and light	0.007	-0.012	0.010	0.002	0.985	0.713	0.070	1.130
Clothing	-0.200	0.047	0.021	0.004	0.951	0.684	0.001	2.362
Foot Wear	-0.083	0.019	0.007	0.001	0.966	2.052	0.019	2.339
Misc. Goods and Services	-0.066	0.029	0.014	0.003	0.949	2.533	0.090	1.450
Durable goods	-0.037	0.009	0.010	0.002	0.898	1.868	0.011	2.195
Food-Total	1.531	-0.164	0.038	0.007	0.982	1.007	0.663	0.735
Non-food Total	-0.531	0.164	0.038	0.007	0.981	1.006	0.337	1.629

Table 11.5: Estimates of Parameters of the Engle Curve with their Corresponding Values of Coefficient of Determination (R^2) in Rural Mizoram on the basis of 43rd Round (1987 - 88) NSS Data

ITEMS	α	β	S.E(α)	S.E(β)	R^2	D	W_i	η
Cereals	0.816	-0.177	0.106	0.019	0.790	2.252	0.165	0.219
Pulses	0.012	-0.009	0.003	0.002	0.891	2.196	0.028	0.978
Milk and Milk Product	-0.052	0.099	0.003	0.003	0.801	0.862	0.045	1.046
Edible oil	0.088	-0.010	0.029	0.004	0.775	1.105	0.036	0.709
Sugar	0.024	0.004	0.010	0.003	0.772	0.946	0.029	0.709
Pan/Tobacco etc.	-0.042	0.012	0.010	0.003	0.772	0.946	0.029	1.076
Fuel and light	0.137	-0.010	0.056	0.004	0.736	1.212	0.162	0.916
Clothing	-0.259	0.056	0.078	0.014	0.770	0.867	0.052	2.710
Foot Wear	-0.236	-0.049	0.047	0.008	0.863	1.196	0.187	3.089
Misc. Goods and Services	-0.024	0.0002	0.019	0.004	0.737	0.753	0.104	1.171
Durable goods	-0.036	0.008	0.009	0.002	0.940	2.679	0.008	1.789
Food-Total	1.377	-0.146	0.104	0.019	0.881	1.213	0.567	0.690
Non-food Total	-0.377	0.146	0.105	0.019	0.881	1.214	0.432	1.410

Table 11.6: Estimates of Parameters of the Engle Curve with their Corresponding Values of Coefficient of Determination (R^2) in Rural Tripura on the basis of 43rd Round (1987 - 88) NSS Data

ITEMS	α	β	S.E(α)	S.E(β)	R^2	D	W_i	η
Cereals	1.254	-0.179	0.065	0.013	0.953	0.934	0.294	0.310
Pulses	0.055	-0.006	0.005	0.001	0.803	1.110	0.024	0.688
Milk and Milk Product	-0.121	0.032	0.020	0.004	0.915	0.497	0.047	1.726
Edible oil	0.051	-0.003	0.014	0.001	0.780	1.524	0.042	0.977
Sugar	0.008	0.003	0.0003	0.001	0.664	1.635	0.013	1.244
Pan/Tobacco etc.	0.064	-0.004	0.002	0.001	0.811	2.089	0.097	0.970
Fuel and light	0.143	-0.014	0.021	0.004	0.672	0.619	0.064	0.836
Clothing	-0.257	0.057	0.016	0.003	0.973	0.673	0.048	3.009
Foot Wear	-0.042	-0.009	0.005	0.001	0.913	0.769	0.006	4.000
Misc. Goods and Services	-0.157	0.053	0.020	0.004	0.954	1.937	0.126	1.694
Durable goods	-0.221	0.045	0.054	0.010	0.803	1.184	0.021	6.403
Food-Total	1.398	-0.131	0.078	0.015	0.900	0.640	0.690	0.826
Non-food Total	-0.399	0.132	0.078	0.015	0.901	0.641	0.310	1.964

Table 11.7: Estimates of Parameters of the Engle Curve with their Corresponding Values of Coefficient of Determination (R^2) in Rural India on the basis of 43rd Round (1987 - 88) NSS Data

ITEMS	α	β	S.E(α)	S.E(β)	R^2	D	W_i	η
Cereals	1.131	-0.166	0.019	0.004	0.995	1.195	0.261	0.354
Pulses	0.092	-0.010	0.002	0.001	0.972	0.898	0.040	0.773
Milk and Milk Product	-0.171	0.049	0.027	0.005	0.927	1.718	0.086	1.791
Edible oil	0.071	-0.004	0.004	0.001	0.871	0.931	0.056	0.986
Sugar	0.009	0.004	0.003	0.001	0.860	0.736	0.029	1.228
Pan/Tobacco etc.	0.060	-0.005	0.002	0.001	0.938	0.320	0.032	0.881
Fuel and light	0.241	-0.032	0.002	0.0004	0.998	1.430	0.074	0.611
Clothing	-0.258	0.062	0.013	0.003	0.985	0.906	0.067	2.664
Foot Wear	-0.031	-0.008	0.002	0.0004	0.976	1.278	0.010	2.291
Misc. Goods and Services	-0.167	0.060	0.016	0.003	0.976	1.478	0.144	1.782
Durable goods	-0.206	0.046	0.031	0.006	0.891	1.252	0.036	4.354
Food-Total	1.265	-0.117	0.042	0.008	0.958	1.006	0.638	0.868
Non-food Total	-0.266	0.118	0.041	0.007	0.957	1.006	0.632	1.893

imply that MBS for necessary goods tend to decline with rise in income and that for luxury items increase.

In the state of Arunachal Pradesh and Meghalaya "β" values are found to be negative in case of sugar indicating it as a necessary item of consumption. It is observed that in case of expenditure on total food, the highest MBS on the item (0.702) is in rural Assam (Table 2) and lowest in Mizoram (0.567) while it is 0.638 in rural India.

In case of cereals, the highest MBS is observed in Manipur (0.3 82) followed by Assam (0.369) while it is 0.261 for all India. The lowest MBS for Cereals (0.165) is observed in Mizoram.

In case of fuel and light, among the states of NER, the MBS is found to be maximum in Mizoram and lowest in Tripura (0.064).

In case of clothing, the share of expenditure in Meghalaya is only (0.001) while, for all India it is (0.067). In case of footwear, the maximum share has been observed in Mizoram (0.187) and minimum in Assam (0.005) against 0.01 for all India.

In case of durable goods, highest share is observed in Arunachal Pradesh (0.067) and lowest in Mizoram (0.008) against 0.036 for all- India.

Considering all the non-food items of consumption at a time, it is observed that the pattern of consumption in non-food items are different in different states.

Highest Marginal Budget Share (MBS), among the non-food items of consumption, are found in case of fuel & light in Arunachal Pradesh (0.097) and pan, tobacco and intoxicants (0.095) for Meghalaya. Lowest MBS are found in case of footwear in the states of Arunachal Pradesh, Assam, Tripura and India, while, it is found to be maximum in Mizoram.

It is to be noted that the share of expenditure on Misc. goods and services, among the non-food items, are found to be maximum in the states of Assam, Manipur, Tripura, and also in all-India.

A glance at the tables shows a considerable degree of variation in the estimated elasticities of the items of consumption in the states of NER.

It is striking to note that in the rural sector, the average elasticities are found to be less than unity only for the items-cereals, pulses, edible oil and food total. These items may be clasified as necessary items of consumption in all the states of NER. For the items milk and milk products, clothing, footwear, Misc. goods and services, durable goods and non-food total, the average elasticities are found to be greater than unity in all the. states of NER and thus may be classified as luxury items.

It is worth while to note that the elasticity of sugar is found to be greater than unity in all the states except in Arunachal Pradesh (0.964) and in Meghalaya (0.956). A minute look at the tables reveal that the elasticity for fuel and light is found to be greater than unity in the state of Meghalaya only indicating there by that fuel and light has turned to be an item of luxury in the household consumption basket.

It is interesting to note that the elasticity for the item pan. tobacco and-intoxicants falls in the category of luxury item of consumption in the states of Arunachal Pradesh, Meghalaya and Mizoram.

References

Bhattacharya, N. (1972) *"The Average Elasticity of a Variable Elasticity Engel Curve"*, presented at the 11th Indian Econometric Conference, Hyderabad, 1972.

Bhattacharya, N. and Mitra, T. 1970) : *"An Analysis of Engel Curves based on NSS Household Budget for 7th to 22 Rounds"*, Technical Report, pp. 2093- 2098, I.S.I, Calcutta.

Choudhury, H. (1979) *"An Analysis of Consumer Expenditure in Assam - An Econometric Study"* Journal of the Assam Science Society, Vol. 22 pp. 37-50.

Choudhury, H. (1984) : *"An Econometric study of Marginal Budget shares of some item Groups of Consumption in*

Rural India", Indian Journal of Regional Science Vol.- 16, No. 1, 1984, pp. 23-24, LI.T. Kharagpur, West Bengal.

Deaton A, and Muellbauer, J. (1980) : *"Economics and consumer behaviour"*, Cambridge University Press, Cambridge.

Gupta, D.B. (1973) : *"Consumption Pattern in India : A Study of Inter regional variations"*, Tata McGraw Hill Publishing Company Limited, Bombay, New Delhi.

Leser, C.E.V. (1963) : *"Forms of Engel Curves"*, Econometrica, Vol. 31, pp. 694-703.

Paris, S.J. and Houthakker, H.S. (1955) *"The Analysis of Family Budgets, ed., 1971"*, Cambridge University Press, Cambridge.

Working, H. 1943) : *"Statistical Laws of Family Expenditure"*, Journal of American Statistical Association, Vol. 38, p. 43.

12

Gender Issues and Development in North Eastern Region of India

"To have access to the resources for a descent standard of living. But, the realm of Human Development extends further into other areas of choice highly valued by people including Participation, Security, Sustainability, Guaranteed Human Rights all needed for being creative and productive and for enjoying self respect, empowerment and a sense of belonging to a community." [UN HUMAN DEVELOPMENT REPORT, 2000]

Introduction

The issue of development has been central in all societies for a long time. Its content, form and meaning had experienced sea changes particularly with the emergence of New International Economic Order (NIEO) and adoption of Liberalisation, Privatisation and Globalisation (LPG). Different indicators have been used by different scholars as the yard stick to measure the human development in different societies. The concept of human development in India is no exception to it. Like developed countries, the policy makers of India have adopted the policy to eliminate gender inequality at all levels by 2015 to target the goals of to be achieved for the empowerment of women in particular and human development in general. As human development moves center stage in the global development debate, gender equality and gender equity are emerging as major challenges because of gender discrimination is clearly visible in all the societies of the world. Both in India and in abroad if one looks at the history of the struggle for women's rights, it constitutes one of the most eventful and momentous in recent times from Mexico to Copenhagen, onto Nairobi and Beijing to other conferences is merely contemporary social history.India's contribution to the global women's debate has been rich, diverse and unique in many respects. The principle of gender equality has been basic to Indian thinking for over a century. The 19th and early 20th century saw a succession of women's movement with social issues like women's education, widow remarriage, property rights for women, women equality etc. The constitution of India not only grants equality to women, but also empowered the states to adopt measures of affirmative discrimination in favour of women. The constitution further imposes a fundamental duty of every citizen to renounce practices derogatory to the dignity of women. Since the commencement of New Constitution of India, the Government of India and various States appointed different committees on the status of women in India and a multi-prolonged strategy have been concede for the development of women in India. Constitution in its 72nd and 73rd amendment Acts passed in the year 1993 advocated 33 per cent reservation of the women in Rural and Urban Local Bodies for the (WACD) was set up under the newly created Ministry of Human Resource Development, Government of India. Besides, the national commission for women was set up to study and monitor all matters relating to the constitutional and legal safeguards provided for women, review existing legislation and to look into complaints involving deprivation of the rights of women. Similar commissions are also being set up in different states of India.

Despite of several welfare measures the women of India are still constitute the largest section of the population living in absolute poverty and they present represent the poorest of the poor. It is widely recognized that women as a group and particularly the poor women have been adversely affected by the process of growth, economic transformation and development. The policies and programmes designed by the Govt. of India and various States are not addressed to the needs of women in poverty. Further, India has embarked upon a course of restructuring its economy and development policy frame work since 1911 and became the member of WTO by adopting LPG in 1992. The policies of stabilization measures and structural adjustment programmes of New Economic Policies (NEP) entailing budget compression, reduction in Government expenditure and devaluation might in the end result in high transitional costs on the poor and such costs tend to be most for poor women. The nature of such costs tend to be in terms of short term drop in employment, greater work load and squeezing out of real incomes forcing women to seek alternative survival of strategies. While expansion of employment opportunities tend to take place in export oriented industries, cash- crop cultivation, agro business, finance and insurance sector and high tech areas, traditional sectors tend to diminish in importance. Therefore it is necessary to integrate the concerns, needs and anticipated threats to poor women, with the basic development objectives of stabilization and structural adjustment policies and to continue to strengthen the Social Safety Net (SSN) which the government has already taken up as a priority measure. Taking all the indicators of present Human Development Index (HDI) such as standard of living, education, Nutrition, Health etc., it is clear that the women are the poorest of the poor in India and worsening situation is visible in North Eastern Region (NER) of the country. As there is paucity of literature on gender issues in this region, this paper is an attempt to address the issues of women in North –East. A plenty of literatures have been reviewed on gender issues in Asian Countries and the countries of Indian Ocean area for the completion of the paper.

Pradhan and Dutta (2003) highlighted that in the era of globalisation women's education in NER is not translated into reality although it is squarely on the development agenda of our country. The authors assigned various psychological, socio-cultural, and economic reasons for the decadence of women's education in the region. Although there are Women's Study Centers at some particular universities of the region, most of these are confined to organization of seminars and workshops without addressing the problems of the women of the region as such. Further, the authors also emphasized that the policy, " Education for Women's Equity", of the Government of India is not corroborating the New International Economic order (NIEO). The literature is most appropriate in the era of globalisation to analyse the miseries of the women in the region.

Das and Pathak (2004) rightly pointed out about the malpractices prevailing in the market against women consumer due to socio- economic status. The authors indicated that there is enough scope to develop consumerism in the north-eastern society. But women are not competent to manage such activities due to their dearth of knowledge regarding their rights and responsibilities. They suggested a course on consumerism in the school curriculum with a view to obtaining a group of alert women consumers of the region in future. They further suggested that the Non-government organization (NGO) should come forward for the training the women by organizing meetings, seminars, workshops etc.

Extensive research **(Roy, Tisdell and Blomquist, 1996; Roy and Clark, 1994; Roy and Tisdell, 1996; Rao, 1991 Roy, Tisdell and Sen, 1992)** on women's socio-economic status in Rural India have found that these women have reached the end of their carrying capacity and that the empowerment of women is a fundamental requirement for sustainable development. The above review of literatures show that gender discrimination faced by women and poverty of rural women would seem to suggest that they suffer from their diminishing access to common property resources, minor forest produces, lack of control over land, lack of command over technology, cultural barriers and above all institutional biases towards men.

Molyneux (1998) pointed out that the women movements along with other social movements have contributed to the process of democratization of the polity and society resulting the reassessment of the concepts related to emancipation, political rights and social justice for women to get the status of full citizen. The review of Molyneux literature establishes the fact that women of the present age are still living in Aristotalian era.

Theron (2001) discussed how the developing countries could seek to reduce poverty by effectively dealing with crime and violence to create a stable environment for economic activity, streamlining government spending revenues and by adopting a brisk privatization programme and flexible market reforms targeted at growth and job creation.

One of the crucial concerns of the contemporary women's movements of India is related to the impact of the global political economy and the developmental policies upon woman. The issues like inflation, displacement, deforestation, unemployment, poverty etc. had been raised by the women's organization as all these issues affected women greatly. These issues are the net result of the process of economic modernization, increasing mechanization, Liberalization and globalization.

The New International Economic Order (NIEO) aims at one unified global market with no barriers to trade and that had faced India like country to follow Structural Adjustment Programme (SAP) with its emphasis on privatization, trade liberalization and cuts in subsidies has long term impact on women. In the backward regions of the country the problem is more acute and clearly visible. The women of NER have been dislodged from their traditional source of employment in the small scale industries as a result of the competition that these industries face from the organized industries and have been forced to work under increasingly exploitative conditions. They have also been facing the Jhuming or deforestation, displacement, unemployment, poverty etc. They are confronting with their basic rights of survival, right to livelihood, right to common property resources, right to identity and the need to regenerate the environment. The question of 'Sustainable development', a global agenda has been confronting the NER women and assumed the shape of a new women movement by giving birth a new concept of "Eco-Feminism".

Roy (2001) discussed gender and poverty issues in the Indian Ocean Rim Countries. He pointed out that about one half of the world population are women and yet in many areas of human endeavour they are well behind men. The UN and World bank Policies have contributed in bringing women's issues in the main stream global policy agenda. Roy argues that in an increasingly globalised economy, dynamics of women's movement has been changing rapidly. In an uneven global economic, social and political environment developing countries in particular, must adopt innovative policies to achieve the movement's objectives. This new environment provides opportunity to women to set their own agenda within the boundaries set by governance and civil society issues and various rights instruments.

Considering all the views of different scholars on the subject, this chapter is an attempt to examine and analysis the gender issues of north- eastern states. For the convenience of the study, the chapter is divided into the following heads.

1 To establish the linkage between gender and development.

2. To study the present status of women in NER.

3. Governmental measures to remove the gender discrimination and biasness.

4. Conclusion and suggestion for the gender equality and equity in the region.

For the completion of the study, statistical information collected from the secondary sources, have been used.

Gender and Development

Gender refers to the social classification of men and women into masculine and feminine and it reflects the existing power relationship in any given society. It is a socio-cultural phenomenon.. Historically, women have been given a lower socio-economic and political status in society and this continues in modern society. Democracy and development are two main areas by which the state, society and institutions in order to guarantee equal and legal rights to both men and women. In this respect women too have put their effort in the movement for restoration of democracy and subsequent development. In the course of the struggle for women's rights, the individual, state and the community are regarded as three main agencies of development. These agencies should play a key role in ensuring the well being of a woman and the development of her capabilities and freedom. While development focuses on technology and training of men, the economic work of women is never accounted for and was considered as non-consequential[1]. All ideas of development usually work against women. Increasing inequalities and depriving them of whatever control they had over the resources of family and community. As a result the United Nations decided that there should be a conscious effort to involve women in development and give them access to the formal sector of the economy. This was Women in Development (WID) approach.

Gender equality was the central theme of the United Nation's Human Development Report in 1995. Equal opportunity to all, particularly to females was the prime concern of the said report. It mentioned that, "Human Development if not endangered is endangered". Some of the important findings revealed in the Report are[2] "Poverty has a woman face"- roughly 70 per cent women in the world live in poverty.

- Removing gender inequality has nothing to do with national income.
- While the doors of education and health opportunities have opened rapidly for women, the door to economic and political opportunities are barely ajar.
- Women receive disproportionately small share of credit from banking institutions. It is as low as 7- 11 per cent in case of Latin America.
- Women receive much lower wages than men.
- All regions have higher rate of unemployment of women
- In developing countries women constitute only 1/7th of the administrative and Management lobs

- Women occupy only 10 per cent seats in Parliament and 7 per cent as cabinet Ministers
- In 55 countries there are no or below 5 per cent women in Parliament
- A major index of neglect reveals that many economic contributions made by women are grossly under valued or not valued at all. The magnitude of this omission is to the tune of $ 11 billion a year.
- Discrimination against women and their devaluation begins even before life begins. It starts early in life and continues through out. 1/3 of women in countries like Barbados, Canada, Netherlands, New Zealand, Norway, and USA report sexual abuse during childhood. Over a million children in Asia and mostly girls, are forced into prostitution every year.
- Violence against women becomes part of marriage. In some countries 2/3 married women suffer domestic violence. Sometimes it is manifested in the form of rape too. In Canada, USA, New Zealand and UK, one out of every six women is raped in her life time. It may end in murder or in suicide.

The report concluded that if half of humanity faces such gender discrimination, any talk about human development excluding women is not only worthless but is also violence against the gender. The report took full note of the gravity of the situation and initiated the process of computing Gender Equity Sensitive Index (GESI) or Gender Related Development Index (GRDI) along with Human Development Index (HDI).

To this added a multitude of feminist movements showing the negative impact of the work done by the state or multinational agencies on the women at local level. These experiences were transferred at the theoretical level and began to be referred to as the Gender and Development (GAD) paradigm. It advocated a look at the decision making structures of development which was structured along patriarchal lines in capable of taking into account the concerns of women in the third world countries. Thus what can be done is empowerment of women to ensure their participation in their own development, focus on small scale women- only projects to avoid male domination and in recent years the need to investigate relationships among gender ideology, women's subordination and operation of social, economic and political power. Hence, gender equity entails the concept that all human beings be it man or woman are free to develop their personal abilities and make choices without the limitation set by the rigid gender roles in socio-economic and political hierarchy and other prejudices. Their different behaviour and aspirations should be treated fairly and favours equally according to their respective needs.

One of the most crucial issues that face the women's question today is the relationship of larger political processes, the idea of justice and the role of women. This close relationship has been reflected in the very high human development indicators from several states in India like Kerala, Himachal Pradesh, TamilNadu etc. where a general improvement in the conditions of Health of Women has led to the general improvement of health of both male child and female child. However, the political processes are extremely male centered in India. Development is seen as the only way possible to bring out a positive change gendered exploitation. During the 1980's India followed welfares approach and efforts were made to make gender an important component in development programming. This was the beginning for 33 per cent reservation for women at the local level administration i.e. Panchayet, so that they could enter into decision making domain. The issue of 30 per cent reservation for women in the Parliament and state legislature was taken up and still pending before the parliament. **Amartya Sen (2000),** the famous economist, called development as freedom where development is the way to provide capabilities to women to bring out her fullest self. This is to be done through providing literacy, health and nutrition and other basic facilities to change her economic standing in the family and society and thereby improve her position in order to wrest decision making powers.

Present Status of Women in NER

Women's movement in the contemporary context, are a part of a new style of politics of the New Social Movements (NSM) that have been become the basis of active participation of the community in public life organized around the issues including those of civil liberties, ecology, identity, ethnicity, education, health and nutrition etc., these movements operate outside the party politics. It is generally observed that in most of the democratic countries of the world, the marginalized and powerless section (women) of the society are left out by the system of power. The NSM giving voice to these marginalized people, create alternative political spaces and fulfill their quest for participation. Hence, the boundary between public and private or between the political and non-political does not exist for the NSM. T he phenomenon of women's movements is universal because it represents the resistance of the women all over the globe and of political, social, economic and cultural in nature.

The women's movement in India were initially organized around the issues of sexual and domestic violence against women but gradually other gender-specific issues were incorporated in the agenda of women's groups. During the period of 1980's and early 1990's the feminist issues related to sexuality of women, right to choice and control over their fertility and bodies reproductive health, violence on the images of women in media also assumed importance. As the women's movement matured in India, they set their own agenda and pursue their own strategy. The contemporary women movements in India have been defined by their autonomous nature and the question of autonomy is also linked with the emphasis on the specificity of gender- issues which aimed at resistance to the patriarchal norms and structures. It is quite interesting to note that the women activity within the political parties are as much a part of the women's movements as the women members of any social movement organized around issues other than gender-issues.

Proper education is the only way to make aware the women

regarding their rights, powers and responsibilities in the society in which they live for any socio-economic development. Further, education is a birth right for every citizen. However, Indian constitution gives the "*Free and Compulsory Primary Education*" under the Article 45 and also through the Articles 15 (1) and 16 (1) which provide the basic rights for all round development of women.

In fact the whole issues of what forms the gender interest of women is not only related to the sexuality of women but also the issues related to their poverty, economic deprivation, social discrimination, emancipation from household- bondages and question of empowerment.

Hence the problem of women in NER can be discussed not only relating to sex but also with variety of socio-economic and political issues, which formed the gender issues. Further, with the advent of LPG, the gender issues can be linked with the issues like those of unemployment, deforestation, displacement and shift from main sector to tertiary sector. To analyse the present status of women in NER indicators like education, employment status, percentage distribution of workers, political participation etc. have been used. As the gender issues are related to the Human Development Index (HDI) the above indicators may reach us in a conclusion whether the women of NER are standing in equal footing with the other regions of the country or not.

Fig. 12-A reveals that in comparison to Indian women (41.42 p.c.), North-East women occupied only 1.74 p.c. in case of general education. It is observed that maximum students took admission in the Arts stream followed by science and Commerce. Only exception is in the state of Mizoram where science (51.06 p.c.) followed by Arts (49.05 p.c.) and Commerce (33.33 p.c.) and Nagaland where Arts (45.23 p.c.) followed by Commerce (33.46 p.c.) and Science (27.17 p.c.). Further, it is remarkable to note that in Arts stream all the States of NER except Arunachal Pradesh (33.82 p.c.) are above all –India Level (44.18 p.c.) while in case of Commerce all the States of NER are below all-India level (36.47 p.c.) and also gender gap

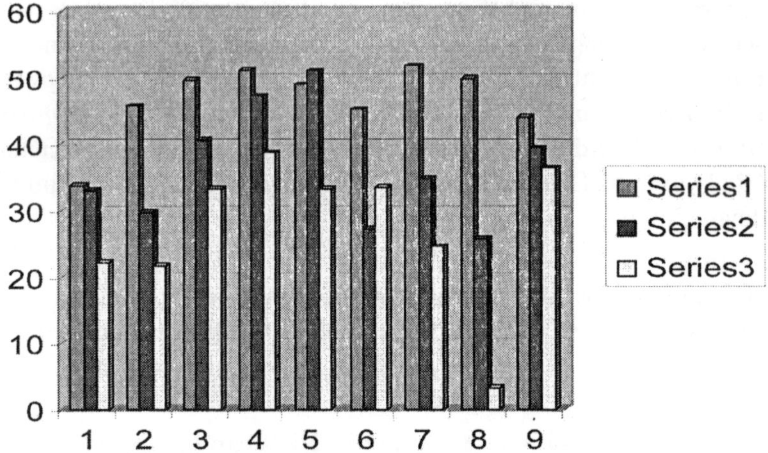

Fig. 12-A: Percentage Distribution of Female Students (General Education) in different Streams (Arts, Science, Commerce), 2000-01

Note 1: Series 1: Arts, Series 2: Science, Series 3: Commerce.
Note 2: Arunachal Pradesh, 2. Assam, 3. Manipur, 4. Meghalaya, 5. Mizoram, 6. Nagaland, 7. Sikkim, 8. Tripura, 9. India.

is well visible in the States of Tripura (minimum with only 3.26 p.c.), Assam (21.67 p.c.) and Arunachal Pradesh (22.26 p.c.) etc. including all India. The Same picture is observed for the States of Assam (29.82 p.c.), Nagaland (27.17 p.c.), Tripura (25.75 p.c.) in case of Science education while Mizoram is the exception (51.06 p.c.).

Table 12.1 shows the percentage distribution of women students out of total students in the NER which proves the fact that women are interested to get admit themselves in the Arts stream rather than Science or Commerce. The percentage of commerce women are very low in all the states of NER which ranges from 0.37 p.c. to 2.75 p.c. which is far below than all India level (7.77 p.c.).

A minute look at the table confirms the fact that in the states of NER, the Female Literacy Rate (FLR) ranges from 44.24 p.c. to 65.41 p.c. It is remarkable to note that all the states of NER, except Arunachal Pradesh (44.24 p.c.), are above all- India level (54.16 p.c.).

Table : 12.1 Percentage Distribution of Female students in different streams and the Female Literacy, Gender Gap and Sex Ratio amongst the different states of NER, 2000-01

	Arts	Science	Commerce	Total	F.P. (in p.c.)	F.L.R	G.GAP	S.R.
A.P.	28.57	3.18	1.30	33.06	47.40	44.24	19.83	901
Assam	36.43	4.03	1.48	41.93	48.24	56.03	15.90	932
Manipur	28.11	15.44	1.78	45.33	49.45	59.70	18.17	978
Meghalaya	39.04	6.72	2.75	48.51	49.36	60.41	5.73	975
Mizoram	45.62	2.28	0.84	48.74	48.40	86.13		938
Nagaland	37.32	2.71	2.51	42.54	47.62	61.92	9.85	909
Sikkim	35.76	7.72	2.15	45.63	46.68	61.46		875
Tripura	36.79	3.85	0.37	41.01	48.73	65.41	16.06	950
INDIA	24.30	9.35	7.77	41.42	48.27	54.16	21.69	933

It is observed from the table that in the year 2001, the Gender Gap (G GAP) in the North Eastern States ranges from 5.73 (Meghalaya) to 19.83 (Arunachal Pradesh) and below the all –India level (21.69). However, it is important to note that, in comparison to 1991, the Gender Gap decreased in all the states of NER in the year 2001. where the range was 7.01 to 24.07 for the states NER and for all- India it was 24.84.

In case of Sex Ratio, it is observed that all the states of NER, except Arunachal Pradesh (901), are above all-India level (933). It should be noted here that with respect to 1991, the Sex Ratio increased in all the states of NER including all- India. The exceptional state in this case is the state of Sikkim (878).

A close look at the table reveals the fact that the percentage of female population in the states of NER lies between 46.68 p.c. (Sikkim) and 49.45 p.c. (Manipur). However, it is to be noted

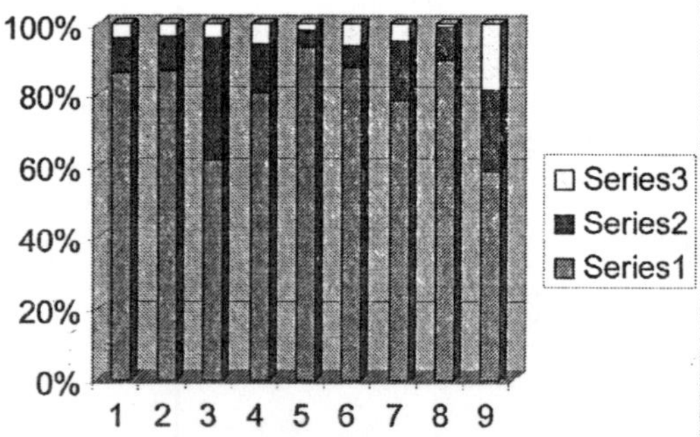

Note 1 :
Series 1 : Arts,
Series 2 : Science,
Series 3 : Commerce
Note 2 :
1. Arunachal Pradesh,
2. Assam, 3. Manipur,
4. Meghalaya,
5. Mizoram,
6. Nagaland, 7. Sikkim,
8. Tripura, 9. India

Figure 12-B: Percentage Distribution of Female Students (General Education) out of Total Women in different Streams (Arts, Science, Commerce) amongst the States of NER, 2000-01

here that the States of Arunachal Pradesh, Assam, Nagaland and Sikim are below all India figure (48.27 p.c.).

Fig 12-B shows the percentage distribution of Female Students in General Education out of Total Women in different Streams. The figure confirms the fact that women are much interested to get admission in Arts stream in comparison to other streams like Science or Commerce. As it is observed that out of total female students (100 p.c.), the percentage ranges from 78.37 p.c. to 93.59 p.c. (except in Manipur, 62.02 p.c.) in Arts stream while in case commerce the range is 0.91 p.c. to 5.89 p.c.

Table 12.2 shows the percentage distribution of female students with respect to total students in different States of NER.

A close look at the table, it may be pointed out that all the states of NER are below the all India level in case of Medicine (43.98 p.c.), Engineering (21.50 p.c.) Education Course. However, Tripura (35.46 p.c.) is the only exception in Engineering Course.

In case of Education, highest percentage is observed in case of Manipur (62.74 p.c.) followed by Meghalaya (58.06 p.c.) and Nagaland (54.38 p.c.) which are above all India level (51.21 p.c.) while lowest is observed in case of Tripura (32.35 p.c.) followed by Arunachal Pradesh (33.02 p.c.).

It is interesting to note that, in case of Law Course, all the states of NER are above the all India women (19.97 p.c.). Among the states of NER, the highest percentage is observed in the states of Sikkim (53.85 p.c.) followed by Meghalaya women (48.37 p.c.) and Tripura (41.01 p.c.) while lowest percentage is observed in the state of Mizoram (23.14 p.c.) followed by Nagaland (24.58 p.c.) and Manipur (29.89 p.c.).

A close look at the table reveals that in case of other Courses (include Agriculture, Veterinary etc.), the percentage of females in all the States of NER are above the all India level (28.64 p.c.).

A minute look at the **table 12.3**, it may be pointed out that total students of Professional Courses, the participation of females are not praise worthy in some of the states like Arunachal Pradesh, Nagaland, Sikkim, Mizoram. Amongstr the professional Courses, the female, in general want to take the course. Education, Law and to some extent in Engineering and Medical Courses.

It is remarkable to note that the percentage of female

Table 12.2: Percentage Distribution of Female Students (Professional Education) in different Sections (Engineering, Medicine, Law and Others) in the States of NER, 2000-01

	Education	Engineering	medicine	Law	Others	Total
A.P.	33.02	13.54	---	--	--	15.50
Assam	46.33	18.93	36.12	35.34	34.49	31.50
Manipur	62.74	20.16	30.28	29.89	34.75	33.70
Meghalaya	58.06	12.50	43.75	48.37	40.00	39.34
Mizoram	40.00	--	--	23.14	---	42.29
Nagaland	54.38	--	---	24.58	34.43	37.12
Sikkim	52.17	16.80	---	53.85	---	26.68
Tripura	32.35	35.46	11.76	41.01	46.05	37.39
INDIA	51.21	21.50	43.98	19.97	28.64	28.69

participation are observed in Engineering Courses in the states of Tripura (19.15 p.c.), Sikkim (12.25 p.c.) and Arunachal Pradesh (12.18 p.c.)while in Assam (11.01 p.c.), Manipur (10.85 p.c.) and in Meghalaya (24.65 p.c.), the maximum percentage is observed in Law Course.

Table 12.4 shows the percentage distribution of arrested female to male persons in connection with different types of Crimes.

It is observed that the percentage of female to male in the states of NER is only 1.77 p.c. which is far below than the all -India level (5.72 p.c.). However, the highest percentage is observed in the State of Sikkim (4.85 p.c.) followed by Manipur (4.02 p.c.) and Nagaland (3.29 p.c.) while lowest percentage is observed in case of Arunachal Pradesh (1.47 p.c.).

Manipur and Mizoram are the States where the percentage of arrested female to male are assumed to be the highest in connection with Culpable Homicide not amounting murder (16.67 p.c.). In connection with Kidnapping (33.33 p.c.) and Cheating (14.29 p.c.), the State of Mizoram is the leader amongst the states of NER. In case of Burglary, the highest percentage is observed in the State of Tripura (8.51 p.c.) while in connection with the Theft and Riots, Manipur stands at the top with 7.41 p.c. and 5.15 p.c. amongst the states of NER.

The percentage of arrested female to male in connection with Rape case assumed to be highest in the states of Sikim (27.27 p.c.) followed by Mizoram (3.23 p.c.) as per the secondary data (published by the Govt. of India) are available so far as the States of NER are concerned. In Assam it is only 0.43 p.c.

Considering all the states of NER as a whole, the percentage of arrested female to male are assumed to be 3.93 p.c. in connection with Kidnapping, 0.59 p.c. in Burgalary, 1.42 p.c. in Theft, 1.63 p.c. in Riots and 2.52 p.c. in connection with cheating. It is to be noted here that all these percentages (NER) are below the all India level. The respective percentages in case of all India level are 5.13 p.c., 1.58, 2.69, 5.52 and 3.59 p.c.

The table 12.5 shows the percentage distribution of female

Table 12.3: Percentage Distribution of Female Students (Professional Education) out of Total Women Students in different Sections (Engineering, Medicine, Law and Others) in the States of NER, 2000-01

	Education	Engineering	medicine	Agriculture	Veterinary	Law	Others	Total
A.P.	3.32	12.18	---	--	--	--	--	15.50
Assam	7.41	2..52	6.14	1.87	1.34	11.01	1.21	31.50
Manipur	10.18	4.95	1.68	3.55	1.05	10.85	1.44	33.70
Meghalaya	7.18	1.99	2.33	0.73	--	24.65	2.46	39.34
Mizoram	7.63	--	20.83	--	--	13.83	--	42.29
Nagaland	16.16	--	--	12.88	--	8.08	--	37.12
Sikkim	4.74	12.25	--	--	--	9.68	--	26.68
Tripura	3.78	19.15	0.23	--	--	6.54	7.68	37.39
INDIA	4.13	9.16	8.54	0.65	0.21	3.94	2.06	28.69

main workers in the States of NER. It shows that except Assam (6.7 p.c.) all the states of NER are above the all India level (8.1 p.c.). It is also important to note that the State of Assam is below the all India level in both the Primary sector (12.3 p.c.) and in Secondary sector (11.5 p.c.). Considering the secondary sector, it is observed that the percentage of female workers in all the states of NER, except in Manipur (25.9 p.c.), are below the all India level (24.9 p.c.). In case of Tertiary sector, the States of Manipur (28.6 p.c) and Mizoram (43.44 p.c.) are below the all India level (52.4 p.c.).

The table 12.6 shows the number of female persons took part in the political decision making bodies like Assam that is in Legislative Assembly Election the percentage of female contestants are being increasing gradually ranges from 2.52 % (in 1985) to 6.92% (in 2006). The percentage of no. of females wining is also increasing steadily which ranges from 10.0% (in 1991) to 18.87% (2001). However, in the current year the percentage decreased to 18.84%.

The percentage of females took part in the Legislative Assembly Election of Tripura are also being increasing gradually ranges from 1.86 % (in 1977) to 5.64 % (in 1983). The percentage of no. of females wining is also increasing steadily which ranges from 1.67% (in 1977) to 6.67% (1983). These proportions are further increased in the year 2003.

Institutional Support Measures

From women's problem to women's issues and finally to women's perspectives, there has been a whole reshaping of paradigms of human development. Considering the new concept of Human Development several remedial measures had been taken by the Goverment of India and various state governments to remove the gender discrimination. Several institutions expressed deep concern over the rights and status of women all over the world. Although the principle of gender equality has been basic to Indian thinking over a century, concretely the new constitution of India, adopted in 1950 granted the status of equality to women and imposed a fundamental duty

Table 12.4 : Percentage Distribution of Females with respect to Male Arrested under Different Crimes in the States of NER, 2001

	Crime	Murder	Culpable Homocide	Rape	Kidnapping	Burglary	Theft	Riot	cheating
A.P.	1.47	4.12	--	--	2.06	1.39	0.76	--	4.55
Assam	1.54	2.44	--	0.43	4.42	0.07	1.40	1.54	0.71
Manipur	4.02	--	16.67	--	3.95	--	7.41	5.15	3.23
Meghalaya	1.61	5.71	--	--	4.26	--	1.26	--	5.26
Mizoram	2.57	--	16.67	3.23	33.33	0.31	0.76	--	14.29
Nagaland	3.39	--	--	27.27	--	1.55	4.08	--	10.34
Sikkim	4.85	3.57	--	--	--	--	2.47	--	--
Tripura	3.16	1,.69	--	--	--	8.51	0.40	3.34	9.38
NER	1.77	2.45	--	--	3.93	0.59	1.42	1.63	2.52
INDIA	5.72	4.78	1.90	2.48	5.13	1.58	2.69	5.52	3.59

Table 12.5: Percentage Distribution of Females Main Workers (URBAN) in the States of NER

	Main Workers	Primary Sector	Secondary sector	Tertiary Sector
A.P.	11.7	22.5	10.7	76.3
Assam	6.7	12.3	11.5	76.3
Manipur	20.8	45.6	25.9	28.6
Meghalaya	16.1	11.81	5.42	82.77
Mizoram	27.8	52.49	4.07	43.44
Nagaland	12.0	34.1	7.8	58.1
Sikkim				
Tripura	8.7	4.3	6.9	88.70
INDIA	8.1	22.8	24.9	52.4

Table 12.6: Total Number of Females contested in Assembly Election in Assam in different Years

	Total No of Contestants	No. of Females Contested	No. of Wining Seats by Female
1985	1153	29 (2.52 %)	4 (13.79%)
1991	1657	50 (3.02 %)	5 (10%)
1996	1228	45 (3. 66 %)	7 (15.56%)
2001	907	53 (5.84 %)	10 (18.87 %)
2006	997	69 (6.92 %)	13 (18.84 %)

on every citizen to renounce practices derogatory to the dignity of women.

Following the tradition, the Govt. of India in 1971 appointed a Committee on the Status of Women in India (CSWI) to examine all questions relating to the rights and status of women in the context of changing social and economic conditions in the country. The committee comprised of some very eminent representatives of the women's movement, who raised the basic questions about the socialization processes inherent in a hierarchal society, about the resource, power and asset distribution patterns and about diverse cultural values of this country. The report also stressed the need for special measures to transform the de-jure equality guaranteed by India's constitution and legal edifice into de-facto equality.

A significant outcome of these policies debates in the Seventies was a seed in recognition from securing women as targets of welfare policies in the social sector to regarding them as critical groups for development. This recognition was reflected in the Sixth Five Year Plan (1980-1985). A chapter on women and Development, for the first time, included in India's Planning history. The plan conceived of a multi-pronged strategy as essential for women's development. The strategies were like employment and economic independence, education, access to health care, support services to meet the immediate gender needs of women and the creation of an enabling policy, institutional and legal environment.

In India, the search for an organizational structure to co-ordinate efforts towards gender equality had commenced right after independence and the concept of national machinery has been evolving ever since. A separate department of Women and Child Development was set up in 1985 under the newly created Ministry of Human Resource Development. The decade since Nairobi Conference has seen the growth of new institutions to interact and add to the network that today comprises India's National Machinery[3].

The country has taken big strides in the first half of the 20th century towards elimination of natural calamities like famine and fighting communicable diseases that took a heavy toll of life. The development of health facilities and establishment of Primary Health centers in rural areas provided the much needed health services. Family Welfare Programme was also launched to check population growth. Government took a number of steps to improve the health status of vulnerable groups, like women. A major initiative was the launching of the Integrated Child Development Services Scheme (ICDS) in 1975-76. By September, 1993, 16.3 million children and 3.2 million mothers were benefiting from it. It has had a significant impact on the nutrition and health status of women. The cumulative impact of all these measures has been to reduce mortality rates. Female mortality has come down from 12.3 during 1980-82 to 9.8 during 1981-91, while infant mortality has come down from 110 in 1981 to 79 in 1992. Female life expectancy has risen fast to overtake that males.

Traditionally, girls in India are married at a very young age, often before attaining puberty. However, the mean age at marriage has been rising significantly and was 19.5 years in 1991 as compared to 18.3 years in 1981. Reduction in fertility is also at a relatively slow pace.

Despite intensive efforts to improve literacy, it is low. The sex differentials are very pronounced. While the male literacy rate in 2001 was 75.85 p.c., female literacy rate was 22 p.c. lower at 54.16 p.c. Rural- urban and Regional disparities continue to be wide vis-à-vis women's literacy.

Girls enrolment in schools has greatly increased at all levels. The percentage of girls in total enrolment has also improved. Though school enrolment ratios have been rising, the problem has been that of high drop out rates among girls.

Employment of women is an index of their economic status. The work participation rate of females has risen steadily from 14.22 p.c. in 1971 to 19.67 p.c. in 1981 and to 22.27 p.c. in 1991. During the 1991 census, conscious efforts were made to count women workers more completely and remove their invisibility. Out of the 22.27 p.c. female work participation in 1991, main workers contributed 16.03 p.c. sand marginal workers 6.24 p.c. It is significant to point out that women constituted 90 p.c. of the total marginal workers. Of the total employment of women, the organized sector employment formed only 4 p.c. A matter concern is the unemployment rates for female workers in recent years. The rate of unemployment is more significant for urban females at 4.7 p.c. compared to 0.3 p.c. for rural females.

Although women have a high life expectancy over men in different age groups like, in age group 40, life expectancy is 34 years over 30.9 years ; in age group 50, it is 25.3 over 22.7; in age group 60, it is 17.7 years over 15.7 years and in age group 70, it is 11.6 years over 10.3 years in the country while for the same age group the figures are observed in Assam (one of the States of NER) the respective figures are 30.7 years over 28.3 years, 22.4 over 20.3, 15.5 over13.8 and 10.1 years over 8.9 years respectively which are lower than all India level. The same trend is observed in the lower age group like at birth, age group 10 years, age group 20 and age group 30 years.

The literacy movement have sought to respond to the needs of the people at grassroots. The decadal growth rate of female literacy in India has shown an increase of 13.67 percentage points during the period 1991 to 2001.The same tend has also been observed in the states of NER which ranges from 7.17 (Nagaland) to 15.76 (Tripura).

The 2001 census counted 495.7 million females against a total population of 1027 million, with sex ratio of 933 and percentage of population in the age group 0 – 6 years is 15.42 p.c. while percentage of female population in this age group is 15.36 p.c.

In 2001, age structure of female population has shown a shift from the very high proportion of children into a higher proportion of adults in the working age group. This pattern of change is similar for both males and females.

It is observed that Primary School Enrolment Ratio, 1995-1999 (NET) is 74: 64 for Male : female. The Secondary School Entrants Ratio, 1995-97 (Gross) is 59 : 39 for male: female. With an average 91 p.c. literacy, Kerala tops the list among the States of India. The only State to have a female to male ratio of 1058 : 1000 (Sex Ratio). It also registered the lowest population growth rate of only 9.42 p.c.

However government has taken several initiatives to improve the status of women. Some of the important initiatives may be highlighted as :

The National Perspective Plan (1988-2000) is a set of recommendations aimed at the welfare and development of women, guided by the principles relevant to the development process. While some recommendations are in the process of implementation, others are being processed for acceptance "SHRAMSHAKTI" (1988) – The report of the National Commission for Self Employed Women and Women in the Informal Sector, examined all related issues concerning women work force in the informal sector and made valuable recommendations for improving their status.

The National Plan of Action for the Girl Child (1991-2000) was formulated for the SAARC decade of the girl-child and built upon a strategy of ensuring survival protection and development, with a special focus on the adolescent girl-child. The National Expert Committee on Women Prisoners (1986) studied the conditions of women prisoners in the criminal correctional justice system and made a series of recommendations suggesting legislation, custodial, correctional and prison reforms relating to women prisoners. Their implementation is being monitored by the National Commission for Women. The National Nutrition Policy (1993) suggests short term and long term measures necessary to improve the nutritional status of the country, especially women and children. It is in the process of operationalisation.

The 72nd and 73rd constitutional Amendment Acts of 1993 mark historic events in the advancement of Indian women as they ensure them 1/3 of the total seats and positions of chairpersons in the rural and urban elected bodies. About 1 million women were estimated to emerge as leaders/ decision makers as grass - roots levels; of these 75000 would be Chairpersons in the rural areas.

The National Commission for Women, set up in 1992, has a mandate to study and monitor all matters relating to the Constitutional and legal safeguards provided for women, reviewing existing legislations, suggest amendments and look into complaints involving deprivation of the rights of women. Similar Commissions are also being set up in the States.

A special cell monitors 27 beneficiary schemes which are women-specific and women related to report directly to the

Prime Minister's Office. It also monitors indicators relating to 'Equality of Women' in the identified priority areas, under the 20 point programme.

The Women's movement in India gave birth to National Commission for Women in 1992 after passing of the National Commission for Women Act in August, 1990. Thereafter the Assam Govt. also promulgated an ordinance for constitution of the State Commission in November, 1993. This prompted the State Government to pass the Act of Assam State Commission for Women in January, 1994. This is a statutory body under the State Act which strives to achieve equity, equality and justice. It provides a platform for realizing the expectation of millions of women in the State and gives them an opportunity to work hand in hand and shoulder to shoulder with the men in the developmental process of the State. The Commission has worked relentlessly since its inception towards this cherished goal-equity, equality and justice for the women folk of the state.

Some of the statutory functions of the Commission and important areas of work are highlighted below :

- To investigate and examine all matters relating to the safe guards provided for women under the constitution and other laws.
- To present to the State Govt. annually and at such other times as the Commission may deem fit, reports upon the working of those safeguards.
- To make such reports, recommendations for effective implementation of those safeguards for improving the conditions of women by the State.
- To take up the cause of violation of the provisions of the constitution and other laws relating to women with the appropriate authorities.
- To give counseling and assistance to women victims of atrocities and women in distress in the State.
- To pursue gender justice through intervention in cases of violation of equality in laws, denial of opportunity

and deprivation of women's rights.

- To undertake promotional and educational research so as to suggest ways of ensuring due representation of women in all spheres and identify factors responsible for impeding their advancement.
- To call for special studies or investigations into specific problems relating to women..
- To look into complaints and take suo-moto notice of matters relating to deprivation of women's rights, non-implementation of laws relating to protection of women, non-compliance of policy decisions, guidelines or instructions ensuring welfare and providing relief to women.

The commission emphasizes and impresses upon the Govt. the importance and necessity of implementation of the recommendations of the Assam State Commission for Women have been incorporated in the first (1994-95) and second (1995-96) annual reports of the Commission and forwarded to the State Government for implementation to remove and control various social evils affecting the women in the society. Some of the important recommendations of the Commission are :

- A forum of National Commission for Women and State Women Commission may be set up for co-ordination of activities and net working in areas of common interest.
- The Commission recommended that the Gauhati University should immediately start the Faculty of Sociology and simultaneously open a department of Sociology in the affiliated colleges under the University of Gauhati.
- Commission recommended 30% reservation for women in all the University Courts.
- A joint conference of Women's Commission, Women's Development Corporation and Departments of Women Welfare should be held to consider issues of common interest to women and evolve integrated strategies.

- The Commission recommended that there should be strong condemnation by Women's Organisation against violence.
- The Commission held that unemployment is a root cause of terrorism. To tackle the problems of unemployment rapid industrialization and industrial development was recommended.
- The Legal Advisory Committee of the State Women Commission recommended recruitment of about 50 Lady Constables and 25 Assistant Sub-Inspectors of Police and suggested that Women Task Force should be attached to each Police Station for attending to Women related criminal offences.
- The Commission may hold discussion with NGOs, MPs and M.L.As from time to time on issues of women's interest.
- The Commission make valuable suggestions on proposed Indian Prisons Bill, 1997 for ensuring safe and secured prison life for women prisoners. The recommendations also relate to improved sanitation, health and hygiene which is far from satisfactory particularly in women enclosures of the jail. The Commission also recommended for minimum training for all prison staff for improvement of prison administration. Vocational training for the women prisoners and improved care and after- care services for the women prisoners were emphasized. It was suggested that Review Committee of the prisons must include women experts and social workers and it was also suggested that prison discipline should be enforced through human approach.
- A list of experts in different areas of women's concern may be prepared both at all India level and State level.
- Small Scale Cottage Industries should be developed for creation of employment opportunities.
- In order to check the growing menace of prostitution in the State Cities, the Commission recommended that

- (a) S.P. City will prepare a list of beauty parlours, possessing license of Municipality Corporations.
- (b) Beauty Parlour Proprietors will also furnish the names of parlour girls to the police authority and municipality authority.
- (c) the Commission suggested that such girls and women who are forcibly engaged in the profession should be rescued immediately and provided with an opportunity to lead an honest and respectable life with gainful economic rehabilitation being trained on vocations and trades suitable to their qualifications, aptitude and other back grounds.

But till today any action taken by the government on the recommendations of the commission is not known.

In the year 1994, the Commission in its meeting expressed serious concern over the victim women of Assam and decided to organize seminar on " Role of Women in Preventing Terrorism and Violation of Human Rights in the Present day Society" and workshop on "Immoral Traffic, Women and Child Prostitution-A Social Menace and its Remedy". They also proposed for constitution of a committee for socio-economic development of women with stress for economic development of the women to assert and establish their position in the society. They visited all the districts of Assam as part of their Awareness Programme and observed 24th November, 1996 as Women's Day during the "Quami Ekta Week". They initiated Mahila Lok Adalat held at Guwahati on 16.03.1997 to finalise the cases relating to women of Assam.

A workshop on "Combating Gender Violence and Atrocities against women" was organised by the National Institute of Public Cooperation and Child Development (NIPCCD) through Tata Institute of Social Sciences at Mumbai on 21-23 October 2001.

As part of the activities of the Women's Empowerment Year, the Department of Women & Child Development sponsored a visit of 30 girls from Madhya Pradesh to visit Nathula Check-post on Indo-China Border in Sikkim to tie Rakhi's to the soldiers on Raksha Bandhan.

Arunachal Pradesh and Assam organised seminars/ workshops on gender sensitisation, meetings of women's groups/ Mahila Mandals, etc. to generate awareness of their rights. Further, District level committees were formed to monitor and take steps to expedite the disposal of cases of atrocities against women at all stages.

Mizoram launched WEY in a special function, which was graced by the Minister of Social Welfare Department. Three female Padmashree awardees were also awarded in appreciation of their contribution. Seminar on legal safeguards for women, Gender Sensitisation workshop on Adolescent Girls Scheme were also organized.

Meghalaya also set up Help lines and Complaints Committees for prevention of sexual harassment of women. A year long plan of action was chalked out for celebrating the Women's Empowerment Year. Further, State/District level committees were constituted to prevent atrocities against women.

Tripura observed the International Women's Week in the State by organizing workshops, seminars at State and Block level. Awareness camp was also arranged in slum areas which was inaugurated by the Minister of Social Welfare and Social Education, Government of Tripura

Conclusion and Suggestion

Human Development has moved to the center of the Global Development Debate. The objective of development is that all people can enjoy long, healthy and creative lives. It is for all practical purposes a synonym of gender equity and equality. It is important to recognize that discourses on planning have not considered women as part of the complexity called " Development Structures". At no stage of formulation or implementation of National Development Plan were their interests adequately reflected and in no development plan the women have achieved equality in allocation of resources or investment targets. Although in the 1980's the needs and interests of women began to be partially recognized, out of 96 countries surveyed by the Un International Research and Training Institute for the advancement of women, in only 6 countries women issues were accorded a place in the text of the development plan. Thus, human development, gender equity and gender equality still remain distant goals.

From the aforesaid discussions, it is clear that the gender issues have never been arrested by the Indian Planners and Policy makers in general and the Planners and policy makers of NER in particular. Further, it is to be noted that although Kerala, Himachal Pradesh, and Tamil Nadu like states have adopted the gender issues as key to the process of Human Development, the policy makers of the states of NER had never paid their attention towards this issue.

Considering the indicators used in the present study, it confirms the fact that gender issues are intertwined with the issue of Human Development for which the states of NER are lagging behind and the women of NER are still poorest of the poor despite of the favourable social customs and tradition.

Hence, following suggestions may be given for the improvement of the status of women in the states of NER and the same may be applied in other regions too.

- It is a general feeling that women participation in public life and decision making process has a significant impact on Indian democracy and development. However, merely increasing representation of women may not lead to greater promotion of women's interest. Nevertheless, number should be large at crucial level for significant and effective exercise of power. But the experience tells that most of the women representatives in rural and urban local bodies are guided by their husband, male relatives or in-laws. Hence, women should also be equipped through suitable means to shoulder these responsibilities so that intention of women's empowerment to be realized and real education is the only solution for this.

- Policies must take cognizance of the needs, problems and choices of women-.so different from those of men- and incorporate this fact in the design of programmes or schemes.
- Improved governance through the promotion of greater participation of women in plans/ programmes is essential, if benefits for women are to actually reach them.
- Historically, in the North Cachar Hills of Nagaland, Gudiallo, affectionately called "Rani", became famous for her role in the Civil Disobedience Movement during freedom struggle in India. She got. involved in very early age of 13, inspired by her male causin "Jadonang" who was active in mobilizing the villagers in Manipur. In 1931-32, Gudiallo led " No Tax" campaign and villagers stopped paying the compulsory levies on portage and started refusing to work as forced labour. At present, in NER, the war against environmental degradation is fought mainly by the Adibasis or sons and daughters of nature. The main stream government of Independent India does not realize that our country is once again getting colonized by the world market forces. Powerful women writers like Arundhati Roy are trudging the "women only" field and taking up the cause of humanism or universal human rights much more forcefully than men. Women are making men realize that their good lies in women's good and that women's good lies in the entire humanity. Thus, both men and women are complementary to each other not only in household activities but also in other fields. That is why Human Development Index in the states of NER should contain the women development as well.
- The last episode in our parliament regarding reservation of women in both the house of parliament and in the State Legislative Assemblies had not only shocked the women folk but also the policy makers and planners of our country. If this trend will continue then women empowerment can not be realized in India and

the dream of our leaders to make India a developed country by adopting LPG can never be fulfilled. Hence, irrespective of party affiliation, all the leaders should come forward for amending the constitution so that women can participate in the political process of the country.

- The tendency in our society to keep male workers in industry and other organizations, lack of confidence on women should be avoided at all cost in the present era of globalization. In order to provide women, justice in political and economic fields the society should stop all kinds of gender based social injustice and to create an atmosphere of equality where women can breath, freedom and justice in its true form. In this respect, apathy towards girl child, removal of illiteracy among women folk, co-operation of husband and male family members for upbringing children if women are employed, encouragement to girls for all kinds of vocational, technical and professional education as per the present needs and inculcating the values of gender equality and gender justice through the syllabuses of schools, colleges and universities etc. will no doubt be regarded as solution for the development of women in general and Humanity in particular.
- One must agree with **Binayak Roy (2001)** that the women's movement despite of some successes is far from achieving many of its objectives, including equity and empowerment. In an uneven global political, economic and social environment there can not be one strategy for all countries as aspects of gender issues are complex and deep rooted in their social structures. A globalised economy requires states and government to follow internationally accepted governance principles which focuses on creation of a strong civil society. This includes international covenants and instruments covering both economic and non-economic issues and equality of sexes and privileges confirmed by the state (World Bank 1994). Signatories to these instruments and covenants feel obliged to comply with them. Hence a new approach to be followed by the leaders of women's movement to

set their agenda and women's issues can be sensitized in a non-threatening way by making coalition with men and removing the rural –urban disparity.

- In Handloom Sector women contribute a considerable segment of the total workforce. Thus special attention should be paid to ensure that a large number of women artisans get benefit in all the development schemes such as training, marketing related award, national awards exhibitions etc.
- It should be focused on qualifying the women's substantial labour contributions not just to crop production in rural areas, but also to the often invisible activities such as tending to live stock, processing food, and weaving clothes in Assam, Manipur etc. These latter activities account for as much as two-thirds of the labour time of women, a fact not often recognized by most policy makers. As in other parts of India, women are paid lower wages than their male counterparts and suffer a greater degree of seasonality in paid work.

Further, it is to be quantified the extent of say that women exercise in various decisions and it is suggested that while women do make important decisions regarding crop production, they have very little say in financial matters.

- To conclude the study it can be said that the gender issues are closely related with the human development of the country and the states of NER should consider it seriously in order to keep a pace with the modern world and other regions of the country. The nature has made the mothers as creator and the creatures should try to nurse them otherwise the day will come when the whole creation will be destroyed.

Note

1. [page 17 : INDICATORS OF HUMAN DEVELOPMENT AND HUMAN DEVELOPMENT REPORTS in India : Democracy and Development, MPS-003, Book-2, Indira Gandhi National Open University School of Social

Science.]

2. Easter Boserup's Work, Women's Role in Economic Development.
3. 4th World Conference on Women, Beijing, 1995 Country Paper- India (A DRAFT), Department of Women and Child Development, Govt. of India, 1994.

Source

1. STATISTICAL ABSTRACT INDIA 2003, CSO., Ministry of Statistics and Programme Implementation, Govt. of India, New Delhi.
2. CENSUS OF INDIA, 2001 : Population Policy of India – Population And Progress In Global Perspective, J. C. Aggarwal.

References

1. Das, D. and M. Pathak (2004) : "Women Consumer Against Malpractices Prevailing in the Market" in Food Security and the Public Distribution System Today : Failures and Success (eds) Amalesh Banerjee.
2. Maxine Molyneux (1998): "Analysing Women's Movements" in Cecile Jackson and Ruth Pearson (eds), Feminist Vision of Development, London, R outledge.
3. Pradhan B.C. and P. C. Dutta (2003) : "Higher Education: A Gap Between Theory and Practice in North East India", Proceedings of the National Seminar on Transition in NER of India S.S. College, Hailakandi
4. Roy. B. (2001) : "Gender Issues, the Women's Movement and the Indian Ocean Rim Countries" in Human Rersources and Gender Issues in Poverty Eradication (eds) Rabin Ghose, Rony Gabby, Abu Siddique, Atlantic Publishers and Distributors.
5. Roy, C.H.H. (1991) : "Rural Society and Agricultural Development in course of Industrialization : Case of India",

Economic and Political Weekly, 24 (11, 12)

6. Roy, K.C. and Tisdell,C.A. and Sen R.K. (1992) : "Economic Development and Environment- A Case Study of India, Calcutta", Oxford University Press.
7. Roy, K.C. and Clark, C. (1994) : "Technological Change and Rural Development in Poor Countries: neglected Issues, Oxford University Press, New Delhi.
8. Roy, K.C. and Tisdell, C.A. (1996) : "Women in South Asia with Particular Reference to India" in Economic Development and Women in the World Community (eds.) Roy, K.C. and Tisdell, C.A and Blomquist H.D., C.T. and London; Praeger.
9. Sen Amartya (2000) : *Development as Freedom*, Oxford University Press, New Delhi.
10. Theron Schalk.W. (2001) : "Poverty and Inequality and the Eradication there of" in Human Resources and Gender Issues in Poverty Eradication (eds) Rabin Ghose, Rony Gabby, Abu Siddique, Atlantic Publishers and Distributors.
11. UNDP, Human Development Reports (Oxford University Press, 1990-2003).

GLOBALISATION, GROWTH AND INEQUALITY IN NORTH EAST INDIA

GLOBALISATION, GROWTH AND INEQUALITY IN NORTH EAST INDIA

(In 2 Volumes)

(Volume-2)

Paritosh Chandra Dutta
and
Ram Krishna Mandal

KALPAZ

Globalisation, Growth and Inequality in North East India

Rs. 1800 (Set)

ISBN: 978-81-7835-876-5 (Set)
ISBN: 978-81-7835-878-9 (Vol. 2)

Published in 2011 in India by
Kalpaz Publications
C-30 Satyawati Nagar, Delhi-110052
E-mail: kalpaz@hotmail.com
Phone : 9212729499

Leser Type Setting by : Square Vision, Delhi
Printed at : Chawla Offset Printers, Delhi

Contents

13. Demographic Changes, Racial and Linguistic Conflicts in Assam of North Eastern Region 359

14. Population Growth and Development in North Eastern Region of India 391

15. Population Dynamics and Socio-Economic Scenario in North Eastern Region 431

16. Impact of Socio-Economic Development with Special Reference to The Problems of Population Growth and Urbanisation 453

17. Economic Development and Environmental Pollution in India with Special Reference to North East Region 497

SECTION-IV: ENVIRONMENTAL DEGRADATION

18. Biodiversity: A Threat Perception to Sustainable Development 537

19. Flora and Fauna: Economic Viability and Sustainability 597

SECTION-V: AGRICULTURAL SCENARIO

20. Changing Agricultural Scenario in North East India 647

21. Impact of Shifting Cultivation on Environment in NER and Its Sustainability 675

Index 691

13

Demographic Changes, Racial and Linguistic Conflicts in Assam of North Eastern Region

Introduction

One of the most debatable topics in the Indian Sub-Continent is increasing tension and turmoil in north-east India arising out of ethnic crisis among the people of the region. The geographical situation in north eastern region of India (NER) has given the region its special position and importance as the region is surrounded by the foreign countries like China, Burma, Bhutan and Bangladesh. Situated in the north-east corner of India, popularly known as the CHICKEN NECK, the NER is like a sentinel of the country and most sensitive as the states of NER have been suffering a state of insecurity since time of independence. It is a meeting ground of the people with different cultures, religions, languages etc. The region is unique in the sense that the migration to the region was mainly from the east whereas migration in the rest of India were from the west to the east. Immigration or influx of foreign nationals into the region is not a recent phenomenon but has a long historical past. The entire North Eastern Region inhabited by numerous ethnic and linguistic groups have grievances, economic, political, cultural and administrative. Planning based on the flow of quantum of money and achievements measured in terms of expenditures incurred remains a matter of criticism by the politicians as well as by the economists. It is the apathy, indifference and neglect by New Delhi which has produced frustration among the growing middle class of people of different ethnic groups. Too much oppression on a particular minority group will help fragmentation with powers hostile to India. The Centre should act with prudence to avert greater crisis. No linguistic or ethnic group should be haunted by a sense of alienation. A very significant fact about the region is the assimilation of Indo-Aryan and Mongolian cultures. However, the present day ethnic composition is something different from the region of the past.

The whole population of NER can be divided into two broad racial types like –(i) the Caucasoid and (ii) Mongoloid as it is not easy to determine the real ethnic affinities of the population of the region. Broadly speaking, scheduled tribe population in the hills as well as in the plains have mongoloid features and the Aryan speaking people in the plains have mainly Caucasoid features. However, in the western side of the plains, there is a blend of Caucasoid and Mongoloid features. The Caucasoid type is represented by the cast Hindus, the Muslims and some professionals.

The Indo-Mongoloids can be identified by yellow brown colour of the skin, stretched or flat wave and coarse hair of the head. The broad face has scanty hair growth, the body hairs are also scanty. After assimilation, most of these communities have not lost their tribal characteristics. The major tribes of the region are – Adi, Aka, Apatani, Bongro, Hill Miri, Khamti, Miji, Mishing, Nishi, Nocte, Sherderphen, Singhpho, Sulung, Tagin, Wangcho, Ashinh, Galong, Minyong, Padam, Tangsa etc in Arunachal Pradesh, Boro-Kachari, Chutya, Dimasa, Karbi, Lalung, Mech, Mishing, Rabha etc. in Assam, Garo, Hajon, Khasi, Jaintia in Meghalaya, Hmar, Mizo, Pawi-Lakhar, Ralte, Kuki, Riang, Lusai etc. in Mizoram, Aimol, Anal, Chiru, Chothe, Hmar, Kabui, Khairao, Maram, Maring, Paite, Purum, Thangkhul, Thadou, Vaithei, Mao, Gangte, Kacha Naga etc. in Manipur Angami, Ao, Chang, Dimasa, Kuki, Konyak, Lhota, Naga tribes, Phom, Rengma, Sena etc. in Nagaland and Chakma, Hollam, Magh, Riang, Noatia, Tripuri, Jaintia, Kuki, Lushai etc., in Tripura. Thus, NER presents a unique picture of multi-ethnic region in India. But since the advent of the 20th century there had been ethnic crisis in the region and due to which the society of the region is in a state of tension and turmoil till the advent of the present century. Sometimes these social tensions pose a serious threat to the unity and integrity of the region by changing its geography and history. Demands have been raised in different ways for autonomy, separate state-hood and secession from the Indian Union and no viable solution to the problems appears to be insight. North-eastern Region of India is the home to peoples of diverse ethnic communities (within as well as between the States) who, while sharing many common historical experiences and cultural orientations follow different religious, speak varied languages, and live in societies with different political and economic structures.

The political history of Assam is a history of annexation of territories and integration of small states. "M. S. Aney ... said that in India, provinces were formed not on scientific basis nor on linguistic affinity but for administrative convenience and on financial expediency" **(page 287, Political History of Assam, Vol. II).** It is clear from the above that the State of Assam was never a homogeneous unit but a composite one of heterogeneous communities and tribes. 'Without any strong linguistic, cultural, economic or any other kind of affinity, "Assam stands out in all India as a miniature League of Nations'. "Assam, originally, meant the land," conquered and consolidated in 1228 by the Shans. When the British, after occupation, constituted the new Province in 1874, they extended the name to the whole territory that came within its purview. Needless to state that history is a record of the past over which lies the foundation of the present.

From the study of formation of Assamese nationality it would appear that the bulk of the population of Assam is of Mongoloid origin. However, most of these communities through assimilation have lost their tribal characteristics. The two broad categories of castes are the Brahmins and the Koch represents a heterogeneous type. Many people believe that after Hinduisation of different tribes, they were included in the Caste-fold Assamese Society. But, the Rajbanshis claimed themselves that they have separate entity since long past. The Assamese muslims are medium saturated having leptorrhine nose and mesocephalic head. With the recognition of the immigrants muslims as the Na-Asamiya, four groups of Muslims are found like the Syeds, the marjas, the Sheikhs and the Na-Asamiyas.

According to the constitutional Amendment Act of 1976, 14 tribes like Chakma, Dimasa, Cachari, Garo, Hajong, Hmar, Kukitribes, Khasi-Jaintia etc, Lakhar, Man, Mizo, Mikir, Naga, Pawi, Syntheng were scheduled in the autonomous districts of Karbi-Anglong and North Cachar. The 9 tribes scheduled in the plains of Assam are like Burmans in Cachar, Bodo and Bodo-Cachari, Deori, Hojai, Cachari and Sonowal, Lalung, Mech, Miri and Rabha. The Ahoms now occupy special position in respect of distribution in Upper-Assam districts. Originally Thai or Shan speaking Ahoms soon become Hinduised and accepted the Indo-Aryan Language- Assamese.

Although the roots of the social tension in the region are traced to the geographic, demographic and socio-cultural distinctiveness of the region by different scholars, the role of foreign countries, Christian and other missionaries involvement in the ethnic conflict are deliberately ignored with. Further, few attempts have been made to define the term "ethnic" or "ethnicity" by establishing a link with the ethnic conflicts and social tension in the region.

In the border areas of Nagaland and Mizoram, there are Naga and Mizo people speaking their respective Naga and Kuki-Chin languages. Broadly speaking, the population of the plains of Brahmaputra and Barak Valley speak Assamese and Bengali of the Indo-Aryan family. Thus, Assam presents a unique picture of multi-ethnic state of India. But since the advent of 20th century and till now there is a crisis of ethnic identity in the state of Assam. Sometime it posses a serious threat to the unity and integrity of the state by changing the geography of Assam. Due to ethnic conflicts, the geographical boundary of the State has been reduced to such extent that present Assam cannot be identified by the readers of other provinces who have gone through the past history.

In this paper an attempt has been made not only to identify various racial and linguistic groups of Assam but also to examine the causes for the growth of resentment and dissatisfaction among these groups. Finally, attempt has also been made to explain the consequences of such conflicts in the state of Assam resulting in the further decadence of the state. The study, based on statistical data and other secondary sources, has been concluded with some findings and suggestions for the minimization of social tension in the state in particular and the region in general.

The concept 'ethnic' and 'ethnicity' are frequently used today by the politicians, sociologists and academicians. But the terms give the impression of meaning different things to different people and in different contexts. While in American society, ethnic groups are meant for minority groups, but in the expression of ethnic conflict the meaning is totally different. The dictionary meaning of the term' ethnic', is like "of or relating to large group of people closed together according to common traits or customs". Thus, the ethnic group is essentially a culture-based entity. In the sense in which the term 'ethnic' is used by sociologists and social scientists today, it refers to a social group, which consciously shares some aspects of common culture and is defined primarily by descent.

Ethnicity is a new concept in social science. It was first used by David Reedman in 1853 as referred to in the 1972 supplement of the English Oxford Dictionary and subsequently by Cynthia, H. Ennloe and in India by J. Dasgupta. Before 1953 other terms like 'ethnic communities' by Caroline E. Ware in the Encyclopedia of Social Sciences of "Ethno-Centriam" by Edward Byron Reuter in a modern hand book of sociology were used. Since 1953, other terms are used "ethnic Groups" by H.S. Morris in the International Encyclopedia of Social Sciences (1968) and other Writers like MaxWeber and Talcot Parsons; " Primordial attachments" by Clifford Geetz; Communal Group by Daniel Dell and 'minority groups' by Preston Valien.

However, all these terms aim at identifying a particular social group and it becomes difficult when we apply the term ethnicity to the communities of north-east India.

Barth (1969) defined ethnic group as a population which-

(i) is largely biologically self perpetuating,

(ii) shares fundamental cultural values, realized in overt unity is cultural forms,

(iii) has a membership which identified itself, and is identified by others, as constituting a category distinguishable from other categories of the same order.

Glazer (1976) observed that ethnicity is something that is determined by the prevailing socio-cultural and socio-political trends. If awareness about ethnicity was formerly handed down consciously but silently from one generation to another, it has today become a matter of open declaration. Ethnicity, as apart of culture, always had to be taught. One group learns from another picks up its language, its demand, its resentments, its form of organization.

Dutta (1985) mentioned that much of anxiety of the smaller ethnic groups, particularly of the tribals of NER has been associated with the identity crisis which they have been facing due to various economic, social, cultural and political factors. In search for their roots sometimes they have been forced to take the agitational path.

Singh (1982) in his study of the ethnic movements in NER found that the first stage of ethnic movement is to assert the identity around certain social problems and the second stage is to criticize the identity by forming an ethnic association. The third stage is to claim separate administrative arrangement so that the group concerned can preserve their cultural heritage, language etc. The fourth stage is to demand a separate administrative unit comprising the areas where the ethno-cultural groups form a majority.

Thus, the above authors left the questions unanswered that whether after formation of the state or achievement of autonomy, common identity has developed or not and whether any chance of ethnic conflict there or not?

One must realize that north-east is a mini-India. There are more than 75 major population groups and sub groups, speaking approximately 400 languages and dialects, of which there are about 168 in Arunachal Pradesh, 95 in Nagaland, 87 in Manipur, 100 in Tripura and 200 in Assam, Meghalaya and Mizoram (Madhab, J, 1999). Thus, the whole north-eastern India is a place with people of diverse races, cultures, languages and various dialects with different traditions. Besides the heterogeneity of geographical and socio-cultural factors, the more striking view of the North-Eastern scenario is the co-existence of the extreme forms of both tradition and modernity.

Hence, in the context of NER, in general and Assam in particular, ethnic groups may be defined as such minorities socio-cultural groups having common origin and background, searching for their identity and to establish their primordial loyalties like ancestry, religion, language race, culture, custom and tradition. As search for identity of different ethnic groups led conflicts in the region and took the path of violence by creating a social tension, the nature and character of such issues may be discussed under the heads of Religion, Language, Ethnicity etc.

The North eastern Region of India (NER) comprises, at present, seven full fledged States like Arunachal Pradesh, Assam, Manipur, Meghalaya, Mizoram, Nagaland and Tripura poetically called 'seven sisters'. Before independence, the region consisted of one province of Assam, two native states like Manipur and Tripura and one centrally ruled area known as North Eastern Frontier Agency (N.E.F.A.).

The share of population of NER to the total population of India as low as 1.70 per cent in 1901. Since then it has been steadily increasing and reached at nearly 3.75 per cent in the census year of 2001 from 2.84 p.c. in the year 1951.The decadal growth rate of NER is always higher than the all-India level during the period 1951-2001. However, the growth rate of NER is decreased from 41.34 p.c. in 1961 to 22.02 p.c. in the year 2001 while at the same time for India the respective rates are 21.64 and 21.35. during the period rate of growth of population for India is 184 p.c. while for NER it is 275 p.c. **(table -14.1).** The share of migrants from Bangladesh was between slightly more than 70 per cent to slightly more than 87 per cent in pre-independence era. In the post independence era it reached to 94 per cent in 1951. However, the share was around 89 per cent in the census year of 1991 and it again shows an increasing trend after 1991. The phenomenal migration is instrumental in creating not only social tension but also jeopardizing the security of the region.

The total geographical area of NER was 2,55,037 sq. km. At the time of independence. But within a span of 40 years in the post independence period, the region has been splinted several times and yet the region is not free from the threat of further split with the most dominant tribes like Bodos, Karbis etc. The state of Nagaland with an area of 16,579 sq.km. was formed in the year 1963. On 2nd April, 1970, the hill state known as Meghalaya with an area of 22,429 sq. km. was inaugurated by the then Prime Minister of India. The states of Mizoram and Arunachal Pradesh were made as Union Territory in the year 1972. In 1986, Mizoram with an area of 21,087 sq. km. became the full fledged state and Arunachal Pradesh with an area of 83,746 sq. km. became an autonomous state in the year 1987. Thus, at present, out of the total geographical area of NER,the state of Assam occupies only 30.75 per cent while Arunachal Pradesh occupies 32.83 per cent. The other states like Manipur, Meghalaya, Mizoram, Nagaland and Tripura occupy 8.75 per cent, 8.79, 8.27, 6.50 and 4.11 per cent respectively.

Religious Issues

The geographical situation of Assam has given the state its special position and importance situated in the north-east (NER) corner of India and surrounded by four foreign countries like China, Burma, Bhutan and Bangladesh. Assam stands like a sentinel of the country in a most sensitive region. It is a meeting ground of the people with different cultures. At the time of country's independence in 1947, Assam attracted attention of the entire nation for foreign national issue. However, this issue is not a trend developed on the eve of independence, it is as old as British occupation of Assam. The products of the New English Education in Bengal by the end of the 19th century over flown into Assam for livelihood. During this time, the dominance of middle class Bengalees in employment by virtue of their cultural superiority started in Assam. During the years of Muslim league ministry under Sir Mahammed Sadullah and before there was a heavy flow of people from East Bengal. It is possible that the Muslim League ministry encouraged the land-hungry peasants from East Bengal to settle in the fertile plains of Assam out of purely communal considerations but in the name of agricultural development of the State. Before independence, there had always been a latent fear in the Assamese mind of being swamped by the Bengali-speaking people and such suspicious were strengthened when Assam was included in the group "C" category by the Cabinet Mission.

Taking language as an issue, the then leaders of Assam headed by Mr. Gopinath Bordoloi committed a serious blunder in Assam's history as a result of which there was every possibility of Muslim dominance in Assam. The separation of Bengali-speaking district of Sylhet from Assam in 1947 through a referendum known as "Sylhet referendum" greatly helped to calm Assamese fears of being outnumbered by Bengali speaking population but the path for future ethnic conflicts were cleared from that day onwards in Assam.

In 1951 census, the rise in the population of Assamese-speaking people was substantial as the migrated Muslim population adopted Assamese as their language leaving their mother tongue Bengali. Meanwhile, the refugees from East Pakistan poured into the State in their thousands leading to an abnormally high rate of population growth in the State. During that time, the Bengali-speaking population in Barak

Valley districts was in majority. To see the political situation of Assam, they started "Purbanchal" movement, which was suppressed when the plan for 'purbanchal' was rejected by the State Re-organisation Committee of 1954.

Before independence Sir Sadullah bore the responsibility for settling the Muslim infiltrators in Assam and after independence task was given to Mr. Fakruddin Ali Ahmed and Moinul Haque Choudhury. The then Newspapers alleged that Moinul Hoque Choudhury was encouraging muslim communalism in Barak Valley districts as a Pro-pakistani and supporter of "Azad Cachar Party", for which he was detained by the then Deputy Commissioner of Cachar under 'Preventive Detention Act' for providing shelter to the muslim infiltrators from Pakistan[1]. During that time the linguistic nationalism of the Bangalees in Barak Valley was at its peak against the Official Language Bill passed in the Assam Legislative Assembly. Besides, the leaders of the Indian National Congress encouraged Muslim infiltrators into Assam for their vote bank, which was clearly manifested in one of the election meetings in which a leading congressman of Assam expressed " so long as Alis and Coolies are with the congress, we have nothing to fear". Later on, the AGP Government of Assam continued to appease the muslims by making them as their vote bank too. On the other hand, to reduce the Hindu Bengalees into minority in Assam, the government of Assam is still trying to impose upon them the process of assamization. The Bengalees as a race has been subjugated on the language issue in different ways even after independence for which communal riots erupted in different parts of the state at different points of time. However, during the period 1951-1991, the percentage of Hindu population in NER decreased from 65.61 p.c. in 1951 to 60.92 p.c in 1991 while at the same time the percentage of Muslim population increased from 20.88 p.c. to 21.56 p.c. The percentage of Christian population has also been increased from 6.34 p.c. to 12.25 p.c. **(table 14.3).**

It is to be observed, in this context, that every successive government in Assam since independence adopted an attitude that can set one community against another, one race against other etc. i.e. an attitude that can sharpen the divide among people in respect to either religion, race, or language. And by doing so, they might wrest political power but the sharp cleavage, once created, has struck its root deep and even after more than five and half decades of independence the level of backwardness in economy, communication, industrial investment etc. is writ large in the face of the region in general and the state of Assam in particular. Unless homogeneity is achieved in heterogeneity, progress lies distant. The political leaders, cutting across party lines, are, it seems, bent on letting loose and inferno for the people of the state and building a Tajmahal for them out of the public exchequer. Again party in power at the center at present can not be escaped from the accusations as NER is deliberately ignored by the central government so far as the problem of security is concerned though it sanctioned thousand crores of money during the last seven years in connection with insurgency problems in the region. But the problems can not be solved unless the governments try to appropriate the money in a proper way.

Language Isues

Assam is a composite state (truncated four times already) is inhabited by various indigenous ethnic groups and mainly two linguistic groups (Assamese and Bengalees) having Indo-Aryan culture. The number of Bengalee Muslims (neo-Assamese) are far more compared to that of Asssamese Muslims. The entire political power was vested since independence into the hands of the Hindu elite of the Brahmaputra Valley who mustered necessary support from Muslims and other ethnic groups not conscious politically during those hey days. This established the Rhodesian regime in Assam. Prior to the partition of the country, the province of Assam was divided mainly into two regions – Surma Valley and Brahmaputra Valley. In Surma Valley, according to 1931 census report, the Bengali speaking people were 28,48,454 and Assamese speaking people were 2,692. In Brahmaputra valley including N.E.F.A. and Hill

Table 13.1: Percentage Distribution of Bangalee and Assamea Population in Assam: Before and After Independence

	Before Independence			After Independence		
	1911	1921	1931	1951	1961	1971
Assamese :	35.31	33.43	32.32	56.29	57.14	60.89
Bengalees :	26.90	27.60	27.56	19.64	17.60	19.71
Assam (popn):	38.49	46.7	55.61	80.29	108.37	146.25 (population in lakhs)

N.B.: No tabulation on language basis due to war economy in the year 1941.

districts, the Assamese speaking people were 19,77,515 the Bengali speaking population were 10,86,258. Thus 73 years ago, Bengali speaking people in Assam numbered 39,60,712 and Assamese speaking people were 19,77,515. This figure in census report was a great headache to the Assamese leaders headed by Mr. Gopinath Bordoloi and others of Indian National Congress. For the domination of Assamese in the politics of Assam they wanted to separate Sylhet from Assam. They persuaded the Central leadership of Indian National congress as a result of which "Sylhet Referendum" took place. Only three and half Police Stations of Karimganj Sub-division remained in India along with the then Cachar district.

The following table shows the percentage of Assamese and Bengalee -speaking population as recorded in different census.

It transpires from above that the number of Assamese –speaking people in the Brahmaputra Valley of Assam has risen twofold in 20 years – from 19,78,823 in 1931 to 59,65,159 in 1951 (total population being 90,43,707) while Bengali speaking people decreased to 8,14,979 in 1951 from 10,86,258 in 1931. This miracle cannot be explained biologically as human being do not multiply at this rate "All this decline" (i.e. sharp fall of percentage of other languages) according o Mr. R.B. Baghiwala, ..., *the superintendent of Census Operation in Assam,"* has gone to swell the percentage of people speaking Assamese in 1951. Thus, there is a striking increase in the percentage of the people who speak Assamese in 1951 (56.7 p.c.) over those of 1931, which was only 31.4 p.c. while during the same period the percentage of Bengalee speaking people decreased from 26.8 p.c. in 1931 to 16.5 p.c. in 1951. With the solitary exception of Assamese every single language or language group in Assam shows a decline in the percentage of people speaking the same. The figures do not fail to reflect the aggressive linguistic nationalism prevails in Assam.

It can be realized the intensity with which this 'aggressive linguistic nationalism' worked when one will compare between the real and the manipulated population figures from 1951 census onwards. In Brahmaputra Valley, the percentage of Assamese- speaking people increased from 42 p.c in 1931 to 73.1 p.c. in 1951 and it is only 73.3 p.c. in 1961 while at the same time in the same valley, the percentage of Bengale-speaking people decreased to 13.0 p.c. in 1951 from 23.0 p.c. in 1931. It is further decreased to 9.8 p.c. in 1961.

Just after independence, disappointment and resentment overtook the Bengali speaking people of Cachar and considering the linguistic, racial and cultural affinities they wanted to integrate Cachar district with Tripura under the New Scheme of "Purbanchal". When the "State Re-organisation Committee" was set up they supplied the facts and figures in support of it. However, the commission rejected the proposal for which the Bengali-speaking people expressed their resentment. Assam is a multilingual state but on 24th October, 1960, the government of Assam declared Assamese as the sole official language of the state. The people of Cachar district launched a movement of non-violent Satyagraha on 19th May, 1961. As a result of brutal police excess, 1 girl and 10 boys were killed. Cachar Zila Sangram Parishad and Bhasa Andolan Samiti launched a non-violent movement demanding Bengali as the second official language of the State. Three language formula called as "Shastri Formula" was evolved by Sri Lal Bahadur Shastri by which "Assam Official Language Act" was amended so far as to make Bengali as the official language in Barak Valley. In 1972, on 12th June, Academic Council of Gauhati University passed a resolution making Assamese as the sole medium of instruction in all the educational institutions of Assam. Tension mounted again in the Barak Valley of Assam. On 18th June, 1972, Cachar Zila Sangram Parishad lodged a protest against the decision of the Gauhati University. On 28th July, 1972, 'Cachar Bandh' was observed and in continuation of the movement, 'Satyagraha Movement' took place in Nov. 1972 and continued till January, 1973, in phased manner, organized jointly by 'Chatra Yuva Sangram Parishad' and 'Cachar Sangram Parishad' with great dissatisfaction of the leaders of Barak Valley due to step motherly attitude of Assam

Government towards the Bengalees of Barak Valley. The "Union Territory Demand Committee" (UTDC) was formed under the leadership of Paritosh Paul Choudhury. The UTDC organized different types of movements to get Barak Valley enrolled as one of the members of North Eastern Council (NEC) for preserving the language and other interests of the people of the valley. Barak Upatyaka Banga Sahitya O Sanskriti Sammelon (BUBSOSS) started different types of movements after its formation through its first conference held at Silchar in January, 1977 and protested against the strategy followed by the State Government towards Barak Valley. In the year 1980, another student organization named "All Cachar Students' Association" (ACSA) was formed and started movement demanding one central University in Barak Valley. Afterwards its name was changed first as "All Cachar and Karimganj Students' Association" (ACKSA) and then "All Cachar Karimganj and Hailakandi Students' Association" (ACKHSA). In the year 1985, a movement again started under the banner of "Cachar Siksha Sangrakshan Samiti" formed in 1973, to protest against the Article- 6 of historic Assam Accord and for the demand of Central University in the Valley. Fresh tension mounted in the valley when the SEBA circular (No.SEBA/AB/Syllabus/1/85-86-1 dated 28.02.1986) imposed Assamese language in the valley. On 21st July, 1986 there was a police firing on students at Karimganj, as a result of which 2 students were killed[3]. On 4th April, 2001, a memorandum submitted to the Deputy Commissioners of three districts of Barak Valley by the BUBSOSS demanding total implementation of Official Language Act for using Bengali in all official works, in the valley. The very attitude of State government towards the Valley in different forms has not stopped till date. Though the demand for Union Territory is suppressed, it may crop up again and may take violent turn if the harmonious relationship between the people of the valley and their counterparts in the government of Assam will not properly be maintained.

In 1979-80, the anti outsider movement was started by the "All Assam Students Union" (AASU), the largest student organization in the state after the revocation of national emergency in 1977, demanding for deportation of foreigners from the State. In its Sibsagar session of 1979, AASU decided to start peaceful democratic and non-violent Gandhian Movement for fulfillment of their demand, which converted into anti foreign national movement. The targets were both Hindu and Muslim Bengalees and they demanded to abandon 1981 census of the State. This students' movement in the state also involved the non students and general people of the state under the banner of "All Assam Gana Sangram Parishad (AAGSP) which was created by AASU in its Dibrugarh meeting on August 27/28 of 1979. The different phases of movement led by AASU and AAGSP later on supported by all section of people living in Assam except the targets. They decided to boycott the parliamentary election of 1980 as the name of the foreign nationals still in the Voter's List. However, election was conducted at the point of bayonet, which led serious communal holocaust and massacre. In the election to the State Legislative Assembly of 1983, the congress party came back to power in an abnormal situation boycotted by the AASU. The AASU did not recognize the legitimacy of the election and the resultant government. As a result the movement continued and on 14th August, 1985, the 'Assam Accord' was signed and fresh election was declared. The Assam Gana Parishad (AGP) came to the power in the state in the election of 1985. All the front-ranking leaders of AASU became the leaders of AGP but the vital ethnic issue is still in a hanging position. The percentage of Bengali speaking people in Assam was 14.77 p.c. according to 1971 census while the percentage increased to 14.89 p.c. in the year 1991 in the whole of North eastern region. **(table 13.2).**

Before dwelling on the validity of charge(s) leveled against the 'foreigners' viz. the Bengalee Hindus in particular that they do not learn Assamese nor do they mingle with the so called mainstream of Assamese culture, it will be relevant to reproduce the extract from a letter appeared in 'AMRITA', a prestigious news magazine of the 'Amrit Bazar Group' of Calcutta, which devoted its August, 24, 1979 number completely to publish a

Table 13.2: Linguistic Composition of the Population in North East Region (in p.c.)

Language	1971	1991
Assamese	45.63	41.08
Bengali	14.77	14.89
Bodo/Boro	2.73	3.75
Manipuri	0.45	3.52
Khasi		2.79
Tripuri		2.05
Garo		1.76
Lushai / Mizo		1.64
Others		28.52

Source : Census of India, Statement No. 3, Paper 1 of 1997 Language,

Note : 1971 Census Data are for Assam alone which included Mizo hills also

bunch of Assamese stories. "This issue presenting Assamese stories is a milestone in the literary spectacle. He expects more Assamese drama, poems and essays and other important writings. The poems may be in original .... Your bold attempt will definitely strengthen ties between the linguistic groups and remove regionalism. There are only 10 millions of Assamese speaking people as against 100 millions of Bengalees in both Bengals. It is our responsibility also to bring their language and culture to the fore" **(B. Das, Cal-31, Amrita, dated September 14, 1979 translated)**. There were many more letters, voicing the same demand and each congratulating the editor on his bold attempt. He was also requested to publish more on Assamese literature and culture.

But, the AGP government of Assam toed the line of the earlier government and continued to appease the muslims by making them as their vote bank too. On the other hand, to reduce the Hindu Bangalees into minority in Assam, the government of Assam is still trying to impose upon them the process of Assamization. The Bengalees as a race has been subjugated on the language issue in different ways even after independence for which communal riots erupted in different parts of the state at different points of time.

Recently, again communal disturbance started in the Brahmaputra Valley of Assam against Hindi speaking persons, in general and Bihari Population in particular. Recently, for the protection of Hindi speaking people in Assam, the organization named as Non-Tribal Youth Union (NTYU) requested one of the MPs of Bihar to place 11-point Charter of demands before the house of the Parliament.

Another language movement in Barak Valley attracted the attention of the politicians, administrators and others in the state is the conflict between Metei and Bishnupuri groups. In 1962, the "Nikhil Bishnupriya Manipuri Bhasha Parishad" (NBMBP) was formed and placed its demands for the recognition of 'Bishnupriya' as 'Manipuri'. Then the movement was spearheaded by the "Bishnupriya Manipuri Andolan Parishad" through peaceful and democratic means. In 1975, the Information and Broadcasting Ministry declared that broadcasting facilities through All India Radio would be extended to Manipuri Language – both Metei and Bishnupriya. In this respect memorandum submitted on 5th August, 1983 to the then Chief Minister of Assam. On 2nd January, 1990, a memorandum submitted to the then Prime Minister of India jointly by 'Nikhil Bishnupriya Manipuri Mahasabha', 'Nikhil Bishnupriya Manipuri Sahitya Parishad' and 'Bishnupriya Manipuri Samaj Sanstha' headed by Monoranjan Sinha. However, the said language has been implemented as a medium of instruction at the primary stage of education in the Barak Valley vide Govt's notification No. EMI.169/74/pt-III/310 dated Dispur, the 14th November, 1983 and No. EDG.459/86/217 dated Dispur, the 21st July, 1989. One of the main demands is the correction of 1961, 1971 and 1981 figures of this linguistic minority and to record correctly this linguistic minority as Bishnupriya Manipuri. A memorandum submitted by NBMSP to the then President of India in this regard. Tension mounted in Barak Valley when the government of India gave the recognition to the language of Metei group as one of the languages in the 8th schedule of the constitution of

India. Since then and till now the Bishnupriya group have lost their faith on the governments – both central and state and their agitational programmes are going on.

Tribal Issues

In the post independence era, some remarkable ethnic conflicts took place which changed the current of Assam's political history. To safeguard the language, culture, customs etc., the different hill tribes through their organizations and leaders have separate themselves from the mainstream of Assam and got the status of statehood. At present, separate states like Nagaland, Mizoram, Meghalaya, and Arunachal Pradesh have been emerged as separate political entity in this region but the problem of ethnicity is yet to be sorted out.

The demand for a separate state of 'kamata' or 'Koch land' in North Bengal as well as some parts of Assam has taken a violent turn during the last few years, organized by 'Kamatapur Liberation Organization' (KLO), 'Koch Rajbanshi Liberation Organization' (KRLO), 'Koch Rajbanshi Liberation Tiger Force' (KRLTF) and 'Koch Rajbanshi Security Force' (KRSF). This movement has received help and assistance from extremist groups of Assam like the outlawed 'United Liberation Front of Assam' (ULFA), 'Bodo Ultra Groups' etc. the movement originated with a view to protecting their rights and interest in Social, Political, Cultural and Economic spheres. The chief aim of these organizations is to win the right of self – determination of Koch Rajbanshi people in North Bengal as well as the western parts of Assam. As a result of their movement, the areas of Assam worsely affected are Dhubri, Bongaigaon, Goalpara, Kokrajhar and its adjoining areas. According to security sources, the KLO, the KRLO, the KRITF, the KRSF have been receiving training with militant groups of Assam in the dense forests and hilly areas of Assam, Bhutan and Bengal tri-junction. The Koch Rajbanshi's fear is that they would loose their ethnic identity because of the steady influx of illegal Bangladesh nationals through the pores of indo-Bangladesh

International Border of Lower Assam and North Bengal. They swear to restore and regain their lost identity which were established in the 15th century Assam by carving out separate state. They also demanded their Kamatapuri language to be included in the 8th schedule of Indian Constitution and separate T.V. center for them. In this respect they have sent eleven point charter of demands to the Govt. of India and their movements are going on[4].

The plain tribals of Assam can broadly be divided into two groups like –(i) the Bodo group and (ii) the Miri and the Michings. The Bodo and the Miri group belong to Mongolian origin and they are ethnologically different from the rest of the Assamese people. They are the earliest known inhabitants of Assam. From time immemorial they had been maintaining their sovereignty till their last king Tula Ram Senapati died in 1854 A.D. The language spoken by the Bodo group of the plain tribals belong to the Tibeto-Burman group and widely differs from the Assamese language. The Bodo groups of the plain tribals of Assam belong to different religious, some of them Hindus, some Christians and some profess tribal religion. Among the hill tribes of Assam the Dimasa and Garos belong to this Bodo stock. The All Bodo Students' Union (ABSU), A student organization of Bodos has been demanding that Assam must be divided fifty-fifty between the tribals and the non-tribals. The present area of Assam is 78,523 sq. km. and half of it becomes 39,261.5 sq. km. Tribals are getting 25,478.1 sq. km. as Union Territory along with 15,222 sq. km. for Karbi Anglong and N.C. Hills Autonomous State totaling 40,700.1 sq. km. together which is slightly more than 50 per cent and non-tribals will get 37,822.9 sq. km. in the rest of Assam. The areas of Union Territory include the whole of Kokrajhar and Lakhimpur districts on Majuli and Sadia Sub-division, northern parts of Dhubri, Goalpara, Barpeta, Nalbari, Kampur, Darrang and Sonitpur districts. They claimed that they had been the master and ruler of Assam at one time and the present Assamese society is formed by the influx from Kanauj, Mithila, Magadha etc. of the central India in the 13th and 14th century only whereas the Bodos and other tribals are the aboriginal people of Assam. They alleged that the Assam government whether the past or present ones are not the government of the people of Assam but it is merely the government of Assamese people. The government of Assam and the administrators are deadly anti-tribal. No progress tribal people can be achieved under this type of government. As such no expected progress of tribals in the dimension of education, economy, language, culture could be achieved even after more than five and half decades of independence of India. The Assamese people and government are having a deep conspiracy to swallow and to assimilate the people of Assam had their distinct linguistic and cultural heritage and hence Assam should be separated on the basis of language and culture. The tribal people want to enjoy he right to political self-determination and separate State would fulfill their desire[5].

Large scale violence in the districts of Kokrajhar, Bongaigaon and Dhubri of Assam in the month of May, 1996 against Adivasis, mainly Santals, rendered more than 1,50,000 people homeless. Riots accompanied by plunder, arson and massacre which occurred then were the 3rd major set of riots against the non-bodo communities in the Bodo Autonomous Council Area of western Assam, which was set up as part of an agreement in 1993. As Bodo Liberation Front (BLF) and All Bodo Students' Union (ABSU) who are spearheading a movement for a separate Bodo-Land, targeted non-Bodo communities to spark violence. The Justice Safique Haque Commission was set up to probe the circumstances leading to the 1996 riots. But the commission's investigations have made little progress. Fresh riots in April, 1998 once again disturbed the fragile peace in Kokrajhar. Both Santals and Bodos have been affected in the current tension.

The year 1993 was a turning point in the political history of Assam when BTC was granted after signing the Accord. The doubts had been expressed that the geography of Assam is going to be further reduced and the fact was established when the Bodo insurgent group, BLT, Central Government and the State Government decided to implement the Accord on the

10th February, 2003. Though the state government was not willing to grant BTC to the Bodos but by the said Accord, the same will be realized as it was happened in case of Meghalaya. At that time no one can resist the Bodos rom their demand of separate statehood and this very demand is due to the repressive attitude of the Assamese people towards the other ethnic groups. BLT, which formed in the year 1996, demanded separate statehood for the people living on the northern side of the river Brahmaputra and also to include the Bodos in the 6th schedule of the Indian Constitution for the Bodo people living in the Karbi-Anglong district of Assam. The step motherly attitude towards the non-Assamese people in case of employment policy and in developmental work and also aggressive policy of Assamisation by the State government of Assam gave birth of dissatisfaction to the Bodo people **(Samayik Prasanga, 10th February, 2003).**

To restore peace and normalcy, the central government invited BLT to the discussion table as a result of which BTC came into being. 12 members under the leadership of Hagrama Basumatari took oath in the presence of the Deputy Prime Minister and the Chief Minister of Assam. Another insurgency group under the banner of NDFB raised its ugly head as they are deprived of power in the newly created BTC.

The Hmars are the inhabitants of Mizoram and a part of Assam in the Barak Valley and North Cachar Hills. The Scheduled Caste and Scheduled Tribes Order (amended) Act of 1976 includes not only the Lusais and other 37 tribes or sub tribes but also Lakher, Pawi and Hmar apart from the Chakma settlers from Tripura. The Mizos or Lusais in general opposed this classification as well as granting of autonomous status to the Lakhers, Pawi and Chakmas. To their great dissatisfaction and under the banner of Hmar Peoples Convention (HPC). Hmars have been carrying on agitations since 1954 for autonomy within or separately to safeguard their interests in Hmar dominated areas. In a memorandum to the Prime Minister of India on 21st January, 1987, HPC raised the demand for a separate Homeland or State called Hmar Ram.

They wanted the recognition of North Eastern States to satisfy their political aspirations. The demand made by the Hmar was unacceptable to the Mizos. They staged agitational programmes and were capable of cutting off the lines of communication to the people of Mizoram as they had their control over a part of the Silchar- Aiwjal Road. In 1989, the State Government of Mizoram decided for granting autonomy to the Singlung Hill Development Council (SHDC) for social, economic and cultural development of the people under its jurisdiction.

One accord was duly signed on 27th July, 1994 and this was followed by an agreement on 8th August, concerning the settlement of SHDC's jurisdiction. A three member Commission verified the SHDC area but the State Government delayed its implementation. The president of HPC, Mr. Hmingchunghenung, complained that a year had passed since the boundary was demarcated but the government of Mizoram had shown total disregard to the findings of the commission, set up to ascertain whether the Hmars are in a majority is the HPC demand area or not. As a result the president of HPC warned that it will take extreme step in this regard. Despite surrender of a number of cadres of the HPC to the government of Mizoram in 1994, some of the dissidents who remained underground had been able to reactive the organization and a nexus between NSCN and HPC has been established. The militants had enabled the Hmars to set up camps in dense forests along Assam- Mizoram border and with their active support extended operations to the Barak Valley and North Cachar Hill region of Assam.

The Mikir Hills and the North Cachar Hills are the only two autonomous Hill Districts remaining in Assam after independence as the Naga Hill District got a full fledged Statehood Status in 1962 and Khasi and Jayantia Hill and Garo hill districts formed the state of Meghalaya. Later on, the Mizoram district got the status of Union Territory and finally become a state under Indian Union. The Karbi Anglong and North Cachar Hill of Assam bounded by the plain district of Nowgong and Sibsagar on the North, Meghalaya on the West,

Nagaland and Manipur on the East and the[3] district of Cachar on the South. During the days of British Rule, North Cachar Hill was a Sub-division under the plain district of Cachar and the Mikir Hill was a part of Nowgong, Jowai and Sibsagar district. These two districts were administered as "Excluded and Partially Excluded Area". On the eve of independence the constituent assembly of India appointed a sub committee of these areas known as Bordoloi Sub-Committee to enquire into the will and aspiration of the tribal people of this area under the new government. The tribal people of this area represented for separate autonomy to safeguard their language, culture, customs and ways of life. Bordoloi sub-committee report was that Autonomous District Council for all the hill districts of Assam will be created under the provision of 6th schedule of the constitution. In 1975, the Mikir Hill, came into being out of the portions of Sibsagar and Nowgong districts of Assam and a new civil district with North Cachar Hill sub-division was formed in 1970, the North Cachar Hill sub-division was raised into the status of a district. The Mikir and Dimassa Kachari are the main tribes living in the Mikir Hills District. While North Cachar Hill District is inhabitant of Dimassa Kachari, Hmar, Kuki, Mikir and other tribes. They have their own languages, cultures and traditions but one thing they have in common is their backwardness, educationally, economically and politically. At the time of State Re-organisation of 1969, the Mikir Hills and the North Cachar Hill District Councils were given option to join the proposed Meghalaya Sub-State but the people of those hills did not see the solution of their problems in joining Meghalaya. On the other hand, they received certain significant assurances from the highest authority of the government of Assam and the APCC (Assam Pradesh Congress Committee). They wanted to develop in all spheres by preserving their own separate entities as tribes.

The main discontent was mounted in this hill district when Assamese was imposed as medium in the University and Secondary level of education. They desire to have their own state enhanced when the erstwhile sister districts enjoyed much larger shares of natural resources and these two districts are lagging behind. The customs, traditions and manners of these two districts differ greatly from the contiguous tribal areas. Considering all these the Mikir hill and the North Cachar Hills Leaders' conference submitted a memorandum for a separate State to the Prime Minister of India in June, 1973. The Central Committee of Karbi Anglong and North Cachar Hill State Demand Committee again submitted memorandum to the Prime Minister of India on 18th January, 1982 for creation of a separate full fledged State. They expressed their desire due to the economic, political and cultural backwardness of their people along with the issue of medium of instruction. Their agitation took violent turn when the Autonomous State Demand Committee (ASDC) and the Karbi Students' Association (KSA) jointly submitted a memorandum to the Prime Minister of India on 18th May, 1987. They proposed English as the official language of the proposed Autonomous State and a separate legislature to be located in Diphu, besides other proposals. Till now, the issue is pending before the Central and State governments. Due to their strikes, demonstrations and Road Blocked, normal life has been paralysed and delay in governments decision into the matter is taking the dangerous turn in these areas.

The most important burning issue of the present day Assam is the extension of Naga Ceasefire to other states of North Eastern Region. The Central government's representative and negotiator, Mr. Padmanabhaiah, has opened a new Pandora box of problems in a highly region, known for insurgency, agitation and bloodletting. On 14th June, 2001, one agreement was signed between Mr. Padmanabhaiah and the general secretary of the National Socialist Council of Nagaland (NSCN), Mr. Muivah at Bankok while the earlier Accords were operating within the Nagaland territory, the fresh ceasefire has been extended to the geographical territories of Assam, Manipur and Arunachal Pradesh where there are Naga inhabitants. It not only affects 9 districts of Manipur for which recently Manipur is burning with fire but also applied to Tirap and Changlang districts of Arunachal Pradesh and Sibsagar, Jorhat, Golaghat, Karbi Anglong, North Cachar districts and some portion of Barak Valley districts of Assam which contain a sizable Naga population. In these areas that is so called greater Nagaland, the NSCN is recruiting fresh cadres establishing larger militant networks and Camps and collecting taxes when the ceasefire is in operation since August, 1997. As a reaction to it various political parties and leaders of Assam and Manipur lodged protest against the centre's decision. The Chief Minister of Assam was not consulted by the central government but only informed about the decision of the ceasefire. The Assam government is not in a mood to give an inch of Assam's land to NSCN leaders for their aspiration of greater Nagaland. Whether the Naga ceasefire will bring peace in the region or not but one thing is certain that the region will face some consequences as happened during the days of partition on the eve of independence. It will change not only the geography of North Eastern Region of India but also the history of the region. On its wake it may bring bloodshed and several new terrorist organizations as it is a great lesson to all other militant groups of the region that the violent activities is the only means to achieve the political aspirations. It would like an epidemic or cancer for the entire North Eastern Region for which heavy price may be paid.

In NER the expenditure to control insurgency has been increasing day by day. But ironically along with the expenditure to control insurgency, insurgency has been increasing by leaps and bounds. Recently, in an NEC published paper a detailed account of expenditure is presented. This paper of expenditure is outside the budget of Defence Ministry and seven State Governments. After so much expenditure, bomb in Chief Minister's Convoy, Kidnapping of Bureaucrats, bombs in buses are regular features.

If anything serious happens, the Chief Ministers of this region make the lame excuse that there are no sufficient Central forces in the region. But, in the last six years, in NER, the central government spent an additional amount of 1,000 crore for deployment of police forces. After spending such huge amount of money, the condition of the region is no better.

In the last seven years, the states of NER have sanctioned crores of rupees in their budget. Side by side an amount of 767 crores of rupees they have spent for police security out of the enhanced amount of Rs. 1,000 crores sanctioned by the Central government. Among these seven states, Assam having an expenditure amounting Rs. 487.8 crore, Tripura having 118 crore and Nagaland having 96 crores are at the top of the list **(table 13.3).** For the modernization of police force another278 crores of rupees has been spend. In this sphere also these three states top the list. The amounts spent are 103 crore, 46 crores and 39 crores respectively **(table 15.3).**

According to an official communiqué of the Home Ministry in the last 12 years only in the state of Assam, 1378 have been killed and 178 security personnel too have been murdered. In this 12 years the Security Personnel could kill 552 Bodo (NDFB) insurgents. In the last six years the total numbers may be arranged in the following way. 763, 73 and 486. From the year 2001, in Assam, Army men killed. 841 insurgents. In the last year, 159 ULFA activists, 125 NDFB activists too were killed. In the last 33 months of the two outfits 1,596 and 606 insurgents of these groups have been murdered by the Army men.

This governmental information made it clear that despite of huge expenditure normalcy cannot be brought in the region. Here both the central State governments are a great failure. According to the Deputy General of Assam Rifles, Lt. Gen. H.S. Konwar, I.S.I is solely responsible for the whole situation.

Conclusion and Suggestion

A review of the above ethnic issues in NER proved that the ethnic conflicts in the region, in general, and in Assam in particular, were due to the religious, linguistic, crisis of ethnic identity of different groups of people living in the region and the repressive attitude of the people in the mainstream of the

Table 13.3: Expenditure in Modernisation of Police Force in North East Region (Rs. in Lakh)

Year / State	1997-98	1998-99	1999-00	2000-01	2001-02	2002-03	Total
Arunachal Pradesh	--	56	386	538	76	541	1597
Assam	1710	664	2272	2245	1821	1561	10,273
Manipur	626	98	554	651	362	1149	3440
Meghalaya	--	122	474	635	325	488	2044
Mizoram	--	67	346	436	365	814	2028
Nagaland	616	108	452	651	593	1588	3908
Tripura	611	133	606	1381	832	1036	4599

region. Through different ethnic movements, the state of Assam is bifurcated into different states and the process of separation is still going on jeopardizing the unity and integrity of the region and threatening the security of the country. Hence, the solution to the problem lies in the realm of a humane approach. An effort should be made to win hearts of the people of different ethnic groups of the region so that they can understand the destructive nature of the foreign hands by which they will not be benefited at all. The tribal and non-tribal gap should be closed in the region at any cost through different governmental programmes by which they should not be segregated from the Indian Society. The society of the region cannot be tension free by granting mere autonomy and self government to the ethnic minorities and hence, the centralized political administrative structure should be removed in order to minimize the external influences to the ethnic conflicts of the region. It is high time to negotiate with the neighbouring foreign countries to ensure that state boundaries do not stand in the way of social, economic and cultural interactions among different ethnic groups of people. As the twin objective of ethnic issues are for autonomy within India and independence from India, the above suggestions can serve the very purpose of reducing social tension in the region.

The ethnic movements in the region initially reflect the ethno-cultural aspirations of the people and finally deviate from the real path by turning the movements into violence of the insurgence for material gains and to search the quick money through smuggling, drug trading etc. Hence, the government should suppress these organizations with heavy hands by saving the entire society of the region from further decadence. A review of the sub-nationalist movements in Assam have resulted in the formation of different states and ongoing movements of the Bodos, Bangalees, tribes of North Cachar Hills and Karbi-Anglong, Koach Rajbanshis etc are very much in the air and day will come when they will secede away from the Assamese mainstream. It is noteworthy to mention that the recently held ceasefire agreement with the NSCN Chief by the representative of the Central Government will pose a serious threat to the Government of Assam. Hence, it may be revealed that due to the lack of foresightedness of both the central and the state governments, the unity and integrity of the state may be jeopardized. In the pre-independence era, the tribals demanded for simply autonomy but the leaders of Assam were adamant in their attitude as a result of which they get themselves separated from the mainstream.

In the conclusion, it may be said that the ethnic conflicts in Assam are due to excess repressive attitude of the government of Assam from time to time. Had the leaders of Assam been liberal to all the ethnic groups and sympathetic to safeguard their languages, customs and cultures, ethnic movements in different parts of Assam would not have taken place.

References

Barth, Prederik (1969) : Ethnic Group And Boundaries., Olso Morris H. S., 1968, International Encyclopeadia of Social sciences

Glazer N. (1976) : Ethnicity – A World Phenomenon, American Review, No. 20, No.2/3 (Abridged from Encounter)

Singh, K. S. (1982) : Tribal Movement in India, *Manohar,* New Delhi

Madhab, Jayanta (1999) : "North East ; Crisis of Identity, Security and Underdevelopment" *Economic and Political Weekly, Vol. 34, No. 1, Feb. 6-12.*

Dutta, B. (1985) : The Reemergence of Folklore in North East India, *Man and Life, Vol. II, No. I & II, Calcutta.*

Note

1. (a) "Ruinous Tendency to Side Track the Main Issue in Assam", Hindusthan Standard Patrika, July 2, 1961.
2. (b) "Pradhan Mantri Ki Balitechen – Kitchu Na Kintu Tadanta Report Ki Chilo – Bengali Hindu Uchechedane Sarbanash Jote – Ekti Aprakashito Dalil", Ananda Bazar Patrika, July 2, 1961.

3. "Certain Aspects of Social Movements in Barak Valley", P. C. Dutta and B.C. Pradhan in Social Movements in North East India (ed.) M.N. Karna, Indus Publishing Company, New Delhi, 1998.

4. "Separate Kamatapur Demand of Koch Rajbanshi", S.C. Chatterjee, The Assam Tribune, June 3, 2001.

5. "Autonomy Movements in Assam : Documents", A memorandum to Rajib Gandhi, submitted by ABSU (ed.) P. S. Dutta, Omson's Publications, New Delhi.

14

Population Growth and Development in NER

The World Summit on Sustainable Development (WSSD) in Johennesburg, South Africa (26 August, 4 September, 2002) was called by the United Nations to consider strategies toward sustainable development in all its dimensions. Its mandate was broader than that of the 1992 United Nations Conference on Environment and Development (the Rio Conference). Population issues have previously been discussed in a separate series of World Population Conference **(Bucharest 1974, Mexico City, 1984, Cairo, 1994)**. Sustainable development aims at improving human well-being, particularly through alleviating poverty, increasing gender equity, and improving health, human resources, and stewardship of the natural environment. Because demographic factors are closely linked to these goals, strategies that include consideration of population have a better chance of success. The International Conference on Population and Development in Cairo in 1994 recognized that population policy should be oriented toward improving social conditions and expanding choices for individuals. In Johennesburg, consideration of sustainable development policies included population growth and distribution, mobility, differential vulnerability, and the empowerment of people, especially women.

Rapid population growth has exacerbated freshwater depletion, climate change, biodiversity loss, depletion fisheries, and degradation of agricultural lands. It can also have important economic benefits by reducing the number of children relative to the working-age population, creating a unique opportunity to increase investments in health, education, infrastructure, and environmental protection. Before the end of this decade, a majority of the world's population will live in urban areas. Urbanisation can improve people's access to education, health and other services. It also creates environmental health hazards, such as water and air pollution, and by increasing consumption levels, can have environmental impacts in distant rural areas also.[1]

The modern theory of human capital came to prominence in economics only in recent decades, but its antecedents can be traced back to the earliest economic writings. The notion that human skills represent economic value comparable to that of capital was clearly articulated by the classical economists, notably by William Petty and Adam Smith. That improvement of skills and increase in the number of persons in whom skills are embodied are sources of economic progress follows from their conceptual clarification. The economic value of the population depends very much on their command over the powers of nature; which they acquire by education.

Addressing an international conference of Islamic scholars (ulema) on *'Population and Development'* on 6th May, 2005 in Islamabad, General Pervez Musharraf, President of Pakistan stressed the need for population policies based on a realistic assessment of socio-economic conditions in Pakistan and more broadly, in the Muslim World (Ummah). He was of the opinion that there should be no doubt in his mind that the main factor retarding economic growth, poverty alleviation and action on joblessness is population growth. Those who do not understand this are living in a world of their own. In the case of Pakistan, from 1951 to the mid 1980s population grew roughly at an average of 3 p.c. per year; from mid 1980s to 2000 it grew at an average of 2.5 p.c. ; from 2000 to 2005, the growth rate as an average of 2.0 p.c. Had we grown at 2 p.c. per year from 1951 onwards our per capita income today would have been $ 920- much more than China's – instead of $650 which we are at now. This is the negative impact and effect of population growth on our economy and on our poverty level. However, history can't be undone but we must wake up..... So our plan is to reduce our population growth rate from 1.9 p.c. to 1.3 p.c. by 2020. We must do it for the sake of our future generation, who will otherwise be poorer. He feels that the Ulema can play an extremely important role in controlling population. But unfortunately, some Ulema here in Pakistan are playing a negative role by giving a fatwa against population control. He acknowledged the role of the Ulema in Iran, Turkey, Indonesia, Egypt and Bangladesh, where they for population control.[2]

Russian president Vladimir Putin's 2005 annual address to the Federal assembly of the Russian Federation, delivered on 25th April was widely noted in the World Press. The President expressed confidence that by creating conditions to "encourage people to have children, lower the mortality rate and bring order to immigration," the size of the Russian population will gradually stabilize. He was also of the opinion that an increase in the population should be accompanied by a carefully planned immigration policy. It is in our interest to receive a flow of legal and qualified workers...... Without any rights, after all, illegal immigration are convenient in that they can be exploited endlessly. They are also a potential danger from the point of view of breaking the law.[3]

China's one-child policy is a major example of social engineering and the subject of human rights concerns. Given the significance of the policy, it is important to ascertain the attitudes of Chinese citizens. Announcing in 1980, China's one-child-per-couple policy was formulated in the wake of the cultural Revolution (1966-76) as an emergency measure to slow rapid population growth and to facilitate modernization goals **(Wang, 2005; Croll, 1984).** This draconian policy met with strong resistance, especially in China's vast rural areas where the peasant family remains the primary locus of economic activity and old-age support. A few years after the announcement of the policy, a quite but significant retreat took place to modify the radical and unrealistic stance. In China's privileged urban sectors, the population continued to be subject to the one-child policy. Couples in rural china were allowed to have two children if they met certain criteria, most notably if they lived in a poor area or had only a daughter. Exemption to the one-child rule often came with a spacing requirement, stipulating a minimum of four or six years between the first and second birth. Modifications to the state policy of population control have been left to each province, under the general principle of slowing down population growth and encouraging only one child per couple[4].

The latest United Nations population projections to 2050 (UN 2005) indicate that the deceleration of world population growth may be even faster than thought only a few years earlier. According to Nikos Alexandratos (2005), the realization that the world is probably on a fairly smooth path of transition toward a near-stationary population in the not-too-distant future influences the debate on the interrelationships between population, development, and sustainability. The notion that the trend toward an ever-growing population, the so-called population explosion, threatens our welfare and the sustainability of our existence (or, at least, the prospect that all people can achieve "acceptable" living standards) seems to be losing currency among the public.

India has for centuries had a rich intellectual tradition concerning both the quantitative and qualitative aspects of population, as well as practical experience in controlling fertility since time immemorial.[5] In fact, Indians had for many years been participating in International debates about population. Following Independence, and after the 1951 census showed continued population growth despite a decade of war, famine, and sectarian strife, Nehru called for the new Planning Commission to convene another population committee. Their report recommended fertility limitation both for the sake of mothers' and children's health and to stabilize population "consistent with the requirements of national economy." It called for free sterilization and contraception when recommended on medical grounds, and suggested that where feasible these methods should be adopted for social and economic reasons as well.[6] Officials were still concerned about population "quality". Control of population growth family planning as a measure for achieving faster economic development has its supporters as well as opponents, of course, supporters are more numerous. India was the first country to obtain family planning advice from the World Health organization. However, India's government was slow to implement a family planning programme. In 1960 Indian officials elevated the family planning programme to "the very centre of planned development [7]."India committed to the goal of reducing the birth rate by 40 p.c. by 1972. It becomes clear that there were always some individuals who fought to defend family planning as a means to promote individual dignity and welfare, rather than to control population growth. The current consensus is not, therefore, just faddish or politically correct, but the fruit of a long struggle, one that is far from over **(Connelly, 2006)**.

The concept of development has been defined as a stage of growth or advancement of a society and the different countries of the world have broadly been classified into two categories viz. 'developed' and 'developing'. The primary object of development is to satisfy the essential material needs of the society, but not at the cost of local environment and people's culture. When people change, the society to which belong also change, and the country moves with them too. But the North-Eastern Region (NER) is an exception while this region is endowed with rich resources of land, water, forests, minerals etc. It appears that it is difficult to establish any relationship between expressed opinion on family size, actual family size and family's economic achievement. The economic development not only brings about changes in the socio-economic and cultural life of a population but it also influences the consumption pattern in the long run. The development is a complex process and has multi dimensional structure depending upon its resources in general and infrastructural facilities in particular **(Dutta,1996)**.

In the era of globalisation rapid socio-economic transformation has been taking place in the economy at international level. The planners and policy makers in India are trying to cope with it. Economic welfare does not merely depend upon the level of development but also on its distributive aspects. In the pluralistic nature of the country, differences in natural resources, climate, topography, vegetation and density of population can be identified easily and the North Eastern Region of India (NER) is no exception to it. Unequal distribution of wealth and resources caused regional disparity in the country as a result of which the states of NER are lagging behind.

One must realize that north-east is a mini-India. There are more than 75 major population groups and sub groups, speaking approximately 400 languages and dialects, of which there are about 168 in Arunachal Pradesh, 95 in Nagaland, 87 in Manipur, 100 in Tripura and 200 in Assam, Meghalaya and Mizoram (Madhab, J, 1999). Thus, the whole north-eastern India is a place with people of diverse races, cultures, languages and various dialects with different traditions. Besides the heterogeneity of geographical and socio-cultural factors, the more striking view of the North-Eastern scenario is the co-existence of the extreme forms of both tradition and modernity.

It is a fact that the urbanisation is the most essential for all round development of the developing nations, as it increases employment, income and standard of living in these countries. But it simultaneously creates a number of socio economic and environmental problems. Urbanisation disturbs the ecological balance by creating air, water and noise pollution through industrialisation. Haphazard growth of urban centres and their ill-planned urbanisation aggravated the pollution problems and deteriorated the environment.

Therefore, environmentalist aptly say that urbanisation-environment relationship is not complementary but contradictory with each other The increasing urbanisation has led to a number of socio-economic problems like crime, suicides, drug abuse, unemployment and poverty, alcoholism, overcrowding, housing shortage, slums, traffic control and pollution etc. At the same time they are also centres of civilisation and culture by helping a lot in the process of modernisation (**Dutta, 2002**).

It is in this context, an enquiry is deemed to be necessary to examine the multi dimensional and complex relationships among some socio-economic and demographic variables of the north-eastern region of India as it is physically located in a backward and disadvantageous position due to its physical geography as well as the social and political conditions prevailing in the region. One of the purposes of the present study is to examine whether or how urbanisation creates the hazardous situation in socio-economic aspects. Further, the study shows how population growth affects over-all environment of the region. The study has been concluded with some valuable suggestions The study is based on secondary sources of data relating to socio-economic and demographic variables for the North-Eastern Region of India. Different rounds of NSS data and Census data, Rural Health Statistics, Ministry of Health and Family Welfare, Govt. of India and other published and unpublished secondary data are used in the present study.

Population Growth and Socio-Economic Characteristics

The total population of the region is about 38.5 million representing 3.75 p.c. of India's total population in 2001 and 40.02 million in the mid year of 2003. It is of great interest to note that India's population exceeded the population of Europe (729 million) comprising 47 countries and was equal to Europe and Northern America including United States of America (310 million). We live in a world of unprecedented demographic change. Global population increased by 2 billion during the last quarter of the 20th century, reached 6 billion in 2000. Changes in population growth, age structure, and spatial distribution interact closely with the environment and with development. Despite government efforts to cut growth rates, India's population which was 238 million in 1947 touched 1.012 billion in March 2001 and is expected to be 1.263 billion by

2016, according to India's health ministry.

The **region's growth rate of population is much higher than the national average.** It is striking to note that India's total population increased by 51.80 p.c. in the period 1951-71, 54.39 p.c. in 1971-91 and 21.35 p.c. in 1991-2001. Whereas for the NER, respective growth rates are 90.86 p.c., 62.11 p.c. and 22.02 p.c. At the same time share of population of NER, in comparison to all-India, increased from 2.84 p.c. in 1951 to 3.75 p.c. in 2001 (table 14.1). As regards the decadal growth rate of population, the highest decadal growth rate (41.33 p.c.)was seen in the decade 1951-61. The decadal growth rate of population in NER were as high as compared to all India level. It is to be noted here that the percentage of population in the region with respect to India was 1.70 in 1901 and 2.70 in 1941. It can be concluded here that population is increasing faster in NER as compared to the country as a whole. It is observed that there is a large variation in the **density of population** among the states of NER (table 14.2). Density of region's population (151) is almost half of the national density (324) in 2001 while it was only 34.19 in 1951. Again within the region it varies from 13 in Arunachal Pradesh to 340 in Assam. The bulk of population of the region (almost 70 p.c. of total population of the region) is concentrated mainly of three sectors viz. Brahmaputra valley and Barak valley of Assam and Tripura. The large variation is caused by the geographical and economic factors, which vary greatly within the region. Population growth in the region has been unusually rapid, mainly due to interstate migration in earlier decades and to immigration from other countries and relatively high fertility among some immigrant groups in recent decades.[8]

The age-distribution in each state of NER is typical of high fertility populations, with a high proportion of the population in the younger age-groups. Manipur, Mizoram and Tripura have the lowest percentage of population below 15 years of age (37 p.c.) and this Percentage is the highest in Arunachal Pradesh (43 p.c.). The proportion of the population of age 60 and above varies from just over 2 per cent in Nagaland to 8 percent in

Table 14.1: Population Trend in North East Region (in'000) **Literacy Rate**

Year / State	1951	1961	1971	1981	1991	2001	Literacy Rate 1991	Literacy Rate 2001
ANP	---	337	468	632	865	1091	41.59	54.74
ASM	8029	10837	14625	18041	22414	26638	52.89	64.28
MNP	578	780	1073	1421	1837	2389	59.89	68.87
MGH	606	769	1012	1336	1775	2306	49.10	63.31
MZM	196	266	332	494	690	891	82.27	88.49
NGN	213	369	516	775	1210	1989	61.65	67.11
TRP	639	1142	1556	2053	2757	191	62.66	73.47
SKM	138	162	210	316	406	541		
N E R	10260	14501	19582	24752	31547	38495		
India	361088	439235	548160	683329	846303	1027015	52.21	65.38
1*	---	41.34	35.04	26.40	27.45	22.02		
2*	2.84	3.30	3.57	3.62	3.70	3.75		

1* Decadal Growth Rate of NER.

2* Percentage of NER with respect to India.

Tripura **(Dutta, 2002)**.

The total number of tribal population is 81.42 lakh which is approximately 25.71 p.c. of the total population. The percentage of Schedule Tribes varies from 13 p.c. (Assam) to 91 p.c. (Mizoram) which are above the country's figure (8 p.c.). However, more than three fourths of the household belong to scheduled tribe in the states of Mizoram, Nagaland (96 p.c.), Meghalaya (89 p.c.), Arunachal Pradesh (76 p.c.) and while in Tnpura (17 p.c.), Manipur (35 p.c.) and Assam, these are below 50 p.c. **(Dutta, 2002b)**.

Sex ratio is an important determinant of population growth. This ratio in a population influences fertility rate. In all developed countries, the ratio is over 1000, while in most developing countries, it is below 1000. It is remarkable to note that the sex ratio in NER has consistently shown excess of males over females as noted for India... In India, there are only 933 females per 1000 males in the total population (table – 2). Amongst the states of NER, it is the highest in Manipur (978) followed by Meghalaya (975), Tripura (950) and Mizoram (938) while other states are lying below the national level. It seems that there is more male migrants in the region lowering the sex ratio of general population.

Education is the main instrument of social change. Normally it has been considered an agency helping economic production through the development of skills and efficiency highly necessary for the said production. "Education is an organic entity, changes, grows with the time, responds to the needs of the society adopts to the environment. It was mostly an ornament in the agricultural civilizations, a tool in economic development in the industrial era and has become today all pervasive resources, a resource that can find substitutes for other resources, but has no substitute for itself.", according to **V.C. Kulandai Swami**.

A minute look at the table 14.1, it is observed that there are some notable features of this region in regard to literacy rate. Except Arunachal Pradesh (41.59 p.c.) and Meghalaya

Table 14.2: Female Literacy Rate, Female Work Participation, Gender Gap in literacy and Density of Population (per sq. km.)

State	Female Literacy Rate (in p.c.)		Sex Ratio			Density of Population (population per sq. km.)			Gender Gap in Literacy	
	1991	2001	1981	1991	2001	1951	1991	2001	1991	2001
AN P	29.69	44.24	862	859	901	--	10	13	21.76	19.83
ASM	43.03	56.03	910	923	932	102	184	340	18.84	15.90
MNP	47.60	59.70	971	958	978	26	82	107	24.03	18.17
MGH	44.85	60.41	954	955	975	27	79	103	8.27	5.73
MZM	78.60	86.13	919	921	938	9	33	42	7.01	-
NGN	54.75	61.92	863	886	909	13	73	120	12.87	9.85
TRP	49.65	65.41	946	945	950	61	263	304	20.93	16.06
NER			921	925	937	40	124	151		
India	39.29	54.16	934	937	933	117	273	324	24.84	21.69

(49.1 p.c.), the literacy level of the region's population is above the national level (52.21 p.c.) accord¬ing to 1991 census while in 2001, percentage of literacy rate in the states of Arunachal Pradesh (54.74 p.c.), Meghalaya (63.31 p.c.) and Assam (64.28 p.c.) are below the national figure of 65.38 p.c.

However, the **female literacy rate** is highest in Mizoram (86.13 p.c.) fol¬lowed by Tripura (65.41 p.c.) and lowest in Arunachal Pradesh (44.24 p.c.) which is the only state in NER below the national level (54.16 p.c.) in this respect (table – 2).

The percentage of population of age 6 and above who are literate varies from 52 p.c. in Arunachal Pradesh to 91 p.c. in Mizoram. It is further to be mention that in every states of NER including India as a whole, a higher percentage of females has completed each level of schooling with few exception.

The SCR Committee Report shows clearly that the literacy and educational status of Muslims is particularly low. There is a significant disparity between the educational status of Muslims and that of other socio-religious categories(except SCs and STs). Muslim enrolment rates are showing steady increase. In 1999-2000, Muslims had the lowest enrolment rate of all socio-religious groups. However, in 2004-05, the Muslim enrolment had improved significantly 25 per cent of Muslim in the 6 to 14 age group have either never been to school or have dropped out at some stage. The reason for the sluggish growth in literacy are not only among Muslims, but also among other deprived communities are not because the average parents do not wish to provide “modern mainstream” education to their children. One of the important reasons for low literacy is abject poverty.

There is a big **gender gap in literacy** (table 14.2) which is one of the major obstacles in attaining total literacy. Enrolment in various stages of education is growing at a fast rate, but the proportion of girls is low and declines sharply at higher stages of education. The highest gender gap has been found in the states of Manipur (24.03 p.c. points), Arunachal Pradesh (21.76), Tripura (20.93) and lowest in Mizoram (7.01) followed by Meghalaya (8.27). However all the states of NER are below all-India (24.84 p.c. points) level. Low female literacy has strong repercussions on other aspects like enrolment of children, population growth, child care and acceptance of family welfare measures.

It is striking to note that per capita expenditure on education in 1997-98 is highest for smaller states of Mizoram (Rs. 1210), followed by Manipur (Rs. 984), Arunachal Pradesh (Rs. 951) and Tripura (Rs. 836) while it is lowest in Assam (Rs.537) among the states of NER **(Dutta, 2002)**. The Kothari Commission has laid special emphasis on higher education and research, as it strongly believed that it is higher education and research that will contribute to economic development, and to bridge the gap between the rich countries and India. It has also recommended a significant expansion of the centrally sponsored sector in education. Above all, it strongly recommended increase in the allocation of resources to education to the level of 6 per cent of GNP (Gross National Product). Unfortunately, while the commission recommended a package of reforms, the government looked at the recommendations as piecemeal suggestions. It is thus a tragedy that the recommendations of the one commission which was directed to look comprehensively at education were considered mostly in a piecemeal fashion, Naik (1997, 1979) observed. While there can be several factors for the inaction of the government, the lack of strong political will seems to be the most important one.

Population distribution according to religion (table 14.3) reveals the fact that although NER is a small part of the country a great variation of demographic characteristics is seen during the period under consideration. The percentage of Hindu population is steadily decreasing in all the states of NER including India as a whole during the period 1951-2001 and the same trend has also been followed in the year 2011 as per estimated value. It is remarkable to note that during the same period, the percentage of Muslim and Christian Population have shown their increasing trend in all the states of NER including India as a whole. The proportion of

Table 14.3: Distribution of Population According to Religion (in p.c.)

States	Year	Hindu	Muslim	Christian	Others
Arunachal	1951	--			
Pradesh	1971	21.99	0.18	0.79	77.04
	1991	37.04	1.38	10.29	51.29
	2001	34.60	1.90	18.72	44.78
	2011*	32.61	2.41	26.67	38.31
Assam	1951	72.08	24.68	2.01	1.23
	1971	71.51	24.96	2.61	0.92
	1991	67.13	28.43	3.32	1.12
	2001	64.89	30.92	3.70	0.49
	2011*	62.12	33.01	4.02	0.85
Manipur	1951	.60.11	6.44	11.89	21.56
	1971	58.47	6.11	26.03	9.39
	1991	57.67	7.27	34.11	0.95
	2001	46.01	8.81	34.04	11.14
	2011*	43.18	10.13	36.22	10.47
Meghalaya	1951	12.12	2.31	39.66	45.91
	1971	18.51	2.61	49.95	28.93
	1991	14.07	3.46	64.58	17.89
	2001	13.27	4.28	70.25	12.20
	2011*	11.89	5.14	74.51	8.44
Mizoram	1951	3.31	0.07	90.51	6.11
	1971	6.39	0.57	86.08	6.96
	1991	5.05	0.66	85.73	8.56
	2001	3.55	1.14	86.97	8.34
	2011*	2.81	2.08	88.34	6.77
Nagaland	1951	4.71	0.24	46.03	49.02
	1971	11.43	0.58	66.76	21.23
	1991	10.12	1.71	87.46	0.71
	2001	7.70	1.76	89.97	0.57
	2011*	6.31	2.22	91.21	0.26

Tripura	1951	75.92	21.43	0.82	1.83
	1971	89.55	6.08	1.01	3.36
	1991	86.51	7.13	1.68	4.68
	2001	85.62	7.95	3.20	3.23
	2011*	84.42	7.75	2.22	5.61
NER	1951	65.54	21.16	6.42	6.88
	1961	63.92	21.01	7.74	7.33
	1971	66.39	19.40	9.12	5.09
	1991	60.95	21.56	13.64	3.85
	2011*	58.35	24.08	14.82	2.75
India	1951	84.98	9.91	2.35	2.76
	1971	82.72	11.21	2.59	3.48
	1991	82.01	12.12	2.34	3.53
	2001	80.46	13.43	2.34	3.77
	2011*	78.03	14.91	2.87	4.19

Source: Census of India, various years.

* Estimated figures.

Hindu population have been declining mainly due to increase proportion of population professing Muslim, Christian religions. As the Christian dominated states viz. Nagaland, Mizoram and Meghalaya recorded a comparatively higher growth rate of population during the last two or three consecutive decades that definitely resulted in an increase proportion of population of Christian religion in North East of India. The same is true in case of Muslim population in the NER while Hinduism was seen as major religion in NER during 1991 as more than 60.95 p.c. of population profess Hinduism followed by Muslim (21.56 p.c.) and Christian (13.64 p.c.). According to 2001 census figure, the percentage of Hindu population in the state of Assam decreased to 64.89 p.c. while the p.c. of population in case of Muslims increased to 30.92 p.c. and Christians to 3.70 p.c.

The decadal growth rate in NER recorded a very slow incase of population professing Hinduism during the study period. During 1971-91, proportion of Hindu population increased at the rate of 47.91 p.c. against the growth rates of 140.89 p.c. for Christian, 79.04 p.c. for Muslims. As for the country (Table

14.4), the decadal growth rate of Muslim population are 30.8 p.c., 22.9, 34.5 and 36.1 p.c. against the Hindu population as 23.7 p.c., 21.3, 25.1 and 20.3 p.c. during the period 1961-71, 1971-81, 1981-91 and 1991-2001 respectively. During the same period, the growth of Christians are 32.6 p.c., 13.7, 21.5 and 22.6 p.c. which shows the fact that the decadal growth rate of Muslims is the highest through out the period. This growth of population was may be mainly due to influx of people from the neighbouring countries as well as for better sex ratio. It is further to be noted here that for the country, the growth rate of Sikhs, Buddhists and Jains during the period 1991-2001 are 18.2 p.c., 24.5 p.c. and 26.0 p.c. respectively while during 1961-71, the respective growth rates were 32.3 p.c., 17.1 p.c. and 28.5 p.c.

While the sex ratio in India as a whole is lower than 1000, it is not altogether surprising that Muslims show a better sex ratio as compared to other socio-religious groups. Further, Muslims have the highest child sex ratio of any social group in the country. Muslims constitute, at present, about 14.6 per cent of the total Indian population. A larger proportion of Muslims live in urban areas (36 p.c.) as compared to the population average (28 p.c.). The community is also geographically concentrated in some specific areas. Fertility rates among Muslims are higher than average. The estimates show that the total fertility rates (TFR) among Muslims declined from 4.3 to 3.6 in 1990s. During the same period the fertility rates for the population as a whole declined from about 3.4 to 2.9. Fertility among Muslims varies with socio-economic characteristics and there are significant inter-regional variations.

Since 2000 AD Christian population has grown exponentially in many regions due to massive conversions. The Christian population in India officially stands at 2.34% which everybody including Christians don't trust Majority of Christians do not report their religion as Christianity for 2 reasons i.e., (a) loss of caste based reservation benefits (b) Church leaders do no want to raise alarm bells with sudden increase in numbers. Indian Christian leaders conveniently use Census data to

Table 14.4: Decadal Growth of Population According to Religion (in p.c.)

	Year	Hindus	Muslims	Christians	Sikhs	Buddhists	Jains
INDIA	1961-71	23.7	30.8	32.6	32.3	17.1	28.5
	1971-81	21.3	22.9	13.7	26.0	23.8	23.1
	1981-91	25.1	34.5	21.5	24.3	35.3	4.6
	1991-01	20.3	36.0	22.6	18.2	24.5	26.0

portray minority status and pursue persecution strategy while using the church count data to show progress and request more funds from foreign donors. According to the Christian estimate collected by Joshua Project which is based on Church membership, Christians account for 6% of Indian population. The Muslim population count is questionable as illegal Bangladeshi immigrants who are in crores are not counted. According to Justice K.M. Yusuf, a retired judge of the Calcutta High Court and Chairman of the West Bengal Minority Commission in an interview said the true percentage is between 20-25 p.c. (published in *The Hindu* October 01, 1999). Further, it is remarkable to note that considering the percentage of Christian population in all the state capital towns of India, Aiwjal stands at the top with 90.03 p.c. followed by Kohima (85.03 p.c.) and Shillong (41.02 p.c.), all belong to NER.

In the developed economics, the process of **urbanisation** has been closely and positively related with the economic development, while in the third world developing countries is a consequential phenomenon. Besides, the pattern of urbanisation in the latter economies has been spatially and structurally imbalanced. The rates of urbanisation vary over time and space. In the later half of the twentieth century the developing countries have been urbanizing very fast and India is no exception. The rate of urbanization during the post independence period has been quite rapid with highest rate,during 1971-81 decade, of 46 p.c. The 1991census reveals a slowing down urban population growth (36.19 p.c.) during 1981 – 91. and 32.61 p.c. during1991-2001. It is the quantum increase in urban population vis-à-vis total population growth is of vital concern.

Coming to the states of NER, the notable point is that **the percentage of urban population to total population (urbanization)** varies from 12.80 (Arunachal Pradesh) to 46.10 (Mizoram). It is striking to note that except Manipur (27.52 p.c.) and Mizoram, all other states of NER are below the national level (25.71 p.c.) according to 1991 census. Urban population growth was always higher than total population growth during the 20th century. The slower tempo of urban population growth during 1981-1991 and longer perspective of guided urbanisation having been considered for future urban population growth. In 2001, the p.c. of urbanization is the lowest in the state of Assam (12.90) followed by Tripura (17.05) and Nagaland (17.74) while highest p.c. observed in the state of Mizoram (49.63), which is the only state above national level (27.81), followed by Manipur (23.88), Arunachal Pradesh (20.75) and Meghalaya (19.58). As per the latest figure available only 15.51 p.c. of the total population of NER resided in urban areas against the country's figure of 27.78 p.c. in 2001 census year. During the early period i.e. 1951-61, the urban population of NER was increased by 139.83 p.c. and after that the decennial growth rate of urban population declined abruptly to 67.44 p.c. in 1961-71, 57.49 in 1971-81, 50.67 in 1981-91 and finally touched at 36.29 p.c. in 1991-2001. The urbanization in India is structurally imbalanced and is going to maintain the same trend unless there is a policy intervention to reorient the urbanization trend in favour of small and medium size towns along with metropolitan decentralization.

Migration

Migration is the driving force of population growth. Migration has long been seen as a means of improving one's career prospects, particularly in developing countries where the distribution of economic opportunities is uneven. In contrast to migration, education has little effect on the rate of occupational change, but it gives a significant boost to the socio economic level achieved after the change. The data base for a complete study of migration in India is weak, and official rigidity in respect of publication of certain information does not help the situation. It is a truism that, in developing countries, an accurate measurement of migration is grossly handicapped by the nature and lack of basic data on events. In most Third World countries today, population registers, an appropriate and key sources of data for migrants and migrations, are almost non-existent. In these countries, the most important sources of migration data is national censuses, usually conducted decennially. Again, in censuses, the information collected on migration is very limited, often restricted to lifetime migration only.

Hendrick and Henkens (2007) concluded that age, education, income and social networks play key roles in triggering immigration. They are also is of the opinion that economic considerations play a role in explaining the intent to immigration but the economic theory of migration is not sufficient to understand immigration. Needless to say, a significant number of migrants- refugees and asylum seekers- are also sometimes forcefully driven by the quality of the public domain in their home country. They considered the perceptions of three aspects of the public domain – viz.

(i) societal problems such as crime, pollution and ethnic conflict

(ii) environmental problems such as loss of natural environments and increasing population density and

(iii) shortcomings in institutions that deal with welfare and social problems, that is the educational system, social security, health care, law and order and old-age pensions.

The assumption that population growth adversely affects economic growth and natural resources came under fire beginning in the late 1970s with the work of **Julian Simon (1977, 1981)**. Simon's view was that moderate population growth is beneficial, not detrimental, because it induces technical innovation. Furthermore, market mechanisms insure substitution away from scarcer to more abundant resources, and thus prevent resource shortage. The report of National Academy of Sciences (NAS) concluded that population growth can have negative effects on some types of environmental outcomes, under particular social, economic and political conditions: Renewable resources, air and water quality, the climate, and species diversity may be harmed by rapid population growth. But the existence and size of these effects depends on the efficacy and efficiency of social institutions that regulate resource use and allocate the costs of externalities **(NAS, 1986)**.

As NER is surrounded by four foreign countries, there is every possibility of influx from these countries in search of food, employment, business etc. The absolute number of the migrants was more than 91 thousand in 1901, since then it has been steadily increasing and reached at nearly 745 thousand in the census year 1991. The share of migrants from Bangladesh was between slightly more than 70 P.C. to slightly more than 87 P.C. in pre-independence era. The post independence era, it reached at 94 P.C. in 1951—the highest among the period, 1901-1991. From 1961 onwards the share started to decline and become around 89 p.c. in the census year of 1991. It is also clear from the statistical information that Bangladesh was followed by Nepal in sending migrants to the NER of India. Again the number of migrants who come from other states of India varied between 0.5 million to around 0.8 million during the pre independence era. But it declined to around 0.4 million in 1951 and reaching slightly more than 0.5 million in 1991. In the recent years the flow of immigration from the neighboring countries shows an increasing trend. This heavy growth of population was mainly due to influx of people from the neighbouring countries or states in search of food, employment, business etc.

However, the share became around 89 p.c. in the census year of 1991, the absolute figure is 745 thousand. Remaining 11 P.C. of the migrants to this region are from Nepal, Myanmer etc. However, total migrants, from outside the country, to this region stands at 834 thousand during 1991. The proportion of foreign migrants from Bangladesh to Assam was around 85 P.C. among the total foreign migrant in the state. The respective percentage for the state of Tripura was more than 99 P.C. according to 1991 Census. This migrant no doubt has some impact on the social, economic, cultural and political sphere of the North- Eastern region.

It is to be noted here that from the pre independence period (table 14.5), the percentage of Muslim population in the state of Assam has been increasing steadily from 16.23 p.c. in 1911 to 30.92 p.c. in 2001 while in case of India it has been decreased from 22.39 p.c. in 1911 to 9.91 p.c. in 1951 but then again it has been increasing steadily and reached at 12.12 p.c. in 1991. This is no doubt due to the effect of population migration from other states of the country and the neighbouring countries to this north eastern states in general and Assam in particular. As a result. In 1951 census, the rise in the population of Assamese-speaking people was substantial as the migrated Muslim population adopted Assamese as their language leaving their mother tongue Bengali. Meanwhile, the refugees from East Pakistan poured into the State in their thousands leading to an abnormally high rate of population growth in the State. During that time the linguistic nationalism of the Bangalees in Barak Valley of Assam was at its peak against the Official Language Bill passed in the Assam Legislative Assembly. Besides, the leaders of the Indian National Congress encouraged Muslim infiltrators into Assam for their vote bank, which was clearly manifested in one of the election meetings in which a leading congressman of Assam expressed " so long as Alis and Coolies are with the congress, we have nothing to fear". Later on, the AGP Government of Assam continued to appease the Muslims by making them as their vote bank too. On the other hand, to reduce the Hindu Bengalees into minority in Assam, the government of Assam is still trying to impose upon them the process of assamization. Political vested interests have obviously played a decisive role in this development, which if allowed to go on unabated will worsen the situation and endanger India's unity and integrity.

In NER the **expenditure to control insurgency** has been increasing day by day. But ironically along with the expenditure to control insurgency, insurgency has been increasing by leaps and bounds. During the period of seven years (1997-2003) the states of NER have sanctioned crores of rupees in their budget. Side by side an amount of 767 crores of rupees they have spent for police security out of the enhanced amount of Rs. 1,000

Table 14.5: Proportion of Muslim Population in India and Assam (in p.c.)

	1911	1931	1951	1961	1971	1991	2001
Assam:	16.23	22.78	24.68	25.30	24.56	28.43	30.92
India:	22.39	23.49	9.91	10.71	11.21	12.12	13.41

Source: Census of India, various years

crores sanctioned by the Central government. Among these seven states, Assam having an expenditure amounting to Rs. 487.8 crores, Tripura having 118 crore and Nagaland having 96 crores are at the top of the list. For the modernization of police force another 278 crores of rupees has been spend. In this sphere also Assam is on the top of the list along with the states of Tripura and Nagaland. The amounts spent for these states are 103 crore, 46 crores and 39 crores respectively. According to an official communiqué of the Home Ministry in the last 12 years only in the state of Assam, 1378 have been killed and 178 security personnel too have been murdered. This governmental information made it clear that despite of huge expenditure normalcy cannot be brought in the region. Here both the central and the State governments are a great failure. **(Dutta and Deb 2005)** and ultimately affected in over all socio-economic development of the region.

Economic Development and Environment

The main and foremost objective of all planning and policies of any country is human development and to improve the quality of life of the human resources of the country. As the second most populous country of the world, India has only 2.5 p.c. of global land whereas it has to provide home for one-sixth of world's population. Thus, living in a country with a high population density and high growth rate of population, which increases pressure on the existing resources of the country, planners perceived that there is a serious threat coming up on the way to achieve developmental goals. Demographic transition is an important phenomenon in this regard. However, demographic pattern has already been studied in the previous sections of this paper.

Population pressure on farmland has long been a concern in the demographic literature. **Foster et al. (1997)** concluded that, in Indian villages, technological change in agriculture "reinforces the destructive effects of population growth on forests" (p.13). But they also found that rural industrialization appears to preserve forest land. Population growth and its relation to economic development has been a matter of debate for over a century. For the developing country like India, population growth is likely to impede economic growth resulting in reduction of per capita income and resources. In addition to this the growth of labour force will add to the unemployment trends. The Tenth Five Year Plan (2002-07) is aimed at achieving the Gross Domestic Product (GDP) growth rate of 8 per cent, doubling the per capita income and creation of 100 million of employment opportunities in next 10 years (Planning Commission 2002). These targets are formulated based on the past growth trends and the vision of making India as a developed country by 2020.

While one of the recognized strengths of demography is its powerful descriptive potential, the discipline also has a long history of causal analysis. Social Science problems often involve multiple causal forces operating within complex, interrelated networks. Complexity can probably better handled by breaking up problems into separate components. However, the criteria can be used with reference to uncertain causal structures, such as the effect of historical changes in climate on population growth, the impact of legislation on demographic parameters (e.g. marriage and divorce), the economic consequences of migration, the demographic effects of particular social policies, or the population and economic growth. Demographers' interest in the environment has generally been enmeshed in broader issues of population growth and economic development. Empirical research by demographers on environmental issues other than natural resource constraints is limited. In his first Essay, more than 200 years ago, Thomas Malthus argued that unrestrained population growth would eventually be limited by fixed natural resources **(Malthus 1798)**. Human activity has radically altered the earth's surface, oceans, and atmosphere, especially over the last 200 years. On the 200th anniversary of this Essay, the relationships between population growth, human welfare, and the natural environment continue to be widely debated **(Livernash and Rodenburg 1998; Lubchenco**

1998). Public and scientific concerns about population and the environment have, of course, varied over time. Vernon Ruttan identified three waves of social concern about the environment since World War II (Ruttan 1993). These waves, each of which focused on a different set of environmental issues.[9]

The first wave, in the late 1940s and early 1950s, centered on whether natural resources (such as land, water and energy supplies) could sustain economic growth and food production in the face of population increase. These issues are similar to Malthus' original concerns.

The second wave, in the late 1960s and early 1970s, added another focus – the environment's ability to absorb by-products of modern technology, such as air and water pollutants, asbestos, pesticides, radioactive waste, and household waste **(Ruttan, 1993)**. This second wave was spurred in part by rising incomes in industrialized countries, which, ironically, increased demand, both for the commodities producing these detrimental by-products and for a cleaner environment.

The third wave, in the late 1980s and the 1990s, added yet another focus- changes occurring on a global scale, including acid rain, global warming, and ozone depletion. The second and third wave issues involve public goods- air, water, and the atmosphere- which have a well-known tendency toward over-exploitation. As the 1997 Kyoto Conference on Global Climatic Change **(UNFCCC 1998; Warrick 1998)** suggests, third-wave problems will be particularly difficult to solve because they involve considerations of equity in the use of public goods among nations **(Das Gupta, Folke, and Maler 1994; Najam 1996)**.

The interaction between economic development and **female work participation** has attracted attention amongst economists, social scientists etc. for more than fifty years. Female work participa¬tion is much higher in the states of north east except in Tripura. In a traditionally bound society like India where male predominates, the inferior image of women has become in¬grained in the minds of men, and finds expression in their day-to-day life. Even though a women can work proficiently as man they are considered inferior and subordinate to man. Bur with the advancement of time, more and more women are gainfully employed.

Food insecurity is a matter of great concern not only to the people of NER but also to the policy makers and planners of NER. In the entire North East, the valley districts of Manipur are among the most productive zones of nation in the production of paddy. However, the same cannot be true about the districts of Assam and lack of assured irrigation seems to be the major factor behind it. The productivity of paddy in Manipur-Tripura Vally and Mizoram is higher than the regional average and also above Assam which alone accounts for more than 70 p.c. of area and output in the region. Mizoram achieved a remarkable growth in the yield rate of paddy since around the middle of 1980 due to increase in fertiliser consumption and new land use policy in Mizoram. Although the paddy productivity is the lowest in Arunnachal Pradesh, the yield of oil seed and pulses is the highest in the states of Meghalaya, Mizoram and the hill districts of Manipur. As the region is classified into hill areas and plain areas, the cropping patterns in the hills districts is more varied and not similar to that of plain areas. The development of infrastructural facilities like road and communications, banking, health are responsible for the above gaps. Further, corruption at the government level and red tapism of bureaucrats are responsible for this problem in the region. The expansion of irrigation facilities, operation and maintenance of irrigation system and distribution of water have not received due attention.

Irrigation sector is today facing twin issues of sub-optimal sector planning and financial management on the one hand and inadequate water management and maintenance on the other. Involving the farmers in the irrigation system is one obvious remedy for addressing the management problems. In comparison to all-India level only 1.4 p.c. of area is under irrigation system in the NER and only 1 p.c. in the state of Assam (5,39,000 hectares). However, percentage of total irrigated area in Assam is 65 p.c. with respect to total irrigated area in NER.

Since north eastern society is dominated by the tribal population, the reference may be made to the tribal method of cultivation. Out of 23.78 lakh hectare of land in the country as a whole 19.91 lakh hectare (83.73 p.c.) of land in the northeast is under shifting cultivation or jhuming adopted in the ancient farming system, which was once considered as a farmer friendly practice has now become an ecological menace. Rapid deforestation over the years 1987-1997 due to the shifting cultivation in the region have reduced the total forest cover amounting to 1312 sq. km. (table - 2). An inevitable consequence of deforestation is increased run off rain water, precipitation and extensive soil erosion resulting in unacceptable deterioration of top soil, degradation of land and sedimentation of water bases resulting in desertification and frequent flooding. The high rate of soil erosion in deforested area in our country ranges from 10 tones per hectare in the plains to about 30 tones per hectare in the north eastern hilly region[10], 10 to 50 times larger than in the forest areas. Extensive deforestation in the region has resulted in increased carbon-di-oxide concentration in the atmosphere. The changes in climatic and rain pattern gradually setting in because of deforestation. Water and soil erosion have affected the maximum lands used for agricultural purpose. The climatic fluctuation and changes in the rain pattern have further compounded the problem of providing adequate food security to our increased population. Gross,neglect of environment also resulted in polluting not only river water but also surface water, making them fertile breeding grounds of many communicable diseases.

The Union Government sanctioned Rs. 68 crore to the eight North Eastern States during the past three years (2000-2003) for modernizing the forest protection force, forest protection system and strengthening the forest management. Tripura and Assam got the maximum amount of Rs. 16 crore each while the other states of the region received 5-9 crore for this purpose. Among the eight NE States, including Sikim, the forest cover had increased in Arunachal Pradesh and Tripura[11].

The expansion of irrigation facilities, operation and maintenance of irrigation system and distribution of water have not received due attention. Irrigation sector is today facing twin issues of sub-optimal sector planning and financial management on the one hand and inadequate water management and maintenance on the other. Involving the farmers in the irrigation system is one obvious remedy for addressing the management problems. In comparison to all-India level only 1.4 p.c. of area is under irrigation system in the NER and only 1 p.c. in the state of Assam (5,39,000 hectares). However, percentage of total irrigated area in Assam is 65 p.c. with respect to total irrigated area in NER. Health is a social goal and considered as an integral component in over all socio economic development. The majority of health problems are the products of illiteracy, poverty, ignorance, over crowding, poor environmental conditions and uneven distribution of health manpower and institutions. It is observed that there are only 4.32 p.c. of public health centres in the states of NER as compared to India's figure.

There is a need to examine the **extent of suicides** and levels in different states as a result of different socio-economic condi¬tions. Table 14.6 shows the comparative study of distribution of suicides in different age groups for two years 1996 and 2001. A minute look at the table reveals the fact that in the states of NER, the highest percentage of suicides occur in the age group 15-29 years (35.76 p.c.) followed by 30-44 years (32.06 p.c.) which is also true for the country in 1996 as well as in 2001 while in the percentage of suicides shifted highest in the age group 30-44 years (38.71 p.c.) followed by 15- 29 years (36.12 p.c.) in the states of NER. However, percentage of Region's total suicides in comparison to the country decreased from 3.67 p.c. in 1996 to 3.53 p.c. in 2001. It is striking to note that in both the periods (1996 & 2001) maximum number of suicides occur in the state of Assam (76.54 p.c. & 69.04 p.c.) followed by Tripura (17.05 p.c. & 22.27 p.c.) among the states of NER

A close look at the table 14.7, it is observed that highest percentage of suicides occur in the state of Assam (75.15 p.c.) followed by Tripura (16.73 p.c.) among the states of NER. It is also striking to note that highest number of suicides occur due to illness (11.64 p.c.) followed by unem¬ployment (4.51 p.c.) and poverty (1.01 p.c.) in 1996 while in 2001, the highest percentage of suicides took place due to unemployment (12.49 p.c.) followed by poverty (6.65 p.c.) and illness (6.04 p.c.) in the state of Assam. The proportion of suicides due to unemployment, poverty and drug abuse in respect to total suicides in NER is 6.45 p.c. in 1996 and 16.68 p.c. in 2001 which are observed mainly in the states Assam and Tripura. In backward areas rapid population growth tends to offset the benefits of development. Rather, it results in family frustra¬tion, dependence burden, employment and social tensions leading to a breakdown of an order society.

Dutta (2002, 2003) observed that due to excessive population growth, there are housing shortage, number of unemployment goes up which creates frustration among the younger generation and ultimately affects the society with creation of civil disorder, crime, drug abuse, health hazards etc. Further, due to illiteracy and poverty, population increases rapidly population explosion creates food shortage, unemployment, poverty, crime, illiteracy. Poverty is an important factor in the development of frustration among the young generation and as a result of which suicide takes place. Again the food shortage may occur due to over burden of the excess population. All these creates social chaos in the society and ultimately the frustrated people raise their ugly faces to create social disturbances through different nasty activities. Thus, terrorism is a multi-causal phenomenon and usually results from multiple causal factors such as economic, political, religious, and sociological factors, among others.

On the other hand, over population affects the nature of bio-sphere and creates ecological imbalance due to over activities of the people. Over activities of people, due to population growth, occur by depleting the nature resources like forest land, agricultural land, water etc. and misusing the energy sources. These also create different types of pollution

Table 14.6: Incidence of Suicides by Age Group (1996 & 2001)

States	By all groups		Up to 14	15-29	30-44	45-59	60+
	Male	Female					
ANP	38	13	1	15	29	6	---
	(76)	(35)	(4)	(47)	(47)	(12)	(1)
ASM	1678	814	157	913	804	501	117
	(1836)	(811)	(54)	(1003)	(976)	(537)	(77)
MNP	16	2	----	8	6	4	---
	(24)	(17)	(1)	(23)	(10)	(6)	(1)
MGH	59	13	2	18	34	12	6
	(69)	(18)	(1)	(33)	(38)	(8)	(7)
MZM	31	3	3	24	6	1	---
	(46)	(8)	(7)	(25)	(12)	(7)	(3)
NGN	26	8	---	16	17	1	---
	(25)	(15)	(--)	(15)	(20)	(5)	(--)
TRP	299	256	37	170	148	124	76
	(463)	(391)	(30)	(239)	(381)	(149)	(55)
INDIA	51206	37503	3404	33925	29138	15393	6381
	(66314)	(42192)	(3007)	(38910)	(36448)	(21579)	(8652)

*No. of suicides (By all groups) in 2001 shown within bracket

Table 14.7 Incidence of Suicides in N E States of India (1996 & 2001)

States	Change in eco Status(1998) / Poverty (2001)		Illness		Dowry		Drug abuse		Unemployment	
	1996	2001	1996	2001	1996	2001	1996	2001	1996	2001
ANP	--	4		3	---	----	---	----	---	---
ASM	11	176	324	160	15	13	24	8	149	336
MNP	---	----	2	---	---	---	2	2	---	---
MGH	--	1	9	18	---	---		---	---	
MZM	----	----	3	---	---	---	5	6	---	2
NGN	----	-----	---	1	---	---				
	4	2	---	---						
TRP	----	16	66	71	3	----	5	---	---	---
INDIA	2352	2549	22071	24098	2517	2414	1221	1414	1745	2734

due to modernization which is the effect of industrialization. Direct threats to human life style are the most obvious aspect of environmental deterioration and of these direct threats, the phenomenon commonly lumped under the term pollution has been contributed by over population and modern industrialisation. A major factor contributing to environmental degradation in most Indian cities and towns is the inadequate provision of safe drinking water and Sanitation.

Conclusion and Suggestion

The objective of development is that all people can enjoy long, healthy and creative lives. It is for all practical purposes a synonym of gender equity and equality. It is important to recognize that discourses on planning have not considered women as part of the complexity called " Development Structures". Human Development has moved to the center of the Global Development Debate. The gender issues have never been arrested by the Indian Planners and Policy makers in general and the Planners and policy makers of NER in particular. Considering the indicators used in the present study, it confirms the fact that gender issues are intertwined with the issue of Human Development for which the states of NER are lagging behind and the women of NER are still poorest of the poor despite of the favourable social customs and tradition.

The abnormal growth of population in the region may be due to heavy influx of people mainly from the neighbouring countries and also to some extent from other states in search of food, employment, business, political and disturbed conditions prevailed in the region and more particularly in the state of Assam. As regard to sex ratio, NER recorded comparatively a lower sex ratio as compared to Country's figure. In regarded to urbanization it can be concluded that the overall process of urbanization in agro-based NER is very slow basically due to it's locational and infrastructural problems. Development of secondary sectors also not up to the mark in this NER resulted in heavy dependence on agriculture sector.

The social and economic implication of population growth are useful for national planning of any country or of a region. Every development plan contains future estimates of a nation's needs as well as for policy formulation for sectors such as labour force, education, health, urbanization, agriculture etc. The GDP per capita will enable us to understand the economic progress of the country. On education, the projection of school going children, requirement of new schools as well as other infrastructure helps us to make the educational planning of the country. The health requirement with respect to health professional including the family planning situation enable us to formulate the health sector planning. The investment has to be made more and more on health and education of the people of the country in general and NER in particular. For adequate and efficient investment on human resource development, the state governments of the region have to give emphasis on improving the quality and coverage of health and nutritional services as well as educational infrastructure. Creation of sufficient employment and skilled personnel should be the targets. More and more importance should be given to meet the needs of old-age dependents in terms of health care, housing facilities, financial as well as social security.

The emphasis should be given more on economic and demographic situation of the region. There is an urgent need for re-examination of pattern of development, particularly of industrialization in the context of balanced regional development in the country. Policy makers should not ignore the heterogeneous identities of people of the region while planning development strategies for the states of NER. Through the development of the rural people the process of Region's progress can be accelerated. The spirit of nationalism should be inculcated in the minds of the people of the states of NER. Efforts should be made to ensure harmonious growth of national and sub-national identities to cure the malady. The root cause of alienation of land and indebtness among the people is poverty. Thus, to uplift the economic condition of the people of the region, the society of each village and of community must protect the economically weaker sections of the region by improving their economic condition. The developmental schemes for their economic upliftment should be implemented sincerely and expeditiously.

The State governments of the region and also the Central government should establish the requisite institutional mechanism and enabling environment at all levels of the society to ensure that population factors are appropriately addressed within the decision making and administrative process of all governmental agencies responsible for economic, environment, and social policies and programmes. There is a need for transparency, monitoring and data availability so that equity-related concerns across Socio-Religious Communities can be assessed on a continuing basis. For this, regular collection of detailed information by SRCs is essential. An autonomous National Data Bank (NDB) can be a repository of this data which should be publicly available. An independent Assessment and Monitoring Authority can be set up to look into participation of all disadvantaged SRCs including Muslims. Nominations of ethnic, linguistic, sex and religious minorities, depending on the context, in local level bodies are essential which can make the link between economic and political spaces.

Development is the process by which we affect the environment. Environment is what is left after development. Environmental awareness programmes at all levels should be sponsored by governmental and non-governmental agencies engaged in environment development. Environmental awareness should be strengthened through formal and non-formal education. Urban authorities should encourage to city dwellers for effective tree plantation nearby their residence. The best agricultural lands with ideal moisture conditions are to be utilised for agricultural purpose only. Industri¬al and urban activities should not be allowed in such areas. Environmental improvement schemes should be incorporated into the integrated urban development plan.

The tendency in our society to keep male workers in

industry and other organizations, lack of confidence on women should be avoided at all cost in the present era of globalization. In order to provide women, justice in political and economic fields the society should stop all kinds of gender based social injustice and to create an atmosphere of equality where women can breath, freedom and justice in its true form. It may be suggested that no Indian woman should be denied access to family planning assistance because of economic condition. It should be established as a national goal the provision of adequate family planning services within the next five years to all those who want them but cannot afford them. In order to achieve this national goal, it will have to increase the amount spending on population and family planning. But success in this endeavour will not result from higher expenditures alone. It needs additional research on birth control methods of all types and the sociology of population growth. Utilizing its Centre for Population Research, the Department of Health, Education, and Welfare Should take the active initiative in developing and expanded Research effort. It also needs more trained people to work in Population and Family Planning Programmes. The effects of population growth on environment and on the total food supply needs careful attention and immediate action. Efforts should be made in providing adequate inputs and to utilize the available abundant natural and human resource of the region to accelerate economic growth and overall development. It is to be noted seriously and sincerely that the Governments should also be very much Spartan in their financial deals in regard to all socio-economic development projects and programmes with direct co-operation of the people. The entire projects should be free from all unwanted and undesirable interruptions from the corrupted Bureaucracy.

To achieve sustainable development and a higher quality of life for all people, governments should reduce and eliminate unsustai¬nable pattern of production and consumption and promote appro¬priate demographic policies. At the same time the governments should implement the reform policies with extreme caution so that it would not arouse the people's emotion and sentiments by interfering in the social laws, customs, traditions et. Hence the slogan should be *'Globalisation within limits or reform in a controlled manner'*.

Note

1. Documents on The Global Science Panel on Population in Sustainable Development, population matters to development and Environment, pp. 367-368, *Population and Development Review*, Vol. 28, Number 2, June 2002.
2. Document on Environmental degradation and human well-being : the President of Pakistan, *Population and Development Review*, Vol. 31 Number 2, June 2005.
3. Document on Environmental degradation and human well-being : the President of Russia, *Population and Development Review*, Vol. 31 Number 2, June 2005.
4. "China's Local and National Frtility Policies at the End Of the Twentieth Century", Gu Bachang, Wang Feng, Guo Zhigang & Zhang Erli in *Population and Development Review*, as Notes and Commentary, pp. 129-147, Vol. 33, Number 1, March 2007
5. Raina, *Planning Family in India*, 1990, pp. 12-79, passim.
6. Raina, Population Policy, 1988, pp. 5-7; and. "Recommendations of the Committee... on Population Growth and Family Planning," 14 April 1951, Reprinted as appendix A2 in Gupta, Sinha and Bardhan, *Evolution of Family Welfare Programme in India,* Vol. 1, 1992.
7. India, Planning Commission, *Third Five Year Plan*, 1961, pp. 25, 72
8. Page 45 of Vol. 35 No.1, Feb. 1998, DEMOGRAPHY.
9. PRESIDENTIAL ADDRESS : Demography and The Environment, Anne. R. Pebley, Demography, Vol. 35(4), Nov., 1998, pp. 377-389.
10. U. R. Rao (1994) : Space For Sustainable Development, G. B. Panth Memorial Lecture, Guwahati.
11. NE News Letter, Vol. 5, No.4, April, 2003.

References

Connelly Matthew (2006) : *"Population Control in India: prologue to the Emergency Period"*, Population And Development Review, pp. 629-668, Vol. 32, No. 4, December 2006.

Croll Elisabeth J (1984) : *"The Single-Child Family : The First-Five Years"*, in Neville Maxwell and Bruce J. McFarlane (eds.), China's Changed Road to Development, New York: Pergamon Press.

Das Gupta, P., C. Folke, and K.G.Maler (1994) : *"The Environmental Resource Base and Human Welfare."* pp. 25-40 in Population, Economic Development, and the Environment, Ed. K. Lindahl-Kiessling and H. Landberg. Oxford University Press, Oxford.

Dutta P.C. (1996) : *"Quality Variation of Some Food Items of Consumption in North Eastern Region (NER)"*, Indian Journal of Regional Science, Vol. 28 (1).

Dutta P.C. (2002) : *"Population Growth and Environmental Crisis in North East India :* Problems and Remedies" in Development Priorities in North East India(ed), B. J. Deb, Concept Publishing Company, New Delhi.

Dutta P.C. (2002) : *"A Study on The Impacts of Socio-Economic Development in North East India with Special Reference to the Problems of Population Growth and Urbanisation On Environment"*- UGC sponsored MRP (2000-2002), Report submitted on 18.03.02

Dutta P.C. (2003) : *"Regional Disparity and its consequences in North Eastern Region of India"* in Economic Liberalization and Regional Disparities in India-Special Focus on the North eastern Region (ed) A. C. Mohapatyra and Chitta Ranjan Pathak, Star Publishing House, Shillong.

Dutta P.C. (2005) : *"Problems of Ethnicity in North East India"* in Perspective of Security and Development in North East India (ed) S. K. Agnihotri (IAS) and B. Datta Ray, Concept Publishing Company, New Delhi.

Dutta P.C. and Y. Deb (2005) : "Problems and Prospects of Peace Process in Assam of North East India", Paper presented in the National Seminar on Prospects of Peace Process in Assam of North East India, NEICSSR, Shillong, December 9-10

Foster, A.D., M.R. Rosenzweig, and J.R. Behrman (1997) : "Population Growth, Income Growth and Deforestation – Management of Village Common Land in India", Unpublished manuscript, Department of Economics, Brown University.

Hendrik P. Van Dalen and Kene Henkens (2007) : *"Longing For the Good Life: Understanding Emigration from a High –Income Country"*, Population and Development Review, pp. 37- 66, Vol. 33, No.1, March, 2007.

Livernash, R and E. Rodenburg (1998) : *"Population Change, Resources and the Environment"*, Population Bulletin 53(4), 1-40.

Lubchenco, J (1998) : *"Entering the Century of the Environment. A New Social Contract for Science"*, SCIENCE 279(23), 491-97.

Madhab, Jayanta (1999) : *"North East, Crisis of Identity, Security and Underdevelopment"*, EPW, Vol. 34, No.1, Feb. 6-12.

Malthus, T.R (1798) : *"An Essay on the Principle of Population as it Affects the Future Improvement of Society"*, Reprint, Harmondsworth, Middlesex, England : Perican Books, 1970.

Naik, J.P. (1997) : "The Education Commission and After" Second Edition New Delhi, (First edition, 1979, APH Publishing Corporation, New Delhi.

Najam, A.(1996) : "A Developing Countries' Perspective on Population, Environment, and Development." Population Policy and Policy Review, 15:1-19.

National Academy of Sciences (1986) : *"Population Growth and Economic Development; Policy Questions"*, Washington DC, National Academy Press.

Nikos Alexandratos (2005) : *"Countries with Rapid Population Growth and Resource Constraints : Issues of Food, Agriculture, and Development"*, Population And Development Review, pp. 237-258, Vol 31, No. 2, June 2005.

Ruttan, V.W. (1993) : *"Population Growth, Environmental Change, and Innovation: Implications for Sustainable Growth in Agriculture"*, pp. 124-56 in POPULATION AND LAND USE IN DEVELOPING COUNTRIES, ed. C.L. Jolly and B.B. Torrey, Washington DC, National Academy Press.

Simon, J. (1981) : *"The Ultimate Resource"*. Princeton, NJ: Princeton University Press.

Simon, J. (1997) : *The Economics of Population Growth*. Princeton, NJ: Princeton University Press.

United Nations Framework Convention on Climatic Change (UNFCCC) (1998) : *Report of the Conference of the Parties on Its Third Session, Held in Kyoto From 1 to 11 December, 1997. Addendum. Part Two : Action Taken by the Conference of the Partiesat its Third Session*. New York: United Nations.

Wang, Feng. (2005) : *"Can China Afford to Continue Its One-Child Policy ?."*, Asia Pacific Issues 17, Honolulu: East-West Centre.

Warrick, J. (1998) : *"Reassessing Kyoto Agreement, Scientists See Little Environmental Advantage."* Washington Post, February 13, p. 14.

15

Population Dynamics and Socio-Economic Scenario in NER

At the Millennium Summit in September 2000, world leaders agreed on a set of goals to guide global development in the 21st century. What have become known as The United Nations' Millennium Development. Goals (MDGs) include: halving extreme poverty and hunger, achieving universal primary education and gender equity, reducing under-five mortality and maternal mortality by two-thirds and three-quarters respectively, reversing the spread of HIV/AIDS, halving the proportion of people without access to safe drinking water and ensuring environmental sustainability. They also include the goal of developing a global partnership for development, with targets for aid, trade and debt relief. Empowering women was recognized as an important end in itself, as well as a key to improving the quality of life of everyone. Without the full and equal participation of women, there can be no sustainable human development.

In the era of globalisation rapid socio-economic transformation has been taking place in the economy at international level. The planners and policy makers in India are trying to cope with it. Economic welfare does not merely depend upon the level of development but also on its distributive aspects. In the pluralistic nature of the country, differences in natural resources, climate, topography, vegetation and density of population can be identified easily and the North Eastern Region of India (NER) is no exception to it. Unequal distribution of wealth and resources caused regional disparity in the country as a result of which the states of NER are lagging behind.

It is a fact that the urbanisation is the most essential for all round development of the developing nations, as it increases employment, income and standard of living in these countries. The increasing urbanisation has led to a number of socio-economic problems like crime, suicides, drug abuse, unemployment and poverty, alcoholism, overcrowding, housing shortage, slums, traffic control and pollution etc. At the same time they are also centres of civilisation and culture by helping a lot in the process of modernization.

India's growth prospect is shared by most international observers who now believe that India now has the potential to achieve sustained growth at 9 to 10 p.c. for the next 20 years. "Our nation is going through a major challenge of uplifting of 220 million people who are below the poverty line and also to give better life for many millions who are on the border line of poverty or just above the poverty line. Our GDP is growing at more than 8 p.c. per annum on an average. Whereas, the economists suggest that to uplift the people from below the poverty line, our economy has to grow at the rate of 10 p.c. per annum consistently, for over a decade", the President of India expressed.[1]

Choudhury and Rajakutty (1999) argued that Social Development Index (SDI) and Infrastructure Development Index (IDI) showed a close association with poverty reduction. Assam along with three other states of India have high backwardness index (meaning that large parts of these States are backward in terms of social and physical infrastructure and social development). He also showed that in Gender Related Development Index (GDI), India's (GDI 0.388) rank is 112 out of 143 countries. In the late 1970s there emerged a cluster of notions according to which China's rapid population growth was self-evident proof of the country's backwardness and a major cause of China's continued failure to achieve its rightful place in the world.**(Susan Greenhalgh, 2003).**

According to the present average of 2.2 children per couple,

China's population will reach 1,300 million in 20 years and will surpass 1,500 million in 40 years.... This will aggravate the difficulties for the four modernisations and give rise to a grave situation in which the people's standard of living can hardly be improved..... Moreover, too fast a growth of population not only creates difficulties in education and employment but will overtax the energy, water, forest, and other natural resources, aggravate environmental pollution and make the production conditions and living environment downright bad and very hard to be improved. **(Central Committee, 1985).**

Education for Women's Equity", of the Govt. of India is not corroborating the New International Economic Order (NIEO). The literature is most appropriate in the era of Globalisation to analyse the miseries of the women in the region. Apart from the distribution of infrastructural facilities, the quality of life depends upon several other factors like geographical, ecological, socio culture etc. which are distributed in an haphazard manner all over the country and thus handicaps the development of relatively backward regions. India's North-Eastern Region is no exception to it.

Dutta (2003) brought out the facts about the regional disparity in NER and concluded that the states of NER are far behind from other states of the Indian Union so far as the basic amenities of life such as health, education, safe drinking water, banking facility, food security, communication etc. are concerned. Iniquitous distribution of national wealth and resources of the country causes regional disparities by giving rise to various types of socio- economic problems.

It is in this context, an enquiry is deemed to be necessary to examine the multi dimensional and complex relationships among some socio-economic and demographic variables of the NER of India as it is physically located in a backward and disadvantageous position due to its physical geography as well as the social and political conditions prevailing in the region. The study has been concluded with some valuable suggestions. The study is being made on the basis of secondary sources of data relating to socio-economic and demographic variables for the NER of India covering a period of 55 years (1951-2005). However, economic studies made by various research workers based on different secondary data have also been used for the purpose.

Analysis

The analysis of the study have been completed under different sections.

Population Growth and Demographic Characteristics

The NER covers an area of 2.63 lakh sq. km. which accounts for 7.9 per cent of total geographical area of the country. The share of population of NER to the total population of India as low as 1.70 per cent in 1901, since then it has been steadily increasing and reached at nearly 3.8 per cent with a total population of 38.86 million, as per 2001 census. According to India's Health Ministry, India's population which was 238 million in 1947 touched 1.012 million in March 2001 and is expected to be 1.263 billion by 2016. The share of population of NER, in comparison to all India, increased from 2.89 p.c. in 1951 to 3.78 p.c. in 2001.

Fig. 15-A and Fig. 15-B shows the population structure of different states of NER in 1951 and 2001 respectively. The figures reveal the fact that Assam (80.29 lakhs and 266.38 lakhs) occupies the highest position followed by Tripura and Manipur while Sikkim (1.38 lakh and 5.4 lakh) is the smallest state followed by Mizoram (1.96 lakh and 8.91

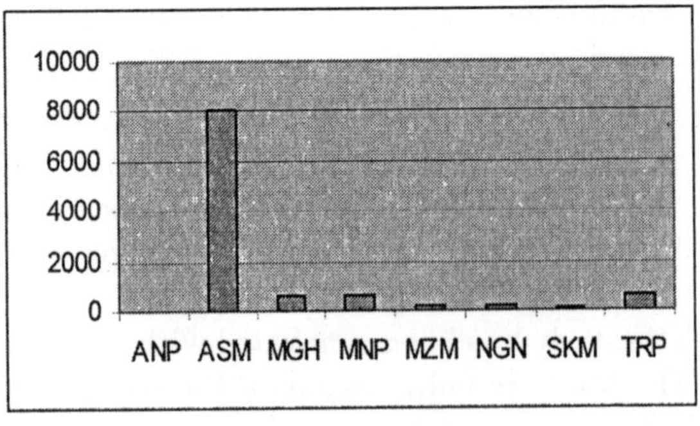

Fig. 15-A: (1951)

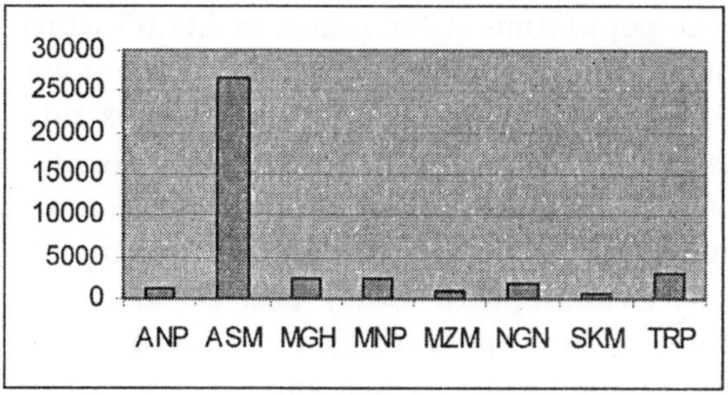

Fig. 15-B: (2001)

lakh) among the states of NER.

Figure-15-C shows the percent decadal variation of total population for different states of NER and India as a whole for the period 1951-2001. It is remarkable to note that highest variation occurred in the state of Tripura (78.7 p.c.) during the period 1951-61 and for Nagaland, it is 64.41 p.c. during the period 1991-2001 which increased from 14.41 p.c. during 1951-61. The decadal growth rate of population (1991-2001) is the lowest in the state of Tripura 16.03 p.c. followed by Assam (18.92 p.c.) and highest in the state of Nagaland (64.53) followed by Sikkim (33.06 p.c.). The region's growth rate of population (21.61 p.c.) is slightly higher than the national average of 21.35 p.c. during 1991-2001. The density of the population varies from 13 in Arunachal Pradesh to 340 in Assam followed by 305 in Tripura.

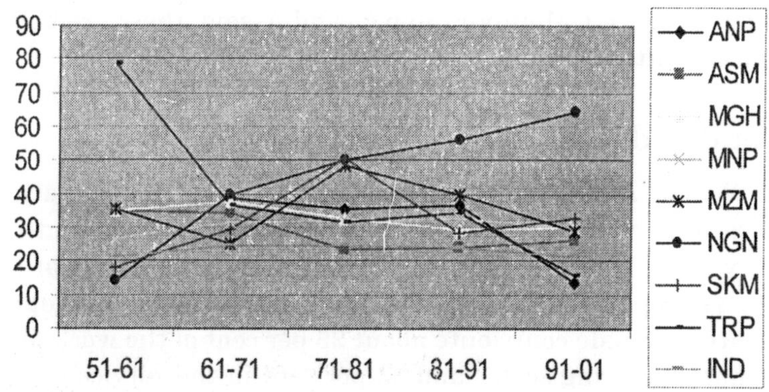

Fig. 15-C: Percent Decadal Variation of Total Population in NER

The density of the population of the region is 147.65 which is almost half of the national density (324) in 2001 while it was only 34.29 in 1951. It is remarkable to note that the sex ratio in NER has consistently shown excess of males over females as noted for India. The bulk of population of the region (almost 70 p.c. of total population of the region) is concentrated mainly of three sectors viz. Brahmaputra valley and Barak valley of Assam and Tripura. The large variation is caused by the geographical and economic factors, which vary greatly within the region.

The age-distribution in each state of NER is typical of high fertility populations, with a high proportion of population in the younger age-groups. Manipur, Mizoram and Tripura have the lowest percentage of population below 15 years of age (37 p.c.) and this Percentage is the highest in Arunachal Pradesh (43 p.c.). The proportion of the population of age 60 and above varies from just over 2 per cent in Nagaland to 8 per cent in Tripura. The total number of tribal population is 81.42 lakh which is approximately 25.71 p.c. of the total population. The percentage of Schedule Tribes varies from 13 p.c. (Assam) to 91 p.c. (Mizoram) which are above the country's figure (8 p.c.).. However, more than three fourths of the household belong to scheduled tribe in the states of Mizoram, Nagaland (96 p.c.), Meghalaya (89 p.c.), Arunachal Pradesh (76 p.c.) and while in Tnpura (17 p.c.), Manipur (35 p.c.) and Assam, these are below 50 p.c. **(Dutta, 2002)**.

Gender disparity

Women account for roughly half the world's population, perform two-thirds of the hours worked, receive one-tenth of the world's income, and have less than one hundredth of the world's property registered in their names [2]. In many developing countries female contribute about 25 per cent of the work force in manufacturing sector and 33 per cent in the service sector. Recent findings suggest that the social benefits from investing in female education are far greater than those from investing in male education. Female education is perceived as an important factor not only in imparting new knowledge and information, skills and values for improving their participation in the labour force or earnings, but also in enhancing their status within and outside their immediate family.

In comparison to Indian women (41.42 p.c.), North-East women occupied only 1.74 p.c. in case of general education. The percentage distribution of women students out of total students in the NER which proves the fact that women are interested to get admit themselves in the Arts stream rather than Science or Commerce. The percentage of commerce women are very low in all the states of NER which ranges from 0.37 p.c. to 2.75 p.c. which is far below than all India level (7.77 p.c.).

A minute look at the figure 15-D confirms the fact that in the states of NER, the Female Literacy Rate (FLR) ranges from 44.24 p.c. to 65.41 p.c. It is remarkable to note that all the states of NER, except Arunachal Pradesh (44.24 p.c.), are above

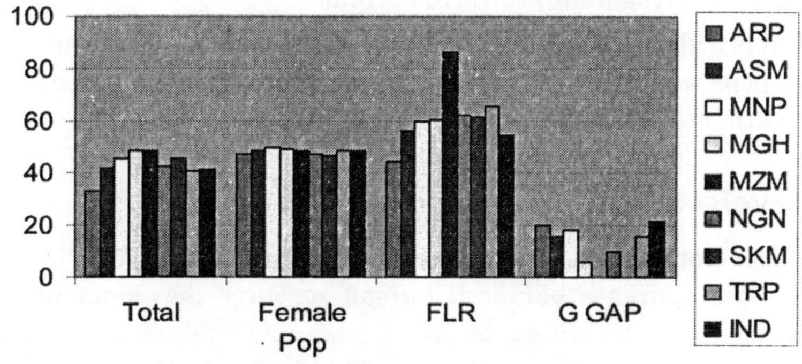

Fig 15-D: Percentage Distribution of Total Female students (in different streams), Female Literacy, Gender Gap and Sex Ratio (2000-01) in different states of NER.

all- India level (54.16 p.c.). It is observed from the figure that in the year 2001, the Gender Gap (G GAP) in the North Eastern States ranges from 5.73 (Meghalaya) to 19.83 (Arunachal Pradesh) and below the all –India level (21.69). However, it is important to note that, in comparison to 1991, where the range was 7.01 to 24.07 for the states NER and for all- India it was 24.84, the Gender Gap decreased in all the states of NER in the year 2001.

In case of Sex Ratio, it is observed that all the states of NER, except Arunachal Pradesh (901), are above all-India level (933). It should be noted here that with respect to 1991, the Sex Ratio increased in all the states of NER including all- India. The exceptional state in this case is the state of Sikim (878). A close look at the figure reveals the fact that the percentage of female population in the states of NER lies between 46.68 p.c. (Sikim) and 49.45 p.c. (Manipur). However, it is to be noted here that the States of Arunachal Pradesh, Assam, Nagaland and Sikim are below all India figure (48.27 p.c.).

The literacy movement have sought to respond to the needs of the people at grass-root level. The decadal growth rate of female literacy in India has shown an increase of 13.67 percentage points during the period 1991 to 2001. The same trend has also been observed in the states of NER which ranges from 7.17 (Nagaland) to 15.76 (Tripura).

It is widely recognized that women as a group and particularly the poor women have been adversely affected by the process of growth, economic transformation and development.

Development

Development is a process, which improves the quality of life. It requires a balanced human resource development in the country. According to latest Human Development Index Report (HDI), India's position is 96 out of 120. The impact of developmental activities cannot be evaluated fully by any single indicator because it is a multi-dimensional process. Hence there is a need of combining the effect of different indicators for assessing the level of development.

The development of an area is best reflected in the quality of life of its people. Quality of life index may be comprised of Literacy Rate (LR), female literacy rate (FLR), sex ratio (SR), Child-women ratio (CWR), female work participation (FWP),

Per capita expenditure (PCE), dependency ratio (OR), Per capita non-food expenditure (PCNFE), Percentage growth of population (PGR), infant mortality rate (IMR), mean age at marriage (MAM), per capita net domestic product (PCNDP) public health centre (PHC), etc.

Positive correlations are obtained for LR with PCE (0.382), MAM (0.892 PCNDP (0.576*), FWP (0.201) while negative correlations are obtained with PGR (-03762), IMR (-0.633).

Thus raising the status of female by education and employment may help the birth control resulting lower growth rate. It has been further observed that there exist a negative correlation between percentage of urban population (PUP) and IMR which is highly significant. It is observed that for some of the demographic variables explain even 73 p.c. of the total variation in PCE. The variables for the different equations are selected on the appropriate knowledge about their intrinsic importance with respect to the dependent variables, even if their association with the dependent variable is reflected to be feeble on the rank correlations. The parameters are estimated under OLS method. The figures in the brackets show the respective standard errors of the regression coefficients.

Regression Equations

1. PCE = 114.61—0.08 SR—0.09 IMR + 0.26 PCNDP

   (4.902) (0.04) (.05) (0.11), $R^2 = 0.70$

2. PCE = 89.86 + 247.16 PCEI—252.87 *PCEIN + 0.228 PCNDP—0.95 L.R

   (16.21) (160.63) (113.16) (0.06)

   (0.94), $R^2 = 0.57$

3. PCE = 62.89 + 149.94 PCEI + 0.33 PCNDP

   (18.36) (105.18) (0.12) $R^2 = 0.73$

4. PCEI = 0.72 + 0.0002 PCNDP + 0.0006 PGR + 0.0022 SR

   (0.04) (0.0003) (0.004) (0.0005),

   $R^2 = 0.47$

Equation -I is straight forward with expected signs of the regression coefficients for PCE (PCE) on Sex ratio (SR) and explains 70 p.c. of the total variation of PCE on sex ratio, Equation -I is straight forward with expected signs of the regression coefficients for PCE (PCE) on Sex ratio (SR) and explains 70 p.c. of the total variation of PCE on sex ratio, infant mortality rate and per capita net domestic product. The coefficient of determination (R^2) is 0.57 for the regression equation of PCE on inequality in PCE (PCEI), inequality in non-food total PCE (PCEIN), literacy rate (LR), and per capita net domestic product (PCNDP) where regression coefficient for PCNDP shows significant indicating that PCE is significant indicating that PCE is influenced by inequalities in non-food total PCE.

The distribution of land holding is another important indicator of an economy. Lorenz ratios have been used to throw light in the matter of distribution of land in the rural economy in the various states of India. The values of Lorenz ratio are found to be lowest in Manipur (0.325) followed by Meghalaya (0.353) and Arunachal Pradesh (0.462). The degree of inequalities in the states of NER are found to be lower as compared to country's figure (0.639). In case of individual land holding, the level of inequality is found to be lowest in Arunachal Pradesh (0.352). It is further observed that land is evenly distributed in the north eastern states of India **(Dutta, 2003)**.

Energy

Energy plays a crucial role in the socio-economic development of a country as growth in energy consumption is intrinsically linked to growth in the economy. There is huge potential for the development of oil, gas and energy prospects in Assam and the NER of India which have not been utilised to their fullest potential and large possibilities have remained unexplored due to lack of trained manpower, lack of organised efforts and a conservative mindset. All this, if properly harnessed, can bring about a radical change to the economy of the region. In the era of globalization, electricity is one of the basic inputs for achieving socio-economic development of a nation. The present per capita consumption of electricity in India is little over 400 Kwh, which is much lower than that of the developed countries (five times lower as compared to world average).

There is a regular feature of the shortage of power in the state of Assam. About 87 per cent of the state population live in rural areas, that is 26,247 villages. Of these, as on March 31, 2006, only 21,586 villages have been electrified of which only 16.54 per cent of the total households in these electrified villages have electricity connection. The development of an area is best reflected in the distribution of basic needs. The North Eastern Council (NEC) has contributed to the North Eastern Region power supply through its power projects. The total installed capacity for power generation in the NER, as on 31st August 2006, is placed at 2404.2 MW. The power generation capacity includes the three sectors viz. the state sector, central sector and private generation. During the past six years or so, the capacity additions made in the power sector in the NER aggregated to 909 MW of which the contribution of the State sector is 148.5 MW (16.30 per cent) and the Central sector was 760.5 MW (83.60 per cent). Cumulatively, 29605 villages have been electrified out of a total of 40377 inhabited villages (as per 2001 census) in the NER up to 31.3.05. Which indicates that 73.32 p.c. of total villages electrified as on 31.03.05 while only 24.26 p.c. of the rural households have electrification in NER. (Source : Rajya Sabha Unstarred Question No. 1863, dated 09.03.2006). It confirms the fact of region's backwardness as it is observed that the per capita consumption of electricity is much lower in the states of NER as compared to the country's consumption (338.5 kwh). Among the states of NER, the highest per capita consumption is observed in the state of Meghalaya (134.5 kwh) and lowest in Tripura (80.4 kwh).

Agriculture

India's total cultivable area is 1,269,219 km^2 (56.78 p.c. of total land area), which is decreasing due to constant pressure from an ever growing population and increased urbanisation. NER as a whole is placed amongst the poorest regions in the country. The per capita income of the region is Rs. 12407 which is less than the national average of Rs.17978 (2001-02). The pattern of agricultural growth has however remained uneven across regions and crops. Although Assam is more industrially developed than the other North Eastern states, it is primarily an agrarian economy with 74 p.c. of its population engaged in agriculture and allied activities. As per 2001 census, 53 p.c. of total work force are engaged in agricultural activities. But during the period 2000-05, the overall scenario of agriculture is not praiseworthy. The contribution of agriculture to Net State Domestic Product of the state is only 31.19 p.c. in 2003-04. The production of winter rice steadily decreased from 2713 thousand tones in 2001-02 to 1800 thousand tones in 2004-05. Same trends are observed in case of Autumn rice. Summer rice, cotton, Jute etc. As per the report of livestock census 2003, the total livestock population in Assam was 140.23 lakh as against 134.67 lakh in 1997. The livestock products as milk, egg and meat are plying a vital role in the economy of Assam. As per the State Directorate of Fisheries, present level of annual fish production is 1.86 lakh metric tones (2004-05) which increased by 15.41 p.c. in comparison to 2001-02.

Agriculture plays an important role in the State's economy and employs more than 50 p.c. of the total workforce of the State of Meghalaya. Agriculture not only supplies raw materials for industries outside the State such as cotton, jute, ginger etc. but also provides inputs to other few small agro-based industries in the State such as turmeric, paddy, maize etc. Production of total cereals and Pulses in Meghalaya was 174.83 thousand tones and 0.70 thousand tones respectively during the year 2004. However, the production decreased by 11.75 p.c. over the last year. Nagaland, like the other states of the NER, is also predominantly an agrarian economy. In Nagaland, almost 75 p.c. of the working population is engaged in the primary sector. Rice is the staple food and occupies about 70 p.c. of the total cultivated area, consisting about 75 p.c. of the total food grain production. Nagaland has been identified as a potential area for development of food processing industries in its geo climatic conditions. The agriculture and allied sectors in Nagaland offer good inputs for development of a host of industries which could include floriculture, horticulture, rubber plantation and allied industries, sericulture, tea cultivation and processing, bamboo shot preservation, mushroom cultivation and processing, piggery, poultry etc. Sikkim's economy is largely agrarian, based on traditional farming methods, on terraced slopes. The rural populace grows crops such as cardamom, oranges, apples, tea and orchids. Rice is grown on terraced hillsides in the southern reaches. Sikkim has the highest production and largest cultivated area of cardamom in India. Because of the hilly terrain, and lack of reliable transportation infrastructure, there are no large-scale industries. The economy of Sikkim is mainly based on agricultural and animal husbandry. Approx. 11 p.c. of the total geographical area is under agriculture. Tripura's economy is primarily agrarian. Agriculture and its allied activities contributes nearly 34 p.c. to the state's NSDP. Agriculture in Tripura includes traditional Jhum (shifting) cultivation. After Kerala, Tripura is the largest producer of natural rubber and the rubber produced is of superior quality. The state also has the distinction of being the highest producer of True Potato Seeds in the country.

The table 15.1 shows the percentage distribution of female main workers in the States of NER. It shows that except Assam (6.7 p.c.) all the states of NER are above the all India level (8.1 p.c.). It is also important to note that the State of Assam is below the all India level in both the Primary sector (12.3 p.c.) and in Secondary sector (11.5 p.c.). Considering the secondary sector, it is observed that the percentage of female workers in all the states of NER, except in Manipur (25.9 p.c.), are below the all India level (24.9 p.c.). In case of Tertiary sector, the States of Manipur (28.6 p.c) and Mizoram (43.44 p.c.) are below the all India level (52.4 p.c.).

A close look at the Fig. 15-E reveals the fact that the Net

Table 15.1: P.C. Distribution of Females Main Workers (Urban) in NER

	Main Workers	Primary Sector	Secondary sector	Tertiary Sector
ANP	11.7	22.5	10.7	76.3
ASM	6.7	12.3	11.5	76.3
MNP	20.8	45.6	25.9	28.6
MGH	16.1	11.81	5.42	82.77
MZM	27.8	52.49	4.07	43.44
NGN	12.0	34.1	7.8	58.1
SKM	7.08	20.1	16.8	43.9
TRP	8.7	4.3	6.9	88.70
INDIA	8.1	22.8	24.9	52.4

State Domestic Product (NSDP) of NER has increased by 20.55 p.c. from Rs. 46521 crores in 2000-01 to Rs. 56082 in 2002-03. During this period, Assam's share (60.75 p.c.) of NSDP in total NER, however, decreased to 59.76 p.c. while Tripura's contribution increased from 10.47 p.c. to 10.78 p.c. in 2002-03. The lowest contribution in NER is observed for the state of

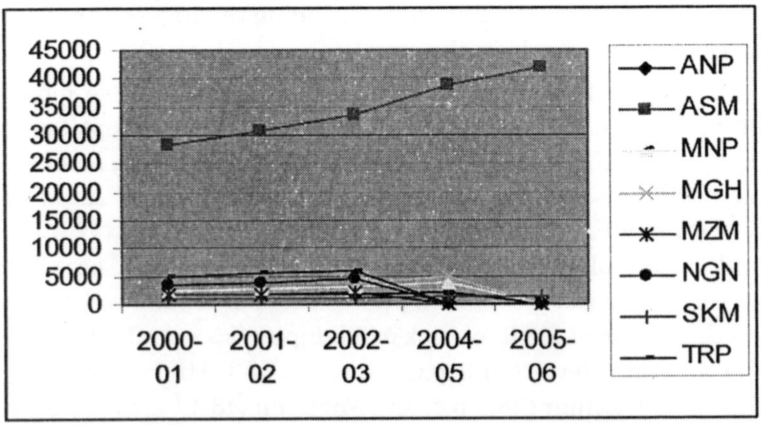

Fig. 15-E : State-Wise Net State Domestic Product (At Current Prices)

Sikkim (1.89 p.c.) in the period 2000-01 which increased to 1.98 p.c. in 2002-03. Again considering the own state development, Assam's NSDP increased by 48.05 p.c. over the years 2000-01 to 2005-06. while for Sikkim it is only 75.51 p.c. Further, the region has one of the lowest gross per capita industrial output at around Rs. 3313, (in Assam) which is much below

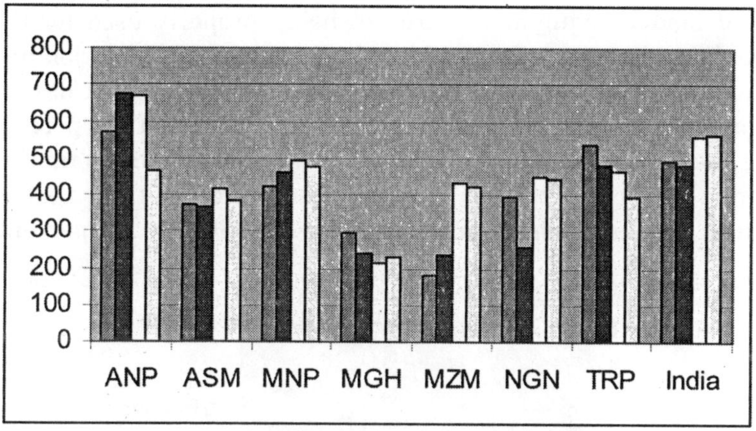

Fig. 15-F: Per Capita Per Day Availability of Food Grains (in Gms.)

the national average of Rs. 9111 [2000-01].

Fig. 15-F gives a picture of per capita per day availability of food grains production for 4 different years namely 1983,1988, 1994 and 1999 where same picture is observed as in case of pulses. It is observed that Arunachal Pradesh, the only state in NER tried to maintain its superiority till 1994 but declined there after.

Fig 15-G shows the comparative study of population and production over two periods 1980-1990 and 1991-2000. The figure reveals the fact that only the state of Mizoram maintains the superiority on production over population growth. The state of Arunachal Pradesh shows the negative growth of production in the period 1991-2000 over the last period 1980-1990. However maximum of the states show the less average growth of production in comparison to average growth of population which is not all praiseworthy.

Thus food insecurity is a matter of great concern not only to the people of NER but also to the policy makers and planners of NER. It is further observed that no proper care has been taken for the development of agriculture to increase production by which the living condition of the society of NER may be a better one. Modern technologies, irrigation facilities, scientific and modern equipments are not being properly used for the real development of agriculture in the age of globalisation and liberalization and for which the region stepping back day by day. It is striking to note that so far as the poorest ten percent of the rural population is concerned the shares of consumption are relatively better in Manipur and Mizoram than that of their counterpart in NER while for the richest ten percent,

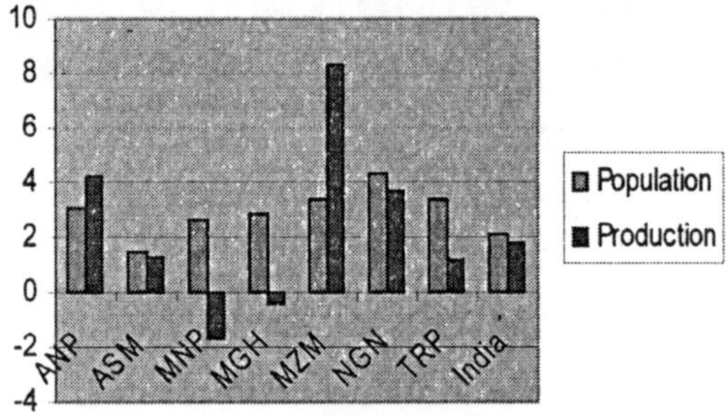

1980-90

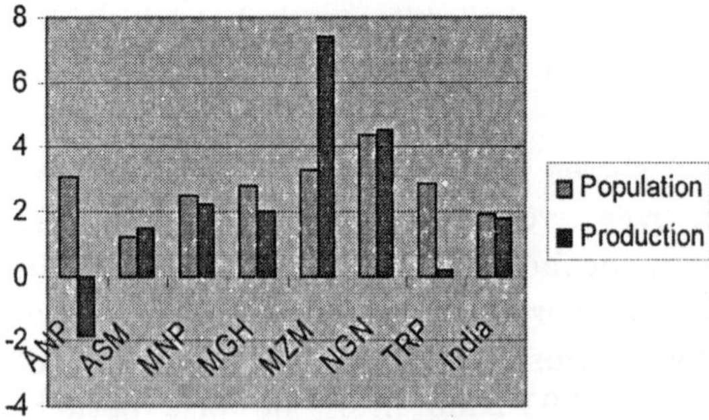

1991-2000

Fig. 15-G: Annual Average Growth Rate of Population and production (Food Grains)

the shares of consumption are relatively better in Assam and Meghalaya (table – 15.2). Coming to the urban sectors of NER, it is worthwhile to mention that the percentage share of expenditure according to poorest ten percent groups of consumers were found to be better in the state of Nagaland and worst in Assam while for the richest ten percent of the consumers, the share is relatively better in Assam among the states of NER.

Dutta and Choudhury (1996) noted that the pattern of consump¬tion is most uneven in Assam and is one of the highest among the states of NER though it is considerably less than the average for all India in the rural sector. It can also

Table 15.2: Percentage share of consumption by extreme two groups (bottom and top 10 p.c) of population in rural and urban areas in the N. E. States.

State	Rural	Rural	Urban	Urban
	Bottom 10 p.c.	Top 10 p.c.	Bottom 10 p.c.	Top 10 p.c.
ANP	3.43	22.13	3.01	25.04
ASM	3.43	23.28	1.15	37.23
MNP	4.74	19.33	4.01	18.66
MGH	3.02	22.79	2.94	25.61
MZM	4.11	17.46	3.92	18.78
NGN	---	---	5.82	18.52
SKM	3.47	22.15	3.87	27.98
TRP	3.92	20.52	3.02	21.76
India	2.65	26.16	1.83	32.02

be pointed out that the poorest section of the society in Assam has been badly affected. Thus it may be pointed out that the poorest section of the society in Assam has been badly affected. The results reveal that the extent of degree of inequality in the level of living in the states of NER is much more than what is taken to guide some of the decision making elements in connection with resource transfer from centre to these north eastern states particularly in Assam.

Poverty

Global income inequality is probably greater than it has ever been in human history. There is some debate about whether it is getting worse or getting better. Currently, the richest 1% of people in the world receives as much as the bottom 57%. The ratio between the average income of the top 5% in the world to the bottom 5% increased from 78 to 1 in 1988 to 114 to 1 in 1993. Inequality is increasing around the world while the world appears to globalize. Even the wealthiest nation has the largest gap between rich and poor compared to other developed nations. Poverty is not just an economic issue, it is also an issue of political economics. People are hungry not because of lack of availability of food, or "over" population, but because they are too poor to afford the food. Politics and economic conditions have led to poverty and dependency around the world. If food production is further increased and provided to more people while the underlying causes of poverty are not addressed, hunger will still continue because people will not be able to *purchase* food.

Monthly Per Capita Expenditure (MPCE) may be accepted as an indicator of standard of living for people, on the basis of minimum calorie intake, suggested by Indian Council of Medical Research (ICMR) which should be 2400 calorie for an Indian working persons in rural India and 2100 calorie in urban India. However, economists and statisticians in the year 2000 estimated the monthly income needed for a rural individual to consume 2,400 calories per day was Rs 567. Considering the economic condition of NER, it is estimated that the percentage of population below the poverty line is higher in respect of all-India level in 1998 and which come out as 56.83 p.c. and 42.33 p.c. for the rural and urban people of NER respectively. As per NSSO's round survey, the poverty ratio has declined in the NER which is 38.01 p.c. in 2000 as compared to 45.01 p.c. in 1993-94. However, as per 2000-01, all the states in NER has much higher levels of population below poverty line (35.13 p.c.) as compared to the national average of 26.1 p.c. Economic growth is an essential but not the sole requirement for success in the fight against poverty. It is equally important to have a social policy that places particular emphasis on meeting basic human needs. The region represents one of the highest rates of unemployment in the country, with an unemployment rate close to 12 p.c., against the national average of 7.7 p.c. [1999-00].

Expenditure to Control Insurgency

Table 15.3: Expenditure in Security Arrangement of Police Force in North East Region (Rs. In Crore)

Year State	1997-98	1998-99	1999-00	2000-01	2001-02	2002-03	Total
ANP	--	--	--	1.00	1.90	0.95	3.85
ASM	131.91	78.86	52.17	63.97	92.86	68.01	487.78
MNP	--	19.43	3.44	14.18	4.00	7.64	48.69
MGH	--	--	--	3.21	0.60	8.35	12.16
NGN	--	35.61	17.88	7.50	12.71	22.42	96.12
TRP	--	28.55	17.53	15.00	27.70	29.85	118.63

Source : The Ananda Bazar Patrika, 28th November, 2003

In NER the expenditure to control insurgency has been increasing day by day. But ironically along with the expenditure to control insurgency, insurgency has been increasing by leaps and bounds. Recently, in an NEC published paper a detailed account of expenditure is presented. This paper of expenditure is outside the budget of Defence Ministry and seven State Governments. In the last six years, in NER, the central government spent an additional amount of 1,000 crore for deployment of police forces. After spending such huge amount of money, the condition of the region is no better.

During the period 1997-2003, the states of NER have

sanctioned crores of rupees in their budget. Side by side an amount of 767 crores of rupees (table 15.3) they have spent for police security out of the enhanced amount of Rs. 1,000 crores sanctioned by the Central government. Among these seven states, Assam having an expenditure amounting Rs. 487.8 crore, Tripura having 118 crore and Nagaland having 96 crores are at the top of the list. For the modernization of police force another 278 crores of rupees has been spend. In this sphere also these three states top the list. The amounts spent are 103 crore, 46 crores and 39 crores respectively. Unless we bring back peace and security to the region, we shall stay far behind the rest of the country in the match towards development and prosperity.

Conclusion and Suggestions

NER had all along been facing various challenges, cutting across the spheres of economy, society and polity towards its all round development. From foregoing discussions it may be inferred that the region requires a holistic and comprehensive approach that can unify the interest of various ethnic groups and synergise the strengths that are inherent in the society, polity and economy and hence the economic development is mismatchingwiththepopulationgrowth.However,development can not take place properly as there are corruption at all levels of society, from governments, civil society, judiciary functions, military and other services and so on.

Following suggestions can be made to address the problems of socio-economic development and population growth in the context of NER.

The ultimate goal should be to achieve rural prosperity and not just poverty reduction. The Planning Commission should monitor not only the allocation and expenditure but also scrutinise whether these expenditures directly result in reduction of poverty or not. The government should develop an economic system that addresses regional economic development which must be in tune with political, cultural and social life and strive to eliminate structural poverty as well as the culture of poverty that affects large segments of the population. It should be based on economic development on the principles of sustainable development with due emphasis on the efficient and sustainable use of natural resources. During the planning, the authority should take into account region's ethnic and religious diversity and demographic conditions, including the vertical and horizontal arrangement that divide society, and minimize the social and economic disparities within and between every group in society.

The government and NGOs of NER should attempt to educate people about the equity and benefits of female education and that public policy should encourage girls' access to schooling by subsidies in order to compensate for the asymmetry in parental incentives to educate sons and daughters.

A globalised economy requires states and government to follow internationally accepted governance principles which focuses on creation of a strong civil society. A new approach to be followed by the leaders of women's movement to set their agenda and women's issues can be sensitized in a non-threatening way by making coalition with men and removing the rural –urban disparity. In the era of globalisation, rich countries need to stop dictating policies that encourage corruption in the first place.

The problem of infrastructure facilities which plays an important role should also have to be taken into consideration in the future study as regard to process of economic development.

However, no policy in the region will be successful unless the people of the region are well conscious about their own health, food, sanitation etc. to upgrade the quality of life in the age of modernization. Hence, people's participation, particularly women, is urgently needed in any development programme of the government. Last but not the least is that government should establish the requisite institutional mechanism and enabling environment at all level of society to ensure that population factors are appropriately addressed within the decision making and administrative process of all governmental agencies responsible for economic, environment, and social policies and programmes.

Note

1. APJ Abdul Kalam, His Excellency the President of India, delivered the Convocation Address on the 2nd Convocation of Nagaland University, Kohima on Thursday, 15th March, 2007.
2. Janet Momsen, *Women and Development in the Third World* (London: Routledge, 1991) 1-2.

References

Central Committee (1985) : "Open Letter from the Central Committee to all the Communist Party and Communist Youth League Members on the Question of Controlling China's Population Growth", in Population Year Book of China, pp. 27-29.

Dutta. P.C. (2002) : "Population Growth and Environmental Crisis in North East India : Problems and Remedies" in Development Priorities in North East India (ed), B. J. Deb, Concept Publishing Company, New Delhi.

Dutta, P.C. (2003) : Regional Disparity and its Consequences in North Eastern Region of India in *Economic Liberalization and Regional Disparities in India – Special Focus on the North Eastern Region* (ed) A.C. Mohapatra and C.R. Pathak, *Star Publishing House, Shillong.*

Dutta P. C. & H. Choudhury (1996) : "*A Note on Inter State Variation in* Per Capita Non-Food Household Items of Consumption in The North East India", *IJRS, Vol. 28 No.2.*

R. C. Choudhury and S. Rajakutty (1999) : India Rural Development Report, National Institute of Rural Development, Rajendranagar, Hyderabad.

Susan Greenhalgh (2003) : "Science, Modernity, and the Making of China's One-Child-Policy", Population And Development Review, Vol. 29, No. 2, pp. 163-196.

16

Impacts of Socio-Economic Development on Environment with Special Reference to the Problems of Population Growth and Urbanisation

Introduction

The concept of change and developed is a dynamic one apprehending each and every aspect of human existence. The primary object of development is to satisfy the essential material needs of the society, but not at the cost of local environment and people's culture. When people change, the society to which belong also change, and the country moves with them too. But North-Eastern Region (NER) is an exception. Interestingly, this region is endowed with rich resources of land, water forests, and minerals. One would have thought that such a typical region would have been the cherised pride of the country; instead it is the backward and undeveloped one.

In recent times many countries have experienced upsurge among different groups. In NER the expenditure to control insurgency has been increasing day by day. But ironically along with the expenditure to control insurgency, insurgency has been increasing by leaps and bounds. Recently, in an NEC published paper a detailed account of expenditure is presented. This paper of expenditure is outside the budget of Defence Ministry and seven State Governments. After so much expenditure made for security purpose, bomb in Chief Minister's Convoy, Kidnapping of Bureaucrats, bombs in buses are regular features. If anything serious happens, the Chief Ministers of this region make the lame excuse that is no sufficient Central forces in the region and also there may be a role of third party and the ISI. But, in the last six years, in NER, the central government spent an additional amount of 1,000 crore for deployment of police forces. After spending such huge amount of money, the condition of the region is no better.

People for preservation of socio-cultural entity and economic and political rights

Apprehensions have been noticed among different groups of people of being outnumbered and swamped away by other groups of people and consequent deprivation from economic and political benefits. This is primarily because of exorbitant growth of population among some groups of people.

Population is a very important factor in the whole process of socio-economic development. Again the growing population in developing aid under developing countries, in particular, is straining social, economic and even political system of the nation. Three inter governmental **World Population Conference** re organised by the United Nations during the 20 years period (1974–1994) all of which focussed on problems of population and development. However, five world population conference have been held so far within the period 1954–1994 under the auspices of the United Nations. At the last conference in **Mexico city (5–13 September, 1994)** 76 decisions were made to improve the standards of living and quality of life for all people among which socio-economic development, the environment and the population, the role and status of women etc. re given the priority.

For the past over 200 years, scholars and policy makers have been debating the question of the relationship between population and development. Realising the negative effect of rapid population growth on development, many developing countries have launched family planning programmes. But in a majority of countries including India, family planning programmes have not been so successful. The macro-level impact of this surging population growth in India is being felt in every walk of life; growing inadequacy of potable water, traffic congestion, air pollution, swelling numbers of dwellers in 'Jhuggi-Jhopadis' in cities and towns, pathetic over-crowding in buses and trains etc. Life in India is becoming terrible to live and according to the statement of Mr. Ram Jethmalani, the urban development minister, **'Delhi is a dying city', he said, 'of the capital's slums and falling standards of quality of life (Times of India, dated 9th May, 1998)'.** It is now well-recognised that a sizable portion of their economic boom can be attributed to their rapid fertility transition.

In the era of globalisation rapid socio-economic transformation has been taking place in the economy at international level. The planners and policy makers in India are trying to cope with it. Economic welfare does not merely depend upon the level of development but also on its distributive aspects. As development takes place, side by side, the force—growth promoting and those distributing the benefits of growth —come in conflict. Consequently, the gap between the development level of resourceful and less resourceful regions goes on widening. **Privatisation, liberalization and globalisation** are going to be introduced in Indian Economy in order to bring socio-economic progress of the country. However, these dreams of our planners and policy makers cannot be fulfilled until and unless the regional disparities are minimized in India. In the pluralistic nature of the country, differences in natural resources, climate, topography, vegetation and density of population can be identified easily and the North Eastern Region of India (NER) is no exception to it. Unequal distribution of wealth and resources caused regional disparity in the country as a result of which the states of NER are lagging behind.

Quality of life is a very complex concept and perceived and interpreted differently by different people depending upon their socio-cultural and religious background, personal preferences and their philosophy of life. The quality of life involves the satisfaction of the emotional needs and social aspirations of the community or society as well as the society's ability to meet the basic needs of food, energy, space, housing etc. by itself. Concern about resources, quality of life etc. in the western world is however, far from new. It dates back to the early 1960s, in which the seminal book by **Rachel Carson (1962)** attracted strong attention by describing the extensive damage of the environment caused by chemicals and industrial process.

The development of an area is best reflected in the quality of life of its people. Apart from the distribution of infrastructural facilities, the quality of life depends upon several other factors like geographical, ecological, socio culture etc. which are distributed in an haphazard manner all over the country and thus handicaps the development of relatively backward regions. Historical and political conditions also affect the socio-economic development of the region. The impact of all these constraints are generally seen in the agricultural, industrial, infrastructural and financial development of the region which directly affect the quality of its people. Due to these reasons, the goals of balanced regional development of the country has not been fulfilled even after more than fifty years of independence. So before formulating and implementing the development policy of any region, it is essential to know such basic characteristics of the region which inhabits the process of development.

Urbanisation, a phenomenon closely related with burgeoning population, has swallowed up approximately 1.5 million hectares of agricultural land in the past 30 years. In addition 1.3 million hectares of forest was lost each year during 1975-82. The shortage of housing is an ever-growing problem. Over one-fifth of the urban population lives in slums. The mounting problems of pollution consequent upon unimaginative interference of human beings with nature have been adversely affecting the quality of life. Forests provide several products of daily use such as food, timber, fire wood, would pulp etc. apart from different medicinal plants which are yet to be explored. The greatest significance of forests, however, lies in their critical role in maintaining ecological processes and life supporting systems **(Singh and Sudarshan, 1996)**. Various studies on Indian urbanisation reveals that, Indian cities are expanding on the one hand and loosing green field areas on the other, with disastrous ecological crisis in our towns and cities. The deterioration of the environmental quality is regarded as the inevitable consequence of urbanisation.

Urbanisation is a process of population concentration. We have conceded the **Kingsley Davisian** view in the 19th Century that ***"it is not possible to have industrialisation without urbanisation"***. It is fact that the urbanisation is the most essential for all round development of the developing nations, as it has increased employment, income and standard of living in these countries. But it has simultaneously created number of socio economic and environmental problems. Urbanisation has disturbed the ecological balance by creating air, water and noise pollution through industrialisation. Haphazard growth of urban centres and their ill-planned urbanisation aggravated the pollution problems and deteriorated the environment. Therefore, **environmentalist aptly say that urbanisation - environment relationship is not complementary but contradictory with each other (Patil, 1998).**

The increasing urbanisation has led to a number of socio-economic problems like crime, suicides, drug abuse, unemployment and poverty, alcoholism, overcrowding, housing shortage, slums, traffic control and pollution etc. At the same time they are also centres of civilisation and culture by helping a lot in the process of modernisation **(Dutta & Pradhan, 1998).** The very pattern of economic development in the third world countries has resulted increasing imbalance in the distribution of per capita national income and large number of people are being relegated to below poverty line. The poor occupy the environmentally vulnerable areas liable to water logging or flooding, other natural hazard, epidemics, fire and chemical pollution. Economic development not only brings about changes in the socio-economic and cultural life of a population but it also influences the consumption pattern in the long run **(Dutta, 1996).**

Exploiting the socio-economic problems of the region, various divisive forces raised their ugly heads under the banner of regionalism to gain the support of the mass people. But sometimes their activities cause a serious threat to the unity and integrity of the nation. The problem becomes more serious as the governments of the concerned states of the NER had to spend huge sums of money, allotted for development activities. As a result, the economy of the region worsened further.

Dutta and Pradhan (2000) observed that the most important problem which creates the hindrance on the way of agricultural development is the problem of population explosion in the region. Although India has emerged as a food surplus state in the world, the NER is still suffering from food deficit. In almost all the states, there are substantial urban-rural and inter district variations, along with the marked variation between tribal and non tribal population within the district, for which it is always a difficult task to measure the nutritional standard of the population living in a particular region and the case of NER is highly apparent.

The study by **Dutta and Pradhan (2001)** brings out the facts about the regional disparity in NER and concluded that the states of NER are suffering from paucity of funds to improve their socio economic backwardness. The study further reveals that the states of NER are far behind from other states of the Indian Union so far as the basic amenities of life such as health, education, safe drinking water, banking facility, food security, communication etc. are concerned.

Poverty is the worst form of environmental degradation because it forces an extremely sub-standard quality of life upon a large segment of society and causes deprivation from such basic needs of human existence as shelter, nutrition, hygiene and health service, education, safe drinking water, sanitation and other physical infrastructure. The rapid increasing of urbanisation has led to a number of socio-economic problems like crime, alcoholism, drug abuse, over crowding, housing shortage, unemployment and poverty, slums, traffic control and pollution. At the same time they are also centres of civilisation and culture by helping a lot in the process of modernisation **(Dutta and Roy, 1998).**

The very pattern of economic development in the third world countries has resulted in increasing imbalance in the distribution of income and large number of people are being relegated to below poverty line. The economic development not only brings about changes in the socio-economic and cultural life of a population but it also influences the consumption pattern in the long run **(Dutta1996).** The development is a complex process and has multi dimensional structure depending upon its resources in general and infrastructural facilities in particular.

The picture of regional disparity was first observed and analysed by **Prof. Hirschman (1958)** in his famous **"Inverted -U- shape theory"**. This theory tells that as an economy grows, regional disparities diverge at first only to converge later. **Adelman and Morris (1973)** after analysing the data from 74 under developed countries for the period 1957-68 concluded that the relationship between the level of economic development and the income share of the poorest 60 percent of population is asymmetrically U-shaped.

Education promotes development in all the sectors of the economy and yield high social and economic returns. Sustainable development can not take place without investments being made in people. It is now widely accepted that the improvements in the quality of people as productive agents must be a central objective of development policies **(Prabhu, 1996; Malhotra, 1997).** The social-sector expenditure plays an important role in supporting economic growth and reducing poverty. Education plays a very important role in promotion of economic, social, political and institutional development. Education promotes development of all the sectors including agriculture, industry and social sector. Rather the social returns to education for more out weigh the economic returns and the social rate of return is highest in case of primary education followed by secondary and higher education **(Pracharopouclus, 1994).**

Higher levels of education may have greater direct impact on economic development but the primary and middle level education are important because they widely distribute the conditions conductive to development. In order to have desired results, there has to be threshold level of investment. Such investment have long gestation period but they also yield returns over a long period because of durability of human capital and its wider implications **(World Bank, 1997).** High teacher-pupil ratio affects the quality of education, which is one of the dampening factors in educational decision. Low levels of educational attainment at primary level, particularly in rural areas are particularly due to low quality of education, which is partly due to over crowding of primary classes **(Malhotra, 1999).**

Ehrlich and Holdren (1971) in a typical formulation has conceived the interrelationship between population and environment which is as follows:

I = (P) (A) (T), where

I = a measure of environment impact.

P = population, A = Affluence (measured by per capita GNP),

T = Technological efficiency (use of energy in the production of per unit of GNP).

This conceptual model identifies consumption and production pattern as proximate factors of environmental deterioration. This has been criticized by Researchers on the ground that the nature of intersections between the variables is not clear **(Mackellar et. al., 1995)**. Further, the model is not explicit about the role of poverty in environmental degradation. The poverty has been recognized as one of the most important aspects of environmental degradation in a conceptual model recently proposed by **UNICEF (1994).** It has been called as

PPE model (Population-Poverty-Environment model) by UNICEF. Recently, the environment issues are also looked upon from gender perspective, known as **'Ecofeminism'** in the writings of environmental issues particularly in the developed countries **(Cutter, 1994).**

It has been admitted that "because ultimate cause are so resistant to change, inte to modify population growth may be the most expedient means of preventing further environmental degradation" **(Asian Development Bank Document quoted in Hossain, 1993).** Thus, the other areas of action excepting population control are left with ease under a perceived resistance by the rich **(Hossain, 1993).**

Aims and Objectives

It is in this context, an enquiry is deemed to be necessary to examine the multi dimensional and complex relationships among some socio-economic and demographic variables of the north-eastern region of India as it is physically located in a backward and disadvantageous position due to its physical geography as well as the social and political conditions prevailing in the region.

In this study, income inequality, share of expenditure by different decile groups of population and some of the demographic characteristics of the population have been studied. The study have also tried to find the relationships of some socio-economic and demographic variables with inequalities in PCE to study whether any significant relations exist among the variables for confirming the fact of existence of relationship between socio economic and demographic variables.

The purpose of the study is to examine whether or how urbanisation creates the hazardous situation in socio-economic aspects. Further, the study shows how population growth affects over-all environment of the region. The study has been concluded with some valuable suggestions.

Data and Methodology

The study is based on secondary sources of data relating to socio-economic and demographic variables for the North-Eastern Region of India covering a period of 50 years (1951–2001). Different rounds of NSS data on consumer expenditure, Rural Health Statistics, Ministry of Health and Family Welfare, Govt. of India, different Census Reports published by the Govt. of India are used in the present study. However, economic studies made by various research workers relating to household consumption based on different rounds of NSS data have been used for the purpose. Various statistical methods viz, inequality in consumption using Log-normal hypothesis, rank correlation coefficients, regression coefficients and various statistical tests for testing statistical hypothesis have been used. Cartographic technique is used to highlight the relationship among Population-Environment and Population-Poverty-Environment.

Profile

The North-Eastern Region comprises the state of **Arunachal Pradesh, Assam, Manipur, Meghalaya, Mizoram, Nagaland and Tripura.** Geographically, the region is lying between 21°5 - north latitude and 85°5–97°5 east longitude covering an area of 2,55,037 sq. km. accounts for 7.7 percent of area and contains 4.04 percent of country's population, of which 70 percent is occupied by the hills and mountains which virtually surrounds the region on all sides, and this is nearly 8 percent of total geographical area of the country. The topography of NER is not uniform. Moreover, rivers and barren hilly terrain remain as problems rather than prospect for development. The region has long international borders with China, Burma, Bangladesh, Tibet and Bhutan and is connected with the rest of the country through a narrow corridor in the North-East Bengal with a width of about 30 km **(called chicken neck).** This has greatly enhanced its strategic importance with respect to the demographic study.

One must realize that north-east is a mini-India. There are more than 75 major population groups and sub groups, speaking approximately 400 languages and dilects, of which there are about 168 in Arunachal Pradesh, 95 in Nagaland, 87 in Manipur, 100 in Tripura and 200 in Assam, Meghalaya and Mizoram **(Madhab, J, 1999).** Thus, the whole north-eastern India is a place with people of diverse races, cultures, languages and various dilects with different traditions. Besides the heterogeneity of geographical and socio-cultural factors, the more striking view of the North-Eastern scenario is the co-existence of the extreme forms of both tradition and modernity.

Analysis

The analysis of the study have been completed under different sections.

Population growth and demographic characteristics:

The **total population** of the region is about 31.54 million according to 1991 census, representing 3.72 p.c. of India's total population. It is evident that there is uneven spatial distribution of population among the constituent states. One of the important problems which creates the hindrance on the way of economic development is the problem of population explosion in the region. The total population of the region is about 38.5 million representing 3.75 p.c. of India's total population in 2001. The **region's growth rate of population is much higher than the national average.** It is striking to note that India's total population increased by 51.80 p.c. in the period 195 1–71, 54.39 p.c. in 1971–91 and 21.35 p.c. in 1991-2001. Whereas for the NER, respective growth rates are 90.86 p.c., 62.11 p.c. and 22.02 p.c. At the same time share of population of NER, in comparison to all-India, increased from 2.84 p.c. in 1951 to 3.75 p.c. in 2001.

Increased population at an alarming rate in the region is due to **immigration** from outside the country as well as from within the country. The population explosion caused by immigration pose serious threat on the natural resources of the region and hence on the economic development.

The **absolute number of the migrants** was more than 91 thousand in 1901, since then it has been steadily increasing and reached at nearly 745 thousand in the census year 1991. The share of migrants from Bangladesh was between slightly more than 70 p.c. to slightly more than 87 p.c. in pre-independence era. The post independence era, it reached at 94 p.c. in 1951—the highest among the period, 1901–1991. From 196lonwards the share started to decline and become around 89 p.c. in the census year of 1991. It is also clear from the statistical information that Bangladesh was followed by Nepal in sending migrants to the NER of India. Again the number of migrants who come from other states of India varied between 0.5 million to around 0.8 million during the pre independence era. But it declined to around 0.4 million in 1951 and reaching slightly more than 0.5 million in 1991. In the recent years the flow of immigration from the neighboring countries shows an increasing trend.

However, the share became around 89 p.c. in the census year of 1991, the absolute figure is 745 thousand. Remaining 11 p.c. of the migrants to this region are from Nepal, Myanmer etc. However, total migrants, from outside the country, to this region stands at 834 thousand during 1991. The proportion of foreign migrants from Bangladesh to Assam was around 85 p.c. among the total foreign migrant in the state. The respective percentage for the state of Tripura was more than 99 p.c. according to 199lCensus. This migrant no doubt has some impact on the social, economic, cultural and political sphere of the North- Eastern region.

It is observed that there is a large variation in the **density of population** among the states of NER (table-i). Density of region's population (151) is almost half of the national density (324) in 2001 while it was only 34.19 p.c. in 1951. Again within the region it varies from 13 in Arunachal Pradesh to 340 in Assam. The bulk of population of the region is concentrated mainly of three sectors viz. Brahmaputra valley and Barak valley of Assam and Tripura. The large variation is caused by the geographical and economic factors, which vary greatly within the region.

The table reveals that Assam, second in terms of area contains 71.05 percent of the region's population while Mizoram less than 3.0 percent (p.c.) of the regional population stands at the other extreme according to 1991 census. It is interesting to note that India's population is increased by 134 p.c. in the period 1951-1991, while for the region the growth was 208 p.c. No doubt existing population of each state is a matter of concern, but the most important is the fast growing population in some of the states of the region. A close look at the table reveals that there is a continuous higher **decennial growth rate** in the region's population, as compared to all India, throughout the period.

The total number of tribal population is 81.42 lakh which is approximately 25.71 p.c. of the total population. The percentage of Schedule Tribes varies from 13 p.c. (Assam) to 91 p.c. (Mizoram) which are above the country's figure (8 p.c.). Nagaland, Meghalaya, Mizoram and quite a substantial parts of Assam and Tripura and overwhelmingly tribal areas inhabited by a vast multiplicity of ethnic groups. About 67 tribes exist present in N.E. India **(Horn and Sharma, 1995).** The Reangs were originally inhabitants of Mizoram, but they have been described as a martial tribes in the oldest histories of Tripura **(Mazumdar, 1980).** However, more than three fourths of the household belong to scheduled tribe in the states of Mizoram, Nagaland (96 p.c.), Meghalaya (89 p.c.), Arunachal Pradesh (76 p.c.) and while in Tnpura (17 p.c.), Manipur (35 p.c.) and Assam, these are below 50 p.c.

Sex ratio is an important determinant of population growth. It is remarkable to note that the sex ratio in NER has consistently shown excess of males over females as noted for India but always lower throughout the period (1971-1991) than the country as a whole.

There is a need to examine the extent of sex ratios difference and levels in different states as a result of differential mortality and selective migration. The sex-ratio in a population influences fertility rate. In all developed countries, the ratio is over 1000, while in most developing countries, it is below 1000. In India, there are only 927 females per 1000 males in the total population. Among the states of NER, it is the highest in Manipur (958) followed by Meghalaya (955) and Tripura (945) while other states are lying below the national level. It seems that there is more male migrants in the region lowering the sex ratio of general population.

The age-distribution in each state of NER is typical of high fertility populations, with a high proportion of the population in the younger age-groups. Manipur, Mizoram and Tripura have the lowest percentage of population below 15 years of age (37 p.c.) and this Percentage is the highest in Arunathal Pradesh (43 p.c.). The proportion of the population of age 60 and above varies from just over 2 per cent in Nagaland to 8 per cent in Tripura.

Soclo-economic characteristics:

In the developed economics, the process of urbanisation has been closely and positively related with the economic development, while in the third world developing countries is a consequential phenomenon. Besides, the pattern of urbanisation in the latter economies has been spatially and structurally imbalanced.

The rates of urbanisation vary over time and space. In the later half of the twentieth century the developing countries have been urbanizing very fast and India is no exception. The rate of urbanization during the post independence period has been quite rapid with highest rate, during 1971-81 decade, of 46 p.c. The 1991 census reveals a slowing down urban population growth (36.19 p.c.) during 1981-91. It is the quantum increase in urban population vis-à-vis total population growth is of vital concern.

Coming to the states of NER, the notable point is that the **percentage of urban population to total population (urbanization)** varies from 12.80 (Arunachal Pradesh) to 46.10 (Mizoram). It is striking to note that except Manipur (27.52 p.c.) and Mizoram, all other states of NER are below the national level (25.71 p.c.) according to 1991 census.

Urban population growth was always higher than total population growth during the 20th century. The slower tempo of urban population growth during 1981-1991 and longer perspective of guided urbanisation having been considered for future urban population growth and it is expected to grow with decadal rate of 35 p.c. during 1991-2001. The urbanization in India is structurally imbalanced and is going to maintain the same trend unless there is a policy intervention to reorient the urbanization trend in favour of small and medium size towns along with metropolitan decentralization **(Pathak, 1998).**

The interaction between economic development and **female work participation** has attracted attention amongst economists, social scientists etc. for more than fifty years. Female work participation is much higher in the states of north east except in Tripura. In a traditionally bound society like India where male predominates, the inferior image of women has become ingrained in the minds of men, and finds expression in their day-to-day life. Even though a women can work proficiently as man they are considered inferior and subordinate to man. Bur with the advancement of time, more and more women are gainfully employed.

With economic progress the death rates begins to decline. The commitment made in the **'National Policy For Children 1974'** got further momentum when Govt. of India endorsed all the child survival goals for the year 2000 agreed by the **'World Summit For Children in 1990'.** The convention on the **'Rights of Child 1992'** of which India was a signatory further enunciated the **child's right as right to survival, right to protection, right to development and the right to participation.**

Of these rights, the most important one is the **right to survival of the child.** In India, the infant death rate is very high being 72 per 1000 live births in 1996 which is 22.5 p.c. as compared to world's total infant death. Coming to the NER of India, it is observed that it ranges from 10 (Nagaland) to 64 (Arunachal Pradesh) per thousand live births which are below the national average (74) according to 1991 census. Death rates are high because of poor diet, primitive sanitation, absence of preventive and curative medical facilities etc. Besides these direct causes, there are factors, cultural, social and economic which contribute to high infant deaths. Those may be are: lower age of mother, order of birth, less interval between two births, large family size, low family income, poor environmental conditions etc. On the other hand, the rate of decline in infant mortality is attributed to improvement in socio-economic conditions, control of communicable diseases, better nutrition, better health awareness among people.

Education is the main instrument of social change. It is the index of social progress and economic development of a region. Normally it has been considered an agency helping economic production through the development of skills and efficiency highly necessary for the said production. ***"Education is an organic entity, changes, grows with the time, responds to the needs of the society adopts to the environment. It was mostly an ornament in the agricultural civilizations, a tool in economic development in the industrial era and has become today all pervasive resources, a resource that can find substitutes for other resources, but has no substitute for itself."***, according to **V.C. Kulandai Swami.**

Considering Rural-urban separately, it is striking to note that in case of female or total population, literacy rates in all the states are higher than the all-India level. The advancement of the region can be well marked by the rate of literacy and other infrastructural facilities provided for the development of the education. Literacy rate is the highest in Mizoram (88 p.c.) followed by Tripura and lowest in Arunachal Pradesh (55 p.c.) followed by Meghalaya and Assam.

The **female literacy rate** is highest in Mizoram (95 p.c.) followed by Nagaland (77 p.c.) and lowest in Arunachal Pradesh (48 p.c.) which is the only state in NER below the national level in this respect.

There is a big **gender gap in literacy** which is one of the major obstacles in attaining total literacy. Enrolment in various stages of education is growing at a fast rate, but the proportion of girls is low and declines sharply at higher stages of education. The highest gender gap has been found in the states of Manipur (24.03 p.c. points), Arunachal Pradesh (21.76), Tripura (20.93) and lowest in Mizoram (7.01) followed by Meghalaya (8.27). However all the states of NER are below all-India (24.84 p.c. points) level. Low female literacy has strong repercussions on other aspects like enrolment of children, population growth, child care and acceptance of family welfare measures.

It is striking to note that **Per Capita expenditure on education** in 1997-98 is highest for smaller states of Mizoram (Rs. 1210), followed by Manipur (Rs. 984), Arunachal Pradesh (Rs. 951) and Tripura (Rs. 836) while it is lowest in Assam (Rs. 537) among the states of NER.

Health is a social goal and considered as an integral component in over all socio economic development. The majority of health problems are the products of illiteracy, poverty, ignorance, over crowding, poor environmental conditions and uneven distribution of health manpower and institutions. It is observed that there are only 4.32 p.c. of public health centres in the states of NER (958 Nos.) as compared to India's figure and only in Assam there are 64 p.c. public health centres among the states of NER, while less than 10 p.c. are in each of the other states of the region. The same patterns are observed in case of sub centres and community health centrtes. Thus, it is high time to make an effort to increase the number of health centres in backward states of NER so that health problems can be minimized to some extent.

A look at the **table,** it is observed that the maximum **amount of water is required** in the states of Assam among the states of NER, which is approximately 2.33 p.c. as compared to India's requirement in 1991, and the figure (0.833 cubic km.) has risen to 2.63 p.c. in 2001. However, there is an increasing trend of water requirement in 2001 over 1991. Regarding the **safe drinking water** facilities, all the states of NER, except Arunachal Pradesh (70.02 p.c.) are less than the national average (62.3 p.c.). It is striking to note that only 16.21 p.c. of total households of Mizoram can drink safe water while **water is the life blood of the environment.** Thus, conservation of water is an important aspect in this regard And the people of NER should take active step for the management of water for the maintenance of the standard of water quality.

There is a need to examine the **extent of suicides** and levels in different states as a result of different socio-economic conditions. **Table 14.6** shows the **distribution of suicides according to different age groups.** A minute look at the table reveals that highest percentage of suicides occur in the age group 15- 29 years (35.76 p.c.) followed by 30-44 years age group (32.06 p.c.) which is true for the country also. Region's total suicide is 3.7 p.c. as compared to the India's figure. Male suicides dominates over the females which is true for the region is also true for the whole country. It is striking to note that maximum number of suicides occur in Assam (76.54 p.c.) followed by Tripura (17.05 p.c.) among the states of N.E.R.

A close look at the **table 14.7,** it is observed that highest number of suicides occur due to illness (11.64 p.c.) followed by unemployment (4.51 p.c.) and poverty (1.01 p.c.). The proportion of suicides due to unemployment, poverty and drug abuse in respect to total suicides in NER is 6.45 p.c. and which is observed mainly in the states Assam and Tripura. The same trend is observed in both the periods 1996 and 1998.

In backward areas rapid population growth tends to offset the benefits of development. Rather, it results in family frustration, dependence burden, employment and social tensions leading to a breakdown of an order society.

Table reveals the fact that total **number of persons**

arrested in connection with cognizable crimes has been decreased only in the states of Manipur, Meghalaya and Tripura over the periods 1996-98 while the number of **IPC cases per civil police person** in the states of Assam, Mizoram and Tripura increased. It is remarkable to note that only in the states of Assam, number of IPC cases per civil police man has been increased from 2.5 in 1996 to 2.6 in 1998 which are greater than the national level of 2.3 cases per civil police man in both the periods.

The development of an area is best reflected in the distribution of basic needs. **Fig. 17-A,** confirms the fact of region's backwardness as it is observed that the **per capita consumption of electricity** is much lower in the states of NER as compared to the country's consumption (338.5 Kwh). Among the state of NER, the highest per capita consumption is observed in the state of Meghalaya (134.5 Kwh) and lowest in Tripura (80.4 Kwh).

In the north-eastern hill areas **food production** is subject to wide fluctuations due to shifting cultivation. Hence estimate of production may not give the true picture. However, during the last two decades per capita production has declining in the states of Assam, Manipur, Meghalaya and Mizoram and are lower than the national average except in the state of Arunachal Pradesh. **While the population** is rapidly increasing in the states of the region, it is observed that in case of Assam, the per capita food production decreased from 158 kg. In 1972-73 and 154 kg. In 1990-91 to 139 kg. In 1997-98. The respective figures for Meghalaya are 120 kg., 87 kg. And 83 kg. Only.

Since North-Eastern Society and dominated by the tribal population, the mode of production and tribal method of cultivation largely retards the growth of agriculture and food production in the region. Out of 23.78 lakh hectares of land in the country as a whole 19-9 1 lakh hectares i.e. 83.73 p.c. of land in the NER is under jhumias, who adopted ancient farming system. Rapid deforestation over the years due to shifting cultivation in the region have reduced the total forest cover as a result of which extensive soil erosion, degradation of land, desertification and frequent flooding etc. are marked. The high rate of soil erosion in deforested areas in our country ranges from 10 tones per hectare in the plain to about 30 tones per hectare in North eastern hilly region, 10 to 50 times larger than in the forested areas The resulting annual sedimentation load from Ganges and Brahmaputra alone exceed 1500 million tones, making them the two larger dumpers of suspended loads anywhere in the world. The environmental extensively affected the capacity of the reservoirs as well as the aquatic eco-system in the inland water, Just as soil erosion, in addition to less of fertility, has drastically reduced the recharging capacity resulting in severe depletion of underground water. Extensive deforestation has resulted in increased carbon-di-oxide concentration in the atmosphere. The changes in climatic and rain pattern gradually setting in because of deforestation. Water and soil erosion have affected the maximum lands used for agricultural purpose. The climatic fluctuation and changes in the rain pattern have further compounded the problem of providing adequate food security to our increased population. Gross, neglect of environment also resulted in polluting not only river water but also surface water, making them fertile breeding grounds of many communicable diseases.

In the entire North East, the valley districts of Manipur are among the most productive zones of nation in the production of paddy. However, the same cannot be true about the districts of Assam and lack of assured irrigation seems to be the major factor behind it. The productivity of paddy in Manipur-Tripura Vally and Mizoram is higher than the regional average and also above Assam which alone accounts for more than 70 p.c. of area and output in the region. Mizoram achieved a remarkable growth in the yield rate of paddy since around the middle of 1980 due to increase in fertiliser consumption and new land use policy in Mizoram. It is also observed from the table that while the government of Assam fixed the amount for expenditure in agriculture sector (Rs. 1557.82 lakhs) as on 1st April, 1998, but disbursed only 23.60 p.c. and 15.9 p.c. of disbursed amount actually utilised (58.67 lakhs). The same is true in the states of Arunachal Pradesh and Meghalaya. On the other hand, the Govt. of Manipur and Tripura not only disbursed more but also utilised 70.25 p.c. and 47.09 p.c. respectively on agricultural sector. Although the paddy productivity is the lowest in Arunnachal Pradesh, the yield of oil seed and pulses is the highest in the states of Meghalaya, Mizoram and the hill districts of Manipur. As the region is classified into hill areas and plain areas, the cropping patterns in the hills districts is more varied and not similar to that of plain areas. The development of infrastructural facilities like road and communications, banking, health are responsible for the above gaps. Further, corruption at the government level and red tapism of bureaucrats are responsible for this problem in the region.

In a study, **Chakraborty and Dutta in Alternative Economic survey, 1998–2000,** it is said that agricultural activities will remain the mainstay of livelihood for the majority of the Indians for another twenty years and even at an estimate assuming that the per capita availability of cereals at the prevalent rate 428.8 gms per day, we would require at least 200 million tones. This implies that another 6 million hectares of land need to be brought under cereal cultivation by the year 2020 at the prevailing rate of yield 1.5 tones per hectare. A study on state wise estimated total problem area treated and balance area yet to be treated shows that it the treatment of yet untreated area of 168.78 lakh hectares will be done, NER can or over fulfill its food need and get rid of its food shortage.

Diet survey data from many parts of India show that almost one-third of the children in poor families do not eat enough food needed for normal growth. On top of this, the poor environmental sanitation around them predisposes them to infection. The magnitude of the problem of anaemia second only to that of protein - energy malnutrition. The problem is less severe in the urban areas than in the rural areas. Anaemia reduces work capacity and productivity, which is particularly important in the context of the agricultural economy of the country.

Despite of several governmental measures, the purchasing capacity of the people of NER has not increased up to that level what our planners and policy makers desired, The statistics of per capita income of the people of NER may be stated as, **in 1992-93 the per capita income of Nagaland and Mizoram was just slightly above the national average (Rs. 5781 at current prices)** whereas in case of Arunachal Pradesh it was marginally below Rs. 5551. Incase of Manipur, it was Rs. 1429, Meghalaya Rs. 1361, and Tripura Rs. 1323. The per capita income in 1980-81 was not only so significantly below the national average (Rs. 1625) but has also shown consistent deterioration in relation to national average over the periods (1980-81 to 1992-93). Only in case of Assam it has shown a fluctuating tendency through at much lower level in relation to national average. At the national level, the inter state regional disparities as measured by coefficient of variation have just marginally been reduced from 31 p.c. in 1980-81 to 30.39 p.c. in 1992-93. At regional (NER) level, however, it has more than doubled from 7.79 p.c. to 18.12 p.c.

A look at the **table 5.4** it is observed that the performance of the north-eastern states in comparison to all-India level, regarding **availability of cereals,** all the states of NER, excluding Arunachal Pradesh and Tripura, are below the national average of 448.4 gms per capita per day in the year 1983. But in the year 1999, all the states of NER are below the all-India level **(522.7 gms per capita per day).** In case of **per capita per day availability of pulses,** it is observed that all the states of NER are below the all-India average over the period 1983-1999.

Table gives a picture of per capita **per day availability of food grains production** where same picture is observed as in case of pulses. It is observed that Arunachal Pradesh, the only state in NER tried to maintain its superiority till 1994 but declined thereafter.

Thus, food insecurity is a matter of great concern not only to the people of NER but also to the policy makers and planners of NER.

The recommended intakes of nutrients of a nation differ from those of international norms setup by **FAO and WHO.** The term used to describe dietary stand is **"recomended Dietary Allowance (RDA).** The **table 8 shows the quantity of items (Recommended Dietary Requirements)** should be consumed by the persons of different sex and age groups. This is the level of intake of essential nutrients considered, in the judgement of the (national or international) committee on dietary allowances, to be adequate to meet the known nutritional needs of practically all healthy persons.

Forests play a crucial rule in maintaining the ecological balance on the earth. Forests are being cut ruthlessly to make towns, roads, dams, which are creating ecological imbalance. Apart from the atmospheric effects, the destruction of forests endangers the several species of plants and animals to their virtual extinction. The entire north-eastern hill region has a prestigious place in the world map of orchid flora. But the continuous exploitation of the orchid has resulted almost extinction of many of a valuable species causing a great concern of the region.

Table 21.4 reveals the fact that o.4 p.c. of the total forest cover area has been deforested over the periods of two years (1991 - 1993). In the same period, out of the total destruction in NER, highest percentage occur in Assam (40 p.c.) followed by Mizoram (25 p.c.) while forest cover gained in the states of Nagaland and Tripura. However, during this period, total loss in the states of NER due to shifting cultivation is 387 sq. km. of which highest in Mizoram (40 p.c.) followed by Meghalaya 27 p.c.).

The expansion **of irrigation facilities, operation and maintenance of irrigation system and distribution of water** have not received due attention. Irrigation sector is today facing twin issues of sub-optimal sector planning and financial management on the one hand and inadequate water management and maintenance on the other. Involving the farmers in the irrigation system is one obvious remedy for addressing the management problems. **In comparison to**

all-India level only 1.4 p.c. of area is under irrigation system in the NER and only 1 p.c. in the state of Assam (5,39,000 hectares). However, percentage of total irrigated area in Assam is 65 p.c. with respect to total irrigated area in NER.

The Border Area Development Programme (BADP) was launched in the 7th Plan period for balanced development of remote and inaccessible areas situated near the borders and for ensuing effective administration in these areas for developmental activities. In the 9th Plan period the programme was extended to all the land borders in response to the demands of the State Governments of NER and the Ministry of Home Affairs. The programme now covers 16 states and which is a 100 p.c. Centrally funded programme. The Planning Commission have allocated Rs. 202 crores under Special Central Assistance under the BADP for annual plan 2000-01 of which only 26.33 p.c. is allocated for the states of NER. However, out of the funds allocated for the NER (53.19 crores) only 27.9 p.c. released indicating the less interest of the government for the development of border states. The road and communication system of Assam is strategically important so far as India's north eastern border is concerned. However, the roads are in miserably condition for which the government submitted a proposal of Rs. 180 crores to the centre for the repairation of 1500 km. of roads and 4000 bridges of the state. The PWD minister of the state expressed that the centre sanctioned Rs. 548.5 crores of which Rs. 137.78 crores have been allocated for the repairations of roads and bridges.

Assistance sanctioned by the **All India Financial Institutions (AIFI)** to North Eastern States has come down from about Rs. 209 crores in 1996-97 to Rs. 174 crores in 1997-98 and Rs. 131 crores in 1998-99. Similarly assistance disbursed by AIFI in NER has come down from Rs. 272 crores in 1996-97 to Rs. 126 crores in 1997-98 and Rs. 81 crores in 1998-99. Assistance by **Small Industrial Development Bank of India (SIDBI)** was lower at Rs. 25 crores in 1998-99 compared to Rs. 33 crores in 1997-98. Disbursemen (during

1998-99 at Rs. 21 crores were also lower compared to Rs. 27 crores in 1997-98. However, during the period 1990-99, the same trend is observed in the states of NER. **Credit-Deposit Ratio (CDR)** in the North-East ranges between 14 p.c. to 42 p.c. compared to All-India average of 55 p.c. Against the total sanctions under **Rural Infrastructural Development Fund (RIDF)** of Rs. 385 crores the disbursement has been only about Rs. 83 crores. The percentage of number of Scheduled Commercial Bank branches in the states of NER is only 2.93 p. c. compared to all-India level (64924). However, in comparison to NER (1900), the percentage of number of branches in the state of Assam is 65.

Thus a region may remain poor and backward in spite of possessing heavy natural resources. This is true in case of NER. While some of the states of India like Punjab, Haryana, Maharashtra etc. are going ahead in economic well being, the NER and particularly Assam is lagging far behind. This distortion caused by inter- regional disparity in wealth and income apparent from the per capita income of the states. In terms of inter regional comparison, while Assam had an annual per capita income of Rs. 8700, the national average was Rs. 14,712 in 1998. If the poverty is defined as **"inability to attain minimal standard of living"** by the World Bank, it can be said with much confidence that the states of NER and particularly Assam are poverty stricken. Recent events in the state have pointed to a system failure in the field of finance and improvement of financial capacity to implement even poverty alleviation programmes due to government of India's reluctance to provide funds for economic development on the grounds of corruption and non-fulfillment of constitutional obligations by the state governments during the past few years.

Per capita net state domestic product, inequality in income (consumption) and poverty:

The chief aim of economic activity is consumption. Consumer may be regarded as the unit of decision making regarding the economies of consumption. Due to various socio economic structure of the population the consumption basket will differ. The existence of wide disparities in the level of living between regions and between classes of people is widely believed to be one of the important causes of social tension and unrest. In this context, per capita expenditure (PCE) data has been taken as proxy for income.

Per Capita Net State Domestic Product (PCNSDP) gives a rough idea about the economic condition of NER with respect to all — India level. It is observed that all the states except Arunachal Pradesh (Rs. 21 19-Rs. 3265) and Mizoram (Rs. 2 119- Rs. 7743) of NER are below the all- India level (Rs. 1857-Rs. 2553) for the years 1985-86 to1994-95. In this respect **Assam's position is the lowest for ever during the period (1990-91 (Rs. 1544) to 1996-97 (Rs. 1628) and also in the period 1980-81 (Rs. 1254).**

The picture shows the economic backwardness of the region in general and Assam in particular. Insurgency has created an atmosphere in which financial accountability and internal resource mobilization has become the main casualties and to the extent insurgency has vitiated the true logic of development.

While **economic poverty and inequality** are nothing new for people in the third world or for people in India and within India it is for the people of NER. It has been accepted by them as a cultural heritage, thus showing cultural poverty. On the other hand, people of NER are indifferent regarding quality of education and health. Occupational mobility of people is nearly absent reminding one of the persistence of a traditional type society characterized by caste, language, custom, prejudice, belief etc. **Monthly per capita expenditure (MPCE)** may be accepted as an indicator of standard of living for people, on the basis of minimum calorie intake, suggested by the **Indian Council for Medical Research (ICMR)** should be 2300 for a person working (staying) in rural India and urban India. Rural poverty line, in terms of level of Consumer expenditure has been defined as an expenditure of Rs. 6400 for a family of 5 at 1983-84 price level which comes to Rs. 106.67 per capita per month in 1983-84 and Rs. 156.25 at 1986-87 prices. Assuming urban poverty level as around 25 p.c. higher the estimated poverty level in urban areas of India may be set at Rs. 133.34 and Rs. 195.31 for the 1983-84 and 1986-87 prices respectively **(Pathak, 1998).** It is further estimated as Rs. 275.75 and Rs. 343.00 for the rural and urban people of NER in the year 1998. Corresponding proportion of rural people below poverty line is 52 p.c. Particularly, for the state of Assam, poverty level for the rural and urban are calculated as Rs. 232.05 and Rs. 212.42 by the expert group as adopted by the lamiing commission. The respective figures for all-India are Rs. 205.84 and Rs. 281.35.i the economic condition of NER, the percentage of Population below poverty line is higher in respect of all-India level in 1998 **(Dutta, 1999). Dutta and Choudhury (1995)** observed that while there was a definite decline in the centrally funded programme. The Planning Commission have allocated Rs. 202 crores under **Special Central Assistance under the Border Area Development Programme (BADP)** for annual plan 2000-01 of which only 26.33 p.c. is allocated for the states of NER. However, out of the funds allocated for the NER (53.19 crores) only 27.9 p.c. released indicating the less interest of the government for the development of the border states. The road and communication system of Assam is strategically important so far as India's north eastern border is concerned. However, the roads are in miserably conditions for which the government submitted a proposal of Rs. 180 crores to the centre for the repairation of 1500 km of roads and 4000 bridges of the state. The PWD minister of the state expressed that the center sanctioned Rs. 548.5 crores of which Rs. 137.78 crores have been allotted for the reparations of roads and bridges.

It may be pointed out that in the rural sector, the **degree of inequality** is found to be minimum in Mizoram while maximum in Arunachal Pradesh. In most of the cases the level of inequalities is found to be less in NER in comparison to all-India level. It has been observed that there has been a declining tendency in the inter-regional disparities in the consumption level of the rural sectors while there is no such tendency in the urban sectors. As regards all-India level, the degree of inequalities has not changed so much in both rural and urban sectors over the rounds **(1965–87).** A perusal at the tables confirm the fact that the inequality in non-food total PCE is relatively greater in urban Assam in comparison to other states of NER and also India as a whole.

It is interesting to note that so far the **poorest ten percent** of the rural population is concerned the shares of consumption are relatively better in Manipur and Mizoram than that of their counterpart in NER while for the **richest ten percent,** the shares of consumption are relativley better in Assam and Meghalaya **(Dutta, 2001).**

Coming to the urban sectors of NER, it is worthwhile to mention that the **percentage share of expenditure** according to poorest ten percent groups of consumers were found to be better in the state of Nagaland and worst in Assam while for the richest ten percent of the consumers, the share is relatively better in Assam among the states of NER.

In 1965-66 and 1970-71, the minimum disparity in household consumption is found in Assam while in other periods viz. 1968-69, 1982-83, 1986-87 and 1987-88, the minimum disparity is found in Manipur and Mizoram in the rural sector. On the other hand, in the urban sector, the minimum inequality is observed in Assam in the periods 1965-66 and 1968-69, in Manipur in 1970-71 and 1982-83 and Nagaland in the periods 1986-87 & 1987-88 **(Dutta & Choudhury, 1996).**

It is evident from the above analysis that while there has been a definite decline in the inequalities in the consumption level of the rural households of NER, there is no such tendency for the urban households. But taking into account both the rural and urban households, it is reasonable to conclude that during the period 1970-71 to 1987-88, the region came closer in the period 1982-83 but after that it diverged to some extent in the period 1986- 87 and then in the period 1987-88.

Thus it may be pointed out that the poorest section of the society in Assam has been badly affected. The results reveal that the extent of degree of inequality in the level of living in the states of NER is much more than what is taken to guide some of the decision making elements in connection with resource transfer from centre to these north eastern states particularly in Assam.

Herrick and Hudson (1989) have defined ***"poverty as a composite phenomenon operating simultaneously on multiple spatial levels, involving a variety of interesting process and requiring a versatibility of analytical approaches, to grasp as in integrated system for effective policy intervention".*** Poverty line refers to qualities of possessions, services and consumables that provide subsistence living standard. But if it is defined as involuntary deprivation then it also incorporates a state of mind and a condition of being that transcend material condition, so poverty has experimental qualities that do not issue clear signals when one crosses a predetermined poverty line **(Kundu, 1993).**

Rural poverty line, in terms of level of consumer expenditure, has been defined as an expenditure of Rs. 6400 for a family of five at 1983-84 price level. This comes to Rs. 106.67 per capita per month in 1983-84 and 156.25 at 1986-87 price. Assuming urban poverty level as around 25 p.c. higher, the estimated poverty level in Indian urban areas may be set at Rs. 133.34 and Rs. 195.31 respectively.

Thus, an estimated people of 46 p.c. in urban India ml 988 were below the poverty line. Corresponding proportion of rural people below poverty line is 52.2 p.c. It is considered the living cost differences in urban areas as 25 p.c. higher than the rural areas. But basic services which are typical urban people oriented, are not available to rural poor.

Choudhury (1996) working on the **National Family Health Survey Data (NFHS, 1992–93)** for India suggested that in controlling fertility, schooling of females in the age-group 6-14 plays a vital role.

It has been further observed that there exist a negative correlation between percentage of urban population (PUP) and

IMR which is highly significant.

The **prime objective of the regression estimate study** is to find the effect of soclo demographic variables on economic variables. It is observed that for some of the demographic variables explains even 73 p.c. of the total variation in PCE.

The distribution of land holding is another important indicator of an economy. Lorenz ratios have been used to throw light in the matter of distribution of land in the rural economy in the various states of India. The values of Lorenz ratio are found to be lowest in Manipur (0.325) followed by Meghalaya (0.353) and Arunachal Pradesh (0.462). The degree of inequalities in the states of NER are found to be lower as compared to country's figure (0.639). In case of individual land holding, the level of inequality is found to be lowest in Arunachal Pradesh (0.352). It is further observed that land is evenly distributed in the north eastern states of India **(Dutta, 2001).**

Population-poverty-environment relationship:

Fig-16-A tries to show the impact of population growth on society as well as on environment. It is observed that multi-dimensional relationship exist between the population, environment and development which is a complex issue Mathematical relationship among the various indicators can not empirically proved due to lack of data. It is obvious that standard of living rises, when more people own cars, two wheelers etc. and which ultimately creates air pollution, sound pollution etc.

However, from the figure it is observed that population explosion creates food shortage, unemployment, poverty, crime, illiteracy. Again, frustration comes due to poverty and unemployment and as a result of which suicide takes place. Over population affects the nature of bio-sphere and creates ecological imbalance due to over activities of the people. Due to excessive population growth, there will be housing shortage, number of unemployment goes up which creates frustration among the younger generation and ultimately affects the

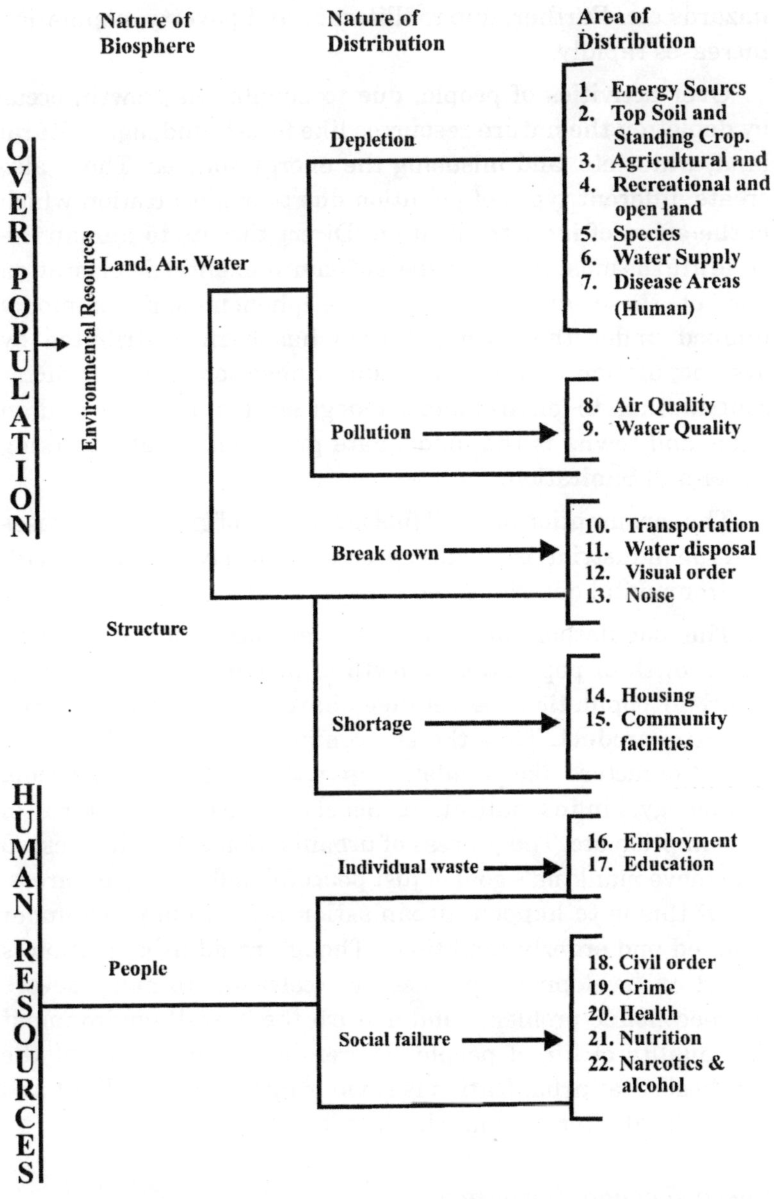

Fig. 16-A : Impact of over population on environment

society with creation of civil disorder, crime, drug abuse, health hazards etc. Further, due to illiteracy and poverty, population increases rapidly.

Over activities of people, due to population growth, occur by depleting the nature resources like forest land, agricultural land, water etc. and misusing the energy sources. These also create different types of pollution due to modernization which is the effect of industrialization. Direct threats to human life style are the most obvious aspect of environmental deterioration and of these direct threats, the phenomenon commonly lumped under the term pollution has been contributed by over population and modern industrialisation. A major factor contributing to environmental degradation in most Indian cities and towns is the inadequate provision of safe drinking water and Sanitation.

The consumption of fossil fuel is a source of greenhouse gases and the industrial production process is closely associated with environmental deterioration.

The population and economic variables include density and growth of population, growth of labour force, percentage of urban population, percentage share of industries in gross domestic product. Thus the environmental crisis is the result of host of factors like population growth, level of urbanization, technology, industrialisation, level of income, pattern of consumption etc. The process of urbanisation can be harnessed to achieve mankind's goal of just peaceful and lasting progress. But if this is to happen, urbanisation must take place under planned and orderly conditions. Though rapid urbanization is a part of development process, it accelerates to many severe socio-economic problems and disturb the overall environment and quality of life of people. Therefore, one must accept the synthesis that urbanization is saviour up to a certain limit and detrimental after without check to it.

Conclusion and Suggestions:

NER of India is currently undergoing demographic, economic,

social, educational, agricultural and health transition. These changes can bring about a substantial change in health and nutrition status of the population in the region. The strategy of achieving improvement in the nutrition status was one of the major objectives of the **Ninth Five Year Plan.** Besides, **National Nutrition Policy and the National Nutritional Action Plan** with emphasis and high priority to increase in food production and to make NER hunger free in the next ten years. It envisages a mission mode approach for planning and implementation with appropriate co-ordination between Centre, State and Panchayati Raj institutions to achieve the goals within the time frame. A high level commission was appointed by the Prime Minister of India for NER in October, 1996 by announcing **"New Initiatives for the NER"** to examine the backlog in respect of **"Basic Minimum services"** in seven sisters. It was also required to look into the gaps in important sectors of infrastructure development in the region. In their report titled **"Transforming the North East"** submitted to the Prime Minister of India in March, 1997, the commission finished a detailed assessment of the funds required to tackle the backlogs in "Basic Minimum services" and Infrastructural Need and made specific recommendations in different important sectors concerning the development of the region. The total requirement of the funds for providing Basic Minimum services was assessed at Rs. 9395.54 crores. The indicative requirement of funds for development of infrastructure was put at Rs. 93,619 crores of which Rs. 17,795 crores was assessed to be requirement of the **Ninth Five Year Plan period (1997-2002).** The Government also required the central ministers to set a part 10 P.C. of their budget allocation for the purpose of the development programmes of the NER. Since the requirement of the region could not be accommodated to the plan proposals, it was decided to provide additional funds for the purpose through the mechanism of a central pool created out of the likely savings from the funds year marked for the NER in the central budget. By the end of the **Seventh Five Year Plan.** the North Eastern Council (NEC) had incurred an expenditure of Rs. 1284.60 crores since its inception. Another Rs. 411.45 crores were spent during 1990-91 and 1991-92. The approved outlay for the Eighth Five Year Plan was Rs. 1,160 crores at 1991-92 prices. This total of yearwise approved outlays, worked out to Rs. 1648 crores. Against this the NEC has incurred an expenditure of Rs. 158 1.28 crores.

With regard to agricultural and allied services for food production, the NEC should focus on introduction of improved technology, empowerment of farmers through training and providing technical infrastructure for imparting technical advice and inputs. The development of market linkages and innovative projects in areas like horticulture, spices, aromatic and medicinal plants should be taken up by the NEC.

To enhance the nutritional status of the common people and to provide adequate diet, steps should be taken by the Government to display the nutritional value or composition of carbohydrates, proteins, fats and vitamins content in each unit of items sold so that price paid for per unit of calorie purchased would be distinguished. Every possible measures should be taken by the Government of India to raise the quality of food grains available in fair price shops and to check the food grains from being deplored.

If the extreme inequalities are to be reduced, the adequate amount of employment opportunities will have to be created. Programmes and projects of employment expansion are a better way of redistributing incomes.

The government must devise a system which ensures equal opportunities to the poor with the rich in obtaining higher education and training or in getting a start in trade and industry or securing employment. Another important measure is the introduction of a comprehensive social security scheme guaranteeing to each individual a minimum standard of living. Government should provide various social services like education, medical aid, labour welfare and other services for social and economic security of the weaker section of the population. Some of the **Indirect Nutrition Programmes** should be initiated honestly and sincerely. Agriculture related programmes which promote food production and schemes which provide subsidized foods to the poorer sections come under the indirect category. **Anti poverty schemes** such as the food for work programme, employment guarantee schemes, other income guaranteeing plans and developmental activities also fall into this category.

The **family welfare programme** is also an indirect nutrition programme since by reducing family size, it will not increase the per capita availability of food but also result in all round facilities including health care.

The women play a vital role to maintain a perfect balance between human activity and environment. Their participation in both rural and urban development will help to maintain a sustainable eco-system as the women are continuously and closely in contact with the forest for fuel and other activities. Thus, to check the population growth and to save the forest from degradation, the employment of the women by proper training is necessary **(Dutta, 2001).**

The sex ratio is declined from 972 **(females per 1000 males)** in 1991 to 933 in 2001. The differentials in sex ratios will lead to many social problems starting from the family itself, creating an impact on the whole society as such. Inequalities and disparities among the two sexes have come out to be detrimental to the female sex. Empowerment of women including protection of rights of the girl child, providing her the same opportunities for growth and development, health care, education and employment opportunities are the responsibility not only of women but mainly of men and the society at large.

Further, in order to enhance the socio-economic status of the rural areas more participation of women in agriculture and industries and in other sectors should be ensured. The main reasons for the non participation of women in the women co-operative societies provided by the state government are low level literacy, suppression, cruelty, mal treatment, exploitation and victimization of other social and economic evils **(Dutta**

and Pradhan, 2001).

The ethnic movements in NER initially reflect the ethno-cultural aspirations of the people and finally deviate from the real path by turning the movements into violence of the insurgence for material gains and to search the quick money through smuggling, drug trading etc. Through different movements, NER is bifurcated into seven sisters and the process of separation is still going on Jeo-pardising the unity and integrity of the region and threatening the security of the country **(Dutta and Pradhan, 2002).** Thus, the governments of NER should take initiative steps honestly, sincerely and should be liberal to understand the sentiment of the ethnic groups,

Improving the nutrition of people is vital for improving the health of the nation and for national development. This can be achieved, not in isolation but as part of a well - implemented package of services which includes all aspects of socio-economic well conceived development.

Development is the process by which we affect the environment, environment is what is left after development. **Environmental awareness programmes** at all levels should be sponsored by governmental and non-governmental agencies engaged in environment development. Environmental awareness should be strengthened through **formal and non formal education.** Urban authorities should encourage to city dwellers for effective tree plantation nearby their residence. The best agricultural lands with ideal moisture conditions are to be utilised for agricultural purpose only. Industrial and urban activities should not be allowed in such areas. **Environmental improvement schemes** should be incorporated into the integrated urban development plan.

Open burning of used raw material bags are desired to be stopped as it causes air pollution. In a word, the present generations should preserve for future generation's natural resources, necessary for sustaining human life and for its development and should ensure that future generations are not exposed to pollution which may endanger their health or their existence itself.

Investment in human resource development, in accordance with national policy, must be given priority in population and development strategies and budgets, at all levels, with programmes specifically directed at increased access to information, education, skill development, employment opportunities, both formal and informal, through the promotion of sustained economic growth within the context of sustainable development in developing countries.

To achieve sustainable development and a higher quality of life for all people, governments should **reduce and eliminate unsustainable pattern of production and consumption** and promote appropriate demographic policies. Government should establish the requisite institutional mechanisms and enabling environment, at all levels of society, to ensure that population factors are appropriately addressed within the decision making and administrative process of all government agencies responsible for economic, environmental and social policies and programmes.

The Government should give priority to set up various technical and professional institutions to enhance the capacity and improve the quality of the education and training of the people of NER along with the projects for the development of transport and communication system for linking NER with the main stream of the country.

While there is an improvement on the understanding of interrelationship between population and environment, more research is still needed on the interaction between population, environment a development for effective planning and action.

However, no policy in the region will be successful unless the people of the region are well conscious about their own health, food, sanitation etc. to upgrade the quality of life in the age of modernization. Hence, people's participation, particularly women, is urgently needed in any development programme of the government.

Last but not the least is that government should establish the requisite institutional mechanism and enabling environment at all level of society to ensure that population factors are appropriately addressed within the decision making and administrative process of all governmental agencies responsible for economic, environment, and social policies and programmes.

References

Ahiluwalia, D (1993): "Public Distribution of Food in India", Food Policy, February, pp. 33-54.

Alternative Economic Survey — 1998-2000, Alternative Survey Group Rainbow Publishers Ltd. June, 2000.

APRET (1998) : "Population Issues-II", Three contributions, Applied Population Research Trust, Bangalore.

Awasthi, Kashyap and Wadhva (1988): "Analysis of Regional Growth Pattern in India", sponsored by the Planning Commission, Govt. of India, Sardar Pate! Institute of Economic and Social Research, Ahmedabad.

Bansil, P.C. (1999): "Demand For Foodgrains Demand in India to 2020", Economic and Political Weekly, December, 27.

Bardhan P. K. (1974): "The Pattern of Income Distribution in India: A Review", Sankhya, Title Indian Journal of Sta Tjs Tics, Vol -36, Series-c, part 2 & 4, pp. 103-108.

Bhalla, G.S. and P.Hazell (1997): "Foodgrains Demand in India to 2020", Economic and Political Weekly, December, 27.

Bhalla,G.S., P.Hazell and J. Kerr (1999): "Pprospects For India's Vereal Supply and Demand to 2020, Food, Agriculture and the Environment", Discussion Paper 29, International Food Policy Research Institute.

Bhattacharya, N (1998): "On Level of Living Surveys in India", Presidential Address, 8?' Indian Science Congress, Section Of Statistics.

Chatterjee G. S. & Bhattacharya N. (1974): "On Disparities in per Capita Household Consumption in India", Sankhya,

Vol-36, Series c, 2 & 3.

Choudhury. H (1996): "NFHS Findings on Nuptiality Pattern and Policy Implications for the states Meghalaya, Mizoram and Tripura based on National Family Health Survey (NFHS) Results"- Paper presented in the Regional Seminar on Dissimination of Findings of NFHS Reports For The N.E.States, 27-29 Nov, Guwahati.

Cutter, S.E.(1994): "Environmental Issues, Green Rage, Social Changeand the New Environmentalism", Progress in Human Geography, Vol. 18 (2).

Daly and Cobb (1989) : "For The Common Goal : Redirecting The Economy Towards Community, The Environment and a Sustainable Future", B OS TON Beacon Press.

DEV, S Mahendra and M.H. Suryanarayana (1991 : "Is PDS Urban Biased and Pro Rich". Economic and Political Weekly, October 12.

Dev, S.Mahendra (2000): "Agricultural Development and PDS - Lack of Major Initiatives", Economic and Political Weekly, March 25.

Dutta, B and B. Ramaswami (2001): Targeting and Efficiency in The Public Distribution System - Case of and Hrapri4desh and Maharashtra", Economic and Political Weekly, May 5.

Dutta B.B. (1994) : "Insurgency and Economic Development in India's North East" in India's North East, The Process of Change and Development, B.R. Publishing, New Delhi.

Dutta P.C. (1999) : "Insurgency and Economic Development in India's North East- The process of Change and Development" (ed) R.K. Samanta, B.R. Publishing Corporation, pp1-38, New Delhi.

Dutta P.C. (1999) : "Population Growth and Environmental Crisis in N. E. India — Problems and Remedies", Paper presented in seminar, NEICSSR, 13-14 Dec.

Dutta P.C. (1999) : "Power Crisis and its Remedies in the Barak Valley Districts of Assam in NER : A Review" in

Energy and Energy Resource Management (ed.) V.S. Mahajan, S.K. Agnihotri and R.P. Athparia, Deep and Deep Publication.

Dutta P.C. (2001) : "The Development of Social Forestry in Assam of North Eastern Region"- Paper presented in the Seminar on Protection, Promotion and Conservation of Forest Resources of North East India, 5th June, NEICSSR, Shillong.

Dutta P.C. & B.C. Pradhan (2000) : "Agricultural Development and Security of Life in North East India"- paper presented in the National Seminar on Food Security, Nutrition and Public Distribution System in the North East India, November 27-28, NEICSSR, Shillong.

Dutta P.C. & B.C. Pradhan (2001) : "Regional Disparity and its Consequences in NER"- paper presented in the 33rd Regional Science Conferences of Regional Science Association, India, October 19-20, held at NEHU, Shillong.

"Dutta P.C. & B.C. Pradhan (2001) : "Issues and Problems of Ethnicity in Assam of North East India" – paper presented in the seminar on Ethnic Issues, Secularism and Conflict Resolution in North East India, Neicssr, 25-26 April, Shillong

Dutta P.C. & B.C. Pradhan (2002) : "Ethnic Issues and Social Tensions in North Eastern Region(NER) of India"- paper presented in Regional Seminar organized jointly by I.S.I., Calcutta and Department of Statistics, Gauhati University, March 2-3, Guwahati

Dutta P. C. & H. Choudhury (1995) : "Per Capita Household Consumption Inequalities in the North Eastern Region of India", Indian Journal of Regional Science (IJRS), Vol- 2 7, NO 1 & 2.

Dutta P.C. & H. Choudhury (1996) : "A Note on Inter-State variation in per capita Non-Food Household Items of Consumption in the North East India", IJRS, Vol.28, No:2

Dutta P.C. & N. Roy (1998): "Socio-Economic Development of North East India with Special Reference to the Problems of Urbanisation". Paper presented and published in the Abstract of seminar on Environmental Problems in North east in India, 6-7" Nov, 1998, Assam University, Silchar.

Dutta P.C. & N. Roy (2000): "Informal Border Trade in North East India and its Socio Economic Impacts- A Case Study of Karimganj District" in Border Trade in North East India (ed) G.Das and R.K. Purkayastha.

Dyson, and A. Hanchate (2000): "India's Demo Graphic and Food Prospects - State Level Analysis", Economic and Political Weekly, November 11.

Kumar, P (1998): "Food Demand and Supply Projections For India , Agricultural Economics Policy Paper, 98-01, Indian Agricultural Research New Delhi.

Gedam, R (1998) : Poverty in India, Deep and Deep Publications, New Delhi, pp. 386-420.

Gupta D.C. (1988) : "Indian Government and politics", page 459-502, Vikas Publishing House, New Delhi.

Koropeckyj I. S (1972): "Equilisation of Regional Development in Socialist Countries an Empirical Study", Economic Development and Cultural Change Vol-21, No. 1, Oct., Pp 68-86.

Madhab, Jayanta (1999) : "North East, Crisis of Identity, Security and Underdevelopment", EPW, Vol. 34, No.1, Feb. 6-12

Mahajan O.P. (1982) : "Economic Planning and Regional Development in India", Ess Publications, New Delhi.

Mahanta, A (2001): "Hunger: Amidst Planty", Assam Tribune, 16 October.

Maiti, A and S. Chakrabarti (2000) : "Globalisation—Yet Another Threat to Food Security and Regional Parity in India"—Paper presented in National Seminar on Food, Nutrition, Food Security, Public Distribution System in the North East India, 27-28 November, Neicssr, Shillong.

Malhotra, N (1999) : "Human Development in India and Inter State Pattern", Indian Regional Science, 31(1), 31-45.

Mazumder, D.N. (1980): "North East India- A Profile" in Eastern Himalayas: A Study on Anthropology and Tribalism (ed) T.C. Sharma and D.N.Mazumder, pp23-61, Cosmo Publication, New Delhi.

Nair K.R.C. (1983): Regional Experience in A Developing Economy , Wiley Eastern Ltd.

Parikh, K (1994): "Who Gets How Much From PDS - How Effectively Does It Reaqch The Poor ", Sarvekshana, January-March.

Pathak C. R.(1998): "Urbanisation and Urban Poverty in Third World Countries: A Case Study of India" in Essays on Regional Science, Regional Development and Planning, Vol-Il, RSAI, Calcutta.

Patil S.Y. (1998) : "Environmental Impact on Urbanisation in India" in Essays on Regional Science, Regional Development and Planning, Vol.II, RSAI, Calcutta-91.

Prakash S. (1977) : "Regional Inequalities and Economic Development with Special Reference to Infrastructural Facilities in India", IJRS, Vol. XI, No. 2, pp 173-195

Procharopouclus G(1994):"Returns to Investment in Education; A Global Update", World Development, pp 1325-43.

Rao,V.R. (1994): "Space for Sustainable Development "G.B. Panth Memorial Lecture, Guwahati

Rao, U.R. (1995): "Global Connectivity Through Telemedicine", Journal of Medical System, 19, 3, 295.

Rao, V.R (1996): "General Presidential Address in 83rd Indian Science Congress, Patiala.

Samanta, R.K. (1994) : "Issues for Agricultural Development in Tribal Dominated North East India "In India's North East - The Process of Change and Development, B.R. Publishing Corporation, Delhi.

Sen A. (1973): "On Economic Inequility" Oxford University Press.

Shah, A (1997) : "Food Security and Access to Natural Resources - A Review Of Recent Trends" ,Economic and Political Weekly, June 28.

Singh U.K. & K.N. Sudharshan (1996) : "Population Education", DPH Education Series, Discovery Publishing House, New Delhi.

Swaminathan, M (1997): "Understanding The Cost of Food Corporation of India ,Onomic and Political Weekly, December, 25.

Visaria L (1985) : "Infant Mortality in India : Level, Trends and Determinants", Economic and Political Weekly, (10th, 17th and 24th August).

Williamson J.G. (1965) : Inequality the Process of National Development", Economic Development And Cultural Change, Vol-13, No-4, Part-II, July.

World Bank (1997) : "Primary Education in India, Development in Practice Series", Washington.

World Development Report–Poverty 1990 World Development Indicators. (Foot Notes 5, 6, 7, 8, 9) And World Development-Investing in Health 1993, World Development Indicators Prepatred By World Bank and Published By Oxford University Press.

Zolotas X (1981) : "Economic Growth And Declining Social Welfare", New York Printing Press, New York, U.S.A.

Basic Statistics of North Eastern Region, 2000 and 2001, Nec, Shillong

Statistical Abstract of India, 1998 and 2000, Govt. of India

Different Issues Of N.E. Newsletter, Ministry of Home Affairs, Govt. of India.

Human Development Report -2001

Census of India : 2001, Population Policy of India, Population And Progress in Global Perspective By J.C.Aggarwal, Doaba House, Delhi.

Carson. R (1962) : "The Silver Spring", Boston, Houghton Miffin.

Dutta P.C. (1996) : "Quality Variation of Some Food Items of Consumption in North Eastern Region (NER)", Indian Journal of Regional Science, Vol. 28 (1).

Ehrlich. A and Holdren J (1971) : "Impact of Population Growth", SCIENCE, 171, pp.1212-1217.

Hirschman, A (1958) : "The Strategy of Economic Development", New Haven, Yale University Press.

Hossain,M (1993) : "Interrelationship between Population, Environment and Development"-Them paper presented in the Fourth Asian and Pacific Population Conference, 19-27 August,1992 and appear in Asian Population Studies Series, NO. 124 (selected papers) United Nations, New York.

Mackellar, F.L. et al (1995) : "Population Households and CO2 Emissions", Population and Development Review, 21(4), PP. 849-65.

PRABHU, K.S (1996) : "Social Sector in Economic Development: Some Issues", Paper Presented in 79th Annual Conference, Indian Economic Association, Gwalior.

Dutta P.C. And B.C. Pradhan (1998) : "Problems of Community Integration in Small Towns of Barak Valley Districts of Assam- A Case Study Of Lala Town", in Urban Development in North East India : Potentiality and Problems Ed. B.Dutta Roy, A.K.Neog & H.K. Mazhari, Reliance Publishing House, New Delhi.

17

Economic Development and Environmental Pollution in India with Special Reference to NER

Gross national product measures neither the health of our children, the quality of their education, nor the joy of their play. It measures neither the beauty of our poetry, nor the strength of our marriages. It is indifferent to the decency of our factories and the safety of streets alike. It does not include the beauty of our poetry or the strength of our marriages, the intelligence of our public debate or the integrity of our public officials. GNP measures neither our wit nor our courage, neither our wisdom nor our learning, neither our compassion nor our devotion to our country. It measures everything, in short, except that which makes life worthwhile.

Senator Robert Kennedy (1968)

The development is a complex process and has multi dimensional structure depending upon its resources in general and infrastructural facilities in particular. The very pattern of economic development in the third world countries has resulted in increasing imbalance in the distribution of income and large number of people are being relegated to below poverty line. The economic development not only brings about changes in the socio-economic and cultural life of a population but it also influences the consumption pattern in the long run.

Sustainable development aims at improving human well-being, particularly through alleviating poverty, increasing gender equity, and improving health, human resources, and stewardship of the natural environment.

Sustainable development, meaning 'meeting the present needs without compromising those of the future' **(WCED 1987)**[1], involves important inter- generational equity considerations, including those related to the environment. Environment is of importance not only because of its effects on the psychic and non-economic welfare, but also because of its impact on production over the long term **(World Bank 2000)**[2]. Urbanisation can improve people's access to education, health and other services. It also creates environmental health hazards, such as water and air pollution, and by increasing consumption levels, can have environmental impacts in distant rural areas also.[3]

In Asia—perhaps more than in any other region—the interplay between population growth, resource depletion, and environmental degradation is cause for concern. The growth in population beyond the optimal size associated by socio-political development and technical revolution results in increased pressure on natural environment as well as on the process of economic development. In order to achieve a better quality of life, care has to be taken to obtain smooth movement in all the systems and sub systems connected with quality of living. The increasing population pressure has given rise to linkages between quality of life, population dynamics and environmental degradation.

Addressing an international conference of Islamic scholars (ulema) on **'Population and Development'** on 6th May, 2005 in Islamabad, General Pervez Musharraf, the then President of Pakistan stressed the need for population policies based on a realistic assessment of socio-economic conditions in Pakistan and more broadly, in the Muslim World (Ummah). He was of the opinion that there should be no doubt in his mind that the main factor retarding economic growth, poverty alleviation and action on joblessness is population growth. Those who do not understand this are living in a world of their own.

Growth rates are seen to be high in India, Indonesia, Iran, Malaysia, Mongolia, Myanmar, the Philippines, and Vietnam. Economically and industrially, Asia is the fastest-growing region in the world. This economic and industrial development is inevitably accompanied by changing patterns of consumption. Primarily as a result of rural-to-urban migration, Asia is the fastest urbanizing region in the world. According to United Nations estimates, the urban population in Asia will nearly double in the next 30 years. By 2030, more than half of Asia's population will live in cities—some 2.6 billion people. By 2015, the urban population of Asia will be larger than the urban population of all the other regions of the world combined **(United Nations 2001b).** This rapid—largely unplanned—expansion of urban areas has robbed many Asian countries of some of their most productive agricultural land and has resulted in serious problems of air, soil, and water pollution.

Like developed countries, the policy makers of India have adopted the policy to eliminate gender inequality at all levels by 2015 to target the goals of to be achieved for the empowerment of women in particular and human development in general. As human development moves center stage in the global development debate, gender equality and gender equity are emerging as major challenges because of gender discrimination is clearly visible in all the societies of the world. The primary objective of development is to satisfy the essential material needs of the society, but not at the cost of local environment and people's culture.

The Eleventh Five Year Plan (2007-12) has been prepared against a backdrop of high expectations arising from some aspects of the recent performance. GDP growth in the post reforms period has improved from an average of about 5.7 per cent in the 1980s to an average of about 6.1 per cent in the Eighth and Ninth Plan periods, and 8.5 percent in Tenth Plan period, making India one of the ten fastest growing countries in the world. The Eleventh Plan has specific focus on key indicators of human development. Malaysia, Republic of Korea and Thailand, among other East Asian countries, sustained annual growth rates at levels equal to, or higher than what India was seeking to achieve in the Tenth Plan for several years, before the outbreak of the east Asian crisis. The People's Republic of China, a large country like India in terms of both area and population, has been one of the best performers among the major economies of the world during the 1980s and 1990s and has been maintaining high growth (7 per cent plus) despite the slowdown in global economic activity.. The experience of India in terms of growth acceleration is also similar to that of countries in East Asia and China

A number of studies were undertaken by different economists to establish a linkage between infrastructure and economic development. **Brutan (1960)** was of the view that infrastructure had a positive impact on the development of an economy by reducing cost of production through economies of scale and thereby increasing its profitability and overall increase in production, employment and hence further expansion. **Ahluwalia (1984)** statistically proved a significant correlation between infrastructure and per capita income of different states of Indian economy. The role of infrastructure in economic growth has been the subject of considerable research in the fields of public policy, economics, and planning.

The central objective of planning in India at the present stage is to initiate a process of development which will raise living standards and open out to the people new opportunities for a richer and more varied life. While the GDP of the country as a whole is growing at 9.2 per cent per annum, the growth rate in the NER as a whole is under 4 per cent. Nearly 98 per cent of the frontiers of the region constitute the international frontier of India and the remaining 2 per cent is connected with the rest of the country. Still the region has virtually no trade relationship with those bordering countries. Physical infrastructure including road, rail and air connectivity is a serious problem in North Eastern Region of India (NER).

Dutta (2004) highlighted that in the era of globalisation women's education in NER is not translated into reality although it is squarely on the development agenda of our country. It is to be noted that although Kerala, Himachal Pradesh, and TamilNadu like states have adopted the gender issues as key to the process of Human Development, the policy makers of the states of NER had never paid their attention towards this issue **(Dutta and Pradhan, 2007).**

In consonance with the above objectives, the present study has been designed under different heads like Population and Demography, Urbanisation, Economic Infrastructure, Social Infrastructure, Industrial development, Per Capita Net State Domestic Product, Inequality in income (consumption) and poverty, Quality of life index, Population Dynamics And Environment, Corruption and its Impact. Lastly the study is being concluded with valuable suggestions. In doing so, correlation coefficients and multiple Regressions along with statistical tests have been made to find out if there is any significant relation exist among the socio-economic and demographic variables However, for the completion of the study, published and unpublished Secondary statistical data along with various reports of the scholars have been used.

Population and Demography

India accounts for 2.4 per cent of the world surface area but it supports 16.7 per cent of the world population. The population of India as on 1st March, 2001, crossed one billion and was enumerated at 1.03 billion (excluding the earthquake affected areas of Gujarat) which was 23.84 crore in 1901, thereby 332.05 p.c. over the period of 100 years. Thus India became the second country in the world after China to cross the one billion mark. According to India's Health Ministry, India's population which was 238 million in 1947 touched 1.012 billion in March 2001 and is expected to be 1.263 billion by 2016. However, as per estimation, the population of India in the year 2008 was 1,132 million.*

The decadal growth of population at 21.34 per cent between 1991-2001 was the sharpest decline in the rate of growth of population witnessed since independence, with the average exponential growth rate declining from 2.14 per cent per annum during the previous decade to 1.93 per cent per annum. India was the first country to obtain family planning advice from the World Health organization. In 1960 Indian officials elevated the family planning programme to "the very centre of planned development."[4] The National Population Policy (NPP) 2000 outlines the long-term objective of achieving a stable population by 2045, at a level consistent with the requirements of sustainable economic growth and social development.

The percentage decadal growth of population in rural and urban areas in the decade 1991- 2001 was 17.9 per cent and 31.2 per cent respectively. Urban population constitutes 27.8 per cent of the total population of the country, which is higher by 2.1 percentage points as compared to the situation in 1991. The density of population has increased steadily from 117 persons per sq.km. in 1951 to 324 persons per sq.km. in 2001. The sex ratio for the country as a whole has improved from 927 females per 1000 males in 1991 to 933 females per 1000 males in 2001. The literacy rate for the country as a whole in 2001, works out to 65.38 per cent for the population aged seven years and over. The corresponding figures for males and females are 75.85 per cent and 54.16 per cent respectively.

Classification of population by economic activity according to results of 2001 census reveals that out of the total population of 103 crore (excluding the earthquake affected areas of Gujarat) in the country, 31.32 crore (30.55 p.c. of total population)were main workers, 8.93 crore (8.71 p.c.) were marginal workers and 62.27 crore were non workers. Among males 45.34 per cent were main workers and 6.59 per cent were marginal workers, while among females 14.69 per cent were main workers and 10.99 per cent were marginal workers. Out of total workers (main and marginal) 31.71 per cent were cultivators, 26.69 per cent were agricultural labourers, 4.07 per cent engaged in household industries and 37.53 per cent were engaged in other economic activities. Thus, about 58.40 per cent working population was engaged in agriculture (i.e. cultivators and agricultural labourers). This proportion was of 73.33 per cent in rural areas.

On the other hand, the NER covers an area of 2.63 lakh sq.km. which accounts for 7.9 per cent of total geographical area of the country. With a total population of 38.86 million, as per 2001 census, it accounts for 3.8 p.c. of total population of India. The share of population of NER, in comparison to all India, increased from 2.89 p.c. in 1951 to 3.78 p.c. in 2001. The region's growth rate of population (21.61 p.c.) is higher than the national average of 21.35 p.c. during 1991-2001. The density of the population varies from 13 in Arunachal Pradesh to 340 in Assam followed by 305 in Tripura. The density of the population of the region is 147.65 which is almost half of the national density (324) in 2001 while it was only 34.29 in 1951.

Urbanisation

Urbanisation is a process of population concentration. We have conceded the **Kingsley Davisian** view in the 19th Century that ***"it is not possible to have industrialisation without urbanisation"***. It is fact that the urbanisation is the most essential for all round development of the developing nations, as it has increased employment, income and standard of living in these countries. But it has simultaneously created number of socio economic and environmental problems. Urbanisation has disturbed the ecological balance by creating air, water and noise pollution through industrialisation.

The increasing urbanisation has led to a number of socio-economic problems like crime, suicides, drug abuse, unemployment and poverty, alcoholism, overcrowding, housing shortage, slums, traffic control and pollution etc. At the same time they are also centres of civilisation and culture by helping a lot in the process of modernisation **(Dutta, 2002).** Therefore, **environmentalist aptly say that urbanisation-environment relationship is not complementary but**

contradictory with each other (Patil, 1998).

In the developed economics, the process of **urbanisation** has been closely and positively related with the economic development, while in the third world developing countries is a consequential phenomenon. The rates of urbanisation vary over time and space. In the later half of the twentieth century the developing countries have been urbanizing very fast and India is no exception. The rate of urbanization during the post independence period has been quite rapid with highest rate, during 1971-81 decade, of 46 p.c. The 1991census reveals a slowing down urban population growth (36.19 p.c.) during 1981 – 91. and 32.61 p.c. during 1991-2001.

Coming to the states of NER, the notable point is that the **percentage of urban population to total population (urbanization)** varies from 12.90 (Assam) to 49.63 (Mizoram). It is striking to note that except Mizoram, all the states of NER including NER as a whole (15.66 p.c.) are below the national level (27.82 p.c.) according to 2001.

Though rapid urbanization is a part of development process, it accelerates to many severe socio-economic problems and disturb the overall environment and quality of life of people. Therefore, one must accept the synthesis that urbanization is saviour up to a certain limit and detrimental after without check to it.

Economic Infrastructure

The term "economic infrastructure" signifies a group of improvements in land-areas which are typified by physical forms of capital investments in the usefulness of land for production and habitation. However, only the indicators like Energy and power, Banking and communication will be discussed in this section.

Energy and Power

Energy is an essential input for the economic development of a country in improving the quality of life of its people. The per capita consumption of the power in the country is much below the consumption levels in developed countries. To achieve the target of providing power to all by 2012, the Centre has initiated a number of steps with the help of the States.

It may be pointed out that in 10th Plan (2002-07), 26.5 per cent of the Plan Outlay was allotted for energy which was amounting to Rs. 4,03,927 crores for the country as a whole **(table 17.1).** It is also to be noted here that during 5 Annual Plans of 2002 – 2007, the percentage of allotted amounts

Table 17.1: 10th Plan Outlay, Energy Development : India, 2002–07 and Annual Plans (2002-03 to 2006-07), Amount (Rs. Crore)

	Tenth Plan 2002-07	Annual Plan 2002-03	Annual Plan 2003-04	Annual Plan 2004-05	Annual Plan 2005-06	Annual Plan 2006-07
Energy	403927.0	44710.0	50199.1	60729.5	71305.8	90498.9
	(26.5)	(21.3)	(22.3)	(23.0)	(20.3)	(20.5)
Power	(N.A)	25280.8	30784.7	34315.5	39939.0	52090.3
		(12.0)	(13.7)	(13.0)	(11.4)	(11.8)
Non	(N.A)	1712.2	1205.3	896.4	719.2	1093.9
Conventional Sources of Energy		(0.8)	(0.5)	(0.3)	(0.2)	(0.2)

Percentage distribution are shown in parentheses.

were ranges from 11.4 p.c. to 13.7 p.c. while in case of non conventional energy sector, the percentages vary from 0.2 p.c. to 0.8 p.c. during the same Plan Periods.[5]

Higher electricity use per capita correlates with a higher score on the Human Development Index (1997). Developing nations score much lower on these variables than developed nations. The continued rapid economic growth and increase in living standards in developing nations with large populations, like China and India, is dependent on a rapid and large expansion of energy production capacity. The present per capita consumption of electricity in India is little over 600 KWh, which is much lower than that of the developed countries. The degree of economic growth is correlated with the generation and consumption of electricity. The per capita consumption (PCC) of electricity in some developed countries as calculated by the International Energy Agency for the year 2004 and gross annual per capita consumption of electricity of different states of NER during the year 2005-06 are as given in **table 17.2** Maximum per capita consumption (17179 KWh) is observed in

Table 17.2: Annual Per Capita Consumption of Electricity (in KWh), 2004

Name of the country	Annual PCC	Name of the States	Annual PCC
Canada	17179	Arunachal Pradesh	297.66
USA	13338	Assam	170.65
Australia	11126	Manipur	215.21
Japan	8076	Meghalaya	517.54
France	7689	Mizoram	250.15
Germany	7030	Nagaland	179.34
United Kingdom	6206	Sikkim	429.81
Russia	5642	Tripura	190.62
Italy	5644	NER (North Eastern Region)	201.44
India	631.41		

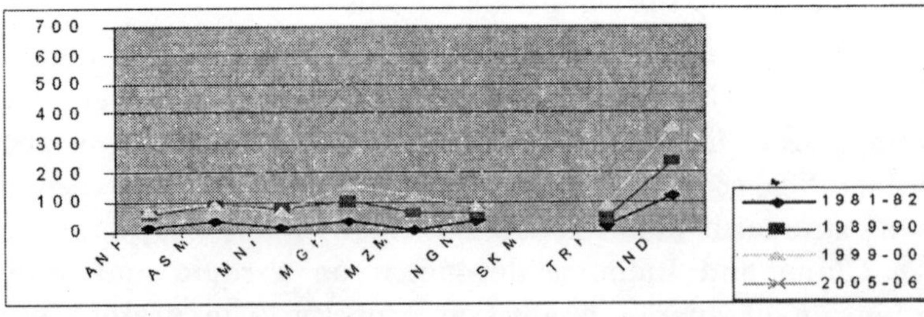

Figure 17-A: Per capita consumption of Electricity in NER (in KWH)

Canada which is 85 times of NER (201.44 KWh) and 27 times of India's per capita consumption (631.41 KWh). However, Canada is followed by U.S.A (13338 KWh) and Australia (11126 KWh). It is remarkable to note that India's PCC is more than three times of NER's PCC while NER is considered as power house of India.

From the **Figure 17-A** it is clear that during the 20 years period (1981-2000), per capita consumption of electricity (in kwh) has increased very little in all the states of NER in comparison to next 6 years period (2000-06). However, during 2005-06, per capita consumption in all the states of NER including NER as a whole (201.44 kwh) are below than the national level (631.41). It is to be noted here that, per capita consumption in the state of Assam is the lowest (170.65) and the highest in the state of Meghalaya (517.54) among the states of NER.

Banking

Financial infrastructure is essential for economic development. Banks have expanded their network extensively particularly during the last two decades in different states of NER. The number of branches of scheduled commercial banks (SCBs) in NER was 1935 in 1996 which gradually increased to 1941 in 2001 but then it decreased to 1915 in 2003. After 2003 it started to increase again and stands at 1952 as on March 31, 2005. With respect to NER (1952), the percentage of number of branches in Assam is 63.27 and with respect to India (28958) it is only 1.81 p.c. However with respect to India (66970 nos.), there are only 2.87 p.c. branches in NER as on March, 2004

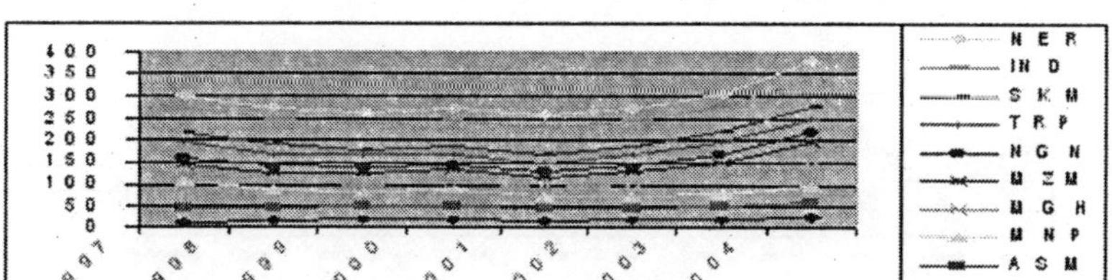

Figure **17-B:** Credit Deposit Ratio of SCBs in the NER

which increased by 1.67 p.c. as on March, 2005. The credit deposit ratio was 24.40 p.c. as compared to the national average of 66 p.c. as on March, 2005. The credit-deposit ratio (CDR) of banks in NER have fallen from 47 p.c. as on end of March 1991 to 26 p.c. as on end March 2003. But after that it has increased to 35 (as against the national average of 66) as on the end of March 2005. The CDR of banks of all the states of NER including NER and India as a whole for the periods 1997-98 to 2004-05 are shown by **figure 17-B.** However, percentage increase in the CD ratio in NER (16.67 p.c.) is low as compared to the all India.

Transport and Communication

The surface transport facilities of the region which includes Road transports, Railways and waterways along with the links with the neighbouring states and the rest of the country are totally inadequate and subject to severe hardships during monsoons. Adequate infrastructural facilities are considered to be the pre-requisite for industrial development. Under the successive Five Year Plans, the plan outlay on transport and communication varied significantly. Although 17 p.c. of the total outlay was allocated on transport and communication during First Plan but the share was declined in subsequent three years and reached to 4.8 p.c. during ad hoc. Plan and again after 4th plan (13. 1 p.c.), the declining trend has been observed up to 8th plan (6.3 p.c).

However, the share has been increased in subsequent two plans. It is to be noted that in the 9th and 10th Plans the share of percentage have been increased to 10.24 p.c. and 10.57

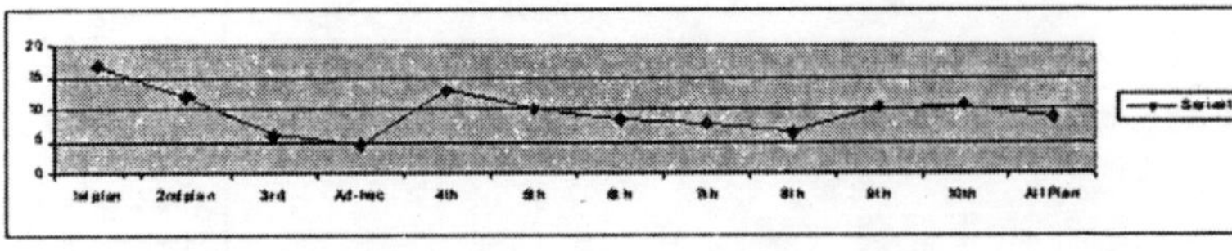

Figure **17.C:** Percentage of outlay on Transport and communication with respect to Total Outlay (1951-2007)

p.c. respectively which are also far below of 1st Plan period **(Fig. 17-C).** The above figure reveals the fact that the transport and communication did not receive much priority under the successive Five Year Plans. The length of National Highways is 2044 kms while state highway occupy 2028 kms and the other PWD roads occupy 29271 KMs. The East West Corridor spans over 713 kms in Assam.

Social Infrastructure

Social infrastructure is the glue that holds a regional community together. The social-sector expenditure plays an important role in supporting economic growth and reducing poverty. There are several key policies and priorities being pursued to support critical social infrastructure (incorporating education, healthcare, cultural facilities and community facilities). However, it is being tried to discuss regarding education and health care in the present study.

Expenditure on social sectors as a proportion of total expenditure, after decreasing from 20.4 per cent in 2002-03 to 19.5 per cent in 2003-04, increased steadily to 22.3 per cent in 2006-07 (RE) and 22.5 per cent in 2007-08 (BE). Expenditure on education as a proportion of total expenditure has increased from 9.8 per cent in 2004-05 to 10.4 per cent in 2006-07 (RE). Share of health in total expenditure has also increased from 4.4 per cent in 2004-05 to 4.9 per cent in 2006-07 (RE).

Education

The vision of a 21st century modern India fast emerging as a global powerhouse has opened its economic regime to immense possibilities and progress. The impact of such reforms should go beyond its economic prosperity and should widen the social opportunities for the masses to create a better capability index. One such vital index is education which shapes human capital, and higher education in particular generates human skills for research and development, training, provide policy advice. **Education is the main instrument of social change.** It is the index of social progress and economic development of a region. Sustainable development can not take place without investments being made in people. Higher levels of education may have greater direct impact on economic development but the primary and middle level education are important because they widely distribute the conditions conductive to development. High teacher-pupil ratio affects the quality of education, which is one of the dampening factors in educational decision.

There are some notable features in regard to literacy rate in the states of NER. Except Arunachal Pradesh (41.59 p.c.) and Meghalaya (49.1 p.c.), the literacy level of the region's population is above the national level (52.21 p.c.) according to 1991 census while in 2001, percentage of literacy rate in the states of Arunachal Pradesh (54.74 p.c.), Meghalaya (63.31 p.c.) and Assam (64.28 p.c.) are below the national figure of 65.38 p.c.

There is a big gender gap in literacy which is one of the major obstacles in attaining total literacy. Enrolment in various stages

Table 17.3: Number of Educational Institutions in NER

Prim + UP	Sec + HS	Arts/Sc. Colleges	Engg.	Medical	Universities	Polytechnics	ITI	IIT
56677	7716	497	6	6	13	18	49	1

Source: Draft Report of the Task force on Development Initiatives for the NER, Sept. 2005.

of education is growing at a fast rate, but the proportion of girls is low and declines sharply at higher stages of education. The highest gender gap has been found in the states of Manipur (24.03 p.c. points), Arunachal Pradesh (21.76), Tripura (20.93) and lowest in Mizoram (7.01) followed by Meghalaya (8.27). However all the states of NER are below all-India (24.84 p.c. points) level. Low female literacy has strong repercussions on other aspects like enrolment of children, population growth, child care and acceptance of family welfare measures. As per 1991 census literacy rate of NER was 58.09 per cent (all India 52.2 per cent), while in 2001 it was 68.5 per cent (all India 64.8 per cent). Mizoram has the second highest literacy rate in India.

It is important to note that with a population of size 388.58 million, there are only 6 engineering colleges, 18 polytechnics and 49 numbers of Industrial Training Institutes along with only one Indian Institute of Technology in NER **(table 1.6).** The figures reveal the fact that the number of technical institutions are very poor while these are essential for producing high skilled technical persons for industrial development.

It is also observed that among the states of NER, highest number of higher level educational institutions are found in Assam which is only 2.37 per cent in comparison to all-India **(table 17.4).** In case of Vocational professional schools, the highest number is observed in the state of Assam (0.55 per cent in comparison to all –India) followed by Manipur and Meghalaya (0.14 per cent). Considering the total number of scholars, it may be pointed out that there are 4.49 per cent of scholars (9830728) in the states of NER out of which 47.65 per cent (4684251) are women scholars which is 4.74 per cent in comparison to the country as a whole.

Health

Health is a social goal and considered as an integral component in over all socio economic development. The majority of health problems are the products of illiteracy, poverty, ignorance, over crowding, poor environmental conditions and uneven distribution of health manpower and institutions. However, there is some debate whether there is an economically or socially meaningful correlation between inequality and aggregate health outcomes or whether it is purely compositional **(Deaton, 2001).**

National Rural Health Mission (NRHM) covers the entire country, with special focus on 18 states including 8 states of NER where the challenge of strengthening poor public health systems and thereby improve key health indicators is the greatest. An updated national health database is essential for proper planning, decision making, monitoring and evaluation of various health programmes and health sector developments.

Table 17.4: Number of Recognised Educational Institutions, Vocational Professional Schools and Total Number of Scholars (General and Technical) in 2003-04

State	Total for Higher Level Education	Vocational Professional Schools	Total Number of Scholars (General and Technical)	
			Male	Female
ANP	12	2	309042	138774
ASM	405	27	6298613	2983531
MNP	74	7	697922	334541
MGH	59	7	734550	368279
MZM	32	1	220543	106831
NGN	44	3	438523	209972
SKM	10	1	139603	69477
TRP	23	4	991932	472846
IND	17062	4877	219088500	98696006

Source: Department of Education, Ministry of Human Resource Development.

It is observed that there are only 4.32 p.c. of public health centres in the states of NER as compared to India's figure and among the states of NER, there are 64 p.c. public health centres only in Assam, while less than 10 p.c. are in each of the other states of the region. The same patterns are also observed in case of sub centres and community health centres. Thus, it is high time to make an effort to increase the number of health centres in these backward states of NER so that health problems of this region can be minimized to some extent **(Dutta, 2008).**

Table 17.5 shows that the number of doctors possessing recognized medical qualification (under I.M.C. Act) and registered with State Medical Council over the years 1991 to 2005 for the state of Assam increased from 10499 to 16401. In comparison to all –India level, the percentages share of doctors decreased from 2.67 per cent to 2.48 over the period considered. During the period for the state of Assam, the number of doctors

Table 17.5: Number of Doctors in Assam and India in the period 1991-2005

Year	1991	2000	2001	2002	2003	2004	2005
Assam	10499	14253	14586	15060	15526	15649	16401
India	393640	555550	577094	607075	625423	643984	660733

Source : Medical Council of India.

Table – 17.6 : Population served per Doctor in NER

State	ANP	ASM	MNP	MGH	MZM	NGN	SKM	TRP
No. of Doctors	464	2160	945	389	89	367	174	860
Population Served Per Docter	2352	11980	2427	5411	10360	5422	3108	3720
Reference year	2002-03	1999-00	2002-03	1998-99	1999-00	2002-03	2001-02	2003-04

Source: Basic Statistics of NER 2006.

increased by 56.21 per cent. The respective percentage for the whole of India is 67.85 per cent.

Table 17.6 shows the number of population served per government doctor in the states of NER. A minute look at the table confirms the fact that the health facility is not good at all in the states of NER. The number of government doctors ranges from 89 in Mizoram to 2160 in Assam. The number of population served per doctor ranges from 2427 in Manipur to 11980 in Assam. The state of Assam is followed by Mizoram where the number of population served per doctor is 10360. However, the data available are not fully comparable since the time periods are not same.

Drinking Water

Water is the life blood of the environment. Although India occupies only 3.29 million sq.km geographical area, which forms 2.4 p.c. of the world's land area, it supports over 15 p.c. of the world's population Thus, India supports about one-sixth of

Table 17.7: Percentage (p.c.) of population with access to safe drinking water, (2000)[12]

Country	P.C.	Country	P.C.	Country	P.C.	Country	P.C.	Country	P.C.
Albania	97	Algeria	89	Azerbaijan	78	Brazil	87	Chile	93
China	75	Cuba	91	Egypt	97	India	84	Indonesia	78
Iran	92	Iraq	85	Kenya	57	Mexico	88	Morocco	80
Peru	80	Philippines	86	South Africa	86	South Korea	92	Sudan	67
Suria	80	Turkey	82	Uganda	52	Venezuela	83	Zimbabwe	83

Note : All industrialized countries (as listed by UNICEF) with data available are at 100 p.c.

world population, 1/50th of world's land and 1/25th of world's water resources. March 22, 2009 was declared as World Water Day.

Health authorities have historically suggested at least eight glasses, eight fluid ounces each (168 ml), of water per day (64 fluid ounces, or 1.89 litres),[6] and the British Dietetic Association recommends 1.8 litres.[7] The United States Environmental Protection Agency has determined that the average adult actually ingests 2.0 litres per day.

The percentage of population with access to safe drinking water in some developing countries is shown in **table 17.7** A close look at the table confirms that Albania (97 p.c.), Egypt (97 p.c.), Chile (93 p.c.), South Korea (92 p.c.) and Iran (92 p.c.) are on top listed countries and Uganda (52 p.c.), Kenya (57 p.c.) and Sudan (67 p.c.) are placed on the bottom of the list. among the countries considered while in India only 84 p.c. have the facility with access to safe drinking water.

In 2006, waterborne diseases were estimated to cause 1.8 million deaths each year while about 1.1 billion people lacked proper drinking water.[8] It is clear that people in the developing world need to have access to good quality water in sufficient quantity, water purification technology and availability and distribution systems for water. Humans can survive for several weeks without food, but for only a few days without water. The exact amount of water a human needs is highly individual, as it depends on the condition of the subject, the amount of physical exercise, and on the environmental temperature and humidity.[9] In the US, the reference daily intake (RDI) for water is 3.7 litres per day for human males older than 18, and 2.7 litres for human females older than 18[10] including water contained in food, beverages, and drinking water.

The Millennium Development Goal of halving the proportion of people without access to safe drinking water between 1990 and 2015 will probably be reached. Globally Only 27 per cent of the rural population has water piped directly to their homes and 24 per cent rely on unimproved sources. Of the 884 million people without access to an improved water source 746 million people (84 per cent) live in rural areas. Sub –Saharan Africa has made the least progress in improved water sources since 1990, improving only 9 per cent to 2006. In contrast the Eastern Asian region saw a dramatic drop from 45 per cent to 9 per cent reliance on unimproved water in the same time period.[11]

It is observed that the maximum amount of water is required in the state of Assam, among the states of NER, which is approximately 2.33 p.c. as compared to India's requirement in 1991, which further risen to 2.63 p.c. in 2001. Thus, there is an increasing trend of water requirement in 2001 over 1991. Regarding the safe drinking water facilities, all the states of NER, except Arunachal Pradesh (70.02 p.c.) are less than the national average (62.3 p.c.). It is striking to note that only 16.21 p.c. of total households of Mizoram can drink safe water. Thus, conservation of water is an important aspect in this regard and the people of NER should take active step for the management of water for the maintenance of the standard of water quality.

Industrial Development

The necessity of industrialization is a means of achieving rapid growth and prosperity has long been recognized in the strategy of development of any region. Industrially, the NER continues to be the most backward region in the country, and the states in the region hardly have any industrial base, except perhaps Assam, because of its traditional tea, oil and wood based industries. Handicrafts and handloom industry has the potential to promote income and employment generation in a big way. Development of small scale industrial sector (SSI), therefore, is the only alternative to the economic backwardness of a state lies in its significance for generation of employment with low capital cost. The Handloom industry plays a vital role in providing employment to a huge no. of population as it is a labour intensive industry. The NER has the highest concentration of household units in the Handloom sector in the country and more than 50 per cent of weavers belong to the NER states.

Table 17.8: Trend of SSI growth in north eastern region

State	1997-98	1998-99	1999-00	2000-01	2001-02	2002-03
ANP	4,456	4,546	4,694	4,750	4,797	5,022
	(7.00)	(2.01)	(3.26)	(1.19)	(1.00)	(4.70)
ASM	34,258	36,482	38,303	40,419	42,947	45,193
	(6.84)	(6.49)	(4.49)	(5.52)	(6.52)	(5.23)
MNP	5,322	5,447	5,587	5,778	5,868	5,974
	(3.08)	(2.35)	(2.57)	(3.42)	(1.54)	(1.81)
MGH	2,982	3,247	3,505	3,778	4,044	4,213
	(8.87)	(8.87)	(7.94)	(7.79)	(7.04)	(4.18)
MZM	3,907	4,313	4,490	4,610	4,970	5,293
	(6.40)	(10.39)	(4.10)	(2.67)	(7.94)	(6.49)
NGN	712	982	1276	1,600	1,969	2,513
	(15.78)	(37.92)	(29.93)	(25.39)	(23.06)	(27.63)
SKM	294	306	322	333	341	351
	(4.60)	(4.06)	(5.53)	(3.08)	(2.39)	(2.92)
TRP	1,798	1,867	1,931	1,967	2,000	2,020
	(3.90)	(3.83)	(3.31)	(1.86)	(1.67)	(1.00)

Note: Figures in brackets are the percentage increase over the previous year figure.

[Source: Basic Statistics of NER 2006]

The high quality traditional handicrafts and handloom products enjoy a good market, both nationally and internationally. The whole of NER contributes 79.58 p.c. Nagaland positioned the first rank with highest production (in value) as 45.19 p.c. followed by Assam with 37.35 p.c. amongst the states of NER. While the number of units observed highest in Manipur followed by Tripura and the same is observed in case of number of Artisans. For providing employment opportunities in the rural areas and thereby strengthening the rural economy, Khadi and Village Industries play an important role.

Table 17.8 shows the trend of growth of Small Scale Industries (SSI) in the states of NER during the period 1997-98 to 2002-03. Over the period (1997-2003) highest percentage of growth rate occurred in the state of Nagaland (252.95 p.c.) followed by meghalaya (41.28 p.c.) and Mizoram (35.47 p.c.) while it is the lowest in both the states of Arunachal Pradesh and Manipur (12.25 p.c.).

Paper Industry

There are two mills in Assam, one at Cachar and the other at Nagaon which have been performing satisfactorily in spite of logistics problems. However, in keeping with the Centre's policy to help accelerate economic development of the North-Eastern States, Hindusthan Paper Corporation (HPC) has finalised an expansion programme for both the mills. The installed capacity of each mill would be raised by at least 25,000 tonnes each, entailing a total investment of around Rs 250 crore. Along with the expansion programme, efforts are being made to upgrade quality of all varieties of paper so that the company could get better prices in the competitive market. Though `cultural' varieties of paper constitute about 50 per cent of HPC's total annual production of about 2,00,000 tonnes of writing and printing paper, it has plans to add value to non-cultural varieties, thereby enabling it to earn more.

Table 17.9: Production, Export and Import of Tea in India

(in million kg).	2000	2001	2002	2003	2004
Production	846	854	826	857	830
Imports	14	17	22	7	25
Exports	207	183	201	173	190
Consumption	653	673	685	697	710

Source: Report of the Meeting of the Committee on Financial Sector Plan for NER, March 2006.

Tea Industry

The tea industry of NER is the world's largest tea growing

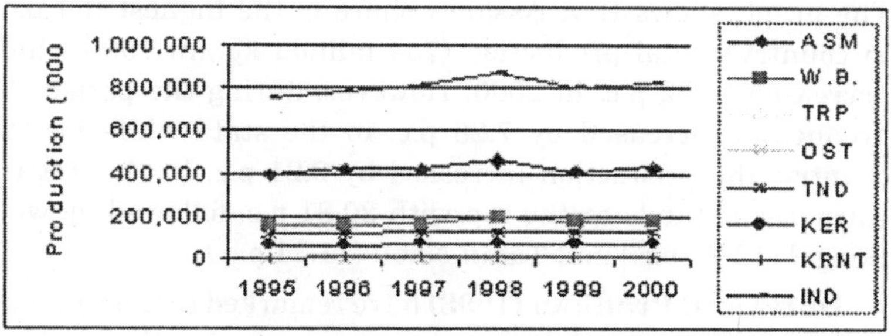

Figure 17-D: Annual State-Wise Tea Production

region having 16 p.c. shares, and is the largest producer and exporter of tea in India (share 55 p.c.). The production of tea in the state of Assam was of the tune of 438.9 thousand tones during the period 2002-03 which increased to 454.1 thousand tones in 2003-04 but decreased to 443.3 thousand tones in 2004-05. In case of tea production in Manipur, it has increased from 76000 kgs in 1998 to 97 thousand kgs in 1999 but it decreased slightly to 96 thousand kgs in 2000. However, Indian tea producers suffered the most in terms of drop in average tea auction price compared with other auction centres around the world between January to October 2002 (**Business Standard-Saturday, January 11, 2003**).

The **table 17.9** shows the picture of Tea industry in India (Annual export) during the 5-year period (2000-04). A cursory view of the table tells the fact that production of Tea has been decreased from 846 million kg to 830 million kg over the period under consideration as a result of which Export quantity has also been decreased over the period. Consumption is also being decreased by 8.73 p.c. Coming to NER, it is observed that the production decreased from 459.9 million kg to 440.3 million kg while area under cultivation increased by 1.09 p.c. (279350 hact. to 282403 hact.) over the period 2000-2002.

The **figure 17-D** shows the annual production of tea in Assam (ASM), Tripura(TRP), West Bengal (WB), other states of North India (OST), Tamil Nadu (TND), Karnataka (KRNT), Kerala (KER) and India (IND) during the period 1995-2000.

The graph shows that Assam's share is the highest (53 p.c.) in country's total production (754 million kg.).in 1995 which decreased to 52 p.c. in 2000. However, during the period the production increased by 7.28 p.c. in the state while for the country, the production increased by 9.21 p.c. In this regard Karnataka stands at the top with 20.81 p.c. followed by west Bengal (12.74 p.c.) and Tamil Nadu (11.34 p.c.).

Dutta and Pradhan (1998) have remarked that only small scale and cottage industries of Assam can solve the problem of unemployment. As Assam is agriculturally based society and the infrastructure for large industries are yet to emerge, agro-based and forest based small industries can upgrade the

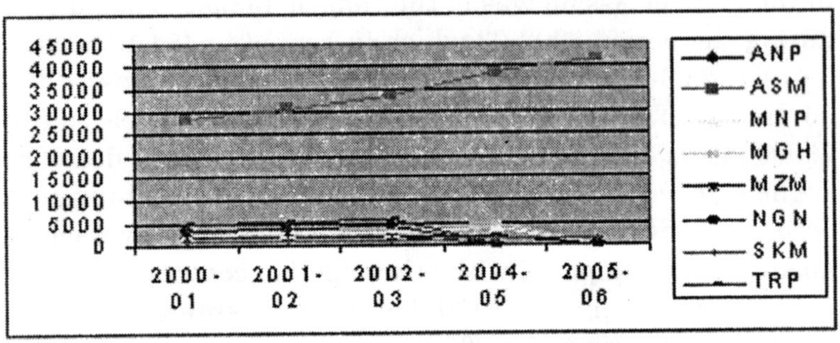

Figure 17-E: State-wise net state domestic product (at current prices)

industrial growth in the state because these are possible with minimum amount of capital.

Per Capita Net State domestic product, inequality in income (consumption) and poverty

The economy of NER is mainly depending on agriculture. The majority of population of region are getting their livelihood from the agriculture sector as they have accepted agriculture as their primary occupation. Thus, agriculture is playing an important role in the economy of NER. The pattern of agricultural growth has however remained uneven across regions and crops. The NER continues to be a net importer of food grains even for its own consumption. In spite of covering 7.7 p.c. of the country's total geographical area, NER produces only 1.5 p.c. of the country's total food grain production. Due to various socio economic structure of the population the consumption basket will differ. The existence of wide disparities in the level of living between regions and between classes of people is widely believed to be one of the important causes of social tension and unrest. In this context, per capita expenditure (PCE) data has been taken as proxy for income.

Per Capita Net State Domestic Product (PCNSDP) gives a rough idea about the economic condition of NER with respect to all — India level. **Fig 17-E** shows the pattern of State Domestic Product (SDP) in the states of NER. The pattern of agricultural growth has however remained uneven across regions and crops. The per capita income of Arunachal Pradesh, since 1996-97, has been lagging behind the national average. The per capita income of the State of Meghalaya has also constantly lagged behind the national average. Nearly 10 p.c. of the total geographical area of Meghalaya is under cultivation. The NSDP of Assam at current prices for the year 2000-01 was 28262 crore which increased to Rs.1783.78 crore in 2003-2004 as against Rs.16788.37 crore in 2002-2003 and Rs. 41842 crore in 2005-06. The NSDP registered a growth of 6.24 p.c. in 2003-2004 over 2002-2003 as against a growth of 3.81 p.c. witnessed in 2002-2003 over 2001-2002.

Inequality

As per World Bank report, 2008, maximum Gini - income inequality is observed in Nigeria (52.2) followed by Pakistan (39.8), Indonesia (39.6), India (36.5) and Bangladesh (33.5) among some selected countries in 1996 **(Table 17.10)**. However, other countries are not comparable as reference period are not same.

Coming to the urban sectors of NER, it is worthwhile to mention that the **percentage share of expenditure** according to poorest ten percent groups of consumers were found to be better in the state of Nagaland and worst in Assam while for the richest ten percent of the consumers, the share is relatively better in Assam among the states of NER. Thus it may be pointed out that the poorest section of the society in Assam has been badly affected. The results reveal that the extent of degree of inequality in the level of living in the states of NER is much more than what is taken to guide some of the decision making elements in connection with resource transfer from centre to these north eastern states particularly in Assam.

It may be pointed out that in the rural sector, the degree of inequality is found to be minimum in the state of Mizoram while maximum in Arunachal Pradesh among the states of NER. In most of the cases the level of inequalities is found to be less in NER in comparison to all-India level. It has been observed that there has been a declining tendency in the inter-regional disparities in the consumption level of the rural sectors while there is no such tendency in the urban sectors. It is interesting to note that so far the **poorest ten percent** of the rural population is concerned the shares of consumption are relatively better in Manipur and Mizoram than that of their counterpart in NER while for the **richest ten percent,** the shares of consumption are relatively better in Assam and Meghalaya **(Dutta, 2001).**

Forest

Forests play a crucial rule in maintaining the ecological balance on the earth. Forests are being cut ruthlessly to make towns, roads, dams, which are creating ecological imbalance. Apart from the atmospheric effects, the destruction of forests endangers the several species of plants and animals to their virtual extinction. The entire north-eastern hill region has a prestigious place in the world map of orchid flora. But the continuous exploitation of the orchid has resulted almost extinction of many of a valuable species causing a great concern of the region.

Table 17.11: India's global position on human and gender development

Country	HDI Rank		GDP Per Capita (PPP US$) minus HDI rank	GDI RANK		HDI rank minus GDI rank	Life expectancy at Birth (years)	Combined GER (Primary, Secondary & tertiary Education	Physician per one lakh people	Infants with low birth weight (in Per cent)
	2000	2005	2005	2000	2005	2005	2005	2005	2000-04	1998-2005
Norway	1	2	1	3	3	-1	79.8	99.2	313	5
Australia	5	3	13	1	2	1	80.9	113	247	7
Sri Lanka	89	99	7	70	89	-1	71.6	62.7	55	22
China	95	81	05	77	73	1	72.5	69.1	106	4
Indonesia	110	107	06	91	94	1	69.7	68.2	13	9
India	124	128	-11	105	113	0	63.7	63.8	60	30
Pakistan	138	136	-8	120	125	-7	64.6	40	74	19
Bangladesh	145	140	0	121	121	1	63.1	56	26	36
Nepal	142	142	08	119	128	-4	62.6	58.1	21	21
Mozambique	170	172	-16	144	150	2	42.8	52.9	3	15
Niger	172	174	-1	146	155	-1	55.8	22.7	2	13

Source: UNDP Human Development Reports 2002 and 2007.

Quality of life index

As per the UNDP's Global Human Development Report (HDR) 2007, in spite of the absolute value of the human development index (HDI) for India improving from 0.577 in 2000 to 0.611 in 2004 and further to 0.619 in 2005, the relative ranking of India has not changed much. India ranks at 128 among the countries with medium human development out of 177 countries of the world as against 126 in the previous year. In terms of Gender Development Index (GDI), India ranks 113 out of 157 countries ranked on the basis of their GDI value **(Table 17.11).** The other indicators related to Health and Education also indicate the same. The situation reinforces the need for greater focus on this area in our development planning. It is this concern that is reflected in the Eleventh Plan which seeks to reduce not only poverty but also the various kinds of disparities across regions and communities by ensuring better access to not only basic physical infrastructure but also health and education services to one and all.

The development of an area is best reflected in **the quality of life** of its people. **Quality of life** index may be comprised of Literacy Rate (LR), female literacy rate (FLR), sex ratio (SR), Child-women ratio (CWR), female work participation (FWP), Per capita expenditure (PCE), dependency ratio (OR), Per capita non-food expenditure (PCNFE), Percentage growth of population (PGR), infant mortality rate (IMR), mean age at marriage (MAM), per capita net domestic product (PCNDP) public health centre (PHC), etc.

Population dynamics and environment

Many analysts blame the environmental crisis on poverty-population growth linkages **(Bucs, 1992).** They maintain that explosive population growth is responsible for environmental degradation. A high growth of population puts a pressure on the availability of resources, which in turn affects the per capita availability of Gross State Domestic Product. As such poverty abetted by ever growing population is the worst pollutant

Table 17.12: Wealth inequality in selected countries

Country	Wealth Gini (2000)	Income Gini(2000)	Year
Argentina	74.0	50.1	2005
Australia	62.2	31.2	2003
Bangladesh	65.8	33.5	1996
Canada	66.3	31.5	2000
China	55.0	44.9	2003
France	73.0	27.8	2000
Germany	67.1	31.1	2004
India	66.9	36.5	1997
Indonesia	76.3	39.6	1996
Italy	60.9	33.3	2000
Japan	54.7	31.9	1998
Republic of Korea	57.9	37.2	1998
Mexico	74.8	49.9	2004
Nigeria	73.5	52.2	1996
Pakistan	69.7	39.8	1996
Spain	56.5	33.6	2000
Taiwan (China)	65.4	33.9	2003
Thailand	70.9	42.7	2001
United States	80.1	46.4	2004
Viet Nam	68.0	37.3	1998

Source: Davies et al., 2008; World Bank, 2008.

in developing world. Without denying the linkage between poverty- population and pollution, it is essential to point out that this formulation does not capture the entire complexity of the economy-ecology inter-connection.

Rao (1995) argued that the Indian State has followed largely a capitalist path of development, which is evident from the policy choices that have been taken in the sources of irrigation, energy and forestry. These policy decisions have contributed heavily to environmental contamination and are

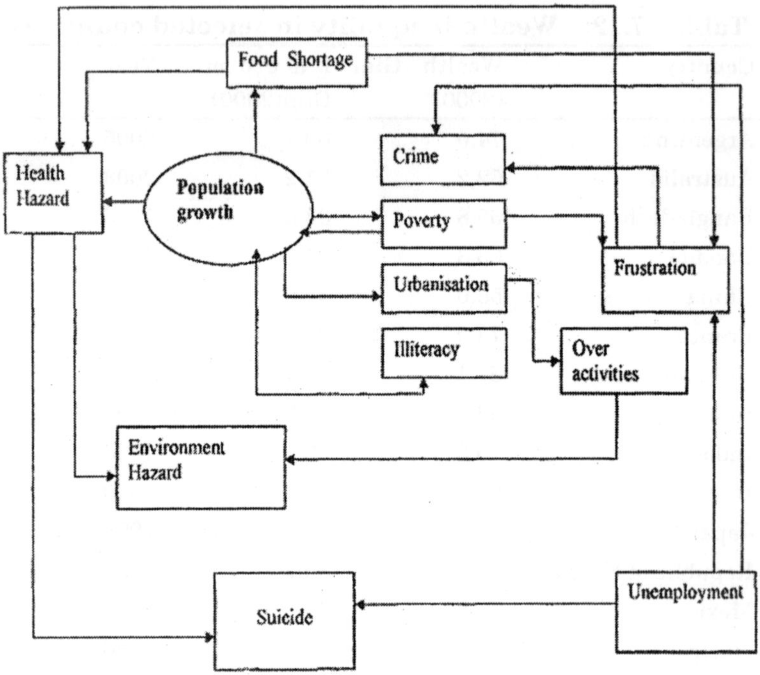

Figure 17.F: Impact of population growth.

clearly indicative of an uneven pattern of development.

Climate change will undermine international efforts to combat poverty. Political leaders around the world gathered to set targets for accelerated progress in human development. The Millennium Development Goals (MDGs) defined a new ambition for 2015. How the world deals with climate change today will have a direct bearing on the human development prospects of a large section of humanity. Failure will consign the poorest 40 percent of the world's population—some 2.6 billion people—to a future of diminished opportunity.

Population-poverty-environment relationship

It **17.F** reveals the complex relationships among population growth, poverty, health and environmental hazards.

Population explosion has led to food shortage, unemployment, health hazard as well as poverty which ultimately creates the environmental imbalance. The root cause of human health hazard is the improper disposal of sewage and wastes. However, poverty is an important factor for health hazard which results in the development of frustration which is the consequence of unemployment and food shortage. Now-a-days drug abuse is a burning problem in the north-eastern states of India which is the result of frustration. Environmental imbalance may also be resulted from urbanisation, food shortage and poverty. Urbanisation is affecting the present environmental scenario through the over-activities of the people. However, urban environment is not a natural environment but a man-made environment. Hence solution lies pertinent to human beings. It is necessary to recast the whole urbanization process and adopt the environment policy in such a way that urbanisation would urge to create environmental balance. Over population affects the nature of bio-sphere and creates ecological imbalance due to over activities of the people (occur by depleting the nature resources like forest land, agricultural land, water etc. and misusing the energy sources.). A major factor contributing to environmental degradation in most Indian cities and towns is the inadequate provision of safe drinking water and Sanitation. The consumption of fossil fuel is a source of greenhouse gases and the industrial production process is closely associated with environmental deterioration. Thus, the direct threats to human life style are the most obvious aspect of environmental degradation which is due to over population and modern industrialisation.

Conclusion and suggestion

Government, both at the centre and the state level has to pay sufficient consideration to the high variation in the magnitude of quality of life indicators across the states in North-East region while assigning priority for their developmental process. This is an inclination towards equity perspective for sustainable development that breaks the vicious circle of poverty.

It is evident that men do influence the uptake of contraception and as such educating men to appreciate the importance of family planning is likely to lead to increased use of contraception. (Letamo and Bainame,2000). Thus, IEC (Information, Education, Communication) component of family planning programmes needs to be strengthened in order to increase the use of contraceptives and there by to control the population growth.

A social dimension of the education, in higher education, is a pre-requisite to enhance the social cohesion and equity. An integrated approach should, therefore, be made for the societal transformation to ensure participation of various sectors such as education, agriculture, energy, healthcare, and information and biotechnology.

The government should give priority to set up various technical and professional institutions to enhance the capacity and improve the quality of education and training of the people of NER along with the projects for the development of transport and communication system for linking whole of NER with the main stream of the country.

One of the main challenges before India is to reduce the problem of unemployment and this would be by the end of 2020. Thus, creation of sufficient employment and skilled personnel should be the targets. Efforts should be made in providing sufficient and proper inputs and to utilize the available human resource to accelerate economic growth and overall development.

It is important to note that poverty is one of the serious problems in India. About 82 p.c. of the total poor lives in the countryside. As a consequence, little attention has been given on the urban poor since independence. The government must devise a system which ensures equal opportunities to the poor, irrespective of caste, with the rich in obtaining higher education and training or in getting a start in trade and industry or securing employment.

The government should develop an economic system that

addresses regional economic development which must be in tune with political, cultural and social life and strive to eliminate structural poverty as well as the culture of poverty that affects large segments of the population. It should be based on economic development on the principles of sustainable development with due emphasis on the efficient and sustainable use of natural resources.

Proper support should be extended to the agricultural sector and small to middle-scale industries to ensure their sustainability. The government has a role in setting standards in the use and management of natural resources and the environment.

One must agree with **Binayak Roy (2001)** that the women's movement despite of some successes is far from achieving many of its objectives, including equity and empowerment. In an uneven global political, economic and social environment there can not be one strategy for all countries as aspects of gender issues are complex and deep rooted in their social structures. A globalised economy requires states and government to follow internationally accepted governance principles which focuses on creation of a strong civil society. This includes international covenants and instruments covering both economic and non-economic issues and equality of sexes and privileges confirmed by the state **(World Bank 1994)**. Signatories to these instruments and covenants feel obliged to comply with them. Hence a new approach to be followed by the leaders of women's movement to set their agenda and women's issues can be sensitized in a non-threatening way by making coalition with men and removing the rural –urban disparity.

There is need of proper planning for the fullest utilization of all the available resources. Unfortunately, the planning and the scheme formulation is done on the dictates of the political players whose vertical interferences may not allow the projects to get the fruits from the projects.

It is most important to develop a balance economic system that is open and transparent and eliminates corruption, collusion and nepotism as well as the monopolistic systems which provide protection and privilege only to a small political and economic elite. To achieve sustainable development and a higher quality of life for all people, governments should reduce and eliminate unsustainable pattern of production and consumption and promote appropriate demographic policies. Hence, a mixed approach may be developed to tackle the situation by promoting quality of life through socially equitable, ecologically viable and economically efficient developmental process.

The nature has made the mothers as creator and the creatures should *try to nurse them otherwise the day will come when the whole creation will be destroyed.* Hence preservation and protection of environment will provide sustainable growth and development in the region. However, no endeavour in this respect will be successful unless and until the people of the region are well conscious and aware of it.

Note

* CIA Factbook: India. *CIA Factbook.* Central Intelligence Agency. Retrieved on 2007-03-10.

1. WCED (World Commission on Environment and Development). 1987, *Our common Future* (The Brundtland Commission Report), Oxford University Press. Oxford, U.K.
2. World Bank. 2000, Entering the 21st Century :World Development Report 1999/2000, Oxford University Press, New York:
3. Documents on The Global Science Panel on Population in Sustainable Development, population matters to development and Environment, pp.367-368, *Population and Development Review,* Vol. 28, Number 2, June 2002.
4. India, Planning Commission, *Third Five Year Plan,* 1961, pp.25, 72.
5. Source : Planning Commission, 10th Plan Outlay by Heads

of Development : Centre, States and Union Territories, 2002-07 and Annual Plans 2002-03 to 2006-07, website: http:/indabudget.nic.in

6. "The Benefits of Water" Cleveland Clinic. http://www.clevelandclinic.org/health/health- info/docs/2700/2731.asp?index=7250. Retrieved 2007-02-19.
7. Greenhalgh, Alison (March 2001). "Healthy living – Water "BBC Health http://www.bbc.co.uk/health/healthy_living/nutrition/drinks_water.shtml. Retrieved 2007-02-19.
8. U.S. Centers for Disease Control and Prevention. Atlanta, GA. "Safe Water System: A Low- Cost Technology for Safe Drinking Water." Fact Sheet, World Water Forum 4 Update. March 2006.
9. Maton, Anthea bj; Jean Hopkins, Charles William McLaughlin, Susan Johnson, Maryanna Quon Warner, David LaHart, Jill D. Wright (1993). *Human Biology and Health.* Englewood Cliffs, New Jersey, USA: Prentice Hall. ISBN 0-13-981176-1.

10 US daily reference intake values.

11. The Millennium Development Goals Report 2009. Referenced 2008-10-20.
12. United Nations Childrens Fund (UNICEF). New York, NY. "Safe Drinking Water" Excerpt from "Progress since the World Summit for Children : A Statistical Review" September 2001.
13. Research Debunks Health Value of Guzzling Water., Reuters, April 2008.

References

Ahluwalia, I.J (1984) : *"Industrial Growth and Stagnation: Infrastructure Constraints",* Paper presented at Institute of Economic Growth, Silver Jubilee Seminar, Delhi, May, 1984.

ADB (Asian Development Bank). 2001. *Asian environment outlook 2001.* Manila.

Buch, M. N. (1992). : "Population and Environment" in V. Gowrikar (ed.) Science and Development, Umesh Communication. Pune.

Brutan, H.J (1960) : *International Encyclopedia of Social Sciences,* Vol.-2, Macmillan.

Choudhury. H (1996): *"NFHS Findings on Nuptiality Pattern and Policy Implications for the States Meghalaya, Mizoram and Tripura based on National Family Health Survey (NFHS) Results"*- Paper presented in the Regional Seminar on Dissimination of Findings of NFHS Reports For The N.E. States, 27-29 Nov, Guwahati.

Deaton, A. (2001): *"Health, inequality, and economic development",* NBER Working Paper No. 8318.

Deaton, A. (2003.) : "Health, income, and inequality", in *NBER Reporter:* (Research Summaries), Spring.

Dutta P.C. (1996): *"Quality Variation of Some Food Items of Consumption in North Eastern Region (NER)",* Indian Journal of Regional Science, Vol. 28 (1).

Dutta P.C. (2002) : A Study on The Impacts Of Socio-Economic Development In North East India With Special Reference To The Problems Of Population Growth and urbanisation On Environment"- *UGC sponsored MRP(2000-2002), Report submitted on 1803.02.*

Dutta P.C. (2004) : *"21st Century Problems and Issues of Higher Education In North East India"* in Education in North East India-Experience & Challenge (ed.) Biloris Lynde and Utpal Kumar De, Concept Publishing Company, New Delhi

Dutta P.C. (2008): *"Some Aspects of Sustainable Socio-Economic Development in The North Eastern Region (NER) of India"* in Society, Culture and Development Essays in Honour of Dr. Basudeb Datta Ray (ed.) Ashok Kumar Ray and S.B. Chakrabarty, Concept Publishing Company New Delhi.

Dutta P.C. and B.C. Pradhan (1998): *"Problems of Community Integration In Small Towns of Barak Valley Districts of*

Assam-A Case Study of Lala Town", in Urban Development In North East India : Potentiality And Problems Ed. B. Dutta Roy, A. K. Neog & H.K. Mazhari, Reliance Publishing House, New Delhi.

Dutta P.C. and B.C. Pradhan (2007): *"Gender Issues and Development In North Eastern Region of India"* in Women Emancipation Focus North East India (ed.) Asok Kumar Ray and Basudeb Datta Ray, OM Publications, New Delhi.

Dutta P.C. and N. Roy, (2006).: *"Socio-Economic Development Of North East India With Special Reference To The Problems Of Urbanisation"* in Modern Trends of Research in Ecology and Environmental Science (ed.) B.K. Dutta and Abhik Gupta, Mittal Publications, New Delhi.

Letamo, G. and Bainame, K. (2000): "Reproductive Decision-making : Do men really matter?" A Paper presented at Fourth International Conference on Social Science in Health entitled Africa Health at Crossroads: Challenges for the next Millennium, organized by the Department of Demography and SOMANet and held at the University of Botswana, Gaborone, 7th-11th August.

Malhotra, N (1999): *"Human Development in India and Inter State Pattern"*, Indian Regional Science, 31(1), 31-45.

Patil S.Y. (1998): *"Environmental Impact on Urbanisation in India"* in Essays On Regional Science, Regional Development and Planning, Vol. II, RSAI, Calcutta-91.

Procharopouclus G (1994): *"Returns to Investment in Education; A Global Update"*, World Development, pp. 1325-43.

Rao, J. Mohan (1995): "Whither India's Environment", Economic and Political Weekly, XXX (13), pp. 677-686.

Roy. B. (2001): "Gender Issues, the Women's Movement and the Indian Ocean Rim Countries" *in Human Rersources and Gender Issues in Poverty Eradication (eds)*

Rabin Ghose, Rony Gabby, Abu Siddique, Atlantic Publishers and Distributors.

United Nations.(2001a.): *State of the environment in Asia and the Pacific:2000.* New York: United Nations Economic and Social Commission for Asia and the Pacific and Asian Development Bank.

United Nations .(2001b) : World urbanization prospects: The 1999 revision. New York: Population Division, Department of Economic and Social Affairs.

Visaria L (1985): *"Infant Mortality in India : Level, Trends and Determinants"*, Economic and Political Weekly, (10th, 17th and 24th August).

Data Sources

1. Basics Statistic of North Eastern Region, NEC, (1982 & 2002).
2. NEDFi Databank Quarterly Journal, January 2004
3. Statistical Abstract, 2005 & 2006.

SECTION-IV
ENVIRONMENTAL DEGRATION

18

Biodiversity: A Threat Perception to Sustainable

Introduction

In a world plagued by the proliferation of weapons of mass destruction, menace of global terrorism, global warming and climate change, owing to environmental destruction and ecological imbalances, global epidemics like HIV/AIDS, and growing incidence of poverty related death as fallout of liberalization, privatization, and globalization (LPG), Gandhi as well as his philosophy appears relevant for ever. Nature had evolved a wonderful pattern in forest environment. Forest is not merely a collection of trees, herbs and shrubs, but it is a complicated structure which is the result of combined influence of climate, soil, biotic interference, topography and time. The components of the natural resources exist in a delicate balance in the ecosystem. A slight change in any of the factors may alter and damage the structure of the ecosystem permanently.

When the whole world is crying for the mercy to get rid of current state of environmental degradation in the form of depletion of ozone layer, global warming and climate change, Gandhiji's very notion of development appears as a savior to the world community. Sustainability is the core to his developmental process which appears to be a best viable alternative model of development in the recent years. Long before the "World Commission on Environment and Development", coined and defined the concept sustainable development, Gandhi talked about the philosophy of the concept but in a different term. Today from United Nations to Government of India, everybody is talking about a form of development which will balance the fulfillment of human needs with the protection of the natural environment so that these needs can be met not only in the present, but in the indefinite future. Now the concept of sustainable development becomes indispensable to the development of the human civilization because of the limited nature of the world's resources. Knowing this inherent limitation of mother earth Gandhi warned the human society not to exploit beyond of its capacity to withstand the exploitation of natural resources for our development. Rather Gandhi advocated for the "optimal utilization" of our natural resources. For him using anything extra is a stealing. Depicting this Gandhian thought very brilliantly Satish Kumar in his article "*Five Elemaents of Ecology*' writes "the crisis of environment comes out of a utilitarian, materialistic, non-sacred, non-spiritual world-view - the Earth is there for us to use, for our comfort, for our convenience." As a consequence we have taken from nature without knowing its limits. When we have a sense of reverence, we shall take from nature only what meets our vital needs. And when we take something, we thank, we show gratitude like we take milk from the mother's breast; the mother is very happy to give her milk in the same way as the Earth is happy to give its fruits as long as we take only what we need. When the baby is full, he or she stops sucking and does not go on sucking. Well, unfortunately we humans go on sucking the Earth.

The environment assumed a central role in India, to a large extent, as a result of the first major international conference on the environment, namely, the United Nations Conference on the Human Environment (UNCHE) held in Stockholm in 1972. In preparation for this meeting, each member country was asked to prepare a report on the state of the environment. India set up a committee on the human environment under the chairmanship of Pitambar Pant, a Planning Commission member. The outcome was three reports, one on the state of the environment, one on the problems of human settlement and one on the possible strategies to manage resources. Environmental goals were subsequently incorporated in the Fifth Five-Year Plan onwards. Legislations such as Wildlife Protection Act, 1972 and the Water (Prevention and Control of Pollution) Act, 1974 were passed soon after as well (Menon, 2006).

What is Biodiversity

Nature has varied forms of creation (plants and vegetation, fauna, insects, birds and microorganism etc.) if all these survive, living would be smooth for all the species on the earth. Thus biodiversity would mean that there is need for diverse biological varieties to co-exist without the threat of extinction. Thus, biodiversity would simply mean "varieties of species right to existence" it also would mean that no one has the right to threaten a species right to existence. Man being the homosapien should restrain from actions that would erode species but do everything to protect them from extinction. This will not only protect the environment but also enable smooth human survival as well. Thus all species are equally important for the sustenance for all human and sub-human species. Hence, there is an urgent need to strengthen the food chain of all living creatures with sustainable and judicious use. Thus, the mantra of the century should naturally be "protect species from perish". This would call for truly holistic concerns. In the nature's scheme of things, all species play complementary and supplementary role for the survival of all living entities. One life supports the other, which is an unalterable law of nature, thus all species have dual role; (a) every species depends on other species and (b) every species adds to the food basket of other species as well. In this sense, all species on this planet could be deduced as food basket. Planet earth is unique in many ways, which is the only one shelter of innumerable species to coexist, though at the same time, each of them is feeding or nourishing one another. Without these diverse varieties putting up together, a few sacrificing in favour of several others, living would have come to a naught. It is for man's smooth existence that he should strive for the maintenance for bio-diversity order. The unlimited greed of man is threatening the healthy and diverse biological order that needs immediate correction. He is exploiting both biological and other precious natural resource beyond the replacement levels, besides polluting them badly thereby posing greater danger to the future generation's smooth survival. In an effort to save erosion of natural resources, several threatened regions are declared as bio-diversity hotspots' which includes the Western Ghats and the Eastern Himalayan that are treasure houses for several flora and fauna. It is time to make man realise the negative impact of nature on 'bio-diversity' and make him act as a 'trustee' or 'conservator' of nature in true sense. Otherwise, a day may not be far off when our future generation would be compelled to face several risks including shortage of food and other requirements. The time is most appropriate to realise importance for biodiversity conservation for the good of all species. It also calls for a well planned strategy to adequately compensate people involved in bio-diversity conservation by foregoing benefits of opportunity costs accruing from commercial crops or exploitation of natural resources.

Forest is the most important resource in Arunachal Pradesh. This can also be called 'primary source' in the words of Norman Myers, the famous ecologist. This resource is the mother of unique culture and traditions of local tribes and is also at the root of abundance of water, biodiversity and soil formation. Forestry is a multi-faceted business and the Department of Environment and Forest is committed to managing forestry resources in a balanced way so that a full range of benefits (economic, social and environmental) are delivered not only today but for generations to come.

Environment conservation and sustainable development are closely interlinked such that one cannot be achieved at the expense of the other. The preservation of natural resources is one of the important components of environmental conservation in the hilly areas. Forests are the most important natural resources in the hilly state and they play an important role in the economic life of the indigenous people in the state. At the same time forest represent a complex economic resource. In addition to their timber value, they are a valuable source of biodiversity, as a carbon store and in reducing the severity of floods.

The broad aim of this paper is to analyze and discuss the factors and issues that are associated with effective operations in degradation of forest and searching the ways for its conservation with the changes of traditional institutions and customary laws that may exist in managing natural resources in a self governed tribal society of Arunachal Pradesh. However, the specific objectives are:

- To examine the real causes of deforestation and its impact in the State including institutional failures.
- To search the possible ways to conserve the forest in the State for sustainable development.

Therefore, this paper is divided into two sections. The first section seeks to an in-depth study to identify the causes of degradation of biodiversity while the second tries to find out the possible ways to conserve the biodiversity under sustainable development and conclusion flows.

Section-I

Causes of Deforestation and its Impact

In Arunachal Pradesh we are destroying a good percentage of forest area every year. Now the question arises what factors are responsible for deforestation. Among the factors we may mention is poverty, inequality in the distribution of land, low agricultural productivity, lack of infrastructural facilities, low level of economic development, industrialization, urbanization and rapid growth of population. Major causes of forest degradation are legal and illegal land-use changes; use pressure from villages inside and outside the reserve in the form of fuel wood collection and grazing of livestock; and institutions that fail to manage the forests. The grabbing of common land by the individual has been observed to a significant extent. In consequence, average distance to be covered by a household to collect CPR products has increased significantly. The size of human and livestock population, scarcity of resources (emergence of new-rich class with commercial interests), distance of the reserve area from the residential area and the quality of the management etc. are some of the important factors that determine the extent of degradation. Market close to the villages cause more severe degradation of forest resources i.e. market plays the promotional role of forest degradation. Scarcity of commons in relation to population leads to its degradation. Though the imposition of a ban on the extraction of forest and forest products by the Supreme Court in 1996 has formally checked the illegal felling of trees, the emerging neo-merchant class are taking the advantages of local power to exploit the forest resources, and in consequence, the state ownership and management have failed to prevent the conservation and degradation of many forests.

A brief analysis of the causes of natural resource degradation and depletion in the region shows that various factors, from a long time, have resulted to the worsening of the situation causing various socio-economic hazards. By this we mean the distribution of total land area among different uses. The pattern of land use, which is a complex phenomenon, in general is the result of the action and interaction of factors like physical characteristics of land, supply of resources like labour and capital, the framework of socio-economic institutions etc. There is virtually no planning in the field of land utilization. The existing pattern of land utilization has evolved over the past few centuries under the pressure of increasing population. So far land use is concerned the North-Eastern Region, like other parts of the country, seems to have no planning virtually in this field and a good portion of land is lying as cultivable waste. In the North-East India even though agriculture is the only source of livelihood to the majority of people, the rational land utilization was not possible because of difficult terrain. Being agricultural backward economy, the productive forces have been arrested by retrogressive agrarian land relations. As a result, more and more area has been brought under cultivation by clearing forests, which meant damage to the ecological balance. In the first place, those who caused this damage were not aware of the repercussions of their actions. There are some major factors which are responsible for destruction of forest and thereby flora and fauna in the state discussed below.

Presently some of the major issues facing the resource managers, researchers, policy makers, international institutions, and some NGOs are: (i) loss of bio-diversity with its yet unknown potential consequences, (ii) increased rate of deforestation and fragmentation, (iii) inadequate knowledge of ecological functioning and complex relationships between and within biotic and abiotic components of the forest biome, (iv) adverse impact on indigenous communities and forest dwellers, (v) inadequate public awareness and lack of transparency (i) resources exploitation. (vi) adverse changes in soil, water and climate due to deforestation.

Shifting Cultivation

However, the problem of natural resources degradation particularly forests in Northeast India appeared to be very serious even during the regime of New Forest Policy explained which envisages that this strategy might have not been implemented with its true spirit. One of the assumptions of the new forest policy was that the forest dependent poor tribal communities are responsible for depletion of these resources as they not only overexploit but also practice shifting cultivation which needs clearing of forests and hence leads to deforestation. Shifting cultivation directly reduces available forest resources and indirectly enhances soil erosion, increases silting of rivers, streams and dams, and causes an imbalance in environmental factors. More specifically, it is argued that the practice of jhum cultivation is the principal factor of deforestation/degradation although a generalized caused and effect relationship between loss of forest and shifting cultivation is misleading because deforestation is a complex socio-economic, cultural and political phenomenon. Moreover, the degradation caused to forests as a result of shifting cultivation depends on the habits and beliefs of the people, the area available, development index, land-man ratio, the population density and the proximity to the market. The forest resources of a specified area may be degraded due to a variety of reasons including government policy of issuing timber permits, market penetration, economic development, and practice of subsistence agriculture and so on. So far management of natural assets is concerned; the question of property rights plays an important role. Most of these resources are treated as open access due to absence or undefined property rights. But unlike other tribal regions, in Northeast India communities and private individuals in most cases enjoy the rights of ownership of forest lands. As a result it seems that the new Bill on forest rights will have little impact on forest condition. Hence the real problem with respect to the management has to be analyzed in the context of socio-economic, cultural, and political set up of the tribal communities in this remote and isolated part of the country. It is argued that the traditional institutional arrangements of tribal communities were effective in sustainable management of local resources for a long time and most likely their breakdown in recent times with the introduction of market economy and development has been behind the present situation of rapid degradation of forest and other natural resources.

The practice of shifting cultivation, cropping of forest areas for a year or two, then clearing another area leaving the first one fallow to revert to scrub forests is widely practiced by tribal communities in the hilly mountainous forest regions. The fallow periods have been gradually shortened with increase in population. If the pressure on land increases, the soil has no chance to regenerate and wider and wider tracts of otherwise productive forests get destroyed. It is noticed that the land under shifting cultivation is still increasing in the north eastern region causing several imbalances in the ecology of the region.

Agriculture occupies an important a major occupation of the people of the state. According to 2001 census, about 79.66% of the state's population is living in rural areas and 58.44% of the total workers are cultivators. Due to scarcity of plain land in the State, the rural people have to practice shifting cultivation, i.e., Jhum cultivation in order to fulfill their minimum requirement for food. The shifting cultivation is called slush and burn method of cultivation. It is labour-intensive process of farming with extensive use of land. The technology being primitive, the level of production and income is very low. It occupies a distinct place in the socio-economic fabric of tribal economy of this state. The man who practices jhum cultivation i.e., shifting cultivation is called jhumia. The jhumia selects the field on the slope of the hill on rotation basis. Due to deterioration in fertility of soil the jhumia is compelled to shift his cultivation on another plot. He keeps the land fallow for a number of years for regeneration of forests. Again he uses the same land after a number of years. That is why, this process is also called shifting cultivation. This practice is not only done in Arunachal Pradesh but also in all north-eastern states due to lack of sufficient plain land. The area under shifting cultivation and number of families are engaged are shown in Table –18.1 in context of North-East States.

Not also are the jhummias facing serious economic problem because the forests in their traditional economic role are unable to sustain them, but society as a whole also has to pay a price for the extensive deforestation in the state in the form of soil erosion, floods and droughts. Therefore, any well-designed forest policy will have to divert the jhumias from jhuming by providing them with alternative occupations in the long run while in the short run, it will have to ensure that the jhumias can derive a higher income from their forest based occupations. Both the long and the short-term measures have two-fold aim to protect the forests and to improve the economic condition of the jhumias. The two aims are complementary because forests cannot be saved without improving the standard of living of

Table 18.1: Shifting cultivation in the North-East Region

State	Annual Area under Shifting cultivation (sq.kms)	Fallow Period (in years)	Minimum Area under Shifting cultivation one time or other (sq. kms)	No. of families practicing shifting cultivation
Arunachal Pradesh	700	3 – 10	2,100	54,000
Assam	696	2 – 10	1,392	58,000
Manipur	900	4 – 7	3,600	70,000
Meghalaya	530	5 – 7	2,650	52,290
Mizoram	630	3 – 4	1,890	50,000
Nagaland	190	5 – 8	1,913	1,16,046
Tripura	223	5 – 9	1,115	43,000
Total	3869		14,660	4,43,336

Sources: The Task Force Report on Shifting Cultivation, Ministry of Agriculture, 1983.

the forest-dwellers and vice-versa. Any policy to be successfully implemented has to be acceptable to the people for whom it is designed. So an exercise is to be carried out in the course of the study on shifting cultivation in Arunachal Pradesh to find out the opinion of the jhumias themselves regarding their preferred occupation. It is found that although the jhumias are aware of the problems of jhum cultivation and the low economic returns derived from this occupation, the majority of them are not willing to give it up at least in the short run. The other forest-based occupations like plantations of coffee and rubber can prove to be very attractive as a source of earning a living for the jhumias. Social forestry and other reforestation schemes will reduce the dependence of the jhumias on the traditional use of forest. These measures, if successfully carried out, will regenerate the economic life of the jhumias as well as the forests of the state.

Deforestation, due to practice of shifting cultivation, is considered world's most pressing land use problem. The effects of deforestation on ecology are too well known. The role of forest in maintaining ground water level, preventing soil erosion and land slide, controlling flood in plains, reducing air pollution have been discussed at length in several publications. The extent of deforestation of tropical forest has caused world wide alarm as tropical forests provide more than 50% of modern medicine. Tropical forests are living museums and laboratories that have yielded only a tiny fraction of their treasures to scientific study. In course of shifting cultivation remarkable varieties of flora and fauna are disappearing, which need immediate attention for extensive and intensive studies.

The type of vegetations destroyed depends upon the length of jhum cycle. A dense forest of long cycle has more tree species than grasses, whereas a forest of short cycle has more number of grasses. All the forest resources are disappearing and become rare due to deforestation and illegal felling of trees. The ecological balance favouring the complete hydrological cycle has been seriously upset over vast areas due to ignorance or lack of appreciation of methods of conserving and managing natural vegetation (whether a forest, grass land or mixed type) and of clearing the vegetation for cultivation. This misuse and destruction of plants cover combined with great increase in human and livestock population has created intense competition for natural resources. In the continued absence of conservation and correctly integrated land use system, overall habitat deterioration has become very widespread.

Forest Grazing

The practice of indiscriminate livestock grazing leads to forest degradation. The excessive and uncontrolled grazing brings about a physical damage to the vegetation and cause erosion of soil, spread of disease, pests and weeds. The unlimited and continuous grazing in the forest interferes with the productive and protective functions of the forest.

Forest Fires for Shifting Cultivation

Forest fires bring widespread damage to the productive capacity and the protective value of forest, destroy wildlife and damage the recreational and the scenic value. The causes may be natural, accidental or intentional etc. The preservation of forest ecosystem demands the elimination of the frequency and severity of the fires. In the months of March and April, the jhumia generally uses fires the forest for jhum cultivation. It is generally seen everywhere in the State even in the surrounding areas of capital city, Itanagar. The Government machinery becomes fails to stop it. After much hullabaloo over the burning of forest in the Capital Complex that led to the formation of an action plan and appeals from Governor Gen. (Retd.) J.J. Singh and Chief Minister Dorjee Khandu, forest burning continues, mocking at the 'action plan' (Arunachal Front, March 21, 2009).

Impact of current development on forest

Urbanization

The North-Eastern States in general and Arunachal Pradesh in particular are proceeding towards the path of development though the progress is slow and uneven. Because of rapidly growing job facilities, business activities, there is a change of interest from agricultural activities to modern enterprises, government jobs, etc. which leads to the speeding up of cities and towns. Those who migrate to cities or towns are in reality pushed out of villages due to economic and social pressures. Generally the immediate outcome of urbanization is that the urban areas become over crowded which leads to congestion. For dwelling of large number of people, for opening and widening of business establishment, forests are destroyed / cleared. Finally, overall pollution (air, water, soil, noise) takes place, which are not only responsible for degradation of natural resources but also of environment. Till 1961 census the State of Arunachal Pradesh was entirely rural. There was no urban centre in the State. Census wise trend in urbanization is shown in the following Table-18.2.

Table 18.2: Censuswise urban centres

Census	No. of census Towns	Name of the census Towns
1961	NIL	–
1971	4	Bomdila, Along, Pasighat and Tezu
1981	6	Bomdila, Along, Pasighat and Tezu, Nharlagun and Itanagar.
1991	10	Bomdila, Along, Pasighat and Tezu, Nharlagun and Itanagar, Ziro, Roing, Namsai and Khonsa.
2001	17	Bomdila, Along, Pasighat and Tezu, Narlagun and Itanagar, Ziro, Roing, Namsai and Khonsa, Tawang, Seppa, Daporijo, Basar, Changlang, Jairampur and Deomali.

Source: Various census Report.

All these towns are administrative centres in most cases. Before the establishment of administrative centres, **these places were full of forest.** According to 1991 census 12.80% people live in ten urban areas while as per 2001 census 20.41 people live in seventeen urban areas. The decennial urban growth rate in the state has been recorded as 139.63 in 1971-81, 167.04 in 1981-91 and 101.24 in 1991-2001.

Rapid Population Growth

Rapidly increasing population in Arunachal Pradesh caused not only by large scale influx of people from Bangladesh and Nepal, but also by natural growth has put immense pressure on the supply of land for various purposes like housing, industrial and other development projects and also for agricultural production and grazing of animals etc. As the available land in the state is insufficient for these myriad purpose, additional land had to be procured by illegal encroachment upon the forest lands, first in the unclassified forest, then in the reserved forest also.

Rapid population growth is one of the major factors of the depletion of natural resources in north-east states in general and in Arunachal Pradesh in particular. Though it is true that population growth is welcome as it initiates and helps in the growth process of any region or country, but it is up to a certain limit beyond which it works adversely. The north-east region is witnessing excessive pressure of population, which acts as one of the causes of natural degradation. Growing population creates extra demand in terms of basic physical requirement of shelter, fuel wood, food; etc. that makes it necessary to exploit forest and other resources directly accelerating the deforestation. The direct impact of the increasing pressure of population has been in terms of absolute decline in the area under forest as forest land that has been converted to agricultural land to meet the growing demand of growing population.

Increasing population coupled with widespread poverty has generated pressure on our natural resources and led to a degradation of agricultural land and forest. The forest resources are threatened due to overgrazing, commercial household needs, encroachment, unsustainable practices like unscientific cultivation (shifting cultivation, burn cultivation etc.) and development activities. Excessive fuel wood removal, indiscriminate felling of trees for timber needs, inadequate natural regeneration have also threatened to the rich biological diversity of 1, 67,486 sq.km. forest cover of North-East India with widest variety of biomass.

The human population census was conducted for the first time in Arunachal Pradesh in 1961. Population increases in 2001 by 326.23 per cent in comparison to the population of 1961. The growth of population and density of population census wise are shown below in Table-18.3.

Table 18.3: Population growth and population density SINCE 1961

Census	Persons	Population Density
1961	336558	4
1971	467511	6 (5.58)
1981	628050	8 (7.50)
1991	864558	10 (10.32)
2001	1097968	13 (13.03)

Source: Census Report, Arunachal Pradesh, 1971, 1981, 1991 and 2001.

Note: (i) Figures in the parentheses show actual values.

(ii)Population Density = Total Population ÷ Area in sq. km.

The decennial population growth rate since 1961 in the State has been recorded as 38.91% in 1961-71, 35.15% in 1971-81, 36.83% in 1981-91 and 26.21% in 1991-2001. It is more than all India average.

We have observed a high trend of growth of population in Arunachal Pradesh. To see the trend of population in the state in future, we can fit a mathematical equation by the method of least square. Let us now construct the necessary table and make necessary computation where we take Y as population and X as year. We take 1981 census year as origin shown in Table-18.4

We put the values in equation (1), we have $Y = 678929 + 191986.7\,X$

After getting this equation, we can find the population strength of any census year.

Suppose for census year 2011, the population, $Y = 678929 + 191986.7 \times 3 = 1254889.1$

For census year 2021, the population, $Y = 678929 + 191986.7 \times 4 = 1446875.8$

And for census year 2051, the population, $Y = 678929 + 191986.7 \times 7 = 2022835.9$

Table 18.4: Calculations for population projection through least square method

Census Year	Y (Population)	X (Year)	X^2	XY
1961	336558	-2	4	– 673116
1971	467511	-1	1	– 467511
1981	628050	0	0	0
1991	864558	+1	1	+ 864558
2001	1097968	+2	4	+ 2195936
Total	∑Y=3394645	∑X=0	∑ X^2 =10	∑XY=1919867

Now, Y= a + bX—— (1) or,

∑Y= na + b∑X —— (2) and

∑XY= a∑X + b∑ X2 —— (3)

We substitute the values shown above in the equations (2) and (3), solving them, we get a = 678929 and b =191986.7

If we compare the population of 1961, the population of 2051 will be six times more. All people especially the rural people have to response to the family programme for their own benefit in particular and for the state in general.

Again with the same procedure we can calculate to see the population density. The population density in 2011, 2021 and 2051 will be 14.80, 17.00 and 23.60.

Growth of Non-tribal Population

The tribal communities in North-east India who constitute a very high percentage of the total population being economically week and socially backward are usually dependent on natural resources for their existence. This is so because the tribal people are basically forest dwellers and from pre-historic age, they have been found to live as a close component of natural resources particularly to forest ecosystem. Forest and tribal people have a symbiotic relationship and the existence of both is mutually beneficial. The life of these primitive people is woven around forest ecology and forest resources. Forest satisfy a great range of human needs which vary from tangible raw materials (economic goods) like fuel and fodder, food and shelter, to intangible environmental benefits. The intangible vary from aesthetic enjoyment to protection against soil erosion and regulation of water supply. The primitive tribal communities collect their livelihood needs through hunting, gathering, and fishing, food production mostly at subsistence level. The forests not only provide them food, material to build house, fuel wood, fodder for the cattle, but also satisfy the deep rooted tribal sentiments. It is also necessary to note that woman and children of these communities are found to be engaged in most of the subsistence activities within the forests. Hence, the management of the forests must be for the satisfaction of the day-to-day needs of the tribals and the forest dwellers in respect of firewood, leaf fodder, small timber, edible fruit, leaves, gums, medicinal plants, resins, etc.

The indigenous people have a unique understanding of tropical forest ecology and resources because their culture has been evolved with the forests. They have learned over the centuries how to utilize the bio-resources in sustainable manner. No other person understands and loves forests as the tribal. Their lifestyle totally depends upon the forests. They are integral part of the forest ecosystem. Their biodiversity management and conservation system has proved to be an ideal system. If we see the census data since 1961, we get the following percentage of tribal people in the state shown in Table-18.5. If the trend keeps its same motion, we can calculate the future trend with the help of Least Square Method taking 1981 as origin shown in Table-18.5.

Table18.5: Tribal population (in %)

Census Year	% of Tribal People
1961	88.76
1971	79.02
1981	69.82
1991	63.65

Source: Different Census Issues.

Transportation

Till 1947, there were only three jeepable roads between Pasighat and Kobo by 35 Kilometers, Sadiya-Tezu-Denzing by 77 Kilometres and still well road 56 kilometers (Source: N.C.A.E.R – Techno-Economic Survey of NEFA, 1967, P.91). So, the total length of roads was only 168 km, till 1947. Before independence the colonial government did not take any effort to initiate the development process and the British indifference towards the area was mainly due to the fact that the area did not possess any readily exploitable resources. After the independence of the country, the Government of India undertook the development of transport and communication with a view to open up this remote state of India and therefore to facilitate the rapid development of the state. In the development plans, the government has been attaching high priority to the construction of roads and as a result the total length of roads constructed in the state stood at about 15021.80 kms. including 399.80 Kms. under National Highway giving the road density of 17.9 kms. per 100 sq.kms. of area at the end of March, 2004. The development of roads and its density (Road length per 100 sq. kms.) are shown in Table-18.6.

Table 18.6: Category-wise length of roads and its density during 9th & 10th plan

Year	Total length of roads	Density of roads (In. Km)
1	5	6
31.03.2000	13982.20	16.70
31.03.2001	13982.20	16.70
31.03.2002	13982.20	16.70
31.03.2003	14450.47	17.26
31.03.2004	15021.791	17.94

Source: Directorate of Economics and Statistics, Govt. of Arunachal Pradesh, Itanagar

Note: Density of Road = Total length of roads ÷ total area.

The impact of road transport is wide ranging which includes agriculture, industry, trade and commerce which cumulatively affect overall development of a region. But at the same time the State has to face deforestation and thereby to destroy the herbs.

Industrialization

At present there are 14 district industries centres in the State. Three DICs provide all possible help and guidance to the prospective entrepreneurs for taking up industrial ventures and provide services for identification of suitable schemes, preparation of project reports, supply and management of raw materials and marketing of finished product, etc. The DICs also organizes trainings at district level to create awareness amongst the entrepreneurs. They also assist entrepreneurs to avail incentive packages and facilities given by both Central and State government. In Arunachal Pradesh at the time of independence, there was almost absence of industry excepting cottage industries in the village. But at present there are 15 medium scale industries which are mostly saw mill, plywood and 11 veneer mills functioning in the State. In spite of many obstacles in the way of development of large and medium scale industries, significant numbers of small-scale industrial units have come up in the State over the year due to active support and positive policy of the government. There were 471 registered small scale industrial units functioning at the end of March 2003 mostly engaged in activities like black smithy, tin smithy, carpet making, carpentry, wool knitting handloom and weaving, cane and bamboo works, printing press, etc.

Mining and querying activities

In North-East Region the unsystematic extraction of minerals is creating environmental problems thereby ruining the region's land, water, forests and air. Mining practices in large scale has made agricultural and forest land into stockyards, townships, roads etc. and also removed vegetation and topsoil. Further, constant air pollution occurs due to disposal of mining waste and mineral dust from mines and also reduces agricultural productivity. Moreover, water resources get polluted, as rain water that passes through mineral wastes, are flowing into rivers and streams. Furthermore, large-scale deforestation, soil erosion result due to mining operation, which is again responsible for various health hazards to the people.

Impact of Deforestation

Environmental Problems

Deforestation and burning of fossil fuels contribute to global warning, which has now become a local issue for every citizen for action. Therefore, restrictive exploitation of forests now in Arunachal Pradesh leads to reduction in Green House Gas emissions which are the main causes of global warming. Reduction in Greenhouse Gas emissions in Arunachal Pradesh will benefit all mankind on planet earth. This State is, therefore, now contributing its bit in fighting global warming.

Deforestation does not take long, while a forest takes a very long time to develop, often hundreds of years, through a series of successive species, before it becomes a self-contained, viable eco-system. The strength of a forest system lies in its variety and the inter-dependence of its various elements. A forest maintains the humidity of the soil, its dry leaves, bird droppings and the remaining of the living organisms to add to its fertility, and the various species to support one another. The animals and insects living in the forest maintain a food chain and a balance in the production of the various species. Without forests, agriculture would die. Forest acts as a pumping station as reservoir, hoards an enormous amount of water in the leaves, stems, and roots of trees during the rainy season, and releases it slowly over the year. Without forests, the agriculture would be without water for most of the year, and there would be nothing to resist soil erosion during the months of heavy rains. Forests are necessary for maintaining the balance in the agriculture system. No less important is the need for a sound statistical base on forests, so that the policy makers are aware of what is going on, and are able to implement a system of forest management which augment the total 'stock' of forests while at the same time producing enough of the annual 'flow' to take care of the needs of the country's economy for forest products. Selection of trees is an equally important matter, and again their impact on other species, animal husbandry, and agriculture would have to be examined, in addition to the revenue generating capacity of those trees. While a commercial approach cannot be avoided, this alone should not be the criterion, regardless of its impact on both the physical and the social environment.

The rich and varied altitudinal and climatic conditions in the territory have given rises to a wide spectrum of vegetation in which several of the important forests occur. These are tropical rain forests, the sub-tropical forests, the temperate forests, the sub-alpine forests. The tribal people depend mainly on forests for their survival, livelihood, occupation and employment. The way they exploit forests has pervasive effect on all other aspects of culture, and the socio-culture milieu emerges as an interlocking system in which case and effect are intertwined in a manner that when one element is significantly altered, it has direct and indirect repercussions on the other parts of the system. The tribal people living near the forest areas depend solely on forests and its produce. A house in a tribal village is almost made of forest produce- the roofing leaves, the posts and the walls made of bamboo and small timber, the tying canes etc. Strips of canes are used as fasteners for the rafters while building houses. The household utensils, the bamboo plates, pipes for carrying water, spoons and ladles, and the drinking cups are all shaped out of the forest produce. The people of the interior areas use beaten barks of forests trees as clothing material for specific uses. They collect many types of tuber, fruits and seeds which help these people to survive during the period of food deficit. The berries, nuts, honey, fruits and roots of all kinds abound and in the process of socializations, the tribal learns to grow which roots, berries and fruits are edible, where these are available, when and for how long etc.

Hundreds of such edible items and the time of their availability are commonly known. He learns how to distinguish between poisonous and non-poisonous edible mushrooms which grow abundantly in the rainy season. Certain organic substances, leaves, flowers, roots are known to have intoxication, catalytic and decomposition and medicinal properties. Some of these are used for intoxicating fish while doing river fishing, for fermenting rice and millet beer called Apung, for making dyes and extracting vegetable fiber. For medicines, the tribal discerningly distinguish between various kinds of plants, weeds and herbs which have therapeutic value both curative and preventive. Some of the folk medicines of the main tribes of Arunachal Pradesh namely Nyishi and the Apa Tanis are very important. Various types of timber, bamboo, cane, leaves and fruits of medicinal value and the bark of the trees are the common items which are collected by the tribal from the forests and are sold to the people of the plains. The forests provide a good amount of animal protein to the tribal people who are now supplemented to a considerable extent by domesticated and semi-domesticated animals and poultry. A bulk of the tribal population is still depended directly or indirectly on forest and forest produce. It will remain so, unless there is drastic change in the way of life. They use herb and medicinal plants to cure their diseases. They have evolved their own system of soil and forest conservation because they are vitally concerned with preservation and continuance of forests and exemplify the age-old pattern of co-existence between man and nature.

The forest provides a good amount of revenue to the state exchequer. Other factors responsible include lack of research and market exploration, incentives to develop logging, lumbering and forest-based industries apart from paper, personnel trained in commercial management of forests and modern equipment. With the growing pressure on natural resources various forms of environmental degradation are evident in different parts of the country especially in the north eastern states. Wild life resources are highly sensitive to such degradations as habitat destruction which leads to extinction of species in the majority of cases. The status of wild life in any area, therefore, may act as a good bio-indicator to measure environmental quality in the natural ecosystem. The important natural resources are land comprising soil, water and associated plant and animal life involving the total ecosystem. Our future depends on the preservation and improvement of the natural resources. Today, on one side we are concerned about the nature and its preservation and on the other side degradation is taking place in land, water, air etc. Soil, water and forest are land-based resources. They exist in a dynamic equilibrium with interaction among all living and non-living components of the ecosystem. Man is the only component of the eco-system which in spite of being a part of the dynamic milieu, tends to place himself 'apart' from it, and by doing so causes great damage. In reality, the effect of humanity on the ecosystem since the dawn of the modern era has so increased that it has now become a bio-geochemical factor itself.

According to Gandhi "there is enough on earth for everybody's need, but not enough for anybody's greed". So need and greed have to be differentiated and, we must not over use or over-exploit the natural resources in the guise of development. Gandhi advises us to contain our greed and to allow our future generation to taste the fruit of real development. Spirituality helps in keeping our greed for materials and resources in check and sustainable development can take place when we use the resources for our needs and not for our greed. His advices are antidote not only to our consumerist culture but also can save the mother earth from most dangerous phenomena called "Global Warming and Climate Change".

Undoubtedly, because of deforestation the area, quality, quantity, and diversity of forest are fast decreasing. This is mainly due to the rate of deforestation, which is alarmingly faster than the natural regeneration. If a vast area is deforested rapidly, re-growth of forest over that area may take a long time depending upon the rate of regeneration in that climatic zone. Moreover, it may or may not reach to climax regeneration in foreseeable time. Due to cutting of trees not only in forest area there occur innumerable changes in the ecosystem, especially related with depletion of plant and animal species. In fact, the clearance of forest has already caused extinction of a number of species and many are either threatened or at verge of extinction. The World Commission of Forests and Sustainable Development (WCFSD) in their report (1999) has mentioned that survival of about 12.5% of the world's 270,000 species of plant and 75% of the world's mammals is threatened by the decline of the forest cover. The decline in the forest cover would also affect 350 million people of the world who depend entirely on forest for their subsistence (Hussain, 2002).

Loss of biodiversity and disturbance of the ecosystem continue to be a major global threat to future development, says the fourth Report of the Global Environment Outlook (GEO) brought out by the United Nations. Disbalance in the distribution of land, fresh water and marine biodiversity is more rapid than at any time in human history. Ecosystem such as forests, wet lands and dry lands are being transformed, in some cases, irreversibly degraded. The rate of species extinction is increasing, and a great majority of them, including the commercially important fish stocks, is declining in distribution or abundance or both. Biodiversity plays multiple roles in the daily lives of people through the supply of ecosystem services. In agriculture, biodiversity contributes in regulating and supporting services through soil formation, nutrient cycling, and pollination. The Report says that poor people in rural and remote areas tend to be most directly affected by the deterioration or loss of ecosystem services. In view of this, many governments have established and adopted the 2010 biodiversity target to reduce the rate of loss of biodiversity at global, regional and national scales. Though there have been local success stories of sustainable use of biodiversity, at a global level, and in most regions of the world, biodiversity continues to be lost because current policies and economic systems do not incorporate the values of biodiversity effectively in either the political or the market systems, and many policies that are already in place, are yet to be fully implemented, says the report (The Arunachal

Times, 2007). North East India is a home of many endemic fauna and flora and many valuable wildlife products which originates from this region. These resources are degrading rapidly due to demand from international trade. Despite strict legislative provisions certain elements resort to illegal and unauthorized wildlife trade. The insurgency and disturbed conditions have made the law enforcement difficult and complicated the matter. Further, ninety eight per cent to the North East India Border is with neighbouring countries. This border is very porous and constant source of smuggling activities. The region is a store house of biodiversity with its species richness of flora and fauna. The NER represents a wide range of physiographic and eco-climatic conditions and is endowed with vast and luxuriant vegetation ranging from tropical to alpine with rich gene pool of both wild and cultivated plant species. The flora of the region basically exhibits an Indo-Malayan affinity. However, the flora elements of other parts of India and far off countries have also contributed to its richness and diversity. India is recognized as one of the 12 mega-diversity centres of the world because of its rich diversity of biological resources. The richness of biological diversity of the NER could be established because of its 650 species of orchids, more than 450 species of grasses, 61 species of bamboo, 65 texa of rhododendrons, 42 species of Impatient, 34 species of Hedychin besides a large number of canes, timber trees, ferns, lichens and wildlife of 15,000 flowering plants (6% of world's total) of India 33% are estimated to be endemic to North-East India. Nearly 500 plant species are threatened. Since North-East India is an area of rich endemism, a large number of endemic plant species of the region are threatened. Mamal fauna comprise of 372 species of which 63% are found in Assam alone and a good number of fauna are threatened due to loss of forest covers (B.K. Sarma, 2002).

The most important natural resources are land comprising soil, water and associated plant and animal lives involving the total ecosystem. Our future depends on the preservation and improvement of the natural resources. Today, on one side we are concerned about the nature and its preservation and on the other side degradation takes place in land, water, air etc. The forest is now under threat. As a result, Loss of biodiversity and disturbance of the ecosystem continue to be a major global threat to future development, says the Fourth Report of the Global Environment outlook (GBO) brought out by the United Nations. Disbalance in the distribution of land, freshwater and marine biodiversity is more rapid than at any time in human history. Ecosystems such as forest, wet lands and dry lands are being transformed, in some cases, irreversibly degraded. The rate of species extinction was increasing, and a great majority of them, including the commercially important fish stocks, are declining in distribution or abundance or both. Biodiversity plays multiple roles in the daily lives of people through the supply of ecosystem services. In agriculture, biodiversity contributes in regulating and supporting services through soil formation, nutrient cycling and pollination. Though there have been local success stories of sustainable use of biodiversity in the state, it continues to be lost because current policies and economic systems do not incorporate the values of biodiversity effectively in either the political or the market system and many policies that are already in place, are yet to be fully implemented.

It is pertinent to mention that Eastern Himalayas including Arunachal Pradesh has been identified as one of the world's to 18 biodiversity hotspots. And after Rio Convention (1992), the global concern for preserving the biological diversity has increased tremendously. Forest has been playing an important role in socio-economic development of this region-specially hill tribal inhabited region, as a source of subsistence, employment, and raw-materials for industry. The indigenous people's role in ecological balance, environmental stability and sustainable development has been recognized in National Forest Policy, 1988. The forest resources of the region are under tremendous pressure due to increasing demand for human and livestock. Too much of extraction has led to forest degradation and disaster in ecological balance in recent time in this region. It is clear that North-Eastern India has been fast losing its pride of place in the matter of environment and ecology. **There has been exodus of population to the hills causing damage to the forest resources.** All these have created severe problems to the whole region in the form of land sliding in the hill and siltage in the rivers. This tells upon not only on the atmospheric condition of the area but also on the livelihood of the people dependent either on forest or on agriculture or on both. Forest dwellers, belonging to different communities, tribes and religion, enjoying for long the traditional and usufractory rights over forest and other natural resources are felling threatened by the forest policies pursued now. There has been a sense of insecurity for the great majority of the rural people who are not only threatened about their present livelihood but also very apprehensive about the future generations. The government, the NGOs and other statutory bodies concerned with improvement of environment should take appropriate and adequate initiatives. All such initiatives should aim at ensuring participation of the broad masses of tribal population. This can only be done by guaranteeing their rights on the forests and lands of the region.

Natural Environment and Ecological Balance

There is a great need today to create a comprehensive awareness of the need to have adequate safeguards against the destruction of the natural environment. The concern for preservation of environment is multi-dimensional and it relates itself to many disciplines and facets of the administration. The protection of environment and ecological balance are the concern of the people all over the globe. The Northeastern region of the country, which forms major part of the Indian portion of the Eastern Himalayas, is not only rich in forest and related natural resources, but also very much rich in bio-diversity. It has myriads of complex problems with distinct constitutional and legal features.

Wildlife in the natural situation constitutes the most important component of the ecosystem, which participates affectively in the energy flow and bio-geo-chemical cycling.

Animal-plant, plant--plant and animal-animal interactions are the basic milestone of the success of an ecosystem and its productivity. As such, the richness of the ecosystem means the capacity of hold high species diversity but deforestation has threatened the very fabric of the survival of wildlife and the ecosystem in the region. Forests are scarce and are becoming increasingly scarce due to pressure on it. It can be attributed to increase in population and demand for forest resources. The forest resources of Arunachal Pradesh are under tremendous pressure due to increasing demand for human and livestock. Too much of extraction has led to forest degradation and disaster in ecological balance in recent time in this region and this led to famous Supreme Court verdict on 12/12/96 banning exploitation of forest resources specially industrial wood in Arunachal Pradesh and other States. Timber extraction in the State was taken up on a large scale till 1995-96. Hence, a large number of woods based industries cropped up. A timber trade in the State had also increased through the operation of tree permits. There was halt on this trade after a Supreme Court Judgment on 12th December, 1996 on a writ petition (civil) No. 202 filed by Shri T.N. Godavarman Thirumulkpad. In recent years, the State's rich biodiversity has increasingly come under threat. The hastening paces of developmental activities in the last three decades, and the improvement in the communication network, have meant increased access. Road building has established communication but the blasting process involved has meant the loss of valuable habitat. The rapid monetization of the barter economies has meant increased trade in timber. A number of hydropower projects have been commissioned, and these projects are at various stages of progress. The urbanization process has meant the destruction of the forest cover adjacent to the new townships that have come up. Another significant threat to the fragile ecosystem and biodiversity of the State is due to the shifting cultivation and the shortening of the jhum cycle and introduction of commercial plantation.

Loss of forest on our live can be interpreted in another way which has a long run implication. Destruction of forest disturbs ecological balance also. The forests regulate the earth's temperature regime, water cycle, control floods and droughts and help to balance the CO2 and Oxygen in the atmosphere. Another cost of deforestation is the loss of biodiversity in the nature. The biodiversity treaty calls for the conservation of ecosystem (Rio-summit, 1992). Because of reckless destruction of forest for domestic fuel and for commercial gains about 17,000 living species are destroyed annually.

In addition, there is the illegal trade of forest projects such as timber, medicinal plants, orchids, animal hide, musk gland and birds, which are smuggled out of the State by poachers. Bio-piracy is a new challenge manifested in a number of ways. Sometimes, the operators enter the State, develop contracts, and smuggle out valuable species, mainly of flora, without the knowledge of the government. Given their highly sophisticated methods of operation, this type of bio-piracy is very difficult to detect. The creation of public consciousness, apart from the enhanced vigilance of the government, can help to control this problem. We know that each of the flora and fauna has its special genetic qualities. Different tree species has specific root system and feeding habits. The Botanical Survey of India has identified 47,688 of plant out of which 10,400 are known for their rich medicinal properties. In the North-East India, as a result of deforestation, about 650 species of plant and 70 species of animal have been listed as endangered. The region has about 50 per cent montane plants species in India of which many are endemic in nature.

Environmental problems in the State may be attributed to two major reasons: (i) due to negative effects of the process of economic growth and development and (ii) due to conditions of poverty and under development. As per the Forest Report of 1997 based on visual and digital interpretation of satellite data pertaining to 1995-96, the total forest cover in India is 6,33,397 sq.km which is 19% of the total geographical area of the country. During the period (1989-1995), forest cover in North-East India (NEI) was reduced by 2,037 sq.km while in the rest of the country it was increased by 933 sq.km. This reduction of forest cover in the NEI is quite alarming.

Medicinal Plants under Threat in the State

Due to the shifting cultivation, growth of urbanization, growth of population, growth of transportation, growth of industrialization and overall development programmes, the hitherto virgin vegetation has become a victim of sudden large-scale changes upsetting the balance of nature. At conference in Guwahati, experts from the State Forest Research Institute, Itanagar, Botanical Survey of India and the G. B. Pant Institute of Himalayan Environment and Development, Itanagar made an assessment of 47 plant species lying under threat. Out of the 47, five are threatened at the global level and are red listed by the International Union for Conservation of Nature (IUCN). This endemic species include Amentotaxus asamica, Coptis teeta, Gymnocladus assamicus, Piper Pedicellatum, P. Peepuloides, Aquilaria malaecensis, Dienia muscifera, Rauvolifia serpentina and smilax glabra are reported to be critically endangered.

Medical tourism exports by India

Now-a-days, India is a position to give world class medical treatment at a low cost in comparison to the developed countries. India has advantage due to low cost of treatment, large number and high quality of Indian health care professionals, world class corporate hospitals (Apollo, Escorts), presence in niche areas. Presently, Patients from developing and developed countries are coming to receive treatment in Indian hospitals. Health tourists from Middle East, CIS countries, neighbouring countries, Non resident Indians in developed countries, foreigners from some developed countries are coming very day. It is ovserved that130, 000 international patients came to India (2003) from South Asia, Africa, Gulf mainly for treatment in India. Again, many foreign patients seek treatment in traditional and alternative medicine (unani, ayurvedic, herbal treatment). The north-eastern region is the home of ayurvedic and herbal medicine. 90% herbal medicine of India is seen in this Himalayas belt. The State like Arunachal Pradesh where almost all of herbals are available has a bright scope to attract health tourists to give treatment at a low cost.

The Central Council for Research in Ayurveda and Siddha, Department of Ayush, Ministry of Health and Family Welfare, Govt. of India has initiated research programmes in this state from the early seventies. Accordingly it has taken up a special survey tour programme to study the traditions, culture, customs, folk medical practices and the extent of availability and the quality of the medicinal plants in the State. Consequently, the council has also initiated other important research programmes, such as clinical research programme in the State and established Regional Research Centre at Itanagar in May, 1979. The status of the centre has been upgraded to Regional Research Institute with effect from 09.09.1999 with the following aims and objectives.

Aims and Objectives of the Regional Research Centre:

- Intensive Clinical evaluation of selected therapies in assigned diseases.
- Specialized ayurvedic treatment is at OPD and IPD level.
- Morbidity, Survey of population, Health Education, Herbal medication and Medical aids in tribal village.
- Medico-botanical exploration of Arunachal Pradesh.
- Collection and compilation of information on local healing practices from rural tribal areas.
- Development and maintenance of Medicinal Plants Garden and supply of genuine drug materials to the research organization working under the Council.
- Advantage due to low cost of treatment, large number and high quality of Indian health care professionals, world class corporate hospitals (Apollo, Escorts), presence in niche areas.

Hydro Power Potential

Arunachal Pradesh, having untapped estimated hydro power potential of 49,000 MW, may emerge as power house of India when this potential is fully harnessed (Source: Deptt. of Power, Govt. of Arunachal Pradesh), this is shown in Table-I. Even if a part of the available hydro potential is harnessed, the state will not only be self sufficient in meeting its own power requirement but at the same time it can earn revenue by supplying power to the other neighbouring states of the country. During 2002-03, 35 numbers of micro/mini hydel projects with an installed capacity of 32.48 M.W. and diesel sets with an installed capacity of 27.12 M.W are the main sources of power supply in the state though the actual power requirement is 95 M.W. So the state is highly deficient in power generation.

Section-II

Conservation of Biodiversity under Sustainable Development

Sustainable Development

It appears that the term Sustainable Development (SD) was first used in the context of environmental degradation across generations (Raskin, 1996). However, it scope has since widened to incorporate the new realities of changing times in almost all areas of human concern. Before elaborating on the various dimensions of SD we first explore its meanings.

The notion of SD is derived from two words – sustainable and development. SUSTAIN means 'to maintain' or 'to uphold' something (e.g., a life, a system, etc.) by providing a minimum necessary support and /or a conducive environment. SUSTAINABLE implies 'capable of maintaining' or 'capable of upholding' and has the objective and subjective dimensions of viability and desirability respectively. Finally, SUSTAINABILITY refers to the capacity or capability of systems for achieving the viable and desirable results from an activity under consideration.

Sustainable Development means 'development that needs the needs of the present without compromising the ability and future generations to meet their own needs. That is, sustainability implies meeting of current human needs while preserving the environment and natural resources needed by future generations. World Bank Report speaks the sustainable development "a process of managing portfolio of assets to preserve and enhance the opportunities people face". Sustainable Development includes economic, environmental, social sustainability which can be achieved by rationally managing physical, natural and human capital. This term being used by economists and politicians all over the world and the term is constantly being refined. 'Intergenerational' equity would be impossible to achieve unless the groups stops exploitation of other groups or community living in other parts of the world.

Historical example reveals that greater economic development was achieved at the cost of inequality, unemployment, weak democracy, loss of cultural identity, over exploitation of natural resources leading to ecological and economical imbalances resulting in a dire threat for both flora and fauna. To be sustainable, we must rely on certain amount of natural resources available in nature to absorb pollution and regeneration of resources.

In Rio de Janeiro in June 1992, United Nations conference on Environment and Development, 1992, Para 2.1, it is declared, "Human beings are at the center of concern for sustainable development. They are entitled to a healthy and productive life in harmony with nature". Sustainable development assumes high substitutability among different, components of national wealth. Depletion of natural resources can be compensated with high investment on education i.e., human development and physical capital development which make ways for replacement of old technology to new technology to have effective usage of non-renewable resources at lesser level.

Economic development comes through the judicious and efficient application of three forms of capital – human capital, physical capital and natural capita. The first two types of capital are known as produced capital whereas natural resources are defined as assets gifted by the nature. Non-renewable natural resources such as mineral resources and some other, though renewable like forests and fish resources, may be exhausted if the rate of exploitation exceeds regeneration rate in the process of economic exploitation. As a result the scope of future development stands limited because of the irreversibility and non-substitutability character of most of the natural resources. To achieving 'sustainable development' i.e., uninterrupted long term development, we have to keep ourselves very alert on our exploitation of our natural resources. Sustainable development does not forbid the use of natural resources but restricts their use in such a way that enough, or as much as possible, is left for the future generation; not only for future but even for day-to-day use. When poor people have little access to the capital available in the 'organized' or market economy, they meet their most basic needs as best they can through subsistence activities. The poor live within a biomass-based subsistence economy; all their fundamental needs (food, fodder, fuel-firewood, cow dung, crop-wastes, fertilizer-dung manure leaf-litter, building materials-timber, thatch, and herbal medicines) are collected (often freely) from the immediate environment.

The traditional knowledge of the biological materials of these tribes is very vast which is often kept secret and passed to next generation through verbal tradition as well as through the individuals gifted with a state of spiritual embodiment possessing quality of rare eloquence and power of observation. The system has tremendous potential to evolve planning strategies for conservation and management of biodiversity and improving indigenous economy as well as environmental security of tribal habitat and thus sustainable development of the state.

Major causes of forest degradation are legal and illegal land-use changes; use pressure from villages inside and outside the reserve in the form of fuel wood collection and grazing of livestock; and institutions that fail to manage the forests. The grabbing of common land by the individual has been observed to a significant extent. In consequence, average distance to be covered by a household to collect CPR products has increased significantly. The size of human and livestock population, scarcity of resources (emergence of new-rich class with commercial interests), distance of the reserve area from the residential area and the quality of the management etc. are some of the important factors that determine the extent of degradation. Market close to the villages cause more severe degradation of forest resources i.e. market plays the promotional role of forest degradation. Scarcity of commons in relation to population leads to its degradation. Though the imposition of a ban on the extraction of forest and forest products by the Supreme Court in 1996 has formally checked the illegal felling of trees, the emerging neo-merchant class are taking the advantages of local power to exploit the forest resources, and in consequence, the state ownership and management have failed to prevent the conservation and degradation of many forests.

1. A periodic exploitation of natural forest should be done on scientific basis. This will help in removing the diseased and unwanted trees to maintain a health density of forest. This, however, should not affect the bio-diversity of the region.

2. People living in and around the forest and largely depending upon the forest resources should be allowed to collect forest products for their subsistence and survival. Even the government is planning to suggest to the Supreme Court to reconsider its decision on the total ban on felling of trees in such areas. In fact, a local need based forest policy can be framed and implemented for forest management, which will keep in mind the interests of the forest and its dwellers. A family depending entirely on forest may even be permitted to collect forest products and sell them to earn enough for their livelihood, of course not for any big commercial purpose. There is a clear-cut distinction between the minimum needs of the family and the commercial exploitation of the forest.

3. Ecosystem based forest management has to be adopted to

maintain ecological balance. For example, cutting of forest of tropical belt is much more dangerous than that of the temperate belt. It is because, the nutrients are looked up in the biomass in the former, and in the soil in the later, i.e., organic cycle and physical cycle, respectively. Hence, cutting of the tropical forest leads to breakdown of the ecosystem itself, giving rise to number of environmental problems. Therefore, forest or trees should be grown in the tropical belt, because here nutrient cycle is 'biological'. In the deforested areas of the temperate zone, crops should be grown, as nutrient cycle is 'physical' here, means all the nutrients are in soil, not in the forest cover. This will give optimum results.

4. Each village, town, industry, and those who need forest products should own tree fields to meet their respective demands.
5. All virgin forest should be declared 'sacred groves' to preserve them for posterity.

Plantation of jatropha: An alternative way for income of rural people and fuel for future

Jatropha curcus is a drought resistant perennial plant growing well in marginal and poor qualitative soil. It is easy to establish, grows relatively quickly and produces seeds for 50 years. The plant produces seeds with an oil content of up to 37% in it. The oil can be combusted as fuel without being refined. It burns with clear smoke-free flame, tested successfully as fuel for simple diesel engine. The by-product is press cake a good organic fertilizer. Its oil contains also insecticide. It is now cultivated in many parts of the country and easily survive with minimum inputs in wastelands. It has also many medicinal values for diseases like cancer, piles, snake-bite, paralysis, etc. A good crop can be obtained with little effort. Oil can be extracted from the seeds after 2 to 5 years after plantation. This can be an important source of income of rural people and thereby diverting the jhumia from their shifting cultivation. But it is not economically viable and very much labour intensive cultivation. But from the ecological point of view only barren land can be used for the purpose.

Incentive and Encouragement to the Poor People

Financial credit, technical assistance and organizational support can help to relieve constraints related to rural poor household's awareness, technology, capacity to invest and local institutional capacity. Co-investment with local communities may be used to mobilize longer term investments through group or micro-credit with labour mobilization or provision of key inputs. Well-organized local participation in project design and management is essential.

Tribal should be encouraged to take up horticulture, floriculture, agro-forestry, growing of medicinal and aromatic plants on hill slope which will not damage the fragile hill ecology. These can play a crucial role in relieving constraints related to a lack of technologies suitable for poor household. Such technologies and resource management systems must raise overall productivity, both increasing household income (to reduce poverty) and protecting or improving the natural resource. Poor rural households have few economic incentives to manage their natural resource more carefully.

Natural Resource Based Entrepreneurship in North-East:

In North-East there is tremendous scope for agro-based industries, agro forestry, horticulture, mushroom farming, herbal, medicinal and aromatic plants, bio-technology, fruit and vegetable processing, handlooms and handicrafts, bee keeping, meat and poultry products, cereal based products, consumer industry, milk and milk based products, food processing, paper products, jute and mestas products, cattle rearing, fishery, edible oil, processing of oils and fragrances, gas based intermediary products, floriculture spices production and processing wood based products, etc.

Explore of Natural Resources in Planned way

People should be made aware of the consequences of the degradation of natural resources due to explore of natural resources and the need to minimize them. Efforts must be made for ensuring optimum utilization and conservation of natural resources which will not only increase national output but also will improve living condition of the people. The schemes of afforestation and tree planting should be extensively done specially by the NGOs and govt. agencies and proper steps should be taken for continuous maintenance of those areas at least in the initial stages. It may be mentioned that though this type of schemes were undertaken earlier but could not give desired result due to lack of proper maintenance.People should also realize the potent dangers of deforestation and take active interest for successful implementation of the afforestation schemes. In this regard Environment Awareness Schemes seem to be fruitful if the message can reach the remotest corner of the region. Efforts should be made to ensure optimum utilization and conservation of natural resources, which will increase both the national output and improve the living standard of the people of the region.

Forestry development in the region can take place through harnessing the community institutions for the purpose of food-fodder, fuel and timber extraction requirement of the people. Further it is also essential to ensure greater coordination between the government machinery, people and voluntary organizations in regard to enhancement of productivity of forest and forest land under protective care and supervision. Private sector investment should be also encouraged upto some extent. Aforestation of identified areas (wastelands, catchment areas of hydroelectric projects and watershed management projects) and regeneration of forest in abandoned jhum land will be helpful in improving the environment sustainability. The centrally sponsored programmes related to agro-forestry, social-forestry, wasteland development and other employment generation programmes should be given more emphasis on this region.

Land Use Pattern

Basically, the land use pattern of a particular region is by and large determined by the nature and general lay out of the physical as well as cultural elements. Primarily, the physical factor like climate, topography set the broad limits upon the capabilities of the land; subsequently, the human factors like length of occupation of the area, density of population, social and economic factors especially, system of land tenure and the technological levels of the people, determine to an appreciable degree the extent to which the physical capacities of land are utilized. Efforts should be made for more intensive people's participation in forest management. It is the people's involvement that will be able to create mass awareness more effectively for preserving the forestry of the region.

Innovations are needed to facilitate poor people's access to natural resources through its more sustainable use whether it is owned or controlled by or shared with others. Land reforms process if taken up in the near future, must ensure secure access by the poor households for both productive and consumptive uses, yet make provision for environmental uses of village commons. Formal arrangements are needed for access to critical resources by the increasing numbers of temporary migrants (e.g., from natural disasters), to limit over exploitation and conflict. Groups of poor people can be involved in land use planning efforts to ensure that their existing use patters and future needs can be met without increasing poverty or resource degradation. Finally, poor households need insurance systems – cash payments, in-kind provisions or public works employment - to provide subsistence needs after crop failures so natural resources are not over-exploited as emergency reserves. Governments, non-governmental organizations (NGOs) and the private sector should to co-invest in the rehabilitation or improvement of productive on-farm natural resources that are assets of the poor households.

Government policy

In order to offset the loss of revenue from forests, the Government of India has given direct fiscal assistance to the State on the recommendations of the Twelfth Finance Commission and is promoting development of non-timber forest products particularly bamboo through a fully funded centrally sponsored scheme. Development of bamboo, cane and medicinal plants are thought to have great potentials for employment generation and economic development. The State should particularly evolve a forest sector development policy, bamboo policy and land use policy before any further delay. These measures would go a long way in improving the environmental governance in the State.

Government's steps

1. The state has to move away from fossil-fuel based, sustainable development processes and adopt alternative sustainable process that provide basic livelihood and social security to all people; this could be done by adopting a clear set of indicators of sustainability (for example, non-conventional energy sources).
2. All leasing of the state's remaining forest areas to mines, industries and other large-scale commercial or development project must halt immediately.
3. Role of NGOs: Government agencies and NGOs need to urgently facilitate communities to derive sustainable forest based livelihoods and provide other sources of employment and livelihood including through the National Rural Employment Guarantee Act. Simultaneously the government has to identify and arrange alternative health, education and other such amenities that do not end up destroying the forest; this can best be done by building on existing traditional knowledge and process of learning rather than completely replacing them.

One of the important components of effective forestry planning is involving the people in the protection and regeneration of forest because forest can never be protected unless the people are made to feel about the necessity of the forest.

In this respect, the N.G.Os can also play an important role in forest conservation and preservation among the people of Arunachal Pradesh. The tribes of Arunachal Pradesh had their own system of forest conservation and management but due to modernization and introduction of monetary economy, much of it has been lost. Hence, it is the NGOs who can make the local people more aware about the age-old tradition of the preservation of forest resources and help them to conserve the forest resources of the state. It should be noted that unless social consciousness about forest promotion and conservation do not grow or revive among the people, the government's efforts will be of no use. It is the NGOs, who can motivate people at the grassroots level.

4. The state and central governments would do well to take care of the increasing signs of unrest and hostility in the regions where unsustainable development is being imposed.
5. **Forest Management:** With the advent of scientific forestry in 1946, the effort of the State Forest Department (now Environment & Forest Deptt.) has been to conserve the forests and wildlife, to maintain the ecological balance, and to promote sustained socio-economic development of the local people. A humble beginning was made with an area of 534 sq. kms. of reserved forests handed over by the Govt. of Assam. Over the years rapid strides have been taken in bringing large areas under scientific management besides associating the people in protection, development and management of the forests. The predominantly tribal population of the State lives in close association with and depends largely on the forest resources. Therefore forest management efforts seek to elicit the involvement and cooperation of the people while safeguarding their customary rights over the land.

Hitherto, forestry has been confined to reserved forests. But now with the growing emphasis on peoples' participation, forestry is gradually catching up as a land use practice even in the traditionally owned community lands under the schemes of social forestry, wasteland development, national afforestation programme and national bamboo mission. These activities are being taken up in joint forest management mode. For this purpose, forest development agencies and village forest management committees have been constituted in various forest divisions (SFRI Information Bulletin No.27, 2008).

Arunachal Pradesh State Pollution Control Board:

Arunachal Pradesh State Pollution Control Board (APSPCB) has been constituted under provisions of the Central Rules - Water (Prevention & Control of Pollution) Act, 1974 by the Government of Arunachal Pradesh on 6th July 1993 in order to regulate the new rules in the State. Due to increasing concerns for environmental issues and realization about the need for protecting the environment from various polluting ingredients, several acts have been enacted and brought under the purview of Environment Protection Act, 1986. The Board is headed by a full time chairman and a senior IFS officer as Member Secretary. The Board is required to be further strengthened. The SPCBs/PCCs, all over the country have been entrusted with the responsibility of monitoring and ensuring the implementation of these acts by various agencies (SFRI Information Bulletin No. 27, 2008).

Arunachal Pradesh Biodiversity Board

The Government of Arunachal Pradesh has constituted Arunachal Pradesh Biodiversity Board in March 2005 with Chief Secretary as Chairman and Director, State Forest Research Institute as Member Secretary and Chief Executive Officer. The Board has other senior officials and scientists as members.

Functions of the Arunachal Pradesh biodiversity board are as follows

(I.) Advise the State Government subject to any guidelines

issued by the Central Government on matters relating to the conservation of biodiversity, sustainable use of its components and equitable sharing of the benefits arising out of the utilization of biological resources.

(II.) Regulate requests for granting of approvals or otherwise for commercial utilization or bio-survey and bio-utilization of any biological resource by Indians.

(III.) Perform such other functions as may be necessary to implement the provisions of Biological Diversity Act 2002, or as may be prescribed by the State Government.

The National Biodiversity Authority provides some financial assistance for setting up infrastructure facilities and towards running expenses of the board. Arunachal Pradesh State Biodiversity Strategy and Action Plan prepared by the State Forest Research Institute have been approved by the Central and State Government (SFRI Information Bulletin No.27, 2008).

Compensatory Afforestation / NPV Scheme

In Arunachal Pradesh many developmental projects are implemented after formal diversion/ de-reservation of forest land under Forest (Conservation) Act, 1980 by the Government of India. The user agencies remit funds for undertaking compensatory afforestation as per the provisions of Forest (Conservation) Act, 1980. The Hon'ble Supreme Court of India vide their order dated 30th October, 2002 and 1st August, 2003 in IA No. 566 in WP (Civil) No. 202 of 1995 ordered realization of Net Present Value (NPV) against the diverted forest land. The user agencies now remit NPV also along with funds for Compensatory Afforestation. The Central Government has constituted a body called the Compensatory Afforestation Fund Management and Planning Authority (CAMPA). The funds received from the user agencies are sent to CAMPA which in turn is released to the State for implementing the Action Plan for NPV fund and Compensatory Afforestation Scheme. Conservator of Forests (Conservation) in the office of PCCF

& Principal Secretary (Environment & Forests) is the nodal agency for dealing with the F.C.A cases including implementing the NPV and Compensatory Afforestation Schemes by utilizing the funds received from CAMPA (SFRI Information Bulletin No. 27, 2008).

All the government rules, regulations and schemes should be strictly carried out. The new Scheduled Tribes and Other Forest Dwellers (Recognition of Forest Rights) Act 2006 is reframed in such a way that community should be given more chance to shoulder more responsibility to manage all the forest regulation acts.

The debates and developments with regard to the draft of National Environment policy (NEP), 2004 and the scheduled Tribes (Recognition of Forest Rights) Bill (STB), 2005 were illustrative in different ways of the manner in which social concerns were dealt with in environmental policy and legislation in India. Yet, while the pros and cons of specific policies and legislations had been Central to the academic debates on the environment, very little attempt had been made to trace the changes in environmental policy making and the way of social concerns still remains problematized.

The government schemes that should have helped communities with securing livelihoods have sometimes done the reverse. For instance, Joint Forest Management (JFM) was meant to create spaces for vulnerable sections of the community to benefit from regenerated forest resources. Certainly in several sites this has helped. However, very often the participation of local people has remained on paper; in any case, the governance framework of JEM is not conducive to power-sharing between the forest department and the communities. In addition to this, JEM has in many cases been superimposed on Community Forest Management (CFM), undermining existing institutions that communities have created.

Community Rights

Our specific focus with regard to social concerns is

community rights to resources – a concern that is central to many of the debates on natural resource management. Three arguments are put forth: (i) that while the environment has at one level assumed a non-negotiable presence in policy, social concerns are only highlighted to the extent that they are deemed not to be environmentally destructive, (ii) that the discursive terrain through which social concerns are deemed harmful is overly simplistic and in need of re-examination and (iii) that the changing nature of environmental discourse can only be understood within the wider shifts in development policy. Although there are many who would claim that the environment itself receives an inadequate attention in development policy, a contention that is at least partly true, we are concerned herewith how emerging policies and legislations tackle social concerns given the socially constructed nature of the environment.

While the discursive thrust of much of environmental policy-making in the late 1970s and early 1980s was on incorporating environmental principles in sectoral planning, something that was matched with legislative intervention, the latter part of the 1980s saw the focus shift towards sustainable development. The importance of this shift was that the link between social and environmental concerns was more forcefully articulated.

The 1988 National Forest Policy (NFP) was the first "environmental" policy document in India that explicitly recognized the linkages between environmental and social concerns in terms of community rights to natural resources. Unlike the previous forest acts that privileged revenue and commercial interests, the NFP was strikingly different. Section 4.6 of the policy highlighted the symbiotic relationship between tribals and forests and the need to involve tribal communities in the management of forests. It also emphasized that domestic requirements of firewood, fodder and minor forest produce should be the first priority of forest management, not commercial or industrial needs.

The 1990 government order on joint forest management (JFM), while giving communities adjacent to reserved forests usufruct rights, was also aimed at improving the protection of forests. As Kolavalli (1995) has argued, citing a number of state-level government orders, JFM was the forest department's way to involve communities in the management of forests as it was incapable of doing it on its own.

But JFM has remained a policy and has not been incorporated into the forest act. Thus, while the NFP recognized the symbiocity of forest dependent (tribal) communities with forest, right afforded to these communities have been limited and often no more (sometimes less) than existing settlement rights.

In 2000, the ministry of environment and forest (MoEF) actually gave an NGO Kalpavriksh, the coordinating role in preparing a national biodiversity strategy and action plan (NBSAP) in consort with 15 members Technical and Policy Core Group. In terms of strategies, the report specified that "empowered local community institutions" should be the implementers of the plan. It would have appeared, therefore, that a good opportunity for decentralized natural resource management where communities were given rights to resources was on the anvil [Kothari, 2004]. However, before the NBSAP was completed in 2003, the National Biodiversity Act, 2002 was passed, although one of the explicit objectives of the act was the recognition of local rights to biodiversity. The National Biodiversity Act, 2002 does recognize the need for local biodiversity committees; the actual powers given to these committees again are mostly managerial in nature. Under section 41, these committees are constituted for "promoting conservation, sustainable use and documentation of biological diversity including preservation of habitats, conservation of land races, folk varieties and cultivars, domesticated stocks and breeds of animals and micro-organisms and chronicling of knowledge relating to biological diversity" [NBA 2004:20].

These three cases have a number of things in common. First, different policies, programmes and laws within particular sectors are often not in consonance with each other in terms of their normative position vis-a-vis community rights. For example, while the National Environment Policy (NEP) has made some headway by recognizing tribal rights to forest produce, JFM as a programme has actually given limited usufruct rights to only those who are part of FPCs. Moreover, the Forest Act has remained un-amended with no room for community-based forest management except in the context of village forests (Menon, 2006).

Conservation of biodiversity

The Convention, which was signed by majority of the Nations during the UNCED Earth Summit held in Rio de Janerio in June 1992, is now an International Law. The World Conservation Strategy takes into consideration the human impacts and the perils that may threaten the future of the world's life supporting systems. It clearly defines three global objectives of living resources conservation:

- to maintain essential ecological process and life support systems
- to preserve genetic diversity
- to ensure the sustainable utilization of species and ecosystems.

Conservation of biodiversity is the management of human use of the biosphere so that it may yield the greatest sustainable benefit to present generation, while maintaining its potential to meet the needs and aspirations of future generations. Conservation includes element of b In this respect, the N.G.Os can also play an important role in forest conservation and preservation among the people of Arunachal Pradesh. The tribes of Arunachal Pradesh had their own system of forest conservation and management but due to modernization and introduction of monetary economy, much of it has been lost. Hence, it is the NGOs who can make the local people more aware about the age-old tradition of the preservation of forest resources and help them to conserve the forest resources of the state. It should be noted that unless social consciousness about forest promotion and conservation do not grow or revive among the people, the government's efforts will be of no use. It is the NGOs, who can motivate people at the grassroots level.

Systematic Study

It is very important to do a systematic study of these forests products to evaluate their nutritional and medicinal values. On the basis of such study the forest planner may consider the viability of growing such plants commercially for use by a wider array of people.

Other preservation and sustainable use, restoration and enhancement

- In situ and ex situ < >conservation of forest genetic resources through establishment of biosphere reserves, national parks and sanctuaries.
- Protection of exceptional and rare trees in preservation plots.
- Creation of Public awareness of rational utilization of valuable forest resources.
- Promotion of Public involvement in the management of protected areas.
- To increase areas under preservation plots to include all forest types and scientifically monitor of the plots.
- Promotion of eco-restoration of degraded forest areas.
- Regeneration of rare and threatened species and introduction of such plants in suitable habitats.
- Establishment of ethno botanical forest parks.
- Vigorous community participation to medicinal and rare plant conservation.
- Creation of State Information and Data Base (SIDB) centres of forest species, medicinal and aromatic species. Wild relatives of cultivated species, wildlife species along with establishment of bioresource centres.
- Identification of traditional knowledge base and species

exploration to conserve diversity in agro-ecosystems and for promoting sustainability in farming systems.

- High raised areas should be developed in National Parks and sanctuaries for protection of wildlife during flood and other natural calamities, so to prevent from migrating wild animals during flood and drought.
- Reduction and replacement of areas under shifting cultivation system by alternative farming systems.
- Environmental educational awareness building and motivation should form strategy in conservation issues.
- Implementation of clear cut forest policy implementation.

Human interference has greatly threatened the natural ecosystem of the region. The forest of the region have dwindled to a great extent due to indiscriminate human intervention resulting into a large number of plant and animal species are endangered or faced extinction.

We have to grow trees for timber, fuel-wood, fodder medicine and other uses on land not meant for agriculture. Trees, especially the timber trees, have to be cultivated on nonagricultural land or 'tree fields'. The grown up trees can be cut to meet the demands. The tree cultivation has to be started in subsequent years in different tree fields, so that annual requirement can be fulfilled from the matured trees in different years. This will enable the tree cultivator to reap the harvest every year or whenever the trees are cut for use. This time-based cultivation of trees would ensure sustainable availability of timber and other forest based products. It is worth mentioning that such practice has already started in various parts of the North-East India.

Local Industries

The absence of local industries to process the forest resources inside the state is another problem. Since no such industries existed or established, the resources have to be exported outside only. If there is local consumption through industries, finished products only will be exported outside and the resources will be able to be utilized in a planned way that will not deplete the natural stock. The Govt. should try as much as possible to establish local industries based on local resources.

Other Forest Management

This task of managing forest resource cannot be done by foresters alone. Local communities have to realize this and have to come forward to join hands with foresters for protecting and conserving this primary source. Arunachal Pradesh has been declared as one of the hotspots of mega biodiversity in the world.

Forest management practices are implemented in the reserved forest and protected forest only and under the control of the state government, that is, through the approved working plans. So, far, the remaining forest of the state under the control of the Autonomous District Councils and private ownership are without working plans which are every essential for sustain harvest and management.

Land tenure system

The state has a peculiar land tenure system where large extent of the land belonged to the community, villages, clans and private individuals. Enforcement of rules and regulation becomes a difficult task. No doubt the system is very good but proper scientific and systematic management is very difficult especially on the part of exploitation and utilization of forest resources.

Lack of awareness

In general, the awareness on the environmental aspect is far from expectation. The rural population is supposed to be the main group which lived and depend on forest resources, but they are unaware of the importance of conservation and utilization. Due to their ignorance they are being exploited to the extent that may be detrimental to their existence.

Publicity

Increase appreciation and awareness of environmental values and importance of conservation have to be promoted in order to get a satisfactory result. Through mass communication, awareness programmes, trainings and interactions, seminar, symposium the people are to be made aware of the things around them. Related institutions both governmental and non-governmental will have to be involved to make the population understanding of the importance of environment.

Forest Protection Force

A handsome amount of fund is required to fully equip the forest protection force with sophisticated arms and ammunition against the fully armed timber smugglers and also to carry out regular eviction operations to drive out the encroachers from lands.

Suggestion

No doubt Management of forest is one of the most important and complicated subject and is guided by the variety of factors. The important factors may be forest resources condition, forest policy, local requirements, industrial commitments, economic and ecological considerations etc. Once the decision about the objectives of management of the forest is taken, the detailed procedure of felling trees, regeneration management systems, control of yield and other operations can be easily worked out.

In the physiographical and socio-economic condition of the region, where tribal communities have to depend heavily on traditional practices of forest exploitation, the right approach to forestry is to plan forest development in such a manner that there would be a net addition to a perpetuating stock even after meeting the essential food, fodder, fuel and timber requirement of the people, as well as, the growing requirement of commercial exploitation. It is also necessary to focus other important aspect namely, the conservation of forest resources and control of harmful exploitation. It is worth while to introduce the basic elements of community forest management strategy with the community as the unit management. This will help forestry to play a significant role in rural development, maintenance of stream flow and preventation of floods in the plains. Strategies will have to be developed for tackling various problems in connection with forest management in the region.

In India, 1972 Wildlife (Protection) Act was introduced with specific provision to control trade and commerce of wildlife and its products. The act has been amended thrice i.e., in 1982, 1986 and 1991. Gradually this trade was discouraged. Initially the act has divided Animals in five schedules. By Wildlife Amendment Act 1991 a new schedule VI was added with imported legislative protection to six species of plants becoming rare and facing extinction. The act as amended till date prohibits trade in all species of animals included in Schedule I and Schedule II (Part II) and increased penalty for violators. No fresh hunting can be done for commercial purpose (Diksit, 2002). But it is a matter of sorry to say that meat of wild animals are sold in open markets of every district head quarters even in capital market, Itanagar till this year,2009.

If villagers are made partners in the use of potential and over the benefits of, they are more likely to take interest in its protection. A food for work programme may be an example for a successful management. Sharing the responsibilities with local communities and NGO's to interact with all user agencies through forest collaboration, can go a long way for sustainable management of forest and development of society. It is realized that poverty, environmental degradation and population growth are inextricably related and that none of these fundamental problems can be successfully addressed in isolation. However a commonly acceptable sustainable development still remains a challenge for all engaged in development process.

One of the important components of effective forestry planning is involving the people in the protection and regeneration of forest because forest can never be protected unless the people are made to feel about the necessity of the forest.

In the pretext of change in forest policy in 1988, the idea of Joint Forestry Management (JFM) came and it was adopted by various states of the country. However, the JFM model will require suitable modifications to be workable in the hill state like Arunachal Pradesh where 62.17% of the total forest areas are mainly under the traditional ownership of local village committees. At the same time, there is enough scope to shift focus from government forests by bringing more virgin USF to J.F.M. network. The concept of Apna Van has received enthusiastic and wide acceptance among some of the local tribes in Arunachal Pradesh.

One of the important components of effective forestry planning is involving the people in the protection and regeneration of forest because forest can never be protected unless the people are made to feel about the necessity of the forest. In the pretext of change in forest policy in 1988, the idea of Joint Forestry Management (JFM) came and it was adopted by various states of the country. However, the JFM model will require suitable modifications to be workable in the hill state like Arunachal Pradesh where 62.17% of the total forest areas are mainly under the traditional ownership of local village committees. At the same time, there is enough scope to shift focus from government forests by bringing more virgin USF to J.F.M. network. The concept of Apna Van has received enthusiastic and wide acceptance among some of the local tribes in Arunachal Pradesh.

Conclusion

In the exploitative development model, the forests were looked upon by man as a resource pool of only timber and other industrial raw materials. This idea has since been changed. Forest now managed also for wildlife, medicinal and other beneficial plants, eco-tourism, and soil and water conservation as well as for meeting the local and industrial needs. However, research efforts are necessary to explore new avenues for development and at the same time for restoration and maintenance of ecosystem. Moreover, large patches of the forest of the world still exist as virgin forests which provide a niche to a large number of species of great biodiversity. These offer an excellent situation for study of ecosystem without human influence. Assessing the economic impact of ecological degradation requires an understanding of the value of ecosystem. Particular attention is required to be given to environmental value of the forest because the ecosystems still continue to contribute to the well being of the people

Given such multi-facet dimension of complexity, conservation and management of forest resources, including eco-development of the region continue to remain a special challenge.

The interests of people depending on the forests products for their livelihood would have to be protected by providing training and employment opportunities in alternative occupations. The population increased and modernization are realities of the day when we plan for the future, new ideological statements are not enough, but one should have proper action plan. It is necessary that a systematic forestation and plantation programmes to be undertaken to increase the forest cover. It is worthwhile to consider allowing barren land to be brought under forest cover by private sector.

For conserving and managing natural vegetation the jhum cultivation and illegal felling of trees, which are the root cause of deforestation, must be stopped immediately but not without rehabilitation of the jhumias. If the government is successful to protect the natural vegetation, the state will be the richest in having the Herbs which can be sold in national and international markets. Hence, it is necessary first to develop the market for Herbs within the state where the local cultivators will be benefited economically. It will give an incentive to the local people to protect the valuable Herbs from extinction.

For the betterment of lives, urbanization, transportation, industrialization are necessary but we can try to minimize the deforestation due to shifting cultivation and illegal failing of trees which are the main cause of disappearance of flora and fauna in Arunachal Pradesh. The Central Government as well as the State Government should give top priority to protect the herbs of economic value in the State which are endowed more than 50% of herbs of the country. Days are not far when the Governments can generate employment as well as earn foreign currency from the export of the State's herbs if they try to take kin interest to protect the existing herbs from disappearance due to impact of the factors mentioned above.

The foresters, wild lifers, conservationists, ecologists, geographers, pedologists and agronomists collectively need to have a good deal of co-ordination with sociologists, and anthropologists for understanding the bad effect of degradation of natural resources and work in the same view for its conservation. A synthesis of traditional knowledge and modern scientific outlook is necessary to evolve a method for improving tribal tradition economy confirming to security.

It is clear that there is a need for conservation of forest in the region. As there are many people maintaining their livelihood from forest, we should chalk out proper aforestation programme which will ultimately satisfy the growing demand for products. But at the time of aforestation we should use multiple species for plantation. Environmentalists have been warning about the damage of planting a single species over a large area. This is because any insect or disease outbreak can wipeout the entire tree plantation, leading to ecological and financial crisis. Monoculture may deplete the nutrients at a particular profile of the soil and cause nutritional deficiency in the long run. The principle behind bio-diversity is to encourage the conservation of a wide range of flora and fauna in a given area to ensure an ideal nutrient cycle, as well as, food chain which are important aspects of ecological balance. Preservation of plants and animals are necessary, because our present knowledge about them is confined to a small number of species and the benefits of the remaining millions of plants and animal species are not known to us today. Nevertheless they play an important role in maintaining the ecological balance **(Hegde, 1994).**

Total comprehension of the problems is essential and this can only emerge if there are attitudinal changes in both the government and the people. Education on environment from lower classes and training at different levels will go a long way to solve some of these problems.

Development of overall environment will be a nursery bed of co-operation and harmony as opposed to mindless competition and conflicts. We must dare act and go beyond and behind nature to seek the main purpose of existence. Saving the tree is only a first step for saving over selves. Only then sons of the earth will repossess the earth and an enjoyable period of time will be ushered in.

It is found that accessible natural forests particularly in the foothills of Arunachal Pradesh are under great pressure to a large scale due to extraction of timber and illegal felling of trees. Although the demand for wood for local consumption is relatively low due to low population of the state but in view of the increasing demand for industrial timber within the state and other parts of the country, the forest in the state are under great pressure. As per the official estimate, the state contributes to nearly 50% of the timber supply made from the North Eastern region of India. At the sometime, it is observed that there is large scale illegal felling of trees, which is many times more than the official permits issued for felling of trees. The tree permit system in unclassified state forest (D.S.F.) which was introduced to enable the local people to earn their livelihood in logging and extraction of timber with a view to generate income has led to the emergence of a 'neo-rich' class in the traditional tribal society to make easy and quick money in collaboration with private forest contractors. There is a growing social and political pressure to over exploit the forest and the protection of forest are becoming increasingly difficult.

China and South East Asian countries have already demonstrated their capability in bio-resource management. China in particular has made great strives in transforming its rural economy through bamboo. Chinese people have replaced wood by bamboo in almost all their industrial, construction and domestic applications. This has considerably reduced pressure on their natural forests. Forest cover in China has increased while India's has remained stagnant. There is, therefore, need for this State to learn about bamboo sector from China particularly in the areas of policy, legal and institutional arrangements which were behind their success story on bamboo (SFRI Information Bulletin No.27, 2008).

References

1. Azad, N.A. (2004): "Poverty and Sustainable Development", S.Bhatt (ed.), Poverty and Food Security in India, Aakar Books, Delhi, PP. 106 – 110.
2. Bhattacharjee, R.P. (2000): Economic Development of Arunachal Pradesh, Himalayan Publishers, Delhi, Itanagar, p.17-18 and p.45-49.
3. Bhattacharjee,R.P.(2006): "Forest Economics in Arunachal Pradesh and its Impact on State Economy", Arunachal Review, Vol.VIII,No.18, June –August, Naharlagun, Govt. of Arunachal Pradesh.
4. B.K.Sarma & et.al.(2002): "Dwinding Forest Biodiversity of North East India" in Roy B.Datta and Alam K: Forest Resources in North East India, Omsons Publication, New Delhi.
5. Diksit, V.K.(2002): "International Wildlife Trade and Its Impact on Wildlife Resources" in Roy B.Datta and Alam K: Forest Resources in North East India, Omsons Publication, New Delhi.
6. Ghosh, A.K. (1990): "Impact of shifting cultivation in Living Natural Resources", in Majumdar, D.N. (ed): Shifting cultivation in North-East India, Omsons, Publications, Guwahati and New Delhi, pp.178 – 197.
7. Govt. of Arunachal Pradesh (2006): Economic Review, Directorate of Economic and Statistics, Itanagar.
8. Govt. of Arunachal Pradesh (2006): Arunachal Pradesh: Human Development Report 2005, Rajiv Gandhi University, P. 171-72.

9. Hegde, N.G. (1994): Biodiversity and Ground Realities, Yojana, February.
10. Hegde, S.N. (1988): "Coptis Teeta Wall (Mishmi Teeta): A Rare Medicinal Plant from Arunachal Pradesh", Arun for News 6(I), pp. 27 – 29.
11. Hussain Zahid (2002): "Tree Cultivation: A Ned of the Hour in Forest Management" in Roy B.Datta and Alam K: Forest Resources in North East India, Omsons Publication, New Delhi.
12. Joshi, M.C. (1997): Role of Herbs and Drugs in Economic Development in Pandey B.B. (ed):Patterns of Change and Potential for Development in Arunachal Pradesh, Himalayan Publishers, Itanagar, New Delhi, pp. 174 -184.
13. Kanjilal, U.N. Kanjilal, P.C. and Das, A. (1934): Flora of Assam, Vol.I, Govt. of Assam, Shillong.
14. Mandal, R.K. (2006): "Sustainability of Medicinal Plants and its Economic Viability in Arunachal Pradesh", Resarun (Journal of the Directorate of Research), Govt. of Arunachal Pradesh, Itanagar, Vol. 31, pp. 1 – 10.
15. Mandal, R.K. (2005): Arunachal Economy: Socio Economic Transformation, Champion Publishing, Itanagar, pp. 116 – 117.
16. Mandal, R.K. (2007): "Flora and Fauna in Arunachal Pradesh: Economic Viability and Sustainability" Arunachal Review,Vol.VIII, No.23, Sept.-Nov., Naharlagun,Govt. of Arunachal Pradesh.
17. Mandal, R.K. (2005): "Arunachal Pradesh Emerging as Power House" Journal of Global Economy, Vol.1., No 4, Research Centre for Social Sciences, Mumbai.
18. Menon, Ajit (2006): "Environmental Policy Legislation and Construction of Social Nature", EPW, January 21 – 27, Vol. XLI, No. 3, p. – 188.
19. Narayana. K.S(2006): "Biodiversity Conservation Should Be The Mantra of the Century". Kurukshetra, December,

Vol.55 No. 2 pp. 3-4.

20. Pandey, H.C. (1988): "Some Healing Herbs of the Monk's Amongst the Minor Forest Produce", Arun for News 6(I), p.1 – 10.
21. Rao, V.M. (2003: Tribal Women of Arunachal Pradesh, Mittal Publications, New Delhi, p. 21.
22. Sharma,T.C.(1976): "The Prehistoric Background of Shifting Cultivation" in Pakem,B, et.al: Shifting Cutivation in North-East India, NECSSR, Shillong.)
23. Wani, Milind and Kothari Ashish(2008): "Globalisation Vs. India's Forest", EPW, September13-19,Vol. XLIII, No.37.
24. The Arunachal Times, Vol.19 No. 154, November 11, 2007.
25. Forest and Forestry in Arunachal Pradesh, SFRI Information Bulletin No. 27, Director, State Forest Research Institute and Mission Director, State Bamboo Mission, Itanagar.
26. Website: www.sfri.org
27. Arunachal Front, March 21, 2009, Vol. 17, No. 201.
28. Sinha, G.N. (2008): Forest and Forestry in Arunachal Pradesh, SFRI Information Bulletin No.27, Issued by Director, State Forest Research Institute and Mission Director, State Bamboo Mission, Itanagar, Arunachal Pradesh.

19

Flora and Fauna: Economic Viability and Sustainability

Introduction

The use of herbs and drugs for treatment of ailments and injuries in the country dates back as early as 4500 B.C., mention of which is found in scriptures (Rig Veda). More than 2000 items are reportedly used for medicine out of which 200 are of minerals origin and the remaining is of vegetative nature. Forest wealth is one of the important natural aids to mankind which should be utilized judiciously. The forests in Arunachal Pradesh are primarily by large and there is vast wealth of plants, grasses, herbs, orchids and others of immense economic, commercial and medicinal values which may not be available in other parts of the country.

In recent years there has been great demand for plant-derived products in developed countries. These products are increasingly being sought out as medicinal products, nutraceuticals and cosmetics. The WHO estimated that about three quarters of the world's population currently use herbs and other forms of traditional medicines to treat their diseases. The European market for phyto-pharmaceuticals in 1995 was reported to be US $ 1,098 million and to US $ 1,375 million in the year 2001 (Fahishi, 1996). The market for botanical health-care remedies in the USA was reportedly US $ 3.24 billion in 1996 with some 60 million people using herbs to treat minor ailments such as allergies, burns, colds, depression, headache, insomnia, premenstrual syndrome and rashes (Johnston, 1997). Surveys carried out in the USA (Eisenberg *et al.,* 1993) and Australia (Maclennan *et. al.*, 1997) indicates that substantial numbers of people are using complementary health treatments including herbs and herbal products. However, inspite of the popularity of the herbal drugs, several questions have been raised in the recent years regarding their efficacy and safety. There is only limited information available in the literature concerning the interaction ofherbal and conventional medicines (Anderson *et al.,* 1985; D' Arcy, 1993). Herbal drugs have been found to report toxic effects as well as show interactions with food and other drugs. The first report of herb-drugs interaction published in 1970s stated that consumption of cruciferous vegetables resulted in lower plasma level of analgesic drug phenacetin. It was suggested that indoles, which are present in such vegetables enormously, could be responsible for interaction (Pantuck, 1996). In this study herb-drug interactions have been reviewed. The rationale for such interactions is often difficult to explain if knowledge regarding the phytochemical constituents of the herbal products understood. It is well established that patients taking herbal drugs along with prescription medicines can experience drug interactions, which may be detrimental to their health (Mehta, 1998).

Arunachal Pradesh is very rich in medicinal flora. In the absence of any sophisticated system of medicine, the indigenous village elders have been claiming the presence of numerous life saving herbs. Simultaneously there are numerous known herbs with deadly poisons which when processed become very potent curing medicines. Good agricultural and collection practices of Herbs can also be potential source of economic development and ecologically safer too to the state. It may also open up a new avenue in commercial cultivation for large production, processing and packaging, marketing and industrial application.

The important types of forests found in the state are Tropical Ever Green, Semi Green, Wet Ever Green, Wet Temperate, Deciduous Mixed Coniferous, Alpine, Bamboo brakes etc. The flora of this remote hill state has medicinal values which are utilized by indigenous people to cure their ailment without any side effects like modern medicines have.

Nature has been exceedingly kind and has endowed this beautiful State of Arunachal Pradesh with diverse forests and magnificent wildlife. The richness of life forms i.e. the flora and fauna that occur in these forests presents a panorama of biological diversity with over 5000 plants, about 85 terrestrial mammals, over 500 birds and a large number of butterflies, insects and reptiles. Such an unparalleled occurrence of life forms can be attributed to the peculiar location of the State which is at the junction of the Paleoarctic, Indo-Chinese, and Indo-Malayan bio-geographic regions. Biotic elements from these regions occur in this State making it very rich in floral and faunal resources. The State offers an ideal agro climate with vast potentials for growing varieties of orchids round the year. Out of about 1150 species of orchids known in India, about 500 species occur only in Arunachal Pradesh. These species occur in varying climatic and habitat conditions in varying concentration from the warm foot-hills to the cool temperate hills in Arunachal Pradesh. Such a diverse climatic situation has favoured the occurrence of the orchids in the State which is a highest number for any state in India thus making it an "Orchid Paradise" of our country. There are over 500 Herbs recorded from Arunachal Pradesh of which 250 are used in various Ayurvedic formulations. Vast climate variations in Arunachal Pradesh have resulted in existence of almost all types of Herbs and timber wealth ranging from tropical teak in foothills jungles to coniferous and alpine of high mountains. The state is very rich flora. It has about 4500 species of flowering plants, 400 species of pleridophytes, 23 species of coniferous, 35 species of bamboos, 20 species of canes, 25 Rhododendron species. Overall, Arunachal Pradesh is, as if, a natural garden of more than 20,000 identified species of medicinal plants and so many still remain unidentified. About 300 plant species out of native flora in North-Eastern India are used for edible purpose. Of these, over 25 provide tubers/rhizomes etc., which are eaten raw or boiled. Over 50 are consumed as green with their leaves/tender shoots cooked as vegetable; about 170 ripe fruits, which are pulpy and sweet/sub-sweet are eaten raw and many of these are used for pickles/vegetables when unripe; about 15 have edible seeds which are eaten raw or roasted.

Like flora, the deeply wooded terrains of Arunachal Pradesh are also rich in fauna. There are believed to be more than 100 species of mammals in its forests. These include four major cats (tiger, leopard, snow leopard and clouded leopard), three antelopes (serow, goral and takin) and the highly endangered hispid hare. The State is home to 8 out of 16 species of primates found in India. Bison or Gaur and Mithun are two important mammals found in the state. Additionally, at least six species of squirrels, mongoose, civet cat are some of the smaller mammals found in the wild. There are four types of deer: Sambar, hog deer, barking deer, and musk deer. Red panda, binturong, black bear, sun bear, sloth bear, wolf, wild boar, wild goat and wild pig, monkey, elephant are the other animal species found in the State. There are about 650 species of birds, including three species of hornbills and the endangered white winged duck and rare pheasants. In addition, there are 105 species of fishes, 42 species of amphibians, besides a large numbers of reptiles, butterflies and other terrestrial mammals.

The land and topography of the state is hilly beginning from foothills to snow-clad zones of alpine region. The elevation of the hills ranges from 150 metres to over 7,300 metres. Out of its 83,743 sq.km., topographically the plains and foothills cover about 10-15%, broad valleys and plateaus about 35%, steep slopes 35%, snow clad peaks and pastoral land 18–20%. The state represents beautiful scenery with irregular mountainous topography. Besides streams, rivers, mountains and peaks, its endless variations in scenic beauty are the first to great sunrise in the country. Rainfall varies from 1000mm. in higher reaches to 5750mm. in the foothill areas, spread over 8-9 months excepting the drier days in winter.

As per the state forest report-1999, published by the Forest Survey of India, forest cover of Arunachal Pradesh is 68951 sq. km. accounting for 82.21% of its total geographical area. The recorded forest area of the state is 51540 sq.kms., which is about 61.5% of its total geographical area. Thus, the State is fortunate to have such high percentage of its area under valuable forests cover against the national percentage of 20.50 in 2001.

Let us take a comparative picture of dense forest area of the State in Table 19.1. We find that in Arunachal Pradesh more area is covered by dense forest as compared to other-States.

We find that in Arunachal Pradesh, more area is covered by dense forest compared to other States. The State, which is the

Table 19.1: Forest classification: A comparative study of Arunachal Pradesh

Sl. No.	State and Category	1991-assessment	1993-assessment
1	**Arunachal Pradesh**	**100.0**	**100.0**
1.1	Dense forest	79.3	79.4
1.2	Open forest	20.7	20.6
2	**North-Eastern States**	**100.0**	**100.0**
2.1	Dense forest	53.5	53.7
2.2	Open forest	46.5	46.3
3	**Rest of India**	**100.0**	**100.0**
3.1	Dense forest	62.6	62.5
3.2	Open forest*	37.4	37.5
4	**All India**	**100.0**	**100.0**
4.1	Dense forest	60.2	60.2
4.2	Open forest*	39.8	39.8

* = including mangrove.

Source:- Govt. of India, "The State of Forest Report, 1993", Table 1.2, Table 1.4, and Table 1.5, pp. 9 – 11.

extension of Eastern Himalayas, is very rich in forest-wealth mainly due to non interference of the forest by mankind. Due to botanical richness, it has attracted many plant explorers in the past. From 1956, the Botanical Survey of India has been actively exploring different parts of the State.

The vegetation has an altitudinal distribution, following the varied nature of the hills and mountains forming the great Himalayan range. However, the stratification is not clearly discernible as the topography is irregular and disturbed by valleys and plateaus of various extents. Broadly, the following main vegetational types can be indicated as follows:-

(i) Tropical Semi-evergreen forests in the foot-hiil regions and adjacent to the Brahmaputra valley upto about 900 m (3000 feet).

(ii) Sub-tropical forests from 900 m to 1900 m (3000 – 6000 feet).

(iii) Humid sub-temperate forests from 1900 m – 3000 m (6000 – 9000 feet)

(iv) Temperate forests from 3000 m to 4000 m (9000 – 12,500 feet) and higher up alpine meadows merging to vegetation-less snow-clad peakes.

There is considerable overlap and mixing up of various species of the different broad zones mentioned below.

Perhaps due to this, Forest Department of Arunachal Pradesh relays more on for set-type mapping using Satellite Remote Sensing Technique and identified the forest. There are as follows:

(i) Hollong Forest,

(ii) Nahar Forest,

(iii) Semi-Evergreen Type – I,

(iv) Semi-Evergreen Type – II,

(v) Sub-Tropical Broad Leaved Forest,

(vi) Sub-Tropical Pine Forest,

(vii) Temperate Forest Type – I,

(viii) Temperate Forest Type – II,

(ix) Coniferous Forest,

(x) Alpine Shrubs/ Grass lands, and

(xi) Bamboo

The Diptero carpus macrocarpus (Hollong) is in pure form in the state specially in the districts of Tirap and Changlang upto altitude of 610 m. Mesua Ferrea (Nahar) is in pure form found in the eastern parts of the State adjacent to upper Assam. The Hollong Forest and Nahar Forest and upper Assam Valley Tropical Evergreen Forest respectively. Other species found in these forests are shorea assamica (Mekai), Altingia excelsa (Jutuli), Artocarpus chaplasha (cham), Amoora Wallichii (Amari), kayea assamica (Sia-Nahar), Terminalia Chebula (Hilika, Hartaki), etc.

The Semi-Evergreen Type–I conforms with Assam Alluvial plains Semi-Evergreen Forests where the important species grown are Amoora Wallichii (Amari), Pterospermum acerifolium (Hatipolia), Altingia excelsa (Jutuli), Bischofia Javanica (Urium), Gmelina arborea (Gomari), Toona ciliate (Jatipoma, Poma), Sterculia villosa (Udal), Terminolia chebula (Hilika, Hartaki), Artocerpus Chaplasha (Cham), Chukrasia tabularis (Bogipoma), Cinnamomum Cecicodaphme (Gon Sorai) etc.

The Semi-Evergreen Type–II forests conform to Sub-Himalayan light Alluvial Semi-Evergreen forest and East Himalayan Moist-Mixed Deciduous Forest. The main species found in this type of forest are phoebe goal parensis (Bonsum), Terminalia myrocarpa (Hallock), Amoora Wallichii (Amari), Artocarpus Chaplasha (Cham), Tetrameles mudiflora (Bhelu, Tula), Bomba ceiba (Dum bolu/ simul), Ailan thus grandis (Borpat) etc. This form is stretched from Bhairab kunda to Sonairupai river in East Kameng District.

The Sub-tropical Board leaved forests conform to East Himalaya Sub-Tropical wet Hill forest. This occurs in lower slope from about 1000 m to 2000 m. A few species of this forest are calophyllum polyanthum (Kurta), Castenopsis Indica

(Hingori), kydia calycina (Pichola) etc.

Sub-tropical pine forest occurs in between 1000 m to 1800 m and the species are Pinus roxburghii, Pinus wallichiana and Pinus armandi.

Temperate Forest type conforms to East Himalaya Wet Temperate Forest and East Himalaya Moist Temperate Forest occurs between 1750 to 2750 m. The species grown in this forest are Quercus lamellosa, Quercus sp., Castonopsis indica (Hingor), Acerhookari, Acer pectina trum, sympolcus spicata and Magnolia chambellii.

The Temperate Forest type-II conform with Naga Hills wet temperate Forest occurs along Myanmar border from 1800m upward. The species grown here are Magnalia species (sopa), Quercus sp., Michulia sp., prunus sp., Betula alnoides (Birch), Acer sp., Bucklandia populnae and Alunus nepalensis.

Coniferous forest resembles with East Himalayan Moist Temperate Forest occurs at an altitudinal zone of about 2300 m to 3000 m and the species grown are Abies sp., and Tsuga brunoniana.

Alpine shrubs/ grass lands includes shrubs/ grass land of sub-Alpine and Alpine areas occurs for about 4000 m to 5500 m altitude. Here only shrub species like Rhododendron sp., Primula sp., Savssura sp. and Saxifraga sp., occur.

And lastly the Bamboo species include Bambusa palida, Bambusa sp., Bambusa Tulda, Dendroncalemus hamilitonni (Kakua), Dendrocalamus hookeri etc.

Forest wealth is one of the important natural aids to mankind which should be utilized judiciously. The forests in Arunachal Pradesh are primary by large and there is vast wealth of plants, grasses, herbs, orchids and others of immense economic, commercial and medical values which may not be available in other parts of the country (Bhattacharjee, 2000).

A great diversity is associated with tropical and subtropical vegetation types. All the useful plant species ranging from medicinal herbs to timber plants are closely linked with the economic life of the people. Arunachal is endowed with about a third (5,000 seed plants) of the 15,000 seed plants found in India, thousands of non-flowering plants, and about 500 exotic orchids. The state is rich in faunal wealth, although it is difficult to get exact figures of animal diversity.

This paper basically attempts an in-depth study about the existence of flora and fauna in Arunachal Pradesh. This paper is divided into four sections. The first section concentrates itself about the investigation and survey done by certain botanists, naturalists, foresters and agricultural scientists in regard of existence of flora and fauna. The second section examines the economic viability of flora and fauna in the national and international market. The third section tries to investigate about the sustainability of flora and fauna due to environmental degradation caused by shifting cultivation, growth of urbanization, growth of population, growth of transportation and growth of industrialization in the State and the fourth section deals with suggestions and then conclusion follows.

Section – I

This section seeks to identify the existence of flora and fauna in Arunachal Pradesh. It is well known fact that more than 80 per cent of the world's medicinal flora is found in the Himalayan ranges of India. Arunachal Pradesh is such type of state which is lying within the Himalayan belt. Since the state has remained a generally inaccessible area with scarce means of communication and transport, very little written record is available about medicinal flora. Mostly the knowledge and information were passed from generation to generation by word of mouth and through folklores. However, under Monasteries of Monpa (Buddhist), there were monks who had expertise and who trained some selected persons in the area of identification, collection and processing, and use of various active parts of the herbs. It is a common knowledge that only certain plants and certain parts of plants like flower, leaf, bark, root are of medicinal use.

The department of agriculture of Arunachal Pradesh during seventies made a positive effort to collect and circulate information on plants of medicinal and economic importance. In pursuance of this, an integrated scheme was also submitted to North Eastern Council for gainful utilization of the medicinal herbs and drugs. Dr. Rajendra Gupta, All India Co-ordinator of Medicinal and Aromatic Plants, Pusa, New Delhi, showed active interest and made some valuable suggestions. Dr. A. S. Rao, Deputy Director, Botanical Survey of India, Shillong, had also undertaken studies of certain plants and orchids of medicinal importance.

In 1976 the upper reaches of Lohit district were explored and the Herbs were listed. The main interest in Dibang Valley came on account of this area being the natural habitat of the prised roots of *mishmi teeta* (coptis) which is a rich source of berberin. Dr. Bordoloi of Regional Research Laboratory (R.R.L.), Jorhat toured different districts of Arunachal Pradesh extensively. During 1976, a team headed by Dr. Jamuwal from RRL Srinagar visited West Kameng District in an expedition to explore the Herbs around Tawang. A valuable inventory of medicinal herbs and drugs was prepared by them in collaboration with the RRL, Jorhat and the Department of Agriculture of Arunachal Pradesh. During the course of their visit the expedition came across patches of lemon grass, growing naturally in hill slopes between Pamaghar and Lumla, beyond West Siang District. The grass has high lemon oil content and rich in vitamin 'A' which the knowledgeable Monpas claim to be a cure for malignant skin diseases including leprosy. Lemon grass oil is of considerable economic significance besides medicinal value.

RRL subsequently surveyed Wangchu area of Tirap district and conducted trials for cultivation of *mentha piperantha* and also undertook multiplication trail for the *solanúm khasyanum* (yellow berries) Manthan yellow berries are the source of solicigin-steroid used as oral contraceptive. This berry was successfully grown in Seneua Farm. There were further trails for diascoreas particularly D.Floribunda, D.Deltoiti etc. which also is a source for steroids. The department of agriculture screened large number of orchids, Herbs and other plants of economic significance. Ethno botanical study is an important part of modern plant science, which will get a unique dimension in India in the exploration process of the ethno botanical wealth of different regions among various ethnic groups. The local tribes of Arunachal Pradesh still prefer to rely on the traditional methods of health care. These people are very familiar with the herbal medicines that are abundantly available from the surroundings. Vast climate variations in the region have resulted in existence of almost all types of Herbs and timber wealth ranging from tropical teak in foothills jungles to coniferous and alpine of high mountains. The state is very rich flora. It has about 4500 species of flowering plants, 400 species of pleridophytes, 23 species of coniferous, 35 species of bamboos, 20 species of canes, 25 Rhododendron species. Overall, Arunachal Pradesh is, as if, a natural garden of more than 20,000 identified species of medicinal plants and so many still remain unidentified. About 300 plant species out of native flora in North-Eastern India are used for edible purpose. Of these, over 25 provide tubers/rhizomes etc., which are eaten raw or boiled. Over 50 are consumed as green with their leaves/tender shoots cooked as vegetable; about 170 ripe fruits, which are pulpy and sweet/sub-sweet are eaten raw and many of these are used for pickles/vegetables when unripe; about 15 have edible seeds which are eaten raw or roasted.

No doubt, Arunachal Pradesh offers an ideal agroclimate with vast potentials for growing varieties of orchids round the year. Out of about 1150 species of orchids known in India, about 500 species occur only in Arunachal Pradesh. These species occur in varying climatic and habitat conditions in varying concentration from the warm foot-hills to the cool temperate hills in Arunachal Pradesh. Such a diverse climatic situation has favoured the occurrence of these species of orchids in the state which is a highest number for any state in India thus making it an "Orchid Paradise" of our country. There are also over 500 Herbs recorded from Arunachal Pradesh of which 250 are used in various Ayurvedic formulations.

Aromatic Oil Yielding Plants

Java-Citronella

This grass grows luxuriantly all along the foothill area of the territory. It is cultivated by planting two to three slips in a hole three feet apart. The oil is extracted through a distillation plant by direct distillation method. The recovery of oil is between 0.8 to 1.0 percent from fresh leaves of citronella. The prices are not much less than the other aromatic oil.

Lemon grass

Lemon grass grows in deep clumps in high hills. Natural patches of these have been found in West Kameng in exploitable quantities. Effort is now being made to grow this grass under cultivated conditions for extraction of lemon oil. Lemon oil, besides being a base for perfumery, has been found to be very effective cure for persistent skin diseases and leprosy. Vitamin 'A' contained in lemon grass is said to have strong healing effects on skin and wounds.

Mentha Piperanta

Mentha oil is of medicinal importance and M/s Glaxo Laboratories have been organizing certain farms and extraction in certain States. For medicinal use menthol has considerable importance.

Musk Dana

There is a plant similar to Bhindi (Okra) plant of malvacceae family which produces musk scented seed known as musk dana. The oils of musk dana is used in high grade perfumery.

Oleoresin Yielding Plants

Ginger, turmeric and Chillies grow widely under varying conditions of soil and agro-climate within the territory. Because of communication and transport limitation these bulky crops hardly attract any significant status. Once oleoresin is extracted from any of these three crops it becomes a low volume high value product and is of great demand in pharmacological industry and for cosmetics. Oleoresin plants will serve as an incentive for extensive cultivation of these crops for economic betterment of the rural communities. Basar, Along, Mebo, Roing, Chowkham, Miao and Bordumsa are potential areas for initiating such extraction plants.

Berberin Yielding Plants

Coptis Teeta: (locally known as Mishmi Teeta):

This is a widely known herb growing just below the snow line as small herb, at altitude between 9,999 to 12,000 ft. altitude MSL. The cultivation of Mishmi Teeta in Dang Valley around Anini was successfully demonstrated during 1975-76. Presently it is being cultivated by a number of enthusiastic cultivators in Dibang Valley. Seeing the successful cultivation of Mishmi Teeta the Adis-Miniyong in Boleng circle of East Siang district have undertaken successful cultivation of coptis teeta locally known as 'Rinko' by the Adis. In Tuting Singa and Gelling Hills, coptis teeta grows naturally in the wild and is being utilized locally for medicinal purposes. It has considerable potential for providing a definite impact on the economy of the people of high hills and also to support a sizeable industry for extraction of berberin for medicinal purpose. Coptis teeta is considered as a vital drug by the village medicine men not only as debility tonic, cure for all kinds of stomach disorder, but also as an eye salve (surma). The use of coptis teetá (memeera) for eye salve is mainly known in J&K Hills of the Western Himalayas.

Tupistra Aurantiasa:

Dipo Tale (Rinte) scientifically known as Tupistra Aurantiasa is another medicinal herb which grows in similar surroundings as coptis teeta but is more hardy with wider adaptations from elevations between 8000 ft. to 12500 ft. altitude MSL. Its leaves are long, fleshy, smooth and provide luxuriant foliage to the plant with characteristic creeping rhizomes. The creeping rhyzome is long fleshy with long internodes, having active bitter berberine content. The village medicine men use small pieces of the rhyzome also as debility tonic and for curing various kinds of stomach disorders and ailments.

Apatani Ricoh

In the higher hills of Apatani plateau there is a climber, the stem of which is widely used as a cure against all stomach ailments and as debility tonic. The plant is known as Ricoh by the Apatanies. The dry stem is equally bitter as the Mishmi Teeta and has medicinal use. Among the Nishyis, the same plant is identified and named as Rik who also use it for medicine.

Aconites

Aconites are some of the oldest well known items of trade between the hill men of frontier tracts and the Ahom rulers of Brahmaputra valley. Aconites provide deadly arrow poison for defense by the local people. Aconites are strong base of Ayurvedic medicine for preparing vital life saving drugs. Presently aconites are widely used under Ayurvedic preparations.

The department of agriculture screened large number of orchids, medicinal plants and other plants of economic significance. Ethnobotanical study is an important part of modern plant science, which will get an unique dimension in India in the exploration process of the ethnobotanical wealth of different regions among various ethnic groups. The local tribes of Arunachal Pradesh still prefer to rely on the traditional methods of health care. These people are very familiar with the herbal medicines that are abundantly available from the surroundings. Vast climate variations in the region have resulted in existence of almost all types of medicinal plants and timber wealth ranging from tropical teak in foothills jungles to coniferous and alpine of high mountains. The state is very rich in fauna and flora. It has 20% of species of country's fauna and about 4500 species of flowering plants, 400 species of pleridophytes, 23 species of coniferous, 35 species of bamboos, 20 species of canes, 25 Rhododendron species. No doubt, Arunachal Pradesh offers an ideal agro climate with vast potentials for growing varieties of orchids round the year. Out of about 1150 species of orchids known in India, about 500 species occur only in Arunachal Pradesh. These species occur in varying climatic and habitat conditions in varying concentration from the warm foot-hills to the cool temperate hills in Arunachal Pradesh. Such a diverse climatic situation has favoured the occurrence of about 550 species of orchids in the state which is a highest number for any state in India thus making it an "Orchid Paradise" of our country. There are over 500 medicinal plants recorded from Arunachal Pradesh of which 250 are used in various Ayurvedic formulations. Some important medicinal plants with their application are listed in Table 19.4.

The vegetation of Arunachal Pradesh varies greatly alongwith the altitude of each separate region. It ranges from a wide belt of swampy rain forests at the foot hills and low lying areas, particularly in the eastern section to the tropical and sub-tropical upto an height of approximately 2,134 metres. The trees of the different species and sizes, cane and bamboo of different varieties, wild banana tree etc. are commonly found in the foot hill belt. Orchids of numerous varieties are also found abundantly for which an Orchid Research and Development Center at Tipi in West Kameng district has been setup by the forest department. The lower elevation area is remarkable for deciduous forest with patches of evergreen tropical vegetables. The Subtropical evergreen tropical vegetations are found at higher elevation too. In the dense forest the common trees are

Holloch, Bola, Semalu, Khoman and Makahi etc. A substantial amount of revenue is earned from these forest products. Wide varieties of medicinal plants are also available. The local inhabitants are well aware of these plants. Between 2134 and 2743 metres, we have the area of deciduous and mixed deciduous forests composed mainly of walnut, oak, Chestnut, pine, spruce and rhododendrons. Further up and continuing upto an altitude of 3,658 metre the wide stretch of area is generally claimed by conifers. Beyond 4,877 m and right upto the snowline, one enters the region of alpine meadow. The Table 19.2 lists the major plants found in the State.

Table 19.2: Floral diversity of Arunachal Pradesh

Sl. No.	Plant species	Number of species (approx.)
1	Rhododendrons	52
2	Hedychium species	18
3	Oaks	16
4	Gymnosperms	29
5	Bamboo	35
6	Canes	20
7	Orchids	500
8	Medicinal plants	500
9	Pteridophytes	452
10	Bryophytes	60
11	Lichens	80

Source: (i) Arunachal Pradesh State Biodiversity Strategy and Action Plan, State Forest Research Institute, 2002.

(ii) Statistical Report: 1999 – 2000, Department of Environment and Forest, Arunachal Pradesh.

Orchids form a dominant group of plants with their attractive and unique blooms. About 500 species of orchids occur in Arunachal Pradesh. These include about 140 species of terrestrial orchids with 15 saprophytes and about 340 epiphytes found in the different forest types. The prominent species are:

Cymbidium ensifolium, C. grandiflorum, Coelogyne corymbosa, Dendrobium aphyllum, D. fimbriatum var occulata, D. densiflorum, Calanthe masuca, Phaius flavus, Paphiopedilum fairieanum, P. venustum, P. wardii etc. (Information Bulletin No. 27, 2008).

Fauna

Like flora, the deeply wooded terrains of Arunachal Pradesh are also rich in fauna. Zoo-geographically, the fauna of Arunachal Pradesh can be categorized under Palaeartic Indo-Chinese and Indo-Malayan elements. With varying agro-climatic and altitudinal condition from tropical to alpine forests and well distributed precipitation with high humidity rising up to 90%, the area is conducive to the luxuriant growth of vegetation, which in turn determines the faunal communities. The richness in faunal diversity would be evident from the following facts:

The state is the home of more than 210 species of mammals out of which as many as 37 species are categorized under Schedule-I of the Indian Wildlife (Protection) Act, 1972.

- The large herbivores in the foothills and adjoining plans are the Elephant (Elephas maximus), Gaur (Bos gaurus), and Asiatic wild buffalo (Bubalus arnee).
- It is the only state which has tree goat antelopes, namely, Goral (Naemorhedus goral), Serow (Naemorhedus sumatraensis) and Takin (Budorcas taxicolor).
- Perhaps it is the only state that harbours four major cats namely, Tigers (Panthera tigris), Leopard (Panthera pardus), Clouded Leopard (Neofelis nebulosa) and Snow Leopard (Uncia uncoa) and many lesser cats namely Golden Cat (Catopuma temmincki), Fishing Cat (Prionailurus viverrinus), Leopard Cat (Prionailurus bengalensis), Marbled Cat (Pardofelis marmarata) and Jungle cat (Felis chaus).
- Seven primates namely Slow Loris (Nycticebus caucang), Hoolock Gibbon (Bunopithecus hoolock), Rhesus macaque (Macaca mulatta), Assamese Macaque (Macaca

assamensis), Pig-taile macaque (Macaca nemestrina), Stump-tailed macaque (Macaca arctoides), and Capped Langur (Trachypithecus pileatus) have been reported from the state. In addition, Arunachal Macaque (Macaca munjala), a species new to science, has been added to the checklist from the state.

- The State has more than 2000 elephants having common corridors with Assam, Bhutan and possibly Myanmar.
- Six species of deer namely Sambar (Cervus unicolor), Indian Muntjac (Muntiacus muntjak), Hog deer (Axis porcinus), Musk deer (Moschus chrysogaster), Black muntjac (Muntiacus crinifrons) and Leaf deer (Muntiacus putaoensis).
- The highly endangered Hispid Hare has also been reported from grassy areas like D. Ering Memorial WLS.
- Among the smaller mammals, as many as 12 species of Moles and Shrews, 71 species of Chiropterans, 53 species of rodents, 13 species of Mustelids, 7 species of Civets etc have been recorded from the state. Of this, the interesting species are Biswamoyopterus biswasi (Namdapha flying squirrel, a new to science from the state), Petaurista nobilis, Marmota bobac, Ratufa bicolor, Myotis longipes, Rhinolophus subbadius, Eonycteris spelaea, Nectogale elegens, Talpa leucura, etc.

The State has amazingly rich avifauna with over 760 bird species. Most of the species are resident and undergo altitudinal migration seasonally, though some winter migrants from the Palearctic region like waterfowls, waders, wagtails etc. are common in wetland areas. The state has the distinction of having rare and endangered species of birds reported no where else in India, such as Ward's trogon (Harpactes wardi), Spotted Longtailed Wren Babbler (Spelaeornis troglodytoides), Austen's babbler (Stachyris oglei) and Mishmi wren (Spelaeornis badeigularis) which occurs nowhere else in the world. It is the richest state of Pheasants with 10 species. Rare pheasants like Mishmi Blood Pheasant (lthagnis cruentus kuseris), Elwe's earred Pheasant (Crossoptilon crossoptilon harmani), Sclater's or Mishmi Monal Pheasant (Laphophorus sclateri), Temmick's Tragopan (Trogopan temmicki) and Tibetan Greybellied Tragopan (Trogopan blythii molesworthi) etc. are found. Many endangered species of birds like White Winged Wood Duck (Cairina scutulata), Black Necked Crane (Grus nigricollis), Bengal Florican (Haubaropsiss bengalensis), Swamp Partridge (Francollinus gullaris) etc. have been reported. Timilinae babblers (Pellorneum sp.), laughing thrushes (Garrulax sp.), Fulvetta, Yuhinas etc. are the family represented by largest number of bird species.

Other vertebrate and non-vertebrate faunal elements also occur in great numbers and forms. The state abounds 49 species of amphibian, 113 species of reptilian and 158 species of pisces and innumerable species of butterflies, moths, beetles and other insects. Some interesting species are Tabanus namdaphaicus, Tabanus shyamarupi, Tabanus tenuifrons (all are new to science from the state), Catapicephala splendens (new to India from the state), Bhagadatta austenia, Lamproptera curius, Delias aealis, Troides aeacus, Troides helena, Appias Iyncida hippoides, Salmostoma boopis, Danio horai, Barilius jayarami, Crossocheilus tirapensis, Aborichthys tikaderi, Noemcheilus arunachalensis, Rhacophorus namdaphaensis, Philautus namdaphaensis, Trimeresurus medoensis, Trimeresurus erythrurus, Calotes mystaceus, Japalura tricarinata, Scinella sikimmensis, Ophisops jerdoni, etc. (Information Bulletin No.27, 2008).

Section – II

This section tries to find out the economic viability of flora and fauna in the State. There is a fundamental and strong bond between the people and the environment; for centuries, the forests and the land have given them all that they need. Plants species, which are used as house building and household materials, are abundant in the tropical and subtropical zones. The cane species grow profusely in the phyto-geographical regions. The over exploitation of certain cane species has meant their disappearance in recent years. Thatch grasses and wild bananas which grow abundantly are often used for roofing.

A remarkable feature of the plant diversity in the state is the occurrence of innumerable wild orchid species. Floriculture is now being promoted in the state and individual entrepreneurs have been quite successful in generating income from floriculture.

Wildlife in the natural situation constitutes the most important component of the ecosystem, which participates affectively in the energy flow and bio-geo-chemical cycling. Animal – plant, plant – plant and animal – animal interactions are the basic milestone of the success of an ecosystem and its productivity. As such, the richness of the ecosystem means the capacity to hold high species diversity, but deforestation has threatened the fabric of the survival of wildlife and the ecosystem in the region.

The Mithun (Bos frontalis), the dearest animal of the people of Arunachal Pradesh, is reared in semi-wild condition. It is a rare bovine species. The highest population of Mithuns in Arunachal is 124,730 in 1998. The animal is an integral part of the socio-economic and cultural life of the people. The wealth of a person is often gauged by the number of Mithuns he possesses. The Mithun is regarded as a symbol of prestige and was traditionally used as a medium of exchange, a means to settle disputes and as the bride price. Mithuns determine social status and are essential part of community feasts. The owners leave the mithuns in the jungles to graze on natural fodder and they are occasionally given a dose of common salt. The mithuns browse over a considerable range in search of fodder and over two dozen species of trees, shrubs, tall grasses, and bamboos form their diet. To maintain these mithuns, the protection of the pristine forest is required, a task that is becoming increasingly difficult.

Majority of the rural poor of Arunachal Pradesh depend on the forest resources for at least four purposes such as food, livestock rearing (grazing and fodder), fuel wood and irrigation of crops. The floral and faunal diversities of the State and the dependence of Arunachal people on natural bio-resources for sustenance have resulted in a rich Indigenous Knowledge System (IKS). These systems have played a pivotal role in the conservation of the unique biodiversity over the centuries. It is imperative that the ethno-medicinal knowledge base of the ethnic groups in Arunachal is documented. Scientific exploitation of some of this rich biodiversity may hold the key to the development of the State. Both the State's biodiversity and its rich IKS are under threat due to the ineffective system of deforestation.

The economic viability of flora and fauna is to protect and preserve the rich wildlife through the creation of awareness among the people on the point of view of tourism. Different varieties of birds migrate from other regions during winter, which enrich the bird sanctuaries. The great Indian Hornbill has attained the status of state symbol. Its feather and beak form an important item of decoration of the traditional headgear of the tribes of the State. To preserve these wild birds and animals a number of sanctuaries and parks have been set up by the State Government. The scheme is implemented in two parts: (i) Protected area network management which includes management of National Parks and Sanctuaries and (ii) Management of Zoological Parks.

There are two National Parks and ten Wildlife Sanctuaries spread over 9528 Sq.Km of its geographical area. The list of National Parks and Wildlife Sanctuaries are given in the Table 19.3.

At present, the important attractions of tourists in the state are the above parks and wild life sanctuaries. On economic point of view, the state has to develop the nature based tourism industry as much as it wants to attract the national and international tourists.

The only one university, Rajiv Gandhi University in the State should establish a Herbal Science Department with following major areas of research as part of teaching and extension programmes.

Table 19.3: National parks and wildlife sanctuaries

Sl. No.	Name of National Parks	Area in sq.km.	Important Fauna	Year of Notification
1	2	3	4	5
A	NATIONAL PARKS AND TIGER PROJECTS			
1.	Namdapha National Park (Tiger Project)	Tiger, Hooloek Gibbon Musk Deer		May 1983
2.	Mouling National Parks	Serow, Black Bear, Takin		Dec. 1986
B	WILDLIFE SANCTUARIES			
1.	Pakui W/L Sanctuary	861.95	Elephant, Tiger, Bear, Sambhar Hornbill and Bison	March 1997
2.	Itanagar W/L Sanctuary	140.30	Elephant, Tiger, Bear	June 1978
3.	D. Ering W/L Sanctuary	190.00	Hog, Deer, Hare	Dec. 1980
4.	Mahao W/L Sanctuary	281.50	Red Panda, H.Gibbon, Takin	Dec. 1980
5.	Kamlang W/L Sanctuary	783.00	Capped, Langur, Bear, Deer	Oct. 1989
6.	Eagle Ness W/L Sanctuary	217.00	Elephant, Tiger, Red Panda	Oct. 1989

7.	Tele W/L Sanctuary	337.00	Clouded Leopard, Deer, Hornbill	July 1995
8.	Kame W/L Sanctuary	55.00	Elephant, Small Cats, Tiger	Sept. 1991
9.	Dibang W/L Sanctuary	4149.00	Trago pan, Kalis, Takin, Pheasan, Mask Deer	Nov. 1991
10.	Ydi-Rebe-Supse W/L Sanctuary	496.15	Capped, Langur, Clouded Leopard, Hornbill, Lesser cats	Feb. 1998

Source: PPCF, Itanagar.

(a) Development of natural products as drugs from living resources.

(b) Standardization of herbal drugs that are already developed.

(c) Validation of commercially available herbal drugs and formulation.

(d) Development of Agrotechnics for herbal plants.

(e) Development of human resources by commencing job oriented short term teaching and training programmes on herbal sciences.

The existing Research Institute (Ayurvedic), Itanagar should be well equipped with enthusiastic field experts who have considerable expertise in dealing with herbal research so as to be awarded national and international patents on herbal products.

Traditional Use

India has one of the richest and most diverse cultural heritages associated with the use of medicinal plants. It represents a striking example of intimate link between biological diversity and cultural diversity. India is one of the 17-mega diversity countries and is home to 7% of the world biodiversity. There are 16 agro climatic zones, 45,000 different plants species of which about 7000 to 8000 species are used in various traditional and folk systems of medicine. The richness of Indian civilization with its glorious past has given the humanity vast knowledge about the usage of plants for food and health care. The strong tradition of health care practised and documented for more than 3000 years in the form of Ayurveda, Unani, Siddha and Yoga & Naturopathy systems of medicine have evolved through centuries of usage and have stood the test of times in providing holistic healthcare to the people and are based on a very intimate and well researched understanding that biotic and non-biotic components of the environment play in promoting holistic health care.

Ayurveda is an ancient philosophy based on a deep understanding of eternal truths about the human body, mind and spirit. It is the science of living, developed meticulously by the devout 'Rishis' of ancient India. This is the study based on the fundamental principles of 'Panchabhootha' (Earth, Water, Air, Fire, and Space) existing in nature and inside man. Ayurveda teaches that the body and the mind are one entity with gross and subtle manifestations. The term 'Ayurveda' is composed of two Sanskrit terms. 'Ayu' means life and 'Veda' means knowledge. Thus, Ayurveda is the knowledge of life or science of life. It is defined as the science, through which one can obtain knowledge about the useful and harmful ways of life, conditions that lead to the above types of life, as well as, the very nature of life.

There is growing interest in the world about the use of these systems and increasingly the developed world is prepared to adopt Indian systems. Today, Yoga has become popular the world over. It is now globally recognized that traditional, alternative complementary systems of medicine provide healthcare to almost 80% of the population in developing and less developed countries. Even in the developed world, there is a growing realization that the modern system of medicine alone is not able to address all the health problems, particularly related to the life style diseases like diabetes, hypertension, AIDS, cancer, etc. It is in this context that scientific wisdom contained in the traditional healthcare system can be used to find solutions to the present day problems. India is fortunate to have inherited rich bio-diversity, both in plants and animals and the ethno-botanical knowledge which need to be explored and researched to find solutions to the health problems. It is this philosophy that the Government of India is very actively promoting for development and promotion of the traditional systems of medicines like Ayurveda, Unani and Siddha. One of the important initiatives in this direction has been to mainstream AYUSH systems of medicine in the healthcare under the National Rural Health Mission (NRHM).

Standardization

A major challenge facing the traditional systems of medicine world over today, however, is the question of standardization, quality and safety. Although traditional systems of medicine have their own science behind them, in order to improve the outreach of these systems, serious attention is being paid to validate the traditional knowledge and bring that in conformity with the modern scientific paradigm. Efforts are being made to strengthen quality control and standardization by evolving pharmacopoeial standards and setting up State Drug Testing Laboratories. Indian Government has also made compliance of Good Manufacturing Practices (GMP) mandatory for Ayurveda, Siddha and Unani drug manufacturing units. Not only this, the GMP norms are being made more and more stringent to ensure compliance with the evolving world standards on GMP. In order to ensure quality of such AYUSH products which use minerals in their preparation, testing for heavy metals has been made mandatory for export purposes with effect from 1st January, 2006 (Kurukshetra, July, 2007, p.27).

If herbal production in the state is known to the rest of the country, it can create an exhaustive job of collecting and collating in all researches and extension studies. It will create a new avenue in the job markets. Different types of medicinal plants grow in different climatic zones. The State may be divided into three zones on the basis of its different climatic conditions: tropical and subtropical zone and temperate and alpine zone. Some important medicinal plants with their botanical and trade names and local uses as medicine for the purposes are shown in Table 19.4.

Table 19.4: Tropical and Subtropical Zone

Habit	Botanical name	Trade name	Purpose
Herb	*Amomum subulatum*	Sthul Ela	Digestion, tonic
	Andrographis paniculata	Kalmegha	Liver disorder
	Asparagus racemosus	Shatavari	Tonic
	Curcuma cassia	Kali Haldi	Joint pain/ sprain
	Curcuma Longa	Haridra	Cough/ pain
	Mimosa pudicaa	Lajjalu	
	Rauvolfia serpentina	Sarpagandha	Hyper tension
	Solanum Khasianum*	Kantakari	Swas cough
	Solanum nigrum	Kakamachi	Digestion
	Zingiber officinale	Ardraka	Cough, arthritis
Climber	Cissampelos pareira	Ambastha/ Patha	Liver tonic

	Tinospora cordifolia	Guduchi	Tonic
Shrub	Abroma augusta	Pishach Karpasa	Gynaecological disorder
	Caesalpinia crista	Lata Karanj	Malaria
	Cassia alata	Dadmardan	Skin disorder
	Euphorbia royleana	Snuhi	Piles; fistula
	Jatroha curcus	Ratnajot	Tonic
	Justicea adhatoda	Vasaka	Cough, swas, pain
	J. gendrussa	Kala Vasak	Cough, swas, pain
	Rauvolfia tetraphylla	Sarpagandha	Hyper tension
	Solanum torvum	Brahati	Cough, swas
	Woodfordia fruticosa	Dhataki	Dysentery, tonic
Scandant Shrubs	Cissampelos pareira	Patha	Tonic
	Embelia ribes *	Via bidang	Worm infestation, liver disorder
Tree	Tinospora cordifolia	Guduchi	Tonic
	Aquilaria agallocha *	Agaru	Aphrodisiac, eye, ear
	Bauhinia purpurea	Kovidar	Throat disorder
	B. Variegata	Kanchanar	Throat disorder
	Bombax ceiba	Semul	Aphrodisiac tonic

	Cassia fistula	Aragvadha	Laxative, purgative, tonic
	Cinnamomum tamala*	Tejpatra	Cough, tonic
	Cinnamomum zeylanica*	Tvak	Cough, tonic
	Gmelina arborea	Gambhari	Cardiac, nervine tonic
	Gynocardia odorata	Chaulmoogra	Skin diseases
	Oroxylum indicum*	Shyonaka	Tonic
	Salmilia malabarica	Salmili	Aphrodisiac tonic
	Saraca asoca	Ashoka	Uterine tonic
	Terminalia arjuna	Arjuna	Cardiac tonic
	T. belerica	Bahera	Digestive tonic
	T. chebula	Haritaki	Purgative
	Zizyphus jujubo	Badara	Digestive, diabetes

Temperate and Alpine Zone

Habit	Botanical name	Trade name	Purpose
	Aconitum heterophyllum*	Visha	Tonic
	Coptis teeta*	Maira	Liver disorder
Herb	Picrorhiza kurroa*	Katuki	Liver tonic
	Swertia chirayita*	Chiraita	Liver disorder
	S.Ciliata*	Chiraita	Liver disorder

	Valeriana hardwickii*	Tagar	Cardiac, hepatic and nervine tonic
	Thalictrum foliolosum	Mamiri	Liver tonic
Shrub	Berberis aristata	Daru Haridra	Liver tonic
	Zanthoxylum alatum	Tumbru	Digestive tonic
	Embelia ribes*	Vai bidang	Worm, liver
Climber	Rubia cordifolia*	Manjishtha	Blood purifier
	Tinospora cordifolia	Guduchi	Tonic
Tree	Taxus baccata*	Talisa	Swas, tonic

Source : Regional Research Institute (Ayurveda), Itanagar, Arunachal Pradesh.

Note : *indicates that these medicinal plants are largely available in Arunachal Pradesh.

Reasons for traditional using of medicinal plants

1. **Lack of Globalization:** Needless to say, India is moving into a new century and a new millennium. In this context, a State like Arunachal Pradesh with continental dimensions should not ignore the changes that are occurring in the rest of the country due to impact of globalization. India initiated the process of globalization and liberalization since 1991. Over the past decade globalization and liberalization in India has been discussed mainly in terms of foreign investment, industrial development, information technology and the tremendous growth of service sector, etc. and there has been substantial media coverage of all these aspects of the Indian economy. The advent of globalization brings with it a marked change in our outlook as far as management of national economy is concerned. Under economic globalization, country after country has

opened up their economies to free flow of finance capital, technology and goods. The death of distance, the service revolution and the mobility of capital are the three pillars of globalization which are present tremendous opportunities for India. **But the good fruits of globalization have not entered the state.**

2. **Lack of Transportation:** After the independence of the country, the Government of India undertook the development of transport and communication with a view to open up this remote state of India and therefore to facilitate the rapid development of the state. The State is the poorest in having roads connecting the urban and semi urban areas. The people living in the remote villages, which lie in hilly and difficult terrain, finds very difficult to bring their patients to health centre for treatment. That is why; many times they depend upon the village Priest and *Vaidya* (Ayurvedician) who are mostly illiterate.

3. **Lack of Medical Facility:** The health care institutions have been shaped in conformity with National pattern. The old health units and dispensaries have been restructured into Primary Health Centres and Health Sub-Centres to ensure comprehensive coverage of preventive as well as curative care. At present (2003–2004), there are 3 General Hospitals, 12 District Hospitals, 31 Community Health Centres,78 Primary Health Centres, 386 Sub-Health Centres, 3 Health units, 17 Dispensaries, 37 Homeo Dispensaries, 3 Ayurvedic Dispensaries and 2 T.B. Hospitals and others functioning in the state (*Directorate of Economics and Statistics, Govt. of Arunachal Pradesh, 2004*). Their total number during 2003-2004 is 581 covering the entire geographical area of the state i.e., 83,743 sq.km. The geographical area per health centre is 144.13 sq.km. The total number of doctors including all registered is 527 during 2003-2004. If we consider the population as per 2001 Census, we get the population per doctor is 2083. Again the doctors are living mostly in urban and semi urban areas. The local doctor posted in health centre located in village areas are hardly living in government allotted quarter. As a result, the village people finding no way depend on locally available herbal medicine.

4. **Believe:** Most of the village people have good faith in village Priest and *Vaidya* (Ayurvedician). Many a times the priest is successful in healing and the *Vaidya* (Ayurvedician) in curing diseases.
5. **Age-old Custom:** There are many age-old customary practices which compel the people, especially village people to use medicinal plants in their suffering. Their ecological adaptation and understanding many a times have proved result oriented. There are many examples in context of this fact. The people of the state are conservative in mind. They want to maintain the age-old custom.

Now-a-days, Herb-drug interactions are a hot topic of debate and herbs are potentially dangerous to patients who are already taking prescription medications. The basic concept of interaction is that consumption of two substances (herbs, drugs) at the same time or within a short interval of each other, will result in physiological effect that are different from a simple summation of the effects (Barbara, 2000)

Section – III

This section tries to bring into notice of authority and policy maker about the sustainability of flora and fauna in the State. In recent years, the State's rich biodiversity has increasingly come under threat. The hastening paces of developmental activities in the last three decades, and the improvement in the communication network, have meant increased access. Road building has established communication but the blasting process involved has meant the loss of valuable habitat. The rapid monetization of the barter economies has meant increased trade in timber. A number of hydropower projects have been commissioned, and these projects are at various stages of progress. The urbanization process has meant the destruction of the forest cover adjacent to the new townships that have come up. Another significant threat to the fragile ecosystem and biodiversity of the State is the shifting cultivation and the shortening of the jhum cycle and introduction of commercial plantation.

Timber extraction in the State was taken up on a large scale till 1995-96. Hence, a large number of wood based industries cropped up. A timber trade in the state had also increased through the operation of tree permits. There was halt on this trade after a Supreme Court Judgement on 12th December, 1996 on a writ petition (civil) No. 202 filed by Shri T.N. Godavarman Thirumulkpad.

In addition, there is the illegal trade of forest projects such as timber, medicinal plants, orchids, animal hide, musk gland and birds, which are smuggled out of the State by poachers. Bio-piracy is a new challenge manifested in a number of ways. Sometimes, the operators enter the State, develop contracts, and smuggle out valuable species, mainly of flora, without the knowledge of the government. Given their highly sophisticated methods of operation, this type of biopiracy is very difficult to detect. The creation of public consciousness, apart from the enhanced vigilance of the government, can help to control this problem.

Impact of Shifting Cultivation

The extent of deforestation of tropical forest has caused world wide alarm as tropical forests provide more than 50% of modern medicine. Tropical forests are living museums and laboratories that have yielded only a tiny fraction of their treasures to scientific study. In course of shifting cultivation remarkable varieties of flora and fauna are disappearing, which need immediate attention for extensive and intensive studies.

The type of vegetations destroyed depends upon the length of jhum cycle. A dense forest of long cycle has more tree species than grasses, whereas a forest of short cycle has more number of grasses. All the forest resources are disappearing and become rare due to deforestation and illegal felling of trees. The ecological balance favouring the complete hydrological cycle has been seriously upset over vast areas due to ignorance or lack of appreciation of methods of conserving and managing natural vegetation (whether a forest, grass land or mixed type) and of clearing the vegetation for cultivation. This misuse and destruction of plants cover combined with great increase in human and livestock population has created intense competition for natural resources. In the continued absence of conservation and correctly integrated land use system, overall habitat deterioration has become very widespread.

Impact of Urbanizations

Till 1961 census the State of Arunachal Pradesh was entirely rural having no urban centre. There were 17 urban centres in the State as per 2001 census. All these towns are administrative centres in most cases. Before the establishment of administrative centres, these places were full of forest. According to 1991 census 12.80% people live in ten urban areas while as per 2001 census 20.41 people live in seventeen urban areas. The decennial urban growth rate in the state has been recorded as 139.63 in 1971-81, 167.04 in 1981-91 and 101.24 in 1991-2001.

Impact of Population Growth

The human population census was conducted for the first time in Arunachal Pradesh in 1961. Population increases in 2001 by 326.23 per cent in comparison to the population of 1961. More population means more shelter, more food, etc. which directly accelerate the deforestation. The decennial population growth rate since 1961 in the State has been recorded as 38.91% in 1961-71, 35.15% in 1971-81, 36.83% in 1981-91 and 26.21% in 1991-2001. It is more than all India average.

Impact of Transportation

Till 1947, there were only three jeepable roads between Pasighat and Kobo by 35 Kilometers, Sadiya-Tezu-Denzing by 77 Kilometres and still well road 56 kilometers (Source: N.C.A.E.R – Techno-Economic Survey of NEFA, 1967, P.91). So, the total length of roads was only 168 Km, till 1947. Before independence the colonial government did not take any effort to initiate the development process and the British indifference towards the area was mainly due to the fact that the area did not possess any readily exploitable resources. After the independence of the country, the Government of India undertook the development of transport and communication with a view to open up this remote state of India and therefore to facilitate the rapid development of the state.

In the development plans, the government has been attaching high priority to the construction of roads and as a result the total length of roads constructed in the state stood at about 15021.80 kms. including 399.80 Kms. under National Highway giving the road density of 17.9 kms. per 100 Sq.Kms. of area at the end of March, 2004. The impact of road transport is wide ranging which includes agriculture, industry, trade and commerce which cumulatively affect overall development of a region. But at the same time the State has to face deforestation and thereby to destroy the herbs.

Impact of Industrializations

Arunachal Pradesh, though endowed with abundant natural resources is still lagging behind in industrial development as compared to other States of the country. Lack of transport and communication, dearth of skilled/technical personnel, poor literacy among local people, and low capital formation for setting up industries in this hilly region are some of the major factors for industrial backwardness. At present the main thrust of the Industry Department is to promote traditional village and small scale industries and there by provide employment opportunities and improve the economic conditions of the people of the State.

Due to the shifting cultivation, growth of urbanization, growth of population, growth of transportation, growth of industrialization and overall development programmes, the hitherto virgin vegetation has become a victim of sudden large-scale changes upsetting the balance of nature.

Medicinal plants under threat in the state: At conference in

Guwahati, experts from the State Forest Research Institute, Itanagar, Botanical Survey of India and the G.B. Pant Institute of Himalayan Environment and Development, Itanagar made an assessment of 47 plant species lying under threat. Out of the 47, five are threatened at the global level and are red listed by the International Union for conservation of Nature (IUCN). These endemic species include Amentotaxus assamica, Coptis teeta, Gymnocladus assamicus, Piper pedicellatum, P.Peepuloides, Aquilaria malaecensis, Dienia muscifera, Rauvolfia serpentina and Smilax glabra are reported to be critically endangered.

Steps taken by the Government

Orchid research cum development centre

Realizing the importance of orchids which are found in abundance in the State, an Orchid Research cum Development Centre has been set up at Tipi in the yea r 1972. Over the last 20 years, the Centre has made considerable progress in conservation, research and development by establishing a good germ-plasm collection of 400 species housed in the Orchidaria at Tipi, Dirang, Roing, Jengging and Itanagar. An Orchid Sanctuary covering an area of 100 sq. km for in situ conservation of 160 species naturally occurring in Sessa area of West Kameng District has been established (Information Bulletin No.27, 2008).

Arunachal pradesh state medicinal plants board

On the directions of the Ministry of Health & Family Welfare in the Department of ISM & H, Govt. of India, a State level Medicinal Plants Board has been constituted under the Department of Health & Family Welfare, Govt. of Arunachal Pradesh vide Govt. notification No. HOMOEO-98/3 dated Itanagar, the 5th February, 2002. Initially the Board was constituted on 7th Nov, 2001 but it started functioning since 5th February, 2002. Now the Board has been fully shifted to the Department of Environment and Forests in July 2007. The Board has a full time chairman and Principal Secretary

(Environment & Forests) acts as Vice-Chairman. Director, State Forest Research Institute, functions as its Member Secretary and Chief Executive Officer. The Board is required to be further strengthened. The Board has following functions:

- Coordination with Departments/ Govt. Organizations for development of medicinal plants.
- Assessment of demand/ supply position relating to medicinal plants both within the state and outside.
- Advice concerned Departments/ Organizations on policy matter relating to schemes and programmes for development of medicinal plants.
- Provide guidance in the formulation of proposals, schemes, programmes etc. to be taken up by agencies.
- Survey, identification, inventorisation and quantification of medicinal plants.
- Promotion of ex-situ/ in-situ cultivation and conservation of medicinal plants.
- Promotion of co-operative efforts among collectors and growers and assisting them to store, transport to market their produce effectively.
- Setting up of data base system for inventorisation, dissemination of information and facilitate the prevention of patents being obtained for medicinal use of plants which is in the public domain.
- Matters relating to import/export of raw materials, as well as value added products either medicine, food supplements or as herbal cosmetics including adoption for quality and reliability in the state of Arunachal Pradesh and outside.

Arunachal Pradesh State Medicinal Plants Board

On the directions of the Ministry of Health & Family Welfare in the Department of ISM & H, Govt. of India, a State level Medicinal Plants Board has been constituted under the Department of Health & Family Welfare, Govt. of Arunachal Pradesh vide Govt. notification No. HOMOEO-98/3 dated

Itanagar, the 5th February, 2002. Initially the Board was constituted on 7th Nov, 2001 but it started functioning since 5th February, 2002. Now the Board has been fully shifted to the Department of Environment and Forests in July 2007. The Board has a full time chairman and Principal Secretary (Environment & Forests) acts as Vice-Chairman. Director, State Forest Research Institute, functions as its Member Secretary and Chief Executive Officer. The Board is required to be further strengthened. The Board has following functions:

- Coordination with Departments/ Govt. Organizations for development of medicinal plants.
- Assessment of demand/ supply position relating to medicinal plants both within the state and outside.
- Advice concerned Departments/ Organizations on policy matter relating to schemes and programmes for development of medicinal plants.
- Provide guidance in the formulation of proposals, schemes, programmes etc. to be taken up by agencies.
- Survey, identification, inventorisation and quantification of medicinal plants.
- Promotion of ex-situ/ in-situ cultivation and conservation of medicinal plants.
- Promotion of co-operative efforts among collectors and growers and assisting them to store, transport to market their produce effectively.
- Setting up of data base system for inventorisation, dissemination of information and facilitate the prevention of patents being obtained for medicinal use of plants which is in the public domain.

Matters relating to import/export of raw materials, as well as value added products either medicine, food supplements or as herbal cosmetics including adoption for quality and reliability in the state of Arunachal Pradesh and outside (Information Bulletin No.27, 2008).

- Wildlife Conservation: Wildlife in Arunachal Pradesh is

not confined to Protected Areas alone. Vast, remote and inaccessible high altitude tracts as well as reserve forests and other areas in the foothills are equally important wildlife habitat. Besides bringing more and more rich and representative wildlife areas under the protected area network, wildlife management has to take into account conservation of biological diversity outside national parks and wildlife sanctuaries. The damage to wildlife in recent years is attributable to habitat degradation, encroachment, fragmentation and poaching.

Hunting has been a part of local tribal culture. Till recent past when the area was virgin and hunting was for self sustenance, the pressure felt on wildlife was not significant. The Wildlife Act of 1972 is applicable throughout the State and wild animals get legal protection outside protected areas also. Of late, it has been realized that wildlife conservation can not succeed without involvement and support of the local people. To seek cooperation from the people living in the vicinity of protected areas, specially designed eco developmental schemes are being contemplated. These schemes aim at development of the areas in the immediate surroundings of national parks and wildlife sanctuaries so that the biotic pressures on protected areas can be minimized.

Namdhapa National Park and Pakhui Wildlife Sanctuary also implement the Central Scheme on Project Tiger. Project Elephant launched by the Central Government in 1991 covers many protected areas, reserve forests and the migratory corridors. The project seeks to stabilize dwindling elephant populations by habitat improvement, corridor linking and control of poaching. Provisions for protection of life and property and compensation for loss of life have been incorporated in the project. The emphasis is on involvement and cooperation of the local people. This Elephant Reserve will be spread in East Kameng and Papumpare Districts covering an area of 1892 Sq. km. This Elephant Reserve harbours Elephant, Tiger, Leopard, Clouded Leopard, Snow Leopard, Red panda etc. A total of 377 Elephants were counted during 2001 Elephant Census.

To impart education, promote awareness and also to keep captive stock of indigenous fauna, the State Zoo at ltanagar and Mini Zoo at Roing and Miao are being developed. At Miao captive breeding of White Winged Wood Duck has been undertaken. The State Zoo at ltanagar houses rare animals like slow loris, binturong, stumptailed macaque etc. It is a captive breeding centre for tiger, barking deer, sambhar etc. Large enclosures and natural way of keeping the animals are noteworthy features of this zoo. The State Wildlife Advisory Board under Chief Minister is also functional in the State. This Board has many senior officials as members SFRI (Information Bulletin No.27, 2008).

Section-IV

In order to harness the vast and varied natural resource endowments of Arunachal Pradesh, the following steps may be suggested. The conservation and sustainable utilization of medicinal plants/ herbs and the conservation of wild lives through community participation can deserves attention. A sustainable management plan for this sector is essential. The plan must analyse the status of medicinal plants/ herbs in the State and identify the threats and opportunities, barriers to markets and investments, recognize indigenous knowledge and practices and help to preserve sacred groves, with the effective use of biotechnology. There is nothing beyond nature, behind nature and other than nature. The key to man's health lies largely in the environment. The purpose of environmental health is to create and maintain ecological conditions that will promote health and thus prevent diseases. The biological and physical environment mostly depends on forest, which needs its preservation and protection. In order to maintain and improve the human quality of life, the renewable natural resources should be conserved. In this regards the following suggestion may be considered.

1. The renewable natural resources are soil, water, air, plants and animals. These are functionally connected to each other and have the capacity to increase under suitable

conditions. Women have a definite role to play in building a free, healthy, prosperous and moral society, because they are much closer to the nature due to their motherhood complex. So, women should be given proper training regarding the conservation of nature based resources.

2. "Nature can meet all the needs of men, not the greed", Mahatma Gandhi said, "Real education is possible only in the lap of the nature", said Rousseau. The greedy nature of the man disturbs the whole environment. There is a dire need to inculcate the feeling of environmental protection among all sections of the people. Environment is our heritage. Hence, it is the – you and I who can save our environment. So, we should adopt environment conscious life.
3. In order to improve the quality of life of the present and future generations we have to establish a system in which resources and human needs are matched and none is being destroyed.
4. For the management of renewable natural resources we should try to establish the best balance between human needs and the resources to satisfy them.
5. Programmes should be developed to raise consumer awareness and promote their active participation to achieve changes in consumption and production patterns.
6. Unauthorized cutting of trees should be strictly restricted.
7. Government should promote the use of solar energy for fuel, light and other purposes.
8. We should recreate the desolated areas by planting more fruit bearing and quality type of trees.
9. Seminar for conservation of animals and plants should be organized in almost very village to grow consciousness among the villagers. The illiterate and innocent hunter should be given allowances and imparted the good effects of conservation of biodiversity. To give punishment the hunter, the informer may be awarded secretly and community hunting is strictly prohibited.
10. A quick survey should be undertaken through a team of

young and enthusiastic field experts borrowed from different organizations dealing with indigenous medicinal herbs and drugs to assess the nature and extent of availability of economic plants and above all to extraction herbs of economic value from the forest should be encouraged.

11. This should be followed by detailed survey for identification, classification and codification of economic medicinal herbs.
12. Considering the market demand both inside the country and the export market, projects should be drawn to cultivate herbs of medicinal value for their desired active ingredients.
13. Bankable projects should be drawn for cultivation and processing of known medicinal herbs.
14. Promotional programmes on the aspect of research and development should be undertaken of selected herbs of known use but unknown economic exploitation for their gainful utilization.
15. The authority should undertake the possibilities for establishment of pharmacological perfumery and other specialized industries.
16. The floral assemblage in the State can cause immediate concern to any investigator. The effects of growth of urbanization, population, transportation, industrialization and overall shifting cultivation on biological resources will have to be assessed on data base and do accordingly for the preservation of natural resources.
17. The only one university, Rajiv Gandhi University in the State should establish a Herbal Science Department with following major areas of research as part of teaching and extension programmes.
    (a) Development of natural products as drugs from living resources.
    (b) Standardization of herbal drugs that are already developed.
    (c) Validation of commercially available herbal drugs and formulation.

(d) Development of Agrotechnics for herbal plants.

(e) Development of human resources by commencing job oriented short term teaching and training programmes on herbal sciences.

18. The existing Research Institute (Ayurvedic), Itanagar should be well equipped with enthusiastic field experts who have considerable expertise in dealing with herbal research so as to be awarded national and international patents on herbal products.

19. Government (Central/State) should sell cooking gas (LPG) at subsidized rate so that the people can use fire wood as least as possible.

20. The women especially village women should be given training how to be preserve bio-diversity in the State, because, in most cases, the women in the State are collecting the fire wood from the forest. Deforestation for domestic fuel supply adds to the environmental crises.

21. Much of the forest wealth of the state is undocumented. A comprehensive Biodiversity Action Plan, beginning with an exhaustive listing of the important plant and animal species of economic value, as well as endangered and rare species, should be the first step towards the conservation and sustainable use of this priceless heritage.

22. For conserving and managing natural vegetation the jhum cultivation and illegal felling of trees, which are the root cause of deforestation, must be stopped immediately but not without rehabilitation of the jhumias. If the government is successful to protect the natural vegetation, the state will be the richest in having the Herbs which can be sold in national and international markets. Hence, it is necessary first to develop the market for Herbs within the state where the local cultivators will be benefited economically. It will give an incentive to the local people to protect the valuable Herbs from extinction.

23. For the betterment of lives, urbanization, transportation, industrialization are necessary but we can try to minimize the deforestation due to shifting cultivation and illegal failing of trees which are the main cause of disappearance

of flora and fauna in Arunachal Pradesh. The Central Government as well as the State Government should give top priority to protect the herbs of economic value in the State which are endowed more than 50% of herbs of the country. Days are not far when the Governments can generate employment as well as earn foreign currency from the export of the State's flora and fauna if they take kin interest to protect them from disappearance due to impact of the factors mentioned under Section-III.

Conclusion

Roy Barman Committee's Report (1982) on Forests clearly stated that banning the practice is not likely to achieve the object in view and it might even provoke reaction. CSE (1985) reports that a number of features have led to the failure of schemes to settle shifting cultivators; low productivity, absence of tools and implements, failure to understand water management in settled cultivation, short term government policies and above all change of socio-cultural ethos, have been listed as probable factors. Question arises if a change is brought looking at the entire terrain conditions of the region, will it be acceptable to the local people and fit into their pattern of life. In this regard it may be suggested that some scientific measures should be taken to put an end to the erosion of top soil and studies should be carried out to explore the possibility of introducing modern innovations on jhum land so as to obtain higher yield per unit area. Besides, replacements of crop cultivation by other types of alternative livelihood like plantations, economic and conservational forestry, horticulture, development of animal husbandry i.e., livestock rearing like poultry farming, sericulture, bee keeping and so on may also be encouraged. The problems arising out of jhuming in Arunachal Pradesh can be solved keeping in view the many facts of shifting cultivation, the socio-cultural life of the people, the feasibility of change over the expenditure involved and the maintenance of a changed pattern. Effects should be so made as to bring the change from within the society. The cultivators should be imparted proper training and education to adopt new innovations. They must also be educated about the danger of jhuming.

Our specific focus with regard to social concerns is community rights to resources – a concern that is central to many of the debates on natural resource management. Three arguments are put forth: (i) that while the environment has at one level assumed a non-negotiable presence in policy, social concerns are only highlighted to the extent that they are deemed not to be environmentally destructive, (ii) that the discursive are deemed harmful is overly simplistic and in need of re-examination and (iii) that the changing nature of environmental discourse can only be understood within the wider shifts in development policy. Although there are many who could claim that the environment itself receives an inadequate attention in development policy, a contention that is at least partly true, we are concerned here with new emerging policies and legislations tackle social concerns given the socially constructed nature of the environment.

The recent debates and developments with regard to the draft of National Environment policy (NEP), 2004 and the scheduled Tribes (Recognition of Forest Rights) Bill (STB), 2005 are illustrative in different ways of the manner in which social concerns are dealt with in environmental policy and legislation in India. Yet, while the pros and cons of specific policies and legislations have been Central to the academic debates on the environment, very little attempt has been made to trace the changes in environmental policy making and the way of social concerns have been still problematized.

Notes and References

1. Agarwala, Padma Guha (2006), "Role of North-Eastern Women in Conservation and Protection of Environment", University News, Vol.44, No. 37.
2. Anderson, L.A. and J. D. Phillipson (1985): Herbal medicine, education and the pharmacist, Pharm. J. 236: 303-305.

3. Barbara, S.(2000), "Is US Health Really the Best in the World? Journal American Medical Association 284(4):483.
4. Bhattacharjee, R.P. (2000): Economic Development of Arunachal Pradesh, Himalayan Publishers, Delhi, Itanagar, pp.17-18 and pp.45-49.
5. Eisenberg, D. M., R. C. Kessler,C. Foster, F. E. Norlock, D. R. Calkins and T. L. Delbanco (1993): Unconventional medicine in the United States. Prevalence, costs and patterns of use. N. Engl. J. Med. 328: 246-252.
6. Fahishi, A. (1996): Complementary medicine. Vol. 1. London: Financial Times and Health care Publishing.
7. Ghosh, A.K. (1990), "Impact of shifting cultivation in Living Natural Resources", in Majumdar, D.N. (ed): Shifting cultivation in North-East India, Omsons, Publications, Guwahati and New Delhi, pp.178 – 197.
8. Govt. of Arunachal Pradesh (2004), Economic Review, Directorate of Economic and Statistics, Itanagar.
9. Govt. of Arunachal Pradesh (2006), Arunachal Pradesh: Human Development Report 2005, Rajiv Gandhi University, pp. 171-72.
10. Harikumar,P.N.and et.el(2007) "Role of Ayurveda Centres in Promoting Backwater tourism in Kerala", Southern Economist,Vol. 46,No. 9,Sept. 1, Bangalore, p. 21.
11. Hegde, S.N. (1988), "Coptis Teeta Wall (Mishmi Teeta): A Rare Medicinal Plant from Arunachal Pradesh", Arun for News 6(I), pp.27 – 29.
12. Jain, S.K. (1987): A Manual of Ethnobotany, Scientific Publishers, Jodhpur.
13. Johnston, G. A. (1997): Market Report. Herbalgram 40: 52.
14. Josh, M.C. (1997): "Role of Herbs and Drugs in Economic Development" in Pandey B.B. (ed), Patterns of Change and Potential for Development in Arunachal Pradesh, Himalayan Publishers, Itanagar, New Delhi, pp.174 -184.
15. Kanjilal, U.N. Kanjilal, P.C. and Das, A. (1934): Flora of

Assam, Vol.I, Govt. of Assam, Shillong.

16. Maclennan, A., D. H. Wilson and A. W. Taylor (1997): Prevalence and cost of alternative medicine in Australia, London: Mintel International Group.
17. Mandal, R.K. (2006), "Sustainability of Medicinal Plants and its Economic Viability in Arunachal Pradesh", Resarun (Journal of the Directorate of Research), Govt. of Arunachal Pradesh, Itanagar, Vol. 31, pp. 1 – 10.
18. Mandal, R.K. (2005): Arunachal Economy: Socio Economic Transformation, Champion Publishing, Itanagar, pp.116 – 117.
19. Mandal, R.K. (2006): "Sustainability and Economic Viability of Medicinal Plants in Arunachal Pradesh, India" Plant Archives: An International Journal of Plant Research, Vol. 6, No. 2.
20. Mandal, R.K. (2006): "Forest and its Sustainability in Arunachal Pradesh", in Josheph, T.M (ed). : New Governance Paradigm: Issues in Development, Kalpaz Publications, Delhi-110 052
21. Mandal, R.K. (2006): "Herbs and their Sustainability in Arunachal Pradesh", Kurukshetra: A Journal on Rural Development, Vol. 56 No. 5, March, Ministry of Rural Development, New Delhi.
22. Mandal, R.K. (2007): "Flora and Fauna in Arunachal Pradesh: Economic Viability and Sustainability", Arunachal Review, Vol.VIII No. 23, Sept.-Nov., Directorate of Information, Public Relations and Printing,Govt. of Arunachal Pradesh, Naharlagun.
23. Mehta D.K., (1998): British National Formulary. British Medical Association and the Royal Pharmaceutical Society of Great Britain. London : The Pharmaceutical Press.
24. Menon, Ajit (2006), "Environmental Policy Legislation and Construction of Social Nature", EPW, January 21 – 27, Vol. XLI, No. 3, pp – 188.
25. Pandey, H.C. (1988), "Some Healing Herbs of the Monk's

Amongst the Minor Forest Produce", Arun for News 6(I), pp.1 – 10.

26. Pantuck E. J. (1996): Stimulatory effect of vegetables on intestinal drug metabolism in the rat. J. Pharmacol Exp. Therapy 198 : 278-283.

27. Rao, V.M. (2003: Tribal Women of Arunachal Pradesh, Mittal Publications, New Delhi, p. 21.

28. Rimo, Y., Tamuk, A. Ranjan, S. & Mishra R. (2004): Some Prominent Medicinal Herbs of Arunachal Pradesh in Mishra, R. (ed): Recent Advances in Environment Biology and Ethnobotany. Sunview Centre, Itanagar, p. 77.

29. Shrivastava, S. R. Barik, N. Mishra, S. Vengurlekar, G. Shrikarthi, S. Revathi, S. Jain (2006): "A Review of Herb-Drug Interactions", Plant Archives: An International Journal of Plant Research, Vol. 6, No. 2, October p. 423.

30. Sinha, G.N. (2008): Forest and Forestry in Arunachal Pradesh, SFRI Information Bulletin No.27, Issued by Director, State Forest Research Institute and Mission Director, State Bamboo Mission, Itanagar, Arunachal Pradesh.

SECTION-V
AGRICULTURAL SCENARIO

20

Changing Agricultural Scenario in North East India

The North Eastern Region (NER) comprises seven states of Indian Territory forming 7.8% of the total land area and about 4% of the total population of the country. More than 70 per cent of total geographical area of NER is covered by hills and about 3 million hectare are estimated to be under soil erosion hazard as a result of practice of jhum cultivation. In Assam alone, 83.2 per cent of area are suffered from erosion of slight (35.3 p.c.), moderate (37.7 p.c.), severe (10.0 p.c.) and very severe (0.3 p.c.) intensity. Improvement of soil conservation and soil fertility is a critical component of low income people. Traditionally, agriculture has been the mainstay of people of this region but the agro-based economy fails to flourish as it should have due to lack of proper involvement and utilization of technological aids. As a result, the stamp of 'backwardness' has been attached to this region suffering from food scarcity, while the country moves ahead from its target of production to food surplus in different phases of the post-Independence era. Increasing the yield of crop in a complex system and in an environmentally positive manner is a challenge that will not be easy to meet in a place like NER.

NER is dominated by the tribal population and the development of agriculture and production of food grains in the region is highly depending upon the custom, culture and the food habit of the tribal people. At the same time, due care should be taken for the protection of the environment of the region and hence sustainable development in agriculture is highly welcomed in the north east.

Our study began as an attempt to evaluate the on going debate regarding the food prospects of India **(Bhalla and Hazell, 1997; Kumar, 1998; Bansil, 1999; Bhalla, Hazell and Kerr, 1999).** This debate is usually depicted as hinging around the issue of future food demand elasticity and the extent to which rise in per capita income will be translated into increased demand for live stock products. As NER is a food deficit area, it cannot be compared with the other states of India, for its peculiar socio-economic and demographic features.

Development has been appropriately conceptualized as a process, which improves the quality of life **(Narain et el., 2003)**. The programmes of development have been taken up in the country in a planned way through various Five Year Plans. The main objective of these programmes is to enhance the quality of life of people as well as effecting improvement in their social and economic well being. The economic growth and uniform regional development are the basic objectives of developmental programmes. The Green Revolution in agricultural sector and commendable progress in the industrial front have increased the overall total production in the country, but there is no indication that these achievements have been able to reduce substantially the regional inequality in the level of development. Although resource transfers are being executed in the backward region of the country, it has been observed that the regional disparities in terms of economic development are not declining over time.

Dutta (2003) observed that the states of NER are suffering from the paucity of funds to improve their socio-economic backwardness. The states of NER are far behind from other states of the Indian Union so far as the basic amenities of life are concerned. He analysed and concluded that the economic development of a country may not be possible without regional development and equitable distribution of wealth and income of the nation among the different parts of the country. Iniquitous distribution of national wealth and resources of the country causes regional disparities by giving rise to various types of socio-economic problems.

T. Dyson and A. Hanchate (2000) concluded that population and food are closely related subjects; yet they are often tackled in relative isolation from each other. Levels of infectious disease can have a major and independent influence upon a population's nutritional status.

M. Swaminathan (1999) observed that in some states, the private traders had lower prices for food grains than the agencies of PDS (Public Distribution system) because of the transportation. The author suggested that an expansion of the geographical coverage of procurement and promotion of decentralized procurement may help to contain the rise in procurement prices.

R. K. Samanta (1994) highlighted the various issues and perspective of agriculture and food production in NER with reference to the tribal culture and eco-friendly activities by which sustainable development can be achieved.

Misra and Rao (2003) examined whether trade liberalization helps to accelerate growth in agriculture and reduce poverty. He observed that the adverse impact of trade policy operating through terms of trade on the rural poor may not entirely attributed to the process of globalisation of Indian economy. It may be noted that factors such as capital stock, net area sown and private investment play very important role in the positive aggregate crop output response. He analysed and concluded that the slower increase in agricultural production during the nineties may be attributed to declining real public investment in agriculture and not the failure of trade and agricultural price policies.

Dutta and Pradhan (2000) observed that the most important problem which creates the hindrance on the way of agricultural development is the problem of population explosion in the region. Although India has emerged as a food surplus state in the world, the NER is still suffering from food deficit. In almost all the states, there are substantial urban-rural and inter district variations, along with the marked variation between tribal and non-tribal population within the district, for which it is always a difficult task to measure the nutritional standard of the population living in a particular region and the case of NER

Dutta and Pradhan (2000) observed that despite several measures taken by the government, the purchasing capacity of the people of north east has not increased up to that level what our planners and policy makers desired.

It was pointed that the poorest section of the society has been badly affected in the states of NER. The extent of degree of inequality in the level of living in the states of NER is much more than what is taken to guide some of the decision making elements in connection with resource transfer from central to these north-eastern states **(Dutta and Choudhury, 1995, 1996).**

Rice is the most important crop grown in India constituting about 44 per cent of the total food grains accounting for about 24 per cent of the total cropped area.

The change in external environment for agriculture came with the setting up of the World Trade Organization (WTO) on January!, 1995 and with the inclusion of agriculture under the multilateral trade discipline for the first time. With this developments and signing of Agreement of Agriculture, it became inevitable that India has no option but to globalise its economy including agriculture **(Kalirajan et el., 2001).**

After the introduction of economic reforms in India, the government neglected the importance of agriculture to the Indian economy and agricultural production started decelerating. We must realize that in India agriculture is a key to rapid and sustained economic growth. The Finance Minister seems to have realized this in his recent budget speech where he indicated that there is a need for agricultural revolution in India, but the strategy for the revolution is not planned out as yet **(Kapila, 2002).**

Agriculture plays a crucial role in the development of

Bangladesh national economy, accounting for 32 per cent of its gross domestic product, contributing about 24 per cent of its exports and employing over 60 per cent of its labour force. The rate of growth of agriculture in Bangladesh was generally low at about 2 per cent per annum between 1975 and 1994, compared to overall economic growth of 3.6 per cent **(Faruqee, R., 1998)**. The author noted that the future of agriculture will depend on how the outstanding issues of key instruments such as agrarian structure, land reform credit and environment, public food distribution system, government policy etc are addressed. He suggested that the future growth of agriculture would require policy changes in four key areas. The important need is emphasized to target the food insecurity and to remove untargeted subsidies that are appropriated, at least partly, by the rich.

The Family Welfare Programme is also an indirect nutrition programme since by reducing family size; it will not only increase the per capita availability of food but also result in all round facilities including health care. The women play a vital role to maintain a perfect balance between human activity and environment. Their participation in both rural and urban development will help to maintain a sustainable eco-system as the women are continuously and closely in contact with the forest for fuel and other activities. Thus to check the population growth and to save the forest from degradation, the employment of the women by proper training is necessary **(Dutta, 2002)**.

In view of the above context, the present study of 'Changing Agricultural Scenario in North East India' is an attempt to focus how the problems of agricultural development can be linked with the social system and the governmental policies of the region. The primary objective of agricultural development is to satisfy the essential materials needs of the society, but the same can not be achieved at the cost of local environment and the culture of the people. Hence, care has been taken to study the tribal way of life and its impact on the agricultural development of the region.

To analyse the agricultural backwardness of the region, some of the social indicators have been chosen. As it is very much customary in this region to blame the rise of insurgency as the major factor which impedes the development of the region in general and the agricultural development, in particular, the study rejects the notion as some of the states of the region made rapid progress in agriculture during the period of insurgency and rise of terrorism.

Finally, the study, based on statistical data and other secondary sources, is concluded with some remedial measures and suggestions for the future planners of the country as well as people of the north-east to cope with the currents of new millennium so that a hunger free north-east can be achieved.

Agricultural Development and Allied Problems

Indian economy is pre-eminently agrarian and North-East India is no exception to it. Agriculture occupies a key position in the economy of NER because of its contribution to:

(a) Overall economic growth through supplies of food, raw materials and export,

(b) Source of livelihood for over 70 p.c. of population and

(c) Providing a large market for non-agricultural goods and services.

Also, it is a source of revenue for the state governments of NER. Agriculture in NER has considerable social and political influence. Agriculture has a vital role to play in the economic development of NER, which is a key factor in the economic growth in absence of mushrooming growth of industries as seen in other parts of India especially in western and southern states. NER produces a wide array of crops although the food crops preponderate over other crops accounting for maximum total cultivated area of the entire region. Among food crops, rice is the major crop followed by maize and pulses. But the slow growth in agricultural sector results the slow growth of north east economy. Again, the policy makers are keener on accelerating industrialization than the development of agriculture.

However, the agricultural backwardness of the region is clearly visible in the context of present day India. While other states of India like Punjab, Haryana, West Bengal are marked by food surplus in the production of rice, wheat, fish etc and they blamed the government of India for not having purchasing capacity and an adequate market facility to supply the surplus food grains, the people of NER are importing two million tones of food grains from other regions of the country at a higher prices.

It is very customary in this region to blame the rise of terrorism as one of the major factors which impedes development of the region in general and the agricultural development in particular. However, during the period of insurgency, the studies show that states of Nagaland, Manipur, Mizoram made rapid progress in the production of food grains[2]. Hence, we can not generalize the problem of terrorism as the greatest hindrance in the development of agriculture and in the production of food grains of the region for which the security of life is always threatened.

Food originates from efficient, effective and environmentally benign production technique and conserve and enhance the natural resource base of crops and animal husbandry, forestry and fishery. In Assam rice production in this year is surplus to the tune of 41 thousand tones. The problem lies in the fact that there is high level of poverty and lack of purchasing power of the poor which reduce the ability to access to food and adequate nutrition. However, economic and ecological access will remain as the main challenge at present.

The impending food crisis over the world is due to increasing population, increasing purchasing power of effluents leading to the consumption of more animal products, increasing damage to the ecological foundation of agriculture, depleting per capita availability of land and water and the absence of technologies that can further enhance the yield of potential of major food crops.

The most important problem which creates hindrance on the way of agricultural development is the problem of population explosion in the region. The total population of the region is about 38.5 million representing about 3.75 per cent of India's total population in 2001. The region's growth rate of population is much higher than the national average. It is striking to note that India's total population increased by 51.80 p.c. in the period 1951-71, 54.39 p.c. in 1971-91 and 21.35 p.c. in the period 1991-2001 whereas for the NER the respective growth rates are 90.86 p.c., 62.11 and 22. 02 p.c. At the same time the share of population of NER, in comparison to India, increased from 2.84 p.c. in 1951 to 3.75 p.c. in 2001 (Table 14.1).

Increased population at an alarming rate in the region is due to immigration from outside the country as well as from within the country. The population explosion caused by immigration poses serious threat on the natural resources of the region and the availability of cultivable lands for the people of NER. As a result, the agricultural production could not cope with the growing population and socio economic changes of the region for which the food grain production is short by 2 million tones of demand in this region.

The absolute number of the migrants was more than 91 thousand in 1901. Since then it has been steadily increasing and reached at nearly 745 thousand in the census year 1991. The share of migrants from Bangladesh was between slightly more than 87 per cent in pre-independence era. In post independence era it reached at 94 per cent in 1951- the highest among the periods 1901-1991. From 1961 onwards the share started to decline and became around 89 per cent in the census year of 1991. It is also clear from the statistical information that Bangladesh was followed by Nepal in sending migrants to the NER of India. Again, the number of migrants who came from other states of India varied between 0.5 million to around 0.8 million during the pre-independence era. But it declined to around 0.4 million in 1951 and reaching slightly more than 0.5 million in 19913. In recent years the flow of immigration again shows an increasing trend.

Since north eastern society is dominated by the tribal population, the reference may be made to the tribal method of cultivation. Out of 23.78 lakh hectare of land in the country as a whole 19.91 lakh hectare (83.73 p.c.) of land in the northeast is under shifting cultivation or jhuming adopted in the ancient farming system, which was once considered as a farmer friendly practice has now become an ecological menace. Rapid deforestation over the years 1987-1997 due to the shifting cultivation in the region have reduced the total forest cover amounting to 1312 sq. km (Table 20.1). An inevitable consequence of deforestation is increased run off rain water, precipitation and extensive soil erosion resulting in unacceptable deterioration of top soil, degradation of land and sedimentation of water bases resulting in desertification and frequent flooding. The high rate of soil erosion in deforested areas in our country ranges from 10 tones per hectare in the plains to about 30 tones per hectare in the north eastern hilly region 4, 10 to 50 times larger than in the forest areas.

The Union Government has sanctioned Rs. 68 crore to the eight North Eastern States during the past three years for modernizing the forest protection force, forest protection system and strengthening the forest management. Tripura and Assam got the maximum amount of Rs. 16 crore each while the other states of the region received 5-9 crore for this purpose. Among the eight NE States, including Sikim, the forest cover had increased in Arunachal Pradesh and Tripura (**N E News Letter, Vol. 5., No. 4, April, 2003**).

The environmental problems caused by increased sedimentation has extensively affected the capacity of the reservoirs as well as the aquatic eco-system in the inland waters just as soil erosion, in addition to loss of fertility, has drastically reduced the recharging capacity, resulting in severe depletion of under ground water. Extensive deforestation has resulted in increased carbon-di-oxide concentration in the atmosphere. The changes in climate and rain pattern gradually setting in because of deforestation. Water and soil erosion have affected the maximum lands used for agricultural purpose.

Table 20.1: Forest Cover in NER of India (Sq. Km.) during the period 1987-1997

State	1987	1989	1991	1993	1995	1997	Total change over decade	Total geographical area of Land (in sq. km.)
Arunachal Pradesh	60500	68783*	68757	68661	68621	68621*	- 162	83578
Assam	26386*	26058	24751	24508	24061	23824*	- 2562	78523
Manipur	17679	17885*	17685	17621	17558	17318*	- 567	22356
Meghalaya	16511*	15690	15875	15769	15714	15657*	- 854	22489
Mizoram	19092*	18178	18858	18697	18576	18775*	- 317	21087
Nagaland	14351	14356*	14321	14348	14291	14221*	- 135	16527
Tripura	5743*	5325	5535	5538	5538	5346*	- 397	10477
NER	**160262**	**166255***	**165777**	**165142**	**164359**	**164943***	**- 1312**	**255039**
India								**3280483**

The Ministry had allocated an amount of Rs. 47.00 crores (10% of Gross Budgetary Support) under various non conventional energy programmes during 2002-2003 including Rs. 1.50 crore for setting up of State nodal agencies in all the NE States for exclusive implementation of various conventional energy programmes. During March, 2003 an expenditure of Rs. 34.23 crore has been incurred, making a cumulative expenditure of Rs. 46.69 crores during April 2002-March, 2003. A total of 323 Family Type biogas plants were installed in Arunachal Pradesh, Manipur, Meghalaya, Mizoram, Nagaland, Tripura and Sikkim, making a total 3841 plants up to February, 2003 during 2002-2003. Under Village Electrification Programme 178 villages were sanctioned for electrification in NE region during 2002-2003.

The climatic fluctuation and changes in the rain pattern have further compounded the problem of providing adequate food security to our increased population. The gross neglect of environment also resulted in polluting not only river water but also surface water, making them fertile breeding grounds of many communicable diseases due to indiscriminate discharge sewage, dumping of solid wastes etc. Further, the tragedy of the commons due to common ownership of the property right also adversely affects not only the loss of fuel and food but also fodder to a large extent.

In the entire north east, the valley districts of Manipur are among the most productive zones in the production of paddy. However, the same can not be said to be true about the districts of Assam. Moreover, the average yield of paddy in Assam is also lower than the regional yield. Lack of assured irrigation seems to be the major factor behind it. The productivity of paddy in Manipur –Tripura Valley and Mizoram is higher than the regional average and also above Assam which alone accounts for more than 70 per cent of area and output in the region. Mizoram has achieved remarkable growth in the yield rate of paddy since around the middle of 1980. It is due to increase in fertilizer consumption and the new land use policy in Mizoram. Also it is observed from the table-9 that while the Government of Assam fixed the amount for expenditure in agricultural sector (Rs. 1557.82 lakhs) as on 01.04.1998 but disbursed only 23.60 per cent while only 15.95 per cent of the disbursed amount actually utilized. The same is true in the states of Arunachal Pradesh and Meghalaya. On the other hand, the government of Tripura and Manipur are not only disbursed more but also actually utilized 70.25 p.c. and 47.09 p.c. respectively on agricultural sector. Perhaps corruption at the governmental level and red tapism of the bureaucrats are responsible for this problem in the states of NER. Although the paddy productivity is the lowest in the state of Arunachal Pradesh, the yield of oil seeds and pulses is the highest in the state along with Meghalaya, Mizoram and the hill districts of Manipur. As the region is classified into hill areas and plain areas, the cropping pattern in hill districts is more varied and not similar to the plain areas. The development of infrastructure facilities like roads, banking, health and communications are perhaps responsible for the above gaps.

The low productivity of food grains explains the shortage of food in the NER and is responsible for poverty of agricultural masses. Agricultural productivity is in inverse proportion in NER to the number of people engaged in it. There is excessive pressure on land resulting in small uneconomic and fragmented holdings. Such small and scattered holdings coupled with defective land tenure system are bound to keep the agricultural productivity very low[5].

Animal husbandry and Diary production is an important subsidiary activity of the people in the north east. Meat consumption is very high but the region draws upon supplies from outside to meet its growing demand. As against the all-India average of 29 cattle for 100 persons, NER has 36 cattle for 100 people. The average number of pigs per 100 people in the north east is 53 as against the all-India average as 1 pig. The same is true of poultry farming.

However, the production of milk and egg is less compared to the population of cows and buffaloes and poultry birds and ducks. The traditional food habit of the people of the region and the poor management practices of the government are perhaps responsible for this.

Fish is an important item of diet of the people of north east. According to an estimate, 203617 hectares of the cultivable water area is available for fish farming in the north east. This is apart from 1,61,713 hectare of water spread area in lakes and beels. However, scientific pisci culture has not yet developed in the region and the availability of fish is much less in comparison to its demand.

A sizable area in the region is in plantation of tea. Its share to the total production of tea in the country in the year 1980 was 53.44 per cent. Many parts of the region are showing good potential for the cultivation of rubber, coffee and a variety of horticultural crops. The region has a total cultivable area of 6.13 million hectare out of which net area sown is only 0.80 million hectare. However, the above production have not reached the target due to various socio-economic problems of the region.

Nutrition and Food Security

It is now a well-known fact that the nutrition plays an important role in physical efficiency of the people and act as a device to determine the food security in a country and in different parts of the country. India is a vast and varied country. There are large differences in per capita income, availability of the food stuffs, purchasing power, dietary habits, habitual consumption of food stuffs, health and nutritional status between different states in the country and even in different areas of a state. In almost all the states, there are substantial urban-rural and inter district variations along with the marked variation between tribal and non-tribal population within the district, for which it is always a difficult task to measure the nutritional standard of the population living in a particular region and the case of NER is highly apparent. It is always a fashion in India to relate food problem with income or private household consumption expenditure. The nutritional value of food items is implicitly or explicitly assumed to be constant. The income elasticity of poor households is supposed to be always less than unity. The income elasticity is sometimes calculated for the sake of deriving relationship with food expenditures. The nutrient intake, household income and working capability of individuals in the household are interrelated. The expenditure incurred on food items is an indication of nutrition intake. Each food item has some calorie value and therefore total calories purchased and consumed as indicated through private consumption expenditure of a household. At the same time it should also possible to say that lower is the consumption expenditure of a household, lower is the calorie intake and that is why intake of calories determines the food poverty. Further, poverty on account of lower intake of calories that are needed to maintain health as the particular household was unable to earn adequate wages or income to purchase the nutrient required. Food provides energy and body spent energy. Once the food intake activity is stopped, the death is certain. Food items are comprised of carbohydrates, proteins, fats, vitamins and minerals. Besides, water is essential for digesting the intake of food ingredients. Although the climatic conditions, food habits, money in hand, age, height, weight and other factors influence the diet and calorie needed, still we can derive the consumption norm based on food items like rice, wheat, pulses, fish, egg, meat, milk and vegetables etc. Hence, the above description may serve as the indicators to determine the nutrition deficit in the population of the NER. The dietary standards differ from one country to another. The recommended intakes of nutrients of a nation differ from those of international norms set up by FAO and WHO. The term used to describe dietary standard is "Recommended Dietary Allowance (RDA)"[6]. The table-8 shows the quality of items (Recommended Dietary Requirements) should be consumed by the persons of different sex and age groups. This is the level of intake of essential nutrients considered, in the judgment of the committee (national or international) on dietary allowances, to be adequate to meet the known nutritional needs of practically all healthy persons.

Education is the main instrument of social change. It is the index of social progress and economic development of a region. Normally it has been considered an agency helping economic production through the development of skills and efficiency highly necessary for the said production. Education is an organic entity, changes, grows with the time, responds to the needs of the society adapts to the environment. It was mostly an ornament in the agricultural civilizations, a tool in economic development in the industrial era and has become today all pervasive resources, a resource that can find substitutes for other resources, but has no substitute for it.

A look into the table 20.1, it is observed that the female literacy rate is highest in Mizoram (95 p.c.) followed by Nagaland (77 p.c.) and lowest in Arunachal Pradesh (48 p.c.) which is the only state in NER below the national level in this respect. There is a big gender gap in literacy which is one of the major obstacles in attaining total literacy. Enrolment in various stages of education is growing at a fast rate, but the proportion of girls is low and declines sharply at higher stages of education. The highest gender gap has been found in the states of Manipur (24.03 p.c.), Arunachal Pradesh (21.76), Tripura (20.93) and lowest in Mizoram (7.01) followed by Meghalaya (8.27).However, all the states of NER are below all-India level (24.84 p.c. points)[8].

The development of an area is best reflected in the distribution of basic needs. Table 20.2 and Fig. 1-B confirms the fact of region's backwardness as it is observed that the per capita consumption of electricity is much lower in the states of NER as compared to the country's consumption (338.5 kwh). Among the states of NER, the highest per capita consumption is observed in the state of Meghalaya (134.5 kwh) and lowest in Tripura (80.4 kwh).

The North Eastern Council (NEC) has contributed to the North Eastern Region power supply through its power projects. The county's third hydel power project and the first in the North East, which is located in the heart of Shillong at Mawprem is all st to be revived after a gap of 81 years since its inception.

The Ministry of Non-Conventional Energy Sources (MNCES) will finance the restoration of the Sonapani Hydel Power Plant, which is expected to light Mawprem and part of Mawlai area. The power plant, which will be "totally unmanned and remote control based" is expected to generate its full capacity of 1.5 Mega Watt for six to seven months especially during the Monsoon and 50% to 62% during other seasons. The unique feature of remote controlling is the first of its kind in the North East and will be managed by the Mawlai 132 KV sub-station.

Drinking water is the most precious commodity in our daily life. Supply of safe drinking water is essential to sustain life. It is remarkable to note that in the state of Mizoram, only 16.21 per cent of households can enjoy the facility of safe drinking water while water is the life blood of the environment (Table 20.2). With a view to ensure community participation in creation and maintenance of source and in the interest of long term sustainability of the sources, Government has introduced reforms in the rural water supply schemes which is called SECTOR REFORMS. West Tripura is one of the 63 districts in the country which have been chosen for implementation of the reforms programme. District Water and Sanitation Mission (DWSM) has been constituted for overall supervision of the project, while District Water and Sanitation Committee (DWSC) and Village Water and Sanitation Committee (VWSC) have been formed for implementation of the programme.

The Centre has constituted a separate cell for the North East in the Ministry of Rural Development to bring the region at par with the rest of the country. The cell, headed by Union Rural Development Ministry Joint Secretary would look after the development of infrastructure in the region besides, generation of employment. The cell has made it mandatory for all the Ministries of the Central Government to allocate 105 of their budget to the region. The Union Rural Development Ministry had also allocated 10% of its budget for the North East since 2000-2001.

Despite of several governmental measures, the purchasing capacity of the people of NER has not increased up to that level

Table 20.2: Per Capita Food Grain Production, Consumption of Electricity and Percentage of Households having Electricity, Safe drinking water in N.E. States

	1*	2*	Per capita food grain production (in kg.)				3*
	1996-97	1991	1972-73	1980-81	1990-91	1997-98	
Arunachal Pradesh	80.8	40.85	104	207	253	186	70.02
Assam	107.6	18.74	158	150	154	139	45.85
Manipur	127.9	50.92	159	205	155	152	38.72
Meghalaya	134.5	29.16	120	116	87	83	36.16
Mizoram	127.8	59.20	244	70	118	123	16.21
Nagaland	88.0	53.42	107	136	160	150	53.37
Tripura	80.4	36.93	116	196	187	152	37.18
India	**338.5**	**42.37**	**172**	**190**	**208**	**198**	**62.30**

1* per capita consumption of electricity (in kwh).

2* percentage of households having electricity.

3* percentage of households having safe drinking water.

Table 20.3: Per Capita Net State Domestic Product (At Current Prices 1980 - 81), in Rs.

State	1980-81	1985-86	1990-91	1994-95	1995-96	1996-97
Arunachal Pradesh	1571	2119	2710	3265	3304	3059
Assam	1284	1510	1544	1585	1606	1628
Manipur	1419	1598	1739	1986	1993	---
Meghalaya	1361	1412	1733	1673	1808	1837
Mizoram	1289	2658	4474	7743	---	---
Nagaland	1448	1653	1916	2270	---	---
Tripura	1307	1240	1646	1898	2113	2197
India	**1625**	**1857**	**2267**	**2533**	**2664**	**2814**

what our planners and policy makers desired. The statistics of per capita income of the people of NER may be stated as, in 1992-93 the per capita income of Nagaland and Mizoram was just slightly above the national average (Rs. 5781 at current Prices) whereas in case of Arunachal Pradesh it was marginally below Rs. 5551 (Table-20.4). In case of Manipur, it was Rs. 1429, Meghalaya Rs. 1361, and Tripura Rs. 1323. The per capita income in 1980-81 was not only so significantly below the national average over the periods (1980-81 to 1992-93).

Per Capita Net State Domestic Product (PCNSDP) gives a rough idea about the economic condition of NER with respect to all-India level. It is observed that all the states of NER except Arunachal Pradesh (Rs. 2119 – Rs. 3265) and Mizoram (Rs.2119 – Rs.7743) are below the all India level (Rs. 1857 – Rs. 2553) for the years 1985-86 to 1994-95. In this respect Assam's position is the lowest for ever during the period 1990-91 (Rs. 1544) to 1996-97 (Rs. 1628) and also in the period 1980-81 (Rs. 1254). The picture shows the economic backwardness of the region in general and Assam in particular (Table 20.3).

Monthly Per Capita Expenditure (MPCE) may be accepted as an indicator of standard of living for people, on the basis of minimum calorie intake, suggested by Indian Council of Medical Research (ICMR) which should be 2400 calorie for an Indian working persons in rural India and 2100 calorie in urban India. This exercise yielded the official or Planning Commission's poverty line (per capita expenditure for 30 days) of rural and urban India at 1973-74 prices as Rs. 49.02 and Rs. 56.64 respectively[7]. Thus an estimated people of 46.02 p.c. in urban India and 56 p.c. in rural India were below the poverty line in the year 1998. Considering the economic condition of NER, it is estimated that the percentage of population below the poverty line is higher in respect of all-India level in 1998 and which come out as 56.83 p.c. and 42.33 p.c. for the rural and urban people of NER respectively **(Dutta, 2003)**. However, as per NSSO's round survey, the poverty ratio has declined in the north east. It has declined to 40.01% in 2000 as round survey,

2000 as compared to 45.01% in 1993-94.

It should be noted that, as for example, the state of Nagaland could not spend the Ninth Plan outlay fully. The Tenth Plan outlay had been projected for Rs. 2227.65 crore which was 11% higher than the Ninth Plan outlay. State Government was advised to have regular monitoring so that tenth plan outlay could be utilized fully. Concern was expressed on the large size bureaucracy eating into resources meant for developmental activities, high rate of population growth, lower literacy in two districts, lower sex ratio, tardy implementation of developmental programmes and absence of banking facilities affecting credit supply in rural areas.

In the north eastern hill areas food production is subject to wide fluctuations due to shifting cultivation. Hence estimate of production may not give the true picture. However, during the last two decades per capita production has declining in the states of Assam, Manipur, Meghalaya and Mizoram and are lower than the national average except in the state of Arunachal Pradesh. While the population is rapidly increasing in the states of the region, it is observed that in case of Assam, the per capita food production decreased from 158 kg. In 1972-73 to 154 kg. in 1990-91 which further decreased to 139 kg. in 1997-98. The respective figures for Meghalaya are 120 kg., 87 kg. and 83 kg. only (Table 20.2).

It is interesting to note that on a global basis, only 8 p.c. increase in food grain production in the last 50 years, has been through expansion of cultivable area, the rest 92 p.c. coming from improved irrigation techniques and use of high yielding cultivates. About 46 p.c. of the global food grain production comes from irrigated area, which has increased from 80 million hectares in 1950 to 240 million hectares in 1993. It will not be possible to increase the total annual food grain productivity in the country beyond 250 million tones, with the present agricultural practices, which totally falls short of the requirement to produce a minimum of 400 million tones by the year 2050 to provide adequate food security to the projected 1.8 billion population[9].

A look at the table-5.4, it is observed that the performance of the northern states in comparison to all-India level, regarding availability of cereals, all the states of NER excluding Arunachal Pradesh and Tripura, are below the national average (522.7 gms per capita per day). In case of per capita per day availability of pulses, it is observed that all the states of NER are below the all-India average over the period 1983-1999.

Table-5.5 gives a picture of per capita per day availability of food grains production where same picture is observed as in case of pulses. It is observed that Arunachal Pradesh, the only state in NER tried to maintain its superiority till 1994 but declined thereafter.

Thus food insecurity is a matter of great concern not only to the people of NER but also to the policy makers and planners of NER. It is further observed that no proper care has been taken for the development of agriculture to increase production by which the living condition of the society of NER may be a better one. Modern technologies, irrigation facilities, scientific and modern equipments are not being properly used for the real development of agriculture in the age of globalisation and liberalization and for which the region stepping back day by day.

Conclusion and Suggestion

The continuous neglect of soil health and fertility exhaustive methods of cultivation must be rectified through appropriate soil conservations methods and efficient use of organic and inorganic plant nutrients through improved soil management practices. Though reduced use of fertilizers is advocated for environmental effects, the use of inorganic fertilizers is a must in the present moment where soil fertility is low and loss of soil and nutrients are more and large section of population are poor and insecure in food supply.

Distribution of improved varieties of crops, arrangement for fertilizer and proper irrigation facilities, availability of these inputs of farmers level, demonstration and training for

Table 20.5: Recommended Dietary Requirement in Grams

Food Items	Adult Male			Adult Female			Children		Boys	Girls
	(1)	(2)	(3)	(1)	(2)	(3)	(4)	(5)	(6)	(6)
Cereals	460	520	670	410	440	575	175	270	420	380
Pulses	40	50	60	40	45	50	35	35	45	45
Leaf Vegetables	40	40	40	100	100	50	40	50	50	50
Other Vegetables	60	70	80	40	40	100	20	30	50	50
Roots& Tubers	50	60	80	50	50	60	10	20	30	30
Milk	150	200	250	100	150	200	300	250	250	250
Oil & Fat	40	45	60	20	25	40	15	25	40	35
Sugar & Jaggery	30	35	55	20	20	40	30	40	45	45

(1): Secondary Worker (2): Moderate Worker (3): Heavy Worker (4): 1-3 years (5): 4-5 years
(6): 10-12 Years

Table 20.6: Agricultural Development in Ner (Rupees in Lakhs)

State	Unutilised amount of money	Amount fixed for Expenditure as on 1.4.98	Amount disbursed	Expenditure
Arunachal Pradesh	421.96	980.32	327.05	94.11
Assam	1440.65	1557.82	365.65	58.67
Manipur	919.52	1538.84	474.90	223.64
Meghalaya	334.20	878.91	523.06	74.01
Mizoram	204.72	1434.17	941.18	283.48
Nagaland	415.22	1799.22	1333.18	574.92
Tripura	537.38	1015.77	438.90	308.34

Table 20.7: Per Capita Output (at Current Prices, In Rs.)

State	1980-81	1986-87	1992-93
Arunachal Pradesh	1561	3274	5551
Assam	1200	2313	4230
Manipur	1429	2362	4180
Meghalaya	1361	2250	4458
Mizoram	1289	2658	5910
Nagaland	1448	2591	5910
Tripura	1323	2108	3569
India	**1625**	**2703**	**5781**
Coefficient Variation:			
India	**31.04%**	**27.84%**	**30.39%**
NER	**7.69%**	**14.31%**	**18.21%**

effective and efficient use of organic and inorganic fertilizers in various farming system through Integrated Nutrient Management System and plant protection through Integrated Pest Management by bio-pesticides etc can be effectively managed in these areas. Besides long term property rights to land, access to credit, marketing facilities of produce and investment in roads and rural transportation system are to be efficiently managed.

Educated youths of the villages must be attracted in farming through spreading science-based precision farming techniques which are both intellectually stimulating and economically rewarding. Increased investment in effective Agricultural research through private sector, NGO's and other agencies is most important NER in particular to achieve household food security and nutritional security.

In the Indian Council of Agricultural Research (ICAR) vision 2020 strategic plan to achieve food and nutrition security it propose to address the issues of bio diversity, natural resource management, farming system approach, rain-fed agriculture, post harvest management, farm mechanization, information networking and effective partnership with other public and private institutions.

It is necessary to improve all the factors employed in agricultural viz. land, labour, capital and enterprise. Poor quality of seeds, non-adoption of modern technologies, non-use of plant protection measures, out-of-date implements, lack of adequate or biased finance (agricultural credit), absence of productive investment in land due to defective land tenure system, poor communication between research and extension or development agencies and lack of irrigation facilities are the low agricultural productivity in the region.

Notes

1. **U.R. Rao (1996):** General Presidential Address in 83rd INDIAN SCIENCE CONGRESS, Patiala.
2. **B. B. Dutta (1994):** Insurgency and Economic Development in India's North East in India's North East – The Process Of Change And Development (Ed.) R.K. Samanta, B.R. Publishing Corporation, pp. 1-38, New Delhi.
3. **S. Bandyopadhyay and D. Chakrabarty (1999):** Migration in the North Eastern Region of India During 1901-1999; Size, Trend, Reasons and Impact in Demography India, Vol. 28(1), pp. 75-97.
4. **U. R. Rao (1994):** Space For Sustainable Development, G. B. Panth Memorial Lecture, Guwahati.
5. **B. K. Sarma and P. P. Pal (2000):** Food Production, Food Problem and Public Distribution System in North East India, Paper presented in the National Seminar on Food, Nutrition, Food Security, Public Distribution System, NEICSSR, Shillong, 27-28 November.
6. **R. Gedam (1998):** Poverty in India, Deep & Deep Publications, New Delhi, pp. 386-420.
7. **N. Bhattacharya (1998):** On Level of Living Surveys in India, Presidential Address, 85th Indian Science Congress, Section of Statistics.

8. **P. C. Dutta (2002):** A Study on the Impacts of Socio-Economic Development in North East India With Special Reference to the Problems of Population Growth And Urbanization on Environment, Report on the U. G. C. sponsored Minor Research Project.
9. **V. R. Rao (1996):** General Presidential Address in 83rd Indian Science Congress, Patiala.

References

Bansil, P. C. (1999): *Demand For Foodgrains by 2020 A.D.*, Observer Research Foundation, New Delhi.

Bhalla, G. S. and P. Hazell (1997): *Food grains Demand in India to 2020*, Economic and Polical Weekly, December 27.

Bhalla, G.S., P. Hazell and J. Kerr (1999): *Prospects for India's Cereal Supply and Demand to 2020, Food, Agriculture and the Environment*, Discussion Paper 29, International Food Policy Research Institute.

Dutta, P. C. (2002): Development Social Forestry in Assam of North Eastern Region, IJRS, Vol. 34, No. 2, pp. 52-62.

Dutta, P. C. (2003): *Regional Disparity and its Consequences in North Eastern Region of India*, (In Economic Liberalization and Regional Disparities in India – Special Focus on the North Eastern Region (Eds.) A.C. Mahapatra and C.R. Pathak, Star Publishing House, Shillong), 179-182.

Dutta, P. C. and H. Choudhury (1995): *Per Capita Household Consumption Inequalities in North Eastern Region (Ner)*, Indian Journal of Regional Science, No. 27 (1 & 2)

Dutta, P. C. and H. Choudhury (1996): *A Note on Inter State Variation in Per Capita Non Food Household Items of Consumption in The North East India,* Indian Journal of Regional Science, No. 28(2), pp. 101-110.

Dutta, P. C. and B. C. Pradhan (2000): Agricultural Development and Security of Life in North East India,

Paper present in the National Seminar on Food Security, Nutrition and Public Distribution System, NEICSSR, Shillong, Nov. 27-28.

Dyson, T and A. Hanchate (2000): India's Demographic and Food Prospects State Level Analysis, Economic and Political Weekly, November 11.

Faruqee, R (1998): Bangladesh Agriculture in the 21st Century (Ed.), The University Press Ltd., Dhaka, Bangladesh.

Kalirajan, K.P., G. Mythili and U. Sankar (2001): Accelerating Growth through Globalization of Indian Agriculture(Eds.), Macmillan India Ltd., New Delhi.

Kapila, Uma (2002): Indian Economy Since Independence (Ed.), Academic Foundation, New Delhi.

Kumar, P. (1998): Food Demand and Supply Projections for India, Agricultural Economics Policy Paper 98-01, Indian Agricultural Research Institute, New Delhi.

Narain, Prem, S.D. Sharma, S.C. Rai and V.K. Bhatia (2003): Evaluation of Economic Development at Micro Level in Karnataka, Journal of the Indian Society of Agricultural Statistics, 56 (1), 52-63.

Misra, V.V. and M. Govinda Rao (2003): Trade Policy, Agricultural Growth and Rural Poor – Indian Experience, 1978-79 to 1999-2000, Economic and Political Weekly, 38(43), 4588-4603.

Samanta, R. K. (1994): Issues For Agricultural Development in Tribal Dominated North East India, in India's North East – The Process of Change and Development, B.R. Publishing Corporation, Delhi.

Swaminathan, M. (1999): Understanding the Cost of Food Corporation of India, Economic and Political Weekly, December 25.

21

Impact of Shifting Cultivation on Environment in NER and its Sustainability

Introduction

The North Eastern Region of India (NER) consists of seven states, namely, Assam, Arunachal Pradesh, Meghalaya, Mizoram, Manipur, Tripura and Nagaland. Large sections of the people in the region are Tibeto-Mangoloid origin speaking variety of languages. The hills constitute about 70 per cent of the total land area, where shifting agriculture, locally called "jhum" is the chief land use (Ramakrishnan, 1996). The Brahmaputra and the Barak Valley in Assam is the largest valley land where settled agriculture is confined. The region covers 7.76 per cent of the geographical area of the country. The ethnical, linguistics and cultural diversities of the region make it a mini-modal for representing the country as a whole. There are hundreds of different tribes in the region differing linguistically and culturally.

Geographical Features

The entire region is more or less geographically isolated from the rest of the country. The only gateway to rest of India for all the seven states is Guwahati, the capital city of Assam. The whole of the region is almost surrounded by international borders with Bangladesh, China and Myanmar. The long stretch of border areas not only creates occasional sense of insecurity but also disrupts the inter-regional communication link. The road communication along the border areas through hilly terrain has become difficult and many places are still inaccessible to vehicular traffic. This has heavily affected the economy of the border areas of every states of the north eastern region **(Barua 1990)**.

Demographical Features

The growth rate of population is much larger in all the states of NER as compared to the all India average. While some states like Assam, Tripura and to some extent Meghalaya and Mizoram have experienced a large scale influx of people from neighbouring countries like Bangladesh and Nepal, the other states are characterised by much higher birth rate than death rate **(Lekhi and Choudhury, 1994)**. As a result the decadal variation in the states of NER seems to be very high as compared to all India average. The decadal variation of the states of the region is shown in Table 21.1.

The Table 21.1 confirms the high rate of decennial variations in the NER as compared to the country as whole. The all India trend shows decline in the variation from 1971-81 to 1981-91, the north eastern states individually or the region as a whole showed an increasing trend during the period. While the average annual exponential growth rate shows that in both the decades 1971-81 and 1981-91 in almost all the states of N.E. region the growth rate becomes higher than all India average. This trend will surely have an impact on the socio-economic condition of the region.

Method of Shifting Cultivation: The forest farmer in the humid tropics has practiced for centuries the method of "shifting agriculture" or popularly known in India as "jhum" (Ramakrishnan, 1996). This is the simplest method of cultivation available to the tribal population living in the hilly region. There is no other alternative way of cultivating the land in the hill areas. The shifting cultivation is the natural way of life to the tribal people in the hill areas. In fact man nature relationship of a community is reflected in its mode of resource use across ideological axis. At a given level of ideology man's material requirements and his perception of nature and natural phenomena determines his interaction with nature and characterises ideal type of the mode of resource use. At this level, ideology acts as determinant variable of mode of resource use and is external to the system. The ideological base of a community, for example, governs production relations forces of production and exploitation of natural resources as well. **(Gadgil and Guha, 1992)**. Use of land resources for shifting cultivation by the different tribes is, however, not indiscriminate, rather it follows certain norms even at ideological level.

The system of shifting cultivation involves a number of operations. First, forest bushes are cut up to the stump level in the months of December-January and small trees and bamboos are felled. Short tree stumps and large tree boles are left intact. The under ground organs of different species are not disturbed. Next, the stumps are allowed to dry, after which they are set on fire. After the burning is completed, the land is cleared and digging stick and seeds of different crops as required are scattered into the holes before the onset of the rains. The cultivation is confined to the area close to the village. After the every crop season of two, the area is left for 25 or 30 years and the cultivator moves to another area to slash and burn and cultivate **(Lekhi and Choudhury: 1994)**. This laborious process often completed by the men from two or three families. Such a joint effort is one of the essential ingredients of a well-knit social organisation. This effort along with the process of allotment of sites for jhum by the village head man who is incharge of overall control of the village community (known as Gaonbura) helps to promote kinship among the members of the village (Ramakrishnan, 1996). However, the system of allotment of lands differs from tribes to tribes.

Paddy is the main crop in jhuming. Among the other crops cultivated are maize, millet, sweet potatoes, leafy vegetables etc. Each family chooses its own cropping pattern according to what it consumes and in quantities enough to meet its own needs. The crops are all rainfed and harvesting starts from August The paddy grown in jhum fields matures earlier than the paddy grown in plain **(Lekhi and Choudhury, 1994)**.

Factors in favour of Jhumming

1. Land Tenure System in Tribal Areas

Communal system of landownership is most suitable for shifting cultivations. Unless there is private ownership of land or cooperative farming, permanent cultivation in the existing economic order is difficult under communal ownership.

2. Law of Inheritance

It makes reparation from joint family early. As there is not much immovable property to inherit, no adult member is required to cling to the family poverty. Because of the free gift of labour under shifting cultivation, a married young man is assisted by the co-villagers to construct separate dwelling house. Villagers also give a young couple some share in the jhume land for cultivation.

3. Religion Belief

Many religions customs, ceremonies and festivals amongst the tribal people are linked with shifting cultivation. There are special ceremonies at the time of clearance of jhume land, harvesting of products; even in case of illness spirit gods are to satisfied in Jhum fields. When jhumming is replaced the rural people must have some alternative mass pooealing ceremonies. It is noticeable amongst the goros converted to Christianity, that althougth they have changed their religion, their habits

Table 21.1: Decadal variation of population in North Eastern Region (in Percentage)

State	Decadal Growth of Population (%)		Change in the growth rate	Average Annual Exponential growth	
	1971-81	1981-91	D.F.	1971-81	1981-91
Arunachal Pradesh	+35.83	+36.83	+1.68	3.04	3.06
Assam	+36.05	+24.24	-11.81	2.12	2.12
Manipur	+32.46	+29.29	-3.17	2.83	2.51
Meghalaya	+32.04	+32.86	+0.82	2.80	2.76
Mizoram	+48.55	+39.70	-8.85	3.99	3.29
Nagaland	+50.05	+56.08	+6.03	4.09	4.50
Tripura	+31.92	+34.30	+2.38	2.79	2.90
N.E. Region	**+33.9***	**+36.3***			
All India	**+24.66**	**+23.85**	**-0.87**	**2.22**	**2.11**

Source: Census of India 1991, Series-i, Paper-2 of 1992.

*Computed figures.

associated with jhumming still prevails.

4. Hill top Dwelling

Because of their age –old preference to have dwelling house on the hill tops, it will be difficult to have such suitable hill top near the valley area suitable for permanent cultivation.

5. Mixed Cropping

Mixed cropping gives the jhumias their daily requirements of food grains and vegetables, in addition to providing in suravce against shortage of one crop by another crop. If only one crop is grown under settled farming, the jhumias will have to depend for their requirements on outsiders. But in the absence of marketing facilities it will be difficult for the jhumias to get their requirements easily.

6. Food Habits

Jhumias have special attachment to the rice varieties and vegetable grown in jhum land. Encouraging permanent cultivation will have to be associated with change of taste.

7. Crop Production

As jhume cultivation is undertaken by whole village in a compact plot of land and as each homestead gets its requirement within the compact block, it becomes easier in the consolidated field to product crop from wild animals (e.g. Elephant, monkey, boars, wild buffaloes) and fires compared to scattered permanent plots in hilly terrain.

8. Capital Investment

Jhuming requires very little capital. If land and human labour is available, cultivation is possible. In permanent cultivation, a pair of bullocks, irrigation, land preparation by manual labour become essential.

In spirit of all these favourable factors for jhum cultivation, because of the pressure of population and progressive deterioration of soil in the hill slopes, it has become invariably difficult to get suitable jhum land on hill slopes. Extension of jhum cultivation in steep slopes will aggravate the problems of soil erosion and the agricultural prospect in hill and plains wil be jeopardized. Hence jhuming as practiced now connot continue owing mainly to the absence of suitable land. Some alternative to jhuming either by fild rotation or improved system of jhuming or by combinations of both settled farming and jhuming must be found out.

Jhum Cycle: In shifting agriculture, cultivator in a particular area for one or two years and then moving into other areas and again returning to the first area for cultivation completes a 'cycle'. The cycle includes the number of years an area is under cultivation plus the years the area is kept under forest fallow. Previously the fallow period was 25 years to 30 years, but it has now come down to 4 to 5 years (Dhar, 1995). Long cycles were possible earlier because population pressures were not heavy and land availability did not limit the cycle. In NER, the average size of a jhum plot varies from 1.0 to 2.5 ha. The average family consists of two adults and three to four children (Ramakrishna 1996).

Agriculture and Environment and Concern for Sustainability

Beyond upland and other less favoured regions, the role of agriculture in the sustainability of rural population and as a means of protection the environment has re ceded in the face of post war farm policies. Agriculture has escaped the mandatory environmental controls applied to other economic sectors, such as the authorization of pollution sources, application of a polluter-pays principle, pollution taxes and so on. Today, such measures are increasingly mooted as means to control modern agriculture, but wide spread changes to landscapes to ecosystem and to natural resources have occurred already. Indeed agricultural modernisation has been predicted upon processes that are inherently damaging to the environment, such as the increasing use of chemical additives, biological and genetic transformation, tree clearance, land drainage and use of heavy machinery **(Nature Conservancy Council, 1984)**. Popular and scientific concern for the environmental effects of agriculture has been slow to emerge. The broad consensus over post-war agricultural development along with a long established belief that agriculture is a "natural" rural activity, has had pervasive effect upon European attitude. Initially, the scale and implications of change brought out by agricultural modernisation took environmentalists and policy makers by surprise. Today, however, the environmental impact of intensive agriculture is a major issue in all European countries **(Buller, 1992)**. The agricultural change and its impact on environment, however, is a growing concern for all the countries of the world, developed or underdeveloped. The remarkable success of green revolution technology in increasing agricultural productivity and improving the food security situation in Asia is hardly debated. It also catalysed investments in agricultural research, institutional development, infrastructure improvement and above all, in extensive development of irrigation facilities. However, these benefits also marked the damage to living environment, physical properties of the natural resources stocks, especially the soil and water and human and animal health caused by indiscriminate use of synthetic pesticides and fertilizers. These concerns have led tone initiatives and policy commitments towards "sustainable development" which basically shifts the emphasis from inputs like seeds and chemical fertilizers to resource management **(A.P.O. Reports, 1997)**.

In fact, there are at least three classes of argument one could make to justify a claim that economic activity should be sustainable. The first argument is a moral one. We, the present generation, have main obligations to those generations which will come after us. The second type of argument is ecological one. Suppose you believe that ecological diversity is an important objective in its own right. Then economic activity that threatens to reduce such diversity is intrinsically undesirable. The third approach to justifying a sustainability goal is an economic one. To develop an economic case, one should need to argue either that sustainable economic behaviour is more efficient than non-sustainable behaviour or that sustainable behaviour is that which maximises inter- temporal social behaviour **(Perman et. al., 1996)**.

Concern for Sustainable Shifting Agriculture in North East Region

The major advantage of the shifting cultivation to the hill people is that it provides a very easy method for the preparing of land for cultivation. Weeds and jungles can be easily cleared by slash and burn process and yield can be obtained within a short period of time. However, the most important evil effect of shifting cultivation is that destruction of forest in the hill area causes heavy soil erosion due to rainfall. Moreover, loss of the "top soil" in the hill areas to the extent of 22 per cent of the total soil due to "jhuming" causes a serious fall in the fertility of the soil and thus it creates a serious problem for the tribal people (Dhar, 1995). In fact, the major problems associated with jhum in the NER are the drastic shortening of the "jhum cycle" to 4 to 5 years during recent years. The important cause for shortening of the cycle is the rapid increase in the tribal population and consequent reduction in the availability of land for cultivation. The obvious effect of shortening of the cycle can be grouped into two classes: (i) Economic effects, and (ii) Environmental effects.

As a result of the reduction in the "jhum cycle" has adversely affected economic yield with gradual decline in yield over a period of time when short cycles are imposed **(Ramakrishnan, 1996)**. The table 21.2 compares the monetary output/input analysis of the jhum under different cycles in the north eastern region.

The reduction in overall economic return is very obvious, when cost is calculated on the basis of prevailing market rates. The decrease in economic return under short cycle of jhum is

Table 21.3: Change in forest cover (1991 and 1992)

State	1991 assessment			1993			Total change in 1993 assessment
	D.F.	O.F.	Total	D.F.	O.F.	Total	
Arunachal Pradesh	54542	14215	68750	54510	14151	68662	-96
Assam	15842	8908	24751	15998	8510	24508	-243
Manipur	5309	12376	17685	5307	12314	17621	-64
Meghalaya	3305	12570	15875	3305	12464	15769	-106
Mizoram	4279	14574	18853	4238	14459	18697	-156
Nagaland	3351	10790	14321	3487	10861	14348	+27
Tripura	1825	3710	5535	1819	3719	5538	+3
Total	**88633**	**77144**	**165777**	**88664**	**76478**	**165142**	**-635**

Table 21.4: Loss/Gain in the forest cover in 1993 assessment as compared to 1991 assessment in the N.E. States (sq. kms.)

State	Loss due to			Gain due to			
	Shifting cultivation	Other reasons	Total loss	Regeneration in abandoned shifting cultivation areas	Other reasons	Total gain	Net (+) Gain (-) Loss
Arunachal Pradesh	70	26	96	-	-	-	-96
Assam	165	190	355	104	8	112	-143
Manipur	28	36	64	-	-	-	-64
Meghalaya	110	2	112	6	-	6	-106
Mizoram	256	-	256	100	-	100	-156
Nagaland	63	-	63	90	-	90	-27
Tripura	10	27	37	15	25	40	+3
Total	**702**	**281**	**983**	**315**	**33**	**348**	**-635**

Note: net loss in forest cover in the N.E. States = 983 – 348 = 635 sq. km.

Source: Govt. India, Forest Survey of India (Ministry of Environment and Forest), 1993, as mentioned in the Basic statistics of North Eastern Region, 1995.

related to reduced soil fertility and increased weed potential of the site.

Table 21.2: Monetary input-output under different jhum cycles in N.E. Region (Rs./hect./yrs.)

	Jhum		
	30 yrs.	**10 yrs.**	**5 yrs.**
Input	2616	1830	896
output	5586	3354	1690
Net gain/Loss	2970	1524	794
Output/input	2.13	1.83	1.88

Note: D.F. : Dense Forest O.F.: Open Forest

Source: Basic Statistics of N.E. Region, 1995, North Eastern Council.

Another most important effect of the shifting cultivation is that it leads to environmental degradation and disturbs the fragile ecosystems in the north eastern region. This occurs as a result of the destruction caused to the surrounding natural vegetation. The environmental imbalance has resulted uneven spread of monsoon rainfall leading to the problem of draught and excessive rainfall resulting flood in the region. In Meghalaya, unabated jhuming has turned the once thick evergreen forest belt of Cherrapunji, a place which used to record the highest rainfall in the world into a dry brown scar. The jhuming practice has caused extensive climatic changes in the state and destroyed rare flora and fauna **(Dhar, 1995)**. The Cherrapunji ecosystem that now stands desertified due to deforestation inflicted sometime in the distant past no refused to recover its original state. Linked with this drastic loss in biological diversity is the human suffering which now is immense. Water is a scarce commodity during the dry months in this high rainfall spot of the world, a contender for being the driest spot on earth along with the near by Mousengram in the Khasi hill of Meghalaya. The tribal who is traditionally bound to the forests has been forced to seek other avenues for survival **(Ramakrishnan, 1996)**. A relative scenario of change in forest cover in the N.E. Region is depicted in Table 21.3 and Table 21.4.

The Table 21.3 and Table 21.4 depicted a detailed picture of forest coverage in the N.E.R. From table 21.3, (it is found that the total loss of forest area in the N.E.R between 1991 and 1993 was 635 sq. km. from the loss and gain accounts. Table .4 -4ndicates that loss due to shifting cultivation accounted to 702 sq. km., while the total loss becomes 983 sq. km. Due to regeneration and other reasons gains amounted to 348 sq. km., totalling a net loss of 635 sq. km. The principal reason for loss of forest area seems to be the practice of shifting cultivation. The net Loss due to shifting cultivation during the period was 387 (702-315) sq. km.

Conclusion and Suggestions

The fact that the Govt. and other agencies have undertaken various measures for controlling shifting cultivation in desired directions. The North Eastern Council and the Indian Council of Agricultural Research has been effectively involved to find way out to solve the problem. From fifth plan onwards different programmes have also been undertaken in this direction. In the Environment report submitted by the Union Environment Ministry to the United Nations in 1992 has mentioned about the practice of jhum cultivation among the tribal people of the North-East India. The report reasoned out why the old practice became enviable and damaging and also states that the increasing population and decreasing availability of land led to the fall in the "jhum cycle" affecting the cultivation process.

Although various attempts have already been made by the State Government and various other agencies in weaning the north-east tribals into modern scientific cultivation but most of these attempts have failed to achieve desired results. A field study of the Department of Sociological Anthropology of the North Eastern Hill University, Shillong in 1994 showed that the tribal hardly used the subsidy given to them for starting a settled way of cultivation. In some cases they sold the land allotted to them, and went back to other old life. The study pointed out that jhuming is an ancient socio-economic tradition that the tribes likes to cling to.

However, tribal resistance to change alone is not the only reason rather lack of whole hearted effort on the part of government agencies is also responsible for such failure. Field surveys in Garo hills of Meghalaya show that some areas selected for terrace cultivation as part of the anti jhuming efforts were unsuitable for food crops. Seeds were often not supplied on time and proper infrastructural facilities required in this connection are also not provided in the resettlement colonies. Such half-hearted official endeavours will hardly stop jhuming silent march in the NER (Dhar, 1995).

The fact that recently jhum around Cherrapunji is banned by the village council is a positive indication of transformation. What needed is an "area-oriented approach" of planning and more patience on the part of the Government agencies and N.G.O's. These will help in making the painful switch to settle agricultural existences. The universities of the region must also come forward in arranging area oriented specific short term motivational programme on the issue.

References

Barua, P.C., (1990): Development Planning of North East India, Mittal Publications, New Delhi.

Buller, J. Henry, (1992): "Agricultural Change and the Environment in Western Europe" in Keith Haggart (ed.), Agricultural change, Environment and Economy, pp. 68-70.

Dhar, P.K., (1995): The Economy of Assam (including Economy of N.E. India), Kalyani Publishers, New Delhi.

Gadgil, M. and Guha, R, (1992): The Fissure Land; An Ecological History of India, Oxford University Press, Delhi.

Goswami, P.C. (1980): "Problem of Jhum Control" in Mathew, T(ed), Tribal Economy of the North-Eastern Region, Spectrum Pub. Gauhati pp. 55-57.

Lekhi, R.K. and Choudhuiy, R.K, (1994): Economy of India Including Assam and North East, Kalyani Publishers, Kolata

Perman R., Ma Yue and Mcgilvray J. (1996): "Natural Resource and Environmental Economics", Longman, London and New York.

Ramakrishnan, P.S. (1996): Shifting Agriculture and Sustainable Development, UNESCO and the Parthenon Publishing Group.

Index

A

A'chik National Volunteer Council (ANVC), 136

ABSU (All BODO Students Union), 134, 135, 379

Academic Council of Gauhati University, 372

Acid Rain, 416

Adivasis, 134

Adivasis Santhals, 134

Africa, 14

Age Distribution, 398, 436, 466

(Population) in North East Region, 436

In NER States, 398

Age-Old Customs, 626, 627

AGP (Assam Gana Parishad), 129, 368, 375, 412

Agrarian Economy, 29, 69, 70, 96, 161

Diversification of-, 29

Agrarian Structure, 651

Agreement On Agriculture, (AoA), 650

Agricultural

Activities, 442

Backwardness, 652, 653

Based Industries, 36

Development, 162, 294, 367, 458, 651-654

Economy, 473

Growth, 441, 519

In North East India, 647-673

Information Networking System, 61, 193

Labourers, 97, 502

Modernization, 681

Plantation, 40

Revolution, 650

Agriculture

In Bangladesh, 651

In North Eastern Region, 210

In Tripura, 69

Agro

Based and Forest Based Industries, 519

Based Economy, 647

Based Food Industry, 211

Based Industries, 69, 95, 101, 210, 442, 573

Business, 325

Climatic Zones, 620

Forestry, 573

Ahoms, 362

Ahom Prince, 119

AIDS, 621

All Assam

Gana Sangram Parishad

(AAGSP), 374

Students Union (AASU), 373, 374

All Bodo Students Union (ABSU), 378

All Cachar

Karimganj—Students Association (ACKHSA),373

Students Association (ACSA), 373

All India Financial Institutions (AIFIs), 298, 476

Alleviation of Poverty, 43

Altitudinal Migration, 614

American Society, 363

Anker, 157

Annual Tea Production in NER, 519

Anthropological Offshoots, 15

Negroid, Mongoloids, -Caucasians, 15

Anti-

Foreign National Movement, 374

India Guerrilla Bases in Bangladesh, 132

Poverty Program, 157

Poverty Scheme, 487

Apung, Rice and Millet Beer, 558

Armed Forces Special Power Act (1958), (AFSPA), 131

Army Operations, 131

All Clear, 131

Blue Bird, 131

Bojrong, 131

Rhino, I, II, III, 131

Shere-Dil, 131

Tiger Heart, 131

Aromatic Oil Yielding Plants, 608-609

Art and Science of Peace Keeping, 117

Arunachal Pradesh

Biodiversity Board, 578

Functions, 578-579

Forests and Magnificent Wildlife, 599

Highest Geographic Area, 19

Junction of-, 599, 613

Indo-Chinese, 599

Indo-Malayan Bio-geographic Regions, 599

Paleoarctic, 599

Medicinal Plant Board, 631

Functions, 632

Tribes, (APT), 15

Adi, 15

Apatani, 15

Dafla, 15

Khampti, 15

Nyishi, 15

Singhpo, 15

Tagin, 15

Wangcho, 15

Orchids Paradise, 599

Rich in Medicinal Flora, 598

Socio-Economic Development, 53

Arunachal Pradesh's Economy, 95

ASEAN

Market, 217

Summit in Bali, (Indonesia), 48

Asia's Population, 499

Asian Countries, 191, 325

Assam

A Troubled Area, 129

Energy Development Agency, 173, 215

Gana Parishad, 374

Industrial Development Corporation, 212, 213

Items, 42

Chaddhar, 42

Dhoti, 42

Gamuchi, 42

Lungi, 42

Mekhala, 42

Khadi and Village Industries Board, 162

Official Language Act, 372

Sahitya Sabha, 131

Small Farmers Agribusiness Consortium (ASFAC), 211

Traditional Tea, Oil, Wood Based Industries, 100

Tribes, 15, 16

Boro, 15

Dimasa, 15

Hajong, 16

Hmar, 15

Kachari, 15

Lalung, 15

Mikir, 15

Rabbga, 15

Assam's

Economic Development, 160

Economy, 161

Assamese

And Bengali 362

Drama, 375

Indo-Ryan Languages, 362

Language, 378

Muslims, 362, 369

Nationality Formation, 361

Official Language, 372

Society, 362

Assam—Mizoram Border, 381

Association of Southeast Asian Nations (ASEANS), 48

ATC (Association of Tea Corp.), 105

Australia, 507

Autonomous

District Council, 382

State Demand Committee (ASDC), 138, 383

Autonomous Status to-, 380

Chakmas, 380

Lakhers, 380

Pawi, 380

Autonomy, 119, 361

Economic and Political, 121

Avifauna, 614

Ayurveda, 567, 620

Ayurvedic Formations, 599

AYUSH System of Medicine, 621

Azad Cachar Party, 368

B

BAC Area (Bodo Autonomous Council Area0, 134

Backward Provinces, 195

Bamboo, 41

Centres, 164

Shot, 96, 442

Shot Preservation, 69

Bangalees in Barak Valley, 368

Bangladesh, 46, 47, 133, 289, 359, 654

And Myanmar, 87

And Nepal, 549, 676

Myanmar and Bhutan, 178

National Economy, 651

Banking, 62, 76

Banking Facilities, 165

Barak (Meghna), 45, 169, 171

Rural Poverty in-, 169

Upatyaka—Sammelan (BUBSOSS), 373

Valley Districts, 119, 367, 368

Valley of Assam, 78, 79, 140, 147, 148, 159, 217, 232, 240, 289

Barapani Project, 214

Barbados—USA, 330

Barking Deer, 600

Barter Economies, 564

Baruah, Paresh, ULFA C-In-C, 131

Basic

Amenities of Life, 458

Infrastructure, 13, 71

Basumatari, Hagrama, 136, 380

BBIMNSTEC (Bangladesh, Bhutan, India, Myanmar, Nepal Srilanka, Thailand Economic Coop), 48

BdSF (Bodo Security Force), 135

Beijing, 324

Beijing Resolution, 38

Below Poverty Line (BPL), 60, 67, 99, 179, 297, 431, 448, 481, 497

Bengalee Muslims, 369

Bengali As Official Language, 372

Berbarin Yielding Plants, 609-612

Bhasha Andolan Samiti, 372

Bhutan, 47, 87, 359

Camps, 136

Bihari Population, 125, 376

Biodiversity, 537-593

Action Plan, 638

Treaty, 565

Biological Diversity, 43

Biomass Gasification, 173

Bio-Piracy, 565

Bio-Reserve Management, 592

Biotic

Interference, 537

Resources, 96

Birth Control, 439

Bishnupriya Manipuri Andolan Parishad, 376

Bison and Mithun, 600

BLT (Bodo Liberation Tiger0, 135, 136, 380

Force, 136

BLT –NDFB, 121, 123

Bodo

And Bodo Cachar, 362

Communities, 145

Group, 134, 136, 378

Insurgent Group, 135, 379

Liberal Front (BLF), 135, 379

Ultra Corps, 130, 377

Bodoland, 135

Bodos, 125

Border Area Development Program (BADP), 51, 298, 476, 479

Bordoloi, Dr Gopinath, 369, 367

Project, 214

Botanical

Health Care Remedies, 598

Survey of India, 602

Brahmins and Koch, 361

Brahmputra, 43, 45, 119

Brahmputra and Barak Valley, 78, 105, 167

Brass Metal, 36

British

Dietetic Association, 515

Occupation of Assam, 367

Rule, 382

British—Jaintia Hills, 119

BTC (Bodo Territory Council), 135-137, 379, 380

BTF (Bengali Tiger Force), 136

Burma, 359

Burmans in Cachar, 362

C

Cachar

Bandh, 372

Sangram Parishad, 372

Siksha Sangrakshan

Samiti, 373

Zilla Sangram, 372

Cachari, 362

Calcutta High Court, 408

Canada, 506, 507

Cancer, 621

Cane and Bamboo Works, 555

Capital Markets, 28

Carpet Making, 555

Cash Crops Cultivation, 325

Caste

Identity, 15

Kinship, Economic Policies and Religion, 18

Caucasoid Features, 360

Ceasefire Agreement, 140, 387

Cement Plants, 51
Central
    Institute of Plastic Technology, (CIPT), 213
    Sector Stations, 71
    Silk Board, 178
Centrally Funded Program, 298
Chatra Yuva Sangram Prashad, 372
Cherrapunji
    Ecosystem, 686
    In Meghalaha, 44
Chicken Neck, 87, 359
Child
    Mortality, 91
    Sex Ration, 406
    Women Ration (CWR), 290, 524
China, 47, 87, 359, 392, 393, 501, 592, 593
    China and India, 196, 504, 505
    Burma, Bhutan and Bangladesh, 123, 366
China's
    One Child Policy, 393, 394
    Population, 432
    Rapid Population Growth, 432
Choudhury, Moinul Haque, 368
Chouthary, Paritosh Paul, 373
Christian Population, 368
CI's Countries, 566
Civil Disobedience Movement, 354
Climate Change, 391, 526, 537, 559
Clouded Leopard, 634
Coffee and Rubber Plantation, 546
Commercial
    Horticulture, 47
    Management of Forests, 558
    Plantation, 564
    Plants, 627
Committee on Status of Women in India (CSWI), 343
Communal
    Ownership, 678
    Riots, 375
    System, 489
Communicable Diseases, 418, 472
Communication System of Assam, 479
Communities
    And Tribes, 361
    Health Centres, 207
Community
    Forest Management (CFM), 580
    Rights, 580, 581
    Villages, 15
Concentration of Tribal Population Zones, (CTPZ), 15
    North, 15
    North Eastern, 15
    Southern, 15

Western, 15
North Eastern, 15
Confederation of Indian Industry (CII), 48, 217
Conservation System, 553
Constitutional Reforms Issues, 192
Consumer Behaviour in India, 307
Consumer's Preferences, 272
Consumption
Inequalities in NER, 255, 270
Of Electricity in NER, 292
Contraceptives, 110, 111
Conventional Energy Sector, 505
Corruption, 158, 177
Of Bureaucracies,--, 121
Cottage
Industries, 36, 182, 211, 555
Match Factories, 164
Cotton, Jute, Ginger, 69
Credit Deposit Rates, 299
Credit-Cum-Subsidy Scheme for Rural Housing (CSSRH), 179
Credit-Deposit Ratio (CDR), 477, 507
Credit-Deposit Ratio in NER, 107
Crimes, Suicides—Pollution, 503
Cross Border Policy, 48
Crude Oil, 45
Cultivation of Rubber and
Coffee, 659
Cultural Identity Crisis, 120
Cultural Revolution, 393
Customs, Traditions, 383

D

Daimary, Ranjan, 137
Dairy Production, 658
Dams, 543
Decentralization of Municipal Governance, 28
Defence Ministry, 143, 144, 383, 449, 453
Deforestation, 81, 327, 418, 471, 541, 543, 544, 547, 550, 556, 555, 559, 564, 565, 574, 616, 628, 638, 655, 686
Causes, 541
Impact of-, 556
Degradation, 543
Of Agricultural Lands, 391, 418, 471, 655
Of Degradation of Land, 418, 471, 655
Of Agricultural Land and Forest, 550
Of Forests, 544
Of Natural Resources, 548
Deka, Kanak Sen, 131
Demographic Features, 676
Density of Region's Population, 289
Deori, 362

Department of North East Region (DONER), 50, 177

Depletion Fisheries, 391

Desertification, 418, 471

Developed Provinces, 195

Development

- Activities, 13
- Funding Pattern, 51
- In NER, 60, 189-224, 391-430
- Planning, 91
- Plans, 353
- Plans Centrally Financed, 50

DHD (Dima Halin Daogah), 121, 123, 131, 140

Dhubri—Kokrajhar, 377

Digboi (Assam), 45

Dima National Security Force (DNSF), 139

Dimasa and Garos, 134, 137-141, 378

Disadvantaged Groups, 194

Disparity in Income, 243, 255

Distribution of

- Consumption, 255
- Water, 297

District(s), 132

- Cachar, 371, 372
- Dhubri—Sonitpur, 378
- East Kameng, 634
- East Siang, 609
- Golaghat, 132
- Hailakondi, 132
- Industrial Centres, (DICs), 555
- Jorhat, 132
- Karbi Anglong, 132, 146
- Kokrajhar and Lakhimpur, 134
- Kokrajhar and Lakhimpur, 378
- Lohit, 606
- Naga Hills, 119, 381
- North Kachar, 132
- Sibsagar, 119, 132
- Sibsagar and Nowgong, 137
- Sibsagar, Jorhad, Golaghat and Karbi Anglong, 384
- Silcher, 132
- Sylhet, 367
- Tinsukhia, 132
- Tirip, 606
- Tirip and Changlang, 384, 603
- Water and Sanitation Mission (DWSM), 662
- West Kameng, 606, 631
- West Siang, 606

Disturbed Areas, 131

Dr. Bordoloi Regional Res. Laboratory Jorhat, 606

Drinking Water, 66, 184, 204, 292, 431, 513, 515

Drug

- Abuse, 457, 459
- Trading, 147

Duck Rearing, 178

Dunken Proposals, 191

E

East
- Asian Countries, 500
- Bengal, 367
- India Company Occupied Districts, (EICOD), 119
  - Cachar, 119
  - Darrang, 119
  - Kamrup District, 119
  - Nagaon, 119
- Pakistan, 367, 412
  - Refugees From, 367
- West Corridor, 79, 509
- West Corridor Project, 217

Eastern Asian Region, 516

Eco-Feminism, 461

Ecological
- Balance, 563, 564, 577, 628
- Crisis, 457
- Degradation, 589
- Imbalances, 522
- Menace, 655

Economic
- Agricultural Backwardness, 543
- And Industrial Development, 499
- And Political Rights, 454
- And Social Development, 300
- Backwardness, 102, 119, 194, 478
- Business of State, 74
- Condition of NER, 200
- Development, 18, 27, 29, 30, 44, 59, 60, 62, 71, 76, 77, 88, 89,106, 118, 120, 124, 125, 127, 147, 159-161, 165, 172, 197, 243, 282, 285, 286, 288 290, 299, 251, 395, 415, 457 460, 463, 464, 468, 498, 504, 507, 509, 510, 541, 544, 569, 598, 648
  - And Environment, 414
  - In India, 497-530S
- Disparity, 66, 286, 302
- Globalization, 625
- Growth, 27, 28, 62, 71, 89, 97, 111, 155, 157, 160, 172, 191, 193 195, 210, 392, 416, 448, 489, 498-500, 502, 505, 506, 565, 648, 650, 652
- Infrastructure, 504
- Policy, 193
- Poverty, 199, 295, 478
- Problems, 231
- Reforms, 189, 190, 194, 218
- Reforms in India, 80, 650
- Restructuring, 158
- Security, 111
- System, 14, 39, 112, 529
- Transformation and Development, 324, 438

Economy, 14, 27, 39, 52, 53, 71, 88, 97, 155, 171, 191, 302, 324, 328, 355, 393, 440, 450, 451, 455, 458, 482, 529, 650
National, 37
Of Assam, 442
Of Barak Valley, Tripura and Mizoram, 79
Of North East, 47
Of North East Region, 87
Of Sikkim, 96
Ecosystem, 35, 537, 559, 560, 562-564, 571, 589, 616, 627, 655
Conservation of-, 565
Eco-Tourism, 589
Education, 39, 67, 91, 92, 154, 158, 159, 167, 174, 193-195, 197, 198, 290, 353, 400, 458-460, 468, 469, 489, 509, 510, 661, 670
And Administration, 217
And Cultural Pattern, 35
And Employment, 432
And Health, 189, 295, 478, 498
And Training, 528
And Training in-, 34
Assam and Meghalaya, 34
For Women's Equity, 432
Educational And Technological Development, 21
Institutions, 372, 511, 512
Electricity
Generation, 72
In Nagaland, 100
Electrification, 173
Electrification in North East Region, 657
Electronic Tourism Platform (ETP), 222
Elephant
Population, 634
Reserve, 634
Elimination of Discrimination against Women, 37
Employment
Generation, 27, 103, 193, 516
Guarantee Scheme, 487
Oriented Schemes, 179
Of Women, 323
Empowerment of Women, 37, 499
Endemic Species, 566
Endogeny, 14
Energy, 171, 440
And Power, 504
Entrepreneurship, 159
Development Program, 211
In North East, 573
Skills, 51
Environment
And Development (Rio Conference), 391
Conservation, 540
In North East Region, 675-689

Environmental
- And Social Policies and Programs, 489
- Awareness Program, 488
- Awareness Schemes, 574
- Crises, 484, 524, 638
- Degradation, 224, 354, 458, 460, 484, 498, 537, 558, 588
- Destruction, 537
- Deterioration, 423
- Education Awareness, 585
- Health Hazards, 392, 498
- Imbalance, 527
- Infrastructure Scheme, 488
- Issues, 461
- Pollution, 432
- Pollution in India, 497-530
- Problem, 224, 392, 410, 556, 565, 655
- Protection Act, 578

Ethnic
- And Linguistic Group, 359
- Associations, 364
- Communities, 361
- Composition, 47
- Conflicts, 121, 122, 128, 145, 362, 365, 377, 387
- Conflicts in Assam, 121
- Crisis, 359, 361
- Defined, 363, 364
- Group and Sub Groups, 20
- Groups, 118, 119, 122, 135, 146, 360, 363-365, 369, 465, 617
- Identities, 118, 121
- Linguistic and Cultural Diversities in NER, 675
- Linguistic Diversity, 125
- Minorities, 145
- Movement, 387
- Movements in NER, 364
- Pluralism, 121
- Region in India, 361

Europe and North America, 397

Excluded
- And Partially Excluded Areas, 382
- Areas, 119

Extortions, 147

F

Fakruddin Ali Ahmad, 368

Family
- Planning, 223, 295, 502
- Planning Program, 110, 111, 395, 455, 502
- Welfare Program, 344

Farm Mechanization, 670

Farming System, 670

Female
- Education, 92, 436
- Foeticide, 223
- Labour in Agriculture, 159
- Life Expectancy, 345

Literacy Rate, 64, 197, 198, 402, 437, 438, 468, 469, 510
Participation Rate, 96
Work Participation, 416
Ferry Services, 78
Fertility, 345
Rates among Muslims, 406
Finance
Commission (12th), 576
Development, 456
Infrastructure, 76, 106, 507
Institutions, 39, 165
First Anglo-Burmese War, 119
Fish Farming, 659
Five Year Plan
(5th), 539
(6th), 344
(7th), 485
(8th), 486
(9th), 485
(10th), 201, 415
(11th), 499
Floods, 167
Flora and Fauna (F&F), 16, 17, 40, 41, 87, 540, 543, 561, 589, 591, 597-643, 686
Economic Viability, 615, 617
Floriculture, 69, 96
Folk
Medicines, 558
System of Medicine, 620
Food
And Agriculture Organization (FAO), 198, 209, 475, 660
For Work Program, 487
Insecurity, 417, 474
Items Consumption in NER, 271-284
Quality Varieties, 271-284
Production, 294
Production in North East, 649
Security, 184, 659
Foreign
Direct Investment (FDIs), 37
Migrants, 464
Migrants from Bangladesh to Assam, 411
Forest
Act, 1980, 579
Based Industries, 558
Classification, 601
Conservation, 577
Degradation, 547, 570, 571
Major Causes, 541
Development Agency, 578
Dwellers, 546, 552, 563
Dwellers Act, 580
Ecology, 552, 553
Ecosystem, 548, 552, 553
Ecosystem Preservation of-0, 548
Fires, 547
Management, 557, 577,

585, 588, 655
Policies, 563
Projects, Illegal Trade, 565
Protection System, 655
Resources, 563
Survey of India, 601
Types, 599
Semi-Tropical Green, 599
Tropical Green, 599
Wet Ever Green, 599
Wet Temperate—
Alpine, 599
Villages, 15
Forestry, 540, 577, 587
And Fishery, 653
Planning, 588
Fossil Fuel, 484, 556
Fresh Water Depletion, 391
Gandhian Movement, 374
Gandhiji (Mahatma), 537, 538, 636
Garo Hills, 119, 136, 381, 688
Gas
Authority of India, 212
Cracker Project, 212, 213
Gauhati University, 372
GB Pant Institute of Himalayan Environment and Development, 566, 631
Gender
And Development (GAD), 330
Discrimination, 198, 323, 326, 328, 330, 341, 499
Disparity, 436
Equality, 59
Gap in Literacy, 402, 469
Gap, 197
Issues, 353
Issues and Development, 323-358
General Assembly of UNO, 36
Generation of Employment, 180
Geographical Features of NER, 675
Global
Global Development, 59
Development Debate, 352
Development Debate, 423
Economy, 224
Income Inequality, 232, 447
Market, 36
Population, 196
Terrorism, 537
Warming, 416, 537, 556, 559
Women's Debate, 324
Globalization, 15, 34-37, 61, 192, 193, 215, 218, 222, 285, 355, 395, 432, 440, 446, 451, 455, 500, 626
Impact on Socio-Economic Life of North East Tribals, 33
And Liberalization, 625, 667
Of Indian Economy, 649

Process, 36, 39
Goalpara and Sylhet, 119
Gogoi, Tarun, Assam CM, 131
Gomati Power Project, 98
Goswami, Dr Indira, Renowned Assam Novelist, 131
Goswami, Mamomi Raisom, 131
Green Revolution in Agriculture, 648
Greenhouse
Gases, 484
Gas Emission, 556
Groups of Muslims, (GM), 362
Marjas, 362
Na-Asamiya, 362
Syeds, 362
Growth
Of Population, 454, 484
Of Urbanization, 26

H

Handicraft, 36, 87
and Handloom Industry, 103, 162, 516
and Handloom, 101
Traditional, 74
Handloom, 36
Handloom Industry, 74, 101, 516
Handmade paper, 74
Hazarikar, Dr. Bhupen, 131
HDPE, 213
Health, 174, 290
And Environmental Hazards, 527
Care and Education, 60
Care Institutions, 626
Centres, 20-7, 209
Education, 567
Education, Safe Drinking Water, 433
Sector, 511
Sub Centres, 626
Herbal
Drugs, 598, 619, 637
Medicine, 567
Medicines of India, 567
And Drugs, 597
Herbs, 607
Around Tawang, 606
Treat Minor Ailments, 598
Allergies, Burns, Colds—Insomnia--, 598
Hill
Area Development Program, (HADP), 51
Economy, 96
Forest Region, 17
Top Dwelling, 680
Tribes, 377
Himalayan Ranges of India, 605
Hindi Speaking People, 124, 125
Hindu
Bengalee, 412
Minority in Assam, 368
Caste System, 18
Population, 368

Hindu/Muslim Bengalee, 374
Hinduisation of Tribes, 361
Hinduism and Heritage in North East States, 42
Hindustan Paper Corporation (HPC0, 380, 381, 518
HIV/AIDS, 59, 431, 537
Hmar, 137, 138, 140, 380, 381
    As Scheduled Caste, 141
    People Convention (HPC), 141
Hog Deer, 600
Hojai, 362
Hollong Forest, Nahar Forest—Bamboo, 603
Home Ministry, 130, 131
Horticulture, 69, 96
Household Industries, 502
HPC (Hmar Peoples Convention), 123
Human Rights of Women, 38
Hunting and Gathering, 553
Hydel Power, 100
    Generation, 72
    Sunapani, 99
    Umium, 99
    Umtru, 99
Hydropower, 17
    Potential, 568
    Projects, 564, 627
HYV Seeds, 167

I

IEC (Information, Education and Communication), 528
Illegal Bangladeshis Immigrants, 408
Immigrant Muslim Liberation Army (IMLA), 136
Immigrants, 303
    Muslims, 362
Immigration, 127, 223, 289, 410, 464, 654
    Or Influx of Foreign Nationals, 359
Impact of Globalization on Women, 37
Imphal Valley, 97
Importance of Plants of Medicinal and Economic value, 606
Income
    And Employment Generation, 162
    Inequality, 231
India,
    A Rural Society, 153
    As a Miniature League of Nations, 361
    Largest Concentration of Tribal People, 14
India's
    Development Strategy, 194
    Growth, 431
    Growth, 62
    Health Ministry, 20, 63, 398, 434, 501
    Human Development
Report, 40
    National Mechanism, 344
    North East, 35

North East Region, 190
Planning History, 349
Population, 20, 434, 465
Rural Cultural Traditions, 394
Total Population (2001), 288
Total Population, 397, 654

Indian
Council of Agricultural Research, 670, 687
Council of Medical Research, 66, 199, 295, 448, 478, 665
Economic Growth, 17
Economy, 37, 189-192, 195, 201, 285 455, 500, 625, 650, 652
Hornbill, 617
Institutes of Technology (it is), 511
Mosaic, 15
National Congress, 368, 371, 412
National Income, 190
Ocean Rim Countries, 328
Planners, 353, 423
Policies, 118
Population, 63, 88, 406
Society, 145, 302, 387
States, Political Administrative Units, 286
Tea Producers, 104
Tribal Societal Population, 14
Tribal Society, 14
Urbanization, 457
Wildlife Protection Act, 613
Women, 436

India—Vietnam, 499

Indigenous Knowledge System, 617

Indira Awas Yojna (IAY), 179

Indirect Nutrition Program, 487

Indo-
Aryan and Mongolian Cultures, 360
Bangladesh International Border of Lower Assam, 378
China Border in Sikkim, 352
Mongoloids, 360

Industrial
and Agricultural Development, 91
and Service Sector Development, 27
and Service Societies, 27
Backwardness, 630
Centres, 28
Corridors, 110
Milli-Jorethank, 110
Ramgpo-Gangtok, 110
Ranipool-Gangtok, 110
Development, 100, 217, 501, 508, 511, 516,

625
Estates in Arunachal Pradesh, 100
Growth, 74, 101
Law Materials, 589
Policy, 110
Scenario of Assam, 44
Training Institutions (IITs), 511
Industrialization, 27, 76, 100, 147, 194, 210, 302, 396, 414, 424, 457, 484, 541, 555, 566, 653
And Infrastructure, 221
Impact of-, 630
Industrialized Countries, 36, 191
Industries, 62, 71, 96, 110, 111, 212, 325
In NER, 74, 100
Middle Scale, 112
Industry and Social Sector, 460
Infant
Death Rate, 468
Mortality Rate, 439, 481, 524
Influx from Kanauj, Mithila, Magadh, 134
Information
Networking, 671
Technology, 22, 625
Technology Services, 218
Infrastructure, 36, 74, 76, 77, 182, 500
Backwardness, 76, 166
Development and NER, 51
Development, 28, 34, 173
Economic, 504
Physical, 459
Social, 501, 509
Facilities, 39, 60, 76, 89, 166, 190, 290s, 432, 451, 456, 497, 508, 688
Services, 59, 88
System, 76
Inland Waterways Transport Assam, 78
In-Migration, 34
Inner Line System, 119, 120
Institutional
Financing, 28
Support Measures, 341
Insurgency, 124, 125, 132, 383, 412, 453, 478, 561, 652
Insurgent Groups, 131
Integrated
Child Development Scheme, 345
Nutritional Management System, 670
Pest Management, 670
Rural Development Program (IRDP), 156, 157, 211
Internal and International Migrants, 30
Arunachal Pradesh, Assam, Mizoram, Mehgalaya- Sikkim, 30
International

Conference of Islamic Scholars, 392
Conference on Population and Development in Cairo, 391
Energy Agency, 506
Law, 583
Union for Conservation of Nature, (IUCN), 566, 631
Inter-State Disparities, 247
Intra-Regional Inequalities, 153
IRA (Islamic Revolutionary Army), 136
Irrawady, 45
Irrigation
Facilities, 297, 419, 445, 475, 667
Potential, 17
Sector, 203
Sector, 297, 417, 475
System, 203, 204, 297, 417, 419, 475, 476
Techniques, 207, 666
ISI, 454
Itanagar State Zoo, 635
IWDP (Integrated Wasteland Development Program), 180

J

Jaintia Ray, 119
Jammu and Kashmir, 47
Jawahar Gram Samridhi Yojna, (JGSY), 180
Jawahar Rozgar Yojna, (JRY), 179, 180
Jethamalani, Ram, 455
Jhum, 443
Corridor, 647
Cultivation, 69, 545, 546, 548
Land, 639
Jhumias, 471, 545, 546, 638, 680
Jhuming, 327
Jhuming, 418, 678, 687
Cultivation, 680, 681, 687
Cycle, 681, 683, 686
Factors in Favour of-, 678
JNH (Jatikhe Naispo Hasom), 140
JNURM (Jawahar Lal Nehru Urban Renewal Mission), 29
Joint Forest Management (JFM), 581-583, 589
Judicial Reforms Issues, 192
Justice Safique Haque Commission, 379

K

Kachari, 137
Kalpvriksha, NGO, 582
Kamatapuri Language, 130, 378
Karbi
National Volunteer, (KNV), 138
People's Force, 138
Students Association

(KSA), 138, 383

Karbi Anglong, 134, 135, 137, 387

And NC Hills Autonomous

State, 123

And North Cachar Autonomous Districts, 362

District of Assam, 380

Karimganj, 371

Kennedy, Senator Robert, 497

Kerala

Agriculture University, 178

Literacy in India, 346

Khadi and Village Industries, (KVI), 102, 162, 164

Board, 164

Commission, 42, 164

Khandsari Centres, 164

Khangchendzonga in Sikkim, 44

Khasi

And Jyantia Hills, 381

Hills, 43

States, 119

KIA (Kachin Independent Army), 129

Kidnapping of Bureaucrats, 454

Kin Groups, 18

KLNLF (Karbi Longri—Front), 138

KLO (Kamatapur Liberation Organization), 130

KLO (Kuki Liberation Army), 123, 377

KM Yusuf, Justice, 408

KNA (Kuki National Army), 123

Kobo, 629

Koch Rajbhanshi (People), 377, 387

Kochland, 130

Kothari Commission, 402

KRLO (Koch Rajbhanshi Liberation Organization), 130, 377

KRLTF (Koch Rajbanshi Liberation Tiger Force), 130, 377

KRSF (Koch Rajbanshi Security Force), 130, 377

Kuki, 137

Kuter Jyoti, Centrally Sponsored Scheme, 99

Kyoto Conference on Global Climate Change, 416

L

Labor Intensive Industry, 101

Lack of Competitiveness, 167

Lalung, 362

Land

Reforms, 180, 651

Tenure System, 586

Tenure System of Tribal Areas, 678

Use Pattern, 575

Language Movement, 147

In Barak Valley, 376

Large

And Medium Industries in Tripura, 102

Scale Industries, 96

Large/Medium Industries, 101

Law of Inheritance, 678

LDPE, 213

Leather Technology Mission, 42

Legal Rights, 329

Lemon Grass, 606

Liberalization, 28, 165, 327, 446-450

Privatization and Globalization (LPG), 80, 190, 191, 193, 195, 212, 218, 323, 325, 333, 355, 455, 537

Linguistic

Groups, 369

Issue, 119

Nationalism, 368, 371

Literacy, 20, 89, 510

And Education, 63, 91

In Kerala, 346

In North East States, 20

Level of Region, 197

Level-Region's Population, 402

Movement, 346 438

Rate, 175, 197, 290, 524

Look East Policy, 47, 48

Low Female Literacy, 290

Lowest Income Group, 255

M

Mahila Lok Adalat, 351

Major

Craft of Meghalaya, 102

Ethnic Groups of North East, 15

Population Groups, 395, 463

Tribes of the Region, 360

Adi—Lushai, 360

Majuli and Sadia, 378

Makum (Assam), 45

Malaysia, 500

Male Sterilization, 223

Manab Adhikar Sangram Samity (MASS), 131

Manipur

And Nagaland, Leather Manufacturing Products of-, 42

And Tripura Valley, 417, 472, 657

Manmohan Singh, Ind PM, 48, 131, 132

Marginal Farmers, 158

Marine

Biodiversity, 560

Economy, 544

Martial

Arts, 87

Tribes, 465

Massacres in-, 147

Chakarchum 147

Dhemaji, 147

Hamren, 147

Nelli, 147

Maternal Mortality, 59

Mawlai Area, 662

Mawprem and Mawlai9, 203

Maximum Inequalities in-, 267

Mizoram and Arunachal Pradesh, 267

Measures of Income Inequality, 231

Mech, 362

Medicinal

And Aromatic Plants, 210

Facilities in Arunachal Pradesh, 626

Plants, 457, 558, 565, 566, 599, 622, 625, 627, 628, 630, 635

Tourism Exports by India, 566

Medicines, 597

Of Mineral Origin, 597

Meghalaya

Meghalaya and Tripura, 24

Small/Medium Industries, 100

Tribes, 16

Garo, 16

Jayantia, 16

Khasi, 16

Meitei Dominated Manipur, 34

Mexico to Copenhagen, 324

Michings, 134

Micro-Enterprises, 212

Migrant Population in Assam, 412

Migrants, 127, 411, 464, 359, 366, 409, 466

And Migrations, 409, 410

From Bangladesh, 127, 464, 654

To North East Region, 654

Migration, 26, 29, 35, 89, 90, 146

Internal, 90

Migratory Corridors, 634

Mikir, 137

Hill Districts, 382

Hills, 119, 137, 138, 382, 383

Militancy, 120, 122, 132

Militant

Cadres, 134

Group, 383

Outfits, (MO), 133

DHD, 133

MULTA, 133

NDFB, 133

RNSR (Rava National Security Force), 133

ULFA, 133

UPDS, 133

Millennium

Development Goals (MDGs), 515, 526

Summit, 59, 431

Mineral

Dust, 556

Resources, 17, 101, 570

Mini-Mission IV, 210, 211

Mining

And Querying, 555

Waste, 556

Ministry of

Health and Family Welfare, 462, 567

Heavy Industries, 220

Home Affairs, 298

Human Resource Development, 324, 344

Non-Conventional Energy Sources (MNCCS), 203, 662

Rural Development, 662

Minor Forest Produce (MFP), 581

Minority, 363

Groups, 360

Miri, 362

Groups, 134, 378

Missionaries, 362

Mithun, 616

Mixed

Cropping, 680

Economy, 190

Mizo Hills, 119

Mizo National Front (MNF), 300

Mizoram,

Industrial Sector of-, 101

Khadi and Village Industries Board, 102

No Entry State. 101

Smallest in Population, 19

Tribes, 16

Garo, 16

Khag, 16

Kuki, 16

Lusai, 16

Modern Technology, 172, 191, 193, 445

Modernization, 26, 27, 423, 451, 457, 577

Modernization of

Police Force, 144

Tourism, 222

Tribals, 120

Mohammad Sadullah, Soz, 367, 368

Monasteries of Monpas, 605

Monetary Economics, 577

Monetization, 564

Mongoloid

Features, 360

Origin, 361

Monopolistic System, 112

Monpas (Buddhist), 606

Monthly Per Capita Expenditure (MPCE), 66

Mortality, 59, 466

And Health Care, 89

And Maternal Mortality, 431

Mother Child Health Care Program, 223

Muivah, 383

Mulberry, Eri, Muga, Tasar, 102

Municipal Act, 30

Muslim

Communities, 368

Infiltrations, 368
Infiltrations in Assam, 368
League Ministry, 367
Population in Assam, 412
Population, 468
World, 498
MWCES, 215
Myanmar, 47
And Bangladesh, 217
Army Operation, 130
ASEAN Member, 49

N

Naga
Ceasefire, 383
Hills, 119
Hills District, 381
Nagaland
And Kuki-Chin
Languages, 362
Medium Scale Industries in-, 101
Most Industrially Backward State,, 101
Shawls and Skirts, 42
Nagas, Tradition of Art and Craft, 102
Nagoan and Dibrugarh, 217
Nairobi, 324
Conference, 344
Nangal Bibra, 99
Narasimha Rao, former Ind PM, 48, 189, 195
Narayana, MK, National Security Advisor, 132
Nathula Check Post, 352
National
Academy of Sciences, 410
Bamboo Mission, 578
Biodiversity Strategy and Action Plan (NBSAP), 582
Censes, 410
Commission for Self-Employment of Women, 347
Commission for Women, 347, 348
Recommendations, 349, 358
Statutory Functions, 348, 349
Commission for Women
Act, (NCWA), 348
Development Council, 286
Development Pram of North East States, 53
Economy, 37, 112, 223
Emergency, 374
Environment Policy (NEP), 81, 580, 583, 640
Expert Committee on Women Prisoners, 347
Forest Policy, (NFP), 581, 562, 582
Handloom Development Corporation, 177
Highways Length, 509

Horticulture Board, (NHB), 46

Institute of Public Cooperation and Child Development (NIPCCB),351

Nutrition Policy, 347

Nutrition Policy, 485

Parks, 585

Parks and Sanctuaries, 617

Parks/Wildlife Sanctuaries Details, 618-619

Perspective Plan, 347

Policy for Children, 1974, 467

Population Policy, 502

Program of Action, 347

Rural Electrification Policy, 173

Rural Electrification Policy, 2004, 73

Rural Employment Guarantee Act, 576

Rural Health Mission (NRHM), 511, 621

Social Assistance Program, (NSAP), 179

Waterways, 78

Nationalized Banks, 165

Natural

Gas Imphal, 214

Rubber, 69, 95, 443

Navigable Rivers of Assam, 78

NC Hills, 119, 137-139, 140, 141, 146, 380-383, 387

Autonomous District Council, 137, 138

Autonomous State, 134, 378

Of Nagaland, 354

State Demand Committee, 138

NDFB (National Democratic Front of Bodoland), 135-137, 139, 144, 380

NEEPCO, 99

Nehru, Pandit Jawahar Lal, 38, 118, 190, 394

Neo-Liberal Economic Reforms, 231

Nepal, 47, 127, 289, 411, 654

Nepotism and Bribery, 112

New

Bill on Forest Rights, 544

Economic Policy (NEP), 62, 189-224, 325

Economic Reforms, 190, 217-219, 221, 222

English Education in Bengal, 367

Forest Policy, 543

Industrial Policy for NER, 51

International Economic Order, (NIEO), 323, 326, 327

Scheme of Purbanchal, 372

Social Movement (NSM), 332

Technology, 569

NHPC, 99

NIEO, 432

Nikhil Bishnupriya Manipuri Bhasha Parishad (NBMBP), 376

NO Tax Campaign, 354

Non-Aligned Movement, 36

Non-Conventional Energy Program, 657

Non-Governmental

Agencies, 488

Organizations (NGOs), 39, 154, 181, 192, 543, 563, 574 577, 583, 584, 588, 670, 688

Of North Eastern Region (NER), 451

Non-Renewable Natural Resources, 570

Non-Transparent Recruitment System, 112

Non-Tribal

Population, 552

Youth Union (NTYU), 125, 376

Non-Violence Movement, 372

North Cachar District, 141

North Cachar Hills, 79 see NC under Hills,

North East

Bengal, 462

Council (NEC), 13, 37, 50, 51, 80, 143, 147, 203, 217, 441

Advisory Body for

Regional

Development

Plans, 13

Re-Organizing Act, 13

Frontier Agency (NEFA), 365, 554, 369

(Present Arunachal Pradesh), 13

Hill Areas, 294

Hill University, 92, 687

India, 13

Communities, 544

Land of Seven Sisters, 13

Seven States, 13

Arunachal Pradesh, 13

Assam, 13

Manipur, 13

Meghalaya, 13

Mizoram, 13

Nagaland, 13

Tripura, 13

India's Socio-Cultural Mosaic, 118

Industrial Policy, 221

Mosaic, 15

Oil Reserve, 45

Reconstruction Act, 1971, 13

Region (NER), 13, 16, 17, 18, 19, 34, 36-46, 48, 49, 51, 53, 62, 65, 66, 67-70, 72-77, 80, 92, 94, 103, 107, 109- 112, 117, 118, 121, 123-125, 131,

143, 144, 147, 167, 171, 172, 177, 192-194, 196- 199,203, 204, 395-398, 400, 403, 405, 408, 411, 412, 417, 420,423, 424, 433-443, 445, 446, 453-455, 458, 463, 464, 466, 467-470, 473, 474, 476, 478 482, 484, 485, 489, 497, 500, 501, 503, 504, 506-508, 510 513, 516, 517, 520-522, 528, 542, 555, 561, 563, 647-650, 652-654, 659, 660, 662, 665, 667, 675, 676-688

Demographic Profile, 63, 90

Educational Scene, 20

Hunger Free, 485

International Borders, China, Burma, Bangladesh, Tibet, and Bhutan, 462

Irrigation Potential, 97 Of Indian States, 365

Arunachal Pradesh—Tripura, 365

Population, 19

Profile, 462

States, 87, 88, 101, 441, 516, 518, 658, 661, 675

Arunachal Pradesh —Tripura,87

Economy, 156

Food Deficit Area, 648

Rural Sub-System, 155

Special Category States, 50

Society, 655

States, 24, 25, 30, 40, 48, 52,61, 130, 161, 381, 418, 545,548, 655

Women, 436

Council, 373, 383, 453, 486, 661, 687

North Eastern

Geographical Area, 16

Region (NER) of India Boundaries, (NERIB), 16

Bangladesh, 16

Bhutan, 16

China, 16

Myanmar, 16

Nepal, 16

Society, 471

Tribes, 121

NS Frontier Tracts, 119

NSCN (IM), 139

NSCN (Nationalist Socialist Council of Nagaland0, 129,

132, 141, 147, 301, 381, 383, 384

Leaders, 384

Numaligarh Refinery Ltd., 212

Nunisa, Dilip, 139, 140

Nutraceuticals and Cosmetics, 597

O

Occupational Mobility of People, 295

Official Language Bill, 368, 412

Oil

And Coal, 51

And Natural Gas Commission (ONGC), 45

India Ltd, 45, 212, 214

Sector, 214

Orchid Research-cum-Development Centre, 631

Orchidaria at-, 631

Dirang, 631

Jengging, 631

Roing, 531

Tipi, 631

Ozone

Depletion, 416

Layer, 537

P

Padmanabhaiah, 383

Pakistan, 392, 393, 498

Panchayati Raj Institutions (PRIs), 179, 155, 181, 485

Panchbhoothas, 620

Paper Industry, 518

Parliamentary Election (1980), 374

Passighat, 629

Patil, Shivraj, HM, 132

Peace

Defined, 115-117

Process in Assam, 115-151

Peaceful Communication Channels, 128

People's

Consultative Groups (PCGs), 132, 133

Republic of China, 500

Pervez Musharraf, Gen. and President of Pakistan, 392, 498

Petroleum Industry, 44

PGCI, 99

Phukon, Reboti, 131

Phyto-Pharmaceuticals, 597

Plain Tribal of Assam, 134

Plain Tribals of Assam, 378

Planned

Development in India, 190

Immigration Policy, 393

Planners, 395, 423, 455

Of North East Region, 417, 474

Planning, 112, 359, 475, 511, 542, 575

And Financial Management,

203, 297, 417
And Policies, 414
Commission, 62, 67, 181, 200, 201, 216, 298, 394, 450, 476, 539, 665
In India, 500
Plant Diversity in Arunachal Pradesh, 616
Plateau of Meghalaya, 41
Plato, 115
PMGY (Pradhan Mantri Gramodyog Yojna), 180
Poaching, 634
Political
And Economic Structures, 361
Assassination, 129
Violence and Insurgency, 146
Pollution, 456, 457, 489, 547
Air, 455
Air and Water, 498
Air, Water, Noise, 396
Chemicals, 458
Problems, 457
Water and Air, 392
Water and Noise, 457
Population, 60, 62, 70, 97
Bihari, 376
Distribution-Religion-wise, (PDR), 403
Christian Population, 403, 405, 406, 408
Hindu Population, 403, 405, 406
Muslim Population, 403, 405, 406
Explosion, 63, 127, 289, 394, 458, 527, 649, 654
Growth, 62, 88-90, 294, 392, 393, 397, 409, 410, 412, 415, 424, 433, 450, 455, 463, 465, 467, 469, 482, 510, 549, 550, 588
Impact of-, 629
Growth and Urbanization, 453-490
Of Assam, 125, 127
Of NER, 360, 433
Policies, 391, 392, 498
Poverty Environment Relationship, 482
Rural, 66, 67
Trend in NER, 19
Urban, 467, 504
Poverty
Alleviation, 211, 392, 498
Reduction, 27
Power
Generation, 72, 172, 441
Hydro and Thermal, 71, 98
Grid Corporation of India, 73
Ministry, 71
Section, 182
Pre-Economic Reform Period, 80
Preventive Detention Act, 368
Primary

Education, 36
Health Centres, (PHCs), 174, 292, 525, 626
Primitive
Society, 39
Tribal Communities, 553
Prison Reforms, 347
Privatization, 327
Problem of Identity, 118
Program of Action (POA), 38
Programmable Time Devices (PTD), 129
Property Rights, 544
For Women, 324
Public Distribution System (PDS), 108, 189, 192, 649
Public Food Distribution System, 651
Public Health Centres, 207
Purbanchal Movement, 368
Purchasing, Power and Parity, 232
Putin, Vladimer, 393
PWD Roads, 77

R

Rabha, 362
Racial Linguistic Conflicts in NER, 359-389
Rail Link Barak Valley--, 79
Railway Route Length in Assam, 78
Rajbhanshis, 362
Rajiv Gandhi
Grameen Vidyutikaran Yojna, (RGGVY) Scheme, 73, 173
University, 617, 637
Rajkhowa, Arobindo, ULFA Chairman, 132
Recommended Dietary Allowance (RDA), 475, 660
Recruitment System, 112
Red
Panda, 634
Tapism, 473
Reforms, 61
Region's
Backwardness, 471
Population, 465
Regional
Development, 285, 303, 648
Development Agencies, 154
Disparity (ies), 300, 301455, 649
Disparities in India, 287
Disparity in North East Region, 285-305
Economic Development, 529
Economy, 51
Research Centre, Aims and Objectives, 567
Regionalism, 123, 192, 285, 300-302
Reid, Sir Robert Neil, Gov of Assam, (1941), 120
Religious
Beliefs, 678
Issues, 366

Renewable Resources, 410
Republic of Korea, 500
Research and Planning, 220
Reserve Forests, 550, 577, 634
Revenue Villages, 15
Rhodesian Regime in Asia, 369
Rights of Child, 467
Rio Convention, 562
Riots, 134
Ritual and Secular Principles, 18
River Brahmputra, 87, 135, 380
Roy Barman Committee Report, 639
Roy, Arundhati, 354
Rubber Plantation, 69, 96
Rural
- Assam, 166, 181
- Barak Valley, 181
- China, 394
- Development, 154-156, 181
- Development Constraints, 166
- Economic Development, 160, 173
- Economy, 41, 162, 592
- Economy of Assam, 159
- Electrification, 99, 172
- Electrification Electrical Policy of Govt.of Assam, 73
- Electrification Policy, 173
- Housing Scheme, 178
- India, 18, 67, 326
- Industrial Marketing, 159
- Industrialization, 161
- Infrastructure Development Fund (RIDF), 299, 477
- Poverty Line, 481
- Regional Banks, 165
- Sectors, 257
- To Urban Migration, 28, 29, 161
- Urban Disparity, 356, 451
- Urban Dualism, 156
- Urban Migration, 499

Russian
- Federation, 393
- Population, 393

S

SAARC Decade, 347
Sadiya-Tezu Denzing, 629
Safe Drinking Water, 59, 62, 204, 458, 470, 662
Saikia, Bhabendranath, 131
Saikia, Hiranya, 132
Saint Augustine, Plato's Follower, 115
Samber, 600
Sampooran Grameen Rozgar Yojna (SGRY), 179
Santals and Bodos, 379
Satellite Remote Sensing Techniques (for Identifying Forests), 602-605
Satyagraha Movement, 372
SAY (Samagra Awas Yojna), 179
Scheduled Caste/Tribes, 179,

109, 169

Order Act, 141, 380

Scheduled

Commercial Banks, 106, 107, 299

Tribes, (ST), 15, 20, 34, 465

Bill, (STB), 580, 640

Population in NER, 20

Scheme

For Surrender of Militants, 133

For Surrender-cum-Rehabilitation of Militants, 133

Scientific Pisci Culture, 659

Sector,

Agriculture, 89, 112, 193, 210, 219, 294, 652, 658

Communication, 76

Energy, 44

Fishery, 95

Handloom, 74, 101, 356, 516

Health, 511

Industrial and Agriculture, 182

Industrial and Service, 27

Irrigation, 417

Petroleum Manufacturing, 44

Railway, 78

Small Scale Industries, 102, 516

Social, 197, 509

Tourism, 41

Sectoral Problems, 288

Security

Agencies, 130

Of Region, 366

Sediment from Ganga and Brahmputra, 472

Self-Help Groups (SHGs), 178, 179, 211, 212

Sen, Amartya, 158

Sericulture, 69, 164

And Community Handloom, 183

Seven Sisters, 365

Sex Ratio, 437, 438, 465, 466, 502, 524

in Arunachal Pradesh,

Nagaland and Sikkim, 25

in Assam, Tripura and Meghalaya, 25

in Manipur, 24

in NER, 400

of North East States, 24

Sexual Abuse, 330

Shans, 361

Shastri, Lal Bahadur, 372

Formula, 372

Shifting

Agriculture in NER, 675, 683

Cultivation, 294, 471, 543-548, 550, 564, 566, 628, 630, 639, 655, 675-689

Impact of-, 628

Cultivation Operations, 677

Villages, 15

Shramshakti, 347
Shukla Commission, 52
SIDBI (Small Industrial Development Bank of India), 299, 476
Siddha, 567, 621, 418
Sikkim, 13, 25, 41, 47, 87, 100, 103, 110, 437, 443, 444, 655
  Tribes, 16
    Bhutias, 16
    Lapcha, 16
    Nepali, 16
Sikkim's Economy, 69, 96, 97, 442, 443
Silcher, 373
Siliguri Neck, 87
Silk Industry, 167
Singlung Hill Development Council, (SHDC), 381
Sinha, Sarat Chandra, 122
SIRD, 178
Skill Training, 39
Small Scale
  And Cottage Industries, 519
  Industrial Units, 555
  Industries, 74, 101-103, 162, 327, 517, 630
  Industries in Tripura, 102
Smuggling, 147
Snow Leopard, 634
Social and Economic
  Disparities, 450
  Security, 486
Social
  Backwardness, 153
  Change, 38, 120, 400, 468, 509
  Customs and Traditions, 81
  Forestry, 578
  Groups, 14, 169
  Infrastructure, 501, 509
  Mobilization, 14
  Safety Net (SSN), 325
  Sectors, 181, 183, 194, 509
    Health and Education, 154, 155
  Security, 194
  Services, 486
  Structure, 18, 153
  System, 119
  Tensions, 361, 362
  Transformation, 26
Society of North Easter Region, 667
Socio-Cultural Entity, 454
Socio-Economic
  Backwardness, 34, 301
  Crisis, 118
  Development, 153-184, 171, 194, 207, 215, 440, 450, 454, 456, 469, 562
    Impact on Environment, 453-490
    In Rural Assam, 153-184
  Development in NER, 59-85, 87-114
  Infrastructure, 27, 109, 157

Issues, 231

Liberalization, 36

Political Development, 34

Problems, (SEP), 285, 396, 433, 458, 459, 484, 649

Crimes, 396

Drug Abuse, 396

Poverty and Alcoholism--Pollution, 396

Suicides, 396

Progress, 122, 123

Transformation, 192, 285, 395, 455

Socio-Political Development, 498

Soil

Conservation, 647

Erosion, 81, 547, 553, 556, 655

Erosion Hazard, 647

Fertility, 647

Solar Photovoltaic, 173

Sonapani Hydel Power Plant, 203, 662

Sonowal, 362

South

Asia Growth Quadrangle, 48

Asian Association for Regional Cooperation (SAARC), 133

East Market, 48

Special Economic Zones (SEZ), 47

Policy, 220, 221

Special Operation Unit (SOU), 130

Species, 539, 540, 560, 562, 599, 600, 602

Board of India, 42

Diversity, 410

Of Hornbills, 600

Of Mammals, 600, 613

Of Orchids, 607

Under Schedule I, 613-614

SSS (Social Security System), 111

Standard of Living, 272

State

Drug Testing Laboratories, 621

Forest Research Institute, 566, 631

Medical Council, 512

Policies, 15

Policy of Population Control, 394

Pollution Control Board, (SPCB), 578

Reorganization Committee, (1954), 137, 368, 372

State's Economy, 69, 95, 442

Status of Women in NER, 332, 353, 356

Structural

Adjustment, 325

Adjustment Program, 62, 190, 327

Changes, 26

Structured Transformation, 88

Sub-

Alpine Forests, 557
Regional Imbalances, 89
Sahara Africa, 516
Subsidy System, 190
Suicides, 457, 470
In NER (Age-Group Wise), 419, 420
Male, 470
Super-national Bodies, 222
APEC, 222
ASEAN, 222
European Union, 222
IMF, 222
UN, 222
Sustainable Development (SD), 60, 391, 498, 538, 540, 541, 568, 569, 570, 588, 648, 649
Swaranjyanti Gram Swarozgar Yojna (SGSY), 179, 211
Sylhet, 371
Referendum, 147, 367, 371

T

Tea
Cultivation, 69, 96
In North Eastern States, 40
In the States of-, (TS), 40
Industry, 62, 75, 104, 518
Industry in North Eastern Region, 104, 518
Technical
Infrastructure, 486
Revolution, 498
Technological
Aids, 647
Transformation of Agriculture in Assam, 167
Technology Aided Articulation, 37
Terrace Culture, 688
Terrorism, 128, 218, 222, 653
Terrorist Organization, 383
Tertiary Sector, 201
Thailand, 500
Thermal Power, 72
Generation, 98
Third World Countries, 60, 88, 409
Tibeto-
Burman Group, 378
Mongoloid Origin, 675
Tiger, 634
Timber
Extraction in Arunachal Pradesh, 628
Permits, 544
Trade, 628
Total Fertility Rate, (TFR), 61, 89
Tourism, 40, 41, 103, 159, 217, 222, 223
In North East India, 41
Industry, 41
Policies, 223
Trade, 218
And Commerce, 555

In North East India, 47
Liberalization, 649
Policy, 649
Traditional
Crafts, 74, 103
Cane and Bamboo Craft, 103
Carpet Weaving, 103
Handmade Paper, 103
Spinning Wool, 103
Thanka Paintings, 103
Cultivation Practices, 294
Farming Methods, 69, 96, 443
Handicraft and Handlooms, 162
Health Care System, 621
Jhum Cultivation, 95
Medicines, 597
Methods of Health Care, 607
Principles of Kinship and Marriages, 18
Rural Industry, 165
Slash and Burn Methods, 88
System of Medicine, 621
Traffic Control and Pollution, 457
Training Programs, 178
In Herbal Sciences, 619
Transparency International, 108
Transport
And Communication, 508
In Arunachal Pradesh, 630
System, 217
Transportation, 554
Impact of-, 629
Infrastructure, 96
System, 76, 166
Tree
Permits, 628
Species, 628
Tribal
Areas, 14
Characteristics, 360, 361
Communities (TC), 15, 120, 543, 544, 552
Arunachal Pradesh, 40
Manipur, 40
Meghalaya, 40
Mizoram, 40
Nagaland, 40
Tripura, 40
Culture, 39, 634, 649
Dominated Nagaland and Mizoram, 34
Dominated States, 17
Arunachal Pradesh, Meghalaya, Mizoram, Nagaland, 17
Economy, 545
Hill Villages, 18
Identity, 39, 120
Insurgency, 120
Issues, 377
Method of Cultivation, 418
Movements, 120

People, Economy and Political Development, 120
Population, 14, 20, 192, 400, 465, 470, 563, 577, 647, 655, 676
Problems of Assam, 12
Regions, 37
Societies, 14, 36, 120
Women, 34-36, 38, 39
Women of North East, 17
Impact of Globalization on-, 17
Tribal/Non-Tribal Population, 458, 459
Tribals of North Eastern Region, 364
Tribe Defined, 14
Tribes
As Notified in Schedule (533), 15
In Meghalaya, 36
Tribes, 147, 362, 540
Apa Tanis, 558
Bodos and Karbis, 366
Bodos—Rajbhanshis, 147
Cachari, 362
Chakma, 362
Dimasa, 362
Garo, 362
Hajoul, 362
Hmer, 362
Khasi Jaintia, 362
Kuki Tribes, 362
Lakhar, 362
Man, 362
Mikir, 362
Mizo, 362
Naga, 362
Nyishi, 558
Pawi, 362
Reangs, 465
Syntheng, 362
Tribes/Sub Tribes of India (573), 14
TRIPS (Trade Related to Intellectual Property Rights), 220
Tripura
Economy, 69, 95, 443
Population, 418
Tribes, 16
Chamma, 16
Kuki, 16
Liang, 16
Lusai, 16
Santhal, 16
Tropical
Forests, 628
Rain Forest, 87, 557
Tropical/Sub-Tropical Zones, 615
True
Potato Seeds, 70, 95, 443
Tura Diesel, 99
Turmeric, 442
Turmeric, 69, 95

U

Ulema in-, 393
- Bangladesh, 393
- Egypt, 393
- Indonesia, 393
- Iran, 393
- Turkey, 393

ULFA (United Liberation Front of Assam), 121-123, 129, 130, 131, 132, 133, 136, 144, 301, 377
- Armed Organization, 129
- Bases, 130
- Centre-Talks, 133
- Extortion and Kidnapping, 129
- Formation, 129
- Leaders, 133
- Leadership, 131
- Militants, 129

UN (United Nations), 328, 329, 37, 221, 391, 454, 499, 538, 560, 687
- Conference, 569
- Conference on Human Environment (UNCHE), 538
- Development Programs, 196, 524
- Environmental Protection, 515
- Global Population Report, 196
- International Research and Training Institute, 353
- Millennium Development Goals, 59, 431
- Population Projections, 394

Unani, 621

UNCED Earth Summit, 583

UNICEF, 460, 461

Universal
- Primary Education, 59, 431

UPDS (United People's Democratic Solidarity), 121, 123, 137
- Cadre, 138

Upper Assam
- Districts, 362
- Valley, 603

Urban
- Centres, 27, 549
- Growth, 29
- Population, 25-30, 240
  - Of Arunachal Pradesh, 30
- Poverty, 26, 95
- Sectors of NER, 521

Urbanization, 25-30, 88, 161, 194, 392, 396, 408, 441, 456, 457, 459, 466, 467, 484, 498, 501, 503, 504, 527, 541, 549, 564, 566, 627
- And Development, 29
- Impact of-, 629
- In Agro-Based NER, 423
- Unplanned, 25

Urbanization-Environmental Relationship, 396

US, 397, 507, 515, 598

US and China, 62

US, New Zealand and UK, 330

UTDC (Union Territory Demand Committee), 373

Uttarakhand, 47

V

Vajpayee, Atal Behari, former Indian PM, 48

Valley

- Districts of Manipur, 417
- Barak, 125, 372, 373, 381, 412, 435, 464
- Brahmputra, 124, 125, 369, 371, 372, 376, 435, 464
- Brahmputra and Barak, 362, 675
- Dang, 609
- Dibang, 606, 609
- Manipur and Tripura, 417, 657
- Surma, 369

Value Elasticity, 281

Versatile Information System for Tourist Attraction (VISTA), 222

Vienna Declaration, 38

Village

- Electrification Program, 657
- Exogamy, 18
- Industries, 36
- Water and Sanitation Committee (VWSC), 662

Violence, 128

- Against Women, 330
- Large Scale, 378
- Political, 128
- Types, 116
  - Cultural, 116
  - Direct, 116
  - Structured, 116

Vivekananda, Swamy, 38

VKI (Village and Khadi Industries0, 162

Vote Banks, 368

W

Water (Prevention and Control of Pollution) Act, 539, 578

Water

- Purification Technology, 515
- Resources of NER, 45, 66, 220

Weapons of Mass Destruction (WMD), 537

Welfare measures, 324

West Bengal Minority Commission, 408

Western Ghats, 540

WHO, 209

WID (Women in Development), 329

Widow Remarriage, 324

Wildlife (Protection) Act, 1972, 539, 588, 634

Wildlife, 548, 558, 559, 563, 577, 585, 588, 616

- Sanctuaries, 617
- Trade, 561

Winter Migrants, 614
Women
  And Child Development, 344
  Consumers of NER, 326
  Empowerment, 355
  Empowerment Year, 351
  Participation, 353
  Participation in Politics, Economy, Social and Cultural Life, 33, 38
Women's
  Development, 344
  Education, 324
  Education in NER, 325, 501
  Empowerment, 224
  Groups, 332
  Literacy, 345
  Movement, 39, 324, 332,
  Participation, 62, 89
  Position—in Society, 92
  Study Centre, 325
World
  Bank Policies, 328
  Commission of Forests and Sustainable Development (SCFSD), 560
  Commission on Environment and Development, 538
  Conservation Strategy, 583
  Economy, 37
  Health Organization (WHO), 395, 475, 502, 597, 660
  Population Conference, 391, 454
  Summit for Children, 1990, 467
  Trade Organization (WTO), 37, 325
  Urbanization, 28
  War II, 416
  Water Day, 515
World's Population, 392
WSSD (World Summit on Sustainable Development), 391
WTO, 650

Y & Z

Yahwah, 115
Yandvaur Treaty, (1814-1826), 119
Yoga, 620
Zoological Parks, 617